To Jack Hamilton
    With best wishes,

May God's richest blessing
be yours as you
teach the Good News

Norm, Carolyn,
    Louise & Patty.

ROMANS

VERSE BY VERSE

ROMANS

Verse by Verse

BY

WILLIAM R. NEWELL

"The only hope of Christianity is in the rehabilitating of the Pauline theology. It is back, back, back, to an incarnate Christ and the atoning blood, or it is on, on, on, to atheism and despair."

—THE LATE FRANCIS L. PATTON, GODLY AND
ABLE PRESIDENT OF PRINCETON UNIVERSITY.

CHICAGO

MOODY PRESS

Author's Note

THE TEXT used is in general that of the Revised
Version, which is much more accurate than that of the Old
Version. At times it is necessary to render literally; and,
in several instances to paraphrase, to make clearer the
meaning.

ROMANS

CHAPTER ONE

Apostolic Introduction. Verses 1-7.

Personal Greetings, and Expressions of Desire to See and to Preach to Saints in Rome. Verses 8-15.

Great Theme of the Epistle: The Gospel the Power of God, — Because of the By-Faith-Righteousness Revealed Therein. Verses 16-17.

The World's Danger: God's Wrath Revealed Against Human Sin. Verses 18-20.

The Awful Course of Man's Sin, and Man's Present State, Related and Described. Verses 21-32.

1   Paul, a bondservant of Jesus Christ, a called
2   apostle, separated unto God's good news, which
    He before promised through His prophets in (the)
3   holy Scriptures, concerning His Son: who was
4   born of David's seed according to the flesh, who
    was declared the Son of God with power accord-
    ing to the Spirit of holiness, by resurrection of the
5   dead,—Jesus Christ our Lord, through whom we
    received grace and apostleship, for obedience of
    faith among all the nations for His name's sake;
6   among whom are ye also,—called as Jesus Christ's:
7   to all those who are in Rome beloved of God, called
    as saints: Grace to you and peace from God our
    Father and the Lord Jesus Christ.

Verse 1: PAUL—We see Paul's name standing alone here—no Silas, Timothy or other brother with him. For Paul is himself Christ's apostle unto the Gentiles, the declarer, as here in Romans, of the gospel for this dispensa-

1

tion. Also, in revealing the heavenly character, calling, and destiny of the Church as the Body and Bride of Christ, and as God's House, as in Ephesians, Paul stands *alone*. When essential doctrines and directions are being laid down, no one is associated with the apostle in the authority given to him.

We dare not glory in a man, not even in Paul, whose life and ministry are by far the most remarkable of those of any human being.* Yet our Lord Jesus said: "He that receiveth whomsoever I send receiveth Me; and he that receiveth Me receiveth him that sent Me" (John 13.20). And Paul was especially *sent* to us Gentiles. At the first council of the Church, recorded in Acts 15, "They who were of repute" (in the church in Jerusalem), said Paul, "saw that I had been intrusted with the gospel of the uncircumcision, even as Peter with the gospel of the circumcision" (Gal. 2.7).

Throughout church history, to depart from Paul has been heresy. To receive Paul's gospel and hold it fast, is salvation,— "By which (gospel) ye are saved, if ye hold fast the very word I preached unto you" (I Cor. 15.1,2, margin).

A bondservant of Jesus Christ—Paul was *bondservant* before he was *apostle*. Saul of Tarsus' first words, as he lay in the dust in the Damascus road, blinded by the glory of Christ's presence, were, "Who art thou, *Lord?*" And when there came the voice, "I am Jesus of Nazareth, whom thou persecutest," his next words were, "What shall I do, *Lord?*"—instant, utter surrender! It is deeply instructive to mark that although our Lord said, "No longer do I call you bondservants, but friends"; yet, successively, Paul, James, Peter, Jude and John (Rev. 1.1), name themselves bondservants (Greek: *douloi*),—and that with

---

*Paul, being really the least, is the greatest of men! The Lord Jesus said, "Among those born of women there hath not arisen a greater than John the Baptist." But He added immediately, "Yet he that is *lesser* in the *Kingdom* of heaven is greater than he." (Matt. 11.11). Paul names himself *"less than the least* of all saints," speaking *in the Spirit.* When John the Baptist speaks of the place he had, it was, as "the *friend* of the Bridegroom"; but Paul, of *his* work, as that of *espousing and presenting the saints as a chaste virgin to Christ"!* We cannot conceive of a higher honor, than that given to this very *least* of Christ's bondservants,—to present *His Church* to Him; as we believe it will be given Paul to do, at the Marriage of the Lamb! (Rev. 19.6-9; II Cor. 11.2).

great delight! It is the "service of perfect freedom"—deepest of all devotions, that of realized redemption and perfected love.*

Paul next names himself **a called apostle,** or "apostle by calling." Three times in these first seven verses the word "called" occurs, and three times more in the Epistle this great word is written: Chapter 8.28,30 (twice). Compare Paul's three other uses of the word: I Corinthians 1.2,9,24; and Jude's: Jude 1; and the one other occurrence: Revelation 17.14. "Called" means *designated* and *set apart* by an action of God to some *special sphere and manner of being* and of *consequent activity.* In the sixth verse of our chapter, the saints are described in the words "called as Jesus Christ's." They were given to Him by the Father (John 17), and connected with Him before their earth-history: "chosen in Him before the foundation of the world"; and in the seventh verse we read that they are "called as saints," or "saints by calling," which does not at all mean that they were invited to *become* saints—a Romish doctrine! But that they *were* saints by divine sovereign calling; holy ones, having been washed in Christ's blood; and having been created in Christ Jesus. It was their *mode of being;* even as the holy angels did not become angels by a process of

---

*It would be well also here, regarding Paul, to apply Mark 10.43,44: "Whosoever would become great among you, shall be your minister." The Greek word for "minister" here is the one we translate elsewhere "deacon" (*diakonos*); but verse 44 goes further and deeper: "And whosoever would be first among you, shall be servant of all." Here the Greek word is the one always used for a slave under bondage—*doulos.* And so we find Paul saying to the Corinthians:

"We preach not ourselves, but Christ Jesus as Lord, and ourselves as your bondservants for Jesus' sake . . . Though I was free from all men, I brought myself under bondage to all (verb form of *doulos*: literally, I became *bondslave* to all), that I might gain the more . . . I will most gladly spend and be spent out for your souls." (II Cor. 4.5; I Cor. 9.19; II Cor. 12.15, Gr.).

No other apostle calls himself "slave of all": Paul got the first place, by our Lord's own word,—not that any who choose to be slaves of all for Christ's sake may not be associated with Paul! But he is "less than the least," even yet!

No wonder, then, that we find Paul speaking with an authority from the Lord such as no other apostle uses. Moses (who had authority in Israel) was "meek above all the men on the face of the earth." The Lord Jesus Himself is seen, when the Kingdom is handed over to Him, as a Lamb that had been slain (Rev. 5.6). He is ever "meek and lowly in heart." Thus Paul says, "I am nothing . . . I am the least of the apostles, that am not meet to be called an apostle, because I persecuted the Church of God." (Here, by the way, was sovereign grace! Christ's choosing His greatest enemy to be His greatest apostle!)

holiness, but were created into the angelic sphere and manner of being. Such is the meaning of the word "called" with Paul.*

Separated unto God's good news—This expression is explained further in Galatians 1.15: "God separated me from my mother's womb and called me through His grace, to reveal His Son in me, that I might preach Him among the nations." In like manner were born Moses, who Stephen says was "fair unto God,"—that is, manifestly marked out to be used by God (Acts 7.20, R.V., margin) ; and John the Baptist, of whom Gabriel said, that he would be "filled with the Holy Spirit even from his mother's womb . . . to make ready for the Lord a people prepared for Him." Likewise were Jacob, Samson, Samuel, and Jeremiah separated even before birth to an appointed calling.

The sovereignty of God is thus seen at the very beginning of this great Epistle. And how well Paul carried out his separation to this high calling, the gospel, the good news about Christ! Yet there are those today, even today, who in ignorance and pride affect to despise the words of this great apostle,—as Peter† warns, "to their own destruction" (II Pet. 3.16).

Now as to this "good news of God," we see in our passage two great facts:

First, that it is **God's good news**. Mark this well! It was *God* who loved the world; it was *God* who sent His Son. Note our Lord's continual insistence on this in the gospel of John (19 times!). Christ said constantly "I am not come of Myself, but My Father sent Me." It is absolutely necessary

---

*The verb to call (*kaleo*), is used in this way of Divine sovereign action about forty times; and the cognate noun *(klesis),* eleven times: always in the sense of Romans 11.29: "The gifts and calling of God are not repented of."

†In the book of Acts, Peter and John, together with others of the twelve, and Philip and Stephen, give witness to our Lord's physical resurrection, and proclaim remission of sins to the Jews and proselytes. Then God, through Peter, (to whom the Lord had given the "keys of the kingdom of heaven") opens the door of faith to Gentiles (Acts 10). Paul, saved outside Jewish bounds, saw the glorified Christ, and heard His voice (Acts 9). He is sent forth by the Holy Ghost (Acts 13), with the gospel which belongs to this dispensation, wholly apart from the Law of Moses: witnessing first in synagogues, and afterwards, at Ephesus, (Acts 19), bringing believers out into separation from rebellious Judaism. Finally, at Rome (Acts 28), through the awful passage of Isaiah Six, he declares the Jews to be judicially hardened, and "this salvation of God sent to the Gentiles." Since that day, Jews are invited to believe,—not as Jews, but as *sinners!*

that we keep fast in mind, as we read in Romans the awful facts about ourselves, that it is *God* who is leading us up to His own good news for bad sinners!

Second, (verse 2), that the good news was **promised through His prophets in holy Scriptures**—These are the Old Testament Scriptures,* with promises, types, and direct prophecies of good news to come, both to Israel and to the nations, concerning His Son. We shall find in Romans 3.21 that there is revealed "a righteousness of God" which had been "witnessed by the law and the prophets": witnessed by the law, in that it provided sacrifices and a way of forgiveness for those who failed in its observance; and witnessed by the prophets directly in such passages as these: "By the knowledge of Himself shall my righteous Servant [Christ] make many righteous" (Isa. 53.11); and, "This is His name whereby He shall be called: Jehovah our righteousness" (Jer. 23.6; 33.16); and again, "The righteous shall live by faith" (Hab. 2.4).

Verses 3 and 4: **Concerning His Son**—Specifically (a) that He died for our sins according to the Scriptures, (b) that He was buried, (c) that He hath been raised the third day according to the Scriptures, (d) that He appeared to various witnesses. The good news Paul preached is therefore scientifically specific, and must be held in our minds in its accuracy, as it lay in that of the apostle. (See I Cor. 15.3-8.)

---

*Compare "holy Scriptures" *(graphais hagiais)* here, with "sacred writings" *(hiera grammata)* of II Timothy 3.15, and with the words, "every Scripture is God-breathed" *(pasa graphē theopneustos)* of the following verse (II Tim. 3.16). We should, in II Timothy 3.16, supply the substantive verb, *"is,"* after "Scripture"; and the words "and is" after the word "God," with the resultant reading: "Every Scripture is inspired of God and is also profitable," etc. The reading in both the English and American Revisions here is a poor attempt at literalness which avoids the evident meaning of the Holy Spirit, and is, furthermore, not a possible translation in view of the Spirit's constant use of the word *graphē* in the New Testament as referring only to the Word of God. To say, "Every *graphē* inspired of God," etc., is to insinuate that there may be a *graphē* uninspired; whereas *graphē* is God's technical word for Scripture, for God's inspired Word, used 51 times in the New Testament as a noun denoting always *inspired writings.* Its first occurrence is Matthew 21.42; its last, II Peter 3.16. Other illustrations are Matthew 26.54,56; John 10.35; and I Timothy 3.16.

We may note also, as to "holy writings," that Paul, if addressing Jews, would have said *the* holy writings, for they had them; but he is writing to Gentiles, therefore omits the article.

These great facts concerning Christ's death, burial, and resurrection are the beginning of the gospel; as Paul says: "I delivered unto you (these) first of all."*

The gospel is all about Christ. Apart from Him, there is no news from heaven but that of coming woe! Read that passage in I Corinthians 15.3-5: "I make known unto you the gospel which I preached unto you: that Christ died, Christ was buried; Christ hath been raised; Christ was seen." It is all about the Son of God! This is the record of Paul's first preaching, after "the heavenly vision": "Straightway in the synagogues he proclaimed Jesus, that he is the Son of God" (Acts 9.20).

Who was born of David's seed according to the flesh, who was declared the Son of God with power according to the spirit of holiness, by resurrection of the dead—We have here two things: first, Christ as a Man "according to the flesh"; and as such fulfilling the promises as to "the seed of David"; second, Christ as Son of God, declared so to be with power by His resurrection,—and that "according to the Spirit of holiness," even that holiness in which He had existed and had walked on earth all His life.† Christ, the Holy One of God had, "through the eternal Spirit offered Himself without blemish unto God," at the cross (Heb. 9.14). God the Father then acted in power and glory, and raised Him (Rom. 6.4,

---

*Let us beware, however, of misapplying I Corinthians 2.2: "I determined not to know anything among *you*, save Jesus Christ, and Him crucified." Paul goes on in verse 6, there, to say: "We speak wisdom, however, among them that are full-grown"; and in 3.1: "I, brethren, could not speak unto *you* as unto spiritual, but as unto carnal, as unto babes in Christ. I fed *you* with *milk.*" *"Jesus Christ and Him crucified"* is the gospel for the sinner and babes in Christ; *Christ Jesus and Him glorified* is the gospel for instructing and perfecting believers (I Cor. 2.6-13).

†"That same energy of the Holy Ghost which had displayed itself in Jesus when He walked in holiness here below, was demonstrated in resurrection; and not merely in His own rising from the dead, but in raising the dead at any time, though most signally and triumphantly displayed in His own resurrection."—W. Kelly.

I have never seen a fully satisfactory explanation of the words (literally) "marked out as the Son of God with power, according to the Spirit of holiness, by resurrection of dead (ones)." The account of our Lord's death in Matthew 27.51-54 remarkably corroborates the truth of this great verse. The rent veil, the earthquake, the rent rocks, and the opened tombs: "And many bodies of the saints that had fallen asleep were raised; and coming forth out of the tombs after His resurrection (ror He was the First-fruits) they entered into the holy city, and appeared unto many." And the awed testimony of "the centurion, and they that were with him watching Jesus, when they saw the earthquake, and the things that were done, feared exceedingly, saying, "Truly this was the Son of God." And as Luke adds: "Certainly this was a righteous man!"

Eph. 1.19,20). Christ was thus irresistibly, eternally "declared to be the Son of God"! Always when prophesying His death, Christ included His rising again the third day as the proof of all. In his last Epistle (II Tim. 2.8) Paul connects these same two facts about our Lord: "Remember Jesus Christ, risen from the dead, of the seed of David, according to my gospel."*

Jesus Christ our Lord—Ten times in Romans Paul uses this title, or, "Our Lord Jesus Christ," that full name beloved by the apostles and all instructed saints from Pentecost onward: for "God hath made Him both Lord and Christ, this Jesus whom ye crucified" (Acts 2.36). *Jesus,* His personal name (Matt. 1.21) as Savior; *Christ,* God's Anointed One to do all things for us; *Lord,* His high place over us all for whom His work was done; and as, truly, Lord of all things in heaven and earth (Acts 10.36).

Verse 5: **Through whom we received grace and apostleship for obedience of faith among all the nations for His name's sake**—Personal grace must come before true service. The grace Paul had received concerned both his personal salvation and his service as the great example of divine favor. Paul's own words are the best comment on this: "I am the least of the apostles, that am not meet to be called an apostle, because I persecuted the Church of God. But by the grace of God I am what I am: and His grace which was bestowed upon me was not found vain; but I labored more abundantly than they all: yet not I, but the grace of God which was with me" (I Cor. 15.9,10); and, "I obtained mercy, that in me as chief

---

*Christ was to be born as Seed of the woman, Seed of Abraham, and Seed of David: as the Seed of the woman to bruise Satan; as the Seed of Abraham, to bring in salvation to the whole household of faith (Gal. 3.16); and Christ was to be the Seed of David, in the actual fulfilment to Israel of all Messianic promises: for He was born into the "house and family" of David. In fact, He is named in the New Testament as Son of David a dozen times. It is from the sixteenth Psalm, concerning David, that Peter quotes in Acts 2.25-36; and Paul calls Christ David's Seed, quoting from the same Psalm in his first recorded sermon (Acts 13.16-41); although he addresses those Jews in Antioch as "children of the stock of Abraham." Christ was the Seed of the woman; He was also the Seed of Abraham; but He was born into this world of a virgin of the family of David (her betrothed husband being also of that family), so that they both went to enroll themselves in the city of David, Bethlehem (Luke 2.4,5).

"There is strong reason to believe that Mary, as well as Joseph, was a descendant f David. This was the persistent tradition of the early Church."—James Orr.

"I do not doubt that Luke's is Mary's genealogy."—Darby.

might Jesus Christ show forth all His longsuffering, for an ensample of them that should thereafter believe on Him unto eternal life" (I Tim. 1.16). Paul's apostleship was marked out by the fact that he had "seen Jesus our Lord" (I Cor. 9.1), and by the "signs of an apostle," in "authority," (II Cor. 10.8; 13.10), in "all patience, by signs and wonders and mighty works" (II Cor. 12.12). Though desperately resisted by the Jerusalem Judaizers, he continually insisted, to the glory of God, upon "obedience of faith among all the nations." To obey God's good news, is simply to believe it. There is now a "law of faith" (3.27); and Paul ends this Epistle with this same wonderful phrase: "obedience of faith" (16.26). Paul was not establishing what is now called "the Christian religion"! Having abandoned the only religion God ever gave, that of the Jews,* he went forth with a simple *message* concerning Christ, to be believed by everybody, anybody, anywhere. And all was "for His name's sake"—Christ's. And why not! The Christ of glory had done the work, had "emptied Himself, taking the form of a servant, becoming obedient unto death, yea, the death of the cross." He was the "propitiation for the whole world" (I John 2.2). We are likely to think of the gospel as something published for our sake only, whereas in fact God is having it published for the sake of His dear Son, Who died. It is sweet to enter into this, as did John: "I write unto you, little children, because your sins are forgiven you *for His Name's sake*" (I John 2.12). Preachers, teachers, and missionaries everywhere, should regard themselves as laboring for Christ's Name's sake, first of all.

---

*By "religion" *(thrēskeia)*: we mean that worship which is conducted through ceremonies. Paul, indeed, calls that worship, in Galatians 1.13,14, Judaism—*(Ioudaismos)*. James (1.26) uses the word *thrēskeia*, which primarily means, fear of the gods. The fundamental thought in "religion" is the performance of duties. In fact, the English word "religion" from Latin, *religio*, a binding, that is, to bind duties on one, and is an accurate setting forth of the original meaning.

Now this was exactly what was *not* done in the gospel. "Religious" duties as such were wholly set aside, and faith in the living Christ substituted. Strictly speaking, a believer is a man who has a Person, not a religion.

The "Judaizers" were those professing to be Christians who were determined to fasten on Christian believers *"Ioudaismos,"* as Paul calls it. The cross ended, all that: the veil was rent, the way to God made wholly open, apart from "religious duties and ceremonies, days, seasons, months and years"!

Verse 6: **Among whom are ye also,—called as Jesus Christ's**—The saints are *connected* with Jesus Christ,—"called as *of* Him"; as we read in Chapter 8.39: Nothing "shall be able to separate us from the love of God, which is *in* Christ Jesus our Lord."

Verse 7: **To all that are in Rome, beloved of God, called as saints***—Note that while God loved the whole world, it is the saints who are called the "beloved of God." They are His household, His dear children. Sinners should believe that God loved them and gave His Son for them; but saints, that they are the "beloved of God." The unsaved are never named God's "beloved." A man, even, may, and should, love his neighbors: but his wife and children are "his beloved."

Grace to you and peace from God our Father and the Lord Jesus Christ—Paul uses practically this same form of address over and over;—and he connects grace with peace in his apostolic greeting to all the saints to whom he writes,—as does Peter. Grace is always pronounced as from "God our Father" as the Source, and "our Lord Jesus Christ" as the Channel and Sphere of Divine blessing. Sometimes grace for the Church is considered in the benediction as wholly from Christ, as in I Corinthians 16.23: "The grace of the Lord Jesus Christ be with you" (see comment on Rom. 16.20). For our Lord Jesus Christ is "Head over all things to the Church"; and life and judgment are distinctly said to be in His hands: "That all may honor the Son, even as they honor the Father" (John 5.21-23). In writing to individuals,—Timothy, Titus, and "the elect lady," (II John 1) Paul and John insert the more personal word, "mercy"; for we are told that we each need mercy (Heb. 4.16). The saints, looked at as a company, *have obtained,* in general, mercy. Like Israel of old, the Church is now God's sphere of blessing. But each individual—even Paul himself—has need of peculiar *mercy* (I Cor. 7.25).

Words fail to express the blessedness of being thus under God's grace, His eternal favor! Such, such only, have peace.

---

*We might render these expressions: "Jesus Christ's by calling," "saints by calling." Calling, in this sense, is always of God the Father, who appoints to each creature its own manner, character, and sphere of being.

All other "peace" than that extended by God and possessed by the saints, will "break up," as Rutherford says, "at the last, in a sad war."

And how wonderful to be of those whose Father is God! to whom the apostle can say in truth, "God our Father." Only those who have received Christ have the right *(exousia)* to become children *(tekna—born ones)* of God (John 1.12).

Grace and peace are eternally proceeding from God the Father and the Lord Jesus Christ,—through and by whom all blessing comes.

8   First of all, indeed, I give thanks to my God through Jesus Christ concerning you all, because your faith is spoken of throughout the whole
9   world! For God is my witness, whom I serve in my spirit in the good news of His Son, how unceasingly
10   I make mention of you, always beseeching in my prayers, if by any means at last I may be so prospered in the course of the will of God as to come
11   unto you. For I long to see you, that I may impart to you some spiritual gift, for your establish-
12   ing: that is, that I with you may be comforted mutually, through each other's faith, both yours
13   and mine. For I do not want you to be ignorant of the fact, brethren, that oftentimes I purposed to come to you (and was hindered until the present time), in order that I might have some fruit in you
14   also, just as among the other Gentiles. To Greeks and to Barbarians both,—both to wise and foolish,
15   I am debtor. So to my very uttermost I am eager to preach the good news to you also in Rome.

Verse 8: **First of all, indeed, I give thanks to God through Jesus Christ concerning you all**—"The apostle pursues the natural course of first placing himself, so to speak, in relation with his readers, and his first point of contact with them is gratitude* for their participation in Christianity," says DeWette. Paul is ever thanking God for any grace he found in any saint. He looks at all who are Christ's, through Christ's eyes, **because your faith is spoken of throughout the whole world.** Not fathered or founded by any apostle, the assemblies that God had Himself gathered from all quarters into the world's capital,† had a faith in Christ which was "spoken of," nay, announced as a wonder, throughout the whole Roman Empire. Announced, too, without steamship, without telegraph, without newspapers, without radio! God sees to it that a real work of His Spirit is published abroad, as it was with the Thessalonians: "From you hath sounded forth the word of the Lord, not only in Macedonia and Achaia, but in every place your faith to God-ward is gone forth." So with every real revival: the whole world soon knows about it.

Verse 9: Paul made unceasing prayer for these believers. He calls God to witness concerning this, as he frequently does when his soul is most exercised. See II Corinthians 1.23; Philippians 1.8; I Thessalonians 2.5,10. The expression, **Whom I serve in my spirit in the gospel of His Son,** is striking and significant. Those who would make man to consist of but two parts, soul and body, cannot properly explain "spirit and soul and body" (I Thess. 5.23); much less "the dividing asunder of soul and spirit" (Heb. 4.12). The constant witness of Scripture is that man exists as a spirit living in a body, possessed of a soul. Paul's service to God was in his spirit, and therefore in the Holy Spirit, and never "soulical" (not *psychikos,* but *pneumatikos*—I Cor. 2.14) : Jude 19, Jas. 3.15. Paul did not depend on music, or architecture, or oratory, or rhetoric. He did not hold "inspirational" meetings to arouse the emotions to mystic resolves. He served God directly, in his spirit. It was the truth in the Holy Ghost he ministered,

---

*"When one puts alongside of this (thanksgiving and prayer) the similar language used by Paul to the Ephesians, the Philippians, the Colossians, and the Thessalonians,—what catholic love, what all-absorbing spirituality, what impassioned devotion to the glory of Christ, what incessant transaction with Heaven about the minutest affairs of the kingdom of Christ upon earth, are thus seen to meet in this wonderful man!"—David Brown.

†Matthew Henry well remarks, "The church at Rome was then a flourishing church; but since that time, how is the gold become dim! The Epistle to the Romans is now an epistle against the Romans."

and the results were "that which is of the Spirit." The spirits
of his hearers were born again; and the Spirit witnessed to
their spirits that they were born-ones of God. Thus it was that
Paul spoke of God's "witness" to him: it was to his spirit God
witnessed. Furthermore, his serving was not by outward forms,
as in Judaism, but in intelligent service (see 12.1), that is,
knowing God and Christ directly by the Holy Ghost.

Verse 10: Paul was pleading with God to bring him, in
His good time, to these Roman Christians. His prayers,
subject to God's will, always tended to this: **unceasingly ...
always beseeching . . . to come unto you.**

Verse 11: His knowledge that he could through the marvelous message entrusted to him, **impart unto them some
spiritual gift, for their establishing,** was the root of his deep
longing to come to them. "Spiritual gift" does not refer to the
"gifts" of I Corinthians 12; but to such operation of the Holy
Spirit when Paul with his message should come among them,
as would enlarge and settle them in their faith. In the words
"some spiritual gift," "we see not only the apostle's modesty,
but an acknowledgment that the Romans were already in the
faith, together with an intimation that something was still wanting in them"—(Lange).

Paul knew that there was in him by the grace of God peculiar
apostolic power, by both his presence and the ministry of the
Word, to "impart a gift" (Greek, *charisma*), or spiritual blessing. "I know that, when I come to you, I shall come in the fulness of the blessing of Christ," he says later (15.29). So it has
been in their measure with all the great men of God, the Augus-
tines, the Chrysostoms, the Luthers, the Calvins, the Knoxes,
the great Puritans, the Wesleys, the Whitefields; and, even in
our own memory, the Finneys and Darbys and Moodys, as
well as the Torreys and the Chapmans; who, by their very
presence, through the spirit of faith that God had given them,
and through the anointing of the Spirit conferred upon them,
have in a wondrous way banished the spirit of unbelief in great
audiences; and made it easy for the saints to run rapidly in
the way of the Lord; to become, as Paul says, "mutually comforted," the preacher and the saints together, each by the other's

faith; with the result that saints became *established,* in the truth and in their walk, as they had not been before.

We today, also, have the written Word and the blessed Spirit of God. We have, in the power of that Spirit, through these wonderful epistles written direct to us, the very words and power of the apostle. As he says to the Corinthians, "For I verily, being absent in body but present in spirit, have already, as though I were present judged," etc. (5.3). For all who are willing to hearken to God, who gave Paul to be the minister of the Church, the body of Christ; and the minister of the gospel of grace and of glory,—to all, I say, who really *hearken,* Paul's voice becomes audible and intelligent.*

Here, then, is the apostle who knew the great secret, the heavenly calling of the Church, writing to the saints at Rome, who, though they were of Christ's Body, and were, therefore, heavenly,—in creation, calling, and character, did not fully know these facts,—longing to see them that he might impart unto them "some spiritual gift, for their establishing"; and, at the end of the Epistle, announcing that God is able to establish them,—but, "according to the revelation of the mystery, which had been kept in silence through aionian times, but was now manifested." (See 16.25-27.)

The burden of Paul's heart, therefore, is to make known to them this heavenly secret: that they were not connected with the earthly, the Jewish calling; but were in the Risen, Heavenly Christ; that, having died to the first Adam with his responsibilities, they were in the Second Man, the Last Adam, by divine creation; and were, therefore, heavenly. True, this heavenly truth is not fully developed in Romans, yet it was according to it that they were to be "established."

Verse 12: His coming, therefore, he says, is, **that I with you may be comforted mutually, through each other's faith, both yours and mine:** but of course their blessing

---

*We must keep the personal-letter spirit of Romans before us, if we are to be truly benefited by it. So we shall seek not only to teach doctrine with Paul, but to exhort response with him. We must not only teach, "Paul said so and so to the Roman Christians"; but, "Paul says so and so to us." And we must remember that as Paul told Timothy to teach, exhort, charge, command, rebuke, to be urgent in season and out of season,—so must we exhort, command, rebuke, who teach Paul to others.

would be unspeakably the greater, because of the mighty gift and grace God had vouchsafed to this apostle for them. Paul's way of speaking here is most humble, gentle, and persuasive.

Verse 13: **Oftentimes I purposed to come to you (and was hindered until the present time)**—He desired them to know this, for he longed for fruit in them, such as he was finding everywhere he went, among Gentiles. In this he is a perfect ambassador of Christ, longing to be used everywhere. That yearning to be used in telling the gospel lies deep in the heart of one who knows it, so if you want to hear some man of God, begin to pray God to send him to you!

As to Paul's having been "hindered" before from getting to Rome, we probably have an explanation in the course of labor that God had appointed to him: "From Jerusalem, and round about [through Asia Minor] even unto Illyricum, I have fully preached the good tidings of Christ . . . Wherefore also I was hindered these many times from coming to you: but now, having no more any place in these regions, and having these many years a longing to come unto you," etc. (15.19, 22,23). Sometimes it was Satan that hindered, (I Thess. 2.18); but here, evidently, superabundant labors, as directed of God, in other parts. Only those carrying God's message of grace to men know fully these great hindrances: the crying need of doors already open; the desperate opposition of the devil at the entrance to every door.

That I might have some fruit in you also—Paul's constant yearning was for fruit unto God in the souls of others. This must characterize all true ministers of Christ. In the degree that this yearning after fruit prevails, is the servant of God successful. "Give me Scotland or I die!" prayed John Welch, John Knox's son-in-law.

Verse 14: **To Greeks and to Barbarians both,—both to wise and foolish, I am debtor.** Greeks* were those that

---

*To the Jew the whole world was divided into Jews *(Ioudaioi)* and Greeks *(Hellenes)*, religious prerogative being taken as the line of demarkation. To the Greek and the Roman the world was similarly divided into Greeks *(Hellenes)* and Barbarians *(Barbaroi)*, civilization and culture being now the criterion of distinction."—(Lightfoot.)

spoke the Greek language and had the Greek culture, which had covered Alexander's world-wide empire; and in which culture the Romans themselves gloried. "Barbarians" were those not knowing Greek, and thus "uncultured." So also the "Scythians" (Col. 3.11) were the especially wild and savage,—as we say, "Tartars."

"Wise and foolish" is more personal, not meaning merely educated and uneducated, but of all degrees of intelligence. Since Paul is debtor to all, he is enumerating all. And he must begin to pay his debt by setting forth the guilt of all; which he does (1.18 to 3.20).

In the words "I am debtor" we have the steward's consciousness,—of being the trusted bearer of tidings of infinite importance directly from heaven; and Paul was "debtor" to all classes. He does not here mention Jews, because, although full of longing toward them, he had been sent distinctly to Gentiles: "The Gentiles unto whom I send thee, to open their eyes," etc., (Acts 26.17). How different Paul's spirit here from that of Moses in the wilderness among murmuring Israel!

> "And Moses said unto Jehovah . . . Have I conceived all this people? have I brought them forth, that Thou shouldst say unto me, Carry them in thy bosom, as a nursing father carrieth the sucking child, unto the land which Thou swarest unto their fathers? . . . I am not able to bear all this people alone, because it is too heavy for me. And if Thou deal thus with me, kill me, I pray thee, out of hand, if I have found favor in Thy sight; and let me not see my wretchedness" (Num. 11.11-15).

We must remember that Moses, beloved faithful servant of God, walked under law. The ninetieth Psalm is the very expression of the forty years in the Wilderness:

> "All our days are passed away in thy wrath:
> We bring our years to an end as a sigh,
> For we are consumed in thine anger,
> And in thy wrath are we troubled.
> Thou hast set our iniquities before Thee,
> Our secret sins in the light of Thy countenance."

But here is Paul, gladly a "debtor" to all, with a message of glorious grace: "God was in Christ reconciling the world unto Himself, not reckoning unto them their trespasses"; "Christ gave Himself a ransom for all"; Christ "tasted death for every man." And not only this, but the hope of the heavenly calling is set before earthly men. We are here seeing "less than the least of all saints," the most wonderful servant God ever had, willing to "become all things to all men to gain some!" But remember, it is not a wonderful *man* speaking, but *Christ in Paul* (Gal. 1.16). Our Lord said of His own ministry: "The Father abiding in me doeth His works." And so of the ministry of the Lord's chief servant!

Now when Paul proclaims himself a "debtor," what does he mean by this word? Was he a debtor in any different sense from what other and all Christians are? For we are all Christ's "witnesses." Let us see.

When Moses had received the tables written with the finger of God, and the pattern of the Tabernacle for Israel, he was bound, he was a debtor, both to God and to Israel, to deliver those tables and that pattern, as given to him by God. To Paul, the risen, glorified Christ Himself had given the gospel by especial "revelation" (Gal. 1.11,12) ; and Paul, as we know, was especially to go to the Gentiles, (as Peter, James and John were to go to the circumcision). Just as definitely as Moses received the Law for Israel, so Paul received the gospel for us, and he was a *debtor,* both to God and to us, till he had that gospel committed to all. How unutterably sad to find many professing Christians shutting their doors in the face of Paul as he comes to pay his debt,—comes to tell them the glories of the heavenly message given to him,—the unsearchable riches of Christ! In his last epistle Paul mourns that "all that are in Asia"—of which Ephesus was the capital!—"turned away from *me.*" So soon! (II Tim. 1.15).

Verse 15: **So to my very uttermost I am eager to preach the good news to you also in Rome**—How blessed is the readiness, yea, eagerness, of this holy apostle to pay his debt, to preach the good tidings to those also in Rome. Rome despised the Jews, and Paul was "little of stature," with "weak" bodily presence; and with "speech," or, as we say, "delivery," "of no account" in the proud carnal opinion of men (II Cor. 10.10). Moreover, he would be opposed by any Jews of wealth or influence in Rome. Furthermore, Rome was the center of the Gentile world: its emperors were soon to demand—and receive—worship; it was crowded with men of learning and culture from the whole world; it had mighty marchings;—great triumphal processions flowed through its streets. Rome shook the world.

Yet here is Paul, utterly weak in himself, and with his physical thorn; yet ready, eager, to go to *Rome!*

And to preach,—what? A Christ that the Jewish nation had themselves officially rejected, a Christ who had been despised and crucified at their cries,—by a Roman governor! To preach a Way that the Jews in Rome would tell Paul was "everywhere spoken against" (Acts 28.22).

Talk of your brave men, your great men, O world! Where in all history can you find one like Paul? Alexander, Caesar, Napoleon, marched with the protection of their armies to enforce their will upon men. Paul was eager to march with Christ alone to the center of this world's greatness entrenched under Satan, with "the Word of the cross," which he himself says is "to Jews, an offence; and to Gentiles, foolishness."

Yes, and when he does go to Rome, it is as a shipwrecked (though Divinely delivered) *prisoner.* Oh, what a story! There, "for two whole years" in his own "hired dwelling" he receives "all that go in unto him" (for he cannot go to them); and the message goes on and on, throughout the Roman Empire, and even into Caesar's household!

And what is the secret of this unconquerable heart? Hear Paul: "Ye seek a proof of *Christ* that speaketh in me." "To me, to live is *Christ";* "It was the good pleasure of God to *reveal His Son in me";* "By the *grace of God* I am what I am"; "I labor, striving *according to Christ's working, who worketh in me mightily";* "I am ready to spend and be spent out (R.V., marg.) for your souls." There was no other path for Christ, nor is there any other for us His servants, but, "as much as in me is," "to my utmost." Those who belong in Paul's company are ever "assaying to go" (Acts 16.7), ever "ready"—to preach or to suffer (Acts 21.13).

16   For I am not ashamed 'of the gospel: for it is the power of God unto salvation to every one that believeth: to the Jew first, and also to the Greek.

17   For God's righteousness on the principle of faith to [such as have] faith is revealed in it [the gospel] : just as it is written, "The righteous on the principle of faith shall live."

Here we have the *text* of the whole Epistle of Romans: First, the words "the gospel"—so dear to Paul, as will appear. Next, the universal saving power of this gospel is asserted. Then, the secret of the gospel's power—the revelation of God's righteousness on the principle of faith. Finally, the accord of all this with the Old Testament Scriptures: "The righteous shall live by faith."

It will assist our study to notice at once the four **"For"**s in the apostle's argument: **"For** I am not ashamed of the gospel,"* **"For** it is the power of God unto salvation," **"For** a righteousness of God is revealed in it"; and the "for" of the next verse, which makes this gospel necessary: **"For** the wrath of God is revealed against all ungodliness, and unrighteousness of men."

Verse 16: **For I am not ashamed of the gospel**—First then, we have Paul's willingness, all unashamed, to go to Rome, mistress of the world, with this astonishing message of a crucified Nazarene, despised by Jews, and put to death by Romans. "The inherent glory of the message of the gospel, as God's life-giving message to a dying world, so filled Paul's soul, that, like his blessed Master, he 'despised the shame.' " So, pray God, may all of us!

---

*"All philosophy is a perfect delusion; intellect has nothing to do with God at all. Faith is never in the intellect; and, what is more, the intellect never knows a truth. Truth is not the object of intellect, but of testimony. This is where the difference lies. You tell me something and I believe you, but the thing that receives truth (on a testimony) is not intellect. Real intelligence of God is in the conscience. The mind is incapable of forming an idea of God, and that is where the philosophers have all gone wrong."—*This word by Mr. Darby is the very truth!*

For it is the power of God unto salvation—The second "For" gives the reason for Paul's boldness: this good news concerning Christ's death, burial, resurrection, and appearing, "is the power of God unto salvation unto every one that believeth." There is no fact for a preacher or teacher to hold more constantly in his mind than this. It is not the "excellency of speech or wisdom," or the "personal magnetism," or "earnestness," of the preacher; any more than it is the deep repentance or earnest prayers of the hearer, that avails. But it is the *message of Christ crucified, dead, buried, and risen,* which, being believed, is "the power of God"! "The word* of the cross is to them that are perishing, foolishness; but unto us who are being saved it *(the word of the cross)* IS the power of God" (I Cor. 1.18).

Again we repeat that it is of the very first and final importance that the preacher or teacher of the gospel believe in the bottom of his soul that the simple story, Christ died for our sins, was buried, hath been raised from the dead the third day, and was seen, IS THE POWER OF GOD to salvation to every one who rests in it,—who *believes!*

The word gospel *(evaggelion),* means good news, glad tidings, —of course, about love and grace in giving Christ; and Christ's blessed finished work for the sinner, putting away sin on the Cross. (There is no other *good* news for a sinner!)

The other word, for "preached," is *kerusso,* which properly means to proclaim as a herald, to publish. And if we would understand Paul's attitude in preaching the good news, we must not forget what he says in I Cor. 1.21: The reading in I Corinthians 1.21 should be, "God was pleased through the fool-

---

*Notice, it is *not the cross.* Romanists put the cross on the top of the cathedral; millions wear a figure of the cross around their necks; but they may never have heard "the *word* of the cross." As Paul says further in I Corinthians 1.23, "We preach Christ crucified, [not the cross, merely] unto Jews a stumbling block, and unto Gentiles foolishness; but unto them that are saved, both Jews and Greeks, Christ the power of God and the wisdom of God."

As one has said,

> "Not to Thy cross, but to Thyself,
>   My living Savior, would I cling!
> 'Twas Thou, and not Thy cross, that bore
>   My soul's dark guilt, sin's deadly sting.

> "A Christless cross no refuge were for me;
> A crossless Christ my Savior could not be:
> But, O CHRIST CRUCIFIED, I rest in *Thee!*"

ishness of the *proclaiming* to save them that believe." The word *(kērusso)* means, to announce as a herald, to proclaim. It does not carry the thought of the proclamation's content, of a glad message, as does the other word *(evangelidzo)*. Therefore God selects the word *kērusso* to show in the great message I Corinthians 1.18-25 how he absolutely passes by the intellect of man, and sets aside all his possible reasoning, ability, philosophy and wisdom—in this amazing way: "by the proclaiming"! Here comes a small and weak Jew upon the assembly of the earth's "wise" at Mars' hill: "proclaiming Jesus and the resurrection." It is "foolishness" to them. Yet "certain men"—including *one* Mars' hill philosopher, and a prominent woman, and others with them, cleave unto him and believe the proclamation, and will spend eternity with God.

No; when you reflect on God's plan of *proclamation*—of Christ, dead, buried, raised, living: it does get right past everything of man. A herald—he does not stop to argue—he has a message; yonder he is; here he comes; yonder he goes—and the message is left. Man is set aside!

It pleased God through the proclaiming to save them that believe! Praise God! Anyone can hear good news!

Therefore the herald does not hearken either to "Jews," who would say, "We have wonderful forms of religion; we have a great temple!" No, the herald proclaims "a Messiah crucified" by these very Jews!—and passes on!

Nor does he hearken to the "disputers of this age"—the "wise," who call to him, "We have a new philosophy to discuss —let us hear *your* philosophical system." No; he proclaims a crucified, dead, buried and risen Son of God, and passes on. And as many as are ordained to eternal life will believe. All others are offended, or stirred to ridicule.

Paul's preaching was not, as is so much today, general disquisition on some subject, but *definite statements about the crucified One,* as he himself so insistently tells us in I Corinthians 15.3-5.

"The power of God unto salvation" is a wonderful revelation! As Chrysostom says, "There is a power of God unto punishment, unto destruction: 'Fear him who is able to destroy both soul and body in hell' " (Matt. 10.28). "The use of the word 'power' here, as in I Corinthians 1.24, carries a superlative sense, —the highest and holiest vehicle of divine power" (Alford). This story of Christ's dying for our sins, buried, raised, manifested, is the great wire along which runs God's mighty current of saving power. Beware lest you be putting up some little wire of your own, unconnected with the Divine throne, and therefore non-saving to those to whom you speak. T. DeWitt Talmadge said at the funeral of Alfred Cookman, one of the most holy, devoted men of God America has known, "Strike a circle of three feet around the cross of Jesus, and you have all there was of Alfred Cookman."

The gospel "is the power of God unto *salvation.*" God does not say, unto reformation, education, progress, nor development; nor "fanning an innate flame." Salvation is a word for a lost man, and for none other. Men are involved either in salvation, or in its opposite, perdition (Phil. 1.28).

To the Jew first and also to the Greek—The Jew had the Law. They had the temple, with its divinely prescribed worship. Heretofore, if a Gentile were to be saved, let him become a proselyte and come to Jerusalem to worship as did the Ethiopian eunuch. Christ came "to His own things" (John 1.11), to Jerusalem, to His Father's house (literally, "the things of My Father"). The apostles were to be witnesses—beginning *from* Jerusalem (Luke 24.47). The Holy Spirit fell upon the hundred and twenty at Jerusalem. Upon the persecution that arose in Jerusalem from Stephen, the disciples "were all scattered abroad throughout the regions of Judaea and Samaria, except the apostles," but Jerusalem was the gospel's first center, then Antioch in Syria, whence Paul and Barnabas, afterwards Paul and Silas, went forth. Afterwards, the center of God's operations was Ephesus, the capital of proconsular Asia, where after being rejected by the Jews in many cities, Paul separates the disciples, and all distinction between Jew and Greek in the assemblies of the saints is gone. Then he goes to Jerusalem to be finally and officially rejected—killed, if it were possible. God waits two years at Caesarea for Jewish repentance: there is none, but the direct opposite. Then the apostle, having been driven into the hands of the Romans by the Jews goes to Rome, the world's center, only to have the Jews reject his teaching (Acts 28). Thereupon it is announced: "Be it known therefore unto you, that this salvation of God is sent unto the Gentiles: they will also hear."

Therefore, in expressing **to the Jew first,** Paul is not at all prescribing an order of presentation of the gospel throughout this dispensation. He is simply recognizing the fact that to the Jew, who had the Law and Divine privileges, the gospel offer had first been presented, and then to the Gentile. As Paul says in Ephesians "And He came and preached peace to you that were far off [the Gentile], and peace to them that were nigh [the Jews]" (Eph. 2.17). We might just as sensibly claim that Ephesians 2.17 gives Gentiles priority because they are mentioned first—"you that were afar" over the Jews who were mentioned last,—"them that were nigh."

To claim that the gospel must be preached first to the Jew throughout this dispensation, is utterly to deny God's Word that there is now no distinction between Jew and Greek either as to the fact of sin (Rom. 3.22) or the availability of salvation (Rom. 10.12). Paul's words in Galatians 4.12 are wholly meaningless if the Jews still have a special place.

The meaning of the word "first" (*prōton*) is seen in verse 8 of our chapter: "First, I thank my God through Jesus Christ for you all." That is, thanksgiving to God was the first thing Paul wrote to the Romans in this Epistle. Then he proceeds to other things. It is an order of sequence; just as the gospel came "first" to the Jew and then to Greek, and now, since the "no difference" fact, is proclaimed to all indiscriminately, Jews and Greeks.

Verse 17: **For God's righteousness on the principle of faith to** [such as have] **faith is revealed in it** [the gospel] **: just as it is written, "The righteous on the principle of faith shall live."**

This third "For" gives another reason why Paul was not ashamed of the good news*: in this message concerning God's Son,—that He died for our sins, was buried, was raised,—there was brought to light,—made manifest—a righteousness of God which had indeed been prophesied, but was really (especially to the Jew under law) absolute *news*:† God acting in righteousness, as we shall find, wholly on the basis of Christ's atoning work,—to be believed in, rested upon, apart from all human works whatever. It was **on the principle of faith**‡ by means of a message, and those exercising faith in the message would be reckoned righteous,—apart from all "merit" or "works" whatever. This is the meaning of "from faith unto faith"—literally, **out of faith** [rather than works] **unto** [those who have] **faith.**

The "For" of verse 17, **For God's righteousness therein is revealed**—in the gospel,—is also a logical setting forth of

*In these days of "respectable" Christianity, with its great cathedrals, churches, denominations, colleges, seminaries, "uplift movements," etc., you may say, Men no longer have any temptation to be "ashamed of the gospel." But lo, and behold, it is not the *gospel* they preach; but a man-reforming, world-mending message of fallen flesh! Who today preaches the wrath of God? But Paul speaks of wrath twelve times in Romans, and says: "If God visit not with wrath, He cannot be the Judge of the world." Who preaches of the awful things we are about to find true of the Gentile world in the end of this chapter? Who preaches, that even among the moral philosophers, the "better" classes (in the first part of Ch. 2); or the "religious" world as represented by the Jew (last part of Ch. 2); or in the whole world (3.10-20), that *"none* is righteous," *"none* doeth good"? Who preaches that the *whole world* is under the Divine sentence of guilt, and that *no man* is able to put this guilt away? that the shed blood of Christ as the vicarious sacrifice for human guilt is *absolutely the only hope of man?* Who preaches this, today? *Here and there, one!* It is blessed for you, brother, if you are preaching the gospel Paul preached, and are not ashamed thereof! It is blessed if you are not sucking the poison-honey of Modernism; nor allured by earth's Kagawas into the fool's paradise of the "social-gospellers"; nor deceived by the Neo-Romanists,—the Man-Confessionalists, the Buchmanites (falsely called the "Oxford Movement"). Better be in prison with Paul, *with Paul's gospel!*

†Note, it is the righteousness of God, not the righteousness of Christ. It is God's acting righteously upon the basis of Christ's redeeming work.

‡A word concerning the preposition *ek* as used in verse 17, "a righteousness of God from *(ek)* faith," etc., or "faithwise." There has been much objection to the translation of *ek* by "on the principle of"; yet that is about the expression nearest to the truth of any we have found, unless it be "faithwise." Literally, *ek* means *out of*, or *from*. We ourselves use "out of" thus: "He acted *out of prudence*,"—(as animated by that principle) or, "He *gave out of kindness.*"

But it is of imperative importance that we get the great fact quickly and forever fixed in our hearts that God declares men righteous not by faith as the procuring cause, for the blood of Christ was that; not by faith as the putting forth of a certain faculty innate in man, much less by the keeping of divine commands, however holy and just; but out of *reliance upon His own word as true,* and on that alone.

the reason why the good news concerning Christ's death, burial, and resurrection is the power of God unto salvation. And this verse is the essence of the text of the whole Epistle: "Therein God's righteousness is revealed."

God could have come forth in righteousness and smitten with doom the whole Adamic race. He would have been acting in accordance with His holiness: it would have been "the righteousness of God" unto judgment, and would have been just.

But God, who is love, though infinitely holy and sin-hating, has chosen to act toward us in righteousness, in a manner wherein all His holy and righteous claims against the sinner have been satisfied upon a Substitute, His own Son. Therefore, in this good news, (1) Christ died for our sins according to the Scriptures, (2) He was buried, (3) He hath been raised the third day according to the Scriptures, (4) He was manifested (I Cor. 15.3 ff),—in this good news there is revealed, now openly for the first time, God's righteousness on the principle of faith. We simply hear and believe: and, as we shall find, God reckons us righteous; our guilt having been put away by the blood of Christ forever, and we ourselves declared to be the righteousness of God in Him!

Habakkuk prophesied of it (Paul quotes him in verse 17); but ah, how little he dreamed of the fulness and wonder of it! It is the *gospel* that brings these to light!

And now in the next section (verses 18 ff) will come Paul's fourth "For": showing man's frightful state of guilt; and his need of the gospel:

18   For there is revealed God's wrath from heaven
      upon all ungodliness and unrighteousness of men,
      who hold down the truth in unrighteousness [of
19   life]; because that which is known of God is man-
      ifest in them; for God made it evident to them.
20   For the invisible things of Him from the creation of
      the world, made known to the mind by the things
      that are made, are clearly perceived,—both His
      eternal power and divinity; so as to render them

21   inexcusable: because, though knowing God, they did not glorify [Him] as God, nor were they thankful [towards Him]; but became vain in their reasonings, and their senseless heart was darkened.
22   Professing themselves to be wise, they became
23   fools, and changed the glory of the incorruptible God for the likeness of an image of corruptible man, and of birds, and of quadrupeds, and of creeping things.

It will not only fail to help us, but will seriously harm us, to study the awful arraignment of God against human sin, unless we apply it to ourselves, thereby discovering *our own state by nature*. Therefore we have sought to make plain these terms which Paul uses, in view of today's sin. Christendom is rapidly losing sin-consciousness, which means losing God-consciousness; which means eternal doom: "As were the days of Noah . . . as it came to pass in the days of Lot . . . they *knew not.*" Because iniquity abounds, the love of many professing Christians is waxing cold; so that we see a Sardis condition everywhere, "a name to live, while dead": on many faces, the horrid lack of spiritual life; the lightless, sightless eyes; the chill,—the corpse-like chill, of the lifeless, the unfeeling.

On the other hand, among God's real saints, those born from above and indwelt by the Spirit of God, there is everywhere, thank God, a gathering, an eagerness, a hunger for His Word, for news from Home,—for their citizenship is in Heaven!

Therefore let all who have ears to hear give the utmost attention to what God says about our state by nature. Do not apply the threefold "God gave them up" of Romans One to "the heathen," as most do. Behold, *we* are those of whom God says: "There is no distinction: all sinned and fall short of the glory of God." ALL are brought under the judgment of God. O saints, beware of the "select" circles, the "we-are-better" societies of pride! For all human beings are alike sinners: for "The Scripture *shut up all things under sin,* that the promise by faith in Jesus Christ might be given to them that *believe*" (Gal. 3.22).

The more you discover yourself to be a common sinner, the more you will realize God's uncommon grace! And the more deeply you despair of man, of *yourself,* the more simple and easy it will be to rest in Christ and in His work of salvation for you.

Verse 18: **Wrath revealed from heaven**—This is the tenor of all Scripture as to God's attitude toward defiant sin. "Jehovah rained upon Sodom and upon Gomorrah brimstone and fire from Jehovah out of heaven," we read in Genesis 19.24. We know that "God has appointed a day in which He will judge the world" (Acts 17.31) ; that He will "visit with wrath" at that time (Rom. 3.5).

However, in the thrice-repeated "God gave them over" of verses 24, 26 and 28, there is to be seen the character, the beginning, and the working of God's wrath *in this world,* in His judicial handing over of rebels to go further into rebellion. But the awful arraignment of humanity in Chapters One, Two, and Three ; together with the particular account of their apostasy and lost condition, however terrible it be, is not a description of the finally damned, but of the at-present-lost : and, "The Son of man came to seek and to save that which was lost." "Such were some of you," says Paul to the Corinthians, after an enumeration of those who "shall not inherit the kingdom of God" (I Cor. 6.11). "Effeminate, and abusers of themselves with men," the very kind of sinners described in our chapter, are in this enumeration. Let us admit, therefore, the judicial "delivering over" of humanity which has "exchanged the glory" of the God they knew for horrid idolatrous conceptions,—a present judicial action of God on earth, where and when He "lets men go their own way." But let us distinguish this apart from the day of the revelation of the righteous judgment of God from Heaven. At the Great White Throne of Revelation Twenty there will be no liberty left to the creature to indulge his lusts as in this present world. The lusts, indeed, will remain, and probably intensify forever : "He that is filthy, let him be made filthy yet more" ; but the ability to indulge lust will be eternally removed, and the damned placed under the visitation of Divine anger.

Thank God, we may still cry with Paul, "Now is the accept-able time; now is the day of salvation!" Grace is still ready to reach the worst wretch on earth!

Note that **ungodliness** is direct *disregard of God,* which to the Jew would connect itself with the first table of the Law, the first four commandments; while **unrighteousness** has reference to *wickedness of conduct,* in itself and toward other men. Note further that it is distinctly said that the human race, in order to live an unrighteous life, **held down the truth.** The meaning of the verb translated "hold down" is seen in its use in II Thessa-lonians 2.6: "Ye know that which *restraineth,*" referring to the present restraining of the sin and wrath of man by the Spirit of God. It is also true, turning this about, that man in his wicked-ness restrains the truth he knows. (See also same word in Luke 4.42, "would have *stayed* Him.") Almost all men know more truth than they obey. They call themselves "truth seekers"; but would they attend a meeting where Paul preached the facts of this first of Romans?

Verse 19: **That which is known of God is manifest . . . God made it evident**—Noah's father, Lamech, was for over fifty years a contemporary of Adam. Knowledge of God was held and imparted by tradition from the beginning. The fact that the "world that then was" became so corrupt as to necessi-tate destruction (Hebrew, "blotting out," Gen. 6.7, margin), only supports the awful account. Not only was the world bad unto judgment at the time of the Flood; but the world after Noah became such that God called out His own (from Abraham on) to a separate, pilgrim life. Sodom, and later the Canaanites, again filled up iniquity's measure and were "sent away from off the face of the earth" (Jer. 28.16). Utter uncompromising, abandonment of hope in *man* is the first preliminary to under-standing or preaching the gospel. Man says, "I am not so bad; I can make amends"; "There are many people worse than I am"; "I might be better, but I might be worse." But God's indict-ment is sweeping: it reaches all. "None righteous; all have sinned; there is no distinction." And the first step of wisdom is to listen to the worst God says about us, for He (wonderful to say!) is the Lover of man, sinner though man be. You and

I were born in this lost race, with all these evil things innate in, and, apart from the grace of God, possible to us. "The heart is deceitful above all things, and is desperately wicked." Only redemption by the blood of Christ, and regeneration by the Holy Spirit, can afford hope.

Verse 20: **For the invisible things of Him from the creation of the world . . . are clearly perceived**—"The heavens declare the glory of God." But humanity today prefers Hollywood's "sound-pictures" to seeing the "things" of the glorious God in the heavens,—beholding His works, and hearing their speech. How long since you have gone out and gazed at moon and stars, made by the blessed God, travelling in such quiet glory, beauty, power, and order? Men know, if they care to know, that an infinite Majesty made and controls this. **Even His eternal power and divinity***—Paul connects the observing of the mighty and beautiful things of the universe with the consciousness of a personal God.† Human science, through its telescope,

---

**Divinity (theiotēs)*—what pertains to God; rather than *deity (theotēs)*—"the state of being God":—the Godhead. That there is divinity, men know from creation; God,—the Godhead, *Deity,* is known by His saints.

†We cannot refrain from quoting here Joseph Addison's beautiful hymn. Would that it were widely learned and sung today!

> The spacious firmament on high,
> With all the blue ethereal sky,
> And spangled heavens, a shining frame,
> Their great Original proclaim.
> The unwearied sun, from day to day,
> Doth his Creator's power display,
> And publishes to every land,
> The work of an Almighty Hand.
>
> Soon as the evening shades prevail,
> The moon takes up the wondrous tale,
> And nightly to the listening earth
> Repeats the story of her birth;
> Whilst all the stars that round her burn,
> And all the planets in their turn,
> Confirm the tidings as they roll,
> And spread the truth from pole to pole.
>
> What though in solemn silence all
> Move round this dark terrestrial ball?
> What though no real voice nor sound
> Amidst their radiant orbs be found?
> In reason's ear they all rejoice,
> And utter forth a glorious voice:
> Forever singing, as they shine,
> "The Hand that made us is Divine."

observes the vast courses of the stars, moving with amazing accuracy in their orbits, but often counts it a mark of wisdom to doubt whether an intelligent Being exists at all! But, "the undevout astronomer is *mad*," as said the great Kepler. No really *great* scientist today supports the Darwinian theory; and many,—and some of the most prominent scientific men are saying, There *must* be a God, a Creator.*

Next the reason for God's wrath is stated: men are **without excuse**—Men had the light, and that from God. His eternal power and divinity were, from creation onward, plain to men, from His works. Napoleon, on a warship in the Mediterranean on a star-lit night, passed a group of his officers who were mocking at the idea of a God. He stopped, and sweeping his hand toward the stars, said, "Gentlemen, you must get rid of those first!" Men secretly believe there is a Power above them, and that their evil deeds deserve the wrath of that Power. In sudden peril, they scream like the guilty wretches they are, "God have mercy!" Knowledge of God, though not acquaintanceship with Him, lay behind Pharaoh's words, "I have sinned against Jehovah and against you" (Ex. 10.16); and behind the words of the Philistines in I Samuel 4.7,8, and 5.7,8,11; and the proclamation of the King of Nineveh (Jonah 3.7-9).

Verse 21: **Because that, though knowing God, they did not glorify Him as God, nor were they thankful**—Every human being knows he ought to give his being over to his Creator's worship and glory, and ought to be continually thankful for life itself, and for its blessings; but men refused both worship and gratitude: they became godless and thankless. But they could not free themselves thus easily from conscience and terrors: so came on *idolatry*. First they resorted to vain speculations and "reasonings," to escape the thought of God and duty. Then the judicial result: as Alford well renders, "Their heart (the whole inner man, the seat of knowledge and feeling), became dark (lost the little light it had), and wandered blindly

*Read *Does Science Support Evolution?* by Dr. E. Ralph Hooper, for many years Demonstrator of Anatomy at the University of Toronto (The Defender Publishers, Wichita, Kansas, U. S. A.; 50 cents). It gives an astonishing amount of accurate testimony.

in the mazes of folly." Think of a whole race of created beings
knowing, but refusing to recognize, their Creator! of their eating from His hand daily, but refusing even one thanksgiving!
Yet such ungodly ones, such unthankful ones, are all about you,
now.

Verse 22: **Professing themselves to be wise, they became
fools**—Rejecting the light of God's knowledge in their consciences, men now arrogated to themselves wisdom, and became
—what? *Fools!** "The fear of the Lord is the beginning"—of
both knowledge and wisdom (Prov. 1.7; 9.10; 15.33; Ps.
111.10; Job 28.28).

The silliness of these "modern" shallow-pan days! How men
are rushing back to the old pagan pit out of which God's Word
and His gospel would have delivered them! They suck up sin;
they welter in wickedness; they profess to be wise! They sit at
the feet of "professors" whose breath is spiritual cyanide. They
idolize the hog-sty doctrines of a rotten Freud:† and count
themselves "wise"! They say, "God is not a person; men
evolved from monkeys; morals are mere old habits; self-
enjoyment, self-expression, indulgence of all desires—this," they
say, "is the path of wisdom." It is the path of those who go
quickly down to the pit and on to judgment! The very morals
of Sodom, as our Lord foretold, are rushing fast upon us, and
God will bring again the awful doom of Sodom (Luke
17.28-31).

Now if someone objects, saying, This is a strange introduc-
tion to the gospel of God's *grace,* we answer, It lies here before
us, this awful indictment of Romans One, and cannot be evaded!
Moreover, until man knows his state of sin, he wants no grace.
Shall pardon be spoken of before the sinner is proved a sinner?
While the evidence is being brought in, the whole attention of

---

*"Fools": "This is Paul, the writer's (that is, to say God's) estimate of the
philosophers and religious leaders of the race. Paul knew the boasted wisdom of
the Euphrates and of the Nile, the learning of Hellas, and of Rome. We know it
today. But there is this difference: there are those in our time who see no generic
difference between these ethnic sages and the prophets of God, while Paul declares
the former to be but 'fools'."—(Stifler).

†*Crucifying Christ in Our Colleges,* by Dan Gilbert, shows the monstrous doctrines of this evil "educator," whose influence is so great with many colleges and
universities in the United States today. May God keep Freud's filthy feet from our
shores!

the court is upon *that*. If the evidence of guilt be insufficient or inconclusive, there is no necessity for a pardon!

Preachers and teachers have soft-pedalled sin, until the fear of God is vanishing away. McCheyne used to say, "A holy minister is an awful weapon in the hands of God." But a preacher who avoids telling men the truth about their sin as here revealed, is the best tool of the devil.

Verse 23: **And changed the glory of the incorruptible God** —Incorruptibility is of the essence of God's being. From the beginningless eternity past to the endless eternity to come, He is the glorious self-existent One. Now came the high insult: having rejected knowledge of God, but unable to escape the consciousness that He exists, men, like Israel later, "changed their glory for the likeness of an ox that eateth grass" (Ps. 106.20). The more you reflect upon the infinite glory and majesty of the eternal God, the more hideous will the unspeakable insult to Him of any kind of idolatry appear to you! Men first likened God to man; but, being given over, they rushed rapidly downwards: a bird, a quadruped; and finally, a reptile!

Vincent remarks "Deities of human form prevailed in Greece; those of bestial form in Egypt; and both methods of worship were practiced in Rome. See on Acts 7.41. Serpent-worship was common in Chaldaea, and also in Egypt, where the asp was sacred." Israel evidently learned calf-worship from Egypt's sacred bull. .

24 Wherefore God gave them over in the lusts of their hearts unto uncleanness, so that their bodies were dishonored among themselves:—such ones as
25 they! who changed the truth of God into the lie! and worshipped and served the created thing rather than the Creator,—Who is blessed unto the ages! Amen.

26   On account of this, God gave them over to
      shameful passions: for their females* changed the
27   natural use into that contrary to nature: and in
      like manner also the males* having left the natural
      use of the females, were inflamed in their lust one
      toward another, males with males working out
      shame, and receiving in themselves the recompense
      of their error which was due.

Verse 24: **God gave them over in the lusts of their hearts.**
This is deeper than the mere lusts of the flesh. Flesh has natural
desires, which may or may not be yielded to. The lusts of the
heart continue after the flesh is dissolved; and even when, in
the tormented bodies of the damned, the lusts of the flesh cannot be conscious or controlling, "the lusts of the heart" will
forever exist.

Notice that when man is delivered from Divine restraint,
the lusts of his heart plunge him into ever deeper bodily
uncleanness, and bodily vileness. History backs up this fact
with terrible relentlessness. What an answer is here to all the
boasting of proud men of a "principle of development" in man;
to the lying claim that man is ever "making progress." The
"Golden Age" of Grecian literature, and that of Roman letters,—in both of them we find remarkable minds; but their
works must be expurgated for decent readers! No printer, even
in this corrupt age, would dare to publish books with literal
descriptions of the orgies of "classical" days.

Verse 25: **For they changed the truth of God into the
lie**—That God is glorious, incorruptible, infinite, is the
truth; that any image whatsoever, be it gold, silver, wood, stone;
picture or symbol, is God,—God here names this *the lie!*† Any

---

*The Greek words used here are not the noble ones meaning *men* and *women;*
but those denoting sex only, as in lower creatures. (For many examples, see *thēleiai*
and *arsenes* in Liddell and Scott's Lexicon.) This passage has deep significance in
this day of the "sex-craze": when, as some one says, "Human beings seem to be just
beginning to realize that they are male and female." The first of Romans warns of
what such a craze will end in!

†The expression in II Thess. 2.11 is exactly the same: God sends them who refuse
the love of the truth "a working of error, that they should believe *the lie*": in this
final case it is the apotheosis of idolatry,—Satan's false Christ, the Antichrist, himself a lost *man,* whom they worship!

such thing, connected with worship, is a fearful travesty of the Divine Majesty. Think of it! They **worshipped and served the created thing rather than the Creator**—who *made* the creature! This is that desperate hiding away from God by wicked-hearted man, called idolatry. (See Appendix III in the author's "Book of the Revelation.")* **Who is blessed unto the ages. Amen.** Paul's adding these humble, worshipful words after "Creator" both glorifies God and also differentiates Paul from the abandoned devotees of sin thronging the dark alley of human history; showing him to be a child of light, as is every real saint of God, though passing through a world of thick darkness.

Verse 26: For the second time we read, **God gave them over**—and now, **unto shameful passions**—There are natural and normal appetites of the body: God is not speaking of these, or even of the abuse of these,—adultery or harlotry—in this verse. He is describing that state of unnatural appetites in which all normal instincts are left behind. And it is significant, that, as originally woman took the lead in sin, so here!

Verse 27: Here men are seen visited with a like condign, judicial "giving up" by God, in which they forget not only the holy relations of marriage, but even the burnings of ordinary lust, and plunge into nameless horrors of unnatural lust-bondage, all, males and females, **receiving in themselves the due recompense of their error.** Compare "among themselves" of verse 24, with "in themselves" of verse 27: "These words bring out," as Godet remarks, "the depth of the blight. It is visible to the eyes of all." And Meyer also: "The law of history, in virtue of which the forsaking of God is followed among men by a parallel growth of immorality, is not a purely natural order of things; the *power of God* is active in the execution of this law."

---

*There is no Scripture record of idolatry before the Flood. The solemn presence of the Cherubim at the gate of Eden, probably continued long. Sin was increasing, but the Spirit was striving with man (Gen. 6.3). Then the 120 years passed; man was given up and the Deluge-judgment came. After the Deluge, came Nimrod, son of Cush (hence Bar-Cush, which becomes Bacchus), and the Satan-invented plan of idols to obscure God,—by demons (I Cor. 10.20). God permitted this as a judgment on a race that did not desire knowledge of Him.

What a fearful account is here! A lost race plunging ever deeper, by their own desire! Left in shameful, horrid bondage, unashamed,—not only *im*moral, but *un*moral, hideous. Missionaries abroad can tell you of what they find; as can the Christian workers in our great cities. But you would be unprepared to believe what exists, in the private lives of many, even in country districts through Christendom. And if God has "made you to differ," thank Him only! It will not do to hold up your hands in self-righteous dismay, and say, These verses do not in any particular describe me. For God will show you and me that this is exactly the race as we were born into it, and out of which the only rescue is being *born again*. All these things pertain to lost, fallen man. Man is a tenant of the earth only by Divine grace, since the Deluge.*

28 And just as they did not approve to have God in [their] knowledge, God gave them over to a mind disapproved [of Him],—to practise things not be-
29 fitting [His creatures]; having become filled with all injustice, destructiveness, covetousness, malice; full of envy, murder, strife, guile, malignant
30 subtlety; secret slanderers, open slanderers, hateful to God, insolent, arrogant, boasters, inventors of

---

*Few, perhaps, realize what is going on right here in America (not Russia) in these last days. Read these two extracts:

From *Children of the Jungle,* by Thos. Minbaugh, Prof. of Sociology, University of Minnesota. (Reprinted in Reader's Digest, 1935):

"Child tramps learn all about life—and who can do that and ignore sex? More and more girls are following their brethren on the bum; about one tribe in ten has female members. About one child tramp in 20 is a girl, disguised usually in breeches, but just as appallingly homeless as the boys, and young—under twenty. They live in the jungles and box-cars, serving as mistresses and maids, sharing the joys and sorrows of life on the roads. They treat all boys and men alike; the girls are available to any and all in the camp. Occasionally a pair of girls travel with a gang for weeks; others prefer variety. They go from jungle to jungle without discrimination; they know they will be welcome."

From *The Disinherited,* by J. Pegano, Scribner's, also reprinted in Reader's Digest:

"I visited the 'jungle,' a mile or so out of town. All men who are 'on the bum' have a certain similarity—a lean and sullen look. [Describes some] . . . and a hatchet-faced man whom I recognized to be what is known among men on the bum, as a *wolf.* A 'wolf' is a man who picks up young boys on the road, for reasons it is not necessary to go into. There are hundreds of 'wolves' on the road, and thousands of boys fall a prey to them."

31 bad things; without obedience to parents, without
    [moral] understanding, without good faith, without
    affection for kindred, without [consent to] truce,
32 without mercy: who, conscious of the righteous
    decree of God that those practising such things are
    worthy of [the sentence of] death, not only keep
    on practising the same, but also are pleased with
    those that are practising them.

Verse 28: Here we have for the third time the judicial
utterance, **God gave them over.** This time it is to a settled
state, **a reprobate mind.** There is such a solemn irony in the
manner of speech in the Greek, that it should be brought out
as well as the English will allow. Alford translates it: "Because they reprobated the knowledge of God, God gave them
over to a reprobate mind." Conybeare renders it: "As they
thought fit to cast out the knowledge of God, God gave them
over to an outcast mind." We might render it: **To a mind
disapproved of God, since they did not approve knowing
God.** And given over to do what? To live lives, think
thoughts, be such creatures, as are **not befitting** the universe
of the blessed God; and most particularly not befitting man,
who was created in God's image.

In the following verses, 29 to 32, three things are seen: first,
some nine phases or developments of human sin (verse 29);
second, the kind of people it makes (verses 29 to 31); and
third, the fearful human conspiracy or agreement of wickedness of man against God (verse 32). Let us mark each carefully. (The student of Greek may well study the roots of these
twenty-two nouns and adjectives, given in the footnote).*

And remember God says men are filled with all these things!
And not only so: they are filled without restraint or limit!
"With all unrighteousness, all destructiveness," etc.

Verses 29 to 31: **1. all injustice**—Selfishness, enthroned
against all rights of others.

*1. *adikia;* 2. *poneria;* 3. *pleonexia;* 4. *kakia;* 5. *phthonou;* 6. *phonou;* 7. *eridos;*
8. *dolou;* 9. *kakoētheias;* 10. *psithuristas;* 11. *katalalous;* 12. *theostugeis;* 13. *hy-*
bristas; 14. *hyperēphanous;* 15. *aladzonas;* 16. *epheuretas kakōn;* 17. *goneusin*
apeitheis; 18. *asunetous;* 19. *asunethetous;* 20. *astorgous;* 21. *aspondous;* 22.
aneleēmonas.

2. **destructiveness**—The same word is used to describe Satan and his hosts: "the evil one," "hosts of wickedness," in Ephesians 6.12,16. It denotes wickedness in hostile activity.

3. **covetousness**—literally, the *itch for more*. "(a) Claiming more than one's due, greedy, grasping; (b) making gain from others' losses; (c) the act of over-reaching by selfish tricks. To take advantage of another's simpleness, to over-reach, defraud."—Liddell and Scott. Lightfoot says, "Impurity and covetousness may be said to divide between them nearly the whole domain of selfishness and vice." Vincent distinguishes between covetousness and avarice: "The one is the desire of getting, the other of keeping." Paul constantly defines covetousness as idolatry, worship of another object than God; and associates it with the vilest sins (I Cor. 5.11; Eph. 5.3,5; Col. 3.5). Many professing Christians are withering in a blight because of this unjudged sin.

4. **malice**—"malignity, maliciousness, desire to injure" (Thayer).

5. **full of envy**—The apostle takes another full breath here, beginning anew this hell-meat catalog. Envy is the hate that arises in the heart toward one who is above us, who is what we are not, or possesses that, which we cannot have, or do not choose the path to attain. "Pilate knew that for envy they had delivered Him." He was holy and good, which they pretended to be, and knew they were not,—nor really chose to be.

6. **murder**—How strikingly the Holy Spirit brings these words, envy, murder, which sound so alike in the Greek,—*phthonou, phonou*—into the order and connection which they constantly sustain in life.

7. **strife**—Literally, beating down in wrangling and contention. How "full of strife," indeed, is this human race!

8. **guile**—Jesus called Nathaniel "an Israelite in whom is no guile" (John 1.47). The Greek word means "a bait for fish," and so, to catch with a bait, to beguile. So in what is called "business" today, men are baited and lured: and "society" lives by it! This is the human heart.

9. **malignant subtlety** — The Genevan New Testament renders it, "Taking all things in an evil sense."

10. **secret slanderers**—By this Greek word of hissing sound *(psithuristas)*, the Septuagint (Greek Old Testament) renders the Hebrew *lahash:* "a snake-charmer's 'magical murmuring.'" Let those privately peddling evil reports, remember that God views their tongue as the slithering of the adder! It is remarkable how secret slanderers can "charm" others (fitted thereto by their evil nature) into believing their slanders. We heard of a modest, excellent young woman secretly slandered by a jealous rival. She could not overcome the falsehood, and died within a year.

11. **open slanderers**—Literally, those who speak against, incriminate, traduce. See its use in I Peter 2.12. Many openly rail at others—especially if their own lives are condemned by theirs.

12. **hateful to God**—Hateful toward God, because haters of God. The word means to show as well as to feel such hatred: "The mind of the flesh is enmity against God."

13. **insolent**—People taking pleasure in insulting others.

14. **arrogant**—Full of haughty pride toward others.

15. **boasters**—The very contrary of Him Who said: "Come unto Me—I am meek, and lowly of heart."

16. **inventors of bad things**—From the days of Cain's city onward (Gen. 4.16-22), men have progressed in evil; until Jehovah said Israel did evil that "came not into His mind" (Jer. 19.5).

17. **without obedience* to parents**—literally, not able to be persuaded by parents. What a photograph of the "youth" of our day! This appalling rejection of parental control is developing amazingly in these last days, just as God said it would (II Tim. 3.1,2). It brings a curse upon whole families, whole

---

*In the six words of which this is the first, God emphasizes the negative, or stubborn quality of badness. Each of these words begins with the Greek *alpha,* which has the force here of *alpha privative:* denial or negation of the quality expressed in the word. Therefore we have translated the first letter in all six "without,"—a rendering consistent rather than elegant, as accuracy of interpretation, rather than "excellency of speech" should be sought here.

communities, and whole lands. Obedience to parents brings promised blessing: "Honor thy father and thy mother (which is the first commandment with promise), that it may be well with thee, and thou mayest live long on the earth" (Eph. 6.2,3).

> "The eye that mocketh at his father,
> And despiseth to obey his mother,
> The ravens of the valley shall pick it out,
> And the young eagles shall eat it."
>
> —Prov. 30.17.

This explains many an early death! Yes; and terrible deaths long delayed.

18. **without moral understanding**—The verb is used in Scripture only of moral and spiritual understanding (Matt. 13.14,15,19,23,51). This adjective (Rom. 1.31) means, without any understanding of Divine things; having no proper moral discernment. That is the awful condition of the human race; and, remember, you and I were born in it.

19. **without good faith**—Faithless, bound by no promise or covenant. This is a very heart-disease! The word denotes that wickedness that does not *intend* to carry out its pledged word, except for selfish ends. Broken business contracts, violated national treaties, light betrayal of personal confidences,— all have this hideous condition as their root.

20. **without natural affection**—Without affection for kindred. Even a third century pagan poet, Theocritus, calls these "the heartless ones." How constantly we see, especially in the selfish lives of graceless "moderns," utter disregard of the natural ties which a kind God has used in "setting the solitary in families." Such are really moral morons; but the possibilities of all these things are in every one of us.

21. **without [consent to] truce,**—literally, not willing to consent to a truce, or cease hostilities. The present ruthless civil war in Spain, and the savagery of Japan in China, are examples. Indeed, only an "armistice," not a peace, was concluded after the World War; and, despite all "treaties" since, there persists

a sort of *international suspicion;* proving that men know, as by instinct, the implacability of human nature.*

22. without mercy—It is said that Nero as a child amused himself in pulling the legs and wings from insects. Perhaps you cry out at this, saying, I have always been tender-hearted towards animals. Indeed? And how about people? Are you tender-hearted towards them? to all of them? Think deeply on this: God "delighteth in mercy"; but "man's inhumanity to man makes countless millions mourn." Consider: A merciful *God!* unmerciful *creatures!*

And now we come to the dark, wilful *conspiracy of evil* of this whole human race. For, remember, what we have been reading is not an indictment of the heathen merely, but of the race. It does indeed depict the progress of human wickedness, and how God gave the race over to those lusts that judicially followed their sin. Yet, as we shall find in the next chapter, it is humanity as such, as thus degraded, of which God is speaking.

Verse 32: Who, conscious that such things are worthy of death, not only keep practising them but approve of others practising them.

Here we are confronted with three terrible realities: (1) They have complete inner knowledge from God (Gr. *epignontes*) that their ways deserve and must have Divine condemnation and judgment; (2) they persist in their practices despite the witness of conscience; (3) they are in a fellowship of evil with other evil-doers!

The Greek word here *(syneudokouso)* which we have rendered "are pleased with," "approve of"; the Revised Version renders "consent with"; Bagster's Interlinear, "are consenting to"; Moule, "feel with and abet." "Not only commit the sins, but delight in their fellowship with the sinner," says Conybeare; "Not only practice them, but have fellow-delight in those that do them"—Darby; "Not only do the same, but applaud

---

*I stood several years ago upon "Starved Rock," near LaSalle, Illinois, a beautiful hill with precipitous sides, where in 1769 the entire tribe of the "Illinois" Indians were starved, almost to the last man, and the tribe practically exterminated, by other Indian tribes besieging the rock. You say, But those were Indians: I am civilized. No, God says, "There is no distinction; for all sinned." And even Paul cried, "I know that in me, that is, in my flesh, dwelleth no good thing."

those that do them"—Godet; "They not only do these things, but are also (in their moral judgment) in agreement with others who so act"—Meyer.

What a description of this world of sinners, this race alienated from the life of God,—at enmity with Him, and at strife with one another! But all in a hellish *unity of evil!*

THE WRATH OF GOD — IN ROMANS

1. The Greek word for wrath *(orgē)* is used twelve times in this book of Romans, and always as connected with God. In all twelve occurrences in Romans it is referred to *God:* "The wrath of God is revealed" (1.18); "Wrath in the day of wrath" (2.5); "Wrath and indignation" (2.8); "God visiteth with wrath" (3.5); "The Law worketh wrath" (4.15); "Much more shall we be saved from the wrath [of God] through Him [Christ]" (5.9); "If God, willing to show His wrath, endured vessels of wrath fitted for destruction" (9.22); "Give place unto the wrath" [of God] (12.19); "Wrath to him that doeth evil" (13.4); "Not only because of the wrath, but also for conscience' sake" (13.5).

Now, the fundamental word for "wrath" is *orgē,* and it always looks, in Romans, toward the final, or last, Judgment; although including, as in 13.4,5, God's governmental actions through present human authorities.

This distinction between the outpouring of governmental wrath which precedes the Kingdom, and the final Assize at the Last Judgment is of primary importance. Paul is dealing in Romans with *eternal* things; with "no condemnation," on the one hand; and with final condemnation on the other. It is not the attitude and actions of God as the dispensational Ruler of *earth's* affairs, but the final Judge dealing with eternal individual destinies, of Whom Paul is writing.

Mark carefully, therefore, that Paul, who is setting forth the gospel of grace, describes the blessedness of those who receive that gospel as forgiven, justified, at peace with God. Romans is *a court book.* God, who adjudged all guilty under sin, gladly declares righteous and safe those who trust Him. Contrariwise, those who reject His mercy and grace are visited by the same

Judge, even God, with wrath. Both the wrath in the one case, and the grace in the other, proceed from *God's personal feeling.* And just as there was personal Divine mercy and eternal tenderness toward the believer, so there is personal Divine wrath and eternal indignation against those who despise His love and mercy, as set forth in the death of His Son. It is *righteous* indignation, certainly; but it is *personal* indignation. Listen carefully to God's own words as to this future visitation of wrath upon the finally impenitent: "Jehovah, whose name is Jealous, is a jealous God" (Ex. 34.14); "Lest there should be among you man or woman whose heart turneth away from Jehovah, to serve other gods, and it come to pass, when he heareth the words of this curse, that he bless himself in his heart, saying, I shall have peace, though I walk in the stubbornness of my heart . . . . Jehovah will not pardon him, but then the anger of Jehovah, and His jealousy, shall smoke against that man" (Deut. 29.18-20); "Jehovah is a jealous God, and avengeth; Jehovah avengeth and is full of wrath; Jehovah taketh vengeance on His adversaries, and He reserveth wrath for His enemies"; "He will pursue His enemies into darkness" (Nahum 1.2,8); "Vengeance belongeth unto Me, I will recompense, saith the Lord" (Rom. 12.19); "It is a fearful thing to fall into the hands of the Living God" (Heb. 10.31); "Can thy heart endure, or can thy hands be strong, in the days that I shall deal with thee? I, Jehovah, have spoken it and will do it" (Ezek. 22.14).

It is fatuous folly to seek to avoid the manifest, necessary meaning of such words. God, who alone has the right to avenge, will avenge! The very first chapter of the Prophets warns any willing to hear: "Ah, I will ease Me of Mine adversaries, and avenge Me of Mine enemies!" (Isa. 1.24). Human justice is to be meted out by juries of men and by judges, uncolored by personal feelings. Not so with God! As is not the case in human courts, it is the Judge Himself who has been wronged. It is *His* light that has been refused for darkness. It is *His* salvation, and that by His Son's blood, that has been despised. And it will not be justice merely, but the infliction of penalty by an outraged Being whose Name is Love, now aroused to a

righteous fury commensurate with the measureless guilt of the
hideous haters of His holiness, the despisers of His mercy—
it will be by the Hand of *the Judge of all, Himself,* that wrath
will fall upon the guilty.

As for the "great" pulpiteers of Christendom, the favorites
of the rapidly apostatizing denominations of this day, the men
who, by their ecclesiastical politics or personal ability, or so-
called "scholarship," are "outstanding" and yet deny or ignore
the wrath of God,—fear them not! They are false prophets,
prophets of "peace,"—which can only be found in the shed
blood of the Redeemer: the blood which they do not preach.

Oh, that Day! that Day!—for these lying preachers of
"peace, peace," who have said, "God is too good to damn anybody." And shall God, in that Day, refuse to remember the
agonies of His Son on the Cross? Shall He change that holy
hatred of sin, wherein He forsook Christ and spared Him not?—
all because miserable guilty Universalists, Unitarians, Millennial
Dawnists, "Modernists," "Christian(!) Scientists(!)"—all the
fawning "Hush, hush" preachers, have promised to men "a God
that would not show wrath against sin!" A God who would
indeed "spare all,—yea, probably, even Satan, finally!"

Let this awful word *Orgē,* Wrath, settle into the conscience
of every soul; for God hath spoken it!

And every Preacher and every Prophet *of God* has warned
of it: Enoch (Jude 14,15); Noah (II Pet. 2.5); Moses (Deut.
32.35); the Psalmists, the Prophets (for example, Isaiah,—all
of Chapters 24 and 34); the Lord's forerunner, John the
Baptist, with his "Flee from the wrath to come"; the Apostles,—
from Romans to Revelation; and the great Preachers and
Evangelists of the Christian centuries,—the men who have won
souls—the Reformers, the Puritans, the Wesleys, Whitefields,
Edwardses, Finneys, Spurgeons, Moodys,—all have told of
man's guilt and danger, of the coming judgment, and of the
wrath of God upon the impenitent and unbelieving.

2. This wrath is here in Romans 1.18 declared to be now, like
the gospel, *revealed from heaven;* and that, now, against *all*
ungodliness; and against *all* unrighteousness of men; in that
they have resisted the truth they know.

Heretofore, as at the Deluge, and that terrible day when "Jehovah rained upon Sodom and upon Gomorrah brimstone and fire from Jehovah out of heaven," God had revealed His wrath on earth when men's cup of iniquity was full; as we read also in the case of the Canaanites (Gen. 15.16; Lev. 18. 24,25). Yet, God "overlooked" much that was evil, even in Israel (Acts 17.30; Matt. 19.8). But now, He "commandeth all men everywhere to repent,"—in view of a revealed coming day of judgment, "by the Man whom He hath ordained" (Acts 17.30,31; Rom. 2.16), and of which judgment He hath given certainty to all men by raising this coming Judge from the dead! The cross brought to an end God's "overlooking" sin, by *judging* it, even to the utter Divine forsaking of Him whom God sent to bear sin. Sin, therefore, is brought into the open; God's wrath from heaven is now revealed against it all! If the blood of Jesus, God's Son cleanseth believers "from *all* sin"; then no sin has been left unjudged at the cross, and no sins will be unjudged upon the lost, at the Great White Throne, nor be "overlooked" today!

This, then, is the first full, formal, and general, announcement of wrath from heaven. For heretofore God had man on trial. While Israel had "the house of God" on earth, and were being tested under law, there was (humanly speaking) the possibility of human recovery. But when they, with the Gentiles, crucified the Lord of glory,—killed the Righteous One, four things came to light: (a) the absolute character of man's sin; (b) the absoluteness of God's holiness which could not spare the Son of His love, when once sin was laid on him; (c) the absoluteness of God's love and grace toward sinners, in publishing forgiveness and righteousness as a free-gift through Christ,—"beginning *from Jerusalem*—where men had crucified His Son! and (c) the revelation from heaven of Divine wrath against all ungodliness, all unrighteousness. It was not that God hated sin less in the past, in "the times of ignorance." But there had been "overlooking, forbearance." Now, with the full revelation of both human guilt and Divine grace by the Cross, there must also be fully announced God's wrath from heaven *against all sin*. It is no longer an earthly, governmental affair,—

as against high earthly offenders, such as Pharaoh, the Sodomites, or the Canaanites; but against *all* ungodliness, *all* unrighteousness. *In grace* God at the cross had come forth; not
in Law or judgment, but *as He was, in His being,*—that is,
absolutely, as *Love,* offering pardon and justification to men.
Therefore, *all He was, absolutely,* in Heaven His dwelling-place,
against the awful thing, sin, must, along with His pardoning
grace, *be revealed!* The days of "winking at" ignorance are
over; for, "He spared not His own Son!" So now, that God is
against all sin must be revealed. The days of that protection
from God's wrath that religion had afforded are over! For had
not Judaism afforded a kind of protection? Jehovah dwelt in
the thick darkness of the Holy of Holies of the tabernacle and
the temple. An outward walk according to external enactments,
secured the nation Israel, amidst which God dwelt. But no
longer! "Your house is left to you desolate," said the Lord to
the Jews. "The blood (for forgiveness), and the water (for
cleansing) followed man's spear of hate thrust into the Redeemer's side." But *by that very fact* we know that there is
absolute wrath against man's sin! Only, flee not from this
wounded Lamb; for here the wrath has struck! There is safety
here,—though nowhere else in the universe!

3. It will fall to other pens than Paul's—to those of Peter
and Jude, and especially to that of John, in the Apocalypse, to
describe the particulars of time and mode of visitation of God's
wrath; together with the places of confinement and punishment
of the wicked, both before and after the Last Judgment. Peter
will write of "Tartarus," where God cast the rebel angels of
Genesis 6 (II Pet. 2.4); and Jude will describe both the "everlasting bonds" of those angels, and also the "eternal fire" that
overtook the sinners of Sodom and Gomorrah; while John will
show the risen Christ with the keys of death and of Hades (the
detention-jail at present of lost human spirits); and John will
describe also that awful "lake of fire" which shall be the final
portion of the devil and his angels, and of those who sided with
him against God. (Compare Rev. 20.10 with Matt. 25.41.)

Paul, however, will set forth the scene as *from God's court.*
Just as his gospel will show a God whose love is such that He

gave Christ for wicked, hateful sinners, and offers to *justify* the ungodly who believe Him; so the contrary of justification—*condemnation,* becomes the portion of the rejecter of mercy.

Since grace is the outpouring of God's "heart of mercy," and is a personal feeling; so despised mercy arouses in God (and how necessarily), the opposite of mercy,—wrath! Paul's words will therefore be: grace, and over against it, wrath. Justification, and over against it, condemnation. Life, and over against it, death. He will say to the saints, "Ye have your fruit unto sanctification, and the end, eternal life." And, of the things whereof the saints are now "ashamed,"—"the end of those things is death!"

4. But be it noted, there is absolutely no foot of Scripture ground to stand upon for those who, refusing the Bible doctrine of a God who "visiteth with wrath," bring in their subtle arguments for the "final restoration of all." Honest readers know that the very opposite is taught throughout the Scripture. *There is no wrath upon believers. There is forever nothing but wrath for unbelievers.* If you value your soul, regard with utter horror all trifling on this question. If you do not believe in Divine wrath, you are not subject to Scripture, and you are in fearful personal danger. The errorists begin very subtly,—as the Bullingerites began with the doctrine of "soul-sleeping." (See footnote to Romans 15.8, found on p. 526.) Then there are the "annihilationists," the "conditional immortality" falsifiers, the Christadelphians, the "restorationists," the Seventh Day Adventists, and all the rest of the rabble. These false prophets are lulling millions upon millions into a deathful slumber from which only the crack of doom will rouse them. There are no "soul-sleepers" or "restorationists" in Hades! They know the truth *now!* And they are in nameless terror of coming Judgment and *final eternal Hell.*

The God of the twentieth century is not the God of the Bible, but the God of the vain imaginations of shallow men,—men who will not look honestly at history (as, e.g., the Flood, or Sodom and Gomorrah); nay, who will not look honestly at present events! Preachers are found by the thousands who pooh-pooh the thought that the great calamities, such as the late war, and that now looming, are judgments of God; that great droughts or floods or storms are sent by Him. Like the hardened wretches whom Ezekiel saw, they say, "Jehovah seeth us not; Jehovah hath forsaken the land."

If Paul, at the beginning of Church days, could write to Roman Christians that terrible arraignment of the human race with which this Epistle begins, and must begin, what shall be the attitude, and what the words, of any faithful preacher or teacher at this, the end of the Church times, after nearly 2000 years of unbelief, heresy, divisions, and general denial of the guilt and danger of lost men!

Merely to give in this book the meaning of the words of Paul,—without applying them to the very soul and conscience of the reader, would, in view of the conditions prevalent today, be both fruitless and cowardly: fruitless, because the present day will not study, and least of all, thoroughly study, Scripture; and cowardly, because shrinking from applying truth would be seeking to be "fundamental" without offending anyone!

"If thou warn the wicked . . . thou hast delivered thy soul," God speaks.

The gospel of Christ is written in letters of heavenly light against the fearful black cloud of human guilt flashing with warnings of coming wrath!

TO THE PREACHERS OF "THE SOCIAL GOSPEL"

This is the doctrine that Jesus Christ came to reform society (whatever "society" may be!); that He came to abate the evils of selfishness, give a larger "vision" to mankind; and, through His example and precepts, bring about such a change in human affairs, social, political, economic and domestic, as would realize all man's deep longings for a peaceful, happy existence upon earth, ushering in what these teachers are pleased to call, "the Kingdom of God."

1. Now, in the first place, Jesus Christ came to save sinners, not "society." He said, "The Son of Man hath authority on earth to forgive sins." Now, sins are individual transgressions against a personal God; there is no such thing in Scripture as these social-gospellers dream of,—a condition of "society" to

be "changed" or "ameliorated." All that really exists is the guilt of a vast number of really guilty sinners. "Society" does not exist before God at all; and it is a vain delusion of the devil that sins are dealt with *en masse*.

2. Sinners, having been pardoned, find themselves in a blessed fellowship, a really heavenly thing, constituted by the Holy Spirit, who indwells each of them. But to confuse this fellowship with what these social-gospellers call "society," is to forget that "except a man be born again he cannot see the kingdom of God."

3. It flatters men's vanity, of course, and shelters them from conviction, to be dealt with as "society," and not as guilty souls *needing personal pardon* through the shed blood of Christ. Therefore this gospel (which is not a gospel, but a lie, a delusion of Satan), draws together vast concourses of unconverted men and women, "church-members" and "non-church-members." Its preachers are plausible and popular, for if "society" is going to be saved in a mass, individual repentance need not be mentioned. The Jesus of these men,—the Stanley Joneses, the Sherwood Eddys, the Frank Buchmans, the Bishop McConnells, the Kagawas, and a whole host of drifters and on-the-fencers, is not the Lamb of God taking away the sin of the world by an atoning sacrifice, not the One despised, forsaken, smitten of God, of the fifty-third of Isaiah! He is not at all the substitutionary Sacrifice drinking the cup of wrath for man's guilt! But He is "the Christ of the Indian Road"—or the American road, the Canadian road, the English road, as you please; walking by the wayside, teaching the multitudes, as in the Four Gospels, *BEFORE HE WAS REJECTED AND DIED.* He is not the RISEN CHRIST, with all power in heaven and earth given unto Him, pouring forth the Holy Spirit and doing mighty works, as in the early church days.

I affirm that the present day popular preachers DO NOT KNOW what human guilt, before God, is! *DO NOT KNOW* that Christ really bore wrath under God's hand for the sin of the world! *DO NOT KNOW* that He was forsaken of God, as the whole race, otherwise, must have been! I affirm that they are preaching as if an unrejected, uncrucified Christ were still being offered to the world! They preach the *"character"* of Jesus, saying "nice things" of Him, and telling people to "follow His example": while the truly awful fact that Christ "bare our sins in His own body on the tree," that He was "wounded for our transgressions," that He was "forsaken of His God"; that "God spared not His own Son, but delivered Him up,"—and that "for our trespasses," *is never told* to the poor, wretched people! Nor are they warned of that literal lake of fire and brimstone into which "every one not found written in the book of life" will be cast, and that *forever*.

One look into the lost eternity to which these last-days "preachers" are leading those who follow them, renders even the briefest consideration of these men who dare to call themselves "preachers of *the gospel*," beyond all enduring. As Jeremiah cries:

> "Concerning the prophets. My heart within me is broken, all my bones shake; I am like a drunken man, and like a man whom wine hath overcome, because of Jehovah, and because of His holy words.

> "Thus saith Jehovah of hosts, Hearken not unto the words of the prophets that prophesy unto you: they teach you vanity; they speak a vision of their own heart, and not out of the mouth of Jehovah. They say continually unto them that despise Me, Jehovah hath said, Ye shall have peace; and unto every one that walketh in the stubbornness of his own heart they say, No evil shall come upon you . . . Behold, the tempest of Jehovah, even His wrath, is gone forth, yea, a whirling tempest; it shall burst upon the head of the wicked . . . I sent not these prophets, yet they ran: I spake not unto them, yet they prophesied. But if they had stood in My council, then had they caused My people to hear My words, and had turned them from their evil way, and from the evil of their doings" (Jer. 23.9,16,17,19, 21,22).

And Ezekiel:

> "And the word of Jehovah came unto me, saying, Son of Man, prophesy against the prophets of Israel that

prophesy, and say thou unto them that prophesy out of their own heart, Hear ye the word of Jehovah: Thus saith the Lord Jehovah, Woe unto the foolish prophets, that follow their own spirit, and have seen nothing! . . . They have seen falsehood and lying divination, that say, Jehovah saith; but Jehovah hath not sent them: and they have made men to hope that the word could be confirmed. Have ye not seen a false vision, and have ye not spoken a lying divination, in that ye say, Jehovah saith; albeit I have not spoken?

"Because, even because they have seduced my people, saying, Peace; and there is no peace; and when one buildeth up a wall, behold, they daub it with untempered mortar: say unto them that daub it with untempered mortar, that it shall fall" (Ezek. 13.1,2,3,6,7,10,11,12-14,15).

And,

"When I say unto the wicked, O wicked man, thou shalt surely die, and thou dost not speak to warn the wicked from his way; that wicked man shall die in his iniquity, but his blood will I require at thy hand. Nevertheless, if thou warn the wicked of his way to turn from it, and he turn not from his way; he shall die in his iniquity, but thou hast delivered thy soul" (Ezek. 33.8,9).

You may say, Those were *Old Testament* prophets—Jeremiah and Ezekiel; and Those were messages to *the Jews*. Wait till you meet, as you will shortly, the God Who inspired these prophets. *Let us see what you will say to Him,—you who profess to preach the gospel of Christ and yet preach it not!*

And Paul saith: "Though we, or an angel from heaven should preach unto you any gospel other than that which we preached unto you, let him be anathema." "For I delivered unto you first of all that . . . Christ died for our sins, according to the Scriptures, . . . that He was buried; and that He hath been raised on the third day according to the Scriptures." This very declaration of the gospel after Christ died, is that atoning death of His. When you leave that out, and prate about the "beautiful life" of Jesus, you are deceived by the devil and are a deceiver of other souls.

4. We know that this "social gospel," the false news that humanity is to be reached in the mass, and not by individual conviction, individual faith, individual new birth by the Holy Spirit, is *a lie,* because Scripture *directly contradicts* any such notion:

Hear Paul: "In the last days, grievous times shall come. For men shall be lovers of self, lovers of money, boastful, haughty, railers, disobedient to parents, unthankful, unholy, without natural affection, implacable, slanderers, without self-control, fierce, no lovers of good, traitors, headstrong, puffed up, lovers of pleasure rather than lovers of God; holding a form of godliness, but having denied the power thereof: *from these also turn away!*" (II Tim. 3.1-5).

Peter also: "In the last days mockers shall come with mockery, walking after their own lusts, and saying, Where is the promise of His coming?" (II Pet. 3.3,4).

Paul again: "Evil men and imposters shall wax worse and worse, deceiving and being deceived" (II Tim. 3.13). And our Lord plainly says:

"In the day that Lot went out from Sodom, it rained fire and brimstone from heaven, and destroyed them all: *after the same manner* shall it be in the day that the Son of Man is revealed" (Luke 17.29,30).

How dare you call yourself a believer of Scripture, while you deny such plain words as these, and preach a fool's dream, that the world, with the devil still here, its prince and god; and man still unregenerate—that the world will by some "social gospel" gradually change in character? It is a lie! and those that preach it, preach a lie. The words of God shall be fulfilled, and not the mouthings of a McConnell or the fumings of a Fosdick.

And, O social gospeller, if you are looking for a changed state of "society," *who is going to help you bring it in?* The *Holy Ghost* will not, for He has inspired men to write that the *very opposite* will occur! that men shall *hate* one another, and that the world will grow worse, to the very return of Christ. And we know that enlightened *Christians* will not go about to bring in what they know from God's Word is not coming in!

And ignorant Christians cannot help you,—for they know not how. And we know that this selfish world will not go about to bring in your social dream: for you and we know they are set on their own interests, and *will remain so*. And Satan cannot do it, if he would!

So, O social gospeller, who would go about to bring in a "new social order," you are left to do it yourself, without that regeneration by the Holy Spirit which alone truly saves men; without any message of pardon for guilty souls through the shed blood of a Redeemer (for you do not preach that!) without the help and prayers of true believers: for, these pray, "Thy Kingdom Come"; but they know that Christ must return to earth to bring in that Kingdom; and they know that all other promises are *false and lying hopes!*

CHAPTER TWO

The Great Principles according to which God's Judgment of Human Action Must Proceed.

1   Wherefore thou art without excuse, O man,— any one judging [others] : for in the very matter in which thou judgest the other man, thou art giving judgment against thy very self: for the same things thou art practising,—thou who art judging!

WE HAVE TRACED the awful history of the human race in iniquity and idolatry, especially since the Flood, and have seen that fearful indictment of above twenty counts which ends Chapter One.

We now enter upon the greatest passage in all Scripture as to the principles and processes of God in His estimate, or judgment, concerning His creatures. If God is "Judge of all," and if the whole world is to be "brought under the judgment of God" (3.19), God will surely take pains to make known the great principles of His action, so that men may know beforehand how He will decide and act. Otherwise, men would "imagine vain things" about the true God, and hug their delusions to their own damnation.

The personal character of God's relations toward men, either in the matter of salvation or of damnation, is rapidly being forgotten by this generation. Yet, if God be God, He must be the Judge of All. Back of the whole revelation of His works and ways, in His Word, is God Himself. And it is only the fool that saith in his heart, "No God." Mark that it is in his heart, his desires, that he speaks; and not in his reason or judgment!

God created man "in His own image." Since we are persons, —so is God. Since we have personal feelings,—so has God.

Now every creature stands in relation to God according to what God is. God cannot change. Daniel Webster, in answer to the question: "What is the greatest thought that ever entered your mind?" said, at once, "My responsibility to my Maker!" You must meet God, and that as He is, not as you might wish Him to be. If you have Christ, you have already met Him! If you have not Christ, you have still to face God in His infinite holiness, and that arrayed against you, at the Judgment Day.

Now this second chapter of Romans deals with those who do not believe that the awful things of the first chapter mean themselves. Consequently, we find two sets of such self-appointed "judges" of others* in Chapter Two:

First, Those who discountenance the "openly bad" of humanity, considering themselves "better"—because of race, civilization, environment, education, or culture; and,

Second, Those who discountenance the bad, thinking themselves "better," because of their religion,—the possession of the Divine oracles: these, of course, were, in Paul's day, the Jews (2.17).

Concerning the first class, the "respectable" sinners, who esteem themselves "better," God lays down six great principles of His estimate or judgment of men; and adds a seventh concerning the second class, the "religious" sinners; of whom God declares that the world itself despises inconsistency between practice and religious profession.

Now just because the history of our race has been so black, as shown in Chapter One ("God gave them up—God gave them up—God gave them up—"), we who read the record are ourselves in peculiar danger, for the doors into the death-chamber of self-righteousness so easily open to us! We readily fall into the delusion that God is speaking in this chapter concerning heathen idolaters, who finally descended to worshiping "creeping things,"—and that He cannot be speaking to *us*!

But will you remember that God comes quickly, through this sad history, to man's *settled state*. For at the end of the history, the announcement concerning men is, "being filled with all unrighteousness!" By and by God will announce that there is "no distinction" as to sinners, and will publish the fact that

---

*Note: The Greek verb for "judging" in the first verse does not mean to estimate a man's value but to condemn his person.

there is but one way of salvation for all men alike,—and that through the shed blood of a Redeemer. But here, as we have above said, God is heading off from escape first the proud "judges" of others, of every sort,—the moralists, and moral philosophers, all the "moral" folks,—the "whosoevers" that "judge"; and, second, those who would escape the consciousness of guilt and judgment by running under a "religious" roof— whether a Jewish shelter, as in Paul's day, or a "Christian" one, in our day.

SEVEN GREAT PRINCIPLES OF GOD'S JUDGMENT

1. God's judgment is "according to truth" (verse 2).
2. According to accumulated guilt (verse 5).
3. According to works (verse 6).
4. Without respect of persons (verse 11).
5. According to performance, not knowledge (verse 13).
6. God's judgment reaches the secrets of the heart (verse 16).
7. According to reality, not religious profession (verses 17-29).

ACCORDING TO TRUTH,—NOT HUMAN IMAGININGS

Verse two of this chapter describes the first principle of God's judgment: it is "according to truth":

2 And we know that the judgment of God is according to truth against them that practice such
3 things. And dost thou reckon this, O man, judging them that practice such things, and thyself doing the same, that thou shalt escape the judg-
4 ment of God? Or dost thou even despise the riches of His goodness and forbearance and long-suffering, not knowing that the goodness of God is meant to lead thee to repentance?

First, then, the judgment of God is "according to truth." Every man is naturally blind to his own state and sins. Not unless mightily convinced by the Holy Ghost, can any man

imagine God's dealing in justice with *him!* The third verse
brings this out. Godet (though seeking to confine this passage
to the Jews) strikingly renders it: "Dost thou reason that thou
wouldst escape,—thou?* A being by thyself? A privileged
person?" And he adds, "The Greek word here used *(logidzomai*—to reason) well describes the false calculations whereby
the Jews persuaded themselves that they would escape the judgment wherewith God would visit the Gentiles."

But Paul does not begin with the Jews as a class until verse
17. Here in the first part of the chapter he is seeking to arouse
all men from that sense of security arising from self-love and
self-flattery.† We must apply these searching sentences to all
"respectable" persons, to all those who, being themselves impenitent, yet "judge" others.

God sees the facts, nay, the motives behind the facts, of the
life of every creature. Of course, this whole second chapter,
and the first part of the third, is meant by God, whose name is
Love, to drive us out of our false notions of Himself and His
judicial procedure, into the arms of our Redeemer, Christ; who
has borne wrath, the wrath of God, as our Substitute. But
whether you are brought to flee to Christ or not, you must face
the facts: God is a God of judgment, and a God of truth. See
how He "spared not His own Son, but delivered Him up." It
is not because God loves to judge and condemn, for He definitely says judgment is "His strange work" (Isa. 28.21).
Nevertheless, He must judge, and it must be "according to
truth," according to the facts, the realities which are, of course,
known to Him. He needs no "jury" to decide any case. He is
Himself Witness, Jury and Judge.

Now, in the next two verses (3 and 4), we see God dealing
with the accursed folly of the deceitful heart of man, who
dreams that by merely judging others (though he practices the

---

*The pronoun "thou" is emphatic in the Greek, indicating a fond conceit about
oneself.

†Bengel, agreeing with Meyer and Godet, gives a searching word here: "Everyone accused, tries to escape; he who is acquitted, escapes." And Meyer: "But it
is not by an acquittal that the Jew (or any religious person) expects to escape; but
by being excepted entirely from the judgment of God. According to the Jewish
notion, only the Gentiles shall be judged; while all Jews, as the children of the
kingdom — of Messiah, — shall inherit it!"

same things), he shall escape God's judgment. Some one says, "We hate our own faults when we see them in others." But this state goes beyond even that, for it puts God right off His throne, and makes Him connive with a guilty sinner, just because, forsooth, this sinner discerns clearly and decries loudly the sins of others,—while committing the same himself.

Furthermore, such a "judge" of others becomes, in his self-confident importance, blind to God's constant mercy toward himself—not feeling the need of it; and in his self-righteous blindness knows not that the "goodness" of God is meant to lead him to personal repentance instead of to judgment of his fellows.*

Note the degrees or stages, also, of God's kindness during the earth-life of such a man: First, it is God's "goodness," in daily preserving him, providing for him, and protecting him. Second, Divine goodness being despised by him, God's "forebearance" is exercised,—God does not smite instantly the proud ingrate, but goes on in goodness toward him, withholding wrath even at times when disease, danger, or death threaten all about him. Third, all God's goodness and forbearance being despised, God's "long-suffering" keeps waiting, even over "vessels of wrath" (see 9.22).

ACCORDING TO ACCUMULATED GUILT

5   **But after thy hardness and impenitent heart treasures up for thyself wrath in the day of wrath and revelation of the righteous judgment of God—**

We have here the second principle, the cumulative character of continued impenitence. This shows how the hardened and impenitent sinner "lays up" during a prosperous earth-life constant "treasures" of wrath,† which will be revealed at the Great

---

*The goodness of God to us, remembered, reflected upon, heartily believed in, moves the heart, and changes the whole attitude toward God. The great preacher of repentance, John the Baptist, cried, "Repent, for the Kingdom" — all you Jews have been hoping for! "is at hand." He was stern, as was his Lord, only with religious pretenders.

†"There is an evident correlation between the phrase, 'riches of goodness,' verse 4; and the Greek word translated 'treasure up.' The latter word, as well as the dative of favor, *seauto*, 'for thyself,' have certainly a tinge of irony. What an enriching is *that!*"—Godet.

Also Bengel: "Note the antithesis between 'despising the riches of goodness,' and 'treasuring up wrath'; between 'hardness' and 'goodness'; between 'impenitent

White Throne judgment of Revelation 20, when all the evil works of the lost will be shown in all their ramifications and evil influences, and effects upon others, as well as in the fearful personal guilt of hardness and impenitence against God's mercy. Not until the last evil result of a life of sin has been marked and weighed, can the final reward of the sinner be shown,—as all will be shown in that "Day." This is the outlook, probably, with most people we meet! How dread and awful that outlook for the sinner who has taken God's earthly gifts and blessings as a matter of course,—no brokenness of heart or contrition toward God! Nay, not even thankfulness! "Behold, this was the iniquity of Sodom: pride, fulness of bread, and prosperous ease" (Ezek. 16.49,50). And our Lord, in speaking of the utter carnal security of the Sodomites, says, "They ate, they drank, they bought, they sold, they planted, they builded; but in the day that Lot went out from Sodom it rained fire and brimstone from heaven, and destroyed them all; after the same manner shall it be in the day that the Son of Man is revealed" (Luke 17.28-30).

So they are today, in these last days: "Treasuring up unto themselves wrath" for that fearful "day of wrath."

Remember, if the goodness of God toward you is not leading you to repentance, then every day, every hour, you live, drops another drop into the terrible "treasure" of indignation which will burst the great dam of God's long-suffering—in the great Day of Wrath, when God shall reveal His righteous judgment! (Of course, if you flee to Calvary, you will "not come into judgment" (John 5.24): for Judgment has already struck there!)

ACCORDING TO WORKS

6 Who will recompense to each one according to
7 his works: to them that by patient continuance in
well-doing seek for glory and honor and incorrupt-

---

heart' and 'repentance,' of verse 4. Also note that it is 'against thyself' thou art treasuring wrath, not against others whom thou judgest. Finally, the unquestionable antithesis between 'forbearance' and 'revelation of judgment.' "

And David Brown: "What an awful idea is here expressed, — that the sinner himself is amassing, like hoarded treasure, an ever accumulating stock of Divine wrath, to burst upon him 'in the day of wrath and revelation of the righteous judgment of God'! And this is said not of the reckless, but of those who boasted of their purity!"

8   ibility, life eternal: but to those who are conten-
     tious, and disobey the truth, being obedient to un-
     righteousness, shall be wrath and indignation,
9   tribulation and anguish, upon every soul of man
     that worketh evil, both of Jew first, and also of
10   Greek; but glory and honor and peace to every soul
     of man that worketh good, both to Jew first, and
     also to Greek.

The third principle then, is, "according to works": "Who
will judge every one according to his works." How could it be
otherwise? You know that when a case comes to trial in courts
of law, men first endeavor, through questioning witnesses, to
discover the facts. Now God knows all the facts about every
one of Adam's race, and His judgment must be in accordance
with them. It is not that God desires you to be damned, but,
contrariwise, to believe on His Son, upon Whom His judgment
for human sin fell at Calvary. Nevertheless, those that come up
at the Last Judgment (Rev. 20.11-15) will be "judged out of
the things which were written in the books, according to their
works" . . . "They were judged every man according to their
works."

But, as we shall see, it is the life as a whole, the *life-choice*,
that is in question here. Consequently, we read here of the two
great classes: the patiently enduring, and the rebellious; those
whose life-practice is good, and those who work evil; those
who obey the truth, and those who reject it in order to remain
in the unrighteousness they love.

Verse 7: The **"patient continuance in well-doing"** is not
at all set forth as the means of their procuring eternal life,*

---

*It must carefully and constantly be borne in mind, as we have said above, that
the question in this chapter is, the principles of God's judgment as Judge of all,
and not the last assize itself, nor any account of the manner in which those said to
be "working good" entered upon that path (which, of course, is always by a publican's trust in a God of mercy). But we are being shown in Chapter 2 how God
must proceed in accordance with His being, toward two classes, — those subject to
Him, and those refusing subjection.

Alford well says: "The Apostle is here speaking generally, of the general system
of God in governing the world, — the judging according to each man's works —
punishing the evil, and rewarding the righteous. No question at present arises,
how this righteousness in God's sight is to be obtained — but the truth is only
stated broadly to be further specified by and by, when it is clearly shown that by
works of law (*erga nomou*) no flesh can be justified before God. The neglect to

but as a description of those to whom God does render life eternal. **Well-doing** is subjection to and obedience to the light God has vouchsafed.* To Abel, "well-doing" meant approaching God by a sacrifice, as a sinner, as he had been taught to do. To Noah, "continuance in well-doing" meant building an ark to save his house and preserve life upon the earth, involving years of labor, and the ridicule of man. To Abraham, it meant leaving his country, his relatives, and his father's house, and becoming a stranger and pilgrim on earth. To Job, it meant his God-fearing, evil-rejecting life; and afterwards, in the midst of his great affliction, bowing before the presence of God in dust and ashes. To Matthew the publican, it meant rising from his business and following the Lord Jesus; to Cornelius the centurion, a life of patient prayer and generosity,—and then believing the gospel at Peter's lips. To Lydia, it meant humble and faithful attendance at "the place of prayer" till Paul came and "her heart was opened" to give heed to the gospel of grace spoken by the apostle,—whence followed her "obedience of faith."

In every age since man sinned there have been those like Jabez, who was "more honorable than his brethren, and called upon God" (I Chron. 4.9,10); and like Joseph, who was "separate from his brethren." There always have been choosers of God and rejecters of God.

Verse 8: We need only sketch in Scripture a few of the **contentious,** the **factious:**† a Cain who was angry, and hate-

---

*God often, in His saving grace, meets an enemy like Saul of Tarsus in the very heat of his opposition to Christ; or saves, and reveals His truth to, young men of wild dissipation like Augustine; or takes up and leads all the way to the Celestial City a profane Bunyan.

Nevertheless, of these also, it could be said, as Paul spake: "I was not disobedient to the heavenly vision." After grace reached them, they too are described as "those who sought for glory and honor and incorruption." We repeat that verses 7 to 10 are not a revelation of the way of salvation, but a general description of the character of those that are saved.

†Literally, it reads here, "those who are of contention"; that is, whose hearts, instead of believing and obeying, rise in opposition to the truth, contending inwardly against the truth and outwardly with them that proclaim it. The word "contentious" here evidently refers to the first conscious risings of man's wicked heart against God's revealed will. " 'Of contention' defines unbelievers, as those who are 'of faith' defines believers" (Hodge).

---

observe this has occasioned two mistakes: (1) an idea that by this passage it is proved that not faith only, but works also in some measure, justify before God; and an idea that by well-doing here is meant faith in Christ. However true it be, so much is certainly not meant here, but merely the fact that everywhere, and in all, God punishes evil and rewards good."

ful at God's accepting Abel's sacrifice; an Esau who despised
his birthright and hated to the end the people of God; a Pharaoh
who said to Moses, "Who is Jehovah that I should hearken unto
His voice?" A Saul who despised the word of Jehovah and
sought to destroy His elect king, David; a Jehoiakim, apostate
king of Judah, who "cut with his penknife" and burned the
prophecies of Jeremiah; scribes and Pharisees, who rejected
John's baptism of repentance,—and, consequently, our Lord's
loving offer of eternal life for sinners through faith in Himself
alone; infidel Sadducees, who **obeyed not the truth,** by
ridiculing it, as Modernists do today. All about us we perceive them,—"the factious," those who oppose to Scripture
their notions or arguments, and continue to **obey unrighteousness.** The world is filled with them, and they will fill
hell shortly!

And now we must faithfully read and believe what God declares will befall these "factious" unbelievers: **Wrath—indignation—tribulation—anguish:*** thus is the fearful visitation of The Great Day upon the impenitent described, with
concise but sweeping comprehensiveness: **Wrath:** this is
"revealed from heaven" as the state of God's mind toward
the unbelieving wicked—"the wrath of God abides upon
him" (John 3.36). **Indignation:** this is vividly described in
Nahum: "Who can stand before His indignation? and who
can abide in the fierceness of His anger?" Or Ezekiel: "I
have poured out My indignation upon them; I have consumed them with the fire of My wrath." It seems to be the
outburst in visitation of wrath stored up. Then (verse 9),
tribulation: Here the visitation strikes its object. The false
peace of his hardened, impenitent earth-life is now horribly
broken up by direct visitation from God in vengeance. Finally,
anguish: which sets forth the result of that tribulation
which meets the lost directly from an angry, indignant Creator and Judge. "I am in anguish in this flame," cried lost
Dives, in Hades (God's prison for the lost until the Day of

---

*Wrath (*orgē*) and indignation (*thumos*) is the true Greek order here. Alford's
comment is excellent: "According to the arrangement, the former word denotes
the abiding settled mind of God, as in John 3.36, towards them; and the latter, the
outbreak of that anger at the Great Day of retribution."

Judgment). What unspeakable horrors, then, will that Day bring!

Verse 10: But God must again, in His heart of love, show in what sweet, heavenly contrast are those working good: glory, honor, peace,—to every such soul, Jew or Greek! The order of the words plainly points to that day when the righteous will be manifest. Then will be manifested in them that glory which they sought; there will be public honor; there will be everlasting peace!

Now remember that although we have not yet come in this Epistle to the unfolding of the way of peace, yet it belongs to your peace to let this great passage we are studying fall full into your heart.

WITHOUT RESPECT OF PERSONS

11 For there is no respect of persons with God.

12 For as many as made a life-choice of sin, though without law, without law also shall perish; and as many as under law made a life-choice of sin, shall be judged by law.*

Verse 11: The fourth principle, then, is, "Without respect of persons." Among men, there is almost nothing else but what James and Jude denounce as "showing respect of persons"—"for the sake of advantage." The rich, the educated, the travelled, the cultured, the prominent, the influential, the pleasing, the strong,—are all sought after. The poor, the ignorant, the weak, are despised and neglected. But not so with God. He sees men through His own eyes of holiness and truth always. He "seeth not as man seeth." It is a terrifying thought to earth's great,—but an infinitely comforting thought to every humble God-fearing soul,—that there is an impartial One, with no respect of persons, with whom they have to do!

---

*Literally: "For as many as without law sinned, without law also shall perish; and as many as under law sinned, through law shall be judged." But the tense of the verb sinned, in both cases is the aorist; and cannot refer to the mere fact that they committed sin; for "all have sinned." The word "sinned" must refer to the general choice of sin as against righteousness and holiness. Therefore have we translated it "life-choice of sin," because the whole life is here looked at as a unit, and that life was a choice of sin, whether by Gentiles without the Mosaic law, or by Jews under it.

Distinction in responsibility, according to privilege enjoyed, is constantly carried through Scripture. But light is light,—not darkness at all. Light is an absolute quality. If persons were lost in a forest at night, the least glimmer of light seen somewhere would attract those who desired deliverance from darkness, and they would hasten toward it; while those that feared light because of works of evil in which they desired to persist, would shrink back farther into the darkness; loving darkness not for its own sake, but, as our Lord said, "because their works are evil."

In both cases, whether of those that do not have the (Mosaic) Law, or of those living, as the Jews did, under it, if they choose sin, there is doom. There will be no respect of persons at all. Those **"without law"** choosing sin **"shall perish"**: those **"choosing sin under law shall be judged by that law,"** and consequently go into more terrible damnation.*

---

*There is a poisonous vagary floating like a miasma through Christendom, that those who do not have the light of the gospel will be saved, either by a "second chance," or by "purgatorial fires,"—because, forsooth, "God is too good to punish sinners." Paul will answer these theories in Chapter 3 by an unanswerable question: "Is God unrighteous who visiteth with wrath? God forbid: for how then shall God judge the world?" Meaning, that wrath is inseparably connected with judgment, whatever the degree of light sinned against may have been.

How indescribably more awful will be the doom of those who now constitute a third company — even those who reject the love and grace of God manifested in His Son! (Heb. 10.28,29).

Always remember that the contemplation of an especially heinous degree of iniquity and consequent judgment is accompanied in the deceitful human heart by the delusion that those not chiefly guilty shall somehow wholly escape. But verse 12 distinctly says as many as chose sin, even though they be "without law" (*anomos* — Cf. I Cor. 9.21 — without externally declared divine revelation), shall also perish.

Now, the word *perish* here is a terrible word! When used in Scripture regarding human beings it never hints of annihilation, but rather the contrary: "And be not afraid of them that kill the body, but are not able to kill the soul: but rather fear Him who is able to destroy both soul and body in Gehenna" (Matt. 10.28). What "destroy both soul and body in Gehenna" means as to time, is shown in Matthew 25.41-46: "Then shall He say unto them on the left hand, 'Depart from me, ye cursed, into the eternal fire which is prepared for the devil and his angels.' And these shall go away into eternal punishment: but the righteous into eternal life," — compared with Revelation 20.10: "And the devil that deceived them was cast into the lake of fire and brimstone, where are also the Beast and the False Prophet; and they shall be tormented day and night unto the ages of the ages."

Note the same word, *aionios*, eternal, concerning life and concerning punishment. "The ages of the ages" is God's constant phrase for the duration of His own endless existence; and for that of Christ, the Son; and for that of His saints. See Galatians 1.5 (the first instance of this phrase,—used 21 times in the New Testament). Revelation 4.9 and 1.18, and 22.5, need to be compared with 20.10, as examples.

ACCORDING TO PERFORMANCE, OR OBEDIENCE, NOT KNOWLEDGE

13   For not those hearing law are righteous before God, but on the contrary those doing law shall be
14   accounted righteous. (For when Gentiles not having law, by nature do the things of the Law, these, not at all having law, unto themselves are law;
15   for such show forth the work written in their hearts of the Law, their conscience bearing joint-witness [to this "work" in their hearts], and their inward thoughts answering one to the other, accusing [them] or else excusing [them].)

Verse 13: **Not those hearing law, but those practising, accounted righteous before God.** The fifth principle is, that hearing God's Word is no advantage without obedience. Paul addresses the Jew directly, beginning at verse 17; but here, in verse 13, the principle is announced in general. It is not yet the Jew as possessing circumcision and the Law, as in verses 17 to 29 (for the word is hearing *law*—not the Law). But it is, in verse 13, the great fact, (true of Jews or Gentiles), that the possession of Divine truth can avail nothing with God apart from subjection and obedience thereto. There is no form of the "deceitfulness of sin" more insidious and more prevalent (because of its subtle power over the self-righteous heart) than that of settling down into false peace because of merely knowing God's truth. Nor does God in this verse say any will be justified by "doing" (for He tells us plainly elsewhere that none will be), but He is saying here that doing, not mere hearing, is what His judgment calls for. We shall find that the gospel will speak of the "obedience of faith": whereas disobedience and unbelief are interchangeable words.

We know that the blood of Christ is the only procuring cause for our being accounted righteous, and faith the sole condition. Yet it is deeply instructive here to quote a passage like that of Luke 1.6, concerning Zacharias and Elizabeth: "And they were both righteous before God, walking in all the commandments

and ordinances of the Lord blameless." Now their walk was
not the ground of their acceptance, although only such as they
are accepted! For they were subject to God's Word, not mere
hearers, but doers. The first verse of the book of Job describes
such another. Indeed, at heart all God's saints are such.

Verses 14, 15: (For when Gentiles [*ethnē**—nations]
not at all having law—that is Law as an external revelation
from God (the Law if you will) : these words alone, although there are many like passages, wholly refute the
claim that God gave the Law to all nations. By nature, the
things of the Law are doing—this does not mean that they
are fulfilling the claims of the Law, for they do not have it,
but that they are unconsciously aware, as moral beings, of
what is right and wrong. These, law not at all having, to
their own selves are law. We are giving the literal rendering of this passage. Note, first, that they do not at all have
law, that is, external Divine enactment. Next, they are by
their moral constitution, not by external enactments, "law
to their very selves." Being such ones, as show out [by
their actions] the work (of the law) written in their hearts
—Here, note most carefully that it is not the Law that is
written, for the word "written" agrees grammatically with
"the work." It is a *work* that is written by God in the constitution of these whom He has "suffered to walk in their own
ways" (Acts 14.16). For "as for His ordinances, they [the
nations] have not known them" (Ps. 147.20). God is describing how He has constituted all men: there is a "work"
within them, making them morally conscious. As we have
said elsewhere, such a "work" would not be contrary to any
succeeding revelation to Israel. Indeed, if the Israelites had
not had this "work" within them, their moral constitution,
the external enactments given by Moses might as well have
been given to the stones of the wilderness. The conscience
of these [nations] bearing fellow witness [with the Law,—
though they have it not] and their inner-thoughts accord-

*This Greek word *ethnē,* translated "Gentiles" in our versions, could always, and
in some cases with great advantage, be translated "nations." It means, like the
Hebrew *goyim,* nations foreign to Israel — not having, as had they, the true God.

ingly one with another accusing or else excusing)—Note that verses 14 and 15 are a parenthesis explanatory of verses 12 and 13: read verses 13 and 16 consecutively to see this fact.

ACCORDING TO HEART-SECRETS

16 —in the day when God shall judge the secret counsels of men, according to my gospel, by Jesus Christ.

Verse 16: The sixth principle of God's judgment here is that it comprehends the very secrets of men. Within every human heart, in hours of consciousness, there is going on a constant dialogue, as we read in verse 15: "Their conscience bearing witness therewith, and their thoughts one with another accusing or else excusing them." There are those, indeed, in whom conscience has been "seared as with a hot iron," so that its voice is no longer heard in protest. In these, also, however, God continually reads the dark, secret things of sin. And in the coming "day" all secrets must come to light. For the wicked, what an outlook! Even the saints, when Christ appears the second time, will come before the judgment seat *(bema)* of Christ (II Cor. 5.10). And, while the question of their works as *sins* will not be brought up at all,—for it is "apart from sin" that He appears to His own (Heb. 9.28),—yet to these, nevertheless, it is said in I Corinthians 4.5: "Judge nothing before the time, until the Lord come, who will both bring to light the hidden things of darkness, and make manifest the counsels of the hearts; and then shall each man have his praise from God." It will be a solemn enough time, even for the saints, to have the works of their lives since their salvation examined, yea, even concerning the "counsels of the hearts," their hidden motives. For the saints will receive only such "praise from God" as is righteously possible for each. But how unutterably awful even the contemplation of appearing *unforgiven* before a God Who will judge the secrets of men by Jesus Christ,—no longer a patient and willing Redeemer, but God's appointed Judge in righteousness! (Acts 17.31).

In this great passage, verses 12 to 16, review carefully these facts:

(a) Absence of degrees of privilege possessed by others, excuses no one.

(b) The greater the privilege, however, the more searching and severe the judgment.

(c) All have committed sin, but it is the *life-choice* of sin, the life looked at as a whole, that is considered, in this place.

(d) Merely "hearing" the Law by a Jew (or, today, by Gentiles, the gospel) justifies no one. The Jew boasted in knowing the Law, but Christ said, "None of you keepeth the Law." Thus, today, millions conscious of "Christian" privilege, and making "Christian" profession are going steadily on to judgment. For the Jew did not obey the Law (which commanded righteousness), and the merely professing Christian has not obeyed the gospel, which commands personal faith in the shed blood of the Redeemer, and confession before men of faith in Christ Risen.

(e) The Gentiles, by their very moral constitution, "by nature," approve the things of the Law: that is, all men know it is wrong to lie, steal, and murder. I asked Chinese who had never heard the Law or the gospel if they knew these things were wrong; they all admitted they did. Consequently,

(f) They are said to be "a law unto themselves, since they show the work of the Law, written in their heart." It is an inner moral consciousness "written" in man's heart, a "work," which while not the Law (though of course not contrary to it), must nevertheless, not be confounded with that operation of God in the future in the hearts of redeemed Israel, when He restores them: "I will put my Law in their inward parts [they will love it], and in their hearts will I write it." [They will not have to try to recollect the Law: they will have it constantly and always before them] for the "stony heart" will have been "taken away" (Jer. 31.31-34; Ezek. 36.24-27). It is then that the (Mosaic) Law will be fulfilled in "every jot and tittle," by redeemed Israel.

But the work of the Law appears in every human being; so that we read,

(g) Man's conscience bears fellow-witness to this law-work in his moral constitution; consequently men daily, hourly, constantly, are having "inward thoughts" which have voices of accusation or approval, according as a man's conduct may be.

To repeat, then, God here declares that there is a righteous "work" Divinely written and maintained in all men's hearts, from which they cannot escape; because their consciences "agree" with it (with this inner working). This "work" is evidently what lies at the root of the human conscience. The Law (of Moses) has never been written in the hearts of the Genties; but a Divine "work" is present in all men. The moral and spiritual constitution of man came 2,500 years before Moses' Law; and the latter could only be the written expression of what existed before as a work, or witness, in man's being, to which his conscience attested.*

ACCORDING TO REALITY, NOT RELIGIOUS PROFESSION

The seventh principle of His judgment, therefore, is, that even a Divinely revealed religion provides no security to its professor if devoid of reality: whether the "Jews' religion" at the beginning of the dispensation, or the "Christian religion" (as it has come to be called), today (verses 17 to 29).

17   But if thou bearest the name of a Jew, and rest-
18   est upon the Law, and gloriest in God, and know-
       est His will, and approvest the things that are

---

*Of course the Sabbath was not a part of this "work" in man's heart. For, although God "blessed" the seventh day (Gen. 2.3), and "hallowed" it, it was because *He* rested from all *His* work on that day. And it was into *His* rest that men failed to enter. For God first revealed the Sabbath to man when He gave it to Israel by means of the manna, and explained it at Sinai (Ex. 19). It was God's special token of a *covenant between Himself and Israel*. No one can read Exodus 31.12-17, with an open mind, and fail to see that the Sabbath was a new revelation to Israel at that time! (Compare Neh. 9.14.)

To Adam was given one simple test of his obedience — not a day, but a tree!

Israel, to whom God's rest was proposed twice, have ever failed to enter it (Heb. 4.3-8).

See further discussion of the Sabbath in Chapter Fourteen.

19 excellent, being instructed out of the Law; and
   art confident that thou thyself art a guide of the
20 blind, a light of them that are in darkness, a corrector of the foolish, a teacher of babes, having in
   the Law the form of knowledge and of the truth:
21 thou therefore teaching another! art thou not teaching thyself? thou, preaching not to steal—dost
22 thou steal? thou, saying not to commit adultery,
   dost thou commit adultery? thou, holding idols in
23 abhorrence, art thou a temple-robber? thou, who
   art glorying in the Law, through thy own transgression of the Law, art thou dishonoring God?
24 For the name of God through you [Jews] is being
   blasphemed among the Gentiles, even as it is writ-
25 ten! For circumcision indeed does profit, if thou
   art a law-keeper: but if thou art a transgressor of
   law, thy circumcision is become uncircumcision.
26 If therefore the uncircumcision be observing the
   moral requirements of the Law, shall not the uncircumcision of such a one be reckoned for circum-
27 cision? and shall not the uncircumcision which is
   by nature, if it keep the Law, rise up in judgment
   against thee, who with the letter and circumcision
28 art a transgressor of law? For he is not a Jew,
   who is one in appearance: neither is that circum-
29 cision which is in appearance, in the flesh! But
   on the contrary, he is a Jew who is one in secret;
   and circumcision is of the heart, in spirit, not in
   letter; whose praise is not from men, but on the
   contrary, from God!

In the above verses Paul directly addresses the Jew. He
shows that the Jew "rested" on The Law,—on having it; and
was proud that the will of the true God had been revealed to
him; that he "knew" that will, and was therefore able to "approve the things that are excellent." He developed a confidence
in himself as a guide, a light, a corrector of the foolish, a
teacher, because in the law he had "the form of knowledge and
of the truth." But did he apply it to *himself*,—his teaching, his

preaching, his saying what folks should be, his abhorring idols, his glorying in The Law? Nay! the name of God was blasphemed among the Gentiles because of the selfishness, the pride, the covetousness, the general wickedness of the Jew!

Paul goes on to declare that Jewish circumcision, which was the mark of that nation's separation to God, was good only if one were thus really separated to God, but that if not, the Jew was really an uncircumcised one; that he was excelled instead, and "judged," by those who, wholly outside circumcision, feared and walked with God. Paul finally declares that a man is not a Jew who is merely one outwardly, and that God does not regard mere outward circumcision: that the only Jew in God's sight is an "Israelite indeed," like Nathaniel, sincere and without guile; and that circumcision is a heart matter, in the real spirit of separation to God and regard for Him. (See the same phrase by which God describes a real Jew [*en tō kruptō*] in Matt. 6.3,6, etc.)

So much for the Jew who was the "religious" man, when Paul wrote Romans. But the "religious" man today is the "professing Christian," and "church-membership" as they call it, has taken the place, in the thought of Christendom, of the Jew's consciousness of belonging to the favored Israelitish race.

If we should thus apply this passage (17-29), must it not read something like this?—"If thou bearest the name of a Christian, and restest on having the gospel, and gloriest in God, and knowest His will, and approvest the things that are excellent, being instructed out of the gospel; and art confident that thou thyself art a guide of the blind, having in the gospel the form of knowledge and of the truth"—Then would follow the searching questions of verses 21 and 22; for do we not know teachers that teach others, but refuse to follow their own teaching? And preachers that denounce stealing, but are accused by the world of being themselves money-grabbers?* So it

---

*The preaching of the gospel is called in the world a "learned profession," along with law and medicine, instead of a high calling of God. The world sneers at the ecclesiastical politics and self-seeking it sees displayed so often. Many professional evangelists, especially, have caused a stench by their reaching after men's pocketbooks.

would read, "Thou who gloriest in the gospel, through thy disobedience to the gospel, dishonorest thou God? The name of
God is blasphemed among non 'church-members'* because of
you! Church-membership† indeed profiteth if thou be an obeyer
of the gospel; but if thou be a refuser of a gospel-walk, thy
'church-membership' is become non 'church-membership.' If
therefore a non 'church-member' obey the gospel, shall not his
non 'church-membership' be reckoned for 'church-membership'?
And shall not non 'church-members,' if they obey the gospel,
judge thee, who with the letter and 'church-membership' art
a refuser of a gospel-walk? For he is not a Christian who is
one outwardly, nor is that 'church-membership' which is outward in the flesh; but he is a Christian who is one inwardly;

---

*Of course we are not referring here to humble, repentant people who may not
have become connected as yet with any company of believers: for we have found
some few of this class. On the other hand, neither do we at all refer, in the questions above, to the cynical, self-righteous, *critics* of the church, and church-fellow-
ship, who complain: "The church is full of hypocrites, therefore, I will have nothing to do with it." The folly of such as these is at once manifest: hypocrites are
going to hell; and these men, who pretend to be shunning the hypocrites on earth,
if they reject personal faith in and public confession of Christ, are on their way to
join them throughout eternity! For whatever the failings of Christians, in their
divisions into sects, their all too manifest weakness of faith, and their inconsistencies, true believers find themselves desirous at once of fellowship with other believers — be the weakness of those believers what it may!

†We repeatedly call attention to the fact which every student of Scripture discovers, that believers are not known in Scripture as *members* of a local assembly,
but *members* of the Body of Christ (Eph. 5.30): "members of Christ" (I Cor.
6.15); and, "members one of another" (Rom. 12.5). This is the only *membership*
found in Scripture.

Although men use the word "member" of this or that local assembly or "denomination," the word should be *fellowship* instead of membership. There is but
one Body: "There is one Body and one Spirit." This should be the constant consciousness of all Christians. To conceive of a Presbyterian *body,* or a Baptist *body,*
or a Methodist *body,* is to defeat at once the one great Body-consciousness which
the Holy Spirit desires to create in all true believers, in answer to our Lord's Great
Prayer in John 17.21: "That they may all be one; even as Thou, Father, art in
Me, and I in Thee, that they also may be in Us."

This, of course, is the very farthest remove from the modernistic cry for
"unity," (as they say), in which they would include all in an outward gathering
together — whether believers, unbelievers (modernists), Jews, or what-not. The
unity of the Body of Christ is in the Holy Spirit, and every believer is a member
of that one Body of which Christ Himself is the Head.

The essence of sectarianism is to be so committed to a system, or to a person,
as to be unable to go on with God, in living faith. No man, no system is fully
right. Only God's Word is perfect. If you are free, you will not be governed in
reading God's Word by what any man may say, however excellent; or what any
system holds. If you must run to this or that "authority," you are a mere sectarian. The Holy Spirit has come! "My children shall be taught of Me," God
has said.

and 'church-membership' is that of the heart, in the spirit not in the letter, whose praise is not of men, but of God."

Now before we proceed, remember yet once again, that God's great announcement of these principles of His throne is given to awaken men out of their false hopes about themselves, unto the truth about themselves; and is to be regarded as a description of God's judgment, as it must be,—in order that men may be *aroused,* and not refuse His truth. But do not confuse Romans Two with Revelation Twenty! At the Judgment Day there will be no such preaching and reasoning with men as Paul here is doing, but damnation only—"according to their works—the things written in the books." O sinner, if God's rebukes are still coming to thee, there is sweet hope for thee! There will be no rebukes in that Great Day: but "visitation" only!

CHAPTER THREE

*The Jews had God's Oracles — a Great Advantage:
their Unfaithfulness Proves, not Hinders, God's Just Judgment. Verses 1-8.*

*Sweeping Fourteen-fold Indictment from Old Testa-
ment Scriptures: All Men, Jews and Gentiles, Brought in
Guilty before God; and so All Mouths Stopped. Verses
9-20.*

*Grace, However, for the Guilty! God's Righteousness
by Another Way than Law — through Faith in Jesus
Christ. Verses 21-31.*

1   What advantage then hath the Jew [over the
    Gentile]? or what has been the profit of circum-
2   cision? Much every way: foremost of all, because
3   they were entrusted with the oracles of God. For
    what if some were faithless to the trust? shall we
    at all think that their faithlessness annulled God's
4   faithfulness? Be it not thought of! Yea, let God be
    true, though every man a liar; as it is written,
        That Thou mightest be justified in Thy words,
        And mightest prevail when Thou comest into
            judgment [by man].
5   But if our unrighteousness commendeth the right-
    eousness of God, what shall we say? Is God un-
    righteous who visiteth with wrath? (I speak after
6   the manner of men). Be it not thought of! for then
7   how shall God judge the world? But if the truth of
    God through my lie abounded unto His glory, why
8   am I also still judged as a sinner? and why not (as
    we are slanderously reported, and as some affirm
    that we say), Let us do evil, that good may come?
    —whose condemnation is just!

72

OR, TO PARAPHRASE this passage: "What preëminence then (if both Jewhood and circumcision are spiritual and inward only), hath the Jew? Or what has the Divine ordinance of circumcision amounted to? Much in every respect! But first and foremost that to that nation the oracles of God were entrusted. For what if some were faithless (to that trust)? Shall their faithlessness render inoperative the faithfulness of God (in carrying out those oracles)? Far be the thought! Yea, let God be found true, and every man, Gentile and Jew (found) false; as it is written (and that by king David, himself, confessing blood-guiltiness):

'That Thou mightest be justified in Thy words,
And mightest prevail when Thou are judged (by
sinful man as to the justice of Thy ways.')

"But (it is further objected) if the unrighteousness of us Jews has proved and publicly commended the righteousness of God both as to His holy nature and as to His truth—(for He plainly prophesied Israel would sin) can we not say that God would be unrighteous to visit us Jews with wrath? (I am speaking thus,—though with horror—because it is the way men talk). Now away with the thought!* For how then (if it were unrighteous for God to visit a Jew with wrath) could God judge the WORLD? (as He indeed will). But (the Jewish objector continues) if the truth of God through my falsity has abounded unto His glory, why am I still judged as a sinner? and why not (since our Jewish evil-doings have in the past been made by God to bring about good)—why not keep doing evil that good may come? They are even slanderously reporting our teaching this awful doctrine!—because we preach righteousness by grace and faith and not by good works. The condemnation of those who bring such arguments is self-evident, and on the very face of it, is just!"

Now to us, at this end of the dispensation, this insistence of God upon moral reality before Him of all, including the Jews

---

*The Greek expression *mē-genoito,* translated in both A. V. and R. V. "God forbid," does not contain the name of God, and should not be so translated. It amounts to, "Banish the thought!" Literally, it is, "Be it not so!" or, "Let it not be conceived of!" Paul uses it frequently,—as much as nine or ten times in this Epistle — to denote instant and horrified rejection of a conception.

themselves, "seems simplicity itself; but it was not so simple to those whom it seemed to strip of all their special and Divinely bestowed privileges." Paul assuredly tells us, in this third chapter, that there is "no distinction" before God between Jews and Gentiles as regards sinner-hood, but he will meet those objections which would arise (vv. 1-8) based in the Jew's mind on (a) the peculiar position of privilege given by God to Israel as Jehovah's separate people; and on (b) the righteous character of God Himself as conceived of by the Jew in his privileged position. These objections* are specious and daring—next to blasphemous: but they must be answered.

The importance of this great passage cannot be overestimated, for if the Jew as that end of the dispensation, or any "religious" person at this end, be allowed to plead special privilege or light as exempting him from judgment, he will spiritually (of course not actually) escape the general sentence of verse 19, where "all the world" is brought under the judgment of God. If a man escapes in spirit from God's pronouncement of "guilty," he will never truly rely upon the shed blood of the Guilt-Bearer, Christ!

Now there are three Jewish questions raised in this passage:

Question I

Verses 1 to 4: What advantage† or preëminence has the Jew and circumcision?

Answer: That nation was entrusted with the oracles of God

---

*Probably Alford is right in viewing these objecting questions "not as coming from an objector, but as asked by the apostle himself anticipating the thought of his reader." I would suggest, however, that the questions beginning in this manner in verse 1 proceed to Paul's thinking Jew-wise in verse 5, and finally, in verse 7, quoting verbally what a Jew (not Paul) would say. This whole passage is generally regarded as one of the most difficult in the whole Epistle. But it will, as we spend work upon it, repay us. Bunyan says:

"Hard texts are nuts — I would not call them cheaters:
Whose shells do ofttimes keep them from the eaters."

†We know that in this dispensation of Grace some Jewish "advantages" become actually a hindrance to one desiring to enter all Divine blessing wholly on grace grounds. This is set forth by Paul in Philippians 3.4-7 ff. There he enumerates seven natural advantages, of which, curiously, circumcision is the first mentioned, zealous persecution of the Church the sixth, and outward legal blamelessness the seventh! These were on the *profit* side (Greek, literally, "gains" side), of Paul's ledger, but he transferred them to the "loss" side: "What things were gains to me, these have I counted loss for Christ."

—inestimable, eternal advantage! despite their unfaithfulness. Every writer of the Bible is, we believe from this, an Israelite. Jewish faithlessness could not annul God's faithfulness in carrying out those oracles (whether of promise, prophecy, or judgment). God must be found true, though every man be false (to whatever God entrusts to him). Paul instances David's most humble confession and ascription of righteousness to God, after David's own great sin had shown David himself faithless to the royal covenant Jehovah had committed to him.

Alford well says: "Because they have broken faith on their part, shall God break faith also on His? Rather let us believe all men on earth to have broken their word and troth, than God His. Whatever becomes of men and their truth, His truth must stand fast."

The "faithlessness" here of the Jew is not his failure to believe God's oracles. (That subject Paul takes up in Chapters 9 to 11.) What is here before us, is the Jew's attitude toward the great primary privilege and responsibility of that nation as the depositary of the Divine oracles. In verse 5, Paul makes the Jews call their conduct "our unrighteousness." It consisted in:

1. National disobedience to God's oracles from Sinai onward.

2. Such neglect of these oracles, that at times (as in Josiah's day), a single copy of the Law was a rarity!

3. Pride, however, over their position as the possessors of these oracles,* even to the despising of nations that had them not, instead of ministering them to others (as Psalm 67 shows was Israel's real business).

---

*As to the expression, "God's oracles" (Gr. *logia*) we quote:

Olshausen: "No doubt in the first place the promises (Acts 7.38; I Pet. 4.11, etc.), and indeed especially those of the Messiah and the kingdom of God, to which all others were related . . . but the whole Word of God is also indicated by this expression. The Divine promises were confided to the Jews, since in what follows it is just this faithlessness (*apistia*) in the possession of these promises which is spoken of. The mention is made of Divine faithfulness (*pistia*) only in connection with this faithlessness."

Tholuck: "Oracles *(logia)* here are primarily, Divine declarations; hence, particularly, promises and prophecies."

Alford: "Not only the law of Moses, but all the revelation of God hitherto made of Himself directly, all of which had been entrusted to Jews only."

Meyer: "Paul means the Holy Scriptures and especially the prophecies of the Messiah and the kingdom. These are not destroyed by the Jews' unbelief."

4. Appalling ignorance of the spiritual meaning of the Divine oracles, and of the "voices of their prophets," so they even killed the Righteous One! (Acts 13.27).

Question II

Verses 5 and 6: If God makes use of human sin to set forth His glory (as He will) would it not be unrighteous to punish that sin with wrath? Here Paul enters into the Jewish con- sciousness: "If our unrighteous Jewish history has commended the righteousness of God, what shall we say? God went right on fulfilling what His oracles said, despite the unfaithfulness of us to whom they had been committed, and, in fact, by means of our sinful Jewish history God's prophecies concerning our dis- obedience were fulfilled before the whole world, from Moses on."

Read here Deuteronomy 31.14 to 32.47. For it is about Israel that Deuteronomy 32.35 to 47 is written. The Jew, knowing well his past disobedient history, yet holds fast to his national place of outward favor, resisting Paul's word of Chapter Two, "He is not a Jew that is one outwardly"; and daring to regard God as "unrighteous" who would "visit with wrath" individuals of His favored nation—for they had only carried out God's predictions!

Paul, in even bringing up such a question as God's acting unrighteously in visiting disobedient Israelites with wrath, in- stantly puts in the reverent parenthesis: "I speak after the man- ner of men"; as, "putting himself in the place of the generality of men, and using an argument such as they would use."

Answer: "Far be such a thought! for then (if God should be unrighteous in visiting a Jew with wrath) how shall God judge the *world?*" The Judge of all the earth will do right, and He will judge the whole world (Acts 17.31) which involves the infliction of wrath upon any and all impenitent, as all Scrip- ture shows.

Note that Paul assumes, and so do even these cavillers, that there will be a day of judgment: "God who visiteth with wrath." What the apostle is attacking is the false hopes of men to evade that judgment. Christ has been judged and smitten in our stead. But, alas, how a man hates to come to the cross as one "to whom that stroke was due" (Isa. 53.8). But if you manage to escape conviction of sin, and thus miss personal faith in the Crucified One, you will go to hell forever.

Question III

Verses 7 and 8: "If God's truth (as to His warnings and promises) was enhanced through my falsity—if He got glory through my (Jewish) sin, why does He find fault with me as a sinner?" Here the very words of the resisting Jew are, as it were, quoted.

Answer: While such cavilling Paul will not deign to answer (for it answers itself!) Paul does return into the gainsaying Jews' teeth the constant slander against salvation by grace,— that it led to license: "The condemnation of such trifling is just! For it is evident both to the hearer and to the asker of such a question that doing evil that good may come, does not change the character of the evil, nor take away its guilt from him who commits it."

"Slander" against the gospel of grace is still going on, and will go on until the Lord comes in righteousness. Moule well says, "The mighty paradox of justification (without works) lent itself easily to the distortions, as well as to the contradictions, of sinners. 'Let us do evil that good may come' no doubt represented the report which prejudice and bigotry would regularly carry away and spread after every discourse and every argument about free forgiveness. It is so still: 'If this is true, we may live as we like'; 'If this is true, then the vilest sinner makes the best saint.' "*

The Jews, deluded by pride, and falsely basing God's favor to their nation upon their own deserts, absolved themselves from judgment. Judgment they relegated to the *"goyim,"* the *"ethnē,"* the Gentiles. Paul himself shows the Jewish consciousness in his rebuke to Peter in Galatians 2: "We being Jews by nature, and not sinners of the Gentiles." And the Pharisees said even of the common, non-religious sinners of the Jewish

---

*Godet says: "God cannot become guilty of any wrong toward any being whatever. Now this is what He seems to do to the sinner, when He at once condemns and makes use of him."

nation: "This multitude that knoweth not the Law, are accursed!" (John 7.49).

But if we, professing Christians, consign this whole passage to the Jew, we fall directly into the same terrible trap. Whole multitudes today in Christendom, sheltered in their imagination by the fact that they have "joined" some church, resent the very doctrines that Paul here insists on. Thousands of so-called "church-members" not only have never been brought under real conviction of sin and guilt and personal danger, but rise in anger like the Jews of Paul's day when one preaches their danger directly to them!

Now if God paid no attention whatever to the claim of the Jew to be exempt from judgment because he was a Jew, neither will He pay any attention to the claim of the "Baptist" or "Presbyterian," "Episcopalian" or "Methodist,"—*as such*. For all men are alike guilty, common sinners! What avails before a holy God the special religious names sinners may call themselves? This book of Romans will do you and me no good if we apply it to Jews or Mormons only!

9   What then? are we [Jews] superior? Not at all!
     For we before laid to the charge both of Jews and
10   Greeks, that they are all under sin; as it is written,
         There is none righteous, no, not one;
11   There is none that understandeth [divine
             things],
         There is none that seeketh after God;
12   They all abandoned the way [of God],
             together they became unprofitable;
         There is none that practiseth goodness,
             no, not so much as one:
13   Their throat is an open sepulchre;
         With their tongues they have used deceit:
         The venom of asps is under their lips:
14   Whose mouth is full of cursing and bitterness:
15   Their feet are swift to shed blood;
16   Destruction and misery are in their ways;
17   And the way of peace they have not known:
18   There is no fear of God before their eyes.

Verse 9: **What then?**—in view of all said of the Jews from Chapter 2.17 to Chapter 3.8.

Are we Jews superior (as we generally think ourselves to be to them—that is, to the Gentiles?) Not at all! Paul here speaks as a Jew,—in sympathy with the Jewish nation, indeed, but rejecting wholly their boast of superiority, in view of the great general indictment of the whole human race, that began in this Epistle at Chapter 1.18 and continues to Chapter 3.20. This is what he means by having **before laid to the charge both of Jews and Greeks, that they are all under sin.** "To be *under sin* means to be under the power of sin, to be sinners, whether the idea of guilt, just exposure to condemnation, or of pollution, or both, be conveyed by the expression" (Hodge).

Now this expression "under sin" is a remarkable and unusual one. We need to note the same expression and context in Galatians 3.22: "The Scripture shut up all things under sin, that the promise by faith in Jesus Christ might be given to them that believe." "All things *under* sin" is a larger expression than "guilty of sin," or, "in bondage to sin." It is a general state described, as of convicts in a prison, or disease-stricken people "under quarantine." An even stronger expression concerning human beings, Gentiles or Jews, asserts: "God hath shut up all unto disobedience, that He might have mercy upon all" (11.32); and the words, "The Scripture shut up all things under sin, that the promise . . . might be given," bear out this fact. Moule says, "Being *brought* under sin, (as the Greek bids us more exactly render), giving us the thought that the race has fallen from a good estate *into* an evil."

That the Jews and Greeks alike, that is, the whole world, are "under sin," is next abundantly shown by Paul from seven Old Testament Scriptures. It will not do to say, as do some, that since the Scriptures were given only to the Jews, therefore the Jews only are in view here, in verses 10 to 18. For we read in Psalm 14, the very first Scripture here quoted:

"Jehovah looked down from heaven upon the children
of men,
To see if there were any that did understand."

"Children of men" is a wider term than Jews. Furthermore, Romans 3.9, which begins this great arraignment, includes both Jews and Greeks as being *"all* under sin." This, therefore, is a world-wide indictment.

FOURTEEN HORRIBLE THINGS ABOUT ALL MEN

We shall find God speaking, in these fourteen counts,* first, as a Judge: verses 10 to 12; next, as a Physician: verses 13 to 15; and third, as a Divine Historian: verses 16 to 18.

I

First, then, as a Judge God describes man's condition:

Verse 10: To begin with, **There is none righteous** [before God], **no, not one** (Ps. 14.1; 53.1; Job 9.2; Eccl. 7.20). No human being has in himself ever been righteous. Even Adam was not righteous: he was innocent—not knowing good and evil. Let us put far from our minds the fond falsehoods of philosophy, science, and human "religions," that there have been men of our race who have attained to a standing before God in righteousness.

Verse 11: Next, **There is none that understandeth** [Divine things]. We have added the words "Divine things" even in the Scripture text, because this verb *(suniēmi)* translated "understandeth" is one of those words which God reserves in Scripture unto a peculiar meaning. (See footnote on 1.31.) Note its use in Matthew 13.13,14,15,19,23,51, as, for instance, verse 19: "When anyone heareth the word of the kingdom,

---

*This awful list of fourteen facts about the human race, quoted from the Old Testament Scriptures, describes, of course, humanity as it is by nature. Therefore if we have believed the gospel, and are thus righteous before God in Christ, we have double reason to study these truths: first, that we may by understanding the facts, as God sees them, about ourselves, have a correct estimate of humanity, which, of course, unenlightened men never gain; and, second, that we may be constantly moved to give praise to God for His measureless grace that reached even such as we were!

Meyer's outline of verses 10 to 18 is: "(1) A state of sin generally (verses 10-12); (2) practices of sin in words (verses 13-14); in deeds (verses 15-17); and (3) the sinful source of the whole (verse 18)."

Haldane thus sums them up: "The first of them, verse 10, prefers the general charge of unrighteousness; the second, verses 11 to 12, marks the internal character, or disorders of the heart; third, verses 13 to 14, those of the words; the fourth, verses 15 to 17, those of the actions; the last, verse 18, declares the cause of the whole."

and understandeth it not." It is used twenty-six times in the
New Testament, the last time in Ephesians 5.17: "Understand
what the will of the Lord is." Now humanity, by nature, "understands" nothing of God. Men think they do, and write vast
books on the subject; but God's sentence remains: "There is
none that understandeth." "In the wisdom of God the world
through its wisdom knew not God." Believe just that: it is
true.

The third of these solemn counts is, **There is none that
seeketh after God.** You say, How can this be possible in
view of pagan lands filled with temples, and worshipers
thronging them? God's answer is: "The things which the Gentiles sacrifice, they sacrifice to demons, and not to God" (I
Cor. 10.20).

Adam, sinning, turned his back and fled from a holy God.
God had to take the place of the seeker: "Adam, where art
thou?" So it has ever been. No human being has ever sought
the holy God. Conscious of his creature weakness, and also
of responsibility and guilt, and filled with terrors of conscience,
or terrors directly demon-wrought; or perhaps under the delusion that some "god" (really, demon) might grant him this
or that favor, man has built his temples and conducts his worship. Banish from your mind the idea that any human being
has ever had a *holy* thought, or love for a *holy* God, in his
natural heart! Grace *"praeveniens et efficax"* (grace "prevenient
and efficacious") is the old phrase expressing the truth that
God Himself takes the place of the seeker, convicter, persuader,
giver, and final perfecter of all man's salvation. His sovereign
grace goes ahead of, and brings into being, all human response
to God.

The fourth solemn count is that of universal human
apostasy: **They all abandoned the way** [of God]. The same
Greek word is used only twice elsewhere in the New Testament: "Now I beseech you, brethren, mark them that are causing the divisions and occasions of stumbling, contrary to the
doctrine which ye learned: and *turn away* from them" says Paul
(Chapter 16.17). The separation was to be absolute, and of
choice. And in I Peter 3.11, the saints are told (quoting Psalm

34): *"Turn away* from evil, and do good,"—again a direct
choice. In Psalm 14.3 it is: "They are all gone aside"; and in
Psalm 53.3: "Every one of them is gone back." To Israel it
was said: "Ye shall observe to do therefore as Jehovah your
God hath commanded you" (Deut. 5.32). But Isaiah speaks
of them (and we know the application becomes universal):
"All we like sheep have gone astray; we have turned every
one to his own way" (Isa. 53.6); while Malachi in the closing sad message of the Old Testament bewails: "Ye are turned
aside out of the way" (2.8).

To understand Romans 3.12, we must conceive of a race of
creatures turned out of God's way, as really as are Satan's
angels, or the demons. The whole race of man is by nature
in that awful case!

As a result you have the fifth count: **They are together
become unprofitable.*** The human race is useless, and worse
than useless, to God. This word translated "unprofitable" was
used by the Greeks concerning rotten fruit, or whatever was
utterly, irrevocably bad, and therefore useless. Ask any house-
wife what can be done with rotten fruit! In Psalms 14.3 and
53.1, from which this is quoted, it is translated "become filthy."
Unless we hold firmly in mind these statements of truth concerning humanity, we shall fail to see what man is, and so
what God's grace sets before him.

The sixth count is, **There is none that practiseth goodness, no, not so much as one.** Corruption rather than holiness, selfishness rather than goodness, cruelty rather than kindness, is the way of apostate mankind everywhere. Thus declares the Judge who looks upon men as they are.

II

Verse 13: Next, God speaks as the all-wise, holy Physician, in diagnosis: **Their throat is an open sepulchre.**
Doctors always insist first on looking down our throats: and
we all know that the throat and tongue denote the state of

---

*It is striking how God uses the aorist tense here and in the previous count. The
race is looked at from Adam down, and as partaking of his guilt, and wilfully in
his path. Note also *hemarton* of verse 23: "all sinned, and are [as a result]
falling short." We shall note this word further, in Chapter 5.12.

health. There could be nothing more horrible than what we have here: death, decay, moral stench, and that not hidden, but open! Unhidden, unashamed putridity:—thus a holy God describes the throat of every one of us by nature! As Bishop Howe says: "Emitting the noisome exhalations of a putrid heart." We must remember we are here seeing man through God's all-holy eyes.

With their tongues they have been using deceit [since man's fall]. The verb is in the imperfect tense, which denotes the habitual practice of the human race. This includes your tongue and mine, reader. But the case is still worse; for the Physician continues:

The venom of asps is under their lips: The fangs of a deadly serpent lie, ordinarily, folded back in its upper jaw, but when it throws up its head to strike, those hollow fangs drop down, and when the serpent bites, the fangs press a sack of deadly poison hidden "under its lips," at the root, thus injecting the venom into the wound. You and I were born with moral poison-sacks like this. And how people do claim the right to strike others with their venom-words! to use their snake-fangs!

Verse 14: **Whose mouth is full of cursing and bitterness** (Ps. 10.7): To prove this, you need only take your stand upon any street, and strike upon the mouth a passerby. As well strike a hornets' nest! How men do curse others! Bitterness is ever ready! What fearful folly for a race speaking thus to imagine that by "being baptized," and "joining the church" they are ready to "go to heaven," and be in the holy company on high, with the meek and lowly Son of God and the holy angels,—and all this without a thought of being forgiven, washed, born again!

Verse 15: **Their feet are swift to shed blood** (Isa. 59.7): I saw a child under two years raise its puny fist against another, crying, "I'll kill 'oo!" Murder is so common, now, that new hideous expressions are invented: "I'll get him"; "Bump him off"; "Put him on the spot"; "Take him for a ride"; or, as the awful Communistic phrase puts it, "Liquidate him." When the restraining grace of God is withdrawn, it will be given to the Red Horse Sitter "to take peace from the earth, and that they should slay one another" (Rev. 6.4). Men's feet, like tigers', are ready and swift for blood-shedding: *"For further details, read your daily papers!"*

III

Third, God speaks as the All-seeing *Historian* of fallen man:

Verse 16: **Destruction and misery are in their ways** (Isa. 59.7). What an epitome of human history. It is said that the ancient Troy of which Homer sang was built upon the ruins of an earlier Troy,—and that seven other Troys, each constructed upon the ruins of a former, have been found! As Meyer vividly renders: "Where they go is desolations (fragments) and misery (which they produce)." Those who so loudly proclaim that the human race is "improving," "progressing," are blind deceivers,—blind to history, blind to present day facts, blind to the rising tide of human violence. "As it was in the days of Noah," our Lord said, "so shall be the coming of the Son of Man." In those days of Noah the earth became "full of *violence*" (Gen. 6.11).

Verse 17: **And the way of peace they have not known.** (Isa. 59.8). It is a terrible thing God here reveals, that not one of the human race knows, or is by nature pursuing, the path of peace. It does not seem to me that the Spirit of God speaks here of that peace with God on the ground of accepted sacrifice which Chapter 5.1 describes (and which is always a direct revelation of God to the soul), but rather in consistence with the context and with the passage in Isaiah 59.8 from which it is drawn: "The way of peace they know not;* and there is no justice in their goings: they have made them crooked paths; whosoever goeth therein doth not know peace." The unregenerate man does not know, follow, or really desire to know the way of wisdom, all whose paths are peace (Prov. 3.17). Thomas Scott well says: "They know not the ways in which godly men walk, at peace with God and their neighbors; and so they go on

---

*This ignorance, of course, is itself a matter of guilt, as is abundantly shown in Leviticus 4.2, 13,22,27: "If any of the people of the land sin unwittingly in doing anything . . . and be guilty."

in those paths which lead to misery and ruin both to themselves and to each other."

Verse 18: **There is no fear of God before their eyes** (Ps. 36.1). This last is the most awful count of all, and explains all the others. "To fear God consists in having such a due sense of the majesty and holiness and justice and goodness of God, as shall make us thoroughly fearful to offend Him. For each of these attributes of God is proper to raise a suitable fear in every Christian mind."

A friend once pointed out to me a champion prize-fighter of America, and I heard another man remark, "How I'd hate to be hit by him!" He could fear a fellow-man. But in a few moments the same man's mouth was using the name of God, and even of Jesus Christ, in profanity! There was "no fear of God before his eyes." It meant nothing to him that God had said, "The Lord will not hold him guiltless that taketh His name in vain." But what will it mean when that man steps out of this life into the realities of eternity! Bengel aptly notes, "The seat of reverence is in the eyes." Godet says: "The words 'before their eyes' show that it belongs to man freely to evoke or suppress this inward view of God on which his moral conduct depends." Haldane comments: "They have not that reverential fear of Him which is the beginning of wisdom, and which is connected with departing from evil. It is astonishing that men, while they acknowledge that there is a God, should act without any fear of His displeasure. They fear a worm of the dust like themselves, but disregard the Most High!" And Calvin says: "Out of the contempt of God cometh all wickedness. Seeing that the fear of God is the fountain of wisdom, when we are once departed from it, there abideth nothing right or sincere. If it be wanting, we are loosed unto all kind of licentious wickedness."

This great passage then, (verses 9 to 18) needs to be pondered, prayed over, thoroughly believed, and preached continually, in these last days, when God-consciousness is dying out. It is no kindness, but a terrible wrong, to hide from a criminal the sentence that must surely overtake him unless pardoned; for a physician to conceal from a patient a cancer that will destroy him unless quickly removed; for one acquainted with the hidden pitfalls of a path he beholds someone taking, not to warn him of his danger!

Verses 19 and 20 concern particularly that nation to whom the Law was given, for Paul plainly in verse 9 applies the passage through verse 18 to "both Jews and Greeks" as "all under sin." But now he turns directly to those who had the Law:

19   Now we know that whatsoever the Law says it is speaking to them that are under the Law [i.e., to the Jews]; in order that every mouth may be stopped, and all the world [Gentile and Jew] may
20   come under the judgment of God; because out of works of law no flesh shall be declared righteous before Him; for through law comes knowledge of sin [not righteousness].

In verse 19, we repeat, and not till then, does Paul turn again to the Jews as those who were under law* to shut off their possible escape from that general arraignment by Scripture of "both Jews and Greeks" beginning at the ninth verse. Thus every mouth was "stopped." Men's mouths keep talking of their own goodness or of someone else's badness, or of both,—as, for example, the Pharisee in the eighteenth of Luke. But the moral history of mankind delineated in Chapter One; and the stern principles of God's judgment which considered neither man's high notions of himself, nor his religious professions, as shown in Chapter Two; and now, in Chapter Three, the fourteen sweeping statements of Scripture concerning the whole guilty human race, with the double conviction of the Jews as not only sinners, but also transgressors of the very Law they

---

*Many insist that the words "the Law" of verse 19 include only all the quotations from Scripture from verse 9 to verse 18; and they would apply it only to the Jews, as alone possessing that Law. But God in verse 9 applies to both Jews and Greeks what is "written" in the following Scriptures (of verses 10-18). We would regard "the Law" in verse 19, then, in a stricter and more confined sense, — as when our Lord said to the Jews, "Did not Moses give you The Law?" Our Lord's general division was "The Law and The Prophets" (Luke 16.16); and in Luke 24.44 He speaks of "the things that are written in the Law of Moses, and the Prophets, and the Psalms concerning Me." In John 10.34 He uses the term "Your Law," covering even the Psalms. And yet, as we said above, the quotation from Psalm 14, includes the whole human race. And if it be argued that this psalm uses God's name Jehovah, His special name for Israel, we reply that in the parallel psalm, the Fifty-third, the name used is God, Elohim, the Creator of the whole earth.

gloried in,—all this stops men's vain mouths! For they are all brought into the presence of their Judge, and the sentence of guilty is upon them all. Not that they are brought in to have their just penalty executed upon them; but that they may be silent while God their Judge announces—astonishing thing!— that He has himself already dealt with the world's sin upon a sin-offering, Jesus, His Son; whom, we shall soon see, He set forth at the cross as a righteous meeting-ground between Himself in all His holiness and righteousness; and the sinner, whether Jew or Gentile, in all his guilt,—through simple faith in the shed blood of this Redeemer!

Verse 20: Now Paul declares what the law cannot do, and what it can do. First, **no one shall be declared righteous [justified] in God's sight by works of law** ["doing right"]; and second, the business of God's Law is rather to **make known to men their sin,** and therefore, their need of a salvation which the Law cannot supply.

In this verse we meet by far the most difficult Divine utterance for the human heart to yield to, that we have met in the entire Epistle. Even those "without law,"—"Gentiles that have not the Law" (of Moses—2.14), we find throughout history so committed to their own ideas of what is "right," and what will propitiate the demons that they worship, that they will desperately fight for their convictions. (See Paul at Lystra, and at Ephesus, in the Acts.) And how much more difficult the task becomes in dealing with those who, as the Jews, know that they have had a direct revelation from God,—"Thou shalt" and "Thou shalt not," and, "He that doeth these things shall live by them." When Paul told the Athenians that he acknowledged them to be "very religious" (their city indeed being filled with idols), but that they were ignorant of God, the Creator, who had raised up from the dead One who would be Judge in righteousness: "Some mocked: others said, We will hear thee concerning this yet again." Now, we say, if men are brought off only with great difficulty from the follies of idolatry, how much greater the task to persuade men to abandon their trust in a holy Law they know to have been given by the true God, from heaven, and on the fulfillment of which all their hopes for eternity have been dependent!* In just the same way Christendom has become fixed in its defense of its "religious" convictions. Scripture names, doctrines and ordinances—falsely explained—have seized hold upon the convictions of men, so that it is more difficult to dislodge them from their position than the heathen themselves. We know from Scripture, for example, that "days, seasons, months and years," do not belong to the Christian position in the least degree, but are Jewish or pagan in origin. Christmas, Lent, Easter, the whole "church calendar," forms, ritualism, the confessional, the mass, clergy,—where are these found in the Epistles of the New Testament? They are not found! Yet try once to dislodge them from those in whose hearts they have been planted! For their heart-hopes are bound up with these false traditions.

None but those taught of God, and they with extreme difficulty and constant watchfulness, escape legal hope. For the question ever before the conscience is, If keeping God's Law avails me nothing for righteousness in His sight, *why did He give it?* WHY DID HE GIVE IT?

And this difficulty becomes all the greater, the more the excellency of the Law is discovered! For our judgment sees these things of the Law to be "holy, and righteous, and good." And we know (if we are honest) that "God spake all these words"—of the Law.

Therefore, the heart's only relief is to hear God's own Word concerning seven questions; to all of which the coming chapters of Romans will give answer: (1) To what nation did He give the Law; (2) Why He gave the Law; (3) What the Law's ministry was; (4) How it was set aside, or "annulled," for another principle entirely; (5) What is meant by the words "under grace"; (6) How the walk "in the Spirit" takes the place of walking by external enactments; and, (7) How that only in those not under law is "the righteous state" *(dikaioma)* of the Law fulfilled!

---

*Someone says, "It is not the good works men have done so much as the good works they persuade themselves they some time will do, in which they hope." For almost all know themselves to have failed; yet they promise themselves that they will be "better"; and the thought of being declared righteous by a work altogether outside of themselves, never once occurs to them!

Now it is apparent that to bring men off from their false hopes in their law-obedience, three things must become evident to them:

(a) That law, having been broken, can only condemn.

(b) That even were men enabled now to begin keeping perfectly any law of God, that could not make up for past disobedience, or remove present guilt.

(c) That keeping law is NOT God's way of salvation, or of blessing.

In connection with verse 20, we will emphasize only the third of these points, for that is what is insisted upon in this verse. We quote in the footnote below verse 20, and then a number of plain statements of Scripture to the same effect, that we may compare Scripture with Scripture:*

The knowledge (or recognition) of sin comes through law, —by (1) its revealing what God approved in man, and what God disapproved and forbade; (2) causing man to undertake obedience; and (3) condemning him for failure to obey.

To all seven of the questions above, the coming chapters of Romans, compared with other Scriptures, will, as we have said,

---

*By works of law shall no flesh be justified in his sight; for through law cometh the recognition of sin (3.20).

A man is justified by faith, apart from works of law (3.28).

To him that worketh not, but believeth on Him that justifieth the ungodly, his faith is reckoned for righteousness (4.5).

Not through the Law was the promise made to Abraham . . . but through the righteousness of faith (4.13).

For if they that are of the Law are heirs, faith is made void, and the promise is made of none effect (4.14).

Through the obedience of the One shall the many be constituted righteous. And law came in alongside, that the trespass might abound (5.19,20).

Ye are not under law, but under grace (6.14).

Ye were made dead to the Law through the body of Christ (7.4).

We have been discharged from the Law (7.6).

Christ is the end of the Law for righteousness to every one that believeth (10.4).

Until this very day at the reading of the old covenant the same veil remaineth, it not being revealed to them that it is done away in Christ (II Cor. 3.14).

A man is not justified by works of law but through faith in Jesus Christ (Gal. 2.16).

If ye are led by the Spirit, ye are not under law (Gal. 5.18).

Law is not made for a righteous man (I Tim. 1.9).

For there is a disannulling of a foregoing commandment [by Him who gave it] because of its weakness and unprofitableness (for the Law made nothing perfect), and a bringing in thereupon of a better hope, [Christ's work] through which we draw nigh unto God (Heb. 7.18,19).

fully give the answers. But it will be wise, perhaps, to look a moment more, in this place, at questions 2, 3 and 4:

As to Question Two, Why God gave the Law, we call attention now, as elsewhere, to the fact that in His dealing with Abraham, and, in fact, in all His ways with the patriarchs, there was not the Law, but simply and only *the promise*. We plainly see in Romans 5.14 that they were not under law. They walked by simple faith, which is, of course, the only principle according to which God has saving relations with man since he became a sinner. But (and this is important) God must show man his sinnerhood and this could not be done but by His revealing His holiness and righteousness, and asking man to conform his life and ways to that holy and righteous rule. God knew he would not and could not do this; but man did not know it, and must discover it through failure. Therefore and thereunto did God give the Law. "By the Law is the knowledge of *sin*."

We have now partly answered Question Three, as to what was the appointed ministry of the Law. But the matter needs to be further emphasized. God names the Law a "ministration of condemnation and death" and not of righteousness. As Paul says in Chapter Seven, "Sin, that it might be shown to be sin, wrought death to me through that which was good" (the Law).

As to Question Four, the Law was set aside or "disannulled." We have God's oft-repeated and most emphatic assertion, that this has been done: "There is a disannulling of a foregoing commandment because of its weakness and unprofitableness (for the Law made nothing perfect), and a bringing in thereupon of a better hope, [Christ's death, burial and resurrection], through which we draw nigh unto God" (Heb. 7.18,19). We repeat this over and over, because that is the way God does—He asserts and re-asserts this great fact: knowing man's self-righteousness will hardly suffer the Law to be taken away.

Now it was not that God changed His plan, though to the thoughtless mind He might seem to have done so: (1) by beginning with man on the faith principle—from Abel onward; then (2) conditioning Israel's relationship and blessing upon their legal obedience; and then (3) "changing back" again, since the cross, to the way of simple faith apart from law. No, there has been no "change" in God. God's way with man has always been that of faith. Neither was the Law a thing additional to faith to secure God's favor; nor was God's "disannulling the foregoing commandment" an evidence that He had been seeking and expecting righteousness in man by the Law; and that now since the Law had failed He resorted to grace, apart from works of the Law. Not at all! The Law came in simply that the trespass might abound,—that is, that by breaking it man might discover his guilt and sinfulness; and his helplessness to relieve himself. Moses had prophesied in Leviticus and Deuteronomy that Israel would utterly fail, and that they would be provoked to jealousy by God's bringing in the Gentiles, "a foolish nation"; and that the remnant of Israel finally, its whole legal hope cut off, would be restored by God in *sovereign mercy* (Rom. 11.31,32).

We know we are saying these things over and over. An old German educator said: "The first principle of teaching is *repetition;* and the second principle of teaching is *repetition;* and the third principle is *repetition.*"

So we come to the next great section of the Epistle, Chapter Three, verses 21 to 31. This will describe God's righteousness through faith in Jesus Christ.

JUSTIFICATION BY FAITH IN CHRIST

21   But now apart from law, God's righteousness hath been manifested,—borne witness to by the Law and
22   the Prophets: God's righteousness, moreover, through faith concerning Jesus Christ unto all them that believe; for there is no distinction [between
23   Jew and Gentile]; for all sinned, and are falling
24   short of the glory of God; being reckoned righteous gift-wise by His grace through the redemption that
25   is in Jesus Christ: whom God set forth a propitiation [mercy-seat] through faith in His blood, unto showing forth His [God's] righteousness in respect of the passing over of the foregoing sins in the for-
26   bearance of God: for the showing forth of His righteousness in the present time,—unto the being Himself righteous, and the One declaring righteous the person having faith in Jesus.

27   Where then is the [Jewish] boasting? It is ex-
      cluded. By what manner of law? of works? Nay:
28   but by a law of faith. For we reckon that a man is
      accounted righteous by faith apart from law-works.
29   Or is God the God of Jews only? [who had the
      Law]. Is He not the God of Gentiles also? Yea, of
30   Gentiles also: if so be that God is one! And He
      shall declare righteous the circumcision on the
      principle of faith [instead of law], and the uncir-
      cumcision through their [simple] faith.
31   Do we then annul law through faith? Far be the
      thought! on the contrary, we establish law!

We now come to the unfolding of that word which Paul in
Chapter One declares to be the very heart of the gospel,—the
reason it is "the power of God unto salvation": namely, "therein
is God's righteousness on the faith-principle revealed to any
having faith" (1.17).

The first work of the apostle, as we have seen in studying
Chapter 1.18 to Chapter 3.20, was to bring the whole world
under the judgment of God, guilty, helpless. His second task
(and it is a blessed one!) is to reveal God's coming out in righteousness at the cross unto us. Let us most diligently read, ponder, yea, and commit to memory verses 21 to 26; for it is God's
great statement of justification by faith. Its first announcement is:

Verse 21: **But now apart from law God's righteousness
hath been manifested,—borne witness to by the Law and
the Prophets**—The first words, "But now," should be hailed
by us joyfully, as beginning an account of something heavenly
different from our guilt and helplessness, detailed in the preceding part of the Epistle (1.18-3.20).

The next phrase is: "apart from law"*—lay it to heart!

---

*The absence of the definite article, *the,* before the word law, in 3.21,28,31;
4.13, etc., shows that it is the abstract principle of law that is before us rather than
the specific, concrete, thing — the Law of Moses, the ten commandments. It will
become evident to us that God is dealing with men now upon a different principle
altogether than that of law: for grace confers the blessing, and lets the fruit flow
from "faith working through love" by the power of the Spirit. Law demands fulfilment of conditions before blessing: grace announces that Christ has fulfilled all
conditions.

Unfortunately, the King James Version misses the emphasis here. For the Greek puts to the very front this great phrase "apart from law" *(chōris nomou)*, and thus sets forth most strongly the altogether separateness of this Divine righteousness from any law-performance, any works of man, whatsoever. Luther's rendering was, "without accessory aid of law." In this revelation of God's righteousness, law was *left out of account*. Righteousness is *on another principle than our right-doing!*

Now the great and most common error in setting forth God's righteousness here, is, to allow law at least some place. Men cannot, it seems, get over reasoning thus: that since God once promulgated the dispensation of law, which called for human righteousness, He must thereafter be bound by it forever. And this despite Divine assurance, over and over and over, that the present dispensation proceeds on an altogether different principle; that there has been a "disannulling of a foregoing commandment" (Heb. 7.18) ; for He who had the right to command had also the right to disannul. It was "because of its weakness and unprofitableness—for the Law made nothing perfect,"—that the "foregoing commandment" was set aside. It had served its purpose—to make the trespass "abound" (5.20).*

It is not that God has not the right to demand legal righteousness from us: but that He does not do it. "Righteousness which is of God" speaks in a way diametrically opposite to man's law-obedience, of any sort whatsoever.

Men who do not see or believe that the whole history of those in Christ ended at the cross (for they died there, with Christ) must hold that God is still demanding righteousness: for "the law hath dominion over a man so long as he liveth!"

The "teachers of the Law" (I Tim. 1.7) say: "Behind God, as He talks with you in 'grace' is His eternal Law. And He must carry out what He has expressed in that Law. But, because you are not able to perform it, He has 'graciously' given Christ, to perform all its requirements for you. And the positive, or

---

*"The Law has no such office in the present state of human nature manifested in history and in Scripture as to render righteous: its office is altogether different, viz., *to detect and bring to light the sinfulness of man*" (Alford).

'active' requirements are, the observance of all the commands of the Law to the letter,—which (these teachers say) Christ has by His perfect life of obedience to the Law on earth, furnished for you. And the negative, or 'passive' obedience, as they call it—that is, the penalty of death for your sins which the *Law* (say they) demanded, Christ has paid on the cross. So that, now your debts cancelled by Christ's death, you have Christ's legal 'merits' as your actual righteousness before God: for God must demand (they say) perfect righteousness from you, as measured by His holy Law,"—etc., etc.

This seemingly beautiful talk is both unscriptural and anti-scriptural.

God says that the believer is not under law, that he is dead to law,—to that whole principle, being in the Risen Christ; and Christ is certainly not under law in Heaven! Believers are "in Him"; they are "not in the flesh" (Rom. 8.9). They were formerly in the flesh (in the old natural life of Adam); but are now "new creatures" in Christ Risen!

If you put believers under law, you must put their federal Head, Christ, back under law; for "as He is, even so are we in this world." To do this you must reverse Calvary, and have Christ back again on earth "under law." For law, we repeat, was not given to a heavenly company, but to an earthly nation. Scripture says it was to redeem that earthly people (Israel) who were under law, that Christ was "born under the Law" (Gal. 4.4). You must thus, if you are "under law," be joined to a Christ belonging to Israel, a flesh and blood Christ; and must consent to be an Israelite—to which nation He was sent. But alas! You find that such a Christ is not here! That He said He must "abide alone,"—like the grain of wheat unless it "fall into the ground and die." To an earthly, Jewish Christ, you therefore cannot be united. And so your vain hope of having Moses and Christ is wholly gone. Therefore you must be united with a Risen Christ, or with none at all! But if to a Risen Christ, it is unto One who died unto sin (6.10); and those (Jewish) believers who were under the Law died with Him unto it (7.4). And you, if you are Christ's, are now wholly, as Christ is, *on* *resurrection ground.* This truth will be brought out fully in Chapters Six and Seven; we can but note it here.*

The words **hath been manifested** (of verse 21) Conybeare lucidly paraphrases, "not by law but by another way, God's righteousness is brought to light." God had always dealt righteously, although His way was not as yet plain. He pardoned many, and He did not seem wholly to judge sin even in the unsaved world. But at the cross "He spared not His own Son." Here was revealed, indeed, righteousness to the uttermost!

Borne witness to by the Law and the Prophets—by the Law, in its sacrificial offerings; by the Prophets, in direct statements: "This is His name whereby He shall be called: Jehovah our righteousness" (Jer. 23.6); and again, "Thy righteousness" —21 times in the Psalms! as, "I will make mention of Thy righteousness, even of Thine only" (71.2,15,16,19,24); and Isaiah: "By the knowledge of Himself shall my righteous Servant make many righteous" (53.11).† Yet it was not brought to light how this should be, until "the fulness of the time" came, and God sent His Son to "suffer for sins, the just for the unjust," to "put away sin by the sacrifice of Himself," that God's righteousness might be "manifested," both in His dealing with sin, and in glorifying His Son in heaven, who had glorified His Father on earth.

It would have been righteous for God to smite Adam and Eve as He did the angels that sinned. He could have revealed Himself in righteousness of judgment in accord with His holiness and justice. He was not obliged to save any man. But it was God's will to reveal *Himself:* for He is *Love.*

Therefore He now comes forth at the cross in love,—albeit He must there come forth also in righteousness,—for He Him-

---

*Your body — you are waiting for the redemption of that. But your body is only the "tabernacle" in which you dwell, — it is not yourself. "That which is born of the Spirit is spirit" (John 3.6). "He that is joined unto the Lord is one spirit" (I Cor. 6.17).

†Peter indeed declares that "God had foreshowed by the mouth of all the prophets that His Christ should suffer" and "to Him bear all the prophets witness, that through His name every one that believeth on Him shall receive remission of sins" (Acts 3.18; 10.43). It is well to remember that Paul reminds his hearers in Pisidian Antioch that it is possible to hear the prophets read and really not understand "the voice of the prophets" nor Him of whom they spake (Acts 13.27).

self must righteously and fully judge sin upon the person of
His own provided Lamb. The sword "awakened against His
Shepherd, the Man who was His Fellow,"—the "fellow" of
Jehovah of hosts! The Shepherd was smitten: "He was bruised
for our iniquity, the chastisement of our peace [that would pro-
cure peace for us] was upon Him." God spared not His own
Son, but delivered Him up, and the penalty for our sin was
visited upon Him, Jesus, God's provided Sacrifice (Zech. 13.7;
Isa. 53.5,6).

God is able to come forth to us now in absolute GRACE,
sending out His messengers "preaching peace by Jesus Christ";
—nay, preaching much more than peace. In effect, God says,
"Utter and infinite oceans of grace shall roll over the place
where judgment and condemnation were!" Forgiving us all our
trespasses, He goes further: having raised up Christ from the
dead, He says, I will now place you in my Son. I will give you
a standing fully and only in Him risen from the dead! Not
only did He bear your sins, putting away your guilt, but in His
death I released you from your standing and responsibility in
Adam the first. You who have believed are now new creatures
in Christ: for I have created you in Him.

And because this is so, it is announced further: "Him who
knew no sin, God made to be sin on our behalf; that we might
become the righteousness of God in Him." These astonishing
words state the present fact as to all believers,—of all those in
Christ: they are the righteousness of God in Him!*

---

*"The resurrection of Christ was not only Divine power in life; there was an-
other truth in it. Divine righteousness was shown in it. His Father's glory, all
that the Son was to Him, was concerned in His resurrection; Christ having perfectly glorified God in dying, and having finished His Father's work, Divine righteousness was involved in His resurrection. And He was raised, and righteousness
identified with a new state into which man, in Him, was brought; and more than
that, indeed, for more was justly due to Him — He was set in glory as man at
the right hand of God. Not only did the blessed Lord meet for us who believe all
our sin as children of Adam, by His death, so as to clear us according to the
glory of God from it all in His sight; but He perfectly glorified God Himself in
so doing. Man, in the person of Christ, then entered into the glory of God. 'Now
is the Son of Man glorified, and God is glorified in Him, . . . and shall
straightway glorify Him.' But all Christ's work was wrought for us; our sin was
put away by it. Christ, as having thus glorified all God is, is our righteousness.
We are thus 'the righteousness of God in Him.'

"Either Christ, in His own present perfectness, risen from the dead, is my
righteousness, His place my place, and I myself absolutely dead and gone as regards the old man; or I am making Christ a completer of my standing, as alive

In the book of Romans, Paul is describing God's action toward a believing sinner in view of the shed blood of Christ. It is as if God were holding court with the infinite value and benefit of the propitiatory sacrifice and resurrection of Christ only and ever before Him. No other apostle will be called upon to set this forth fully as does Paul. Of course it could not be stated by the Old Testament writers in its fulness and clearness; for our Lord had not then offered Himself, and all the Law and Prophets could do was to declare sin temporarily "covered" (Heb., *kaphar*) from God's sight; and so the Old Testament believer was one who rested on what God *would* do, in view of these types and shadows and promises.

John the Baptist, however, pointing to Christ, said, "Behold the Lamb of God that taketh away the sin of the world," something that had never before been! Therefore, after the cross, it is written, "Once in the consummation of the ages, hath He [Christ] been manifested to put away sin by the sacrifice of Himself."

In the Old Testament, we repeat, sin is *covered*,—which is the meaning of the word *kaphar*, "atonement,"—used only in the Old Testament, and there constantly (some 13 times in one chapter—Leviticus 16), to express the covering from God's sight of sin: though the sin remained untaken away until Christ died. In the New Testament, therefore, sin is said to be put away by Christ's sacrifice.*

God can, therefore, not only forgive the sinner, but also proceed to declare the believing sinner righteous, not at all meaning that he has any righteousness of his own, or that "the 'merits' of Christ are imputed to him" (a fiction of theology);

---

*We call attention to the error in the King James Version at the end of Romans 5.11 where those translators render "atonement" when it should be "reconciliation" (*katallangē*). Therefore, properly speaking, the idea of covering up sin ("atonement," *kaphar*, of the Old Testament) is entirely absent in any mention in the New Testament of the effect of Christ's sacrifice, which does not cover up but *puts away* sin from God's sight forever.

---

in the old man. Scripture teaches me that I am not alive as a child of Adam in this world. 'If ye died with Christ . . . why as though alive in the world?' says Paul.

"And now I am in Christ, risen and ascended; and have no righteousness to make out, but to glorify God as His child, being the righteousness of God in Christ already. My defects have nothing to do with my righteousness. They have with respect to my living to God and enjoying communion with Him" (Darby).

but that God, acting in righteousness, reckons righteous the ungodly man who trusts Him: because He places him in the full value of the infinite work of Christ on the cross, and transfers him into Christ Risen, who becomes his righteousness.

We may look at the term **God's righteousness** from God's own side; then from that of Christ; and, finally, from that of the justified sinner.

1. From God's side, the expression "God's righteousness," must be regarded as an absolute one. It is His attribute of righteousness. It can be nothing else. He must, and ever will, act in righteousness, whether it be toward Christ, toward those in Christ, or toward those finally impenitent, whether angels, demons, or men.

2. From Christ's side, it is His being received by God into glory according to God's estimation of His mediatorial work. Our Lord had said that when the Spirit would come, He would "convince the world . . . of righteousness, because I go unto the Father, and ye see me no more" (John 16); and, He had said, "I glorified Thee on the earth, having accomplished the work Thou gavest me to do. And now, Father, glorify Thou me with Thine own self, with the glory I had with Thee before the world was" (John 17). In answer to this prayer Christ was "raised from the dead through the glory of the Father" (Rom. 6.4), and was "received up in glory" (I Tim. 3.16). Now our Lord was man, as well as God. And when the Father glorified Him "with His own self," with that glory Christ "had with Him before the world was," it was as man that God thus glorified Him. So that, at God's right hand, Christ set forth publicly the righteousness of God; for (a) as the slain Lamb He shows the holiness of God and God's righteousness fully satisfied,—since God had "spared not His own Son" when sin had been laid upon Him. The truth of God as to the wages of sin had been shown in Christ's death; thus the majesty of the insulted throne of God had been publicly vindicated, so that Christ's being raised and "received up in glory" set forth the righteousness of God; for it were unrighteous that Christ should not be glorified! And (b) Christ not only thus set forth the righteousness of God, but being God the Son, as well as man, He

was that righteousness! Christ dead, risen, glorified, is the very righteousness of God!

3. From the believer's side, the justified sinner's side, what do we see? The amazing declaration of God concerning us is, "Him who knew no sin God made to be sin on our behalf, that we might become the righteousness of God in Him" (II Cor. 5.21). The saints are said to be the righteousness of God, in Christ. Of course self-righteousness simply shrivels before a verse like this! All is in Christ: we are *in* Christ—one with Him!

The expression "God's righteousness" then signifies:

1. God Himself acting in righteousness (a) toward Christ in raising Him from the dead and seating Him as a man in the place of absolute honor and glory; (b) in giving those who believe on Christ the same acceptance before God as Christ now has, inasmuch as He actually bare their sins, putting them away by His blood, and also became identified with the sinner—was "made to be sin for us" and, our old man was thus "crucified with Him." Just as it would have been unrighteousness in God *not* to raise His Son after His Son had completely glorified Him in His death; so it would also be unrighteous in God *not* to declare righteous in Christ those who, deserting all trust in themselves, have transferred their faith and hope to Christ alone.

2. Thus Christ, now risen and glorified, is Himself the righteousness of believers. It is not that He acted righteously while on earth, and that that is reckoned to us. This is, we repeat, the heresy of "vicarious law-keeping." He was indeed the spotless Lamb of God; but He had no connection with sinners until His death. He was "separate from sinners." "Except a grain of wheat fall into the earth and die, it abideth by itself alone." It is the Risen Christ who is our righteousness. "Christianity begins at the resurrection." The work of the cross of course made Christianity possible; but true Christianity is all on the resurrection side of the cross. "He is not here, but is risen," the angel said.

3. Thus Christians find themselves spoken of as the righteousness of God in Christ. Not as "righteous *before* God," for that would be to think of a personal standing given to us, on

account of Christ's death, rather than a federal standing, as *in* Him, united to Him,—which we are! John Wesley said a wise thing indeed: "Never think of yourself apart from Christ!"

Now to be or become "righteous *before* God"; to have or obtain a standing that will "bear God's scrutiny," is the fond dream of very many earnest Christians. But however stated, and by whomsoever stated, that idea of our obtaining a "standing *before* God" falls short, and that vitally, of Paul's gospel of our being made *the righteousness of God in Christ*. It denies that we died with Christ; and that we have been made dead to the whole legal principle in Christ's death (7.4). Thus it leaves us under the necessity of "obtaining a standing" before God; whereas believers federally shared the death of Christ, and Christ Risen is Himself now our standing!

Negatively, then (as Paul begins to declare in his first recorded discourse, Acts 13.39), "Every one that believeth on Him is justified *from* all things";—"justified in His blood" (Rom. 5.9); and

Positively, Christ was "raised for our justification" (4.25): that we might receive *a new place,* a place in a Risen Christ,— and be thus the righteousness of God in Him, as one with Him who is that righteousness.

God declares that He reckons righteous the ungodly man who ceases from all works, and believes on Him (God), as the God who, on the ground of Christ's shed blood, "justifies the ungodly" (4.5). He declares such an one righteous: reckoning to him all the absolute value of Christ's work,—of His expiating death, and of His resurrection, and placing him *in Christ:* where he is the righteousness of God: for Christ is that!

Does Christ need something yet, that He may stand in acceptance with God? Then do I need something,—for I am in Christ, and He alone is my righteousness. If He stands in full, eternal acceptance, then do I also: for I am now in Him alone,—having died with Him to my old place in Adam.

Earnest and godly men, wonderfully used of God, have brought out, as did the Reformers, that we are justified by faith, not works: without, however, going on to show, as does

Paul, our complete deliverance, in Christ, from our former *place* in Adam, and from the whole principle of law.

The Reformation statements were as follows:

Luther: "The righteousness of God is that righteousness which avails before God." This means a "substantive righteousness,"—a quality bestowed which "avails." But I am not in these words seen as dead, and now in Christ only.

Calvin: "By the righteousness of God I understand that righteousness which is approved before the tribunal seat of God." Here again is a quality, not Christ Himself, who is made righteousness unto me, and I myself "of God," in Him (I Cor. 1.30). And according to Calvin I must stand before God's "tribunal"! But Christ at the cross met all the claims of God's "tribunal,"—and that forever; and I am now in Christ Risen!

Again, Calvin, writing on II Corinthians 5.21, concerning our being made or becoming "the righteousness of God in Christ," says: "In this place nothing else is to be understood than that we stand supported by the expiation of Christ's death before the tribunal of God." Here is still the thought of a future (or present) "tribunal." Only the negative side—expiation of guilt, is brought out. But this text in II Corinthians is positive: we *are* God's righteousness in Christ! Believers are not seen by Calvin as having died with Christ, and having no connection at all with Adam's responsibility to furnish a righteousness and holiness before God's "tribunal." Believers, says Paul, are not now "in the flesh" in their standing,—they are seen by God in Christ only! (Rom. 8.9). Calvin, and all the Reformers, and the Puritans after them, placed believers under the Law of Moses as a "rule of life"; because they did not see that a believer's history in Adam *ended at the cross*. But Paul, in Galatians 6.15,16, says that those in Christ are to walk as "new creatures": they are a new creation! "And as many as shall walk by this rule, peace be upon them!" This is God's prescription for your walk, whatever men may teach!

We do quote Luther, that great man of God, in connection with Chapter Seven, in the expressions of his wonderful personal faith, as saying: "These words, 'am dead to the Law'

(Gal. 2.19) are very effectual. For he saith simply, 'I am dead to the Law'; that is, I have nothing to do with the Law . . . Let him that would live to God come out of the grave with Christ." (Luther on Galatians; in which book is often shown a vigor and boldness of faith hardly to be matched since Paul!)

Dr. Scofield in his note on Romans 3.21, says that the righteousness of the believer "is Christ Himself, who fully met in our stead and behalf every demand of the Law." Yet Scripture says that the Law was given to Israel; and that Gentiles are "without law," as contrasted "with Israel," who were "under the Law." Paul's words to us in Romans 6.14: "Ye are not under law, but under grace," do not mean that we were once under law (as were the Jews) and have now been delivered; but rather mean that we, having died with Christ (our old man crucified with Him, and our history in Adam closed forever before God), are not placed at all under law! It is unfortunate that Dr. Scofield goes on to quote beloved Bunyan: "The believer in Christ is now, by grace, shrouded under so complete and blessed a righteousness that the Law from Mt. Sinai can find neither fault nor diminution therein. This is that which is called the righteousness of God by faith."

Now it is at once evident that such a statement as Bunyan's leaves "the Law from Mt. Sinai" master of the field, lord over us. According to this the Law remains Inspector General of those in Christ! We are not "discharged" from it. We are still on earth, under legal trial, men "in the flesh." The gospel, however, is that we are, in Christ, not under the law-principle at all! "Ye are not in the flesh, but in the Spirit." Those who believe are not now under law, but under grace, being "in Christ." We are now in a Risen Christ, who as such "lives unto God"; and it is unthinkable that He is under law! The Word of God says that Christ was "born of a woman,"—thus reaching the whole race; and "born under the Law, that He might redeem them that were under the Law,"—that is, Israel. But to maintain that the Risen Christ is "under law" in Heaven, is both to deny Scripture (Rom. 6.4) and also to close our eyes to the manner of His risen life (6.10). Christ in Heaven lives under no legal conditions, but freely, in love, unto God. And God has sent forth "the Spirit *of His Son*"—mark that!—into our hearts. This means not only the witness that we are adult sons *(huioi)* of God, but that the very same emotions of relationship and nearness to the Father belonging to Christ, God's Son, are ours,—witnessed in our hearts by the Spirit of His Son!

We find hardly any writers except indeed certain devoted saints among the "Friends of God" of the fourteenth century; and, later, certain among the mystics like Tauler, Ter Steegen, Suso, and the "prince of German hymnists," Paul Gerhardt; together with many early Methodists; and in the nineteenth century, certain of those remarkable men whose followers were later called "Plymouth Brethren," who have seen or dared believe our complete deliverance before God from Adam the First: that is, from our former place "in the flesh," "under law." The last, the Brethren, indeed speak with more Pauline accuracy. But these earlier saints, though much persecuted, exhibit marvelously in their lives and testimony that heavenly freedom of those taught of God their place in Christ! Hear one of them singing:

"Thou who givest of Thy gladness
    Till the cup runs o'er—
Cup whereof the pilgrim weary
    Drinks to thirst no more—
Not a-nigh me, but within me
    Is Thy joy divine;
Thou, O Lord, hast made Thy dwelling
    In this heart of mine.

"Need I that a law should bind me
    Captive unto Thee?
Captive is my heart, rejoicing
    Never to be free.
Ever with me, glorious, awful,
    Tender, passing sweet,
One upon whose heart I rest me,
    Worship at His Feet."

—Gerhard Ter Steegen.

The Law was given to man in the flesh; not to those on resurrection ground. Our relationship now to God is that of standing in the same acceptance as Christ; and we have the same Spirit of sonship as Christ!

Now, Christ was raised from the dead through the glory of the Father, and the life that He now liveth, He liveth unto God. And He lives unto God as man. He is God; but He is also a Risen Man.

It is into this Risen Christ, thus glorified, that God has brought us.*

We do not need therefore a personal "standing" before God at all. This is the perpetual struggle of legalistic theology,—to state how we can have a "standing" before God. But to maintain this is still to think of us as separate from Christ (instead of dead and risen with Him), and needing such a "standing." But if we are in Christ in such an absolute way that Christ Himself has been made unto us righteousness, we are immediately relieved from the need of having any "standing." Christ is our standing, Christ Himself! And Christ being the righteousness of God, we, being thus utterly and vitally in Christ before God, have no other place but in Him. We are "the righteousness of God in Christ."

Not to the cherubim, not to the seraphim, not to the elect angels, has been given such a place as this! They may be sinless,—they are. They may be holy,—they are. They may be glorious,—they are. But they are not "the righteousness of God"; for they are not *in Christ*. They were never cut off, as we have been, by a death that ended completely their former history and standing, and then placed *in Christ!*

And so we come to a verse the very reading of which has been used to save and bring into the light thousands:

Verse 22: **God's righteousness, moreover, through faith concerning Jesus Christ unto all them that believe—If it**

*The "righteousness of God" in the justification of the sinner, is His own attribute of righteousness; that is, His acting in accordance with His own holy nature; manifested, however, not in demanding righteousness from the sinner, but in setting the believing sinner in His own presence, because of the righteous judgment of his sins already visited by God upon his Substitute, Christ. And God is not only *Himself righteous*, in remitting the penalty of sin; but He sets the sinner in the *very standing in which Christ is*, with Him!

were man's righteousness, it would be through something man accomplished. But it is *God's righteousness;* it is apart from our right-doing—that is, law-keeping altogether; for keeping law would be the only way man could get a righteousness of his own.

But the moment we mention righteousness here, people can hardly be restrained from the notion that they are to have a new *quality* bestowed upon them. Since they have themselves lost this quality of righteousness, they are anxious to get it back,—the consciousness of it. But this is really self-righteousness,—and that at its worst.

For we read here the words, "through faith in [or concerning] Jesus Christ." And people rush to talking of Christ's "merits" becoming theirs, being "imputed," or reckoned to them: so that they are, thereby, in a righteous state!

But we shall see in Chapter 4.5 that God accounts righteous the believing *ungodly as such;* not those who are first to be in any wise "changed," and *then* reckoned righteous; not those to whom certain "merits" of Christ are to be given, so that they are thereby righteous—not at all. But the *believing ungodly* are to be reckoned righteous—while they are *still ungodly*: it is that fact that makes the gospel!

Justification is God's reckoning a man righteous who has no righteousness,—because God is operating wholly upon another basis, even the work of Christ. If Christ fully bore sin for man, and has been raised up by God, a believing man has reckoned to him by God all that infinite work of Christ!

Thus, no change in the ungodly man is necessary for justification.* He believes, certainly. But faith is not a "meritorious" work. It is simply giving God the credit of speaking the truth in the gospel about Christ. It is Christ's shed blood, and that alone, which is the procuring cause of God's declaring an ungodly man righteous: while God's grace is the reason for it. Our faith is simply the instrumental condition. God counts

---

*Of course, God will — does — give him *life*: it is "justification *of life,*" in Christ. But he is justified, accounted righteous, while ungodly; and only by the blood of Christ. God will also finally, indeed, present him faultless. But he declares him righteous upon believing — while he is ungodly! If God changed him first, he would not be "ungodly."

our faith for righteousness, because by it we give God and Christ the full glory of our salvation. Faith in God also brings the heart into His light; for, when "with the heart man believeth unto righteousness," the heart, in thus believing, is turned to God directly, in the simplicity of a little child. When Adam sinned, he fled from God; when a sinner believes, he comes back!

Now concerning this chiefest revelation of Romans, we must go to Scripture only. It will never do to accept men's writings as "authorities," or as "standards,"—as men call them. For to do this is not to interpret the Scriptures, but to proceed along Romish lines. Nor will it do to rely on men's devotedness to God, however real, as proof of their reliability in statements of Divine truth.

Take the Reformers: God brought them back, in principle, to the Scriptures as their only guide. (Would that there were the same devotedness and zeal today!) But, after mounting up to Heaven as it were, in personal grasp and use of the truth of justification by faith apart from all works, yet the Reformers put Christians back under Moses as a "rule of life," under law! "What is required? and what is forbidden?" in this Mosaic commandment, or that, is the burden of Christian living, according to this theology.

Godly and earnest men have thus held; but the only question is, what are the words of Scripture? We must "prove all things" men write, in the light of Scripture: for God says we are not under law: and that the "rule of life" is, that we are a new creation (Gal. 6.15,16). Is the Pauline revelation that we died with Christ from all earthly "religious principles" (Col. 2.20), (such as God declares the Mosaic system now to be: Gal. 4.9)—is this glorious fact once set forth in all the reformed "standards"? By no means! Believers were not seen by the Reformers as having had their history ended at the cross, and being now wholly in a new creation. Neither did the Puritans enter into this truth. This Pauline doctrine was not fully recovered until God wrought,—again in a reviving, almost a Reformation power, through godly and devoted servants of His, 300 years after Luther and Calvin. Truth is truth: and those seeking God's truth welcome it wherever they find it! Revealed Truth belongs to the whole Church, to every believer. Those attached to, and entrenched in *tradition,* will always be found fighting for *that.**

Simple faith, then, receives "God's testimony concerning His Son," and rests there. They used to say of Marshall Field in Chicago, "His word is as good as his bond." It was no credit to the merchants that trusted Mr. Field, but it was a great credit to him! It gave him the public honor of his integrity.

God's righteousness, moreover, through faith concerning Jesus Christ—Here we must study carefully. The King James Version reads, "by faith of Jesus Christ." "Through faith" is more accurate, as the preposition is, *dia,* "through," as the Revised Versions, both English and American, read. Concerning the form, *"of Jesus Christ,"* see Mark 11.22, Acts 3.16, Gal. 2.16, Jas. 2.1 where the same Greek construction appears.

The expression "faith concerning Jesus Christ," literally, "faith of Jesus Christ" must be regarded either as:

1. Faith in the gospel of God concerning Jesus Christ, as set forth at the beginning of the Epistle, involving of course appropriation of Christ with all His benefits for oneself; or,

2. Trust in Christ. But Christ has already died for sin, for

---

*We are glad to note, in Sanday and Headlam's *Romans,* this word regarding William Kelly's *Notes on Romans:* "His *Notes* are written from a detached and peculiar standpoint; but they are the fruit of sound scholarship, and of prolonged and devout study, and they deserve more attention than they have received." This is a fair and honest admission. For its irrefutable setting forth of truth, its Christian fairness and love, and its brevity, make Kelly's *Notes* invaluable.

Men prefer "belonging" to a system: (1) Because where faith is not vigorous it comforts the flesh to find oneself among a party. (2) Where direct personal knowledge of Scripture is lacking it is a comfort to the heart to be told "authoritatively" what to believe — what the party to which one belongs, holds. (3) It is abhorrent to the flesh to walk by the Spirit. It is infinitely easier to be occupied with the "Christian duties" practiced or prescribed by your sect. (4) The flesh cannot bear to be little, despised, but desires to be of those that have the regard of "the Christian world" (an awful phrase!). (5) Even among the most earnest Christians the temptation and the tendency have always been to seize upon those truths emphasized by the leaders of the sect they follow and claim those truths and principles as their own! But this in effect denies the unity of the Body of Christ, and that all truth belongs to the whole Church of God.

Now all this is of the very essence of Sectarianism. If your Christian consciousness is of anyone but Christ as Head over all things to the Church, and of any *body* but the Body of Christ, of which all true believers are members, and you members of them — then you are on forbidden, sectarian, "carnal" ground: "For when one saith, I am of Paul; and another, I am of Apollos; are ye not men . . . are ye not carnal, and do ye not walk after the manner of men?"

the world; and trust, here, would mean relying on Christ to do something for the soul; either to put forth power to deliver; or, as they say, to become one's "personal Saviour"; or, "to see one through to the end," or the like. This is in accordance with man's gospel: "Jesus Christ *will* save you *if,*"—rather than in accordance with Paul's gospel of believing God's Word concerning Christ as having accomplished *for us* a work that was finished once for all on the cross.

3. The rendering received by many today in certain circles which would make "the faith of Jesus Christ" mean *Christ's own believing on our behalf!* which, they explain, is "exercising His own mighty faith," instead of calling upon the strengthless hearts of men to believe. But this avoids our responsibility to believe God. They quote here Mark 11.22: "Have faith in God," as, "Have the faith of God"; a grotesque, unbiblical, impossible meaning! Our Lord said, "If thou canst believe, all things are possible to him that believeth." He did not say, "I will believe for you." Again He did say, "This is the work of God, that ye believe on Him Whom He [the Father] hath sent" (John 6.29).

4. Finally, some have thought to render, "the faith of Jesus Christ" as His faithfulness to us; which is not the meaning of the Greek, is out of place, and is contrary to the apostle's usage.

We believe that the first meaning we have indicated—that is, faith in the gospel of God concerning Jesus Christ as set forth at the beginning of the Epistle, is the true one here; for it accords perfectly with this first great expansion in Chapter Three, of the announcement of Chapter 1.1-3, "the gospel of God concerning His Son": the power of which is that "therein is revealed God's righteousness on the principle of faith."

Faith is not trust, and must be carefully distinguished therefrom, if we would have a clear conception of the gospel. Faith is simply the acceptance for ourselves of the testimony of God as true. Such faith, indeed, brings one into a life of trust. But faith is not "trusting," or "expecting God to do something," but relying on His testimony concerning the person of Christ as His Son, and the work of Christ for us on the cross. So faith is "the giving substance to things hoped for." *After saving faith, the life of trust begins.* In a sense that will be readily perceived by the spiritual mind, trust is always looking forward to what God will do; but faith sees that what God says has been done, and believes God's Word, having the conviction that it is true, and true for ourselves.

In saving faith, then, you do not trust God to do something for you: He *has* sent His Son, who *has* borne sin for you. You do not look to Christ to do something to save you: He *has done it* at the cross. You simply receive God's testimony as true, setting your seal thereto.* You rest in God's Word regarding Christ and His work for you. You rest in Christ's shed blood.

It is GOD that justifieth (8.33), as it is God against whom we sinned. And it is God whom we find in Chapter 3.25 setting forth Christ on the cross as a righteous meeting-place (between the sinner and God) through faith in His blood. And again: "To him that worketh not, but believeth on Him [God] that justifieth the ungodly" (on the ground, of course, of the blood of Christ). "Righteousness shall be reckoned unto us who believe on Him that raised Jesus our Lord from the dead" (4.5 and 24). This, it seems, is what the Lord meant in His last public message to the Jews, John 12.44: "Jesus cried and said, He that believeth on Me, believeth not on Me, but on Him that sent Me." Faith, indeed, lays claim to Christ and possesses Him, but it is through believing the testimony of God the Father concerning His Son.

And this seems to me the meaning of the words in Chapter 3.22, "through faith concerning Jesus Christ." Peter also says not only that we have "the answer of a good conscience toward God, through the resurrection of Jesus Christ" (I Pet. 3.21), but: "through Him [Christ] ye are believers in God, that raised Him from the dead, and gave Him glory; so that your faith and hope might be in God" (I Pet. 1.21). Thus also, he says, "Christ also suffered for sins once, the righteous for the unrighteous, that He might bring us to God" (I Pet. 3.18).

---

*I often quote I Timothy 1.15 to inquiring sinners: "Christ Jesus came into the world to save sinners." In response to my question, they confess that "came" is in the past tense. Then I say, "How sad that you and I were not there, so that He might have saved us, for He has now gone back to heaven!" This shuts them up to contemplate the work Christ *finished when He was here;* upon which work, and God's Word concerning it, sinners must rest: *that is faith.*

We must remember that it is the "gospel of God" (Rom. 1.1) in its general aspect, which we are now studying; and that it is "concerning His Son." Christ says also in John 5.24, "He that heareth My word, and believeth Him that sent Me hath everlasting life and cometh not into judgment."

Now we believe concerning Jesus Christ: (a) that He is the Son of God, (b) that He has put away sin by His blood (as Paul will soon show); and (c) that He is and has become through simple believing our very own, so that what He has done was really done for us.

You may say, this is simply "believing on the Lord Jesus Christ." Yes; but it is believing God concerning Christ. In Chapter Four we find that Abraham believed God, and righteousness was reckoned unto him. We also "believe on Him that raised Jesus our Lord from the dead, who was delivered up for our trespasses, and was raised for our justification." Here the faith is in God, and is made possible by His raising Christ, upon whom He had placed our sins. Sanday says: " 'By faith of Jesus Christ': that is, by faith which has Christ for its object." In the gospel of God concerning Christ, God announces not only Christ's person as Son of David, and Son of God; but also His finished work, that He has been set forth by God as a propitiation, a righteous meeting-place between the sinner and God. It is therefore God whom the sinner believes; and in believing God he appropriates Christ, and His saving work.

There is another question in this 22nd verse which must be answered. The King James Version adds, after "The righteousness of God by faith of Jesus Christ unto all," the words "and upon all them that believe." The Revised Version omits "and upon all." This, we believe, is the correct reading. The righteousness of God is not put "upon" any one. That is a Romish idea,—still held, alas, among Protestants who cannot escape the conception of righteousness as a something bestowed upon us, rather than a Divine reckoning about us. But the best authorities omit these words "and upon all," as do the oldest manuscripts, and both the English and American Revised Versions. The words, "God's righteousness through faith concerning Jesus Christ unto all them that believe," describe it all, and fully.

I know people argue that "unto all" describes the "direction of the blessing"; and "upon all" those who (as they put it) have the blessing actually "conferred upon them." But please notice the present passage is setting forth the fact of a new, present revelation—God's righteousness by faith in Christ, as over against man's legal righteousness. Since we find this righteousness is God's accounting or holding righteous a man who believes, rather than a conferment of a quality upon a man, we must read the passage thus. It sets forth this present by-faith righteousness. It is God accounting a man (even as he is, "ungodly"—4.5) righteous in His sight. Do not destroy the gospel by adding to Romans 3.22 words which evidently have been supplied by some one ignorant of the truth. It is simply "God's righteousness through faith about Jesus Christ."*

---

*I have found Mr. Darby's explanations of "God's righteousness" more clear and illuminating than those of any other. It is therefore unfortunate, as it seems to me, that he adds to verse 22 the confusing phrase, "and upon all." I ask, *what* is "upon all"? If, as Mr. Darby holds, the act of justification is a forensic one, a declaration about a sinner who believes, accounting him righteous (although he is not intrinsically so), then why add that this righteousness is "upon" him? For the human mind is unable to conceive of a meaning for such a phrase other than something that a man does not possess being placed upon his person. But this is the exact meaning that Mr. Darby so constantly and justly wars against!

The very thing Mr. Darby so assiduously avoids, that is, the bestowal on a person of a quality, (or of, as he says, "a quantum of righteousness"), he opens the way to, in retaining the phrase "and upon all." Bishop Moule, for example, remarks: "As to 'unto all and upon all,' the Greek phrases respectively indicate destination and bestowal. The sacred pardon was prepared for all believers, and is actually laid upon them as a 'robe of righteousness.'" We would expect such a comment as this from a churchman, or any one of the Reformation theologians, but it is the very thing that Paul does not say; and it darkens all counsel concerning justification.

The expressions "the righteousness of Christ," "the merits of Christ," though not in Scripture, are continually in the mouths even of earnest men, who do not see that our history in Adam ended at the cross, that we died with Christ, and now share His risen life; and that we therefore do not need to have anything whatever "put upon" us, nor any qualities or "merits" of Christ made the basis of God's blessing us. We were in Adam: we are now in Christ, standing in the full, the infinitely complete acceptance of Christ's own Person!

We gravely fear that some brethren, in their resentment against the Revised Version (which we well know is not perfect, though incomparably more accurate than the King James), have kept this phrase "and upon all," in spite of the fact that the earliest manuscripts do not have it. Bishop Gore well remarks, "It is not an exaggeration to say that, in this and very many places of the epistles, the Revised Version for the first time renders the thought of the apostles again intelligible to the English reader. And if the Revised Version is not popular, this is, I fear, only a sign that the majority of English Christians do not really care to under-

Righteousness is a court word. Righteousness is reckoned by God to them that believe. The faith of the ungodly man who believes is "counted for righteousness" (4.5).

The words that close verse 22, **"for there is no distinction,"** should be joined with verse 23: "for all sinned, and are falling short of the glory of God." Pridham well says, "The all-important point to be regarded here is the complete setting aside of the creature-title." That there is no difference as to the fact of sin, between Jews and Gentiles, is, of course, primarily before us in the words "no distinction." Exactly the same expression is found as to the availability of salvation in Chapter 10.12: "no distinction between Jew and Greek." We may well apply it to everybody, as does Pridham in his "no creature title." There is no distinction between sinners—between great offenders and small, with respect to this matter of sinnership. Not the degree of sin, but the fact of sin is looked at here. If you should visit a penitentiary, you would find some imprisoned for terrible crimes, and others for lesser offences, but you would find, in the eyes of the law, no innocent men!

Verse 23: **for all sinned, and are falling short of the glory of God**—Note the difference in the tenses: "all sinned" is in the past tense, while "falling short" of God's glory is stated in the present tense. When Adam had once sinned, in Eden, he continually fell short, outside of Eden, as did all his race, by him and after him.

While it is true, as both the old Version and the Revised translate, that "all have sinned"; yet I am more and more persuaded that inasmuch as the Spirit of God uses in verse 23

stand the meaning of the message with which, as a matter of words, they are familiar."

Mr. Darby himself says that neither the Reformers nor any other human teachers, are an authority for him, so we, agreeing, say that Mr. Darby is in no sense an authority for any Christian. "Prove all things," said the Apostle.

F. W. Grant admits that the earliest manuscripts omit "and upon all." He then says, "The earliest of all is corrected." But why was the earliest manuscript "corrected"? Some hand of legal unbelief "corrected" that manuscript, we certainly believe.

Sanday frankly says: "These words, 'and upon all,' are wanting in the best manuscripts, and should be omitted." As also agrees an excellent Plymouth Brother: "The best Uncial mss. omit 'and upon all.' The context confirms the correctness of this, for the Apostle is writing of those who are justified (verse 24)" (C. E. Stuart).

the same Greek word and tense as in Chapter 5.12, *hēmarton*: that is, "all *sinned*" (aorist, not perfect, tense), God is looking back even here at Adam's federal headship involving us all. He looks at the race as fallen and lost and gone, in their federal head; and then as individually continuing in sins.*

As a natural consequence, all that race "are falling short" of His glory. This "falling short" may mean (1) to fail to earn God's holy approbation (compare John 12.43); or (2) to come short, because of the loss of all spiritual strength through sin (Rom. 5.6), of that estate God prescribed for and must demand of man; or (3) guilty inability to stand before Him or in His glorious holy presence. Probably all these and more are included in the thought. We know that those now justified by faith in Christ "rejoice in hope of the glory of God,"—meaning that state of being glorified together with Christ, which is the high, heavenly hope of the Christian. It is in and through Christ alone

---

*Godet remarks, "The aorist *hēmarton*, 'sinned,' transports us to the point of time when the result of human life appears as a completed fact, the hour of judgment." With this Burton agrees, calling it a "collective aorist." See Sanday.

This word is a verb, second aorist tense, meaning, in Paul's epistles, to miss the mark; then, to err, to wander from the path of righteousness; then, to do or go wrong; then, to violate God's law, — to *sin.* As we all know, the aorist is a statement of past fact, not of present condition or fact; neither does it have the force of the perfect, — that is, of the finishing of prolonged action.

The King James version translates the same verb-form in 5.12 also: "all have sinned." It is our contention that this too is an incorrect translation, beclouding the meaning of Scripture.

It is remarkable in 3.23 that a past tense should be used for the verb sin, and a present tense for the universal consequent result! As we find throughout Scripture, the sin of Adam is evermore in the Divine view. "Thy first father sinned," is God's continual testimony. The consequent translation of this aorist *hēmarton* in 5.12 is, "all *sinned*," — that is, in Adam's act; and also in 3.23: "all *sinned* [in Adam] and [consequently] are falling short of the glory of God": the history of the whole race since.

Of course it will be objected that individual sins and transgressions are treated in the first three chapters of Romans, and federal sin not until the second part of Chapter Five, where the two federal men, Adam and Christ, are set forth, and the effects of their representative acts contrasted. This is true, but why the same aorist form in both 3.23 and 5.12?

Even if Paul used *hēmarton* in 3.23 as summing up in one word the actions of both Gentiles and Jews as detailed in 1.18 to 3.18, we must still note that it is the aorist and not the perfect tense that he uses. It would then resemble the use of the same aorist, *hēmarton*, in 2.12: "as many as sinned without law," — the aorist here expressing the life-choice, looked at in the day of judgment as a past act (as see Godet above). This would make 3.23 say: all made the life-choice of sin, — which we know is not true of those whom God saves and delivers. So that it seems best to read "all *sinned*," — as God's view of men looked at as being sinners, indeed; but their sin a past fact — soon to be connected definitely with Adam! (5.12, ff.)

that sinners ruined in Adam, and daily falling short of the glory of God, find redemption from sin's guilt and deliverance from its power.

How sad and awful, then, man's condition! Suppose I should say, for example, to a New York audience, "Let us all go down to the Battery and jump across to England." Some vigorous young man might jump over twenty feet, but he would "fall short" of England. And some little old lady might not jump one foot. But all would "fall short" of the coast of England. And, for that matter, the one who leaped the farthest would be in the deepest water! Paul, the chief of sinners, leaped to the farthest distance of self-righteousness, only to cry, "Wretched man that I am!" and to find he must put his faith only in Christ!

We now come to the greatest single verse in the entire Bible on the manner of justification by faith: We entreat you, study this verse. We have seen many a soul, upon understanding it, come into peace.

Verse 24: **Being declared righteous giftwise by His grace through the redemption that is in Christ Jesus**—God having brought the whole world into His court-room and pronounced them guilty (vs. 19),—"under sin," now exhibits Himself in absolute sovereign grace towards the guilty!

Being declared [or accounted] **righteous**—Justification, or accounting righteous, is God's reckoning to one who believes the whole work and effect before Him of the perfect redemption of Christ. The word never means to make one righteous, or holy; but to account one righteous. Justification is not a change wrought by God in us, but a change of our relation to God.

Declared righteous giftwise—The Greek word *dorean* means, for nothing, gratuitously, giftwise, as a free gift. Paul, for example, uses the same word in reminding the Corinthians of his labors to make the gospel "without charge." "Freely [*dorean*] ye received, freely give," said the Lord to the twelve (Matt. 10.8). "I will give unto him that is athirst of the fountain of the water of life freely" *(dorean)*,—for nothing (Rev. 21.6) ; and it occurs in almost the very last verse of the Bible:

"Let him take of the water of life freely" (Rev. 22.17). Perhaps the most striking use of this word, *dorean,* is by our Lord: "They hated me *without-a-cause" (dorean)* (John 15.25). The cause of the hatred was in them, not in Christ. Turning this about: the cause of our justification is in God, not in us. We are justified *dorean*—freely, gratis, gratuitously, giftwise, without a cause in us! This great fact should deliver just now some reader who has been looking within, to his spiritual state, or feelings, or prayers, as a ground of peace.

By His grace—We get our word "charity" from the Greek word translated "grace" here *(charis).* True, our word "charity" has been narrowed down in our poor thought and speech to handing out a dole to the needy. But as used by God, this word grace *(charis),* means the going forth in boundless oceans, according to Himself, of His mighty love, who "so loved the world that He gave His only begotten Son." The grace of God is infinite love operating by an infinite means,—the sacrifice of Christ; and in infinite freedom, unhindered, now, by the temporary restrictions of the Law.

Through the redemption that is in Christ Jesus—Remember that everything connected with God's salvation is glad in bestowment, infinite in extent, and unchangeable in character. Christ's atoning work was the procuring cause of all eternal benefit to us. Concerning the Greek word translated "redemption" here *(apolutrōsis)* Thayer says: "Everywhere in the New Testament this word is used to denote deliverance effected through the death of Christ from the retributive wrath of a holy God and the merited penalty of sin."

The effect of redemption is shown in Ephesians 1.7: "In whom we have our redemption through His blood, the forgiveness of our trespasses." Otherwise we were unpardoned and exposed to Divine wrath for ever. Compare Colossians 1.14: "In whom we have our redemption, the forgiveness of our sins"; as also Hebrews 9.15: "A death having taken place for the redemption of the transgressions that were under the first covenant." Here Thayer's interpretation of this word "redemption" is again excellent: "Deliverance from the penalty of transgressions effective through their expiation."

Before you leave verse 24, apply it to yourself, if you are a believer. Say of yourself: "God has declared me righteous without any cause in me, by His grace, through the redemption from sin's penalty that is in Christ Jesus." It is the bold, believing use *for ourselves* of the Scripture we learn, that God desires; and not merely the knowledge of Scripture.

Verse 25: **Whom God set forth a propitiation through faith in His blood, unto showing forth His [God's] righteousness in respect of the passing over of the foregoing sins in the forbearance of God**—This verse looks back to the whole history of human sin before it was judged at the cross,— the vast scandal (so to speak) of the universe!—a holy God letting sin pass for four thousand years, from Adam to Christ. God had been righteous in thus passing over* human sin, both in pardoning without judgment, the sins of the Abels, Enochs, Noahs, and the patriarchs,—even all whom He knew as believing Him; and not only so, He was righteous in forbearing with the impenitent, His enemies: for He purposed both sending Christ to become the propitiation for the whole world; and He would also deal in due time in righteous judgment with those rejecting all His goodness.

But now, in the gospel, His righteousness in all this is publicly shown forth; and the ground of it all seen—even the Lamb "foreordained, indeed, from the foundation of the world, but now manifested," and sacrificed. At the cross was sin seen at its height; and also the righteousness of God in dealing in judgment† with it. It was not until the gospel that all this was manifested. Although God had been dealing righteously in the past ages, it was first seen clearly when He judged human sin openly in the Great Sacrifice: where His own Son was *not spared!*

Whom God set forth a propitiation—Let us consider now this word "propitiation," concerning the meaning of which there is much uncertainty in many hearts.

---

*"Passing by or over"; Xenophon uses this word thus: "A trainer of horses should not let such faults *pass by unpunished*" — Hipparchus 7.10.

†There are, respecting human sin, three judgment-days: (1) of the human race, in Eden; (2) of human *sin*, at the cross; and (3) of human *rebels,* at the Great White Throne of Revelation 20.

Inasmuch as Christ died for our sins "according to the Scriptures" (I Cor. 15.3), we must go to those Scriptures (Old Testament, of course) to find what is there set forth concerning His death.

Now the two goats, on the Great Day of Atonement, represent two great effects of Christ's sacrifice. To quote: "Aaron shall take the two goats, and set them before Jehovah at the door of the tent of meeting. And Aaron shall cast lots upon the two goats: one lot for Jehovah, and the other lot for Azazel" ("removal"—the goat of removal of sins)* (Lev. 16.7,8).

On the great Day of Atonement (Leviticus 16) the high priest presented before Jehovah these two goats: one was slain, and its blood brought by the high priest into the tabernacle, through the holy place, and past the second veil into the holy of holies. There the high priest sprinkled the blood upon "the mercy-seat" (the covering of the ark of the covenant, where the Shekinah glory of God's presence was above the cherubim), and also before the mercy-seat, seven times. This was the blood of the goat upon which the lot fell "for Jehovah"; therefore we have here first the holy and righteous claims of the throne of God as to sin completely met. The golden covering of the ark was called the "mercy-seat" (Hebrew, *kapporeth*). In the Septuagint, the Greek translation of the Old Testament, this golden covering of the ark is always called by the same Greek word, *hilastērion,*† which we find translated "propitiation" here in

---

Azazel, the Hebrew word, means goat of dismissal, or departure, figuring most vividly the effect for Israel of the blood shed by the first goat: for the two goats are one in representing Christ's work in its double effect. First, as answering all the claims of the being and throne of a holy, righteous God; and, second, in removing the transgressions from the people "as far as the east is from the west."

†The meaning of the Greek word *hilastērion,* translated "propitiation" in Romans 3.25 plainly is, propitiatory sacrifice. How else could it be for "the showing of God's righteousness"? If we translate it only "mercy-seat," we forget that it was the propitiatory sacrifice, in its death, which made a mercy-seat possible. It was the slain goat, on the Day of Atonement, (in Lev. 16.15), the blood of which was brought in to be sprinkled upon and before the mercy-seat. The righteousness of Jehovah was proclaimed in the offering's death, and in the meeting, on the ground of this shed blood, of Jehovah and man, at the mercy-seat. Therefore righteousness is set forth in the death of the victim; mercy in its effect at the "mercy-seat."

It will be noticed that all explanations (of *hilastērion*) rest on the thought that "Christ's death was sacrificial and expiatory; a real atonement, required by something in the character of God, and not merely designed to effect moral results in man. We may not know all that this propitiation involves, but since God Himself

verse 25; and "mercy-seat" in the only other New Testament occurrence of the word, Hebrews 9.5.

Does "propitiation" *(hilastērion),* here in Romans 3.25, then, mean that the death of Christ made expiation for human sin? Or does it mean also that Christ, having thus died, therefore becomes to the soul the "mercy-seat" where God in all His holiness, and the sinner in all his guilt, may meet?

The latter may be included; for the type is thus carried out; inasmuch as the blood was sprinkled upon the mercy-seat (Lev. 16.14), the covering of the ark of the covenant, which was called the mercy-seat; the "mercy-seat" thus calling attention to the effect of the sacrifice as affording a righteous meeting ground between the sinner and God. But in Chapter 3.25 it was to show forth God's *righteousness* that Christ was "set forth," —the fact that God, though forbearing 4000 years, had not forgotten or abated His wrath against sin: so that it is Christ's actual death *as an expiation of human sin* that is seen here as showing God's *righteousness.* We may well read, "God set forth Christ propitiatory": thus showing Himself righteous, and also a gracious Justifier of sinners.

The other question connects itself with what we have just said: Should we regard our faith as making the propitiation actual? Of course, the expiatory death of Christ becomes effectual only for those who believe, who rest upon it. But the expiation was made to God for human sin and the propitiation effected, apart from any man's faith therein! This is a plain fact of revelation. Christ "tasted death for every man." "He gave Himself a ransom for all"—whether any avail themselves

---

was willing to instruct His ancient people, by types, of this reality, we ought to know something positive respecting it. The atoning death of Christ is the ground of the 'reconciliation,' since it satisfies the demands of Divine justice on the one hand, and on the other draws men to God. Independently of the former, the latter could not be more than a groundless human feeling" (Schaff and Riddle).

"All that God was in His nature, He was, necessarily, against sin. For, though He was love, love has no place in wrath against sin, and the withdrawal of the sense of it — consciousness in the soul of the privation of God, is the most dreadful of all sufferings, the most terrible horror to him who knows it: but Christ knew it infinitely. But God's Divine majesty, His holiness, His righteousness, His truth, all in their very nature bore against Christ as made sin for us. All that God was, was against sin, and Christ was made sin. No comfort of love enfeebled wrath there. Never was the obedient Christ so precious; but His soul was to be made an offering for sin, and to bear it judicially before God" (Darby).

of it or not. Faith does not have any part in the propitiation, though it avails itself of it. *Propitiation is by blood alone.*

It is forgotten that our God is a consuming fire. Many there are who, in the blindness of unbelief of the last days, proudly say, "We reject the Jehovah of the Old Testament." It is "the Jesus that loved little children," and "went about doing good," who "taught us to call God, Father":—this is the one in whom people say they believe. But will you remember that this same Jesus is called in the Old Testament Jehovah's Servant, and that under Jehovah's smiting hand of wrath He poured out His blood on Calvary and was laid in a tomb, dead, and that it is this Jesus, the Son of God, dead and risen, upon whom you are called to believe?

Now, why did He thus die? or, if you wish, Why must He die, at all? Death is the wages of sin, and He had none! *Why should He die?*

The answer to this question, false teachers crowd to give you. But we must find the answer in what Scripture says, or risk our eternity! For Jesus Christ is the only Savior, and His death is His one saving act. Concerning His person, therefore, and His death, you must learn what God says from His own Word, and believe it. I find thousands of people ready to say, "Christ died for us, to save us"; thousands, I say, who speak thus, but who are able to give no account whatever of salvation; who exhibit, upon being questioned, the most awful ignorance of the character and attributes of God, and of where lay the necessity for Christ's death, and what it really accomplished.

The shed blood on the Day of Atonement witnessed that a death had taken place. The person for whom the blood was shed could not approach or stand for a moment in the presence of the infinitely holy God. When the high priest came in before Jehovah on the Great Day of Atonement, carrying the basin containing the poured out life blood of the slain goat, he swung the censer, and the cloud of incense filled the holy of holies, covering from all human sight or approach, the mercy-seat where dwelt, upon the cherubim, the Shekinah Presence of God. He approaches and sprinkles the blood upon the mercy-seat, and before the mercy-seat seven times, and retires.

Now, what does this witness? Not an angry, vengeful God,* but infinitely the opposite—One who would send the Son of His bosom as the spotless Lamb to pour out His blood for us sinners, and then ascend to His God and Father,—and, unspeakable grace, now our God and Father also!

But, this laid-down-life witnesses that all approach to God on our personal part is impossible forever! To be made nigh unto God *in the blood of Christ* means that we come as those whose Substitute has been smitten unto death,—and that under forsaking and wrath by God Himself. There is peace through this blood, but a peace that leaves for us in our own right, no place whatever. Herein is the "offense" of the cross. Shall Christ be smitten for my sin? Then I deserve such smiting. Shall Christ be forsaken? Then I should have been forsaken. Shall Christ give up the ghost? Then all my hopes *in myself* have perished forever; for He who stood in my place has been smitten, forsaken; has died.

All this men hate and will not hear.

The essence of the truth concerning what men call "atonement," is that God's wrath fell upon Christ bearing our sins. Man's unbelief has sought in every way to avoid or mitigate this awful truth. But if Divine wrath fell not upon Christ, *it must fall upon us;* for God can not let sin pass. The preacher must study the Scriptures until he sees for himself from God's Word this most solemn of all Divine revelations: in the coats of skins—obtained by death as a covering for Adam and Eve in God's presence; in Abel's accepted sacrifice; in all the offerings of the patriarchs; and afterwards in those prescribed to Israel in Leviticus,—where neither remission of the penalty of sin to the offender nor the bringing of man into God's presence was possible except through blood-shedding; and alike strikingly in the Psalms of Christ's sufferings,—as 16,22,40,69,88,102,109;

---

*"The doctrine of atonement produces in us its proper effect when it leads us to see and feel that God is just; that He is infinitely gracious; that we are deprived of all ground of boasting; that the way of salvation, which is open for us, is open for all men; and that the motives to all duty, instead of being weakened, are enforced and multiplied.

"In the gospel all is harmonious: justice and mercy, as it regards God; freedom from the Law, and the strongest obligations to obedience, as it regards men" (Hodge).

and in the prophets: "It pleased Jehovah to *bruise* Him," "The *chastisement* of our peace was upon Him"; "Awake, O sword against My Shepherd, against the Man Who is My Fellow, saith Jehovah of Hosts"; and in the gospels—"The Son of Man must be lifted up"; "The cup [of what but wrath?] that my Father hath given Me, shall I not drink it?" "My God, My God, Why hast Thou forsaken Me?" Throughout the New Testament, as in the Old, this is taught, that God's wrath for sin fell upon Christ upon the cross.

It has ever been the first step to heresy—the denial that Divine wrath for sin fell on Christ. It was, indeed, certainly not anger at Christ's Person—He was obediently drinking a cup His Father had given Him. Nor was it anger at the sinner: "God so loved that He gave." But it was wrath against sin,— the going forth of the infinitely holy nature of God against sin. Alas, how little we feel its awfulness! How poor our knowledge of it; how weak our hatred of it! But wrath against it fell full on Christ. We beseech you, hold this fast. "God spared not His own Son, but delivered Him up for us all."

God is holy in His being: He is righteous in His character. Righteousness appears in His dealings with others. The term righteousness is a relative one; it assumes the existence of others. It is a word of relationship: whether in attitude or in government, God will ever be righteous. But holiness is not a word of relationship, but of nature, of being. God is holy: if there were no creatures He would yet be holy, the Holy One, "Whose *Name* is Holy."

It is in this holiness of God that we must look for the necessity of propitiation. That there must be propitiation does not indicate, primarily, that God is offended and must be appeased; but that God is holy and cannot by sinful creatures *be approached*. Only holy beings (like the seraphim, the cherubim of glory, and the elect angels) can possibly abide in His presence. Sin cannot come nigh Him. It is not that He hates sinners (He gave His Son to ransom them!) but it is that He is holy and cannot look upon sin. And if there be sin, there must be wrath against it: not merely the vindication of God's offended government, but the infinite abhorrence of His holy nature! He "dwelleth in light unapproachable." *It is death to draw nigh*: not because God is vindictive,—He is love: but because He is holy, and we are sinful, unclean, unholy.

True, we are also *guilty:* the *penalty* of sin is upon us. And that means judgment, and the infliction of wrath. But behind this, and deeper than even our guilt, is the abhorrence of a holy God of our sin itself. It is the abominable thing His holy being hates. We must be banished under wrath from His sight! Let all those who think to stand in the day of judgment before God think on this. The atonement arises out of a necessity in the nature of God Himself.

Now in the type of the great Day of Atonement of Leviticus 16, we have the two goats setting forth two great facts, which we must not confuse: First (and most important) the blood of the slain goat brought into God's presence in the holy of holies: the sprinkled blood being the witness that there has been death, a life laid down:* and no effort to come otherwise into God's presence,—no Cain-way, which does not recognize sin, or that holiness of God which was wrath and death toward sin. The blood of the goat sprinkled on the mercy-seat was the witness that all the claims of God, His holiness, His truth, His righteousness, and the majesty of His throne, had been admitted and met by a substitute which had laid its life down.

Then, second, there was the transferring in type of the actual sins,—all of them, to the head of the scape-goat (the "goat of dismissal"), which was then led to the wilderness, never to be found again: thus setting forth the *result* of the death of the first goat,—for the two are really one, in that the two set forth the effect of Christ's death: (1) toward God; and (2) toward sinners.

It is this latter phase of Christ's work,—His taking away our sins forever, that we so constantly find in our hymns (and rightly). But it is the first phase that the Word of God calls "the lot for Jehovah" (Lev. 16.8,9,15). It is of first importance that God should be glorified where sin had so dishonored Him! Sin outraged His holiness, insulted His Majesty, defied

---

*"The great idea in all these offerings (of Leviticus) was that the life of the victim was accepted for the life of the offerer" Angus-Green

His righteous government. And the cross made good all this, and publicly, before the universe. This was first. And second, God could now let sinners, in all their guilt, turn to Him! And we should learn to look at the cross as first of all *glorifying God;* and not solely from the viewpoint of the blessed and eternal benefits accruing to us thereby!

It is the character of God and the character of sin that are before us in Leviticus 16, in the Great Day of Atonement. *"That I die not"* (verse 13) was upon the mind of the high priest as he swung the censer when entering the presence of Jehovah, the Holy One, to sprinkle the blood, "to make atonement for the holy place, because of the uncleannesses of the children of Israel, and because of their transgressions, even all their sins." Note here that it is "uncleannesses" that are mentioned, even before "transgressions" or "sins"! Read carefully Leviticus 16,—especially verses 15 and 16.

Taking *the blood* in before God, in the holy of holies, was not a gift to God! Nor was it that God "delighted in bloodshed"—the monstrous claim of God's enemies. Christ's blood witnesses that a life has been *laid down* (though that of a Substitute, a Lamb, God Himself in love has provided). So that a sinner, unable to be in God's presence at all, and guilty, might, in the Name and Person of that Substitute, be in God's presence, pardoned and justified. So that the blood witnesses at once the infinite holiness and righteousness of God, and also His fathomless love! The words "made nigh in Christ's blood" should be in the constant consciousness of every Christian!

Now in order that these things may be impressed on our hearts, we quote a few of the ever recurring references in Scripture to the holiness of God: its effect in godly fear upon the saints, and also its effect upon the wicked. We have placed these passages in a footnote. We beg you to stop and humbly read them; for the God of the Old Testament is the God of the New. Indeed, that great passage in the Sixth of Isaiah in which the seraphim veil their faces, crying, "Holy, holy, holy, is Jehovah of hosts," is directly declared in the Twelfth of John to have been spoken of the Lord Jesus Christ: "These things said Isaiah, because he saw His glory [Christ's] and he spake of Him" (John 12.39-41). The fact that the Son of God has come, sent by a God of love, and has borne sin for us, so that we who believe shall not come into judgment, but draw near to God by Christ's blood, *does not at all change the character of the holy God;* but, on the contrary, *reveals His holiness as nowhere else!**

Therefore we see in the word translated "propitiation" a propitiatory sacrifice that has expiated guilt; and therefore the "mercy-seat" where God is in all His holiness, and the effect of Christ's expiatory sacrifice, in the bringing into God's holy presence sinners, the defiled and guilty,—whose Substitute has borne their defilement and guilt, His blood becoming the witness thereto before God.

We know that we read in Hebrews 9.8 concerning the sacrifices in that first tabernacle: "The Holy Spirit this signifying, that the way into the holy place hath not yet been made manifest, while the first tabernacle is yet standing." Besides, we also read in Hebrews: "Having therefore, brethren, boldness to enter into the holy place by the blood of Jesus, by the way which he dedicated for us, a new and living way . . . let us draw near with a true heart, in fulness of faith" (Heb. 10.19,22). God's

---

*Ex. 3.5: Put off thy shoes from off thy feet, for the place whereon thou standest is holy ground.

19.22: And let the priests also, that come near to Jehovah, sanctify themselves, lest Jehovah break forth upon them.

24.1, 2: Worship ye afar off, and Moses alone shall come near unto Jehovah; but they shall not come near; neither shall the people go up with him.

24.17: And the appearance of the glory of Jehovah was like devouring fire on the top of the mount in the eyes of the children of Israel.

Lev. 9.7: And Moses said unto Aaron, Draw near unto the altar, and offer thy sin-offering, and thy burnt-offering, and make atonement.

10.1-3: Nadab and Abihu offered strange fire before Jehovah . . . And there came forth fire from before Jehovah, and devoured them, and they died before Jehovah. Then Moses said unto Aaron, This is it that Jehovah spake, saying, I will be sanctified in them that come nigh me, and before all the people I will be glorified. And Aaron held his peace.

Deut. 4.24: For Jehovah thy God is a devouring fire, a jealous God.

5.4, 5: Jehovah spake with you face to face in the mount out of the midst of the fire . . . ye were afraid because of the fire, and went not up into the mount.

Isa. 33.14: The sinners in Zion are afraid: trembling hath seized the godless ones: Who among us can dwell with the devouring fire? who among us can dwell with everlasting burnings?

Heb. 12.29: For our God is a consuming fire.

being and character do not change. The cross is the deepest witness of all to that fact!

In every great revival in church history, as in the Old Testament, there has been a coming back into the consciousness of being guilty, lost sinners, dependent on the shed blood of a Redeemer. If the world has gotten past being recalled to that blessed sinner-consciousness in the presence of a God of mercy at the cross—there is nothing left but judgment!

Verse 26: **For the showing forth of His righteousness at this present season: that He might be Himself righteous, while declaring righteous the person having faith in Jesus.**

Both in verse 25 and verse 26 it is the effect of Christ's sacrifice, as displaying the Divine righteousness, that is before us. From Adam to Christ God had "passed over," not judged and put away, sin. The word translated "passed over" *(paresis)* in Chapter 3.25, is not the word for "remission," of Matthew 26.28, which is used fifteen times for the active pardon of sins; whereas the present word *(paresis)* is used in Romans 3.25 only. This word carries, in a sense, almost the same thought as the word "overlooked," in Acts 17.30. Of course there had to be, before the cross, such displays of Divine government as the Flood, the destruction of Sodom and Gomorrah, the plagues in Egypt, and the dispersion of rebellious Israel. Nevertheless, God did not take up man's sin for judgment according to His own being, until the cross. There He held the public Judgment Day of human *sin,* displaying His absolute righteousness in not sparing His own Son. Before the cross, as Bengel says, "the righteousness of God was not so apparent, for He seemed not to be so exacting with sin as He is, but to leave the sinner to himself, to regard not." But in the atoning death of Christ, God's righteousness was fully exhibited in His wrath against sin as it was in His holy sight. He was shown righteous, at the very moment He was, in love, working out the deliverance of the sinner from the wrath due. He was the Justifier, and yet just!

In the words, "at this present season," God directs our gaze back to the cross, where Christ was publicly set forth and judged for our sin; and also He covers this whole "season" of mercy, the present dispensation. Old Testament believers looked forward: they were forgiven on credit. But "this present season," is better. It is characterized by a righteousness already displayed in God's judging our sin at the cross; and therefore by God as the righteous Justifier of all who believe.

Now our faith is that one act of our hearts that appropriates the work of Christ; and we stand, by virtue of that work alone, in the immediate presence of the infinitely holy God. The words "most holy" occur about forty times in describing the sanctuary matters of the Old Testament; but faith in the once-for-all sacrifice of Christ who fulfills all those shadows, takes the place of all this: therefore, in the New Testament, our faith is called "our most holy faith"! (Jude 20).

Verse 27: **Where then is the [Jewish] boasting? It is excluded. By what manner of law? of works? Nay: but by a law of faith.**

Where then is the [Jewish] boasting? It is plain all through this discussion that Paul has the religious position and opposition of the Jews in mind. Boasting "was excluded at the moment when the law of faith, that is, the gospel, was brought in."*

In view of this new gospel-revelation of the finished work of Christ, who did the whole work for us on Calvary, and that by God's appointment, everything is seen to be *of God,* and not at all of man. Therefore, even the Jews, to whom the Law had been given, had their mouths completely stopped, "because there was no work done," and no ground for boasting!

By what manner of law? of works? Not at all! but by a law of faith. "Law" in this instance is rule, or plan. This "law," or principle, of faith, applies not only to our justification, but to every aspect of the believer's life thereafter,—"building up yourselves on your most holy faith." "That life which I

---

*As one has quaintly said, "The Feast of Mercy was on, and the damsel Grace was at the door, admitting everyone who came on the ground of mercy alone. Old Mr. Boasting, in a high hat and fine suit, presented himself. 'Oh,' said Grace, as she quickly shut the door in his face, 'There is no room for you here! The people here are feasting on the free gifts of God.' So Mr. Boasting was shut out!"

now live in the flesh I live in faith, the faith which is in the Son of God."

Verse 28: **For we reckon that a man is declared righteous by faith, apart from works of law**—This verse is not a conclusion arrived at, but a reason given why boasting is excluded.

Verses 29 and 30: **Or is God** [the God] **of Jews only?** [who alone had the Law]. **Is He not** [the God] **of Gentiles also? Yea, of Gentiles also: since it is one God who shall declare righteous the circumcision on the principle of faith, and the uncircumcision through faith.** To paraphrase: "Or is God the God of the Jews only? (as He must be, if justification is by the Law: for only to the Jews did God give the Law). Is He not the God of Gentiles also? Yea, of Gentiles also: since God is One (in His being, and alike to all nations). And He shall justify the circumcision (Jewish believers) out of simple faith (and not by their keeping Moses' Law though they had it from God), and the uncircumcision (Gentiles, who had nothing) through their faith (apart from His giving them the Law)."

Verse 31: **Do we then annul law through faith? Banish the thought! on the contrary, we establish law.**

It is the constant cry of those who oppose grace, and most especially that declaration of grace that our justification is apart from law—apart from works of law—apart from ordinances, that it overthrows the Divine authority. But in this verse Paul says, "We establish law" through this doctrine of simple faith.

To illustrate: In the wilderness a man was found gathering up sticks to make a fire on the Sabbath day. Now, the Law had said, "Ye shall kindle no fire throughout your habitations on the Sabbath day." How, then, was this Law to be "established"? By letting the law-breaker off? No. By securing his promise to keep the Law in the future? No! By finding someone who had kept this commandment always, perfectly, and letting his obedience be reckoned to the law-breaker? No, in no wise!

How then, was the Law established? You know very well. All Israel were commanded by Jehovah to stone the man to death. We read:

> "And they that found him gathering sticks brought him unto Moses and Aaron, and unto all the congregation. And they put him in ward, because it had not been declared what should be done to him. And Jehovah said unto Moses, The man shall surely be put to death: all the congregation shall stone him with stones without the camp. And all the congregation brought him without the camp, and stoned him to death with stones; as Jehovah commanded Moses" (Numbers 15.33,ff).

Thus and thus only was the commandment of Jehovah *established*—by the *execution of the penalty*.

Paul preached Christ *crucified:* that Christ *died* for our sins, that "He tasted *death* for every man." And that Israel, who were under the Law, He redeemed from the curse of that Law by being made *a curse* for them. Thus the cross established law ; for the full penalty of all that was against the Divine majesty, against God's holiness, His righteousness, His truth, was forever met, and that not according to man's conception of what sin and its penalty should be, but according to God's judgment, according to the measure of the sanctuary, of high heaven itself !

The Jew, prating about his own righteousness, went about to kill Paul, crying that he spake against the Law; whereas it was that very Jew who would lower the Law to his own ability to keep it, instead of allowing it its proper office ; namely, to reveal his guilt, curse him, and condemn him to death, and thus drive him to the mercy of God in Christ, whose expiatory death *established law by having its penalty executed !**

---

*As to the "modernist," being more shallow by far than even the Sadducees of our Lord's day, he is not even exercised in his conscience concerning the Law, or the difference between law and grace as a means of righteousness, — of righteous standing with God. For, forsooth, the "modernist" has already a "character," an "innate nobility," though where the poor fellow gets these things, alas, who can discern? We know from Scripture that his first father was Adam; and that this "modernist," was, like David, "shapen in iniquity and conceived in sin." We have immeasurably more respect for a Jew, who is at least endeavoring by his imagined law-keeping to attain righteousness, — which presupposes that he knows he has it not! Even the Seventh Day Adventists, with their unscriptural bondage to law, are worried in conscience: the "modernist" is smugly secure, for what means *Thus saith the Lord* to him? But wait — till he faces the Great White Throne!

RIGHTEOUSNESS WITHOUT WORKS

If God announces the gift of righteousness apart from works, why do you keep mourning over your bad works, your failures? Do you not see that it is because you still have hopes in these works of yours that you are depressed and discouraged by their failure? If you truly saw and believed that God is reckoning righteous the *ungodly* who believe on Him, you would fairly hate your struggles to be "better"; for you would see that your dreams of good works have not at all commended you to God, and that your bad works do not at all hinder you from believing on Him,—that justifieth the *ungodly*!

Therefore, on seeing your failures, you should say, I am nothing but a failure; but God is dealing with me on another principle altogether than my works, good or bad,—a principle not involving my works, but based only on the work of Christ for me. I am anxious, indeed, to be pleasing to God and to be filled with His Spirit; but I am not at all justified, or accounted righteous, by these things. God, in justifying me, acted wholly and only on Christ's blood-shedding on my behalf.

Therefore I have this double attitude: first, I know that Christ is in Heaven before God for me, and that I stand in the value before God of His finished work; that God sees me nowhere else but in this dead, buried, and Risen Christ, and that His favor is toward me in Christ, and is limitless and eternal.

Then, second, toward the work of the Holy Spirit in me, my attitude is, a desire to be guided into the truth, to be obedient thereto, and to be chastened by God my Father if disobedient; to learn to pray in the Spirit, to walk by the Spirit, and to be filled with a love for the Scriptures and for the saints and for all men.

Yet none of these things justifies me! I had justification from God *as a sinner,* not as a *saint!* My saintliness does not increase it, nor, praise God, do my failures decrease it!

CHAPTER FOUR

Abraham and David, in Whom the Jews Specially Gloried, Accounted Righteous by Faith, not by Law or Works. Verses 1-8.

Righteousness is also Apart from Ordinances (as Circumcision). Verses 9-12.

Abraham's "Heirship of the World," not at All by Law but by Promise; and So, Only, Believers Are All Made Certain of its Blessings. Verses 13-17.

The Way and Walk of Faith Wondrously Exemplified in Abraham the Father of All Believers. Verses 18-22.

The Connection of Our Justification with Christ's Resurrection. Verses 23-25.

1   What then shall we say that Abraham our fore-
2 father according to the flesh hath found? For if
   Abraham was justified on the principle of works,
   he hath whereof to boast. But [we find] he is
3 unable to boast before God: For what saith the
   Scripture? And Abraham believed God, and it [his
   faith] was reckoned unto him as righteousness.
4 Now to him that worketh the reward is not reckoned as of grace but, on the contrary, as a matter
5 of debt. But to one not working, but believing
   upon the God that justifieth the ungodly,—his faith
   is reckoned for righteousness.

THE JEWS ESPECIALLY gloried in Abraham and David, —just as we all naturally glory in the assumed personal righteousness of great saints, as the ground of God's favor to them. But whatever blessing, says Paul, Abraham obtained, Scripture forbade the thought that he could glory before God; because he simply believed what God told him, that his seed should be in

130

number like the stars of heaven. (Read Gen. 15.6.) Abraham gave God His proper glory as the God of truth. We cannot conceive of Abraham as boasting before his house and before the Hittites that he had performed an act creditable to himself in believing God!

Paul now answers Jewish objectors to the doctrine of justification by simple faith; and he uses as examples those two great men of faith whose names were constantly on Jewish tongues,—Abraham and David.

The question about Abraham, **What has Abraham our fleshly forefather found?** is practically the same as in Chapter Three, "What advantage, then, hath the Jew?" We do well, while standing absolutely with Paul, to understand with sympathy the state of mind of the Jew, who had the Old Testament Scriptures, and a national history of marvelous Divine instruction and providence, and also remarkable religious prominence everywhere, in Paul's day. "To Israel pertained the fathers" (9.5); Paul here in Romans 4.1, places himself, therefore, among the Israelites, and says, "Abraham our forefather according to the flesh."*

Verses 2, 3: Now argues Paul, **if Abraham had been declared righteous before God on the works principle, he** would indeed have had **something to boast of!** But the Scripture record showed there was nothing of which he could boast before God. For concerning Abraham more definitely and directly than of any other human being, God's word was specific: **Abraham believed God, and it [his faith] was reckoned†** to him as righteousness.

---

*The doctrine of Abraham as being the "father of all that believe," has yet to be announced, — as is done later in this same chapter.

†"It was *reckoned* unto him as righteousness"; here the word "reckoned" is *logidzomai*, a great word with Paul, used 41 times in the New Testament, 35 of which are in Paul's epistles, 11 of these here in Chapter Four. Where it is used as in verse 3, here, of God, it is always a court word, God acting as Judge and accounting or holding as righteous those who, as Abraham, believe in Him; or the contrary, as is implied in verse 8: "Blessed is the man to whom the Lord will *not* reckon sin," — implying that there are those to whom He will reckon sin and its guilt.

In Chapter 4.5, we see what is reckoned by God as righteousness: "his faith is reckoned as righteousness." This does not mean that faith is a meritorious act, as indeed it could not be, — being simply extending credence to One who cannot lie! Therefore, without being itself righteousness, it is *reckoned as* righteousness; the ground of such reckoning being of course the work of Christ on the cross. (Compare on this word the note on Chapter 5.11.)

To discover that the greatest saints have no other standing
than the weakest saints, is a lesson that is difficult for all of us!
So now for the Jew to find that great Abraham has nothing in
the flesh, but must be justified by simple faith, like any sinner,
is a great shock. There was no honor, no "merit," in Abraham's
believing the faithful God, who cannot lie. The honor was
God's. When Abraham believed God, he did the one thing that
a man can do without doing anything! God made the statement,
the promise; and God undertook to fulfill it. Abraham believed
in his heart that God told the truth. There was no effort here.
Abraham's faith was not an act, but an attitude. His heart was
turned completely away from himself to God and His promise.
This left God free to fulfill that promise. Faith was neither a
meritorious act by Abraham, nor a change of character or nature, in Abraham: he simply believed God would accomplish
what He had promised: "In thee shall all the families of the
earth be blessed" (Gen. 12.3).

Verses 4 and 5: **Now to him that worketh the reward is
not reckoned as a matter of grace, but, on the contrary, as
a matter of debt. But to one not working, but believing
upon the God that justifieth the ungodly,—his faith is reckoned for righteousness.**

Here Paul writes two verses which every believer should
commit to memory: for they state what no mind of fallen
man ever imagines; for do not people naturally believe that
the way to be saved is to "be good"?

To him that worketh—To a man that works for wages,
the wages are due as a debt. That is a simple enough principle. But do not seek to apply it to salvation! No one ever
got righteousness by work or worth! Righteousness is not
by doing right, strange and impossible as that may seem.

But to him that worketh not—to him who "casts his deadly
doing down"; who, seeing his guilt, and his entire inability
to put it away, ceases wholly from all efforts to obtain God's
favor by his own doings, or self-denyings,—even by his
prayers: **but believeth on the God that declareth righteous
the ungodly**—not the godly or the good! But, you say, God
cannot do that! God cannot declare a man godly if he is really

ungodly. Now God did not say "godly," but He said *righteous,*
—"declareth *righteous* those ungodly who believe." *God can do
that!* For God can reckon to an ungodly man who dares cease
trying to change himself, and relies on God just as he is, a sinner,—God can and does reckon to such a one the glorious benefit
of Christ's death and resurrection on behalf of sinners. And of
such a believing sinner, God declares his faith is counted as
righteousness.

It cannot be too much emphasized that the words, "the ungodly," in verse 5, wholly shut out any other class from justification. If we say, God, indeed, has in some special cases justified
notoriously, openly, evidently ungodly ones; while His general
habit is, to justify the godly (which is what human reason demands), then we at once deny all Scripture. For God says,
"There is no distinction; for all sinned; there is none righteous,
—not one." And if you claim that God justifies the godly, we
ask, on what ground? If you say on the ground of their godliness, you have left out the blood of Christ,—on which ground
alone God can deal with sinners; and you have really denied
this so-called "godly" man to be a sinner before God at all, since
he is to be justified on another ground than is the openly ungodly
sinner,—the shed blood of Christ.

Do you not see that all this distinction between sinners is an
abomination before a holy God? What does it matter whether
you are a nobleman or a knave, if God has said He declares
sinners righteous by Christ's blood? What matter whether you
are an honorable woman or a harlot, if God says you are a sinner (and He does!) and that the only ground of being declared
righteous is the blood of His Son?

The burning question is, have you and I been so really convinced of the fact of our sinnerhood and guilt, and of our utter
helplessness, and lost state, as to be able to believe on a God who
can and does "declare righteous the UNgodly—those who believe, as ungodly, on Him?

A child, without Christ, is "ungodly," in this sense. "Ye
were by nature children of wrath," is an awful word, but a true
word,—going back to our mother's womb, who, "in sin conceived us!" We were born into a lost, guilty race,—we were

born part of that race! And it was written of all of us, concerning Adam's sin: "Through the one man's disobedience the many were made sinners."

We are all ungodly! And when we place our faith in the God who is in the business of declaring righteous the ungodly who trust Him as they are,—on the sole ground of the shed blood of Christ,—then we are justified,—accounted righteous, by God.

No, it is not the regenerate, the born again man, who is declared righteous,—it is the ungodly. It is not the penitent man, or the praying man, as such, but the ungodly. It is not the professing Christian who has "escaped the defilements of the world" (II Peter 2) through certain spiritual experiences (it may be of a high order), but the ungodly, who believes, as such, on the God who declares righteous the ungodly who believe on Him—AS SUCH!

And of course it is not the "church-member,"—Baptist, Methodist, Presbyterian, Episcopalian, Roman Catholic, or Plymouth Brother, as such,—but, *the ungodly*. This is not, either, putting a premium on ungodliness, but telling the truth! If you have not relied on God as an ungodly one, you have yet to be declared righteous; for He is the God who *declares righteous the ungodly who believe on Him.**

---

*We beg the reader's permission to relate below an experience of our own, as illustrating "To him that worketh not, but believeth on Him that declares righteous the ungodly":

Years ago in the city of St. Louis, I was holding noon meetings in the Century Theater. One day I spoke on this verse, — Romans 4.5. After the audience had gone, I was addressed by a fine-looking man of middle age, who had been waiting alone in a box-seat for me.

He immediately said, "I am Captain G————," (a man very widely known in the city). And, when I sat down to talk with him, he began: "You are speaking to the most ungodly man in St. Louis."

I said, "Thank God!"

"What!" he cried. "Do you mean you are glad that I am bad?"

"No," I said; "but I am certainly glad to find a sinner that knows he is a sinner."

"Oh, you do not know the half! I have been absolutely ungodly for years and years and years, right here in St. Louis. I own two Mississippi steamers. Everybody knows me. I am just the most ungodly man in town!"

I could hardly get him quiet enough to ask him: "Did you hear me preach on 'ungodly people' today?"

"Mr. Newell," he said, "I have been coming to these noon meetings for six weeks. I do not think I have missed a meeting. But I cannot tell you a word of

So we have seen in verses four and five the working method **and** the believing method contrasted. What a place heaven **would** be if men were allowed to pay their way! They would

what you said today. I did not sleep last night. I have hardly had any sleep for **three** weeks. I have gone to one man after another to find what to do. And I **do** what they say. I have read the Bible. I have prayed. I have given money **away**. But I am the most ungodly wretch in this town. Now what do *you* tell **me** to do? I waited here today to ask you that. I have tried everything; but I **am** so ungodly!"

"Now," I said, "we will turn to the verse I preached on." I gave the Bible into **his** hands, asking him to read aloud: "To him that worketh not."

"But," he cried, "how can this be for me? I am the most ungodly man in St. **L**ouis!"

"Wait," I said, "I beg you go on reading."

So he read, "To him that worketh not, but believeth on him that justifieth the **u**ngodly."

"There!" he fairly shouted, "that's what I am, — ungodly."

"Then, this verse is about you," I assured him.

"But please tell me what to do, Mr. Newell. I know I am ungodly: what shall **I** do?"

"Read the verse again, please."

He read: "To him that worketh not," — and I stopped him.

"There," I said, "the verse says not to do, and you want me to tell you some**thing** to do: I cannot do that."

"But there must be something to do; if not, I shall be lost forever."

"Now listen with all your soul," I said. "There was something to do, but *it has been done!*"

Then I told him how God had so loved him, all ungodly as he was, that He **sent** Christ to die for the ungodly. And that God's judgment had fallen **on** Christ, who has been forsaken of God for his, Captain G————'s, sins there **on** the cross.

Then, I said, "God raised up Christ; and sent us preachers to beseech men, all **ungodly** as they are, to believe on this God who declares righteous the ungodly, **on** the ground of Christ's shed blood."

He suddenly leaped to his feet and stretched his hand out to me. "Mr. Newell," **he** said, "I will accept that proposition!" and off he went, without another word.

Next noonday, at the opening of the meeting, I saw him beckoning to me from **the** wings of the stage. I went to him.

"May I say a word to these people?" he asked.

I saw his shining face, and gladly brought him in.

I said to the great audience, "Friends, this is Captain G————, whom most, **if** not all of you, know. He wants to say a word to you."

"I want to tell you all of the greatest proposition I ever found," he cried: "I **am** a business man, and know a good proposition. But I found one yesterday **that** so filled me with joy, that I could not sleep a wink all night. I found out **that** God for Jesus Christ's sake declares righteous any ungodly man that trusts **Him**. I trusted Him yesterday; and you all know what an ungodly man I was. **I** thank you all for listening to me; but I felt I could not help but tell you of this **w**onderful proposition; that God should count me righteous. I have been such **a** great sinner."

This beloved man lived many years in St. Louis, an ornament to his confession.

boast all through eternity, one about this, another about that. But the works method and the grace method are mutually exclusive. Each shuts out the other. Men must cease even seeking; they must cease all works—weeping, confessing, repenting, even earnest praying, and simply believe God laid their sins, their very own sins, all of them, on Christ at the cross. *There comes a moment when a man ceases from his own works, hearing that Christ finished the work, paid the ransom, at the cross.* Then he rests! Such a soul believes,—knowing himself to be a sinner, and ungodly,—but he believes on God, just as he is, and knows he is welcome!

Note that Scripture does not say that God justifies the praying man, or the Bible reader, or the church member, but the *ungodly*. Have you yourself believed on the God that accounts righteous the ungodly? Have you ever really seen yourself in the ungodly class, a mere sinner, and *as such* trusted God, on only one ground, the blood of Christ?

6   Even as David also pronounceth blessing upon the man, unto whom God reckoneth righteousness
7   apart from works [saying],
        Blessed are they whose iniquities are forgiven,
        And whose sins are covered.
8   Blessed is the man to whom the Lord will not reckon sin.

Verses 6 and 7: Now David also, in the Spirit, sets his seal to this blessed doctrine with great joy: saying twice in the beautiful Hebrew of Psalm 32: **Oh, the blessednesses of the man!** Of what man?

First, of the man **whose iniquities are forgiven**—Forgiveness is more than mere remitting of penalty. Even a hardhearted judge might remit a man's fine if it were paid by someone else, but forgiveness involves the heart of the forgiver. God's forgiveness is the going forth of God's infinite tenderness toward the object of His mercy. It is God folding the sinner, as the returning prodigal was folded, to His bosom. Such a one is blessed indeed!

Then, **whose sins are covered**—"Covered" is the Old Testament word, (Heb. *kaphar*); for those sacrifices could never "take away" sins, but only "cover" from sight. "In those sacrifices there is a remembrance made [not a removal] of sins year by year" (Heb. 10.11,3). There was a type of Christ's coming work, but the sins were yet there before God till Christ took them away on the cross. If then, one like David could pronounce blessed the man whose sins were "covered," out of God's sight in His mercy (though not yet removed), much more should we rejoice to know that Christ has been manifested "to *put away* sin by the sacrifice of Himself"! (Heb. 9.26).

Verse 8: The third element David here describes, in "righteousness without works," is the inflexible purpose of God never to bring up again the sin of the "blessed" man: **Blessed is the man to whom the Lord will not reckon sin.** (Again the Hebrew repeats "Oh, the blessednesses!"—Ps. 32.2). Many believers indeed, like David and Peter, have sinned deeply. But, as Nathan said to David on the very occasion of the announcement of both the King's sin and its being "put away," celebrated in this 32nd Psalm: "Jehovah hath put away thy sin; thou shalt not die." So have many been forgiven. High offences were David's indeed: adultery, hypocrisy and murder. But they were not "reckoned" against David. True, the king was chastened: "The sword shall never depart from thy house." At Nathan's parable David's indignation (how righteously indignant we can become at our own sins when we see them in others!) called for a four-fold payment by the rich man who took the poor man's lamb (II Sam. 12.5,6). And God allowed four sons of David's to be smitten: the child of Uriah's wife, then his first-born, Amnon; then fair Absalom; and, last, goodly Adonijah. Nevertheless, God had not "reckoned" the guilt against him! No wonder he pronounces blessed the man to whom God reckons righteousness apart from works!*

---

*This world hates the God of David, because it hates *grace*. The world rather likes David's taking Uriah's wife (for that is the world's manner of life!). But for Jehovah *not to reckon* this sin as damning guilt, and freely to forgive David, — and that so fully as to give "her that had been the wife of Uriah" another son, and bestow His special love on him (Solomon) to the extent of giving him a personal name, Jedidiah "for Jehovah's sake" (II Sam. 12.24, 25) and placing this woman Bathsheba in the official genealogy of Christ (Matt. 1.6); and, above all, for God to call David a man "after His own heart," — all this rouses the ire of a vile, self-righteous, neighbor-judging, blind, grace-ignorant, impenitent world, — a world that has neither repented, nor means to repent, of the very sins, into which David fell, and of which he repented most deeply. God's record of David is "a

Next we have the fact that even Divine ordinances like circumcision have nothing to do with righteousness,—any more than have good works; that even Abraham's circumcision was merely a seal of the righteousness of a faith he before had.

9   Is this blessing [of righteousness without works] pronounced upon the circumcision, or upon the uncircumcision also? for we say, To Abraham [a circumcised man] his faith was reckoned as righteousness.
10   Under what circumstances, then, was it reckoned? When he was in circumcision, or in uncircumcision? Not in circumcision, but, on the contrary, in uncircumcision! And he received the
11   sign of circumcision, a seal of the righteousness of the faith which he had while he was in uncircumcision: that he might be the father of ALL them that believe, though they be in uncircumcision,— that righteousness might be reckoned unto them;
12   and the father of circumcision to them who not only are of the circumcision, but who also walk in the steps of that faith of our father Abraham which he had in uncircumcision.

Verses 9 and 10: Paul had to have Jews in mind, just as we today have to have "professing Christians" in mind. The Jew relied upon and boasted in the outward mark of circumcision (which God, in Genesis 17, prescribed to Abraham and his fleshly seed), entirely forgetting that God, fourteen or fifteen years before circumcision (Gen. 15.6), had accounted Abraham righteous wholly apart from circumcision.* Circumcision was an outward sign or symbol, both to Abraham and to the world about him: to Abraham, that God was his God; to the world, that Abraham was separated from the world unto God. Just so

---

*"Paul has turned the Jew's boast upside down. It is not the Gentile who must come to the Jew's circumcision for salvation; it is the Jew who must come to a Gentile faith, such faith as Abraham had long before he was circumcised . . . When Isaac was saved, he was not saved by his circumcision any more than was his father before him. God never promised salvation except to faith. He never promised a perpetual nationality except to circumcised men who believe" — Stifler.

---

man that will do all my purposes" (Acts 13.22, margin). How about it, critic of David's God? Have you repented? Do you desire to do all God's purposes? If not, — well, you will shortly meet the God of whom your false mouth has prated!

baptism today is an outward sign that we are Christ's in faith and identification, and that we no longer belong to the world: but how deadly is the delusion that baptism in itself amounts to anything before God!*

After the same manner with the Jews, the vast majority of those calling themselves Christians place reliance, alas, today, on some ordinance (or, as it is called, "sacrament"), saying, "Christ told us to repent and be baptized, did He not? Christ commanded us to take the Lord's supper." But remember that God justifies NOT those observing ordinances, but the ungodly who believe. If you are still regarding baptism, or the Lord's supper, or "the mass," or "christening," or "confirmation," as having anything whatever to do with God's declaring you righteous, you do not understand being declared righteous as an ungodly one. And in the gospel, since the cross, you are not told first to cease being ungodly, and then believe; *but, as ungodly, to believe!*

Neither baptism nor the Lord's supper (upon both of which, in distorted form, thousands have rested, as "sacraments" commending them unto God), has power to give any standing whatever before a righteous God: that belongs only to the shed blood of the Redeemer of guilty and hopeless ones such as are we all!

Note that here, first, *human works* are set aside as a ground of righteousness; and then *Divine ordinances* also are just as fully set aside. Circumcision had been commanded to the Jew. The Jew trusted in it, and became utterly blind to the fact that even Abraham, "the father of circumcision," had been declared righteous on another principle,—by simple faith, years before his circumcision! Uncircumcised, then, a common sinner (a "Gentile"—if there had been at that time "Jews"), Abraham just *believed* God: gave Him the honor of being a God of truth. And be it so that God saw that one day He would make Abraham as righteous in glory as He in that past day reckoned him in grace; yet it remains that God reckoned him what he was not,

---

*"The sacraments and ceremonies of the Church, useful when viewed in their proper light, become ruinous when perverted into grounds of confidence. What answers well as a sign, is a miserable substitute for the thing signified. Circumcision will not serve for righteousness, nor baptism for regeneration" — Hodge.

as yet, in experience; and that Abraham stood before God thus
righteous *the moment he believed!* And not what Abraham
would become, but what Christ would do on the cross for him,
was the ground of God's reckoning!

Each year I live I become more impressed with the solitary
grandeur of this great friend of God. Behold him! Late come
from the very home of idolatry, he walks among the Hittites as
a "Prince of God"—their name for him (Gen. 23.6). Behold
him, to whom "the God of glory" had appeared in his old place,
Ur of the Chaldees; and to which blessed God he is so drawn
by the cords of trust and love, that his whole life is as *God's
friend*—walking with Him, ever learning of Him more and
more; taking a mark of absolute separation to Him; ever building altars to Him, and calling on His name. Behold him, called
to part with Isaac, his only son, readily giving him up to God!

Verses 11 and 12: It was in order to become **the father
of ALL them that believe** that Abraham received the sign
of circumcision: that is, he would have been the father of
uncircumcised believers apart from his own circumcision
(for he himself believed while uncircumcised); but God
desired a circumcised separate nation, and so would have
Abraham **also the father of circumcision** to those who **not
only had circumcision, but also** (rare thing among the
Jews!) should **walk in the steps of that faith of their father
Abraham which he had while yet uncircumcised.** How few

---

*These "steps of faith" of the uncircumcised Abraham would embrace all
Abraham's story from his "call" in Genesis 12 to his circumcision in Genesis 17,
— when he was 99 years old: (1) The revelation of the God of glory to Abraham,
while yet in Ur of the Chaldees, and his evident turning from idols to Him. (2)
Obedience to the command to get out of his country, from his kindred, and from
his father's house (Gen. 12.1-4); tarrying indeed at Haran on his way until his
father died (Acts 7.4; Gen. 11.31). (3) The altar-worship of Jehovah in Canaan
(Gen. 12.7, 8). (4) Choosing his portion with God: Lot's separation from Abraham (Gen. 13), and Abraham's arrival at Hebron ("fellowship"). (5) The victory over the kings (Gen. 14). (6) Accepting through Melchizedek the new revelation of "God Most High, Possessor of Heaven and Earth," and the rejection of
riches from men (Gen. 14). (7) Believing God's bare word concerning his seed,
and being thus "accounted righteous" (Gen. 15).

Notice that in the seventh of these steps, there is the peculiar element of counting on God, as God, to do the impossible. On the God who calleth the things not
being, as being!

No doubt, there were further walkings and testings until the offering of Isaac
in Chapter 22, after which we find no more testings: Abraham's faith had become perfected. So James writes (see above), "The Scripture was *fulfilled* that

Jewish teachers or preachers can challenge Gentiles with the freedom and truth of the apostle Paul: "I beseech you, brethren, become as I, for I also am as ye" (Gal. 4.12). The Galatians were raw Gentiles, "without law." Paul cries, "I am as ye are: I have no reliance on circumcision; if ye Gentiles receive circumcision, Christ will profit you nothing!"

The blessing of righteousness, then, comes not only without works, but also without ordinances, whether Jewish or Christian. And we see that only those Jews are really accounted circumcised in God's sight, who have heart-belief, as mere sinners, in the Redeemer. Faith, like true circumcision, is "that of the heart" (Rom. 2.29 and 10.10). According to this, there are very few real Jews on earth; yea, and relatively few true Christions, also; if righteousness be wholly by faith, apart from works, and apart from ordinances.

13   For not through law was the promise to Abraham or to his seed that he should be heir of the world, but, on the contrary, through righteousness
14   of faith. For if they which are of law be heirs, faith is made empty, and the promise is made useless:
15   for law works out wrath [to sinful man]; but where there is not law [to transgress], there is no trans-
16   gression [of it]. On this account the inheritance is

saith, Abraham believed God, and it was reckoned to him for righteousness." This word "fulfilled" is deeply significant. There was and always is, the prophetic, as well as the declarative element in justification, (that is, in God's accounting a sinner righteous. It is "the God who calleth the things that are not as though they were," (Rom. 4.17) who acts in justification. The moment He declares sinners righteous, they are so, having immediately the standing of being in Christ before Him. But they will also be manifested, by and by, and be glorified with Christ. "Glorified" they are already in God's mind (8.30). What James insists on is that there will be a living walk, fulfilling the Divine declaration that the man is righteous.

This living walk also is before Him whom we believe, even God (4.17). It has no reference whatever to men. The explanation by some that Abraham was "justified by faith before God and by works before men" is trivial! Both in Genesis 15.6, when God accounted him righteous, and in 22.15 to 18, Abraham was alone with his God. When James says, "By works was faith made perfect," he is expanding the statement, "Faith wrought with his works." Paul has almost the same phrase: "In Christ Jesus, neither circumcision availeth anything, nor uncircumcision; but faith working through love" (Gal. 5.6). Of course saving faith is a living, acting thing, as against mere opinion or profession; and this again is what James is insisting on. Works are the result of a true faith; but they are not, like faith itself, a condition of salvation. What "works" did the dying thief perform? You say, None: he cast himself on Christ as he was. Good. So must you and I: *only that!*

on the principle of faith, in order that it may be according to grace: so that the promise [which could not be broken], **might be made sure to all the seed** [of Abraham] : **not to that which was of the Law only, but also to that which** [although not having had Moses' Law] **was yet of the faith of Abraham;**

17   **who is the father of all of us** [believers] **(as it is written, I made thee father of many nations) in the sight of Him whom he believed, even God** [the God], **who makes alive the dead, and calls things not existing, as existing.**

Verses 13 to 17: Here the further question of Abraham's "inheriting the world" is considered, and this again is only through the righteousness of faith: this expression not meaning that faith is a righteous, meritorious thing, but that, as explained before faith, not law, is the Divine mode of blessing.

Verse 13: **For not through law was the promise to Abraham or to his seed that he should be heir of the world, but, on the contrary, through righteousness of faith.** "Heir of the world": Behold, then a new order of all things! Adam had failed, and his fleshly seed were fallen. Abraham has succeeded, to become the father of spiritual seed,—"of all them that believe": it will be a believing seed, not a natural seed. This man and that seed shall enter into the inheritance Adam forfeited for headship! What can "heir of the world"* mean? Nay, what shall it not mean? "The meek shall inherit the earth." And who are they? Not Adam's but Abraham's seed. Bishop Moule beautifully says: "Then and there, perhaps side by side with his Divine Friend manifested in human form, Abraham is told to count the stars under the glorious canopy, the Syrian 'night of stars'; and he hears the promise, 'So shall thy seed be.' It was then and there, that as a man uncovenanted, unworthy, but called upon to take what God gave, he received the promise that he should be 'heir of the world.' In his 'seed,'—that childless

---

*Dean Alford with his usual clearness says: "The inheritance of the world then is not the possession of Canaan merely, either literally, or as a type of a better possession, — but that ultimate lordship over the whole world which Abraham, as the father of the faithful in all peoples, and Christ, as the Seed of Promise, shall possess: the former figuratively indeed and only implicitly, — the latter personally and actually."

senior was to be a King of Men, Monarch of continents and oceans. 'All nations,' 'all the kindreds of the earth' were to be blessed in him, as their patriarchal Chief, their Head, in covenant with God."

How hardly do we banish the thought of human "merit" in God's great saints! ("Merit" is a Romish term: away with it!) Faith is the ground of God's blessing. Abraham was a blessed man, indeed, but he became heir of the world on another principle entirely—simple faith.*

Verse 14: **For if they which are of law be heirs, faith is made empty, and the promise is annulled**—Here Paul enlarges, that for God to bless the merit-folks,† would make God's promise-method impossible, and so our faith in His promises, empty and void.‡ Faith and law are contradictory principles, the apostle shows: absolutely diverse means of blessing.

---

*Now Paul completely shuts out the legalists from heirship with Abraham's seed. Because, as Weiss says, "If those persons were the possessors of the promise, who on the basis of a law had entered upon this inheritance of their father Abraham, (on the ground that it had been offered to them as a reward for the fulfillment of this law), then faith, which according to its essence is a confidence in the attainment of salvation, would be rendered void, and the promise, which has full assurance of that which is promised, would be made of no effect. For the law, in view of the sinful condition that prevails, can be completely fulfilled by none, and necessarily produces wrath. But the bestowal of that which is promised presupposes the continuation of the graciousness of Him who made the promise; and this graciousness becomes equally impossible, as does the believing confidence — if law must be fulfilled to secure it!"

When law comes in, it conditions everything upon obedience to it. It had to be "disannulled" when a better hope was brought in! (Heb. 7.18,19.)

†The reason God hates your trust in your "good works" is, that you offer them to Him instead of resting on the all-glorious work of His Son for you at the cross.

Reflect:

1. What it cost God to give Christ.
2. What it cost Christ to put away sin,—your sin, at the cross.
3. What honor God has given Him "because of the suffering of death."
4. What plans for the future God has arranged through Christ's having made peace by the blood of His cross, to reconcile "things upon the earth and things in the heavens, unto Himself."

Now, by that uneasiness of conscience on account of which you keep doing "dead works," you neglect *all God is, has done, and desires,* for you, and substitute your own uncertain, fearful, trifling notions of "works that shall please God." You would make God come to your terms, instead of gladly accepting His great salvation and resting in the finished work of Christ.

It is ominously bold presumption, when God is calling all to behold His Lamb, to be found asking God to behold your goodness, your works!

‡Greek, *katargeo,* from *kata,* "down from"; and *ergon,* "work"; literally, therefore, to *put out of work,* or *out of business,* to *render ineffective;* a word often used by Paul, and most important in his exposition. Its uses in Romans are seen

Verse 15: **Law,** Paul explains, given to sinners, simply **brings forth God's wrath,**—for sinners in the nature of the case will transgress. Law gives no life, and has no power over the flesh. So Paul calls law a "ministration of death and condemnation" (II Cor. 3.7,9). Alford well says, "From its very nature, law excludes promise,—which is an act of grace, and faith, which is an attribute of confidence." **Where law is not, neither is there transgression.** This brings out several things: First, that it takes law to bring forth transgression of it,—though sin may be present. There can be no transgression of a law which exists not. The absence of law is the absence of transgression. The entrance of law (in the case of a fallen being) is the entrance of transgression. Second, that there may be Divine dispensations where law is not the principle of relationship with God. Third, that to come into a spiritual place where there will be "no transgression," men must be removed completely from under the principle of law. (This will appear in Chapters Six and Seven. God indeed has an entirely different manner of life for those in Christ than being under the principle of law!) Fourth, that only the place of freedom from law is the place of the inheritance.

Verse 16: Here we see anew God's great kindness. He desired that all the seed of Abraham, whether Jewish or Gentile believers, might have security,—**that the promise might be sure to all the seed.** Now if you introduce man's works (for man always says, "I must do my part"), you introduce an element of insecurity and uncertainty. For no man, trying to "do his part," is ever certain that he has done, or *will* do, his "part." Salvation is of God, not of man. It is of faith, and so, of grace; and thus, of God. For faith is unmixed with the vain promises and hopes of man to accomplish "his part"; but looks *to what God has done,* in sending His Son, to do a *finished work* on the cross; and to the fact that God has raised up Christ; and that Christ is our unfailing High Priest in heaven.

---

in Chapters 3.3,31; 4.14; 6.6; 7.2,6. It occurs in his epistles 26 times, and elsewhere only once, but that once is illuminative: "Cut it down: why doth it also *cumber (katargei)* the ground?" (Luke 13.7). The ground was unchanged, but rendered wholly unproductive through the shade of, and the use of all the moisture by, the fig tree. This is the exact meaning: a result otherwise to be expected is by some hindering power *annulled*. Remember this word!

Abraham is declared to be "the father of us all,"—of all who *believe*. Believers will come from all nations of the earth, and Abraham is called "the heir of the world"; which he will be openly seen to be in the millennial kingdom that is shortly coming: "Ye shall see Abraham and Isaac and Jacob, in the kingdom of God" (Luke 13.28).

Verse 17: (as it is written, I made thee father of many nations) in the sight of Him whom he believed, even God [the God], who makes alive the dead, and calls things not existing, as existing. The words "Abraham, who is the father of us all" in verse 16, are to be connected with "before Him whom he believed" in verse 17, the intervening words being a parenthesis. There is a great household of faith! Whether believers realize it or not, they are sharing Abraham's inheritance. The mighty promises of God to Abraham and to His Seed, Christ (Gal. 3.16), should be studied deeply and often by all Christians. "For if ye are Christ's then are ye Abraham's seed, heirs according to promise" (Gal. 3.29). God lodged the promises in Abraham: Christ fulfilled the conditions (of redemption), and we share the benefits! Abraham got us by promise; Christ bought us by blood. Abraham is the "father of all them that believe," whether his earthly seed, Israel; or his heavenly seed, the Church; or any who shall ever believe. As to our regeneration, of course, God is the Father of all believers. But as to our relation in the household of faith, Abraham is our father: Abraham believed *for us all*. That is, he believed a promise that included us all.

Believers may indeed be said to have a three-fold fatherhood: (1) that of Abraham, of the whole household of faith; (2) that of the teacher of the gospel who was used to win them to Christ ("For though ye have ten thousand tutors in Christ, yet have ye not many fathers; for in Christ Jesus I begat you through the gospel"—I Cor. 4.15); (3) that of God, who is our actual Father, who begat us by the Holy Spirit through His Word. The first two fatherhoods, of course, are fatherhoods of relationship, so to speak; the last only is of life and reality. Yet the first two fatherhoods are also real, and should be recognized, —especially that of Abraham.

Let us hold fast in our hearts the great revelation about God which closes verse 17: "God, who makes alive the dead, and calls the things not existing as existing." The translation in both the King James and the Revision Version surely comes short of the meaning here. The Greek literally is, **God making alive dead ones, and calling things not being, being!** It is as when God spoke to the darkness, back in Genesis One (Hebrew), the creative word, *"Let light be!*—and light was." It shone, too, "out of darkness"—not a ray that was projected from already existing light! His *word* was a creative *fiat;* and, answering it, "out of darkness" sprang the heretofore non-existent, now created, light!

Note that it is the God who makes alive* dead ones;—not those with some faint and feeble existence, but actually dead ones, those utterly gone! It is the God who calls non-existent things existent,—not, "as though" they existed, a translation which, not reaching the Divine view, really involves *doubt.* "Not being, being," is what the text reads. It is as when God says of His words, "I make all things new,"—"they *are* come to pass!" (Rev. 21.5,6). This is the God whose word Abraham trusted. It was in this character, that of Life-Giver to the dead, and the Caller of not-things existent, that he trusted Him. Thus Abraham was nothing (but dead), and the seed, non-existent! Yet Abraham believed God's word that he should be "Father of a multitude"; and obediently changed his own name from Abram to Abraham!

Therefore the actual process and progress of Abraham's life of faith in such a God, is vividly set before us as our pattern. We should study it over and over. The character of faith will be the same, with this consideration: Abraham believed on God in view of what He said He *would* do; we believe on Him who *has* raised up Jesus our Lord from the dead.

*This remarkable compound word (*zoē*, life, plus *poieō*, make) is translated in the King James Version by the poor word "quicken." The Revised Version is right. The King James Version uses the same feeble word, "quicken" to translate the mighty word of Ephesians 2.5, a marvelous word of three components: a preposition, ("together with," — *sun*) — plus our compound word, "make-alive," of Romans 4.17, above, — the whole really meaning, "made-alive-together-along-with" — Christ! God *enlifes* us in Him, — us who once were in the other Adam, dead in sins! "Quicken" is not only pitiful, but lamentable in such a verse, as it hides the fundamental truth of a believer's *union* with Christ in life and position

So, in His counsels and reckoning the believer, in Chapter Eight, is seen already glorified! Of course, in counting things not being as being, God is committed to bring into outward actuality all that He reckons; thus the believing ungodly not only is accounted righteous, but will one day be publicly manifested as the very "righteousness of God"! Indeed, justification *involves* God's giving him *life,* as see 5.18. But that is not the ground of his being reckoned righteous—that some day he will be in experience as righteous as he is now reckoned—any more than that he is accounted righteous on the ground of his own good works. For justification is a sovereign, judicial—not creative-act of God, based wholly upon the death and resurrection of Christ. When a sinner is to be justified, then, righteous is that which he is not! But, he believing, God counts him, holds him as righteous. He has no more righteousness *(as a quality)* than when he a moment ago, believed. But he stands in all Christ's acceptance by the act of God, the Judge! Though we have said, God will make this standing good in glorious manifestation, yet no degree of sanctification or glorification is the basis of his being declared righteous, but the blood of Christ only, and His resurrection,—the sacrifice of Christ and God's sovereign act in view of it.

For God to call the things not being as being; to extend to a man the complete value of Christ's atoning work and "reckon" him justified and glorified in His sight, although not yet so in manifestation, is God's own business. Let us praise Him for His grace!

18 Who against hope in hope kept on believing, to the end that he might become a father of many nations, according to what was spoken: So shall
19 thy seed be! And not at all weakened in his faith, he took full account of his own body, as in a dead condition (he being about a hundred years old), and
20 also the deadness of Sarah's womb, but, looking unto God's promise, he wavered not through unbelief, but on the contrary became inwardly strength-
21 ened through faith, giving glory to God, and being
22 full of assurance that what He had promised, He

was able to perform. Therefore also it [his faith] was reckoned to him as righteousness.

23   Now this was not written for his sake only, that
24   it [his faith] was thus reckoned to him: but for our sakes likewise; for it [our faith] will be reckoned [for righteousness] to us also who are believing on Him who raised Jesus 'our Lord from
25   the dead; who was delivered up for our trespasses, and was raised for our justifying.

Here, then, in verses 18 to 25 we have the difficult, though blessed and glorious, yea, and God-glorifying path of faith, exemplified in Abraham. He kept on in hope, believing contrary to all human hopes! There were many trials to his faith, the essence of the difficulty, however, always being to "look unto the promise of God" alone, and not to circumstances, or to the impossibility, according to the flesh, of the promise's being fulfilled.

We inherit what Abraham believed for and received. Mark down two points, naming the first "A" for Abraham; and the second, "C" for Christ. Now draw a line from "A" to "C" and then onward, and let that line represent the line of God's blessing. The promises of blessing were lodged in Abraham, and all conditions of blessing were fulfilled by Christ; and you and I merely step into the line of blessing from Abraham through Christ. It is good to be born into a good family on earth; how blessed to be in the great family of faith, the family of God, along with Abraham!

Satan hates active faith in a believer's heart, and opposes it with all his power. The world, of course, is unbelieving, and despises those who claim only "the righteousness of faith." The example of professing Christians generally is also against the path of simple faith. Among the "seven abominations" that Bunyan said he still found in his heart, was "a secret inclining to unbelief." "Against hope," against reason, against "feeling," against opinions of others, against all human possibilities whatever, we are to *keep believing*.

This is the very article and essence of faith,* that it *reckons as God does*,—that is, upon God as described here, giving life not to the feeble, but to the dead, to those who cannot be "recovered" or "helped" or so wrought upon or patched up as

*I cannot refrain from quoting John Bunyan's *Come and Welcome to Jesus Christ*, in his contrasts of faith and unbelief:

"Let me here give the Christian reader a more particular description of the qualities of unbelief, by opposing faith unto it, in these particulars:

1. Faith believeth the Word of God, but unbelief questioneth the certainty of the same.

2. Faith believeth the word, because it is true, but unbelief doubteth thereof, because it is true.

3. Faith sees more in a promise of God to help than in all other things to hinder; but unbelief, notwithstanding God's promise, saith, How can these things be?

4. Faith will make thee see love in the heart of Christ when with His mouth He giveth reproofs, but unbelief will imagine wrath in His heart when with His mouth and word He saith He loves us.

5. Faith will help the soul to wait, though God defers to give, but unbelief will snuff and throw up all, if God makes any tarrying.

6. Faith will give comfort in the midst of fears, but unbelief causeth fears in the midst of comforts.

7. Faith will suck sweetness out of God's rod, but unbelief can find no comfort in the greatest mercies.

8. Faith maketh great burdens light, but unbelief maketh light ones intolerably heavy.

9. Faith helpeth us when we are down, but unbelief throws us down when we are up.

10. Faith bringeth us near to God when we are far from Him, but unbelief puts us far from God when we are near to Him.

11. Faith putteth a man under grace, but unbelief holdeth him under wrath.

12. Faith purifieth the heart, but unbelief keepeth it polluted and impure.

13. Faith maketh our work acceptable to God through Christ, but whatsoever is of unbelief is sin, for without faith it is impossible to please Him.

14. Faith giveth us peace and comfort in our souls, but unbelief worketh trouble and tossings like the restless waves of the sea.

15. Faith maketh us see preciousness in Christ, but unbelief sees no form, beauty, or comeliness in Him.

16. By faith we have our life in Christ's fulness, but by unbelief we starve and pine away.

17. Faith gives us the victory over the law, sin, death, the devil, and all evils; but unbelief layeth us obnoxious to them all.

18. Faith will show us more excellency in things not seen than in them that are, but unbelief sees more of things that are than in things that will be hereafter.

19. Faith makes the ways of God pleasant and admirable, but unbelief makes them heavy and hard.

20. By faith Abraham, Isaac, and Jacob possessed the land of promise; but because of unbelief neither Aaron, nor Moses, nor Miriam could get thither.

21. By faith the children of Israel passed through the Red Sea, but by unbelief the generality of them perished in the wilderness.

22. By faith Gideon did more with three hundred men and a few empty pitchers than all the twelve tribes could do, because they believed not God.

23. By faith Peter walked on the water, but by unbelief he began to sink.

Thus might many more be added, which, for brevity's sake, I omit, beseeching every one that thinketh he hath a soul to save or be damned to take heed of unbelief, lest, seeing there is a promise left us of entering into His rest, any of us by unbelief should indeed come short of it."

to become something that they were not before; but who are absolutely hopeless, *dead!*

That God should call the things that are not as *being,* is what faith rejoices in! Only God could call things thus. Abraham becomes before our eyes the particular shining example of this.

Verse 19: **His own body as in a dead condition**—"he considered"* it, and knew it to be thus, and was therefore wholly hopeless in himself. Moreover, Abraham knew Sarah was "past age," unable to bear a child. He had before him, then, himself as dead, and **the deadness of Sarah's womb.** But he also had before him the promise of God: "Thou shalt become a father of many nations"; "So shall thy seed be."

Verse 20: It was plainly and only a question of the veracity of God, and of His ability to carry out what He had promised. Abraham, therefore, *believed†* in Jehovah (Gen. 15.5,6); and

---

*The King James Version along with certain commentators reads "considered not." William Kelly says: "There is excellent and perhaps adequate authority of every kind (mss., versions and ancient citations) for dropping the negative particle." It is remarkable in this nineteenth verse that whichever reading we adopt, the resultant statement is not inconsistent with the context, though the two readings are opposite as can be.

†The moral grandeur, yea, sublimity, of Abraham's position cannot be put into human description.

Alone (except for Melchizedek) in a world that had left God, Abraham became by his faith, the silver thread that bound his seed to the God the world had deserted! Out from Eden man had gone, and then away from God's presence, to found, in Cain's city, a state of human affairs *with God left out.* Condemned and judged by the Deluge, they had built their proud Babel-tower. Scattered, again by Divine judgment, over the earth, they set up wood and stone "gods," and sacrificed to demons, glorifying the very lusts of their degradation: such was man's state, without God and without hope, in the world.

And then — Abraham!

Walking by a principle the world could not know, direct faith in God *as He is,* — as He reveals Himself step by step to this friend of His, Abraham comes quietly, but how wondrously, upon the scene. Even the Hittites, though they said of him, "Thou art a prince of God among us," yet *knew* him not, — neither Abraham, nor his blessed God.

Faith in God cannot be understood, nor those who have it known, except by the men of faith. And because real faith in God enters into all the walk and ways of a trusting soul, such a one becomes, like Abraham, a "stranger and pilgrim on earth."

The Lots, the Ishmaels, one by one, withdraw from Abraham. He dwelt at "Hebron," which word means "communion." Lot, though saved at last, walked as a worldling, — "by sight." Ishmael, as after him Esau, knew nothing of God.

But Abraham knew, and progressed steadily in knowledge of his God, even to the ready offering of Isaac upon the altar.

There was a seven-fold revelation of God to Abraham: First, it was as "the God of glory" that He appeared first in Ur of the Chaldees (Acts 7.2). Second, He revealed Himself to him as Jehovah (Gen. 12.8; 14.22; 15.2, 8),—although

he wavered not through unbelief, but became inwardly
strengthened through faith, giving glory to God; and also
even Sarah herself "counted Him faithful who had promised;
and received power to conceive seed."

We find in Genesis 17.17 that Abraham not only considered
the natural deadness of his body, but also brought up the question before the Lord: "Shall a child be born unto him that is a
hundred years old? and shall Sarah, that is ninety years old,
bear?" But, Jehovah having answered his objection with a
definite promise, Abraham thereafter refused to have his faith
weakened by any natural thought of himself and Sarah, but set
God's promise only before his mind, without wavering,* as
"double-minded" people, in their doubting, do (James 1.6-8,
R.V.). Indeed, his constancy was such that it evidently

---

*The word translated "wavered" (Rom. 4.20), originally means to discriminate;
then to learn or decide by discrimination; then to dispute or contend inwardly;
then to be at variance with oneself, to hesitate, doubt. See Thayer's Lexicon,
where he finally translates: "Abraham did not hesitate through want of faith."

Uncertainty, inward balancings and strugglings of faith with unbelief (as the
father of the demoniac cried, "Lord, I believe; help thou mine unbelief") such was
not the state of Abraham's soul. Having committed himself to God's promise,
which was wholly beyond human possibility, he went steadily forward. This had
the double result of giving glory to the God whom he believed, and of making
Abraham himself stronger and stronger in faith.

Two travelers on their way home came to a river frozen over, but evidently not
as yet with thick ice. One said, "I am afraid that ice will not bear my weight,"
and he sat down in the cold. The other said, "I am going home," and strode forward over the ice with steady step. He had committed himself! He refused to
look at circumstances; and every step strengthened his resolve to go ahead. He
reached the other bank, and eventually his home. The other man stayed back in
the cold.

Mr. Moody used to say, "Unbelief sees something in God's hand, and says, I
wish I had that. Faith sees it, and says, I will have it! — and gets it."

As one has said:

"The steps of faith fall upon the *seeming* void,
    And find the rock beneath!"

---

not opening to him, as afterwards to Moses in Israel the meaning of that
Name (Ex. 3.15); third, as El Elyon, God Most High, "Possessor of heaven and
earth": and the Disposer of lands, and kings: (Gen. 14.19 to 22; Dan. 3.26; 4.2;
5.18,21); fourth, as Lord (Adonai, Jehovah — 15.2,8); fifth, as El Shaddai, the
Almighty God (17.1); sixth, as "the Everlasting God" (21.33); and seventh, as
"Jehovah-Jireh" (22.14): The God who will *Provide,* — Especially, a *Lamb for
Sacrifice* (22.8).

Christ, in His ministry on earth, said "Your father Abraham rejoiced to see my
day; and he saw it, and was glad!" And, finally, Paul tells us in Hebrews 11
that this great man of faith "looked for the city which hath the foundations,
whose Architect and Maker is God" (Heb. 11.10), — that is, the New Jerusalem
of Revelation 21 and 22. Thus Abraham was taken into God's complete confidence
— as he himself had had complete confidence in God!

"The Friend of God" — what a title! No angel or seraph had that name!

wrought upon the doubting Sarah, who learned that He was "faithful who had promised."* Sarah's incredulous but eager laugh (Gen. 18.12,13,15) Jehovah charged her sternly with; for He had before when Abraham laughed (Gen. 17.16-19), named the son whom she was to bear "Isaac"—which means laughter! Thus both Abraham and Sarah thought this thing "too good to be true"; but God in faithfulness brought it to pass. And we remember the happy laughter into which Sarah finally entered: "Sarah said, God hath made me to laugh; every one that heareth will laugh with me" (Gen. 21.5-7). Every time she spoke the name "Isaac" she could remember her doubt, and how gracious Jehovah had been to her.

Verse 21: **Being full of assurance that what He had promised, He was able to perform.** What a blessed assurance of faith, resting wholly upon God's performance of what He had promised,—how that puts us to shame! Since Abraham's day we have the written Word; and Christ has come. Yet how often we doubt!†

Verse 22: Now God tells us that His word concerning Abraham, that "his faith was reckoned as righteousness," was written not for him only, but for us, also,—for all Abraham's children. There is no more striking description of the principle and process of faith than in this passage. Look at the "also" of verse 22: **Wherefore also it was reckoned unto him as righteousness.** That evidently looks toward Genesis 22; at the end of Abraham's testing time, when he offered up Isaac. Let us see what is here:

(1) We are not told that Abraham was reckoned righteous because of the vision of the God of glory that was vouchsafed

---

*God let Abraham wait many years, over thirteen at least (compare Gen. 16.16 with Gen. 17.1) before He began to let him realize the promises in the birth of Isaac.

†"We have also a precious suggestion of some *reasons* (if we may say so) *why* God prescribes Faith as the condition of the justification of a sinner. Faith, we see, is an act of the soul which looks wholly away from 'self' (as regards both merit and demerit), and *honours the Almighty and All-gracious* in a way not indeed *in the least meritorious* (because merely reasonable, after all), but yet such as to 'touch the hem of His garment.' It brings His creatures to Him in the one right attitude — complete submission and confidence. We thus see, in part, *why* faith, and only faith, is the way to reach and touch the Merit (value and power) of the Propitiation" — Moule.

to him in Ur of the Chaldees (Acts 7.2). Nor do we read that he was reckoned righteous because he forsook his own land and was brought to the land of Canaan, nor because he built altars to Jehovah and worshipped him; nor because he had such high courage as to slaughter the kings and deliver Lot. All these things occurred before the amazing scene of Genesis 15: where God proposed to him something absolutely impossible of accomplishment, except in God Himself.

(2) Abraham was *reckoned righteous* when he "believed in Jehovah," in His word, to bring about concerning Abraham something that could not humanly be—that he should be a "father of nations." God came to him years after this (Genesis 17), commanding him to change his name from Abram, "high father" (but desolate, like a lonely peak), to Abraham, "father of a multitude." And Abraham obeyed, and changed his name thus; although God had just rejected Ishmael, the only offspring he had in sight, from being the seed of promise and covenant!

(3) Abraham "gave glory to God," because he counted on God's bringing to pass His word, about that which only His glorious power could effect; a thing completely outside human possibility, but which all God's faithfulness and truth were pledged to accomplish. Thus Abraham let God in upon the scene, to act according to His own truth and power. Probably at that time he was the only man on earth who was giving God His due praise as the God of truth, who has "magnified His Word above all His Name" (Ps. 138.2). Our reason, yea, and our conscience also, keep telling us that *right living* is essentially better than *right believing;* but both conscience and reason are wrong!*

---

*Ernest Gordon in the *Sunday School Times* says, "A French Unitarian preacher, M. Lauriol, in speaking at the recent synod of Agen, said, 'Purity of heart and life is more important than correctness of opinion,' to which Dean Doumergue answers shrewdly, 'Healing is more important than the remedy, but without the remedy, there would be no healing.' "

Faith is the only faculty by which we can lay hold of God. "Let him take hold of My strength," is God's command (Isa. 27.5). But we cannot reach His greatness — we are dust. We cannot look upon His face, for He dwelleth in light unapproachable. We cannot apprehend His wisdom, for it is infinite, incomprehensible, — "reasonings of the wise, (regarding God) are vain." Then how shall we lay hold of God at all? By *believing* Him! The weakest of men can *believe what God tells him!* Praise be to His Name! Faith, simple faith, connects us with the Mighty One! Paul says, "The faith of God's elect" involves *"the knowl-*

(4) Jehovah reckoned Abraham righteous not because he was either righteous or holy, but acting absolutely, and entirely according to Himself—who "giveth life to the *dead*" (Abraham was dead: he could beget no seed); and "calleth the things that are *not*" (Abraham was a sinner, not righteous in himself) "as though they were."

(5) The purpose, then, of God concerning Abraham, Abraham thus allowed God to fulfil. Some day you will see Abraham just as righteous and holy in character and in evident fact, as His God, in that far day, reckoned him. It was not, however, on the ground of what God would make him in the future that He reckoned Abraham righteous when he believed Him. The ground, as we see plainly in Chapter 3.25, was Christ set forth as a propitiation,—through faith in Christ's blood. For "God set Him forth as a propitiation . . . because of the passing over of the sins done aforetime" (that is, by Abraham and by all who lived before Christ's death).

God had His own foreknown ground, Christ, as the Lamb "without blemish and without spot," foreknown "before the foundation of the world" (I Pet. 1.19,20). We keep repeating these things because of the continual tendency of our wretched hearts to find some cause in ourselves, or in our own faithfulness, for God's reckoning us righteous.

(6) Verses 23 and 24: **Now it was not written for his sake only, that it was reckoned unto him, but for our sakes likewise, for it** [our faith] **will be reckoned** [as righteousness] **to us also who are believing on Him that raised Jesus our Lord from the dead.** This is a blessed and sweet revelation for believers, that we, like Abraham, have righteousness reckoned to us; and that the story in Genesis was "written for our sake." The Old Testament is a *living* book for God's real saints!

---

edge of the truth which is according to godliness" (Titus 1.1). "Purity of heart and life" without the correct, accurate, constant teaching of doctrine, — "the *doctrine* which is according to godliness" (I Tim. 6.3) — is simply a philosopher's speculation or a Romanist's lie, or a "Modernist's" imagination.

But we must remember that God's methods with faith are always the same. Abraham's faith was tried: are not we also told to expect the trial of our faith?*

There is also a beautiful message in the literal rendering of verse 24, that can scarcely be supplied in English: **It was on account of us also, unto whom it** [righteousness] **is about to be reckoned, to those who believe**—as if God were eager (as indeed He is) to write down righteous those who believe His testimony concerning His Son!

Note two things here: First, it is upon *God* we believe. The very God who was, in the opening chapters of the Epistle, bringing all of us under His judgment, without righteousness and helpless to attain it, is here believed on; as our Lord Jesus indeed said in John 12.44: "He that believeth on Me, believeth not on Me, but on Him that sent Me."

But, second, it is upon Him as having raised Jesus our Lord from the dead that we believe on God in verse 24. It is not merely on the God who set forth Christ to be a propitiatory sacrifice for our sins, but it is on the God who has set a public seal to the truth of our Lord's last words, "It is finished," by raising Him from the dead. "He is not here, but is risen," was the angel's word that thrilled those saints early at His tomb. And since then He has been received up in glory, and the Holy Spirit has come, witnessing to the amazing fact that the One who hung on a Roman cross, numbered with transgressors by men, and forsaken of God in the just judgment of our sins,

---

*Satan, our deadly foe, has one target at which he constantly aims, — the *faith* of a believer. We believe that Satan's whole effort is engaged directly against faith in Christ. Millions of demons — unclean spirits, dumb spirits, lying spirits — swarm the air of this earth to carry on, together with those angelic principalities and powers who fell with Satan, the terrible program, with its "lusts of the flesh" and "of the eyes," and "the vainglory of life," called in Ephesians 2.2 "the course of this world" (literally, — the *aion* of this *cosmos,* that is, the present stage of this world-order). But Satan himself, filled with hellish jealousy against the Son of Man who came and spoiled the strong man's house (in the wilderness temptation); and triumphed over all Satan's hosts at Calvary, when He put away the sin of the world from God's sight (a fact which is true already, as Satan, and instructed saints, well know, and which will be made good openly soon, in the new heavens and new earth), — Satan himself, we say, is at present chiefly occupied in blinding men to the redemption and glory that are in Christ, and in preventing and hindering the progress of every believer. Every one who confesses the Lord Jesus is openly challenged by the prince of this world. It is well that "the God of peace shall bruise Satan under our feet shortly!" But God meanwhile says, "Whom resist, steadfast in your faith!"

was raised and glorified by the same God who forsook Him on Calvary. This glorious fact should be held fast by our hearts. For not only does God's raising up Christ prove our sins to have been put away; but a Risen Christ becomes a new place for us! We were justified from all things by His blood; we are now set by God in Christ Risen!

And thus we are prepared for the last great verse in this blessed chapter.

Verse 25: **Who was delivered up for our trespasses, and was raised for our justifying.** Here we have Jesus our Lord delivered up for our offences. Now the Greek word for "delivered up" occurs again in Chapter 8.32: "God spared not His own Son, but delivered Him up for us all." The meaning is evident: on account of our trespasses, of what you and I have done, our Lord was delivered up by a holy God to bear our sin, with its guilt and penalty, even to God's forsaking His Son: for He must otherwise have forsaken us forever!—yea, to His smiting our Substitute instead of smiting us: "He was bruised for our iniquities."

And was raised for our justifying—This must be the sense here: for we are not justified till we believe. Furthermore, if Christ's resurrection was merely to prove that we had been justified (as some teach) a verb-construction would have been used, which would signify, on account of our having been justified. But God uses the noun-construction *(dikaiōsis)* meaning, "the act of justifying"; showing that Christ's resurrection was for the purpose of justifying us, *positively*, in a *Risen* Christ, (Compare 5.10.)

Matthew Henry says: "In Christ's death He paid our debt; in His resurrection, He took out our acquittance." But Scripture goes much further in this matter of justification than the satisfaction of all claims of God's justice against us. We are set in a new place of acceptance, the Risen Christ, that has nothing to do with our old place. God will now go on to "create us in Christ Jesus." It will be "justification *of life*," as we shall see in Chapter Five.

Only, we repeat, let us always remember that we are justified as ungodly, and now we are "new creatures in Christ Jesus."

Here, indeed, is a great mystery. God does not declare us righteous as connected with the old Adam—old creatures, we might
say. Nor does He declare us righteous because we are new creatures. But God that calleth the things not existing as existing,
acts in justification, declaring the ungodly who believe on Him,
righteous: not because of any process of His operation upon the
creature, but by His own fiat, reckoning to the beliving one the
whole work of Christ on his behalf. This involves God's giving
this ungodly believing one a standing in Christ Risen; and God
will go on by an act of creation, to cause him to share Christ's
risen life, which is justification of life. But it is as ungodly
that he is declared righteous. We must hold fast to this, the
first point of the gospel (I Cor. 15.3).

We are indeed said to be justified by or in His blood (5.9),
but if there had been no resurrection, His death would have
availed us nothing. So Paul says that both Peter and he were
"justified *in* Christ" (Gal. 2.17): that is, in the Risen Christ, in
view, of course, of His finished work on the cross. When our
Lord said, "It is finished," He announced the penalty paid for
every believer that shall be. But He lay under the power of
death for three days and nights, His body in Joseph's tomb and
His spirit in Paradise.

Now justification involves not only, negatively, the putting
away of our guilt; but, positively, a new place and standing.
For the old Adam was utterly condemned, as his history, and
the law, and finally the cross, fully showed. If I am a sinner,
and my sins are transferred to the head of Christ my Substitute,
and He bears the penalty of them in death, *then where am I,*
if Christ be not raised? His death and resurrection are one and
inseparable as regards justification. Christ being raised up, God
announces to me, "Not only were your sins put away by Christ's
blood, so that you are justified *from* all things; but I have also
raised up Christ; and you shall have your standing *in Him.*
I have given you this faith in a Risen Christ, and announce to
you that in Him alone now is your place and standing. Judgment is forever past for you, both as concerns your sin, and as
concerns My demand that you have a standing of holiness and
righteousness of your own before Me. All this is past. *Christ*

is now your standing! He is your life and your righteousness;
and you need nothing of your own forever. I made Christ to
become sin on your behalf, identified Him with all that you
were, in order that you might become the righteousness of God
in Him."

I must here quote the vigorous, triumphant words of Martin
Luther, from his commentary on Galatians, touching these
words, "delivered up for OUR trespasses": "Christ verily is the
innocent, as concerning His own person, and the unspotted and
undefiled Lamb of God, and therefore He ought not to have
been hanged upon a tree: but because, according to the law of
Moses, every thief and malefactor ought to be hanged, therefore Christ also, according to the law, ought to be hanged. For
He sustained the person of a sinner and of a thief: not of one,
but of all sinners and thieves. For He being made a sacrifice
for the sins of the whole world, is not now an innocent person,
but a sinner which hath and carrieth the sin of Paul, who was a
blasphemer, an oppressor, a persecutor; of Peter, who denied
Christ; of David, who was an adulterer and a murderer; and,
briefly, Christ, who hath and beareth the sin of all men in His
own body, not that He Himself committed them, but for that
He received them, being committed or done of us, and laid upon
His own body, that He might make satisfaction for them with
His own blood. Therefore whatsoever sins I, thou, and we all
have done and shall do, hereafter, they are Christ's own sins, as
verily as if He Himself had done them. To be brief, our sin
must needs become Christ's own sin, or else we shall perish
forever.

"Also learn this definition diligently ('Who was delivered
for OUR trespasses'), that this one syllable being believed, may
swallow up all thy sins: that thou mayest know assuredly, that
Christ hath taken away the sins, not of certain men only, but
also of thee. Then let thy sins be not sins only, but even thy
own sins indeed.

"Thus may we be able to answer the devil accusing us, saying,
Thou art a sinner, thou shalt be damned. No, say I, for I *flee
unto Christ* who hath given Himself for *my* sins. Therefore,
Satan, thou shalt not prevail against me in that thou goest about

to terrify me, in setting forth the greatness of my sins, and so to bring me into heaviness, distrust, despair, hatred, contempt, and blaspheming of God. Yea, rather, in that thou sayest, I am a sinner, thou givest me armour and weapons against thyself, that with thine own sword I may cut thy throat, and tread thee under my feet; for Christ died for sinners! Moreover, Satan, thou thyself preachest unto me the glory of God; for thou puttest me in mind of God's fatherly love toward me, wretched and damned sinner: 'Who so loved the world that He gave His only begotten Son, that whosoever believeth on Him shall not perish, but have everlasting life' (John 3.16). And as often as thou objectest that I am a sinner, so often thou callest me to remembrance of the benefit of Christ my Redeemer, upon whose shoulders, and not upon mine, lay all my sins; for the Lord hath 'laid all our iniquity upon Him' (Isa. 53.6). Again, 'For the transgressions of His people was He smitten' (53.8). Wherefore, when thou sayest I am a sinner, thou dost not terrify me, but comfortest me above measure."

So Paul closes his setting forth of this great resurrection side of our salvation, saying, **He was raised for our justifying.** Doubtless other, and eternal ends were in view in God's raising up Christ; but lay fast hold of this, that in your case it was for the purpose of declaring you who believe righteous, that God raised Christ. And further, of giving you a hitherto unheard of place, to be *in* Christ, one with Him before God forever, loved as Christ is loved, seen in all the perfectness and beauty of Christ Himself, glorified *with* Him, associated *with* Him as companions, that He might be the First-born among many *brethren!*

There is no limit to God's favor toward those in Christ!

JUSTIFICATION—A REVIEW

I *What It Is Not*

1. It is not regeneration, the impartation of life in Christ, for although it is "justification of life"—meaning God will give life to the justified, he is justified as *ungodly*.

2. It is not "a new heart," or "change of heart,"—indefinite expressions at best, but having in them no proper definition of justification.

3. It is not "making an unjust man just," in his life and behavior. The English word *justified,* as we all know, comes from the Latin word meaning to make just or righteous; but this is exactly what justification is *not,* in Scripture.

4. It is not to be confused with sanctification; which is the state of those placed in Christ,—"sanctified in Christ Jesus"; and consequently the manner of their walk in the Spirit.

II *What It Is*

1. It is a declaration by God in heaven concerning a man, that he stands righteous in God's sight.

2. God justifies a man, on the basis or ground of the "redemption that is in Christ Jesus" (3.24). See 5.6: We are "justified by [or in] His blood";—the blood the procuring ground, or means; God the acting Person.

3. God who has already acted judicially, in pronouncing the whole world guilty (Rom. 3.19), now again acts judicially concerning that sinner who becomes convinced of his guilt and helplessness, and believes that God's Word concerning Christ's expiatory sacrifice applies to himself; and thus becomes "of faith in Jesus" (3.26, margin): God's judicial* pronouncement now is, that such a believing one stands righteous in His sight.

4. Justification, or declaring-righteous, therefore, is the reckoning by God to a believing sinner of the whole value of the infiinte work of Christ on the cross; and, further, His connecting this believing sinner with the Risen Christ in glory, giving him the same acceptance before Himself as has Christ: so that the believer is now "the righteousness of God in Him" (Christ).

---

*"Wherefore as condemnation is not the infusing of a habit of wickedness into him that is condemned, nor the making of him to be inherently wicked who was before righteous, but the passing of a sentence upon a man with respect to his wickedness; no more is justification the change of a person from inherent unrighteousness by the infusion of a principle of grace, but a sentential declaration of him to be righteous" (i.e., in his standing before God) — John Owen.

Negatively, then, God in justifying a sinner reckons to him the putting away of sin by Christ's blood. Positively, He places him in Christ: he is *one with Christ forever before God!*

> Wondrous prize of our high calling!
>   Speed we on to this,
> Past the cities of the angels,—
>   Farther into bliss;
>
> On into the depths eternal
>   Of the love and song,
> Where in God the Father's glory
>   Christ has waited long;
>
> There to find that none beside *Him*
>   God's delight can be:
> Not BESIDE HIM, NAY, BUT IN HIM,
>   O BELOVED ARE WE!
>
> —C. P. C., in *Hymns of Ter Steegen.*

CHAPTER FIVE

The Glorious Results of Justification by Faith: Peace With God, a Standing in Grace, Sure Hope of Coming Glory, Present Patience, Joy in God. Verses 1-11.

The Two Representative Men, Adam and Christ, Contrasted: Condemnation and Death by Adam to All in Him; Justification and Life by Christ to All in Him. Verses 12-19.

By the Law, Sin Became Trespass; but GRACE TRANSCENDED ALL! Verse 20.

Grace Now Reigns, "Through Jesus Christ our Lord." Verse 21.

THIS GREAT CHAPTER naturally falls into two parts:

In the first eleven verses we have the blessed results of justification by faith, along with the most comprehensive statement in the Bible of the pure love and grace of God, in giving Christ for us sinners.

In the second part, verses 12 to 21, God goes back of the history and state of human sin, (which in Chapters 1.21 to 3.20 have been before us) to Adam, as our representative head, who stood for us, and whose sin became condemnation and death to us; and shows us Christ, as the other representative Man (whom Adam prefigured), by His act of death on the cross bringing us justification and life. The emphasis in this great passage will be in each case upon the fact that the act of the representative, and not of the one represented, brought the result to pass.

1 Therefore having been declared righteous on the principle of faith, we have peace towards God,
2 through our Lord Jesus Christ: through whom also we have obtained access into this Divine favor

162

wherein we are standing: and we exult in hope of
the glory of God.

3   And not only so, but we also exult in the tribulations [which beset us]: knowing that tribulation
4   is working out endurance; and endurance [a sense
of] approvedness [by God]; and [the sense of]
5   approvedness works out [a state of] hope: and
[our state of] hope does not make us ashamed:
because God's love [for us] is poured out in our
hearts through the Holy Spirit which has been
given to us.

6   For Christ, we being yet helpless [in our sins],
at the appointed time died for ungodly ones. For
7   hardly for a righteous man will any one die: for
perhaps for a good [generous] man some one might
8   venture to die. But God commends His own love
toward us, in that, while we were yet sinners,
9   Christ died for us! Much more then, having been
now declared righteous by [means of] His blood,
10   shall we be saved through Him from the [coming]
wrath. For if, being enemies, we were reconciled
to God through the death of His Son, much more,
being reconciled, shall we be saved by His [risen]
life.

11   And not only so, but we even exult in God
through our Lord Jesus Christ, through whom we
have now received the reconciliation.

Verse 1: Therefore having been declared righteous on
the principle of faith—We must note at once that the Greek
form of this verb "declared righteous," or "justified," is not the
present participle, *"being* declared righteous," but rather the
aorist participle, *"having been* declared righteous," or "justified." You say, What is the difference? The answer is, "being
declared righteous" looks to a state you are in; "having been
declared righteous" looks back to *a fact that happened.* "Being
in a justified *state"* of course is incorrect, confusing, as it does,
justification and sanctification. "Whatsoever God doeth, it shall
be forever." The moment you believed, God declared you

righteous, never to change His mind: as David says, "Blessed is the man to whom the Lord will not reckon sin" (Rom. 4.8). If therefore you are a believer, quote this verse properly, and say, "Having been declared righteous on the principle of faith I have"—these blessed fruits and results which are now to be recorded.

The Epistle takes on a new aspect in each chapter: in Chapter Three, Christ was set forth as a propitiation for our sins; in Chapter Four, Christ was raised for our justification; in Chapter Five, we have peace with God through Christ, a standing in grace, and the hope of the coming glory.

We have three blessings, then, in this first part of our chapter: (1) peace with God, in looking back to Calvary where Christ made peace by His blood; (2) a present standing in grace, in unlimited Divine favor; and (3) hope of the glory of God—of being glorified with Christ when He comes.

We have peace with God through our Lord Jesus Christ —"Peace" means that the war is done. "Peace with God" means that God has nothing against us. This involves:

1. That God has fully judged sin, upon Christ, our Substitute.

2. That God was so wholly satisfied with Christ's sacrifice, that He will eternally remain so: never taking up the judgment of our sin again.

3. That God is therefore at rest about us forever, however poor our understanding of truth, however weak our walk. God is looking at the blood of Christ, and not at our sins. All claims against us were met when Christ "made peace by the blood of His cross." So "we have peace with God."*

> "If Thou hast my discharge procured,
> And freely in my place endured
>   The whole of wrath Divine:
> Payment God will not twice demand,
> First at my bleeding Surety's hand,
>   And then again at mine!"

---

*As to the Greek text having the subjunctive in verse 1, we believe that the Authorized Version and the American Revised Version are correct in reading "we have peace" rather than the English Revised Version, "Let us have peace." See Jamieson, Fausset and Brown, Darby, Meyer, Godet and many others. The whole context proves that "we have peace" is correct, for the passage is not an exhortation, but an assertion of facts and results, true of all those declared righteous or justified.

Our peace with God is not as between two nations before at war; but as between a king and rebellious and guilty subjects. While our hearts are at last at rest, it is because God, against whom we sinned, has been fully satisfied at the cross. "Peace with God through our Lord Jesus Christ" does not mean peace through what He is now doing, but through what He did do on the Cross. He *"made* peace" by the blood of His cross. All the majesty of God's holy and righteous throne was satisfied when Christ said, "It is finished." And, being now raised from the dead, "He *is* our peace." But it is His past work at Calvary, not His present work of intercession, that all is based upon; and that gives us a sense of the peace which He made through His blood.*

This peace with (or towards) God must not be confused with the "peace *of* God" of Philippians 4.7, which is a subjective state; whereas peace with God is an objective fact—outside of ourselves. Thousands strive for inward peace, never once resting where God is resting—in the finished work of Christ on Calvary.†

"I hear the words of love,
 I gaze upon the blood;
I see the mighty Sacrifice,
 And I have peace with God.

" 'Tis everlasting peace,
 Sure as Jehovah's name;
'Tis stable as His stedfast throne,
 For evermore the same.

---

*The Romanist will go to "mass" and "confession"; and the Protestant "attend church"; but neither will find peace with God by these things. Prayers, vows, fastings, church duties, charities—what have these to do with peace?—if Christ "made peace by His blood"!

†The difference may be brought out by asking ourselves two questions: First. Have I peace *with* God? Yes; because Christ died for me. Second, Have I the peace of God in quietness from the anxieties and worries of life in my heart? We see at once that being at peace *with* God must depend on what was done for us by Christ on the cross. It is not a matter of experience, but of revelation. On the contrary, the peace of God "sets a garrison around our hearts and thoughts in Christ Jesus," when we refuse to be anxious about circumstances, and "in everything (even the most 'trifling' affairs) by prayer and supplication with thanksgiving let our requests be made known unto God." Every believer is at peace *with* God, because of Christ's shed blood. Not every believer has this "peace *of* God" within him; for not all have consented to judge anxious care and worry as unbelief in God's Fatherly kindness and care.

>   "My love is oftimes low,
>   My joy still ebbs and flows;
>   But peace with Him remains the same,
>   No change Jehovah knows.
>
>   *   *   *
>
>   "I change, He changes not,
>   God's Christ can never die;
>   His love, not mine, the resting-place,
>   His truth, not mine, the tie."
>
>   —(Bonar)

Verse 2: Look a moment at the second benefit: **Through whom also we have had our access into this grace wherein we stand**—The word "also" sets this blessing forth as distinct from and additional to that of peace with God. Through Christ, in whom they have believed, there has been given to the justified "access" into a wonderful standing in Divine favor. Being in Christ, they have extended to them the very favor in which Christ Himself stands. Notice that the words "by faith" (as in A. V.) here should be omitted. It is not by an additional revelation, and acceptance thereof, that believers come into this standing in grace. It is a place of Divine favor given to every believer the moment he believes. In Chapter 6.14 we are to be told that we are *under grace,* not *law.* It is a glorious discovery to find how fully God is *for us,* in Christ.*

Now, as to this third great matter: **We rejoice in hope of the glory of God.** This is the future of the believer: to enter upon a glorified state, glorified together with Christ, as it is in Chapter 8.17. It is not merely to behold God's glory, but to enter into it! "When Christ, who is our life, shall be manifested, then shall we also with Him be manifested in glory" (Col. 3.4). "The glory which thou has given Me I have given unto them" (John 17.22). We shall speak of this further,

---

*Sanday quotes Ellicott's translation: "Through whom also we have had our access," and adds, " 'have had' when we first became Christians, and now while we are such."

And Darby comments: "We are not called on to believe that we *do* believe, but to believe that Jesus is the Son of God, by whom we have access, and are brought into perfect present favor, every cloud that could hide God's love removed; and can rejoice in hope of the glory of God."

in its place in Chapter Eight. The translation "exult" rather than "glory," or "boast," suits Paul's meaning here. So in the next verse, we exult in our tribulations. It is an inner, joyful confidence, rather than an outward glorying or boasting before others, although this latter will often necessarily follow!

Verses 3 and 4: **And not only so, but we also exult in the tribulations** [which beset us] : **knowing that tribulation is working out endurance: and endurance** [a sense of] **approvedness** [by God] ; **and** [the sense of] **approvedness works out a state of hope**—So now we find that not only does the believer look back to peace made with God at the cross; at a God smiling upon him in favor; and forward to his coming glorification with Christ, but he is able also to exult in the very tribulations that are appointed to him. Paul constantly taught, as in Acts 14.22 and II Thessalonians 3.3, that "through many tribulations we must enter into the kingdom of God," and that "we are appointed unto afflictions." The word means pressure, straits, difficulties; and Paul had them! "Pressed on every side, perplexed, pursued, smitten down"; "in afflictions, in necessities, in distresses, in stripes, in imprisonments, in tumults, in labors, in watchings, in fastings; by evil report, . . . as chastened, and not killed; as sorrowful,— yet always rejoicing; as poor, yet making many rich; as having nothing, and yet possessing all things!" (II Cor. 4.8,9; 6.4-10). He regarded these as "our light affliction" said he, "which is for the moment, and is working for us more and more exceedingly an eternal weight of glory," (II Cor. 4.17) ; and so Paul "took pleasure" in them! (II Cor. 12.10).

We need to take a lesson from the martyrs, who lived in the freshness and strength of the early faith of the Church of God, who often sang in the midst of the flames! We hear today of just the same courage where persecution and trial are greatest. We can but give here a testimony from Russia that will reach all our hearts. It is a classic on suffering for Christ's sake.*

---

*A letter that lately came out of Northern Siberia, signed "Mary," reads: "The best thing to report is, that I feel so happy here. It would be so easy to grow bitter if one lost the spiritual viewpoint and began to look at circumstances. I am learning to thank God for literally everything that comes. I experienced so many things that looked terrible, but which finally brought me closer to Him. Each time circumstances became lighter, I was tempted to break fellowship with the

The Divine process is as follows: God brings us into tribulations, and that of all sorts; graciously supplying therewith a rejoicing expectation of deliverance in due time; and the knowledge that, as the winds buffeting some great oak on a hillside cause the tree to thrust its roots deeper into the ground, so these tribulations will result in steadfastness, in faith and patient endurance; and our consciousness of steadfastness—of having been brought by grace through the trials,—gives us a sense of Divine approval, or approvedness, we did not before have; and which is only found in those who have been brought through trials, by God's all-sufficient grace. This sense of God's approval arouses within us abounding "hope"—we might almost say, hopeful*ness,* a hopeful, happy state of soul.

Verse 5: **And [our state of] hope does not make us ashamed: because God's love [for us] is poured out in our hearts through the Holy Spirit which has been given to us.** Furthermore, then, no matter how much the world or worldly Christians may avoid or deride us, this hopefulness is not "ashamed," or is not "put to shame": because there is supplied

---

Lord. How can I do otherwise than thank Him for additional hardships? They only help me to what I always longed for—a continuous, unbroken abiding in Him. Every so-called hard experience is just another step higher and closer to Him."

Another recent letter from "Mary" reads, "I am still in the same place of exile. There is a Godless Society here; one of the members became especially attached to me. She said, 'I cannot understand what sort of a person you are; so many here insult and abuse you, but you love them all' . . . She caused me much suffering, but I prayed for her earnestly. Another time she asked me whether I could love her. Somehow I stretched out my hands toward her, we embraced each other, and began to cry. Now we pray together. My dear friends, please pray for her. Her name is Barbara."

In a letter a month later, "Mary" writes: "I wrote you concerning my sister in Christ, Barbara. She accepted Christ as her personal Savior, and testified before all about it. We both, for the last time, went to the meeting of the Godless. I tried to reason with her not to go there, but nothing could prevail. She went to the front of the hall, and boldly testified before all concerning Christ. When she finished she started to sing in her wonderful voice a well-known hymn,

'I am not ashamed to testify of Christ, who died for me,
His commandments to follow, and depend upon His cross!'

The very air seemed charged! She was taken hold of and led away."

Two months later, another letter came from "Mary": "Yesterday, for the first time, I saw our dear Barbara in prison. She looked very thin, pale, and with marks of beatings. The only bright thing about her were her eyes, bright, and filled with heavenly peace and even joy. How happy are those who have it! It comes through suffering. Hence we must not be afraid of any sufferings or privations. I asked her, through the bars, 'Barbara, are you not sorry for what you have done?' 'No,' she firmly responded, 'If they would free me, I would go again and tell my comrades about the marvelous love of Christ. I am very glad that the Lord loves me so much and counts me worthy to suffer for Him.' " *The Link*

the inward and wonderful miracle of the consciousness of God's love shed abroad in our hearts through that second mighty gift of God to us (Christ Himself being the first),—**the indwelling Holy Spirit.**

Paul now takes up this "love of God" in what is, as regards God's sheer grace, the highest place in Paul's epistles. It is the greatest exposition in Scripture of God's love, as announced in John 3.16: "For God so loved the world that He gave—." Ephesians unfolds the marvelous heavenly calling into which God's grace has brought us. But, as to God's love itself, what it is, we must come to the present verses of Romans: as John says, "Herein is love, not that we loved God, but that He loved us, and sent His Son to be the propitiation for our sins" (I John 4.10).

First of all, the indwelling Holy Spirit, given freely to all believers, sheds abroad in our hearts this love of God—making us conscious of it in a direct inner witness: and that especially in times of trial or need.

A THREE-FOLD VIEW OF GOD'S LOVE FOR US—SINNERS

Next, we see three stages of our sinnerhood, each connected in a peculiar, fitting, and touching way with God's love.

1. Verse 6: **For Christ,—we being yet helpless [in our sins], at the appointed time died for ungodly ones**—The fact of man's total moral inability is stated here in the gentlest possible terms. It is a bankruptcy of all moral and spiritual inclination toward God and holiness, as well as of power to be or do good. Yet into a scene of helplessness like this, God sends His Son,—for what? To die for the "ungodly." No return or response is demanded: it is absolute grace—for the *ungodly.*

Verse 7: **For scarcely for a righteous man will anyone die: though perhaps for a good man some one might even venture to die**—Paul proceeds with his wonderful pean of praise concerning God's love: Among men, while for a sternly honest man no one would die, yet some one might be found to venture death for a "noble" person, one of generous-hearted goodness. But what of *God's* love?

2. Verse 8. **God commendeth His own love toward us, in that, while we were yet sinners, Christ died for us**—Now "sinning" is a stronger word than "strengthless": but it is strong in the wrong direction! Strengthless indeed toward God and holiness, we were all; yet vigorous and active in sin. And what did God do? What does God here say? It was while we were thus sinning that Christ died for us! And thus doth God "commend"* His peculiar love toward us. It is most astonishing, this announcement that God is "commending" this love of His for us,—a love "all uncaused by any previous love of ours for Him."† Salesmen "commend" their wares to those whom they deem able and willing to buy them. God "commends" His tender love to us; for He loved us as wretches occupied in sin, unable and unwilling to pay Him or obey Him. This is absolute grace.

3. Verse 10: **For if, while we were enemies, we were reconciled to God through the DEATH of His Son, much more, being reconciled, shall we be saved in His LIFE.**

Now, "enemies" is a much worse word than either "strengthless" or "sinners"; it involves a personal alienation and animosity. "The mind of the flesh is enmity against God . . . not subject to the law of God, neither, indeed, can it be." What a condition! And yet, while we were going about avoiding and hating God, that same God was having His Son, Christ, meet all the Divine claims against us by His death on Calvary!

Mark that, **while we were enemies,** He did this. No change of our hateful attitude was demanded by God before He sent His Son. "Herein is love, not that we loved God, but that God

---

*"Proves, as in 3.5" (Meyer); "establishes" (Godet); "confirms" (Calvin); "manifests" (Haldane); "gives proof of" (Alford); "demonstrates" (Williams); "commendeth" (Sanday). The English word "commendeth" happily covers the double meaning of the Greek: (1) approving or establishing *things,* and (2) recommending *persons* (16.1).

†"In sovereign grace He rises above the sin, and loves without a motive, save what is in His own nature and part of His glory. Man must have a motive for loving. God has none but in Himself, and 'commendeth His love to us' (and the 'His' is emphatic as to this very point), in that, while we are yet sinners, Christ died for us; the best thing in heaven that could be given for the vilest, most defiled, and guilty sinners" (Darby).

loved us, and sent His Son to be the propitiation for our sins."
Grace, brother, *grace,*—unasked, undesired, and, of course, forever undeserved,—Divine *kindness!* "When the kindness of God our Savior, and His love toward man appeared, not by works which we did ourselves, but according to His mercy, He saved us."

Here, then, whoever you are, read your record: strengthless, sinning, hating: then you can begin to conceive of, if you will believe, this sovereign, uncaused love which God here in this great passage "commends" to you. Do not try to be "worthy" of it; for offers to pay, by an utter bankrupt, are not only worthless, but an insult to *grace!* Self-righteousness seeks to discover in *itself* some cause for that Divine favor that God declares has its only source in Himself and His love. "Strengthless"—"sinners"—"enemies"—such were we all, and God sent His Son to die for us as such!

Now let us not dare try to get God to be reconciled to us through our prayers, our consecration, our works. We were reconciled to God while His enemies, through the death of His Son. One who has believed is overwhelmed to find that this reconciliation was effected while he himself was an enemy to God; and so the "much more" gets hold of his heart: I was reconciled by His death while I was an enemy: how much rather, now that I have accepted this reconciliation and share Christ's own risen life, shall God pour His salvation-favor upon me! I was an enemy then, and God gave Christ for me; now that I am God's friend, He cannot do less!*

---

*To illustrate reconciliation:

Suppose I am the master of a school and I make a rule that there is to be no profane swearing. I write that rule on the blackboard, and the whole school sees and hears it. The penalty I announce, too: there is to be a whipping if any one breaks the rule.

Now, there is a boy named John Jones in my school, a boy I am fond of. At recess-time he swears. Everybody hears him; I hear him; everybody knows I hear him. When I call the school to order, all the scholars are looking at me to see what I will do.

I have a son of my own in that school room, a beloved son, Charles. I call him, and we go outside to counsel, while the school waits. I say, "Son, will you bear John Jones' whipping for him? He doesn't believe that I love him. He thinks I hate him because he has broken my rule. There must be a whipping. I must be true to my word, but you know how I love John." My son says, "Yes, father, I'll do anything for you that you wish. And I love John Jones, too."

I bring my boy, Charles, out before the whole school, and I say, "This is John Jones' whipping I am giving to my son Charles. The law of the school was broken

This is the important thing to see, in the matter or reconciliation: it was necessary for us to be reconciled to God Himself, to that holiness and righteousness in God, that was infinitely *against sin.* This was brought about in Christ's death.

So, we read, "God was in Christ reconciling the world unto Himself" (II Cor. 5.19). "While we were enemies, we were reconciled to God by the death of His Son." All sin is contrary to God's holiness, righteousness, truth, and glory, but sin was put by God on Christ, and God "spared Him not." And now God says to His messengers: "Go be ambassadors on behalf of Christ. Tell sinners that I have smitten Him instead of them. Tell them I forsook Him on the cross, that I might not forsake them forever!"

THE FOUR "MUCH MORES"

There are in this remarkable chapter four "much mores" which it is interesting and profitable to note. Two are in this first section; and two in the second. First, we have the two "much mores" of future safety; verses 9 and 10; then the two "much mores" of grace's abundance: verses 15 and 17, which are developed in the other section of the chapter.

Verse 9: **Much more then, having been now declared righteous by** [means of] **His blood, shall we be saved through Him from the** [coming] **wrath**—God *has* done the harder thing: He *will* do the easier thing. He has had Christ die for us while we were "yet sinners"; "much more" will He see that we, being now believers and accounted righteous in

---

by John Jones. I am putting the penalty on my boy. He says he will gladly do this for me, and for John." Then I whip my son Charles; and I do not spare him. I whip him just as if he were John Jones, just as if he had broken the rule himself.

When the whipping is over, I say to some scholar, "Go and tell John Jones I have nothing against him,—nothing at all. And ask him to come and give me his hand." This breaks John Jones up, and he comes forward, in tears, and says, "I didn't know you loved me that much! I thank you from my heart!"

Now he is reconciled from *his* side, to *me.* But you see I reconciled him to myself, *first.* I had to deal with his disobedience, *or be myself unrighteous.*

view of Christ's blood, shall be saved from the coming wrath through Him (Christ).*

Notice that *shed blood is the justifying ground, the procuring cause,* of our being accounted righteous; and that instead of our being uncertain of preservation from the wrath which is coming at the Last Judgment, the fact that Christ died for us while were were *still sinners* should give us a constant state of calm security!

Verse 10: **Much more, being reconciled, shall we be saved by His [risen] life**—Again, God has done the harder thing—

*Concerning Christ's bearing in our place God's wrath against sin, let us say:

To regard God as "angry," or as demanding that Christ suffer "the exact equivalent of all the agonies the elect would have suffered to all eternity," is to miss the whole meaning of propitiation.

1. Remember it is God Himself who "loved us and sent His Son to be the propitiation for our sins." God held no enmity against us. God loved us.

2. Therefore, strictly speaking, it was not *punishment* which Christ bore on the cross, but *wrath.* Punishment is personal,—against the offender; but wrath upon Christ was against the thing—*sin.* Christ bore that wrath which God's being and nature always and forever sustains toward sin. The sinner cannot come nigh Him, but must die, must perish in His holy presence,—not because God hates him, but because God is the Holy One. Therefore did Christ die,—and that forsaken of God under wrath—because He was bearing our sins in His own body on the tree. So it was, that, sin being placed on Christ, judgment and wrath fell upon Him. So it is, also, that the believer has not been "appointed unto wrath" (I Thess. 5.9): the wrath has fallen on Christ.

3. The conception that Christ on the cross was enduring all the agonies of the elect for all eternity grew directly out of the Romish legalism from which the Reformers did not escape,—to wit: that we still have connection with our responsibilities in Adam the first; that our history was not ended at the cross. But the shed blood brought in before God on the Day of Atonement simply witnessed that a life had been laid down, ended. "The sufferings of all the elect for all eternity" could never take the place of the *laid down life* of the great Sacrifice. God did not ask for *agonies;* sin simply could not approach Him! There must be banishment of the sinner from His presence—unless a substitute should come, who, taking the place of the sinner, and bearing his sin, could lay down his life. Such was Christ. He "laid down His life that He might take it again." But remember both parts of this great utterance: (a) "He laid down His life," bearing our sin, putting it away from God's presence forever. But even Christ, when bearing our sin, could not, as it were, come nigh God, but was forsaken, under holy wrath against sin. Not the agonies of Christ could avail, but that, bearing sin, He laid His life down, poured out His soul unto *death.* Thus He owned God's holiness to be absolute and infinite, and said, "It is finished." (b) Now in taking up His life again, it was not that life which, according to Leviticus 17.11, was "in the blood," because the blood was "all one with the life" (Lev. 17.14), and therefore "given to make atonement for souls,"; "it was not the blood-life" which He took up, but "newness of life" in resurrection!

God indeed permitted man to inflict the terrible sufferings of crucifixion upon His Son. But those sufferings were not "the cup" that His Father had given Him to drink. The cup was the cup of Divine wrath against sin, and it involved His being "cut off out of the land of the living" under the hand of *Divine judgment.*

delivering Christ to death to reconcile us to Himself. He will certainly—much more! do the lesser thing for us: He will see that we share Christ's risen life forever; and thus, even in the hour of visitation upon the wicked, we shall be "saved by His life." (This will more fully come out in Chapter Eight, where the blessed Spirit supplies that life which is in Christ to us, as a very "law of life.")

We were reconciled to God by God's having Christ meet in His death all the claims of His throne,—His majesty, His holiness, His righteousness, His truth. "Much more," being from our side reconciled, shall we be saved now and in the future by and in Christ's risen life which we now share!

This "saved by His life" evidently looks forward to the coming Day of Judgment referred to in verse 9* as the coming wrath, into which judgment our Lord has told us we shall not come (John 5.24). Indeed, Paul writes in I Thessalonians 1.10,—"Jesus, who delivereth us from the wrath to come"!

And now the apostle closes up this section of the Epistle with a note of highest exultation:

Verse 11: **And not only so, but we also exult in God through 'our Lord Jesus Christ, through whom we have now received the reconciliation**—He says, **We exult in God.** How great a change! Three chapters back, we were sitting in the Divine Judge's court, guilty—our mouths stopped, and all our works rejected! Now, "through our Lord Jesus Christ" and His work for us, we are rejoicing, exulting, *in* Him who was our Judge! This is what grace can do and does! And we see that it is simply by receiving the reconciliation that has been brought in by Christ. For the word here is not "atonement," which means to cover up, and is applied to the Old Testament sacrifices. The word reconciliation here *(katallaga)* is simply

---

*The Greek preposition *en* in verse 9, is not fully or exactly rendered by the English word "in"; for the Greek *en* here includes: in the shed blood of Christ (vs. 9), as the ground before God of our justification; in view of that blood's power as seen by God the Justifier; in the eternal availingness of that blood before God; and the consequent eternal redemption it has procured.

Likewise, in the same construction in verse 10, we translate, "in His life": meaning that the believer shares that risen life of Christ; that in the power of that endless life the believer will abide both now and forever: as John says, "we may have boldness in the day of judgment; because as He is, even so are we in this world."

the noun form of the verb "reconcile," in verse 10. Compare "God was in Christ reconciling the world unto Himself, not reckoning unto them their trespasses (II Cor. 5.19).

To "receive" a complete, accomplished reconciliation,—how simple! We have seen men and women exult in God, thus! Every believer has this great right of exultation. This is a "song of the Lord" that lasts forever—"through our Lord Jesus Christ."

GOD'S PLAN: THE "REIGN OF GRACE" THROUGH CHRIST

Romans 5.12-21.

THE TWO MEN

$\left. \begin{array}{l} ADAM \\ CHRIST \end{array} \right\}$ Verse 14.

THE TWO ACTS

ADAM—one trespass: Verses 12, 15, 17, 18, 19.

CHRIST—one righteous act (on the cross): Verse 18.

THE TWO RESULTS

By ADAM—Condemnation, guilt, death: Verses 15, 16, 18, 19.

By CHRIST—Justification, life, kingship: Verses 17, 18, 19.

THE TWO DIFFERENCES

In degree
Verse 15
$\Big\{$ God the Creator's grace by Christ, abounds beyond the sin of the creature, Adam.

In kind or operation
Verse 16
$\Big\{$ One sin, by Adam—condemnation and reign of death.
Many sins on Christ—justification and "reigning in life" for those accepting God's grace by Him.

THE TWO KINGS

SIN—reigning through Death: Verse 17.

GRACE—reigning through Righteousness: Verse 21.

THE TWO ABUNDANCES

$\left. \begin{array}{l} \text{OF GRACE} \\ \text{OF THE GIFT OF RIGHTEOUSNESS} \end{array} \right\}$ Verse 17.

THE TWO CONTRASTED STATES

CONDEMNED MEN, SLAVES OF DEATH, BY ADAM

JUSTIFIED MEN, REIGNING IN LIFE, BY CHRIST

12   Therefore it [salvation through Christ's work]
      is just as when through one man sin entered the
      world, and through the sin, death: and in that
      way death passed to all men, for that all sinned
13   [in Adam]: for before the Law [of Moses] sin was
      in the world: but sin is not put to account if there
14   is not law [against it]. Notwithstanding, death
      reigned-as-king from Adam until Moses, even over
      those not having sinned after the likeness of the
      transgression of Adam,—who is a type of the
      Coming One [Christ].
15   But not as the trespass, so also is the grace-
      bestowal *(charisma)*. For if by the trespass of the
      one the many died, much more did the grace of
      God, and the free-gift *(dorea)* of the One Man.
16   Jesus Christ, abound unto the many! And not as
      through one that sinned, so is the act of giving
      (dorema): for the judgment came out of one
      [trespass] unto condemnation; but the grace-
      bestowal *(charisma)* came out of many trespasses
      unto a righteous [or justifying] act *(dikaioma)*
      [at the cross].
17   For if by the trespass of the one, death reigned-
      as-king through the one, *much more* those accept-
      ing the abundance of grace and of the free-gift
      (dorea) of righteousness, shall reign-as-kings in
      life through the One, Jesus Christ!
18   So then just as [the principle was] through one
      trespass unto all men to condemnation; even so
      also [the principle is] through one righteous [or
      justifying] act [*dikaioma*] unto all men to justi-
19   fication of life! For just as through the dis-
      obedience of the one man the many were set down
      as sinners, even so, through the obedience of the
      One the many shall be set down as righteous.
20   Law, moreover, came in alongside, that trespass
      [of law] might abound. But, where the sin
      abounded, the grace overflowed!
21   In order that, just as sin reigned-as-king by

means of death: grace might reign-as-king, through righteousness, unto life eternal, through Jesus Christ our Lord.

THE GREAT DOCTRINE OF THE TWO MEN

We have seen, in Chapters One to Three, the fact of universal human guilt, that all thus are "falling short of God's glory"; and we have seen Christ set forth by God as a "propitiation through faith in His blood." We also found that believers were declared righteous; and seen connected with a Risen Christ, in Chapter Four. Then we saw, in the first part of Chapter Five, the blessed results of this "justification by faith."

When we come to Romans 5.12, a new phase or view of our salvation appears. (Although note our comments on Chapter 3.23.) A general view of the passage will be helpful.

The two men, Adam and Christ, with their distinct federal* or representative consequences, are before us. It is no longer what we have done—our sins, but the one trespass of Adam that is in view. And it is the work of Christ, also, looked at as an "Adam,"—His "righteous act" of death; with its effect of justification for us. So now we look back to the act that set us down as sinners, instead of to our own deeds; and to the act that sets us down righteous, apart from our own works.

There is no more direct statement in Scripture concerning justification than we find in verse 19: **Through the obedience of the One shall the many be constituted righteous** [before God]. It is true that up to verse 11 the question has been one of sins rather than the thing sin itself. It is true also that in verse 18, in the expression **justification of life,** the resurrection-side of salvation is before us. But we need to mark that God, in the great passage from verse 12 to verse 21, grounds our justification wholly in the work of Another than ourselves, even Christ; showing also the incidental place that the Law had—"that the trespass might abound"; thus opening the flood-gates of Grace!

Federal: in this book we use this word as indicating the action of one for all in a representative manner; or for the consequences of such action.

The key word of this great passage is *"one."* You will find it as follows (14 times in all):

"*One* man"—"*one* man"—"*one* man"—verses 12, 15, 19.

"The *one*"—"the *one*"—"the *One*"—verses 15, 17, 19.

"*One*"—"*one*"—"*one*" (trespass) "*one*" (righteous act)—verses 16 (twice), 18 (twice).

"Through $\begin{cases} \text{\textit{one} trespass"—verses 15, 17, 18.} \\ \text{\textit{one} man's disobedience"—verse 19.} \end{cases}$

"Through $\begin{cases} \text{\textit{one} act of righteousness"—verse 18.} \\ \text{the obedience of THE \textit{ONE}"—verse 19.} \end{cases}$

It will never do to go about counting ourselves justified in the sense merely of having our own trespasses, those we have committed, forgiven; for this would amount to counting ourselves as innocent before we personally sinned, and to have become guilty merely because we personally sinned. But this is to forget that we all were made sinners by Adam's act,—not our own. Nor does this mean that we got a "sinful nature" from our "first parents": *"By nature"* we were, indeed, "children of wrath," Paul tells us in Ephesians Two; and David declares: *"In sin* did my mother conceive me." But Romans Five does not talk of a nature of sin received by us from Adam, but of our being *made guilty* by his *act.* We were so connected with the first Adam that we did not have to wait to be born, or to have a sinful nature; but when Adam, our representative, acted, we acted. Verse 19 plainly says, **Through the one man's disobedience the many were set down as sinners,** while the preceding verse says the principle was, **through one trespass—unto all men to condemnation.**

"Condemnation" is a forensic word, it belongs to the court, not to the birth-chamber.

The same Divine principle is illustrated in the fact that "through Abraham even Levi," Abraham's great-grandson, "who receiveth tithes, *hath paid tithes,* for he was yet in the loins of his father when Melchizedek met him" (Heb. 7.9). God says of Levi, who was not yet born, whose father was not yet born, whose grandfather (Isaac) was not yet born: "LEVI PAID TITHES!"

The great truth of Romans 5.12 to 21 is that a representative acted, involving those connected with him.

We see immediately how Paul in a seven-fold way insists on the fact that Adam's act of sin affected his race:

1. **Through one man sin entered into the world** (vs. 12a).

2. **So in that way death passed unto all men, for that all sinned,** [when Adam sinned] (vs. 12b).

3. **By the trespass of the one the many died** (vs. 15).

4. **The judgment came out of one** [trespass] **unto condemnation** (vs. 16).

5. **By the trespass of the one, death reigned-as-king through the one** (vs. 17).

6. **Through one trespass** [the effect was] **towards all men to condenmation** (vs. 18).

7. **Through the one man's disobedience the many were set down as** [or made to become] **sinners** (vs. 19).

On the other hand, as regards Christ, we find:

1. That He is also an *Adam*—a representative or federal Man who acts for all, and in whom all in Him are seen. Adam is called a figure [Greek: *typos*—type] of Him that was to come—Christ (vs. 14).

2. That by the One Man Jesus Christ, **the grace of God, and the free-gift** [by that grace] **did abound unto the many** much beyond the evil results of Adam's sin (vs. 15).

3. That through our Lord's **one righteous act** [His death on the cross] the free-gift goes out **to all men to justification of life,** just as through [Adam's] **one trespass the judgment came to all men to condemnation** (vs. 18).

4. That through the **obedience** [unto death] **of the One** [Christ] the many [those who received the gift] **shall be set down righteous** [before God] (vs. 19).

5. That those who receive the abundance of [God's] **grace and of the gift of righteousness shall reign-as-kings in life through the One, Jesus Christ,**—much beyond death's reigning through the one [Adam] (vs. 17).

We may now consider this passage briefly, verse by verse:

Verse 12: This whole plan of salvation,—by Christ's work, not ours, which we have been considering in Chapters Three, Four, and Five, gives rise to the "therefore" which introduces this verse: **Therefore** [this plan of salvation of all by a single Redeemer], **is on the same principle as when through** [the other] **one man sin entered the world;** and, with it, its wages, **death.** Paul proceeds to emphasize that it was in that way,—that is, by one man, that death passed to all men, because when Adam sinned, all sinned. It was a federal representative act. Evidently physical death is primarily in view. "Man's breath goeth forth, he returneth to his earth; in that very day his thoughts perish" (Ps. 146.4). And read carefully the note below.* **So death passed unto all men, for that all sinned**—The word "so" refers to the sin of the one man, but the words **all sinned** must not be read "all have sinned" (as the King James Version unfortunately mistranslates). The whole point is that *all* acted when Adam acted: *all* sinned. We have remarked on the aorist tense, "sinned" (Greek: *hēmarton*) in connection with its use in Chapter Three. To translate it here (5.12) "have sinned" is utterly to obscure the Scripture, making man's "sinnership" to depend on his own acts rather than on Adam's—which latter is the whole point of the passage.

Verses 13 and 14: Now comes the remarkable statement that although **sin was in the world** during the first 2500 years, from Adam to Moses, **it is not put to account when there is no law.** The Greek word "put to account" used

---

*Death is a Divine decree: "It is appointed unto men once to die and after this cometh judgment." Death involves four consequences:

First, the utter ending of what we call human life.

Second, falling consciously into the fearful hands of that power under which men have during their lifetime lightly lived, unprotected from the indescribable terrors and horrors connected therewith.

Third, being imprisoned in Sheol or Hades—in "the pit wherein is no water," as was Dives in Luke 16. Compare Zech. 9.11.

Fourth, exposure to the coming judgment and its eternal consequences.

Of course, the believer is rescued from all this—even physical death,—from bodily "falling asleep," if Christ comes during his lifetime! while it is true of all saints, those who keep Christ's word, that they shall "never see death" (John 8.51). Death and judgment are past for the believer, Christ his Substitute having endured them.

Nevertheless, in this day of mad pleasure-seeking, it certainly behooves all of us to reflect on *the fearful realities connected with death!* (See also comment on Chapter 6.23.)

here occurs only one other time—Philemon 18. It signifies to charge up something to anyone as a due. (The wholly different word "reckon" in Chapters 3.24 and 4.23, 24 regards the *person;* this word in 5.13 regards some *item* put to one's account.) It was to Adam, not to us, that God said: "In the day that thou eatest thereof thou shalt surely die." It was to Israel through Moses that God gave the ten commandments. The general argument of the apostle here is to show the effect of a federal or representative sin, in which an Adam acted, bringing an effect upon the individuals connected with him. Paul is about to prove that **death passed to all men** not because they sinned, but because Adam sinned. He is also about to show (verse 18) that all men were condemned by Adam's act,—were made to *become sinners.*

To understand, therefore, the force of the words, **sin is not put to account where there is no law,**—or, as Conybeare enlighteningly paraphrases, "Sin is not put to the account of the sinner when there is no law forbidding it,"—we must remember:

1. That sin was in the world, between Adam and Moses.

2. That, according to Chapter One, the race had rejected light and were without excuse; though they were "without law" (*anomos*): for God's definition of sin is not "transgression of law" (I John 3.4, A.V.), but *anomia,* which means refusal to be controlled—self-will.

3. That there was a "work" (working) written in their hearts, to which their consciences bore witness, either accusing or else excusing them; and that this working necessarily corresponded morally to any law to be afterwards revealed by Jehovah.

4. That condign judgments, such as the Flood, and the overthrow of Sodom, and the destruction of the Canaanites, followed the "filling up of the cup of iniquity" at such times: for such sinners both trampled on their own consciences, and inherited the previous generations of guilt.

5. That, nevertheless, the sins between Adam and Moses did not bring about the *sentence of death* upon humanity, however much individuals or nations might hasten death's over-

laking them. For these people, though they sinned, **had not sinned after the likeness of Adam's transgression,** which was a wilful violation of a direct command of a revealed God; as was Israel's making, through Aaron, the calf at Sinai: involving judicial consequences to others besides themselves. For we read in Exodus 32.34 of a set future "visitation" on Israel, because of that sin at Sinai of their fathers: "In the day that I visit, I will visit their sin upon them"; this will be in "the time of Jacob's trouble," in the Great Tribulation—long after the calf-worship; indeed, still future!

6. We therefore must regard the human race as under a sentence of death they did not bring upon themselves: **death reigned from Adam until Moses** (vs. 14). Unlike Adam, and unlike Israel after Moses, those who lived between the two had no positive outward Divine law, the breaking of which would be a direct transgression and a threatening of death therefor. Nevertheless "death reigned"—even over them. Constantly before our eyes is the attestation to the same truth: babes that know nothing of right or wrong, die. Every little white coffin,—yea, every coffin, should remind us of the universal effect of that sin of Adam, for it was thus and thus only that "death passed to all men."

We see then, that from Adam until Moses, death "reigned-as-king"* on account of Adam's sin. Paul has said (Rom. 4.15), "Where there is no law neither is there transgression"; so that those between Adam and Moses, not having direct commands of God, consequently had not transgressed known commands as Adam had done. Nevertheless, Adam's transgression had involved his whole race.

Verse 14: Here Adam is declared **a type of the One who was to come**—that is, of Christ, the last Adam. We cannot sufficiently urge the study of this great passage: until the mind sees, and the heart understands—and that gladly, *condemnation by the one,* and *justification by the Other.* It is just as necessary to see this *"by the one"* doctrine regarding our spirits, as regarding our bodies. As to the latter, Paul says, "As in Adam

---

*We say, "reigned-as-king," because the Greek word means that. Not the power of sin to hold in bondage, as in Chapter Six, is here meant; but the royal word, *basileuo,* is used, denoting sovereignty, not mere lordship.

all die, so also in Christ shall all be made alive"; "The first man is of the earth, earthy; the second Man is of heaven . . . And as we have borne the image of the earthy, we shall also bear the image of the heavenly" (I Cor. 15.22,47,49). To discover that we are even now no longer connected with that first Adam in which we were born, but with the Risen Christ, the last Adam—this will be our joy in Chapters Six to Eight. But the foundation of this blessed truth is laid here in the Doctrine of the Two Men.

We find in verses 15 to 17 a sort of parenthesis in which the results of Adam's trespass and Christ's act of obedience are shown to differ in two respects (but not at all in the principle of the one involving the many). In the first case (verse 15) there is the difference of degree in the result, because of the infinite chasm between the creature Adam, and the Creator— God and His Son Jesus Christ! So we read:

Verse 15: **For if by the trespass of the one [Adam] death came to the many; MUCH MORE did the grace of God, and the gift by the grace of THE ONE MAN, JESUS CHRIST, abound unto the many!** It takes faith to esteem this true now, seeing, as we do, the cemeteries all about us; death on every hand,—the general dire results of sin; but we must believe that the free gift will finally be seen, in its results, to be as far beyond the results of the trespass, as God and Christ are greater than the creature Adam!*

Verse 16: **And not as through one that sinned, so is the act of giving: for the judgment came out of one unto condemnation; but the grace-bestowal came out of many trespasses unto a righteous act.** This tells us that out of Adam's

---

*David Brown (in Jamieson, Fausset and Brown's excellent commentary) disagrees here, saying: "The 'much more' here does not mean that we get much more of good by Christ than of evil by Adam (for it is not a case of quantity at all); but, that we have much more reason to expect,—or, it is much more agreeable to our ideas of God, that the many should be benefited by the merits of one; and, if the latter has happened, 'much more' may we assure ourselves of the former."

But after all this does not disagree with what we have above said, for it is Adam, the sinning creature, on the one hand; and the infinitely great and good God, and His grace by His Son Christ, on the other. Measure, quantity, must enter in: as, indeed, in saying of God "we have much more reason to expect," Dr. Brown tacitly admits. "Much more," says Paul, "did the grace"—of whom? GOD. This emphasizing *God* brings out everything!

one trespass came judgment, but that out of many trespasses laid upon Christ came *not* judgment, but a righteous act *(dikaioma)*.* In short, all men acted,—sinned in Adam's act of sin. **They that receive** is on the principle of "the one for the many," but manifestly does not include all men, because some reject; although we find in verse 18 that the free gift "came" unto them,—"unto all men."

Note what it is that believing ones "receive":

First, **abundance of grace:** The cross having met righteously all the claims of the Divine being, and the Divine throne, against sinners, God has now spoken to us *as He is,* in abounding grace, for "God is *Love.*" Over and over are "abound," "abundance" used here to express God's attitude; and the free motion, since the cross, of His infinitely loving heart toward sinners, in *gracious kindness.* Those who "receive" God's grace give Him the honor of His graciousness.

Second, Those that "receive" this abundance of grace have therewith the **gift of righteousness.** What a gift! Apart from works, apart from the Law, apart from ordinances, apart from worthiness, an out and out *gift* of righteousness from God! Many times in teaching this passage to Bible classes I have asked them to repeat three times over each of these expressions: "The *abundance* of grace," "the *gift* of righteousness." We earnestly commend this to you, dear reader! *Try* it.

Alas, how few believers have the courage of faith! We have looked so long at our unworthiness that the very thought of pushing away from the shore-lines and launching out on the limitless, fathomless ocean of Divine grace makes us shrink and waver. When some saint here or there does begin to believe the facts and walk in shouting liberty, we say (perhaps secretly), "He must be an especially holy, consecrated man." No, he is just a poor sinner like you, who is *believing* in the *abundance* of *grace!* And if we hear some one praising God for the gift of righteousness, because he is now righteous in Christ before

---

*To the student of Greek (and to others, also), it is most instructive to note Paul's use of the words connected with righteousness: *dikaios* means righteous; *dikaiosune* means righteousness; *dikaioō* is to declare righteous; *dikaiōsis* means justification, or the act of declaring one righteous; *dikaiōma,* the "righteous act," that makes justification possible.

God, we are ready to accuse him of thinking too highly of himself. No, he is just a poor sinner like you and me, but one who has dared to *believe* that he *has received* an outright *gift* of righteousness, and is rejoicing in it.

Verse 17: **For if by the trespass of the one, death reigned-as-king through the one,** *much more* **those accepting the abundance of grace and of the free-gift of righteousness, shall reign-as-kings in life through the One, Jesus Christ!** It is not only that you have life, and that eternal life, in Christ: but here in verse 17 we find two kingdoms:

First, **By the trespass of the one death reigned-as-king through the one.** And is that not true? I travelled around this world from west to east, beginning from Chicago. As we went eastward to the older parts of the States, we saw the stones thicker and thicker in the cemeteries. Then in England and Scotland, still more cemeteries, with still more monuments to the reign of death. But when we got out to old China, I was literally appalled at the number of the tombs and the coffins! Surely *death has reigned,* through Adam!

But second (for the fourth time in this chapter), God now uses the words "much more," applying them to those who accept the abundance of His grace and of His gift of righteousness, saying these **shall reign-as-kings in life through the One, even Jesus Christ.** Look now at this expression, **reign-as-kings in life.** I am writing this during the week of the coronation of George VI of England, and have heard of the splendors with which the ceremony was attended; and we do thank God for the British Empire, and honor, with her subjects, her monarch. But, ah, believer, look closely at these words of Paul, **reigning in life.** Here is a kingdom before which all of earth is *dust.* And who are the kings here? Believers! Those whose humble faith has "received the abundance of grace and of the gift of righteousness": these shall reign-as-kings through Jesus Christ.

God has "the ages to come" in which to manifest fully this mighty reigning! But it is *already begun* for those *in Christ.* Gideon, speaking of certain Israelites, asked the kings of Midian, "What manner of men were they?" "As thou art, so were they," they answered; "*each one resembled the children of a king.*" "They shall *reign* forever and ever," is God's description of the saints of the New Jerusalem (Rev. 22.5). And their reign has already, in this life, begun; because they are *in Christ,* the mighty *Victor!* Satan would fain keep from your ears this news, believer, that you stand in the *abundance* of God's grace; that you have received *the gift* of righteousness in Christ; and that you are to *reign-as-a-king-in-life* now and forever, through the One, Jesus Christ. May God awaken us to the *facts!** Satan is deathly jealous of the Church of God, which is already in the heavenlies, from which he is soon to be cast out. He knows that the Church will share Christ's throne and soon reign with Him in indescribable glory. Therefore he will blind you, if he can, to your present place of royal power of life in Christ. It will, we are sure, be a matter of fathomless regret to many Christians, at Christ's coming, that their lives on earth were characterized by doubt, defeat and depression; rather than by victorious reigning in life in Christ. God has no favorites. Each one who is in Christ has a complete Christ. The exhortations of the Epistles are addressed alike to all. David Livingstone early wrote in his diary, "I have found that I have no unusual endowments of intellect, but I this day resolved that I would be an uncommon Christian." Concerning such it is written, "Considering the issue of their manner of life, imitate their faith" (Heb. 13.7). Let us refuse to be content with a Christian existence that cannot finally be summed up as "He *reigned* in life through Jesus Christ,"—over sin, Satan, the world, difficulties, adverse surroundings and circumstances. Let us remember the apostles, the martyrs, Reformers, godly Puritans, the holy Wesleys, and Whitefields, the Havergals and Crosbys; and the humble saints we know, whose existence is described by Paul's glorious phrase "reigning in life through our Lord Jesus Christ."

---

*When Israel inquired of the Lord about Saul, the son of Kish, who had been anointed as their king (for they could not find him), the Lord answered, you remember, "Behold, he hath hid himself among the stuff." "And they ran and fetched him thence" (I Sam. 10.22-23). How sad if some of us who have received the abundance of grace and of the gift of righteousness, and whom God desires to be *reigning in life* in Christ, have gotten ourselves hidden "among the stuff,"—of earthly goods, and ambitions, "religious" traditions, and the literature of this world!

Verse 18: **So then, just as** [the principle was] **through one trespass unto all men to condemnation; even so also through** *one righteous* [or justifying] *act* [the principle is] **unto all men to justification 'of life! Through one trespass** [it was] **unto all men to condemnation—**The expression "the many" in verses 15 and 19 indicates the principle of the evil effect of the act of the one going forth to others; the expression "all men," of verse 18, emphasizes the extent of the application of that principle: absolutely all human beings were condemned when Adam sinned.

Now do not question either God's right or His wisdom here, or His love. He had the right to have a judgment day of our whole race in Eden, in our head, Adam; and He did so. He always does right. Furthermore, He knew that creatures would ever fail,—there is no sufficiency in the creature, but only in the Creator. You and I would fail, as did Adam! and God desired that believers should be secure forever, by *Christ's* work. It was in love He held that judgment day in Eden. In love He judged us, condemned us, in our federal head, Adam, that He might justify us in the work and Person of the other federal Head, Christ!

The ordinary conception of justification does not go beyond the pardon of sin. This indeed is first; and we should also have confidence that our sins will never be reckoned against us— whether they be past, present, or future sins. This is seen in Chapter 4.7,8; and in Chapter 5.9, we see ourselves "justified in His blood," "justified *from* all things," as Paul says in Acts 13.39. But this leaves the believer without a positive standing. We do not come to "justification of life"* until Chapter 5.18.

Now it is *Christ Risen* who is made our "standing": so that, as we see elsewhere, we do not need aught else: for we are *in Christ*. Justification provides therefore not only release from

---

*The expression "justification of *life*" seems to stand over against that condemnation and death which came by Adam's trespass. It is a *characterizing* word: What is offered unto all men, through Christ's act of righteousness at the cross is not only a cancellation of guilt, but life in the Risen One. For, since Adam's sin, there was only spiritual death in his race. The words of John 1.4, regarding Christ, "In *Him* was life," describe the only source of life for man. And justification must be *of life*: for those justified are most certainly taken out of their place of death **in Adam**, and given a place of life in Christ.

the penalty of sin, but also a place in the Risen Christ Himself. This begins to be indicated in Chapter Four, where righteousness is reckoned to those who "believe on Him who *raised* Jesus our Lord from the dead." It is, of course, necessarily comprehended in the astonishing phrase IN CHRIST JESUS,—used first in Chapter 6.11! And it is amplified and developed through the rest of Paul's epistles. In I Corinthians 1.30 we see that Christ Himself, Risen, was made unto the believer, righteousness. Paul also in Galatians 2.20,21 directly connects his having been "crucified with Christ" with *righteousness*. That is, the history in Adam of believers was ended at the cross. (Yet always remember that it was as ungodly ones that they believed!)

In Colossians 1.12 we read: "Giving thanks unto the Father, who made us meet to be partakers of the inheritance of the saints in light." Then hear again that most stupendous utterance of all: "Him who knew no sin He made to be sin on our behalf; that we might become *the righteousness of God in Him*" (II Cor. 5.21). It is this glorious revelation, which men have been loathe to read, teach, or refer to, which we must apprehend by God's grace, and by that grace believe!

Now, how, in what sense, are we "the righteousness of God" in Christ?

It is at once evident that to set us in His own presence in Christ as He has done, God must (1) reckon to us the infinitely perfect expiation of Christ in putting away our sin by His blood; (2) make us one with Christ in His death; and (3) place us in Christ Risen, even as Christ is received before Him. All this He has done; so that He says we are *the righteousness of God in Christ*. If we are in Christ, we are before God in Christ, "even as He,"—"accepted *in* Him."

Verse 19: **For just as through the disobedience of the one man the many were set down as sinners, even so, through the obedience of the One the many shall be set down as righteous.**

Set down as sinners—the word "sinners," here, is not an adjective (sinful), but a substantive,—*sinners*.* Verse 19 first sums up the doctrine of our federal guilt by Adam's sin, then sums up our justification by Christ's death.

The whole emphasis of verses 12 to 19 is upon the fact that the effect, whether in the case of Adam or in the case of Christ, was produced by a federal head acting apart from any actions of those affected. There was a judgment held in Eden, by the righteous God, the pronouncement of which is, "unto all men to condemnation."† This, of course, has no reference to eternal damnation, which is a consequence of the rejection of "the Light which has come into the world"—men loving darkness rather than light "because their deeds are evil." But it does assert a judgment of *sinnerhood,* by the guilt of Adam's action, *upon the whole human race.*

The whole lesson of this passage is, that just as we have Christ only as our righteousness, we have Adam only as sin and death to us. (God's Word, however, puts Adam's act and its effect first, as a *type* of Christ's work.) We repeat these things over and over, because of their importance, both for our settled peace, and also for our enjoyment of the normal, joyous Christian life.

Even so through the obedience of the One—This was our Lord's death, as an act of obedience:‡ "He became obedient unto death, yea, the death of the cross." He was of course always obedient to His Father, but it cannot be too strongly emphasized that His life before the cross,—His "active obedi-

---

*The Greek word *(hamartōlos)* means not merely one possessed of a sinful nature or tendency, but one who is regarded as having *committed sin.* The same word is used in 3.7 and 5.8.

"Substantive, *hamartōlos,* a sinner; common acceptance, LXX, New Testament, etc."—Liddell and Scott. This word is used in N.T. to designate sinners 41 times, beginning with Matthew 9.10; five times in Luke 15, and four times in John 9; and only four times in an adjectival sense (Mark 8.38; Luke 5.8; 24.7; Rom. 7.13).

†Human reasoning is futile and dangerous here. Men form themselves into "schools of theology" over this subject, each founding a "system" upon his notion of how Adam's trespass affected all. But that a man may act before he is born in person of his responsible forbear is evident, as we have shown, in the case of Levi, in Heb. 7.9.

‡Vaughan (as so frequently) gives a rendering of startling accuracy concerning disobedience and obedience in verse 19: "The one *(parakoees)* is properly, mishearing; the other, *hupakoees,* submissive hearing." Disobedience in its essence is refusal to hearken; and obedience is bowing the ear to submissive listening.

ence," as it is called, is not in any sense counted to us for righteousness. "I delivered to you," says Paul, "first of all, that Christ *died* for our sins." Before His death He was "holy, guileless, undefiled, separated from sinners." He Himself said: "Except a corn of wheat fall into the ground and die, it abideth alone; but if it die, it bringeth forth much fruit." Do you not see that those who claim that our Lord's righteous life under Moses' Law is reckoned to us for our "active" righteousness; while His death in which He put away our sins, is, as they claim, the "passive" side, are really leaving you, and the Lord too, *under the authority of the Law?*

"Justified in (the value or power of) His blood," and of that alone, gives the direct lie to the claim that man must have "an active righteousness" as well as "a passive righteousness." The specious assertion is, that "inasmuch as we have all broken the Law (although God says that Gentiles were 'without law'—and those in Christ are not under it!) and inasmuch as man cannot by his works himself recover his righteous standing, Christ, forsooth, came and kept The Law in man's place (!); and then went to the cross and suffered the penalty of death for man's guilt so that the result is an 'active righteousness' reckoned to man:—that is, Christ's keeping The Law in man's place; and, second, a 'passive righteousness,' which consists in the putting away of all guilt by the blood of Christ."

Now, the awful thing here is the unbelief concerning man's irrecoverable state before God. For not only must Christ's blood be shed in expiation of our guilt; but we had *to die with Christ.* We were connected with the old Adam; and the old man—all we had and were in Adam, must be crucified—if we were to be "joined to Another, even to Him that was raised from the dead." Theological teaching since the Reformation has never set forth clearly *our utter end in death with Christ, at the cross.*

The fatal result of this terrible error is to leave The Law as claimant over those in Christ: for, "Law has dominion over a man as long as he liveth" (7.1). Unless you are able to believe in your very heart that you died with Christ, that your old man was crucified with Him, and that you were buried, and that your history before God in Adam the first came to an utter end at Calvary, you will never get free from the claims of Law upon your conscience.*

I say again, that the Law was *given to neither Adam.* The first Adam had life: God did not give him law whereby to get life! Not until Moses did the Law come in, and then only as an incidental thing to reveal to man his condition. The Law was not given to the first Adam, nor to the human race; but *to Israel only* (Deut. 4.5-8; 33.1-5; Ps. 147.19,20). Again, the Law was not given to the Last Adam! "The Last Man Adam became a life-giving spirit": this is Christ, Risen from the dead, at God's right hand, communicating spiritual life. *Is He under law?* It is only the desperate legality of man's heart, his self-confidence, that makes him drag in the Law, and cling to the Law,—even though Christ must fulfil it for him! "Vicarious law-keeping" is Galatian heresy!

Our Lord said plainly that His work in this world was *to die:* "The Son of Man came to give His life a ransom"; and indeed, "through the Eternal Spirit He offered Himself without blemish unto God." True, He must be a *spotless* Lamb. But for what? For *sacrifice!* He did not touch our case, had no connection with us, until God laid our sins upon Him and made Him to become sin for us at the cross. Christ was not one of our race, "the sons of men": He was the Seed of the woman, not the man. He was the Son of Man, indeed, for God prepared for Him a body (Ps. 40; Heb. 10), by the power of the Holy Spirit (Luke 1.35). But, though He moved among sinners, He was "separated from sinners," and had no connection with them until God made Him their sin offering at the cross.

Christ Himself, Risen, is our righteousness. His earthly life under the Law is not our righteousness. We have no connection with a Christ on earth and under the Law. We are expressly told in Romans 7.1-6, that even Jewish believers who have been under law were made dead to the Law by the Body of Christ, that they might be joined to Another, even to Him

---

*"Both Calvinists and Arminians think that the flesh is not so bad that it cannot be acted on for God by Christ using the Law of God and giving it power through the Spirit"—This is Wm. Kelly's shrewd and correct comment.

who was raised from the dead. One has beautifully said, "Christianity begins with the resurrection."

Verse 20: **Law, moreover, came in alongside** [of sin] **that the trespass** [of law] **might abound**—The reference to law here shows that Paul has justification from guilt, and not our state of sinfulness, in view. "Law entered alongside" *(pareisēlthen)** not, in this connection, to reveal sinfulness, but that the trespass of law,—the *act* of law-breaking might abound. The Law, being given to neither Adam, came in alongside sin,— after sin had been there 2500 years, that vain self-confident Israel (as a public example for us all!) might see God's standard for those in the first Adam, and promising to obey it, fail; and thus know sin in order that Grace might *overflow.* That so, where sin had reigned, Grace might *reign-as-king,* through the righteous work of Christ on the cross, unto eternal life, through Jesus Christ our Lord.

Thus neither our sins nor our "sinful nature" has, in this passage, anything to do with our condemnation: *but Adam's act only.* And not our new life in Christ, nor our walking in the good works unto which we are created (Eph. 2.10), has anything to do with constituting us righteous, but *Christ's act of death only* (vv. 18, 19). As we have said, law "came in alongside,"—not as in any sense a means of salvation, but that Israel (and through Israel, all of us) might discover guiltiness by breaking law; for law gives no power to keep law!

But, where sin abounded, grace did completely overflow. Grace began to work for Israel immediately after the Law was broken! For instead of cutting off Israel as a nation, God appointed Moses a mediator; and when sin came to a climax with the Jews' crucifying their Messiah, the Lord's words were, "Father, forgive them." And as we shall read in Chapter Eleven, God will indeed yet forgive them,—will take away their sins and "bring in everlasting righteousness." Grace will yet over-

---

*It is very striking to note that in verse 12 where we read "through one man sin entered into the world," the word for *entered* is *eisēlthen;* and now law enters *alongside,*—the word being the same—*eisēlthen*—with the preposition *para,* alongside, prefixed. And so, "through law is the knowledge of sin." Sin entered, and law, entering alongside, revealed the sin.

flow for Israel, nationally, as it has now overflowed to us as individual sinners, both Jews and Gentiles.

"Where sin abounded, grace overflowed," for such is ever the result of the work of the cross. Paul, who had been Christ's greatest enemy, the chief of sinners, declares himself to be the great example of mercy and grace: "I obtained mercy," he says, "that *in me as chief* might Jesus Christ show forth all His long-suffering, for an example of them that should hereafter believe on Him unto eternal life." And again: "By the grace of God I am what I am" (I Cor. 15.10; I Tim. 1.16).

We might turn to David and Manasseh in the Old Testament as examples of the overflowing heart of mercy of God. Or we might call up such examples in Church History as the reckless profligate Augustine, whom God made a shining light in His Church; or John Bunyan, the profane tinker, who wrote his wonderful experience of the Divine goodness in "Grace Abounding to the Chief of Sinners"; or John Newton, once a libertine and infidel, "a servant of slaves in Africa," as he wrote of himself for his epitaph,—whom God transformed into one of the great vessels of mercy of the eighteenth century, and whose hymns of praise all the saints sing. It was Newton who wrote:

> "Amazing grace! how sweet the sound
> That saved a wretch like me."

and who told his own experience—so really that of all the saints—in the words of the beautiful hymn:

> "In evil long I took delight
> Unawed by shame or fear,
> Till a new object met my sight,
> And stopped my wild career.
>
> "I saw One hanging on a tree,
> In agonies and blood;
> Who fixed His languid eyes on me,
> As near His cross I stood.
>
> "Sure, never till my latest breath,
> Can I forget that look;

It seemed to charge me with His death,
    Though not a word He spoke.

"My conscience felt and owned the guilt,
    And plunged me in despair,
I saw my sins His blood had spilt,
    And helped to nail Him there.

"Alas, I knew not what I did,
    But all my tears were vain;
Where could my trembling soul be hid,
    For I the Lord had slain!

"A second look He gave, that said,
    'I freely all forgive!
This blood is for thy ransom paid,
    I died that thou mayest live.' "

On November 18, 1834, Robert Murray McCheyne, of St. Peter's Free Church, Dundee, Scotland, whose memory is like ointment poured forth, wrote his remarkable confession that *his* sins had caused Christ's death. The title, *"Jehovah Tsidkēnu,"* is the Hebrew for "The Lord Our Righteousness." Let it serve our use also, as it has that of thousands:

JEHOVAH TSIDKĒNU

"I once was a stranger to grace and to God,
I knew not my danger, and felt not my load;
Though friends spoke in rapture of Christ on the tree,
Jehovah Tsidkēnu was nothing to me.

"I oft read with pleasure, to soothe or engage,
Isaiah's wild measure, and John's simple page;
But e'en when they pictured the blood-sprinkled tree,
Jehovah Tsidkēnu seemed nothing to me.

"Like tears from the daughters of Zion that roll,
I wept when the waters went over His soul;
Yet thought not that *my* sins had nailed to the tree
Jehovah Tsidkēnu—'twas nothing to *me*.

"When free grace awoke me, with light from on high
Then legal fears shook me, I trembled to die;
No refuge, no safety, in self could I see,—
Jehovah Tsidkēnu my Savior must be.

"My terrors all vanished before the sweet Name;
My guilty fears banished, with boldness I came
To drink at the fountain, life-giving and free—
Jehovah Tsidkēnu is all things to me.

"Jehovah Tsidkēnu! my treasure and boast;
Jehovah Tsidkēnu! I ne'er can be lost;
In Thee I shall conquer, by flood and by field—
My cable, my anchor, my breastplate and shield!"

We might multiply examples like these: but these words, "Where sin abounded, grace did completely overflow," with the salvation of Saul of Tarsus as the Scripture example, will suffice. I stood on the bluff at Memphis, Tennessee, and saw the mighty Mississippi, normally a mile wide, stretch over forty miles in flood, covering deep under its multitude of waters the land as far as I could see. So, where sin abounded, the grace of God overflowed everything.*

---

*Two entirely different Greek words are translated, in the Authorized Version, "abounded." But the first, used of sin, means to increase, be augmented; while the second, used of grace, means to *abound beyond measure*, to overflow. See Thayer. These words come from entirely different roots, and should have been so distinguished in translation. But one who undertakes to express in English the depth of the Hebrew, and the extent of the Greek language, will soon discover the frequent poverty of the English tongue. Hebrew seems to be the language in which God first spoke with men; it is the vehicle of praise. But to the Greeks He gave that great intellectual development of their "Golden Age" in which their endeavor to perfect their language extended even to public assemblies where the most exact possible phrasing to express an idea was decided by contest. So when our Lord came as "the Savior of the World," that coming, according to the grand old Hebrew prophecies, was recorded in the Greek, which Alexander the Great had spread throughout the known world. The Romans, to whom had been given the power to govern, themselves admitted that they must borrow from the Greeks not only their philosophy, but also their method and manner of literary expression. Then also when the Roman Empire went into collapse, and the dark "Middle Ages" came in, the so-called Renaissance was the bringing of the Greek classics into crude Europe after the fall of Constantinople in 1453. And above all, the translation directly from the Greek New Testament manuscripts of our English Scriptures; for men had so long depended upon the faulty Latin (or Vulgate) translation.

Perhaps the greatest wonder the last century and a quarter has seen is the translation into over 800 tongues and dialects of these same Hebrew and Greek Scrip-

Verse 21: **In order that, just as sin reigned-as-king by means of death: grace might reign-as-king, through righteousness, unto life eternal, through Jesus Christ our Lord.** This verse unfolds God's great object: that Grace should have a kingdom where Death had had its kingdom: and that, of course, through righteousness,—that is, that all Divine claims should be first righteously met at the cross, and thus that all should be "through Jesus Christ our Lord."

The question of justification is still on in Chapter Five, and not until Chapter Six is "our old man"—all we were from Adam—brought in. Furthermore, to bring into Chapter Five our sinful state by nature, is to confuse our sinful condition with that condemnation which over and over God says was brought about by Adam's single act, and by that only. "The judgment came of ONE TRESPASS unto condemnation," etc.

Now if you and I were condemned in Adam's sin, it is plain that to be justified we must be cleared not only of our own sins, but of our condemnation in Adam: our justification must cover all our condemnation.

Our justification, is, therefore, in this great passage, related not to our personal sins, as in Chapters Three and Four; but to our guilt by and in Adam, from which we are cleared by Christ's death. And Christ being now raised, we, connected with Him at the cross, now share His life: so that our justification is called "justification of life" (vs. 18).

It is true that we are not spoken of as "in Christ" until Chapter Six, where death with Christ is unfolded and our history in the first Adam, and our relation to sin, ended. But Paul speaks of being "justified in Christ" (Gal. 2.17). And certainly the subject in the last section of Chapter Five is justification:

---

tures,—with such transforming power that it is written of one Bible-bearing missionary, a man of God, in the South Sea Islands: "When he came, there were no Christians; when he left, there were no heathen."

How wonderful that God should have a language of spiritual praise and worship—the Hebrew; and a language exact, intellectually rich,—the Greek, in which He could express the great doctrines concerning His Son! And both languages capable of being reproduced as to their spirit and meaning, not only in English, German, and French, but in the dialects of the most benighted heathen tribes,— "every man in his own language."

condemnation by Adam's trespass, and justification by Christ's righteous act of death.

Thus, not until we come to Chapter Six is our walk, our sanctification, taken up. It is true that the doctrine of the two men (5.12-21) makes possible of understanding the great fact of Chapter Six,—that we *died with Christ*. But the subject of the latter section of Chapter Five is condemnation by Adam, justification by Christ.

CHAPTER SIX

We Died with Christ: Our Baptism being Witness; and are to Reckon Ourselves Dead unto Sin and Alive unto God in Christ Jesus. Verses 1-11.

Presenting Ourselves to God as Risen Ones, not under Law but under Grace, Sin Loses Its Dominion over Us. Verses 12-14.

Grace Not to be Abused, for Sin Always Enslaves, and would End in Death; Obedience brings Freedom, with the End, Eternal Life,—God's Free Gift in Christ Jesus Our Lord. Verses 15-23.

1   What then shall we say? Are we to keep on in
2   sin in order that grace may be abounding? Far be the thought! Such ones as we,—who died to sin! how shall we any longer be living in it?
3   Or [in the very matter of our baptism] are ye ignorant that all we who were baptized unto Christ
4   Jesus unto His death were baptized? We were buried therefore [in figure] with Him through that baptism unto death; in order that, just as Christ was raised from among the dead through the glory of the Father, thus also we might be walking in newness of life.
5   For if we became united with [Him] in the likeness of His death, so shall we be also [in the
6   likeness] of His resurrection: coming to know this, that our old man was crucified with Him, in order that the body of sin might be annulled, that
7   we might no longer be in slave-service to sin: for the person who hath died [as have we] is justified from sin.

8   But if we died with Christ, we believe that we
     shall also be living with Him [in this world]:
9   knowing that Christ having been raised from
     among the dead dieth no more: death over Him no
10   longer hath dominion. For in that He died, unto
     sin He died once for all; but in that He is living,
11   He is living unto God. Thus do ye also reckon
     yourselves dead indeed to sin, but alive to God, in
     Christ Jesus.

WE COME NOW to the second part of Christ's work for
us—our identification with His death.*

It is not until we come to Chapter Six that the question of
a holy walk as over against a sinful walk, comes up. For the
blessed verses which describe the results of the discovery of
peace with God, and of "justification of life" and "reigning
in life" through Christ, as revealed in Chapter Five, are things
of experience, of rejoicing,—even in the hope of the glory
of God Himself! But the question of a holy walk under this
"abounding grace" is now brought up, in Chapter Six, in the
answers to two questions: First, Shall we keep sinning that
grace may keep abounding? and, Second, The fact having been
revealed that we are not under the principle of law but under
that of grace, shall we use our liberty to commit sin? That
is, Shall we use our freedom from the law-principle for selfish
ends?

The answer to the first question is, that for all who are in
Christ, the old relationship to sin is broken,—for they federally
shared Christ's death to sin, and are to reckon it so, and walk

---

*There are five parts to our salvation:

1. Christ's propitiatory work toward God through His blood: bearing the guilt
and condemnation of our sins.

2. Christ's identification with us as connected with Adam, "becoming sin for
us," releasing us from Adam, our federal head: "our old man" being crucified
with Christ.

3. The Holy Spirit's whole work in us, as "the Spirit of grace," involving conviction, regeneration, baptism into Christ's Body; being in us as a "law of life"
against indwelling sin, the Witness of our sonship; our Helper, Intercessor, and,
finally, the mighty Agent in the Rapture.

4. Christ's present work in Heaven: leading our worship and praise as our Great
High Priest: and protecting us should we sin, as our Advocate with the Father (as
against our accuser).

5. Christ's second coming to redeem our bodies, and receive us to Himself in
glory: The Rapture.

in "newness of life" unto God. The answer to the second question is, that anyone "yielding his members" becomes *servant* to that to which he yields,—whether of sin unto death, or of righteousness unto sanctification.

Verse 1: **Are we to* remain in sin that grace may be abounding?** This question arises constantly, both in uninstructed believers, and in blind unbelievers. The message of simple grace, apart from all works, to the poor natural heart of man seems wholly inconsistent and impossible. "Why!" people say, "If where sin abounds grace overflows, then the more sin, the more grace." So the unbeliever rejects the grace plan.

Moreover, the uninstructed Christian also is afraid; for he says, "If we are in a reign of pure grace, what will control our conscious evil tendencies? We fear such utter freedom. Put us under 'rules for holy living,' and we can get along."

Another sad fact is that some professing Christians welcome the "abounding grace" doctrine because of the liberty they feel it gives to things in their daily lives which they know, or could know, to be wrong.

Verse 2: **Such ones as we, who died to sin! how shall we any longer be living in it?**

Here we have, (1) **such ones as we** (*hoitines*). This is more than a relative pronoun: it is a pronoun of characterization, "placing those referred to in a class" (Lightfoot). Paul thus has before his mind all Christians, and he places this pronoun at the very beginning: "such ones as we!"

(2) He characterizes all Christians as those **who died.** The translation, "are dead" is wrong, for the tense of the Greek verb is the aorist, which denotes not a state but a past act or fact. It never refers to an action as going on or prolonged. As Winer says, "The aorist states a fact as something having taken place." Note how strikingly and repeatedly this tense is used in this chapter as referring to the death of

---

*It is what is called the deliberative subjunctive here; "May we?" or "Should we?" But best rendered in English by the form we have chosen: "Are we to—is such the path?" And so in verse 15.

which the apostle speaks:* Mark most particularly that the apostle in verse 2 does not call upon Christians to die to sin, but asserts that they shared *Christ's* death, they *died* to sin!

(3) Paul here therefore affirms that it was in regard to their relationship to sin that believers died. He is asserting concerning Christians that they died—not for sin, but unto it.

(4) Paul now asks the question: "How shall those whose relationship to sin has been broken by their dying, be still, as once, *living in sin?*" The answer to this can only be, It is an impossibility. In this second verse, therefore, the apostle is not making a plea to Christians not to live unto sin; but asking how they who died to sin could go on living in it. It is as if one would say, Those who died in New York City, shall they still be walking the streets of New York City?

This does not mean that all Christians have discovered, or walk in, the path of victory over sin; for in this second verse Paul is answering directly the bald bold insinuation of verse 1—that grace abounding over sin warrants and enables one believing that doctrine to go right on in his old life! We know from other Scriptures the impossibility of this: "Whosoever is born of God doth not practise sin, because His [God's] seed abideth in him, and he is not able to practise sin, because he is begotten of God."†

Note the repeated declarations in this Sixth Chapter of our actual identification with the death of Christ:

Verse 2: "We who died to sin."

Verse 3: "We were baptized into His death."

---

*Verse 2, "We *died to sin*" (an aorist tense,— definite past fact).

Verse 6: "Our old man *was crucified* with Him" (another aorist tense); not "*is* crucified," as in the Old Version, which expression is a relic of Romanism, and the meaning of which no one knows.

Verse 7: "The one *having died*" (aorist again; and meaning anyone in Christ) "is declared righteous from sin."

Verse 8: "If we *died* [aorist] with Christ."

Verses 10 and 11: "The death that He *died*, He *died* unto sin, once for all." (Aorist tenses, the second specially emphasized by "once for all.")

†Of course, John deals with the new life; Paul, with the new relationship, the new creation. See II Corinthians 5.17: "If anyone is in Christ,—a new creation! the old things are passed away; behold, they are become new." The seed of God, the new creature, being of *God* does not consent to sin: however weak and ignorant of the truth of the deliverance of the cross they may be, there is always the absolute difference between those in Christ and those not in Christ.

Verse 4: "We were buried with Him through baptism into death."

Verse 5: "We became united with Him in the likeness of His death."

Verse 6: "Our old man was crucified with Him."

Verse 7: "He that hath died is justified from sin."

Verse 8: "We died with Christ."

Verse 11: "Reckon yourselves dead unto sin, but alive unto God in Christ Jesus."

Verse 13: "Present yourselves unto God as alive from the dead."

The same great federal fact is brought out in Colossians 2.20: "If ye *died* [aorist tense, past fact, again] from the religious principles of the world"; and Colossians 3.3: "For ye *died* [aorist tense again] and your life is hid with Christ in God."

It is most evident that the apostle is not here speaking of some state that we are in, but of a federal fact that occurred in the past, at the cross.

It was upon this federal fact that Paul's whole life hung, as he testified to Peter: "I have been crucified with Christ, and it is no longer I that live, but Christ liveth in me" (Gal. 2.20).

Such ones as we, who died to sin! How shall we go on living in it? Paul expresses his very soul in that opening word—"Such ones as we!" Believers were seen by him as risen ones,—dead with Christ to sin. How shall we any longer be living in sin—if indeed we died to it? This perplexes many, this announcement that we died to sin,—inasmuch as the struggle with sin, and that within, is one of the most constant conscious experiences of the believer. But, as we see elsewhere, we must not confound our relationship to sin with its presence! Distinguish this revealed *fact* that we died, from our *experience* of deliverance. For we do not die to sin by our experiences: we did die to sin in Christ's death. For the fact that we died to sin is a Divinely revealed word concerning us, and we cannot deny it! The presence of sin "in our members" will make this fact that we died to it hard to grasp and hold: but God *says* it. And He will duly explain all to our *faith*.

Verse 3: **Or** [in the very matter of our baptism] **are ye ignorant that all we who were baptized unto Christ Jesus unto His death were baptized?**

Here the apostle turns them back to their baptism, that initial step in public confession of the Lord upon whom they had believed. Did they not realize the significance of that baptism—that it set forth their identification with a crucified and buried Lord? For in their baptism they had confessed their choice of Him, as against sin and the old life. But Christ having been "made sin on our behalf," had *died unto* sin; had been *buried,* and had been *raised* from the dead through the glory of the Father; and now lived unto God in a new, resurrection life.

Therefore they could see in their baptism the picture of that federal death and burial with Christ which Paul sets forth so positively in the second verse: "Such ones as we, who died."

We must first of all receive the statement of our death unto sin with Christ (verses 2 and 11) as a *revealed federal fact;* and then allow the Apostle to press the *symbolical* setting forth of that federal death by the figure of water-baptism. For these early Christians had not been befuddled regarding the simple matter of baptism,—as later generations have been! To them it was a vivid and happy memory,—the day they dared step out, against the whole world, and often in the face of persecution and even death, and confess the Lord Jesus, definitely and forever, as their own Savior and Lord.

Now, says Paul, in that very matter of your baptism, you set forth what I am teaching you, that you who are Christ's *died with* Him. Not only so, but your baptism set forth further that you were buried with Him: for was it not a vivid portrayal of your death and burial, when you went down into the waters which signified—not cleansing, but *death?* "Water," says Peter, "which *after a true likeness* doth now save you—even baptism: *not* the putting away of the filth of the flesh, but the answer of a good conscience toward God through the resurrection of Jesus Christ." Eight souls, Peter here says, were saved in Noah's day in the Ark—type of Christ. For those eight were, in the Ark, brought safely through the waters of judgment which drowned the world; as we were brought, through Christ, safely through the judgment of sin at the cross; and now have "a good conscience toward God"— through God's having raised up Christ: all of which, baptism sets forth—"after a true *likeness*" (I Pet. 3.20,21).

Scripture here connects baptism with death, not with cleansing; with burial, not with exaltation; with the ending of a former connection that we may enter a new one.

Or [in the very matter of our baptism] **are ye ignorant that all we who were baptized unto Christ Jesus unto His death were baptized?**

We find therefore, here in Romans 6.3:

1. That Paul, along with all believers of his day, had been **baptized**. He offers no explanatory word, thus showing that the matter of having been baptized was a common consciousness among Christians.

2. That it was **unto Christ Jesus** that believers had been baptized. The preposition "unto" *(eis)* seems best rendered here as in I Corinthians 10.2, where we read that the fathers of Israel were all "baptized unto *(eis)* Moses." Those Israelites were not baptized into Moses, but were indeed judicially associated by God with the Mosaic economy,—"into a spiritual union with Moses, and constituted his disciples." So believers are baptized unto Christ Jesus, which we believe, must be the meaning here. They were indeed so "baptized unto the name of the Lord Jesus" (Acts 19.5), that they thereafter bore His Name (James 2.7, marg.). But we must not confuse this water-baptism of Romans Six, which stands for the identification of believers with Christ in death, burial, and resurrection; with that Holy Spirit baptism of I Corinthians 12.13. For our identification with Christ-made-sin, and our death in and with Him, must never be confounded with what follows our Lord's ascension and the coming of the Holy Spirit,—baptism into the one Body. These are two absolutely different things. One has to do with taking us out of our old man, justifying us *from sin,* as well as from sins. The other, the Spirit's

baptism into "one Body," has to do with the glorious heavenly position God gives us in a Risen Christ.

To seek to have a man baptized by the Spirit into Christ before he has been identified with Christ at the cross in death and burial, is really to ignore man's awful state in the old man, which God had condemned to crucifixion with Christ made sin. So with the Bullingerites and many others: they do not distinctly see or solidly preach our identification with Christ *in death and burial*. "Buried with Him in baptism"—how can these words of Colossians 2.12 possibly apply to the work of the Holy Spirit? *We beg all to consider this.* Death to sin, and burial with Christ, water-baptism, *and that alone,* sets forth.

3. **Unto His death were baptized.** Neither must we confuse baptism unto Christ Jesus here with that actual identification in Christ's death of which baptism is a symbol. That our old man was crucified with Christ is one thing; baptism, quite another. However much baptism portrays our death with Christ, it in no wise brings about that death. If we had not died with Christ, there would be no meaning to baptism.

Certainly baptism sets forth the fact of our death with Christ. Christian baptism in water is the Scripture picture,— not of our being cleansed, nor of our being introduced into the Body of Christ by the Holy Spirit (which is an entirely different matter); and not, of course, of our regeneration. But it is a setting forth of the great fact that we federally died and were buried with Christ, unto sin, unto the world, and unto all of the old creation; and are now raised with Him and share His risen life;—on new ground altogether.

Verse 4: **We were buried therefore with Him through the baptism unto [His] death.** Here the apostle declares that all believers by the very matter of their baptism, proclaimed themselves as having been so identified with Christ's death that they were buried: that their past was ended,—not, of course, by the ordinance, though the ordinance confessed and proclaimed it.* And now the object of our identification

---

*Godet remarks: "Burial is the act which consummates the breaking of the last tie between man and his earthly life. This was likewise the meaning of our Lord's entombment. Similarly, by baptism there is publicly consummated the believer's breaking with the life of the present world, and with his own natural life."

And he relates this striking incident, which proves how these sayings of the

with Christ's death is set forth: **in order that, just as Christ was raised from among the dead through the glory of the Father, thus also we might be walking about in newness of life.**

Christ on the cross not only bare our sins in His own body, but He was also made to be sin,—to be the thing itself. Then God the Father, through His glory, raised Him from the dead,—"that working of the strength of His might which He wrought in Christ when He raised Him from the dead." This was the most marvelous display of glorious, Divine power ever known. The words "through *the glory* of the Father," bring into action all that God is. Christ had fully glorified God in all that He is, in His earthly life, and on the cross (as we saw in Chapter 3.24 and 25). Then God raised Christ from the dead in glorious triumph. And thereafter Christ walked for forty days on earth "in newness of life." He was "the First-born from the dead." He was the Last Adam, now become (though having His flesh and bones body) "a spirit making [others] alive," the Second Man, "a new starting point of the human race." The old man was crucified with Christ, and all that belonged to "man in the flesh" was ended before God there on Christ's cross. Now the "glory of the Father" is put forth in raising Christ and placing Him in that risen "newness of life" never known before, and in receiving Him up in glory!

Walking in newness of life. Note that walking presupposes the possession of life. The literal translation of this word is seen in I Peter 5.8, "walking about."* Now mark in this verse that it is Christ who is raised from the dead, and the saints are to walk, consequently, in "newness of life"—showing

---

*Unfortunately, we do not have this word "walk" in this Pauline sense in ordinary English use. Men have substituted the word "live," and that in a *legal* sense: *"Live* the Christian *life," "Live* as you ought to *live,"* etc.

---

apostle, apparently so mysterious, find an easy explanation under the light of the lively experiences of *faith*:

A missionary was questioning a converted Bechuana as to the meaning of a passage analogous to Romans 6.5,—namely, Colossians 3.3. The Bechuana said to him: "Soon I shall be dead, and they will bury me in my field. My flocks will come to pasture above me. But I shall no longer hear them, and I shall not come forth from my tomb to take them and carry them with me to the sepulchre. They will be strange to me, as I to them. Such is the image of my life in the midst of the world since I believed in Christ."

at once their union with Him; that as He was raised, so also they, when they are placed in Him, walk about in *newness of life.*

Note that it is *life*—not a mere manner of living. Then, it is *newness,* or a new kind of life, for that is the meaning of the word. Resurrection life was never known until Christ was raised from the dead. Lazarus, and the widow of Nain's son, and Jairus' daughter, were brought back into this present earth-life. Indeed, it is written concerning Jairus' daughter, that when the Lord said, "Maiden, arise!" her "spirit returned," and she rose up instantly. The spirit had left the body, the earth-life had ceased; it was now resumed.

But in Christ's resurrection this was not so. He was the First-born from the dead, the First-fruits of them that slept. It was not back into the old flesh and blood earthly existence that He came. He had, indeed, His body: "Handle Me and see." "Have ye here anything to eat?" Yet He had poured out His blood. The life of the flesh was in the blood (Lev. 17.11). He had laid that life down. He is now a heavenly Man. He is in the heavenlies. And He is there as to His human body: "God . . . wrought in Christ, when He raised Him from the dead, and made Him to sit at His right hand in the heavenlies." Poor human reason attempts to follow here; but this revelation is addressed to faith only. The disciples "were glad when they saw the Lord." Into the upper room He came, and stood in the midst; and "He showed unto them His hands and His side." And Thomas was told, "Reach hither thy finger, and see My hands; and reach hither thy hand, and put it into My side: and be not faithless, but believing"; and further, "Blessed are they that have not seen, and yet have believed."

It is in this newness, this new kind of life, which they now share,* that believers are to walk about in this world. They are

---

*Many quote Paul's words in I Corinthians 15.31: "I die daily," to prove the Romish idea of our "dying daily to sin." But we need only remember that the great message of I Corinthians 15 has to do with the *body,* to refute this. Indeed the preceding verse and the following verses (30 and 32) show what Paul meant by "dying daily." "We stand in jeopardy every hour,"—meaning the physical dangers that beset his ministry. And, "If after the manner of men we fought with beasts at Ephesus,"—referring to the terrible outward trials he had faced and yet would face.

To make the words "I die daily" mean an inward spiritual struggle with sin, is to falsify Paul's plain testimony: "I *have been* crucified with Christ"; "Our old

one with this Risen Christ! Being "joined unto the Lord," they are *"one spirit" with Him* now; and shall have bodies, shortly, conformed unto the body of His glory (I Cor. 6.17; Phil. 3.20,21).

Verse 5: **For if we became united with [Him] in the likeness of His death, so shall we be also [in the likeness] of His resurrection:** Here Paul looks back to verse 2, to the *fact* he declared true concerning all believers, that they *died* to sin; and he now insists that that death is a fact about *true believers only*—those who have been vitally enlifed with Christ. The word means to *grow together**—as a graft in a tree, so that the graft shares the tree's life. The meaning of Verse 5 may be paraphrased: If we became actually united with Him, which, in our baptism—the "likeness of His death," we profess; so we shall also be united in the likeness of His resurrection: (so therefore to be walking in newness of life!). Conybeare well remarks concerning verse 5: "The meaning appears to be, *If we have shared the reality of His death, whereof we have undergone the likeness*" (in baptism).

Now when the apostle says we are to be united with "the likeness of His resurrection," he refers to the walking in "newness of life" just spoken of in the preceding verse. (For this verse explains that.) To be joined in life with the Risen Christ, and thus daily, hourly, to walk, is a wonder not conceived of by many of us. But it is the blessed portion of all true Christians. They shared Christ's death, and now are "saved by [or *in*] His life"—as we read in Chapter 5.10. But not only saved: we walk here on earth by appropriating faith, in the blessedness of His heavenly "newness" of resurrection life! This is what Paul meant when he said, "To me to live is Christ"; "our inward man is being renewed day by day"; "I

---

*The Greek word is *sumphutoi*—used only here. It was confounded by the King James translators with *sumphuteuo*, translated in Rom. 6.5, "planted together," whereas the proper word means to be actually enlifed together with.

---

man *was* crucified with Him"; "He that *hath died* is righteously released from sin"; "Reckon ye yourselves *dead* unto sin."

Paul indeed says he desired to be *"conformed unto"* Christ's death (Phil. 3.10); but as one who *had federally shared it*: and not as one who sought to approximate, or imitate, Christ's death! This last is Romanism. But Paul was a *believer*,—in the work of the Cross!

was crucified with Christ; Christ liveth in me . . . the life I now live in the flesh I live by the faith of the Son of God."

Of course this fifth verse may look on, also, to that day when our bodies will share this resurrection-life,—as we have seen in the verse before; but the context here shows Paul is speaking of our "walking about in newness of life" in Christ, today!

We reap the exact effect of what Christ did. Did Christ *bear our sins* in His own body on the tree? He did. Then we bear them no more. Was Christ made *to be sin* on our behalf, and did He die unto sin? Truly so. Then Christ's *relation to sin* becomes ours!

Verse 6: **Coming to know this, that our old man was crucified with Him, in order that the body of sin might be annulled, that we might no longer be in slave service to sin.** The word translated "coming to know," means, in the Greek, coming into knowledge ,—a discriminating apprenhension of facts. See note below.*

Our old man—This is our old selves, as we were in and from Adam. It is contrasted with the new man (Col. 3.9, 10)—which is what we are and have in Christ. The word *our* indicates that what is said, is said of and to all those who are in Christ. The expression "our old man," of course is a federal one, as also is "the new man." The "old man," therefore, is not Adam personally, any more than the "new man" is Christ personally. Also, we must not confuse the "old man" with "the flesh." Adam begat a son in his own likeness. This son of Adam, as all since, was according to Adam,—for he was *in* Adam; possessed of a "natural" mind, feelings, tastes, desires,—all apart from God. He was his father repeated. Cain is a picture before us of the meaning of the words, "the

---

*The Greek word for "know" (*gignōskō*) here, means to *get* to know, come into the knowledge of, become acquainted with the fact. It is an entirely different word from the one translated "knowing" in verse 9 (*eidō*), meaning "a clear and purely mental conception, in contrast both to conjecture and to knowledge derived from others" (Thayer). In this latter verse the fact spoken of is a matter of common knowledge. We, by God's word here, *come to know* (verse 6) that our old man *was crucified* with Christ; whereas we know as a necessary thing that Christ, being raised, dieth no more (verse 9). This is not a fact we "*come* to know," as in the matter of our vital connection with His death, verse 6. The manner in which we "come to know" our old man was crucified is by faith in God's testimony to the fact!

old man." Moreover, since man's activities were carried on in and through the body, he is now morally "after the flesh." Inasmuch as his spirit was now dead to God, sin controlled him, both spirit and soul, through the *body*. And thus we read a little later, in the Sixth of Genesis, upon the recounting of the horrible lust and violence that filled the earth, God's statement: "In their going astray, they are *flesh!*" (R. V. margin.) What a fearful travesty of one created in the image of God, and into whose Divinely formed body God had breathed the spirit of life, so that he was "spirit and soul and body" (I Thess. 5.23); and with his innocent spirit able to speak with his Creator! with his unfallen soul-faculties, and with body in blessed harmony.

When we are told, for instance, in Colossians, that we have put off the old man, we know that we are being addressed as new creatures in Christ, and that the old man represents all we naturally were,—desires, lusts, ambitions, hopes, judgments: looked at as a whole federally: we used to be that—now we have put that off. We recognize it again in the words "Put away as concerning your former manner of life the old man" (Eph. 4.22).

1. First, then, our old man was crucified (Romans 6.6). That is a Divine announcement of fact.

2. Those in Christ have put off the old man.

3. He still exists, for "the old man waxeth corrupt after the lusts of deceit" (Eph. 4.22).

4. He is to be put away as belonging to our former manner of life: for we are in Christ and are "new creatures; old things are passed away; behold they are become new" (II Cor. 5.17).

Now as regards the flesh:

1. While our old man has been crucified, *by God,* with Christ at the cross,—the *federal* thing was done; yet of *the flesh* we read, "They that are *of Christ Jesus* have crucified the flesh with the passions and the lusts thereof" (Gal. 5.24).

2. The flesh has passions and lusts.

3. It has a *mind* directly at enmity with God.

4. As we shall see in Chapter Seven, the flesh is the manifestation of sin in the as yet unredeemed body. "Our old man,"

therefore, is the large term, the all-inclusive one—of all that we were federally from Adam. The flesh, however, we shall find to be that manifestation of sin in our members with which we are in conscious inward conflict, against which only the Holy Spirit indwelling us effectively wars. Our bodies are not the root of sin, but do not yet share, as do our spirits, the redemption that is in Christ. And as for our souls (our faculties of perception, reason, imagination, and our sensibilities),—our souls are being renewed by the indwelling Holy Spirit. Not so the body. "The flesh," which is sin entrenched in the body, is unchangeably evil, and will war against us till Christ comes. Only the Holy Spirit has power over "the flesh" (Chapter 8.1).

Our old man was crucified—The matter of which we are told to take note here is the great federal fact that our old man was crucified with Christ. Perhaps no more difficult task, no task requiring such constant vigilant attention, is assigned by God to the believer. It is a stupendous thing, this matter of taking note of and keeping in mind what goes so completely against consciousness,—that our old man was crucified. These words are addressed to faith, to faith only. Emotions, feelings, deny them. To reason, they are foolishness. But ah, what stormy seas has faith walked over! What mountains has faith cast into the sea! How many impossible things has faith done!

Let us never forget, that this crucifixion was a thing *definitely done by God at the cross,* just as really as our sins were there laid upon Christ. It is addressed to faith as a revelation from God. Reason is blind. The "word of the cross" is "foolishness" to it. All the work consummated at the cross seems folly, if we attempt to subject it to man's understanding. But, just as the great wonder of creation is understood only by faith: ("By faith we understand that the worlds have been framed by the Word of God,"—Heb. 11.3) so the eternal results accomplished at the cross are entered into by simple faith in the testimony of God about them.

No, it is no easy or light thing that is announced to you and me, that all we were and are from Adam has been rejected of God. Scripture is not now dealing with what we have *done,* but with what we *are.*

And really to enter spiritually into the meaning of this awful word, **Our old man was crucified,** involves, with all of us, deep exercise of soul. For no one by nature will be ready to count himself so incorrigibly bad as to have to be *crucified!* But when the Spirit of God turns the light upon what we are, from Adam, these will be blessed words of relief: "Our old man was crucified."

Now here is the very opposite of the teaching of false Christianity about a holy life. For these legalists set you to crucifying yourself! You must "die out" to this, and to that. But God says our old man, all that we were, has been already dealt with,—and that by *crucifixion with Christ.* And the very words "with Him" show that it was done back at the cross; and that our task is to believe the good news, rather than to seek to bring about this crucifixion ourselves.

The believer is constantly reminded that his relation to sin was brought about by his identification with Christ in His death: Christ died unto sin, and the believer shared that death, died with Him, and is now, therefore, dead unto sin. This is his relationship to sin—the same as Christ's now is; and believing this is to be his constant attitude.

Difficulty there will be, no doubt, in taking and maintaining constantly this attitude: but faith will remove the difficulty, and faith here will grow out of assiduous, constant attention to God's exact statements of fact. We are not to go to God in begging petitions for "victory,"—except in extreme circumstances. We are to set ourselves a very different task: "This is the work of God, *that ye believe.*" We may often be compelled to cry, with the father of the demoniac, "Lord, I believe; help Thou mine unbelief!" But it is still better to have our faces toward the foe, knowing ourselves to be *in Christ,* and that we have been commanded to reckon ourselves dead to sin, no matter how great and strong sin may appear. Satan's great device is to drive earnest souls back to beseeching God for what God says has already been done!

"Our old man *was* crucified with Christ." This is our task: to walk in the faith of these words. Upon this water God commands us to step out and walk. And we are infinitely better off than was Peter that night, when he "walked on the water to come *to* Jesus"; whereas we are *in* Christ. And our relationship to sin is His relationship! He died unto it, and we, being in Christ Risen, are in the relationship Christ's death brought about in Him, and now to us who are in Him: whether to sin, law, death, or the world.

If I did not die with Christ, on the cross, I cannot be living in Him, risen from the dead; but am still back in the old Adam in which I was born!

Christ died once—once for all, unto sin. He is not dying continually. I am told to reckon myself dead—in that death of Christ. I am therefore not told to do my own dying, to sin and self and the world: but, on the contrary, to reckon by simple faith, that in His death I died: and to be "conformed unto His death." But, to be conformed to a death already a fact, is not doing my own dying,—which is Romanism. If you and I are able to reckon ourselves dead—in Christ's death: all will be simple.

That the body of sin might be annulled—The word for "annulled" is *katargeo*. See note on Chapter 4.14. The meaning is, to "put out of business." The "body of sin" refers to our bodies as yet unredeemed, and not delivered from sin's rule; as Paul says in the Eighth Chapter: "If Christ be in you, the body is dead because of sin." Now we shall find that we have no power to deliver our body, our members, from "the law of sin" (See Chapter 7.8-24). But since our old man has been crucified with Christ, all the rights of sin are gone; and the indwelling Holy Spirit can **annul** "the body of sin"; thus delivering us from sin's bondage. We know the Spirit is not mentioned here (as He will be constantly in Chapter Eight); but inasmuch as it is His work to *apply* all Christ's work to us, we speak of His blessed *annulling* of the power of indwelling sin. It is blessed to know that we do not have to crucify the old man: that was done in Christ's federal death at the cross. Nor do we have to "annul" the "body of sin": that is done by the blessed Spirit as we yield to Him.

Verse 7: For he that hath died hath been declared righteous from sin!

We must seize fast hold of this blessed verse.

Let us distinguish at once between being justified from *sins*—from the guilt thereof—by the blood of Christ, and being justified from *sin*—the thing itself.

"Justified from sin" is the key to both Chapters Six and Seven and also to Eight! It is the consciousness of being sinful that keeps back saints from that glorious life Paul lived. Paul shows absolutely no sense of bondage before God; but goes on in blessed triumph! Why? He knew he had been justified *from all guilt* by the blood of Christ; and he knew that he was also justified, cleared, from *the thing sin itself:* and therefore (though walking in an, as yet, unredeemed body), he was *wholly heavenly* in his standing, life and relations with God! He knew he was as really justified *from sin itself* as from *sins*. The conscious presence of sin in his flesh only reminded him that he was *in Christ;*—that sin had been *condemned judicially,* as connected with flesh, at the cross; and that he was *justified* as to sin; because he had died with Christ, and his former relationship to sin had *wholly ceased!* Its presence gave him no thought of condemnation, but only eagered his longing for the redemption body. "Justified from sin"—because, "he that hath died is justified from sin." Glorious fact! May we have faith to enter into it as did Paul!*

It is the deep-seated notion of Christendom that *gradually* we become saints,—*gradually* worthy of heaven: so that sometime, —perhaps, on a dying bed, we will have the right to "drop this robe of flesh and rise."

But Scripture cuts this idea off at once, by the declaration that we *died,* and that we are now, here, *justified from* sin!

---

*"Justified from sin" does not mean "sinless perfection,"—but something utterly different, and infinitely beyond that! It is different, in that it does not refer to an "experience" of deliverance from sin, but a *passing beyond,* in *death with Christ at the cross, the sphere where the former relationship to sin* existed! We are justified, accounted wholly righteous, with respect to the thing sin itself! This, therefore, is infinitely beyond any state whatever of *experience*. It is a newly-established relationship to sin, which the saints have because they died with Christ: in which they stand in Christ *as He is* toward sin. They are "meet to be partakers of the inheritance of the saints in light." They are heavenly. Their old relation to sin is over *forever*. They are justified *from* it. They rejoice, indeed, and have a most blessed "experience." But they do not say sin is gone from their flesh: but that they, having died, are *declared righteous* from it; that they are *cleared,* before God, of all condemnation because of sin's presence in this unredeemed body; and delivered from all sin's former rights and bondage over them.

"Giving thanks unto the Father, who *made* us meet to be partakers of the inheritance of the saints in light." The saints in
light are those in glory, and they are there *for one reason alone:*
the work of Christ on the cross.

How unspeakably sad is our little faith! And I am speaking
of true believers, certainly.

1. Many have turned truly to God, but not knowing the
finished work of Christ, that is, that He actually bare their sins
and put them away, are never sure of their own salvation.

2. Many have appropriated gladly Christ's finished work, as
respects the guilt of their sins, and they no longer have apprehensions of judgment, knowing that He met all God's claims
against them on the cross. But as to their relation to sin itself,
it is an "O-wretched-man" life that they live, for they see
honestly their own sinfulness and unworthiness, but have never
heard how they are now *in a Christ who died to sin,* and that
they share His relationship now, dead to sin and alive to God
(6.10,11).

3. Thank God, there are some who have seen and believed
in their hearts that their relationship to sin itself was completely
changed when God identified them with Christ in His death.
Their relationship to sin was broken forever; and they present
themselves unto God as *alive from the dead,* and, through an
ever increasing faith, walk about on earth *in newness of life;*
knowing that the same God who declared them justified from
the guilt of their sins through Christ's shed blood, has now
declared that, in being identified with Christ in His death to
sin, they are themselves *declared righteous* from sin itself!*

As we have elsewhere remarked, relief from guilt and danger,
through the shed blood of Christ, comes first. And the conscience concerning judgment being relieved, the heart ever rests
in the blood of Christ. But to have God tell us further, that we,
having died with Christ, are declared righteous *from sin itself,*
is a new, additional, and glorious revelation, which sets us in
the presence of God not only declared righteous from what we
have done, but declared righteous from what we were—and as
to our flesh, still are! We should have no more dejection and

---

*The Greek word is the perfect tense of the verb *dikaioō,* to *declare righteous.*

self-condemnation when we see our old selves; for we have
been *declared righteous* from that old state of being, as well as
from what we had done! Very excellent and godly men, not
recognizing this blessed fact, have spent much time before God
"bemoaning the sinfulness" of their now revealed old nature.
But this was really not to recognize the Word of God that we
have been *justified, declared righteous, from the old state of
being, from sin itself!**

If Gabriel, the presence angel, were to appear before you,
your natural thought would be, He is holy, sinless; and I am
unholy, sinful. Therefore, I am not worthy to stand in his
presence. But this would be completely wrong. If you are in
Christ, you stand *in Christ,*—in Christ alone,—even as He! The

---

*The author many years ago edited a little book called *Extracts from the Journal
of David Brainerd*—the wonderful missionary to the Indians in New Jersey in the
eighteenth century, whose prayer-life has inspired hundreds; whose devotion to
Christ was sublime. But many, many pages of his diary were found to be occupied with bemoaning (often alone on the room-floor, or in the forest, before God)
his sinful *state*.

For example, "May 13, 1742. Saw so much of the wickedness of my heart, that
I longed to get away from myself. I never before thought there was so much
spiritual pride in my soul. I felt almost pressed to death with my own vileness. Oh
what a body of death is there in me! Lord, deliver my soul.

"May 15. Indeed I never saw such a week as this before; for I have been almost ready to die with the view of the wickedness of my heart. I could not have
thought I had such a body of death in me.

"June 30. Spent this day alone in the woods, in fasting and prayer; underwent
the most dreadful conflicts in my soul that ever I felt, in some respects. I saw
myself so vile, that I was ready to say, 'I shall now perish by the hand of Saul.' I
thought, and almost concluded, I had no power to stand for the cause of God, but
was almost afraid of the shaking of a leaf. Spent almost the whole day in prayer,
incessantly. I could not bear to think of Christians showing me any respect."

God forbid that we should disparage in the least such a very saint as Brainerd,
whose Memoirs draw out our hearts with their sincere godliness as do almost no
other uninspired writings. Yet Paul's attitude is the Divine example. He believed
what he wrote—that he had been justified from sin itself. So that all struggles
from self-condemnation were over. He knew that in him was "no good thing"; but
that he had been justified from even indwelling sin.

George Whitefield used to say, "When I see myself I seem to be half devil and
half beast," and again, as he passed through great crowds on his way to preach:
"I wondered why the people did not stone so vile a wretch as myself."

You may say, This is just the Seventh of Romans, and Paul had that experience.
Yes, Paul had it; and found that in him, in his flesh, there was no good thing.
But, having come to this vision of himself, and agreeing with God as to the evil of
the flesh, he found deliverance in Christ and afterwards rejoiced in Him alway.
There is no hint in his epistles of a continued struggle, nor of the slightest con-
sciousness of Divine condemnation because of the presence of the flesh within. He
walked in the consciousness of justification not only from guilt, but from sin itself!
Therefore, the Risen Christ, rather than ill thoughts of his old self, filled his vision!
The trouble with most of us is, we do not believe we are *utterly* bad. Or if, like
Brainerd or Whitefield, we see and own it, we do not see ourselves where God sees
us, *only in Christ*.

presence of sin in the flesh has no more power to trouble your conscience, than have your *sins:* for both were dealt with at the cross! Your old man was crucified, sin in the flesh was *condemned* (8.3) at the cross. And Paul definitely declares that we have *now come* "to the innumerable hosts of angels," as well as that we have been made meet to be "partakers of the inheritance of the saints in light"!

One of the most astonishing things (and yet, why astonishing?) that came to us in the study of the book of the Revelation was, that once the apostle John had "fallen as one dead" at the feet of the glorified Christ, in Chapter One, and the Lord had "laid His right hand" upon him, saying, "Fear not, I am the First and the Last, and the Living One, and I became dead, and behold I am alive for evermore, and I have the keys of death and of Hades" (Rev. 1.17,18)—after that, John, all unconsciously, but really, fears nothing, and no one! Not even the vision of the glorious throne in heaven before which the four living ones and the four and twenty elders are falling down, crying, "Holy, Holy, Holy," stirs John with the least emotion of fear or shrinking. In fact, he is found weeping because no one can take the sealed book. Not once is he concerned about his own moral or spiritual condition. He goes boldly up to the mighty angel in the Tenth Chapter, requesting according to Divine direction, that he give him the little book in his hand. Twice he falls at the feet of the angelic messenger that is revealing these glorious things to him, but it is not on account of a sense of moral or spiritual unfitness, but rather a being enraptured, overwhelmed with the glory of the scene.

Now why is this? Or how could Paul be caught up to the *third heaven,* into Paradise, and hear *unspeakable words?*

Simply because the work of the cross was complete! Not only were sins put away by the blood of Christ, but our connection with Adam was ended, our old man was crucified, we died to sin; our former history was completely over, before God. Thus it is written, as we quoted, "Giving thanks unto the Father who made us meet to be partakers of the inheritance of the saints in light" (Col. 1.12).

Now as to the *fact,* all this is as true of us here on earth, as it will be in the ages to come. Our realization of the truth may be small; yea, sad to say, our faith may be weak; but the fact is the same!

How utterly marvelous, then, to know that we have been justified *from sin itself.* Not only has it lost all right and power over us, but we are declared righteous from the hideous thing itself; we are standing with God, in Christ, outside the region of sin, "children of light," yea, even called "light in the Lord" (Eph. 5.8).

Verse 8: **But if we died with Christ, we believe that we shall also be living with Him** [in this world].

Here we *take it for granted* that we died; that our old man was crucified *with* Christ. And we go on to the expectation of a blessed life *in* Christ. For it is not only that we shall "live with Him" in resurrection glory when He comes, but even now we walk in newness of life in Him, as verses 10 and 13 set forth. This is no uncertain confidence, because "Christ, being raised from the dead, dieth no more." The brief lordship of death over Him is ended forever, and it is His death and life we share.

Meyer well paraphrases: "Whosoever has died with Christ is now also of the belief that his life, i.e., the positive, active side of his moral being and nature, shall be a fellowship of life with the exalted Christ; that is, shall be able to be nothing else than this." And Rotherham: "If we jointly died with Christ,—we believe that we shall also jointly live with Him." And Conybeare: "If we have shared the death of Christ, we believe that we shall also share His life."

This word, **shall also be living with Him,** must finally include, doubtless, the consummation of our salvation at the coming of Christ, and the fashioning anew of our mortal bodies. But the word refers directly to that expressed by Paul in Galatians 2.20: "I have been crucified with Christ, and it is no longer I that live, but Christ that liveth in me." Here in Romans Six it is called a living *with* Him, as over against our death with Him. Hodge well says: "The future tense is used here, referring not to what is to happen hereafter, so much as to what is the certain consequence of our union with Christ." And Alford: "The future ('we shall also live with Him') as in verse 5, is used, because the life with Him, though here begun, is not here completed."

And now the reason for this assurance that we shall keep on sharing the risen life of Christ, is given:

Verse 9: **Knowing that Christ having been raised from among the dead dieth no more: death over Him no longer hath dominion.**

Knowing—"This participle justifies the 'we believe' of verse eight." We know *(eidotes)* both that our present spiritual participation in Christ's risen life will continue, and also that our mortal bodies will be finally delivered, in view of the fact we are conscious of, that Christ has been once and irrevocably raised; that God "loosed the pangs of death"; that "He raised Him up from the dead, now no more to return to corruption,"—for it was written, "Thou wilt not give Thy Holy One to see corruption." Sin *never* had dominion over Him; and death could have had no dominion except that our sin was transferred to Him! Death, therefore, the "wages," had a brief dominion, but now that is *ended forever;* and we are in Him,—*also forever!* Therefore death with its dominion is for the believer forever passed away. Our identification with Christ in death at the cross made possible of fulfillment His wonderful promise in John 8.51, "Verily, verily, I say unto you, If a man keep my word, *he shall never see death.*" If a believer falls asleep (God's word for a believer's physical death) his spirit goes to be with Christ: there is no "dark valley." On the tomb of an early Christian were these words: "I sinned, I repented, I trusted, I loved; I slept, I shall rise, I shall reign!"

It is a terrible thing to contemplate—that death once held the Prince of Life, the Lord of all. Yet behold the Lord of Life, under the dominion of death! But He is not making atonement during those three days and nights,—that was all *finished* on the cross.* And now, praise God, we read, **Death no more**

---

*Our Lord's last words were, "Father, into thy hands I commend my spirit." As Peter writes: "Being put to death in the flesh, but made alive in the spirit, in which [quickened spirit] He went and preached unto the spirits in prison," etc. [I Pet. 3.18, 19). Christ's human spirit, we know, from His own word, was to be

hath dominion over Him. He liveth unto God, in a glad resurrection life which shall never end. This is the life that we share, for we shared His death.

Verse 10: Therefore we must go on to verse 10 and read God's statement of Christ's death *unto* sin: **For in that He died, unto sin He died once for all; but in that He is living, He is living unto God.**

Now we beseech you, do not change God's word "UNTO," here! Do not confuse with this passage those other Scriptures that declare that Christ died FOR our sins. For this great revelation of Romans 6.10 is that Christ died UNTO sin! There is here, of course, no thought of expiation of guilt. That belongs to Chapters Three to Five. Here, the sole question is one of relationship, not of expiation. Christ is seen dying *to* sin, not *for* it, here.

What is meant by that?

In II Corinthians 5.21, God declares: "Him who knew no sin God made to *be* sin on our behalf; that we might *become* the righteousness of God in Him." Christ is made to be what we were, that we might become, in Him, what He is! Might not Christ, the Sinless One, bear the *guilt* of our sins and that be all? Nay, but we were connected federally with Adam the first—with a race proved wholly unrighteous and bad. And that we might be released from that Adam-state, there must be not only our sins borne, but we ourselves released from the old-Adam headship,—all we had from Adam: which involved the responsibilities we had in him—responsibility to furnish God, as morally responsible beings, a perfect righteousness and holiness *of our own*.

Now God's way was, not to "change" the old man, but to send it to the cross unto death, and release us from it. *No one who remains in Adam's race will be saved!* "Ye must be born again!" should sound the tocsin of alarm, yea, terror, to every one not yet *in Christ*. For God's method was to set forth a Second Man, a Last Adam,—Christ; (with whom indeed all God's eternal plans were connected), whom God would not only

---

"three days and three nights (Matt. 12.40) in the *heart* of the earth." This of course does not refer to His body, which lay in Joseph's tomb on the surface of the earth.

set forth to make expiation of guilt, but would make *to become
sin itself:* thus to get at what we *were,* as well as what we *had
done.* Our old man would thus be crucified with Christ, so that
all the evil of the old man, and all his responsibilities also, would
be completely annulled before God for all believers. For they
must righteously be released from Adam, before they are
created in Christ, another Adam! And this must be by *death.*

Thus God would say to believers, to those in Christ, "Your
history now begins anew!" just as He said to Israel at the
Passover: "This month shall be unto you the beginning of
months: it shall be the first month of the year to you." So Paul
triumphantly writes, "If any man is in Christ, he is a *new
creature:* the old things are passed away; behold, they are
become new." What a day was that when Christ, made to be
sin itself, died *to* it, and was forever done with it! So that now
He lives *unto God* in light and joy eternal without measure!

Verse 11: Therefore the eleventh verse becomes a necessity:
God must say to us: **Thus** [because of the facts of the preceding verse] **do ye also reckon yourselves dead, indeed, to
sin, but living to God, in Christ Jesus!*** Your relationship
to sin is exactly the same as Christ's! Why? Because Christ
is now your only Adam: you are *in Him!* His act of death unto
sin involved all who are connected with Him.

Thus, in His death, all Christ's connection with sin was
broken, ended, forever. Not only did He no longer bear sin;
but He had died *unto* sin. When He was raised, it was as One
who lived unto God, in an endless life with which sin had
nothing to do,—resurrection-life, newness of life!

And, because believers were united with Him in His death,
they too died to sin in and with Him. And their relationship to
sin is now exactly His relationship: they are dead to it. They
are also "alive unto God" in Christ Jesus.

This is not a matter of "experience," but of *fact.* The truth
about believers is, that they are dead to sin and alive to God,

---

*The A.V. translation, *"through* Christ Jesus,"* is unfortunate, as it does not, as
does God's Word, emphasize the *place* of blessing in which we now are—*in* (Gr.
en) Christ Jesus. It is not, in this verse, what shall be done *through* Christ for us;
nor only what *has* been done through Him; but *the place of federal blessing in which
we now are,* that is in view: we are *in* Him who died to sin, and His death was
ours.

being in Christ! And they hear it said by God, and are asked to reckon it so! Their path of faith is plain: "Reckon* ye also yourselves to be dead unto sin, but alive unto God, in Christ Jesus."

John Wesley truly counselled:
> "Frames and feelings fluctuate:
> These can ne'er thy saviour be!
> Learn thyself *in Christ* to see:
> Then, be feelings what they will,
> Jesus is thy Saviour still!"

Lay to heart the very words of the eleventh verse: **Reckon yourselves dead indeed to sin, but living to God, in Christ Jesus.** There are two words signifying death in this passage. The word for dead *(nekros)* here in verse 11, does not refer to the act or process of dying, but to the state or effect produced by death. The other word *(thnēsko)* signifies the act, and occurs in verses 3, 4, 5, 7, 8, 9 and 10; and is used when Christ's dying, or our dying with or in Him, is set forth. It is, therefore, with the *already accomplished death* unto sin of our great Substitute and Representative, Christ, that believers—those now in Christ—find themselves connected; and as we said above, the believer is to reckon himself dead *(nekros)* unto sin, but alive unto God,—*because* he is in Christ Jesus, who died unto sin once for all; but now, in resurrection life, is living unto God. You will realize anew the meanings of these two words for death, when you notice, in verses 4 and 9, that Christ, having died *(thnēsko)* was raised "from among *dead ones*" *(nekroi)*. Christ's body lay in Joseph's tomb. He was not now dying: that was over. He was dead. And so we are not told

---

*This word "reckon" is a favorite word of Paul's in Romans, where he uses it 19 times, and only 16 times in all his other epistles. The Greek word *(logidzomai)* might be called both a court word and a counting-room word. Paul uses it as a court word as to God's action in accounting the believer righteous. In this sense it is used 11 times in Romans Four alone—where it should be studied: see verses 3, 4, 5, 6, 8, 9, 10, 11, 22, 23, 24.

Again, this word *logidzomai* is used to express man's belief and consequent attitude as illustrated in Romans 14.14: "To him that reckoneth anything to be unclean, to him it is unclean." Here, we repeat, an expression of belief, and of an attitude in view of that belief, is included in this word. This is its meaning in Chapter 6.11: "Reckon ye also yourselves to be dead unto sin." The belief of the fact and the attitude in view of the belief, are both involved in the word "reckon" in this verse. (Consult note on Chapter 4.3.)

to die to sin: because we are in Christ who did die to it; and therefore we also are *dead* to it, in His death; and reckon it so.

This should make the believer's task simplicity itself. The only difficulty lies in *believing* these astounding revelations! That we should be dead to sin, and now alive unto God as risen ones, sharing that newness of life (verse 4) which our Lord began as "the First-born from among the dead," is at first too wonderful for us. We see in ourselves the old self-life, the flesh—and straightway we forget God's way of faith, and turn back to our "feelings." We say, Alas, if I could escape from this body, I would be free. But that is not at present God's plan for you and me. We *wait* for the redemption of our body. This body is yet unredeemed. Nevertheless, we are to *reckon* ourselves dead unto sin and alive unto God. Not dead to sin, notice, through prayers and strugglings, nor dead to sin in our feelings or consciousness; but *in that death unto sin which Christ went through on the cross,* and which we *shared,* and *in that life* which He now lives in glory!

Indeed, when we come down to verses 12 and 13, we shall find Paul's definite directions to us to present ourselves unto God *"as those that are alive from among dead ones."* (All out of Christ are of course "dead ones," in God's sight.)

This is really the heart of the struggle in the matter of our walk,—of our having our "fruit unto sanctification." It is hard to reckon and keep reckoning that we shared Christ's death to sin, and that we are alive unto God *in Him.* Yet, *there is no establishing of our souls along any other line!* To turn back from this sheer faith that we died with Christ and now are alive to God in Him, is to turn back—to what? to the weary, hopeless struggle Paul tells us in Chapter Seven he "once" went through to make the flesh obey God; or else back to groanings before God, begging Him to give us personal deliverance. And all the time God is saying, *The word of the cross* is the *power of God.* It is God's word as to what was there done that will establish your heart. God says you died with Christ. *Reckon it so.* "If ye will not *believe,* surely ye shall not be established" (Isa. 7.9).*

---

*On our way to the Far East, out in the Indian Ocean, our ship entered on what has always seemed to me the blackest night I have ever known. It was the dark of

Now if the declaration in verse 2 that we died to sin meant that sin is now absent from our flesh, there could be no exhortation in verse 11 to "reckon" ourselves dead to sin. If the fact that we died to sin with Christ means that sin is gone from these bodies of ours, there would be no thought of "reckoning." The statement would simply have been, "Sin is absent,—no longer a present thing with you!" The word *reckon* is a word for *faith*—in the face of appearances.

The same place for faith is left in the matter of our justification. Christ is "the propitiation for the whole world" (I John 2.2). But in Romans 3.25 it is said, "God set Him forth as a propitiation *through faith* in His blood."

So in Romans 6.2 it is said that we *died to sin,* while here in the eleventh verse we are told to *"reckon* ourselves dead to sin." The reckoning does not *make* the fact, but is commanded in view of the fact.

It has pleased God to call for our faith, both in connection with salvation and with deliverance. Therefore, if we would obey and please God, let us follow His method! Let us learn to *reckon ourselves dead,*—that Christ's death to sin was our death; and is the present relation of us who are *in* Christ, unto sin.

The path of faith is always against appearances,—or, if you will, against human consciousness. God says certain things; and we, obeying the "law of faith," say the same things; like Abraham, not regarding our own body, which says the contrary thing. Facts are facts: and these are what God reveals to us. Appearances, or "feelings," are a wholly different thing from facts! God says, "You died to sin: reckon yourself dead!"

---

the moon, and the clouds had hung heavy all day, and now the very pall of darkness! One of the ship's officers invited me to the bridge. Answering the captain's greeting, I said to him, "Do you know where you are?"

"Yes," he said. "We have sailed by 'dead reckoning' all day, and now I will show you where we are." And he took me into the chart room. Bending over the chart, he said, "We are within several miles of where my finger points. We have a watch aloft, of course; but the sea is very deep here; there are no obstacles. We shall sail on through by 'dead reckoning.'"

I laid the lesson to heart. It is difficult to accustom ourselves to "dead-reckoning,"—right through the darkness, in what seems so untrue to the facts of our consciousness. But, obeying God, we reckon ourselves dead to sin, and alive unto Him in Christ Jesus. And God will bring us through!

Obedient souls do so, and enter the path of deliverance in experience. Doubting souls fall back on their "feelings," and turn back to prayers and struggles, avoiding *faith*.

Now note carefully again: the apostle does not tell us to reckon sin dead, but *ourselves* dead to *it*. We are now in Christ, and His history becomes ours. He died unto sin (verse 10), and left the whole sphere of sin forever. It is not said even concerning Christ that He reckoned sin dead, but that being made sin, the thing itself, He *died unto it,* and now liveth unto God. It seems to us most unfortunate that some very excellent teachers fall into the manner of saying that "*sin* is to be reckoned dead" and that "our old man is counted dead and gone," and so forth. One of the clearest teachers of Pauline gospel that I know, though generally speaking accurately, in Paul's language, that we ourselves died to sin, and that the old man is to be regarded as having been crucified with Christ, yet sometimes lapses into such expressions as "we are to hold the old man as dead and gone."

Yet the old man, though having been "crucified with Christ," and having been *"put off"* by the believer, still exists; and believers are commanded to "put away, as concerning your former manner of life, the old man, that waxeth corrupt after the lusts of deceit." We have spoken of this elsewhere. It is of course the intense desire of a saint truly exercised by the Spirit to be quit of the consciousness of the old man. This has been so in all ages. But the temptation is very strong in Christians, in times of great spiritual uplifting, to regard the old man as having disappeared.

But it is the very essence of a holy walk according to Scripture, to receive God's testimony concerning the old man's having been *crucified*. To *reckon* ourselves dead to sin while conscious of sin in our members, is faith indeed; and is walking according to God's Word, instead of according to our feelings. "Those that are of Christ Jesus have crucified the flesh and its lusts": because they know that the federal thing, the "old man," *has* been crucified (Gal. 5.24). It is in the power of the faith that God *has* dealt with all that we were, that we are able to deal with the manifestations of the self-life.

Nevertheless, this life in this present world, is not the Christian's place of resting. Christ will bring him rest at His second coming (II Thess. 1.7).

It is to those who are described in the opening chapters of Romans,—guilty, under Divine judgment; and also in the flesh, under the old man; far from God, without hope,—to such the gospel message has come! These statements that we belong up there, in Christ, are issued by the High Court of Heaven, itself. God says that no matter how things may seem, *we died with Christ,* and *share His newness of life;* and we are to present ourselves unto God as those alive from the dead.*

---

*A *solemn question*:

To those who refuse or neglect to reckon themselves dead to sin as God commands, we press the question, How are you able to believe that Christ really bare the guilt of your sins and that you will not meet them at the judgment day? It is only *God's Word* that tells you Christ bare your sins in His own body on the tree. And it is *that same Word* that tells you that you, as connected with Adam, died with Christ, that your old man was crucified, that since you are in Christ you shared His death unto sin, and are thus to reckon your present relation to sin in Christ—as one who is dead to it, and alive unto God.

If we claim that this is too difficult, because we feel the consciousness of sin dwelling in us, then reflect that it is only by faith that we know that our sin's guilt was borne by Christ. And it is by faith alone that we are to reckon ourselves dead to sin.

Let us beware, then, lest we be found making a secret truce with indwelling sin, while yet hoping to be saved from the guilt of the sins we have committed by Christ's shed blood.

Again, we repeat, if we are in Christ, we are in a Christ who was made to be sin on the cross and died unto it. This, therefore, is our relationship to sin; and God expects all of us to assert by simple obedient faith this revealed fact,—*to reckon ourselves dead unto sin and alive unto God, in Christ Jesus.*

A danger to be avoided:

It is not as having died with Christ that we are justified from the *guilt* of sin; but it is after we have been justified by His blood, as ungodly, that we are told this second great truth,—that our old man was crucified with Christ—that we died with Him. I have seen professing Christians begin to be exercised in conscience regarding the guilt of sin, who, when they heard that those in Christ were *dead* to sin, immediately seized hold of this latter truth, and that with great relief. This false peace lasted, in some cases, a good while, and gave its possessors much complacence and sweetness of spirit, for they went on in secure Christian profession. But, not having been previously really convinced of their personal guilt before God, and consequently not having fled for refuge to the shed blood of Christ, they became finally the very chiefest targets of the devil, and were sometimes driven back into black despair itself.

God had announced, long before, their common guilt with the worst wretches: "None righteous,—no, not one"; "All under sin." But these had somehow slipped in past that message; and had taken hold of this, that they were "dead unto sin." For a true believer, this is a blessed word of deliverance. But for one who is Christianly religious, who has not really rested, as a guilty ungodly one, in Christ's shed blood, this is a truth dangerous above all. And when Satan attacks such souls, what shall they do? They cannot plead "I am dead to sin," against the *devil!* Saints overcome him only by the *blood* of the Lamb. Only the blood of Christ will avail against Satan, or as a real ground of peace, in your own con-

The glorious promise follows: "Sin shall not have dominion over you: for ye are not under law, but under grace." We have not been brought to a Sinai, to a hard, demanding master, but are under the sweet *favor* in which Christ Himself is, being ourselves in Him, yea, the very *righteousness of God in Him!*

> 12 Let not sin, therefore, be reigning-as-king in your mortal body, that ye should obey the desires
> 13 of it [the body]. Neither be presenting your members unto sin as instruments of unrighteousness. But on the contrary present yourselves to God as being alive from among the dead; and your members to God, as instruments of righteous-
> 14 ness. For sin shall not have lordship over you. For you are not under law, but, on the contrary, under grace.

Verse 12: **Do not, therefore, be allowing sin to reign-as-king in your mortal body, that ye should obey the desires of it** (the body):—and the Greek is emphatic: "Be *not at all* allowing sin to reign!"

1. Notice first, our present body is mortal, that is, subject to physical death. We are *waiting* for the redemption of the body, at Christ's coming.

2. Sin is present in our members, and ready to reign-as-king, if permitted. That is, our bodies have not yet been redeemed from the possibility of sin's being king, if we permit such kingship.

3. It is through the lusts or desires of the body that sin is ready to assume control. The body has many desires not in themselves evil. Paul, speaking of foods, says, "All things are lawful for me; but I will not be brought under the power of any" (I Cor. 6.12). It is when natural desires are yielded to in self-will or self-indulgence, that sin uses the desires of the body to assert sin's power and establish its reign.

science (Heb. 9.14). Christ made peace *by the blood of His cross.* If you have not yet learned to rest *in that only,* for eternal peace with God, and as the answer to all Satan's power, let all else alone until you have learned this: if it be at the cost, even, of confessing openly that you have never known true peace before!

4. The believer is directed to reject this reigning of sin, which would involve our obeying the desires of the body.

5. Note the important word, "therefore." This looks back at the first part of Chapter Six, in which our death with Christ unto sin has been asserted, our relationship to sin being now the same as Christ's—we have done with it in death and burial. Notice that these present verses of exhortation are built wholly upon the fact that we died with Christ: we reckon ourselves dead because we participated in Christ's death. Therefore we dare refuse sin's dominion. We owe sin nothing. We are dead to it; justified from it, and living in another sphere!

Verse 13: **Neither be presenting your members unto sin as instruments of unrighteousness. But on the contrary present yourselves to God as being alive from among the dead; and your members to God, as instruments of righteousness.**

The moment we come to exhortation, we have to do with the *will;* whereas believing is a matter of the heart: "With the *heart* man believeth." In learning that I am dead to sin, all I need to do is to listen to God's marvelous unfolding of the fact that I was identified with Christ in His death, and in my heart believe it. My will has nothing to do with that. When God says, "Your old man was crucified with Christ," that is Divine testimony. It is a revealed fact. I hear it and from my heart believe it, because God is true. I reckon myself to be "dead unto sin and alive unto God in Christ Jesus," because God has said that I was.

But when it comes to the *application* of this stupendous fact, my will is addressed: "*Let* not sin therefore reign." Well, some one asks, if I am dead to it, how can it still reign? We answer, By your presenting your bodily members unto sin for sin to use, as "instruments of unrighteousness." Your tongue, for instance, which James calls "an unruly member,"—you have only to hand it over to sin, and it will talk angrily, lyingly, filthily.

Now, what is God's way? *Present yourselves unto God,* as those in a Risen Christ, those "alive from among the dead." Of course, this will test your faith: you will not *feel* dead to sin. Your old man will seem anything but crucified. But the path of true faith is always one of obedience; and God has *commanded* you to reckon yourself dead unto sin, and alive unto Him (as a risen one) in Christ Jesus. It is in this character, of being *alive from the dead,* that you are commanded to *"present* yourselves unto God."

Now two things about this word "present":

First, as to its meaning here: it does not in Chapter Six signify *consecration*: but the taking of an attitude in accordance with the facts. In Chapter Twelve, it is true, the same word is used to signify consecration to God (12.1). But here, "present" (A.V., "yield"), signifies an attitude to be taken in recognition of the facts: "Present yourselves as those alive from among the dead." We are not here looked at as *giving* ourselves to God, but as believingly assuming the aspect toward God of those *in Christ*—those who *died* to sin in Christ's death, and are now alive in Christ unto God.

If the colonel of a certain regiment of soldiers,—say the One Hundredth, should give notice to all his regiment to repair to his headquarters at a stated hour for review, they would "present" themselves there as members of the One Hundredth Regiment. It would be *as such* and in that consciousness that they would come. So believers are to take the attitude toward God of risen ones because they *are* risen ones. They are in Christ, they are alive from among the dead. This is the *fundamental consciousness* of a *believer,* as described in the Pauline Epistles: "If then ye were raised together with Christ, seek the things that are above, where Christ is . . . For ye died, and your life is hid with Christ in God" (Col. 3.1, 3). If you do not have risen life, you are not in Christ; for those in Christ are all *alive from among the dead*.

Second, the command to present ourselves thus unto God is in the aorist tense, which indicates a *definite entering* upon this attitude of presenting ourselves as risen ones to God. As to sin it is, "Do not be presenting (present tense of habitual and continued action) your members unto sin." The exhortation is believingly to take the attitude of a risen one in Christ, and thus present yourself once for all to God. Whether in prayer or thanksgiving, or praise or service, *you are alive from the dead.* It is not that you make yourself alive by presenting yourself unto God; but that since you are *in Christ,* you are alive to God in risen life, and you thus present yourself. And it becomes an habitual attitude,—you keep on presenting your members unto God as a habit of life. He will now use them as "instruments of righteousness"; as, before,—you well remember! your members were instruments of sin.

Then comes a glorious promise, and also a royal pronouncement:

Verse 14: **For sin shall not have dominion over you, for ye are not under law, but under grace.**

Note the two "fors." The first "for" announces the Divine decree that sin's lordship over us shall be ended. The second reveals the happy condition of things in which such a release is possible: we are not under the legal principle,—which first demanded *duty,* and *then* offered blessing; but we are under the grace principle,—which *confers blessing first,* and, behold, fruits follow!

It is deeply significant here that even to us, new creatures in Christ, and recipients of the Holy Spirit, it is definitely announced to us that we are *not under law,*—else bondage and helplessness would still be our lot. Note, God does not say we are not under *the* Law,—the Mosaic Law: (Gentiles never were!) But, God says we are not under *law,*—under the legal principle. In the opening part of Chapter Seven, Paul will show the Jewish believers, (who had been under law), that only death could release them from their legal obligation; and that they had been made dead to the Law, through being identified with Christ in His death.

Only when we believe that our history in Adam, with all its responsibilities and demands to produce righteousness, ended at the cross, shall we find ourselves completely free to enjoy these words of heavenly comfort—UNDER GRACE!*

---

*Many honest souls cannot believe that obedience to God can be secured in any other way than by law. They say, "Set a man completely at liberty, and you cannot control him." But consider:

1. No human being has ever been really controlled by the principle of law. Israel, whom God placed under law, and that "with marvelous and glorious mani

Study carefully the contrast between Romans 6.14 and I
Corinthians 9.21. Paul declares in the former passage, "We
are not under law." The Greek here is, *hupo nomon*. This
expression evidently indicates placing one under external enactments—under that principle. Now in I Corinthians 9.21, Paul,
in describing his ministry to souls, says, "To those without
law (*anomois*), I became as without law (*anomos*), not at all
being without law Godward, but, on the contrary, en-lawed
(*ennomos*) to Christ,"—as the members of a body to the head,
controlled naturally by the one spirit and will.

There is every possible difference between the two,—between
being "under law," and "en-lawed." Israel under law, placed
under the Law at Sinai, with a veil between them and God,
had to think of their behavior, in all its details, as *affecting
their relationship* to God. The Law was "written on tables,"
by the hand of Divine authority. It was external to them:
there was no union between them and Jehovah; nor was the
Holy Spirit within them (although He was upon certain of
them, for certain service, at certain times).

But, with us, all is different. We are in Christ, *members*
of Christ. The Spirit of God's Son, also, has been sent forth
into our hearts, crying, "Abba, Father!" We are "no longer

---

festations of His own presence and authority," immediately renounced the obedience which they had promised.

2. Consider the relationship of a bride and a bridegroom: it is one of love, and
delighted seeking of mutual benefit. It is not a relationship of enactments of law
at all. The husband does not go about the house tacking up rules for the wife to
"observe": and upon the observance of which the relationship shall continue! Such
rules are for servants! Yet, you find the wife eagerly asking the husband what he
would like for dinner, and how, in any other way, she can make him comfortable
and pleased. And all this arises from the principle of love, not law!

3. Now God declares, and that repeatedly, that we have been removed from under the principle of law "in Christ's death." And now, being under grace, we bring
forth "fruit to God." We serve in "newness of the spirit": which can only mean
that, (like the wife thrilled with delight at the prospect of pleasing her husband),
the very *spirit* of service, which is *personal devotion,* animates the believer.

4. But we really have no hope of any person's willingness or ability to see the
power of this newness-of-spirit plan, this love-plan of God's, until such a one has
seen and believed that he died with Christ,—that he was so bad that his entire "old
man" was sent to the cross to be crucified; so that now he is married to Another,
to Him that was raised from the dead, that he may bring forth fruit unto God.

That God can be a Savior-God and not be a Law-giver, is beyond the reach of
the human mind to conceive, and is to be received by faith alone. That in those
not under law is brought about all—and much more! than the Law demands, is fool
ishness to all but faith!

bondservants, but adult sons" (Gal. 4.4-7). Our relationship is settled.*

"Walking by the Spirit," who indwells us, takes for us today the place that observing the things written in the Law had with Israel. "Being dead to the Law, and discharged therefrom," says Paul, "we bring forth fruit unto God"; "We serve in newness of spirit and not in oldness of letter" (7.4, 6).

When Paul says (as above) in I Corinthians that he was "en-lawed to Christ," the Greek word *ennomos* signifies that blessed control by the Holy Spirit proceeding from Christ as the Head, which corresponds to the control of our natural bodies by our physical heads. This, of course, is the very opposite of being "under law" in the sense of verse 14. To speak of a believer's being "under *the* Law to Christ," would be no more true, than to say that your hand has a set of external rules by which it obeys your head and seeks to render itself pleasing to you! No, your hand is *en-lawed* to your head, in that it is one with your head; your spirit dwells in every member of your body, and the head intelligently directs every member.

I am more and more inclined to the belief that in order to a consistent interpretation of the New Testament, we must scrupulously regard *Israel only* as having been placed under

---

*Seven things believers enter into *since the cross,* and *the coming of the Holy Spirit* that were not true of believers before, may be stated here:

1. Sin has been *put away* on the cross. (It had been only "covered" year by year before that.)

2. Our old man has been crucified with Christ,—opening the way for complete deliverance from the power of sin, by the indwelling Spirit.

3. Christ has been glorified (Acts 1.3; John 7.39).

4. The Holy Spirit has been given, at Pentecost, dispensationally; and upon hearing and believing the gospel, individual believers are hereafter sealed by this "Holy Spirit of promise" (Eph. 1.13); who witnesses in them, as "the Spirit of God's Son," their adult sonship.

5. God began at Pentecost to create "new creatures in Christ Jesus" (II Cor. 5.17): "a kind of first-fruits of His creatures" (Jas. 1.18). Christ, the First-born from among the dead, is the Head of this new creation.

6. Believers were, at Pentecost and thereafter, "baptized into one Body," the Body of Christ,—becoming members of Christ and members one of another, a marvelous thing and a new!

7. After Pentecost the "house of God" was not at Jerusalem, but "in the midst" with believers anywhere,—even of twos or threes gathered in Christ's Name: for there He Himself is (Matt. 18.19,20); and there the Holy Spirit is (I Cor. 3.16; Eph. 2.21,22).

The Law, though doubtless all men have moral responsibility.
See Paul regarding this below.*

Whether then it be the Jew under law, or the race of Adam
under conscience, the freedom that is in Christ means deliverance from trying to "be good" to be accepted of God. Sinners
are accepted freely on account of Christ's sacrifice, and placed
in Him Risen. For such, therefore, as are in Christ, the walk
is one of rejoicing *faith,—appropriating Christ,*—and nothing
else. *The Law of Moses has nothing to say to a believer!* We
know the legalists and the pretenders to human righteousness
will cry out at this. But God says about the Law two things
that cannot be escaped:

First, that the Gentiles were not under Moses' Law, that
Law having never been given to them, but to Israel only.

And, second, that God, who gave to Israel the "foregoing
commandment"—the Law—has "disannulled" the same, and
brought in by another way, even simple faith in Christ, "a
better hope," through which alone all believers, Jew or Gentile, "draw nigh to God" (Heb. 7.18,19).

Not *behaving,* but *believing,* is God's way: behaving *follows*
believing!

I know that true faith is a living thing, and has two feet,
and will walk; but it will be *"walking* in works"—not *working*
in works!—"Good works that God afore prepared." Walking
by faith in "prepared" works; discovering in this walk of faith,
the beautiful will of God day by day; treading this fresh and
living path, is the believer's great secret! The children of Abraham all follow their father in walking by faith!

---

*"We [Jewish Old Testament saints, contrasted with Gentile believers] were
kept under the Law . . . The Law was our tutor to lead us unto Christ
—to be justified by faith. But now that faith is come, we [Hebrew believers] are
no longer under a tutor" (Gal. 3.23, 24).

"Ye are severed from Christ, ye who would be justified by the Law; ye are
fallen away from grace" (Gal. 5.4).

"If ye are led by the Spirit, YE ARE NOT UNDER THE LAW"! (Gal.
5.18).

"Christ abolished in His flesh the enmity [between Jew and Gentile], the Law
of commandments contained in ordinances" (Eph. 2.15).

". . . For there is a *disannulling of a foregoing commandment* because of its
weakness and unprofitableness, (for *The Law* MADE NOTHING PERFECT), and
a bringing in thereby of a BETTER hope, through which we draw nigh unto
God" (Heb. 7.12, 14, 18, 19).

The believer is not under law, not under external enactments, not under conditions; but he has already an eternal standing in grace,—that is, in already secured Divine favor, by a sovereign act of God; which has not only reckoned to him Christ's atoning work, but has placed him fully in the place of Christ's present acceptance with God!

The believer today is neither in the Old Testament with the Patriarchs, nor with Israel at Sinai; nor walking with the disciples during our Lord's earthly life and kingdom ministry! The believer lives now *after* the cross, and in the full right and power of all that Christ did there. God gave Israel at Sinai a Law,—a holy, just and good Law, but they kept it not. The Lord Jesus when on earth said to His disciples, "If any man will come after Me, let him deny himself, and take up his cross, and follow Me"; but they all failed and fled. Why? Man was still under testing. The cross ended that; revealing, as it did, utter wickedness in man; and, also, complete weakness in the disciples,—in God's saints!

Then what? Christ is raised from the dead through the glory of the Father: that we may walk in *newness of life*. Not only are our sins forever put away by His blood, but we ourselves find our history in Adam over, we being dead with Christ, crucified with Him.

Then the Holy Spirit is given at Pentecost as the power of this new, heavenly walk. Men were then, for the first time, transferred *into* the Risen Christ. They shared His risen life; for they had been identified with Him as an Adam, a federal man, in His death, at the cross; and were now placed by God in Christ Risen: yea, they were "created," now, in Him; and even made members of His Body,—which, of course, is an additional favor, based on their identification with Him, as an Adam, at the cross.

Now Paul could say, in triumph, "I through law died to law!" "I have not [desire not] the righteousness of law; yet I know nothing against myself." "Thanks be to God, who always leadeth us in triumph in Christ"; "For me to live is Christ"; "Thanks be to God who giveth us the victory through our Lord Jesus Christ." And he could say this right in the

teeth of sin, and of the Law which gave sin its power! (I Cor.
15.56,57). *Both sin and the Law had passed away for Paul,*
at the cross, as victors over *him!*

Yet, alas, most believers are not walking on the resurrection
side of the cross, and by the "new creation rule" of Galatians
6.14,15: "Far be it from me to glory, save in the cross of our
Lord Jesus Christ, through which the world hath been crucified
unto me, and I unto the world. For neither is circumcision
anything, nor uncircumcision, *but a new creation.* And as many
as shall *walk by this rule,* peace be upon them, and mercy!"

If you had been in heaven fifty years, and were then sent
down by God to earth to live and witness for fifty years, then
to be taken back to Heaven:—*how would you live?* Would
you fall under daily doubt as to whether you should count
yourself as belonging to Heaven? Would you not, rather, be
a constant witness, both in walk and word, that you really belonged in and to Heaven?

Now God says He has "made us alive together with Christ
and raised us up with Him, and made us to sit with Him in
the heavenlies in Christ Jesus" (Eph. 2.5,6). Are you going
to try to add to that glorious heavenly calling *the Law,*—that
was given to Israel down here on earth to make them know
their sin? A Law under which God says you are NOT? May
God forbid such folly in any of us! For we all *tend* toward it.

May Colossians 1.5 and 6 be fulfilled in us all: "The word
of the truth of the good news which is come unto you; even
as it is also in all the world bearing fruit and increasing, as
it doth in you also,—since the day ye heard and knew THE
GRACE OF GOD IN TRUTH"!

15   **What then? Are we to sin because we are not
      under law but under grace? Be it not thought of!**

16   **Do ye not know that to whom ye present your-
      selves as bondservants unto obedience, his bond-
      servants ye are whom ye obey,—whether of sin
      unto death, or of obedience unto righteousness?**

17   **But thanks be to God, that whereas ye were
      bondservants of sin, ye became obedient from the**

heart to that pattern of doctrine [salvation by the
cross] unto which you were handed over [by God

18 in the gospel]. And being set free from sin, ye
were made bondservants to righteousness.

19   I am speaking in human terms on account of
the [moral] strengthlessness of your flesh: for just
as ye did present your members as bondservants
to uncleanness, and to lawlessness unto [further]
lawlessness, so now present your members bondservants to righteousness unto sanctification.

20   For when ye were bondservants of sin, ye were
21 free in regard of righteousness. What fruit then
had ye at that time in the things whereof ye are
now ashamed? For the end of those things is

22 death! But now, being made free from sin, and
being put into bondservice to God, ye have your
fruit unto sanctification, and the end, eternal life!

23   For the wages of sin is death; but the free gift
of God is eternal life in Christ Jesus our Lord.

Verse 15: **What then? Are we to sin, because we are not
under law but under grace? Far be the thought!**

Here Paul warns against the abuse of that liberty which the
believer has: He shows that those who commit sin come under
the bondage of sin as *master;* even as the Lord said in John
8.34: "Every one that committeth sin is the bondservant of
sin."

The two questions in Chapter Six: "Are we to continue in
sin that grace may abound?" (verse 1); and, **Are we to sin
because we are not under law but under grace?** (verse 15);
are distinct, but not really diverse, questions. For each con-
siders that same lawlessness, that same independence of the
Creator, which is ever the creature's great temptation. The fact
that these two questions are *written down* here is the proof of
this. Now Paul, with holy abhorrence, repudiates at once both
these thoughts:

The answer to the first question is: We are in the Risen
Christ, and we shared His death; our relation to sin is broken
forever; we walk "in newness of life."

Verse 16: **Do ye not know that to whom ye present yourselves as bondservants unto obedience, his bondservants ye are whom ye obey,—whether of sin unto death, or of obedience unto righteousness?**

And the answer to the second question is: God has set believers free, to serve *Himself*. The only other master is *sin*. And bondage to sin results from serving sin. But the Word of God says to the believer, **Ye are not under law, but under grace.**

Many people who have been convicted of the guilt of sin and have relied on the shed blood of Christ as putting away that guilt, have not yet, however, seen a state of sin as abject *slavery*. The strength of sin is just as real as its guilt. No creature can free himself from the bondage of sin. Sin brought to fallen man the inability to do anything else but sin (Gen. 6.5). Although contrary to conscience, to reason, to desire for liberty; in spite of the terror inspired by the tragic examples about them,—yea, despite awful warnings and expectations of personal impending ruin, men *continue in sin* and its *bondage*.

But there is another "obedience,"—that unto righteousness. And the case turns on the words, **to whom ye present yourselves as servants.** Although we cannot free ourselves, or change our own spiritual condition, the great fact of human responsibility is plainly written here. God, who would have all men to be saved, is always ready to have them present themselves to Him. And it is by means of the gospel that we do so, —whether to take our place as sinners, in the first instance; or, after we have believed, when we present ourselves to Him and our members as instruments of righteousness.

We all know this, be our theological training what it may. We all know we are doing wrong if we do not obey the gospel of God concerning His Son. "When He, the Spirit of truth, is come, He will convict the world in respect of sin . . . because they believe not on Me" (John 16.8,9).

Let us remember then, that the obedience unto righteousness of verse 16, is "the obedience of *faith*," always.

Verses 17, 18: **But thanks be to God, that whereas ye were bondservants of sin, ye became obedient from the**

heart to that pattern of teaching [salvation by the cross]
unto which ye were handed over [by God in the gospel].
**And, being set free from sin, ye were made bondservants to
righteousness.**

Now, our becoming obedient from the heart to the Word of
the cross involves a work of Divine wisdom and power far beyond that involved in the creation of the world! For how shall
a creature remain, and behold his utter judgment on the cross?
How shall he despair eternally of himself, and yet find hope?
How shall he continue a free being and yet consent to be
bound forever,—"with cords of a Man, with bands of love"?
How shall he walk with confidence into the Court where very
thoughts come into judgment? Moral and spiritual impossibilities are greater than physical impossibilities. It was impossible that where nothing at all existed the physical universe
should leap into being—out of nothing but God's word! Man,
having sinned, ran from God. Men yet sin and flee from
God. Now God's holy nature, His infinite righteousness, bar
the way back. But Christ comes, sent of the Father. And
there is the blood of the cross. And from the North and South,
and East and West, men, women,—and children, too, come,
obeying from the heart this impossible news: of peace by the
blood of His cross,—peace for those whose sins slew Christ!
They come to be gladly bound with the unbreakable "bands
of love, the cords of a Man"—Christ Jesus! (See Hos. 11.4.)

And we see that mighty work of response to *grace* in such
hearts abide and endure. We see God's willing "bondservants"
pouring out their lives in glad service, in all lands, to all
limits!

Now, this becoming **obedient from the heart to that
pattern of doctrine** of salvation by the blood of the cross,
and the freedom from sin that goes with it, may be enjoyed
even in this life, "without stint or limit." For "all things
are possible to him that *believeth."*

Note that the Old Version misses the entire sense of this
seventeenth verse in translating: "that form of doctrine which
was delivered unto you," whereas the true rendering is,
that form of doctrine unto which ye were handed over (or,

delivered). For the verb is in the plural—*ye were delivered over!* This statement instructs us deeply in the
Divine arrangements. The Israelites, for example, were
delivered over to Moses and the Law. It was not only that
the Law was delivered by Moses to them; they were themselves delivered over to a legal dispensation—to a "mold of
doctrine," which had the Ten Commandments as the foundation, and the "ten thousand things of the Law" spoken in
accordance therewith. The Jews knew they were *under* the
Law. They had been handed over to it, to its demands, and
to its whole economy. Likewise, believers now are *delivered
over* to a form or pattern of teaching. Summarily, this is *the
Gospel,*—particularly, *the work of Christ on the cross.* Believers have been handed over by God to the mighty facts,
not only that their guilt was put away on the cross, but that
they, as connected with Adam, died with Christ; that their
history in Adam is thus entirely ended before God; and that
they now share the risen life of Christ, and are before God
as risen ones (Romans 6.10, 11). And all believers are comprehended in these great truths, whether they apprehend them
or not! It is the first duty of every teacher of God's saints
to open to them the glorious *facts* already true *about* them,
and unto which great mold or form of doctrine, they have
been "delivered over" by God.*

Now in verse 17 we see that these Roman believers had
**become obedient from the heart unto this mold of doc-
trine,**—that of salvation by Christ on the cross. They had
yet much to learn concerning their salvation, (and Paul
was coming to "establish" them). But they had seen and

---

*The word "delivered" is the word constantly used, for instance, of our Lord's
being handed over to His enemies (Matt. 20.18, 19; John 19.11, 16); and of the
disciples' being delivered over to councils (Matt. 10.17, 19). It is used of the
Jews' being "delivered over to serve the host of heaven," in Acts 7.42 (most significant as to its force in Rom. 6.17); and I Corinthians 11.23 contains the word
in both its significances: Paul *delivered over* to the Corinthians directions concerning the Lord's supper; Christ was *delivered over* to His enemies. It is the same
Greek word in both cases.

This distinction is vital, because people conceive of the Gospel as something delivered to them to "live up to," or to lay hold of by their own wills, rather than
as of a body of truth *unto which they, as believers,* have already been blessedly
handed over! "Obedience of faith" can be nothing else than walking in the light
of *facts Divinely revealed.*

accepted redemption by the blood of the despised Lamb of God: which involved *everything*,—of separation from a sinful world, as well as of safety from Divine judgment.

Verse 18: **Being set free from sin, ye were made bond-servants to righteousness.** It will help us to note carefully that in this verse is the first description of "experience" in this Sixth of Romans. But it is the result of that "obedience of faith" in which these believers had received the good news of their salvation by Christ crucified; for lo! they found themselves thereby "set free from sin,"— sin was no longer their *master*.*

Verse 19: **I am speaking in human terms on account of the [moral] strengthlessness of your flesh**—Paul here explains why he is using this word "bondservants" throughout this passage. He declares the "infirmity of our flesh" to be such, that we *must* necessarily be *in bondservice*—either to sin or to God. Rome was full of slaves,—indeed, many of the Christians to whom he was writing were slaves, as seems to be indicated in Chapter Sixteen (which see). In the Roman Empire, freedom was a most difficult thing to secure (Acts 22.28). So Paul speaks **in human terms,** "after the manner of men," and he says that we are strengthless naturally, that we must be servants, either of God or of sin.

Man hates this fact. He boasts his independence, whether it be in the realm of intellect—"free thought!" in the matter of private wealth—"independent!" or in the manner of government—"free!" But it is all really a delusion. We indeed rejoice at the intellectual shackles thrown off at the Renaissance, and at liberty of thought and expression, wherever found among men. We also honor those who, like Boaz, are "mighty men of wealth,"—for God has permitted it to be so; and we re-

---

*To make the words "free from sin" of Chapter 6.18 denote what is called "eradication of the sin-principle," a sinlessness in the flesh, is a terrible perversion. Paul constantly preached and testified the contrary. Our bodies will not be redeemed (no matter how much we may be blessed or filled with the Holy Spirit) until "the redemption of the body" at Christ's second coming. Till that time, sin will be in the flesh, although those who "obey from the heart" in simple faith that word of the cross unto which they have been delivered, will find themselves in a state of blessed relief from sin's bondage. For Scripture does teach *heart*-cleansing, a "pure heart," as we have elsewhere shown.

joice at that relief from governmental tyranny which is yet found in some parts of this earth.

But what we most earnestly assert is that not only Paul here, but our Lord Himself, and Scripture generally, sets forth that *only those that know the truth and walk therein, are free.* The Jews (in John 8.33 ff) horribly rebel against our Lord's saying: "If ye abide in My word, then are ye truly My disciples: and ye shall know the truth, and the truth shall *make you free! . . .* Every one that committeth sin is the bond-servant of sin. . . If the Son shall make you free, ye shall be free indeed." There is no freedom out of Christ. "Whose service is perfect freedom" is the beautiful expression of obedience to God.

We must see this necessity of service to God or service to sin for our own lives. When John wrote to believers, "We know that we are of God, and the whole earth lieth in the evil one" (I John 5.19),—what a revelation was *that!*

These Roman Christians had formerly, like the pagans among whom they lived, **presented their members bond-servants to uncleanness** [in every inward thought], **and to lawlessness unto** [further] **lawlessness** [in outward practice]. A blacker page of iniquitous abominations history does not write than that of the Roman Empire of Paul's day. And out of these fearful states of sin, God had delivered these believers! Compare I Corinthians 6.9 to 11.

Verses 20 and 21: **For when ye were bondservants of sin, ye were free in regard of righteousness. What fruit had ye at that time in the things whereof ye are now ashamed? For the end of those things is death!**

And in those former evil days, they had been, as Paul says, **free in regard of righteousness.** They were altogether given to iniquity, without any check whatever.* And those were **fruitless days of which they were now ashamed.** Free and fruitless! what a pair of words to describe the life of one who is going on daily toward eternity! Let each believer look back to those days when God was

---

* "There seems to be a grave but cutting irony in this allusion to their old condition, when the only freedom they knew was in respect to righteousness! They were slaves of sin, and had nothing to do with righteousness!"

"not in all his thoughts." The pleasures and treasures of sin we sought—free in regard of righteousness, like the beasts which perish. What saved one can say of his unsaved life, I can treasure this or that as fruit? of any particular iniquity, I cherish good results from it? **What fruit had you? Shame,** only: **things of which ye are now ashamed.** Furthermore, we were going on steadily in that path unto the end, which was death, and that eternal. Remember the relentless but true description of sin's horrid birth and end, in James 1.14,15.

Now from all this, God has in sovereign grace rescued us, and should we not, do we not, gladly enter upon the path of loving service, yea, bondservice, to Him?

Verse 22: **But now,** having been freed from the fearful Master, Sin, and brought into a sweet, willing bondservice to God, there was not only the daily delightful fruit, which those given over to sanctification were ever bearing; but there was the consciousness that every day brought nearer, the full realization of that blessed **eternal life,**—which they already possessed, but the full enjoyment of which was **the end** of the path of God's saints!

They were now and would be forever under the domination of that motive which is the strongest of all,—LOVE. Their service to God would be no longer one of seeking to fulfil certain enactments by Him (as under law) but a glad willingness, such as Christ expressed toward His Father in the prophetic words of Psalm 40.8: "I delight to do Thy will, O my God!" There is no relief comparable to this surrender to the all-wise and all-loving *will* of God! Our Lord prescribes for those "laboring and heavy-laden," first, to come to Him, and He will *give* them rest (that is, salvation); and then, having come, to *take His yoke upon them* (the yoke of Him who is meek and lowly in heart) and they shall *find* rest to their souls (that is surrender)!

Verse 23: For sin, which they had once served, was a *terrible Paymaster*! **Sin's wages was death,**—appointed so by God Himself. What a hideous employer—Sin! What a horrid service! What hellish wages! Yet sin is the chosen master of all but Christ's "little flock"! Of sin's flock, it is written: "Death shall be their shepherd."

Death, as we read in verse 23, is the "wages of sin." Men speak of it lightly. But it is indeed "the king of terrors" for the natural man (Job 18.14). A well-known writer says: "Man finds in Death an end to every hope, to every project, to all his thoughts and plans. The busy scene in which his whole life has been, knows him no more. His nature has given way, powerless to resist this master (death) to which it belongs, and who now asserts his dreadful rights. But this is far from being all. Man indeed, as man alive in this world, sinks down into nothing. But why? Sin has come in; with sin, conscience; with sin, Satan's power; still more with sin, God's judgment. Death is the expression and witness of all this. It is the wages of sin, terror to the conscience, Satan's power over us, for he has the power of death. Can God help here? Alas, it is His own judgment on sin. Death seems but as the proof that sin does not pass unnoticed, and is the terror and plague of the conscience, as witness of God's judgment, the officer of justice to the criminal, and the proof of his guilt in the presence of coming judgment. How can it but be terrible? It is the seal upon the fall and ruin and condemnation of the first Adam. And he has nothing but this old nature.

"But Christ has come in. He has come into death—O wondrous truth, the Prince of life! What is death now for the believer? 'Death is ours,' says the apostle, as all things are. By the blessed Lord's entering into it for me, death,—and judgment too, is become my salvation. The sin, of which it was the wages, has been put away by death itself. The judgment has been borne for me there."

But the grace-bestowal (*charisma*) of God—here is the same dear word as in Chapter 5.15 and 16. It is the expression which describes what is behind God's gift,—his *grace* (Greek, *charis*). And what is, here, God's grace-bestowal? **Eternal life in Christ Jesus our Lord!** What a bestowment of grace is this! Sins borne, pardoned, gone,—and more! A welcome in Heaven,—and more! Life granted to a lost soul dead in sins,—and more! *Eternal* life,—to last as long as God

its Giver. But more,—life in Christ Jesus our Lord Himself!
Sharing His life, who is the Well-Beloved of the Father,
sharing "the love wherewith God hath loved Christ." Life,
eternal life, in Christ Jesus,—God's grace-gift!

The wages of sin as over against **the free gift of God!**

Mark this, that God will *keep the contrast constantly before
us,* even at the end of this chapter, between what is *earned*
and what is *given.* In verses 21 and 22, "the end" of two paths
is seen: one, **death**; the other, **eternal life.** But it must
finally be said here, at the chapter's close, that while death
is earned wages, *eternal life* is a **FREE GIFT!**

And also note the blessed Sphere of this Eternal life:
In Christ Jesus our Lord. Every advance in the glorious
truth of salvation is marked by Christ's own Name!—from
His being "set forth" by God as "Christ Jesus,—a propitiation
through faith in His blood (3.24,25); raised as Jesus our
Lord from the dead (4.24); our exulting in God through our
Lord Jesus Christ (5.11); and grace reigning through right-
eousness and eternal life through Jesus Christ our Lord
(5.21); reckoning ourselves dead unto sin, but alive unto God
in Christ Jesus (6.11); and now the gift of God, eternal life
in Christ Jesus our Lord (6.23). And victory will come, in
Chapter 7.25: "I thank God through Jesus Christ our Lord."
And, at last, no separation "from *the love of God which is in
Christ Jesus our Lord"!* (8.39).

A FEW WORDS ABOUT GRACE

I

The Nature of Grace

1. Grace is God acting freely, according to His own nature
as Love; with no promises or obligations to fulfil; and acting
of course, righteously—in view of the cross.

2. Grace, therefore, is *uncaused* in the recipient: its cause
lies wholly in the *GIVER, in GOD.*

3. Grace, also is *sovereign.* Not having debts to pay, or
fulfilled conditions on man's part to wait for, it can act toward
whom, and how, it pleases. It can, and does, often, place the
worst deservers in the highest favors.

4. Grace cannot act where there is either *desert* or *ability*: Grace does not *help*—it is *absolute, it does all.*

5. There being *no cause* in the creature why Grace should be shown, the creature must be brought off from *trying to give cause* to God for His Grace.

6. The discovery by the creature that he is truly the object of Divine grace, works the *utmost humility*: for the receiver of grace is brought to know his own absolute unworthiness, and his complete inability to attain worthiness: yet he finds himself blessed,—*on another principle, outside of himself!*

7. Therefore, *flesh has no place* in the plan of Grace. This is *the great reason why Grace is hated* by the proud natural mind of man. But for this very reason, the true believer rejoices! For he knows that "in him, that is, in his flesh, is no good thing"; and yet he finds God glad to bless him, just as he is!

II
The Place of Man under Grace

1. He has been accepted *in Christ,* who *is* his standing!
2. He is not "on probation."
3. As to his life past, *it does not exist* before God: he *died* at the Cross, and *Christ is his life.*
4. Grace, once bestowed, is *not withdrawn:* for God knew all the human exigencies beforehand: His action was independent of them, not dependent upon them.
5. The failure of devotion does not cause the withdrawal of bestowed grace (as it would under law). For example: the man in I Cor. 5.1-5; and also those in 11.30-32, who did not "judge" themselves, and so were "judged by the Lord,—that they might *not* be condemned with the world"!

III
The Proper Attitude of Man under Grace

1. To *believe,* and to consent to be *loved while unworthy,* is the great secret.
2. To refuse to make "resolutions" and "vows"; for that is to trust in the flesh.

3. To expect to be blessed, though realizing more and more lack of worth.

4. To testify of God's goodness, at all times.

5. To be certain of God's future favor; yet to be ever more tender in conscience toward Him.

6. To rely on God's chastening hand as a mark of His kindness.

7. A man under grace, if like Paul, has no burdens regarding himself; but many about others.

IV

Things Which Gracious Souls Discover

1. To "hope to be better" is to fail to see yourself *in Christ only*.

2. To be *disappointed* with yourself, is to have *believed* in yourself.

3. To be *discouraged* is *unbelief,*—as to God's purpose and plan of blessing for you.

4. To be *proud,* is to be *blind!* For we have no standing before God, in *ourselves*.

5. The lack of Divine blessing, therefore, comes from *unbelief,* and not from *failure of devotion*.

6. Real *devotion* to God arises, not from *man's will* to show it; but from the discovery that blessing *has been received* from God while we were yet *unworthy and undevoted*.

7. To preach devotion first, and blessing second, is to reverse God's order, and preach *law, not grace*. The Law made man's blessing depend on devotion; Grace *confers undeserved, unconditional* blessing: our devotion may follow, but does not always do so,—in proper measure.

Baptism in Romans not Baptism by the Spirit

As to the Holy Spirit's "baptizing us all into one Body" (I Cor. 12.13): we are said indeed to be baptized by Him into the Body,—but only *after* we died with *Christ made sin:* —a theological distinction, no doubt, but a most necessary one.

Christ as Head of the Body, the Church, comes after Christ as the Second Man, the Last Adam. It would not be accurate, or indeed, possible, to speak of Christ as the Head of the Body bringing about our death with Him, any more than to say that Christ as the Head of the Body had borne our sins. The Body, the Church, came *after Christ,* as the Last Adam, had put away our sin, and by His "one act" constituted us righteous; and after we had died with *Christ made sin.*

In a man's history before God, he is not made a member of Christ's Body before he has died with Christ made sin! Let us trace this:

1. An ungodly man, as such, believes on God about Christ, and is justified,—declared righteous.

2. His justification, however, involved the resurrection of the Lord Jesus Christ, who was "delivered up for his trespasses, but was raised for his justifying" (Romans 4.25).

3. His justification, therefore, becomes what is called in Chapter 5.18 "justification *of life.*"

4. Now, it is not as a member of Christ's mystical Body that we can assert justification of him. Doubtless he *is* made member of Christ Risen, but,

5. When he is told to reckon himself dead unto sin and alive unto God in Christ Jesus, it is not as a member of Christ's Body that he is thus to reckon, but as one who was in Adam, on whose behalf Christ was made to be sin and died unto sin.

6. Doubtless by one Spirit we are all baptized into one Body, and are made to drink of the one Spirit; but this truth of I Corinthians 12 is not *fundamental* truth, but *positional* truth. A man cannot say, Because I am a member of Christ's Body, therefore I am made dead to sin. But he can say, I was in Adam the First, guilty, a man "in the flesh," in "the old man." But by God's grace I am now in *Christ,* the Last Adam. This is *fundamental* truth. And it is fundamental truth that Romans contemplates. As we state elsewhere, there will be saved Israelites, and others, besides Church saints, who will partake of the benefits of Christ's death and resurrection; but who will not be of the Body of Christ.

7. Therefore, in carrying out the believer's walk as directed in Roman's Six to Eight, we must go back of and beyond our consciousness of the Body of Christ, to *Christ as an Adam,* **a** *federal, representative* Man. Our *standing* is in Christ as the Last Adam; our *membership,* in that blessed corporate company called the Body of Christ, Christ being the Head.

In other words, we had no right to be put into Christ the Head of the Body until we had died with Christ made sin, died to our position in the other Adam. You will notice when Paul describes his personal manner of life, he says: "I have been crucified with Christ, and it is no longer I that live, but Christ liveth in me." This is not Body truth, but federal truth, which is fundamental. Body truth comes after federal truth. Federal truth has to do with our relationship to God. We are either in Adam or in Christ, before God.

Only in Romans 12.4, 5 is the Body of Christ referred to; for Romans is fundamental, and deals with our relation to God,—as in Adam or in Christ; and therefore does not deal with the corporate character of the Church as such.

CHAPTER SEVEN

Release from the Legal Principle Illustrated: Jewish Believers, to whom the Law of Moses was given, Dead to that Law by Identification in Death with Christ Made Sin; now joined to the Risen Christ: thus Bearing Fruit to God and Rendering Glad Service. Verses 1-6.

Paul's Vain Struggle to be Holy by the Law,—Before he knew of Indwelling Sin and his Helplessness against it; and that he had Died with Christ to Sin, and to the Law, which gave Sin power. Verses 7-24.

Deliverance seen through Christ; and the Flesh declared Hopeless. Verse 25.

1 Or are ye ignorant, brethren (for I speak to men acquainted with law), that the law rules over a man as long as he liveth?

2 For the woman that hath a husband is bound by law to the husband while he liveth; but if the husband die, she is discharged from the law of the

3 husband. So then, if while the husband liveth, she be joined to another man, she shall be called an adulteress: but, if the husband die, she is free from the law, so that she is no adulteress, though she be joined to another man.

4 Wherefore, my brethren, ye also were made dead to the Law, through the body of Christ, that ye should be joined to Another,—to Him who was raised from among the dead, that we might bring forth fruit unto God.

5 For when we were in the flesh, the passions of sins which were through the Law wrought in our

6 members to bring forth fruit unto death. But now we have been annulled from the Law, having died to that wherein we were held: so that we serve in newness of spirit, and not in oldness of letter.

HERE WE HAVE a chapter of two sections,—(1) verses 1 through 6; and (2) verses 7 through 25: both of which we are prone to misunderstand and misapply, unless we exercise much prayerful care.

In the first section, God shows how those that were placed by Him under law were released from that relation by sharing in the death of Christ; so that, joined to a Risen Christ, they bear fruit; and, released from law, they give glad and willing service.

In the second section, we have Paul describing his struggle under the Law, as a converted Israelite, before he knew the great facts of this first part,—that in Christ he was *dead* to the Law: "I was alive apart from law *once*." It is the struggle of one that is born again, and "delights in the Law of God," seeking to compel the flesh to obey God's Law. The end, of course, is a cry of utter despair (for the Law was a "ministration of death") ; and a new view of Christ, as the One through whom is found deliverance from sin's power and from the Law that gave it that power !*

The Gospel-Announcement of Chapter Seven: Dead to and Discharged from Law

Verse 1: Or—the opening word of verse 1 connects the first six verses of Chapter Seven directly with verse 14 of Chapter Six, "Ye are not under law but under grace." (For the last part of Chapter Six is parenthetical,—a warning against abuse of our "not under law" position.) Therefore connect these words "Ye are not under law" with the "Or" of verse 1, Chapter Seven. Conybeare aptly paraphrases: "You must acknowledge what I say, (that we are not under law) or be ignorant," etc.

---

*"I," "me," "myself" are used 47 times in the 19 verses of Chapter Seven,—capital "I" 28 times! In Chapter Eight, "me" occurs once; and that, "Christ made *me* free"; "I" twice, and that, "I reckon that the sufferings of this present time are not worthy to be compared with the glory which shall be revealed to us-ward"; and, "I am persuaded that nothing shall be able to separate us from the love of God."

In Chapter Eight "we," "us," "our," and like words occur 41 times! For in Chapter Eight we are conscious at last of the blessed indwelling Spirit: and so, *of all other saints.* While the *legal* struggle is carried on in a terrible loneliness.

The King James, by its failure to translate the chapter's opening word "Or," to which God gives the emphatic position in this argument, obscures the whole meaning of the passage and context. Unless we connect Chapter 7.1 with Chapter 6.14, (as the proper translation "*or*" does), we cannot properly understand the passage.

Are ye ignorant, brethren—Some one remarks that when Paul uses this expression concerning the saints, it often turns out that they are ignorant! (Compare Rom. 6.3; 11.25; I Thess. 4.13, etc.)

(For I speak to men acquainted with law)—In this first verse it is law in general,* because this whole verse is connected with Chapter 6.14: "Ye are are not under law," (not under that principle) referring, of course, to all believers.

That the law rules over a man as long as he liveth—Paul here declares that the claims of law endure throughout a man's life,—death being the only deliverance. The Roman world well knew the reach and authority of human law—of which Paul is here speaking.

Verses 2,3: **For the woman that hath a husband**—Here Paul uses the fundamental law of domestic relationship to illustrate the fact that only death breaks a legal bond. This is the evident, simple meaning in this passage. This husband-and-wife illustration is marvelously chosen. It is of world-wide application—instantly understood everywhere; and it sets forth perfectly what the apostle desired—that is, to describe the dissolution of a relationship by death, thus making possible a new relationship.

Now the simple, and to me obvious path of interpretation is to proceed immediately to the fourth verse, spending no more time on verses 2 and 3 than will suffice to appreciate their force as an illustration of the fact announced in verse 1, that only death breaks a legal claim. We should proceed, therefore, according to the principle illustrated in verses 2 and 3, to the application of the principle in the case of those

---

*When "law" as a principle is spoken of, we have used the small "l"; when the Mosaic Law is evidently meant, a capital "L"; and when the use of the latter is emphatic, we have several times written it "The Law."

believers who had been openly placed by God under a *law:* that is, Jewish believers.

For, in the example of the woman and her husband, there seems no real intention on Paul's part, other than to set forth the fact that death ends a relationship, and sets one free to enter upon a new relationship; as we have, to Christ Risen.

If Adam was our federal head, Christ now is so. And this was made possible by *our death with Christ made sin.*

The obligation that governed our former condition as in Adam, no longer calls for righteousness or holiness of our own in the flesh: we have died as to that place in Adam; and are in the Second Man, the last Adam, Christ,—who is Himself our righteousness and sanctification.

If we undertake to apply verses 4 to 6 directly to any but Jewish believers, we encounter this difficulty: that it is distinctly said, and that repeatedly, that the Jews, being under the Law, were in contrast to the Gentiles, who were "without law." These verses then must first be applied to those who were under the Law, knew themselves to be under it, and were exercised by its commands. Otherwise verse 5 becomes unintelligible:

When we [Jewish believers] **were in the flesh** [they were now in Christ, and so in the Spirit] **the arousings of sins which were *through the Law* wrought in our members to bring forth fruit unto death.**

These words would not be written by Paul concerning Gentiles, but they express exactly the state of Jewish believers as exemplified in the latter part of our chapter.

And now for the gospel, which lies in verses four and six:

Verse 4: **Wherefore my brethren, ye also were made dead to the Law through the body of Christ.**

As touching Gentile believers, this latter fact was to be reckoned on for the disannulling (Chapter 6.6) of "the body of sin," relieving them of sin's bondage. But for the Jewish believer, there was the additional fact that he was under the Law, which bound his conscience, and gave sin very peculiar power over him. For he must obey the Law, for it had been given his nation by Jehovah, and they had covenanted at Sinai to let their obedience be the condition of their relationship to Him.

To the Jewish believer, then, the announcement is now directly made that he was **made dead to the Law through the body of Christ, in order to be to Another, to the risen Christ, thus to bring forth fruit to God;** and that **he has been** [verse 6] **discharged from the Law** [literally, annulled with respect to the Law], thus bringing him out into **service in newness of spirit.*** This was the startling announcement made to those who, for 1500 years had known nothing but the Law: they had died to it all; the Law knew them no more.

Now what Paul affirms in Romans 6.14 covers, of course, both the Gentile and Jewish believer: "Ye are NOT UNDER LAW": that is, not under that principle in **any** sense. The Gentiles had moral obligations as responsible children of Adam, though not under the Law, indeed, "without law." There was the work of the Law in their hearts (as we saw in Chapter Two), with which their consciences bore witness. To Gentiles, therefore, the announcement that in Christ they are not at all under the principle of law, sets them free to delight in Christ, and to surrender to the operations of the Holy Spirit within them. The additional announcement is made to those under the Mosaic Law that they have the same liberty, **having died to that wherein they were held.**

The great lesson which each of us must lay to his own heart, is, that those in Christ, whether Jew or Gentile, are not under law as a principle, but under *grace,*—full, accomplished Divine *favor*—that favor shown by God to Christ! And the life of the believer now is (1) in faith, not effort: as Paul speaks in Galatians 2.20: "The life which I now live in the flesh, *I live in faith,* the faith which is in the Son of God"; (2) *in the power of the indwelling Spirit;* for walking by the Spirit has

---

*The expressions dead to the Law (vs. 4) and discharged from the Law (vs. 6) cannot possibly be referred directly to Gentiles, who had never been alive to the Law—it never having been given to them; and who could not be discharged therefrom, because they were not under it.

taken the place of walking by external commandments; and (3) exercising ourselves to have a good conscience toward God and men always: particularly, not wrongly using our freedom.

While the form of the language in the first six verses makes it evident that the Mosaic Law was before Paul's mind, at the same time it is of profit to us because: (1) We all have a moral responsibility to produce a righteousness and holiness before God and we cannot; (2) Both Jew and Gentile are included in the tremendous statement of Chapter 6.6, "our old man was crucified."

Through the body of Christ—This is a peculiar manner of speech. God speaks not here of propitiation or justification, which are through the blood of Christ (Rom. 3.25; 5.9; Eph. 1.7). But God speaks here of that identification with Christ in which, in God's view, all believers were brought to the end of their history at the cross, so that their former relationships (to sin, law, the world), are ended. It is to be noted that both concerning Christ's death *for* us, and our death *with* Christ, Christ's own body is mentioned. As to the first, we remember I Peter 2.24: "Who His own self bare our sins in His body upon the tree." And as to the second, the present verse: **made dead . . . through the body of Christ.***

That ye should be joined to Another, to Him who was raised from among the dead. The great lesson to learn in this whole passage lies in what we might call the two Christs: first, there is "the body of Christ," of *Christ made sin,* and our old man crucified with Him: our history in Adam thus ended before God; and, second, *Christ raised from the dead.*

---

*To any one who has examined their writings, there is the inescapable conclusion that the Reformed theologians—truly godly men—have kept the vision of believers confined generally to the propitiatory work of Christ, not seeing—at least, not setting forth clearly, the ending of our history in identification with Christ,—thus freeing us from sin, law, and the old creation, and setting us wholly on resurrection ground, in Christ Jesus.

God's identifying us with Christ in His death was just as sovereign an act as was God's transferring our sins to Christ. It did not proceed from His incarnation: for He was "holy," and "separated from sinners." There was absolutely no union with sinful humanity except at the cross! There was no "union with humanity" with Christ in His earthly life! We would be horrified at the teaching that Christ was bearing our sins from His incarnation! But, if these were "laid on Him" at the cross, so also was "our old man" then, at the cross, and not before, so identified with Him as to be crucified with Him. It was God's sovereign, inscrutable act, in both matters: done at the cross, not before!

It is this latter Christ to whom we are now vitally united, to Him only.

That we might bring forth fruit unto God. In this Risen Christ, as we saw in Chapter 6.22: "Ye have your fruit unto sanctification"; or Philippians 1.11; "being filled with the fruits of righteousness which are through Jesus Christ," brought about—made to bud, blossom, grow and ripen, through the indwelling Spirit: or "the fruit of the Spirit is love, joy, peace, longsuffering, kindness, goodness, faithfulness, meekness, self-control" (Gal. 5.22)—what a cluster of grapes that is: fruit unto God, indeed!

Now—however the principle may apply to all believers—Paul evidently, in verses 4, 5 and 6, has the Jew under the Law definitely before him; for he says "Ye were made dead to the Law." It is implicitly asserted here that those under law could not bring forth fruit to God. Because, in order to bring forth such fruit, they had to be made dead to the Law. This cannot be sufficiently emphasized, for all about us we find those who are earnestly seeking to bear fruit to God, while "entangled with the yoke of bondage," not knowing themselves dead to the legal principle.

But before our very eyes those publicly placed under law, yea the Mosaic Law directly from God, did not bring forth fruit in that condition. Else would God have had them die wholly out of that position with Christ on the cross?

No, it is only those who see themselves to have died with Christ and to be now joined to a Risen Christ in glory, that fully bring forth fruit to God.

It is a glorious day when a believer sees himself only in a Risen Christ—dead, buried and risen; and can say with another, "I am not in the flesh, not in the place of a child of Adam at all, but delivered out of it by redemption. The whole scene of a living man, this world in which the life of Adam develops itself, and of which the Law is the moral rule, I do not belong to, before God, more than a man who died ten years ago out of it."

Verse 5: For when we were in the flesh, the passions of sins which were through the Law wrought in our members

to bring forth fruit unto death. Now in this one verse is seen the whole of the great struggle detailed by the apostle in the latter part of this chapter: **When we were in the flesh**—Note, it does not say, in the *body,* for we are all that! Being in the body has no moral significance, but the words are, **in the flesh**—the condition of those not saved, as we see from Chapter 8.8, 9: "For ye are not in the flesh but in the Spirit, if so be that the Spirit of God dwelleth in you." This does describe a moral state or condition,—absence of life, absence of the Holy Spirit, and control by the fallen nature.

The passions of sins which were through the Law—To those in the flesh controlled by the evil nature through a body dead to God, legal restraint was intolerable. As we shall see in the last part of the chapter, sin was there, but quiescent, until the Law came, demanding obedience and holiness. Thus came **the arousings** [or passions] **of sins**—sins of all sorts. It is evident that the Jew who had the Law, is distinctly and especially before the apostle's mind here. For these words could not be written of "Gentiles who have not the Law" (2.14, 15); although these very two verses assert that there was a "work" written in the hearts of the Gentiles, which is called "the work of the Law," unto which their consciences bear fellow-witness. (See carefully, comment on Chapter 2.14.) Nevertheless, it cannot be said that verse 5 describes accurately any but an Israelite to whom the Law was given, and in whom the commandments of that Law directly aroused the opposition of sin in the flesh.

Wrought in our members to bring forth fruit unto death —Even in the last part of the chapter, in Paul's great struggle—after he is saved, we find a law of sin in his members, against which he is powerless, and which would have engulfed him in everlasting hopelessness, except for the revelation of deliverance in Christ. Here, in verse 5, where an unsaved man, a man in the flesh, is in view, **fruit unto death** is brought forth by those "arousings of sins" which came through the Law.

Verse 6: **But now we have been annulled from the Law, having died to that wherein we were held: so that we serve in newness of spirit,and not in oldness of letter.**

This word which we have rendered **annulled**, is Paul's old word *katargeo*,—"put out of business." In Chapter Six we read that "our old man was crucified with Him in order that the body of sin might be annulled"—put out of business. That blessed message could be given to all believers, Jew or Gentile. For it is a federal one, as the words "our old man" reveal. But the Jew had not only the body of sin: he had distinctly given to him the Mosaic Law. Therefore it is written, in Chapter 7.6, that he has been annulled, put out of business, from that Law, having died* to it.

The Law which once "held" him now had nothing to do with him, for he had been put out of the Law's domain, out of the place of business in which the Law operated, that is, on natural children of Adam, on men in the flesh. What a glorious deliverance!

Now let us who are Gentile believers most carefully note two things: (1) that the Jewish believer, who was put publicly, and under sanctions of death, under the Law, by God at Sinai, has been declared by that same God to have died to that wherein he was held, so that the Law has no more business with him. (2) That therefore, however deeply taught by tradition that we Gentile believers are under law, we must throw that tradition all away. For if the Jew, who was Divinely placed under the Law, has been made dead to it and discharged therefrom, put out of the sphere and domain of the Law, then what presumption for a Gentile to claim that he is under that Law before God!

So that we serve!—Wonderful paradoxes of the gospel! In verse 4, having died, they bear fruit; and here, having been discharged, they serve. What an unspeakable satisfaction filled the apostle's heart, at finding himself serving God, in all the capacities of his love-filled being, the more he felt his complete freedom from that Law that once

---

*Note that the King James Version **wrongly** renders that the Law died. But the verb number is plural, as the Revised Version and all the best mss. read. It was believers who died, not the Law!

"held" him. In the old days, it was, "I verily thought I ought to do"; now it is, "I delight to do." As we say elsewhere, the instructed believer finds himself doing the will of God *as it is in heaven,* that is, in the very spirit of service, and not by forms, or ordinances — which are earthly "rudiments." **Oldness of letter** it once was—minute particulars of legal observances according to the tradition of the fathers; **newness of spirit** it had become when the apostle learned that he had died out to the whole legal sphere, to the Adam-position—man in the flesh,* unto whom the Law had been given at Sinai.

Truly Paul could say to his Jewish fellow-believers, God has here, concerning the Law, conferred on us a heavenly degree of D.D.: "Dead, Discharged." (Beware that you do not turn into an LL.D. and go about "desiring to be teachers of the Law, understanding neither what you say, nor whereof you confidently affirm!" (I Tim. 1.7.)

---

*But inasmuch as the endeavor is widely made to make the Law "the first husband," it seems well to urge the fact that this would be to depart from the illustration entirely.

For the fact to be illustrated is, that law rules humanity till death. The illustration is this universal one of a woman bound *by law* to a husband: not *to the Law* as a husband! Death now intervenes, and "the law of the husband" binds her no more. The Law was seen only as governing a relationship,—between husband and wife. A common conception would make the Law the husband! But the husband and wife are both ruled over by law: and if we make the Law the husband, what law would be over *that* Law? Furthermore, it is said, "if the husband die." This word excludes all idea of the Law being a husband: for God's Law does not die. God would not speak thus.

And again, if we are to carry out this illustration, we must find one with whom the person to be set free (here called "the woman") is lawfully connected, and that connection broken by death. Now who, or what, is this?

Does not the whole passage—from Chapter 5.12 onward tell us plainly? With whom were we first connected except Adam the first? All our standing and our responsibilities were in him. Our relation to him was such as nothing but death could break! We were responsible to furnish God a perfect righteousness and holiness in the flesh. No matter if we *could not*: we *ought* to do so. Our inability does not at all diminish our responsibility.

Now, what did God do? "Our old man was crucified." We shared Christ's death as made sin for us. We died to our whole position in Adam, and to our obligations connected with him.

However, inasmuch as the Mosaic Law was a complete economy under which God placed His chosen nation, we do not wonder that many who carry the illustration to its limits have regarded the Law as the "first husband." We do not desire to quarrel with these expositors: only let them confine the Mosaic economy where God confined it—to Israel. Let Israel's deliverance therefrom be to the Gentile believer a glorious illustration of his own blessed position—not under law as a principle, but under grace (6.14).

Now unto us Gentile believers, what a breeze from the delectable mountains this passage is! For our poor consciences are always—sad to say—ready to hear of some new "duty" or "path of surrender," or "dying out" to this or that: not satisfied with God's plain announcement that we died to sin, are not under law: that even those whom He placed under The Law had died to it, and been discharged therefrom! And that we are to present ourselves to Him as "alive from the dead, and our members as instruments of righteousness unto God— 'whose service is perfect freedom.' "*

Paul's Law-struggle—before he knew the Gospel-revelation, that he had died to the Law

7 What shall we say then? Is the Law sin? Banish the thought! On the contrary, I had not become conscious of sin, except through law: for I had not perceived evil-desire, except the Law

8 had said, Thou shalt not have evil-desire. But sin, seizing occasion through the Commandment, wrought out in me all manner of evil-desire. For apart from law sin is dead.

9 And I was alive apart from law once. But upon the coming of the Commandment [to my con-

10 science] sin sprang into life, and I died. And the Commandment, which was unto life, this I found

11 to be unto death: for sin, seizing occasion, through the Commandment beguiled me, and through it slew me.

12 So that the Law indeed is holy, and the Commandment holy, and righteous, and good.

13 Did then that which is good become death unto me? Banish the thought! But sin, that it might appear as sin, by working out death to me through that which is good;—that through the Commandment sin might become exceeding sinful!

---

*Note carefully that it is to God that we are to present ourselves, and that as in Christ (Rom. 6.11,13). We are not told to present ourselves to Christ, for we are already vitally *in Him.*

14   For we know that the Law is spiritual: but I
       am carnal, sold under sin. For that which I am
15   working out, I do not own: for not what I am
       wishing this am I doing: but what I am hating—
16   this I am practicing. But if what I am not wish-
       ing, I am practicing, I am consenting unto the Law
       that it is right.
17   So, therefore, no longer is it I that am working
18   it out, but sin which is dwelling in me. For I
       know that there does not dwell in me, that is, in
       my flesh, a good thing: for the wishing is present
       with me, but the working out that which is right,
19   is not. For not what I am wishing am I prac-
       ticing—that is, the good; but on the contrary,
       what I am not wishing—that is, the evil, this I
20   am doing! But if what I am not wishing, this
       I am practicing, no longer is it I that am working
       it out, but on the contrary, sin which dwelleth
       in me.
21   I find then the law, that to me, desiring to be
22   practicing the right, the evil is present. For I de-
       light in the Law of God after the inward man:
23   but I see a different law in my members, warring
       against the law of my mind, and bringing me into
       captivity under the law of sin which is in my
       members.
24   Wretched man that I am! who shall deliver me
       out of the body of this death?
25   I thank God, [for deliverance] through Jesus
       Christ our Lord.
       So then, I myself with the mind, indeed, serve
       God's Law; but with the flesh sin's law.

Before beginning the study of this great struggle of Paul's,
let us get it settled firmly in our minds that Paul is here
exercised not at all about pardon, but about deliverance: "Who
shall deliver me from this body of death?" The whole question
is concerning indwelling sin, as a power; and not committed
sins, as a danger.

Mark also that while (as we shall show) the indwelling Holy Spirit is the Christian's sole power against the flesh, He is not known in this struggle; but it is Paul himself against the flesh—with the Law prescribing a holy walk, but furnishing no power whatever for it.

Even the fact of deliverance through Christ from the Law (described in the fourth and sixth verses), is most evidently not known during this conflict with the flesh. (This fact itself marks the conflict as one that preceded the revelation to the apostle of his being dead to the Law, not under law: for such knowledge would have made the struggle impossible.)

Therefore this conflict of Paul's, instead of being an example to you, is a warning to you to keep out of it by means of God's plain words that you are not under law but under grace.

But now you will adopt one of two courses: either you will read of *and avoid* the great struggle Paul had, under *law,* to make the flesh obedient by law,—with its consequent discovery of no good in him, and no strength; with his despairing cry, "Who shall deliver me?" and the blessed discovery of deliverance through our Lord Jesus Christ and by the indwelling Spirit: and this is, of course, the true way,—for you are not under law. It is the God-honoring path, for it is the way of faith. It is the wisest, because in it you profit by the struggle and testimony of another, written out for your benefit.

The second course, (and alas, the one followed by most in their distress and longing after a holy life), is to go through practically the same struggle as Paul had,—until you discover for yourself experimentally what he found. In this latter course you will be like Bunyan's pilgrim who fell into the Slough of Despond. You will enjoy reading the quotations below from Bunyan's *Pilgrim's Progress.* We suppose you have this priceless book: but quote, to save the trouble of reference.

If we (as Gentiles who were not put under the Law by God), were able to believe, simply to believe, I say, that we died federally with Christ, we should enter into the blessed state of deliverance belonging to a risen one, who knows both that he died and that he is in Christ—*not under law*: and the "struggle" would be avoided. Rather, there would be a walk of faith, both in Christ's work, and the Holy Spirit's indwelling power.*

And, if we can learn from Paul's struggle in this Seventh Chapter, the lessons Paul seeks to teach us—of the fact that we cannot be what we would, because of the inveterate, incurable evil of our flesh—of "the sin that dwelleth in us," and that deliverance is "through Christ Jesus our Lord,"—through faith in Him, as having become identified with us as we were, and having thus effected our death, with Him, to sin, and all the "I must" claims of our old standing: so that we count ourselves dead to sin, and alive unto God *in Christ Jesus,*—it will be well! We shall be blessed!

---

*Wherefore Christian was left to stumble in the Slough of Despond alone; but still he endeavored to struggle to that side of the slough that was furthest from his own house, and next to the Wicketgate; the which he did, but could not get out because of the burden that was upon his back. But I beheld, in my dream, that a man came to him, whose name was Help, and asked him, What he did there?

Sir, said Christian, I was bid to go this way by a man, called Evangelist, who directed me also to yonder gate, that I might escape the wrath to come: and as I was going thither I fell in here.

HELP: But why did you not look for the steps? [The great and precious promises of God.]

CHRISTIAN: Fear followed me so hard, that I fled the next way and fell in.

Then said Help, Give me thy hand; so he gave him his hand, and he drew him out, and set him upon sound ground, and bid him go on his way.

Then I stepped to him that plucked him out and said: Sir, wherefore, since over this place is the way from the City of Destruction to yonder gate, is it that this plat is not mended, that poor travelers might go thither with more security? and he said unto me, This miry slough is such a place as cannot be mended: it is the descent whither the scum and filth that attends conviction for sin doth continually run, and therefore it is called the Slough of Despond: for still as the sinner is awakened about his lost condition, there arise in his soul many fears and doubts, and discouraging apprehensions, which all of them get together, and settle in this place. And this is the reason of the badness of this ground.

It is not the pleasure of the King that this place should remain so bad; his labourers also have, by the directions of his Majesty's surveyors, been for above these sixteen hundred years employed about this patch of ground, if perhaps it might have been mended: yea, and to my knowledge, said he, here hath been swallowed up at least twenty thousand cart-loads; yea, millions of wholesome instructions, that have at all seasons been brought from all places of the King's dominions, (and they that can tell, say, they are the best materials to make good ground of the place), if so be it might have been mended; but it is the Slough of Despond still; and so will be, when they have done what they can.

True, there are, by the direction of the Lawgiver, certain good and substantial steps placed even through the very midst of this slough; but at such times as this place doth much spew out its filth, as it doth against change of weather, these steps are hardly seen; or if they be, men through the dizziness of their heads step besides; and then they are bemired to purpose, notwithstanding the steps be there: but the ground is good when they are once got in at the gate.

But if we refuse to learn the lessons Paul would teach us here—of the great facts of our deliverance in Christ from "the power of sin which is the Law" (I Cor. 15.56), we shall not only fail of personal deliverance from sin's power, but we shall soon be traducing all the glorious doctrines of Paul, and be sinking to the doctrine that we must expect to go on sinning and getting forgiveness "till we die,"—which is, of course, putting our own death in the place of Christ's death: for God says we died *with Him,* and are now free in Him Risen!

Verse 7: **What shall we say, then? Is the Law sin?**— Paul has been telling us in Chapter Six of having died to sin, and now, in the first section of Chapter Seven, he tells us of having been made dead to the Law and discharged therefrom. His enemies (and he must always keep them in mind—the enemies of *grace*)—would immediately accuse him thus: "You say we died to the Law; therefore you class the Law with sin." **Banish the thought!** is Paul's answer—his usual holy, horrified rejection of what is false. **On the contrary, I had not become conscious of sin except through law:** That is, forbidding a thing to one who cannot abstain from that thing, is the way to make him know his bondage—his own helplessness. "By the Law is the knowledge of sin."

For I had not perceived evil-desire, except the Law had said, Thou shalt not have evil desire—Here Paul begins to show the spiritual character and reach of the Law. He will proceed through the rest of the Chapter to show in detail the spiritual effect of the Law on him.

The direct reference in this word "desire" is to Deuteronomy 5.21, where the correct translation is, "Neither shalt thou *desire* thy neighbor's house, his field, or his man-servant, or his maid-servant, his ox, or his ass, or anything that is thy neighbor's." Now, Saul of Tarsus had been occupied with the outward things, positive and negative, of the Law. But when God quickened to his heart the real meaning of the word covet, or desire—showing him that "desire not" forbade the reaching out of the heart after anything other than loving God with all the heart, soul, and mind, and his neighbor as himself; he discerned for the first time that such desire is sin. For desire, in a creature, for aught else but God's glory, is sin. Imagine Gabriel in God's presence entertaining desire for something for himself*: It would be the beginning of another Lucifer!

It will be well, by the way, for all legalists—for those who seek either righteousness or holiness through the Law, to HEAR the Law: "Thou shalt not have evil desire"!

Verse 8: **But sin, seizing occasion through the Commandment, wrought out in me all manner of evil-desire. For apart from law sin is dead.**

That indwelling sin which was in Paul's members,—left there by God, had no means of making itself known to Paul, except by a quickened Law that became direct Divine *Commandment* to his very self. Then, indeed, when God revealed to Paul, (already renewed but not knowing the incurable evil of the flesh) the spiritual nature and character of His holy Law, together with the demand on his conscience to fulfil it,— then came Sin's chance! Paul had no strength,—only the renewed will: Let Paul undertake—as he will—to fulfil what was commanded! Then it will be seen that "the strength of sin is the Law": that sin will prove itself stronger than Paul, through the Commandment!

Wrought out in me all manner of evil-desire. This discovery that desire is sin would not be confined to the letter of the tenth commandment, "Thou shalt not desire, or covet": but would in Paul's inner consciousness extend itself through the whole Decalogue: For the Law is one!

To illustrate the words **apart from Law, sin is dead**: Suppose a man determined to drive his automobile to the very limit of its speed. If (as is not quite yet done!) signs along the road would say, No Speed Limit, the man's only thought would be to press his machine forward. But now suddenly he encounters a road with frequent signs limiting speed to thirty miles an hour. The man's will rebels, and his rebellion is

---

*The word *epithumia* (desire) is used 37 times in the New Testament,—in all but three of these passages denoting evil-desire. The three exceptions, however, indicate that the context must determine the meaning in any case. (Luke 22.15; Phil. 1.23; I Thess. 2.17: contrasted, for example, with Mark 4.19; John 8.44; Rom. 1.24; Titus 2.12; James 1.14; I John 2.16; II Pet. 3.3).

aroused still further by threats: Speed Limit Strictly Enforced. Now the man drives on fiercely, conscious both of his desire to "speed," and his rebellion against restraint. The speed limit signs did not create the wild desire to rush forward: that was there before. But the notices brought the man into conscious conflict with authority.

For apart from Law, sin is dead—Sin, like a coiled serpent, is in the old nature, but cannot get at the conscience to condemn it: for indwelling sin has no means of "springing into life," *as sin,* apart from law: it is quiescent, dormant, "dead."

Every impulse of the flesh, the old natural life, is sin. Take desire, or coveting: who is to know that this inward, universal, natural desire is sin, till the Law says to the conscience, "Thou shalt not covet"? This command not to covet does not remove the covetousness, but rather calls attention to it. And in forbidding it, immediately puts into conflict the renewed human will with the power of indwelling sin,—in this case with covetousness.

Now, however quickened or renewed the human will may be, strength, power against sin, does not reside in the human will. Furthermore, human strength is not God's way to overcome indwelling sin. That power resides always and only in the indwelling Holy Spirit.

Verses 9, 10: **And I was alive apart from law once: but when the Commandment came, sin revived, and I died; and the Commandment, which was unto life, this I found to be unto death:**

The words **alive apart from law once**—to what stage of his life does this refer? We have noted that the Law had not come as a spiritual thing, as commandment, to him in his unregenerate state. Now let us mark that it was not "the Commandment" that came to save him: it was Jesus of Nazareth, in absolute *grace,* who appeared to him on the Damascus road. Surely if absolute grace ever met a man, it met Saul of Tarsus that day! And the questions that came out of his mouth, "Who art thou, Lord?" "What shall I do, Lord?" have nothing whatever to do with law. He has met a Person, not a code! And when Ananias comes to Saul as he prays, in

Judas' house in Straight Street, he speaks nothing to Saul of law: but, "The Lord, even Jesus, who appeared unto thee in the way which thou camest, hath sent me, that thou mayest receive thy sight, and be filled with the Holy Spirit."

Then Saul immediately begins his joyful, triumphant testimony in the synagogues in Damascus that "Jesus is the Son of God." That was no time for the Commandment to come. God is not speaking to him yet of indwelling sin, but of full and free pardon and justification, through the shed blood of a Redeemer. This fills his soul during the first stage of his Christian life.

Then he goes away into Arabia, and God begins to exercise him, evidently—as we have shown—no longer concerning sins, for they are pardoned; but concerning indwelling sin.

It is to that happy, first stage of his Christian life, we believe, that Paul refers when he says, "I was alive apart from law *once*." He says, "I was alive." Paul would not affirm that a man dead in trespasses and sins was "alive"!

But let us go over the ground very carefully.

Apart from law—these words "apart from law" (Greek, *choris nomou*) are exactly the same as in Chapter 3.21 concerning justification! They indicate therefore, a state of no connection with law. Justification was on grounds where law did not come; and Paul's first condition after salvation was also thus, as we shall see.

Paul connects with this word "once" the Law's becoming quickened to his soul: **When the Commandment came.** No: this could not have been during the Tarsus, or Gamaliel, or persecuting days: for Paul says of those very days, "I verily thought I ought to do many things contrary to the Name of Jesus of Nazareth." There was no hint there, surely, of a conflict with indwelling sin! But only a steady certainty that he was right. Those who would make the struggle of Romans Seven *in any sense* that of an unregenerate Jew under the Law should remember that for a Jew there was no such struggle! An unregenerate Jew was occupied with outward things, and rested there! If he were ceremonially "clean," and kept the "feasts, new moons, and Sabbath days," there was no "struggle" in his heart. Why should there be? Was he not of the chosen people? and walked he not "according to the ordinances"? Paul was a Pharisee—"a Pharisee of Pharisees"—being "more exceedingly zealous for the traditions of the fathers." Let him alone at that! There was no "struggle." He was satisfied, serene, apart from any spiritual knowledge of the Law! The Law was a terrible thing. It was a "fiery Law." When Israel heard it, at Sinai, they stood afar off, in terror, and said to Moses, "Let not Jehovah speak with us any more, lest we die"!

The Jews, in Paul's day, (as today) held it in *the letter*. They knew nothing of its holy, "spiritual" character. They were occupied with the length of a "Sabbath day's journey"; or the question of how many nails a man could have in his sandals without "bearing a burden on the Sabbath"; and of "washing their hands to the elbows" before eating (Mark 7.3, marg.). There is not the slightest reason for differing Saul of Tarsus from those other Pharisees who would let the sick, palsied and demon-possessed remain under Satan's bondage—if only their Sabbath were observed their way! (There is nothing so merciless as self-righteous religion: witness all History!) See Saul holding the clothes of Stephen's murderers! See him "breathing out threatening and slaughter"—mark it—slaughter, wholesale murder, toward "any that were of the Name" of Jesus.

What perfect theological folly to conceive that the struggle of Romans Seven had been all along in Saul's heart! That such a monster of murder was at the same time "delighting in the Law of God after the inward man"! No, no! That was before the holy Law, with its "Commandment" for an inner personal holiness,—free, even, from unlawful desire *(epithumia)* had been quickened to him! Saul of Tarsus could have headed the Spanish Inquisition, and have had no qualms of conscience! He was on his way to Damascus as a regular, merciless Duke of Alva, to crush Christ's confessors,—with a good conscience: "I verily thought I ought to do."

Paul certainly distinguishes here between his early Christian life of rejoicing in the new-found Redeemer, and that later experience in which God exercises him about indwelling sin and deliverance therefrom.

But upon the coming of the Commandment [to my conscience] **sin sprang into life, and I died.**

Here is seen that crisis described by so many godly saints. It is what some people call "coming under conviction for holiness." "Ye are yet carnal," Paul wrote to the Corinthians. Here he is discovering that state in himself. To Paul, converted, but still thinking himself under law, God uses *"the Commandment."* He discovers to Paul the spirituality of the Law and lets it command him to be and do. This Paul undertakes, not knowing of the sin dwelling in his members. So, **Sin sprang into life,** with the result that,—**I died,** as the following verses describe: it is the death of all hopes in himself, in his flesh.

And the Commandment, which was unto life, this I found to be unto death—its proper ministry, condemnation and death (II Cor. 3.7, 9)—to all hopes in flesh, even in the flesh of people born again, as Paul was.

Verse 11: **For sin, seizing occasion, through the Commandment beguiled me, and through it slew me.**

Sin is personified all through this passage: Let Paul, says Sin, undertake to fulfil this Commandment! Let him keep on trying it!

How wonderful the consistency of Scripture! Paul was not under Law, being in Christ. God was not "beguiling" Paul in commanding what He knew Paul could not fulfil. But God permitted Sin to "beguile" him, by leading him to rely on his own power to obey, that Paul might find his utter powerlessness, and finally despair of delivering himself.

And through it slew me—That is, killed off all his hopes in himself, his "flesh." We all know how endlessly "resolutions" are formed by earnest Christians—honest resolutions to be "better" Christians, to "quit" this or that sin or bad habit: and what failure and despair is the result of relying on our own wills!

But to Paul, failure was terrible: for there was the Law, the Law of Moses, given by God, under which he had been born and brought up, and constantly instructed. The Law was his hope. And now it helps him? Not at all! Indeed, it becomes the very means by which Sin attacks him. And Sin slays him—that is, all hopes in himself lie vanquished, dead! And that by means of a holy instrument! for, Paul cries:

Verse 12: **The Law is holy, and the Commandment holy, and righteous and good**—Here Paul positively refutes the charge that he dishonored God's Law. Nay, more, the Commandment *(entolē)*, the direct application to him of the Law, with its fatal consequences to himself, to his self-hopes, he defends. This is the mark of a saint: he upholds God, and condemns himself.

Verse 13: But now he answers the further question: **Did then that which is good become death unto me?** And again his answer is, **Banish the thought!** But it was indwelling sin that wrought death to me,—using indeed, **that which was good. Through the Commandment**, thus, **Sin was shown to be sin.** The more fully and widely the Law resolved itself in new and fresh commands to Paul's soul, the more intense and desperate became indwelling Sin's horrid opposition to it. Thus was Sin's hideous countenance seen in full! It became **exceeding sinful!**

In general, we may say that in verses 14 to 17, the emphasis is upon the practicing what is hated,—that is, the inability to overcome evil in the flesh; while in verses 18 to 21, the emphasis is upon the failure to do the desired good,—the inability, on account of the flesh, to do right.

Thus the double failure of a quickened man either to overcome evil or to accomplish good—is set forth. There must come in help from *outside, beyond himself!* This, of course, is the indwelling Spirit, as the eighth chapter so vividly portrays.

In narrating in particular the account of his great struggle in verses 14 to 23, we find the apostle arriving at three definite conclusions.

First, In doing what he is not wishing, but practicing what he is hating, his conclusion is: "If what I am not wishing, that

I am doing, I am consenting unto the Law that it is right."
Verses 14 to 16.

Second, It is indwelling sin, and not his real self, that is
working out this evil: "But if what I am not wishing, this
I am practicing, no longer is it I that am working it out, but
on the contrary, sin which dwelleth in me." Verses 17 to 20.

Third, There is the terrible revelation of a positive *Law* (or
settled principle) of sin in his members, defeating him despite
his inward delight in the Law of God:—"bringing me into
captivity under the law of sin which is in my members."
Verse 23.

**For we know that the Law is spiritual: but I* am carnal,
sold under sin. For that which I am working out, I do not
own: for not what I am wishing this am I doing: but what
I am hating—this I am practicing.**

The Law is spiritual: but I am carnal—"Spiritual" may
include:

(1) Addressed to man by God, who is "spirit";

(2) To "the spirit of man that is in him" (I Cor. 2.11);
Therefore:

(3) Consisting of communications adapted to and only un-
derstandable by beings of a spiritual realm or sphere.

(4) "Spiritual," also, in the moral sense; holy because communicated by a holy God.

Thus Law is *spiritual*.

But I am carnal: Paul speaks of himself here as he is by
nature. He does not say body-ish (*sema*, body, as opposed to
pneuma, spirit) but "carnal": The word *sarkinos*, translated
"carnal," comes from the root, *sarks*, "flesh."

1. If Paul had been speaking of himself before being quickened, he would have used the word *natural*: "the natural man
receiveth not the things of the Spirit of God" (I Cor. 2.14).

---

*"The apostle does not say, 'We know that the Law is spiritual and *we* are carnal.' Had he done so, it would have been to speak of Christians, as such, in their
proper and normal condition."

"Romans Seven is not the present experience of any one, but a *delivered* person
describing the state of an undelivered one. A man in a morass does not quietly
describe how a man sinks into it, because he fears to sink and stay there. The
end of Romans Seven is a man out of the morass showing in peace the principle
and manner in which one sinks in it" (Darby).

2. "Carnal" is not used to describe an unregenerate person, but a Christian not delivered from the power of the flesh: "I, brethren could not speak unto you as unto spiritual, but as unto carnal, as unto babes in Christ" (I Cor. 3.1).

3. In this connection, note that while Paul's condition at the time of this struggle was that of being carnal, there are those that are spiritual: "He that is spiritual judgeth all things" (I Cor. 2.15). "Ye who are spiritual, restore" (Gal. 6.1).

4. Therefore, by the word "carnal" Paul was describing a state out of which there was deliverance.

We know that **carnal, sold under sin**—is evidently meant by the apostle in this fourteenth verse to indicate the state of human nature as contrasted with God's holy spiritual Law.

Sold under sin: This is slave-market talk: and it describes all of us by nature. Instead of being spiritual and therefore able to hearken to, delight in and obey God's holy spiritual Law, we are turned back, since Adam sinned, to a fleshly condition, our spirits by nature dead to God, and our soul-faculties under the domination of the still unredeemed body. Now Paul, though his spirit was quickened; and his inward desires, therefore, were toward God's Law; found to his horror his state by nature "carnal," fleshly, "sold under sin." How little humanity realizes this awful, universal fact about man—"sold under sin"!

"Sold under sin" is exactly what the new convert does not know! Forgiven, justified, he knows himself to be: and he has the joy of it! But now to find an evil nature, of which he had never become really conscious, and of which he thought himself fully rid, when he first believed, is a "second lesson" which is often more bitter than the first—of guilt!

For that which I am working out, I do not own [as my choice]: for not what I am wishing this am I doing*, but what I am hating, this I am practicing.

---

*Three Greek verbs expressing conduct are used in these verses: (1) *prasso,* do; (2) *poieo,* practise, make a business of; (3) *katergadzomai,* work out to a result (whether by personal choice or nature). By translating literally we can better get the vivid sense of the original.

We must constantly remember throughout this struggle that it is not a description by the apostle Paul of an experience he was having when he wrote this Epistle! but an experience of a regenerate man before he knows either about indwelling sin, or that he died to sin and to the Law which gives sin its power; and who also does not know the Holy Spirit, as an indwelling presence and power against sin. God let Paul have this experience. And he now writes about it that we may read and know all the facts of our salvation: not merely of the awful guilt of our sins, and our forgiveness through the blood of Christ; but also of the moral hideousness of our old selves; and our powerlessness, though regenerate, to deliver ourselves, from "the law of sin" in our members.

Therefore Paul said that in that struggle he found himself "working out" a manner of life he refused to "own"— to admit as his real choice. For, he says, **Not what I am wishing, that am I practicing.** The word "wish" or "desire" is not quite strong enough for the Greek word here, *(thelo)*; but the word *will* is too strong; for "will" has come in English to have the element of carrying a purpose through; which Paul was unable to do. His holy wish never mounted the throne of *I will*.

Verse 16: But now he gains a further step: **But if what I am not wishing, I am practicing, I am consenting unto the Law that it is right.** The wicked man does what he is wishing; and is willing to condemn God's Law if it interferes with him. But Paul cries in this struggle, "I have just discovered that I am not at all in my heart opposing the Law; but am in my heart of hearts consenting that it is right." And that is a very real step. In the matter of forgiveness, the thief on the cross took that step, in saying to his fellow, "We receive the due reward of our deeds." And Paul, forgiven but undelivered, cries, The Law is right! My heart consents to God's Word and God's Way,—however far I am from following it! And now he pursues his advantage:

So therefore, no longer is it I that am working it out, but sin which is dwelling in me.

Verse 17: "No longer I!" That was a wonderful discovery! For a forgiven Saul, who had gone on in joy awhile without inward trouble, it was indeed a terrible awakening to become again convicted—not now of sins, but of *indwelling sin,* of a hateful power that seemed one's very self—but was really "our *old* man."* But he is making discoveries about himself—amazing things, brought out for the first time in Scripture. He is going much further than "consenting to the Law that it is right" (verse 16) ; for now, instead of being completely overwhelmed by this holy, righteous Law; he arrives at (and writes down for us!) a conclusion that is daring: Since I am doing what I am not wishing, there must be another and evil principle working within me. For it is not my real self that is working out this evil, but sin which dwelleth in me. An unwelcome, hateful presence!

Verse 18: **For I know that there does not dwell in me, that is in my flesh, a good thing: for the wishing is present with me, but working out that which is right, is not.**

Here is that man who wrote in Philippians Three, "If any man hath whereof to glory in the flesh, I yet more!" And he gave there seven facts he could glory in,—beyond the greatest Greek, or Roman, or English, or any Gentile—"I yet more"! but now saying, "In me dwelleth *no good thing.*" And also: "I can will, but cannot do!" This great double lesson must be learned by all of us! (1) There is no good thing in any of us—in "our flesh"—our old selves. (2) We cannot do the good we wish or will, to do. Most humbling of all confessions. Renewed, desiring to proceed—we cannot! We are dependent on the Holy Spirit as our only spiritual *power,* just as on Christ as our only *righteousness!*

Alas, how incompletely are these two facts taught and learned! We have seen hundreds of eager young believers who

---

*For, though our old man was crucified with Christ, put in the place of certain, though not instant death—we find, though we have "put him off" (Col. 3.9) we must "put away," as to every thing of the former life, "the old man" (Eph. 4.22). And, to be put away, he must be discovered to us, and this is what is so vividly set before us in this struggle.

Note, it is never said the old man is dead, but that we died. We were federally identified with Christ, and passed on with Him into burial, and now share His Risen life. The old man is not to be "counted dead" (as some very dear brethren have put it): but to be counted crucified—his place being there only.

are being told to "surrender to Christ," that all depended upon their yielding, etc. But these dear children, what did they know of the tremendous truths Paul has taught in the early part of Romans, before asking that believers present themselves to God as alive from the dead? (Rom. 6.13). He has taught the terrible, lost *guilty state* of all men; their *inability* to recover righteousness; then Christ set forth as a propitiation *through faith in His blood* as their only hope; then *identification,* as connected with Adam, *with Christ in His death;* and the command to reckon themselves *dead to sin,* and alive to God *in Christ Jesus;* together with the fact that they are *not under law, but under grace.*

All this *before* the real call for surrender for service, in the Twelfth Chapter is given at all!

Our hearts are weary with the appeals to *man's will,*—whether the *will* of a sinner to "make a start," "be a Christian," etc.; or the appeal to the *will* of believers who have not yet been shown what *guilt* is, and what indwelling *sin* is. For God's Word in Romans 7.18 tells us that while to will may be present with us, to work that which is right *is not* present. Paul told those same Philippians that believers were such as had "no confidence" in the flesh, and that it is *God* that worketh in us, *"both to will and to work,* for His good pleasure."*

Verse 19: For not what I am wishing am I practicing—that is, the good; but on the contrary, what I am not wishing—that is, the evil, this I am doing.

---

*The author must be permitted to say that he had part in the Student Volunteer Movement for foreign missions of fifty years ago; that he saw hundreds of earnest and honest students "volunteer" for the mission field.

But afterwards, in teaching the book of Romans, especially in China, he had many a missionary say, "We never knew this gospel before." It is nothing short of tragic to send men and women out against the hosts of hell in heathendom without teaching them through and through and through and through this mighty gospel Paul preached!—which gospel he says is "the power of God unto salvation." And he comes to further detail in saying, *"The word of the cross* is the power of God." Education, medication, sanitation, and general sweetness—what does Satan care for that? *The word of the cross* is the great wire along which runs the dynamic of God—and it runs along no other wire. If God is permitting great investments of money, men and time along other lines to be swept away, let us remember that the real Church of God, having the Holy Ghost, does not need great outward things. Paul built no colleges, schools, or institutions—which may be useful, never essential. But Paul's last epistle, just before his martyrdom, says "The Lord stood by me and strengthened me; that through me THE MESSAGE *might be fully proclaimed,* and that all the Gentiles *might hear."*

Now this verse must not be for one moment misapplied, that is, it must not be made to describe Paul's "manner of life in Christ Jesus," which was, as we know, victorious, and fruitful, and always rejoicing. But verse 19 does indeed express concerning Paul, and all of us, all the time, our utter powerlessness in ourselves (though Christians) against the evil of the flesh: whether we are consciously under Moses' Law, as was Paul, or convicted by the power of an awakened conscience that we ought to have deliverance from our sinful, selfish selves, and walk in victory in Christ. Verse 19 is not normal Christian experience, certainly. But it may describe our very case, if we have not learned God's way of faith.

Verse 20: **But if what I am not wishing, this I am practicing, no longer is it I that am working it out, but on the contrary, sin which dwelleth in me.**

Paul reasserts the blessed fact (which is, alas, no comfort to him as yet!) that it is no longer the real "I," but indwelling sin, that is **working out** this hated life of defeat.

Verse 21: **I find then the law** [or principle] **that to me, desiring to be practicing the right, the evil is present.**

He now states as a settled conclusion, what he has experimentally discovered. And we all need to consent to the fact—even if we have found God's way of deliverance, **that evil is present.** It is the denial of this fact that has wrecked thousands of lives! For evil will be present until the Lord comes, bringing in the redemption of our bodies.

Verses 22, 23: **For I delight in the Law of God after the inward man: but I see a different law in my members, warring against the law of my mind, and bringing me into captivity under the law of sin which is in my members.**

Here is first, delight, second, discernment, and third, defeat.

1. First, *delight*: in God's Law, Paul **delights**—this is a strong and inclusive word. And, **after the inward man,—** thus revealing himself as regenerate throughout this struggle: No unregenerate man would say, (unless profane) "It is no more I that do it, but sin which dwelleth in me:" For,

(1) An unregenerate man is not conscious of a moral power

which is not himself: for he has but the one nature,—he is "in the flesh."

(2) An unregenerate man could not say, "What I hate, that I do." For only born-again people hate evil. "Ye that love Jehovah, hate evil" (Ps. 97.10), and David could say of himself, "I hate every false way" (Ps. 119.104). But of the wicked he wrote, "He abhorreth not evil" (Ps. 36.4).

(3) An unregenerate man could not say, "What I would not, that I do,—I consent to the Law that it is good." An unregenerate man resists the Law, that he may "justify himself." A regenerate man consents to the Law's being good, no matter how it judges what he finds himself doing! (verse 16).

(4) The unregenerate man could not say, "I delight in the Law of God after the inward man." For by nature all men are "children of wrath," "alienated from the life of God"; and "the mind of the flesh is enmity against God, not subject to the Law of God." Before his conversion, Saul, as we saw, could help to stone Stephen,—"verily thinking he ought" to do it; but Paul was not then seeking holiness (as the man in Romans Seven is), but was secure in his own righteousness as a legalist.

(5) The unregenerate man could not say, "Wretched man that I am!" For he could not *see* his wretchedness! His whole life was to build up that which was the flesh.

(6) If you claim that the "wretched man" of Romans Seven is an unregenerate man under conviction of sin, the complete reply is, that this man of Romans Seven is crying for deliverance,—not from sin's guilt and penalty, but from its power. Not for forgiveness of sins, but help against indwelling sin. This man is exercised, not about the day of judgment, but about a condition of bondage to that which he hates. The Jews on the Day of Pentecost, and the jailor at Philippi, cried out in terror, "What shall we do to be saved?" It was guilt and danger they felt. But this man in Romans Seven cries, "Who shall deliver me" (not from guilt) but, "from this body of death?" No one but a quickened soul ever *knows* about a "body of death"!

(7) But perhaps the most striking argument of all is in the closing words of Chapter Seven—verse 25: "Therefore then I myself with the mind, am subject to God's Law, but with the flesh to sin's law." Here we have both spiritual life and consciousness; also, discernment and discrimination of both his real true new self, which chooses God and His will, and of the flesh which will continue to choose "sin's law": and all this conclusion *after* he has realized deliverance from the "body of death" through our Lord Jesus Christ!

2. Second, *discernment*: **I see a different law in my members.** It is the unwillingness to own this different law, this settled state of enmity, toward God, in our own members, that so terribly bars spiritual blessing and advancement. As long as we think lightly of the fact of the presence with us of the fallen nature, (I speak of Christians) we are far from deliverance. In the law of leper-cleansing (Lev. 13.2 ff), "if a man shall have in the skin of his flesh a rising," or even "a white rising"—he was unclean. (See the various degrees of the plague.) But, "If the leprosy break out abroad in the skin, and the leprosy cover *all* the skin of him that hath the plague from his head even to his feet, as far as appeareth to the priest; then the priest shall look; and, behold, if the leprosy have covered *all* his flesh, he shall pronounce him *clean* that hath the plague: it is *all* turned white: he is clean"! It is significant that at the conclusion of the Sermon on the Mount, (Matt. 8.1-4) two things should be there: (1) A leper —showing the Law could cleanse no one. (2) A leper, as Luke the physician tells us, *"full* of leprosy" (Luke 5.12). It is because people do not recognize their *all-badness* that they do not find Christ all in all to them.

3. Third, *defeat*: There is no strength or power in ourselves against **the law of sin which is in our members.** God has left us as much dependent on Christ's work for our deliverance as for our forgiveness! It is wholly because we died with Him at the cross, both to sin and to the whole legal principle, that sin's power, for those in Christ. is broken.

Verse 24: **Wretched man that I am!** The word here translated "wretched" meant originally, "wretched—through the exhaustion of hard labor," (Vincent). But the word reads in the Septuagint of Isaiah 33.1, Jeremiah 4.30 "desolate, bound for destruction," as also in Revelation 3.17. The hopelessness of Paul's condition, unless he be delivered, is thus appallingly revealed!

Who shall deliver me out of the body of this death? Note now at once that all self-hope has ceased! It is not, How shall I deliver myself? or even, How shall I be delivered? But it is a frantic appeal for a *deliverer!* **Who shall deliver me?** Instinctively and absolutely Paul knows that no *process* will deliver him. The awful shallowness of the "Christian Scientist," who would get rid of all evil by "demonstrating" with the human will against it is seen at once! So is the silly (and damning) folly of the Buchmanites, the "life-changers." Where do such folk come in, in such a struggle as this of Paul with **this body of death?** They simply do not come in, for they know nothing of it. The Holy Spirit is not in their vain self-processes, any more than in the mumblings of human priests,—pagan or popish.

The body of this death—what a fearful description of the body!—unredeemed, unchanged, under the law of sin in all its members. No matter what the "delight" of the quickened human spirit in the things of God may be, to dwell undelivered in such a body is to find it a "body of death."

Verse 25: **I thank God,** [for deliverance] **through Jesus Christ our Lord.** Ah! The answer to Paul's self-despairing question, "Who shall deliver me?" is a *new revelation,*—even identification with Christ in His death! For just as the sinner struggles in vain to find forgiveness and peace, until he looks outside himself to Him who made peace by the blood of His cross, just so does the quickened soul, struggling unto despair to find victory over sin by self-effort, look outside himself to Christ—in whom he is, and in whom he died to sin and to law! Paul was not delivered 'by Christ, but *through* Him; not by anything Christ then or at that time did for him; but through the revelation of the fact that he had died with Christ at the cross to this hated indwelling sin, and law of sin; and to God's Law, which gave sin its power. It was a new vision or revelation of the salvation which is in Christ—as described in verses 4 and 6 of our chapter.

The sinner is not forgiven by what Christ now does, but by faith in what He did do at the cross, for, "The word of the cross is the power of God." Just so, the believer is not delivered by what Christ does for him now; but in the revelation to his soul of identification with Christ's death at the cross: for *again,* "The word of the cross is the power of God."

It will be *by the Holy Spirit,* that this deliverance is wrought in us; as we shall see in Chapter Eight. *Through* our Lord Jesus Christ, and *by* "the law of the Spirit of life in Christ Jesus," is God's order.

To sum up Paul's Great Discoveries in this Struggle of Chapter Seven:

1. That sin dwelt in him,—though he delighted in God's Law!

2. That his will was powerless against it.

3. That the sinful self was not his real self.

4. That there was deliverance through our Lord Jesus Christ!*

I thank God [for deliverance] **through Jesus Christ our Lord!** Paul had cried, Who shall deliver me? The answer is,—the discovery to his soul of that glorious deliverance at the cross! of death to sin and Law *with Him!* So it is said, "Through Jesus Christ our Lord." The word of the cross—of what Christ did there, is the power of God—whether to save sinners or deliver saints!

But ah, what a relief to Paul's soul—probably out yonder alone in Arabia, struggling more and more in vain to compel the flesh to obey the Law, to have revealed to his weary soul the second glorious truth of the Gospel—that he had died with Christ—to sin, and to Law which sin had used as its power!

---

*Archbishop Leighton, on Romans 8.35, says, "Is this he that so lately cried out, 'Oh wretched man that I am! who shall deliver me?' that now triumphs, O happy man! 'who shall separate us from the love of Christ?' Yes, it is the same. Pained then with the thoughts of that miserable conjunction with a body of death, and so crying out, who will deliver? Now he hath found a Deliverer to do that for him, to whom he is forever united. So vast a difference is there betwixt a Christian taken in himself and in Christ!"

And now the conclusion—which is the text of the whole chapter! So then—always a *quod erat demonstrandum* with Paul! I myself, with the mind, indeed—this is the real *renewed self,* which the apostle has over and over said that "sin that dwelleth in him" *was not!* "With the mind" —all the spiritual faculties including, indeed, the soul-faculties of reason, imagination, sensibility—which even now are "being renewed" by the Holy Spirit, day by day. Am subject to God's law [or will]—all new creatures can say this. But with the flesh sin's law. He saw it at last, and bowed to it,—that all he was by the flesh, by Nature, was irrevocably committed to sin. So he gave up—to see himself wholly in Christ (who now lived in Him) and to walk not by the Law, even in the supposed powers of the quickened life— but by the Spirit only: in whose power alone the Christian life is to be lived.

PAUL'S STRUGGLE NOT CHRISTIAN DOCTRINE

It is of the utmost importance clearly to see that the great struggle of the latter part of Romans Seven is neither a purely Jewish one, nor a normal Christian walk, nor a necessary Christian experience.

It is not a purely *Jewish* struggle. Jewish struggles are set forth in the Psalms, and are a conflict with outward enemies, or the questioning cry (as in Psalm 88) as to why God seems far off, or even, for the present, seemingly against the suppli-cator (typically—the Remnant in the Last Days). But not even in the deepest Psalm of trouble is there ever a hint of *two natures* within the struggler! (For example, Psalm 10, or 88, or 77, or even such Psalms as 51 and 32.)

Neither is this struggle a normal *Christian* experience. For (1) there is no mention of Christ until the legal struggle is ended in self-despair,—and (2) There is no mention whatever of the Holy Spirit—whose recognized presence and power make possible proper Christian experience: which is "walking by the Spirit."

That it is not a normal Christian walk, we have also shown from Paul's own triumphant life.

And that it is not a *necessary* Christian experience, is seen from the fact that Paul is, in this struggle, occupied with the *Law,*—under which God says believers are *not!* (6.14.) The complete Gospel believed, makes such a struggle unnecessary and indeed impossible. For the gospel reveals (as in Romans 6.1-11 and 7.1-6, and all Chapter 8) (1) that we died with Christ and are now alive unto God in Christ Risen; (2) that those under Law were made dead to and discharged from the legal economy; (3) that the Holy Spirit indwelling the believer has taken over the conflict with the flesh; and is the whole power of a triumphant walk; (4) that therefore there is no condemnation to those in Christ Jesus, and no separation from God's love to those in Him!

Doubtless we often see other Christians having a Seventh-of-Romans struggle, and shall easily find ourselves falling into such a struggle. But as the gospel concerning our death with Christ both to sin and to the legal principle becomes clear to us, and our faith therein becomes strong; and our reliance upon the Holy Spirit becomes more constant, we shall walk as Paul did:—"Thanks be unto God who always leadeth us in triumph in Christ."

The path of faith is the most hateful path possible for the flesh. Faith gives the flesh no place—leaves no "part" for man's will and energy. The flesh will go to any degree of religious self-denial, or self-inflicted sufferings—anything but death!

But faith begins right there: *we died with Christ, we live in Him!* We have no righteousness, no strength,—and desire none: Christ is our righteousness, and "when we are weak, we are strong."

Thus the walk of simple-hearted faith is indeed in another realm from the struggle of Romans Seven. God give us to have faith "as a little child," a cloudless, unmixed vision, as had Paul at last!

When the demand, however, arises in our hearts that we *be* what we find written in the Epistles, the effect is the same exactly as in Paul's case as regards the discovery of powerlessness. The "Holiness" people call it, as we said, "becoming convicted for holiness." The conscience becomes suddenly awakened. We see that we have been content with a righteous standing, without a really holy walk. If we have seen that we died with Christ; and are properly instructed, we shall, upon such awakening,

(1) Know that there is deliverance in Christ for us, whether we are yet able, or not, in living faith to reckon that we are dead unto sin and alive unto God.

(2) We shall be, or become, willing to have God show us how, or wherein, we are still holding fast to any sin, or any indulgence of the flesh.

(3) We shall be brought, by God's grace, to agree to the sentence of death that has already been pronounced on this particular thing, when our old man,—all our old self, was crucified with Christ.

(4) Then we shall enter into the place of reckoning ourselves *dead* to sin, and to this darling sin, and to all sin,—as God commands His saints who have died with Christ.

(5) We may have, if necessary, a struggle here: as James shows:

"Ye adulteresses, know ye not that the friendship of the world is enmity with God? . . . God resisteth the proud, but *giveth grace to the humble. Be subject* therefore to God; but resist the devil, and he will flee from you. *Draw nigh to God, and He will draw nigh to you!*"

And now see his following words:

"Cleanse your hands, ye sinners" — those saints indulging known sin. "And *purify your hearts,* ye doubleminded"— those believers who have been half for the world, while half for heaven. *"Be afflicted,* and *mourn* and *weep."* (Not that God is unwilling, but that we are!) "Let *your* laughter" (which has been the fool's laughter of this condemned world!) "be turned to mourning, and *your* joy" (which has been the joy of worldlings, not of heaven-bound saints) "to heaviness. Humble yourselves in the sight of the Lord, and He shall exalt you!"

This is the path for *worldly* Christians. Not that the grace of God is insufficient: but they have been rejoicing with a condemned world! And they must come out of that, though in bitterness.

However, the bitterness need not be,—if we are willing! "If ye be *willing and obedient,* ye shall eat the fruit of the land." *And nothing will persuade our hearts like the goodness of God, in the gift of His Son, and the work of the cross, already accomplished on our behalf.*

Whether, then, it be a soul under law, or one in greater light: there will be the discovery of our own utter powerlessness, and of deliverance—from sin and self, in our Lord Jesus Christ! And this is the object of the revelation of Paul's great struggle,—not mere information, but application of these lessons to ourselves. For if we go through Chapters Six and Seven unexercised of soul, how shall we learn the blessed walk in the Spirit of Chapter Eight?

For "the flesh" is there—in Chapter Eight—all unchanged! And unless we *practically* learn,—learn for and regarding our own selves—the great lesson that in ourselves, in "the whole natural man," there is no good; that even when we will to do good, evil is yet present, and dominant! and that help for us, for our very selves, must come from *without*: unless we learn this holy self-despair; we will not enter into actual spiritual deliverance in Christ: but will only be "puffed up" by our study. For mere knowledge "puffeth up." But we all know that Paul was not puffed up when he cried, "O wretched man that I am!" And if Paul found a body of death to be delivered from, you and I have that same body of death! And we too must be brought to say, "I thank God through Jesus Christ our Lord." It may be that you will be found like the remarkable case below, related by Mr. Finney*: and be ready

---

*In his remarkable *Autobiography* Mr. Charles G. Finney relates the case of a lady who had always been marked for simplicity and uprightness of spirit. She had been, when a young woman, very highly regarded, but when she heard the gospel, she believed it, immediately entering fully into the admission of her guilt before God, and trusting Him implicitly on the ground of the shed blood of Christ. But in Mr. Finney's meetings she heard that God had commanded her to yield herself to Him and be filled with the Holy Spirit. She instantly complied again. And her husband came to Mr. Finney saying, "I cannot understand my wife. She was the most perfect creature I ever knew, when we were married. Then she was

to step immediately into any new revelation of blessing in Christ.* It should be a true illustration of every believer!

---

*But if you find yourself not spiritual, not even ready of heart to become so, you can at least pray the prayer Mr. F. B. Meyer—of blessed memory! taught so many:

"Lord, make me willing to be made willing!"

There is a blessed walk in the Spirit for you! Believe that. And cast yourself upon the grace of God! He will bring it to pass!

---

converted, and has been absolutely exemplary ever since. But she says now that at your meeting the other night she yielded herself in a new way to God; and I myself can see the most astonishing change, but cannot account for it at all." (We relate from memory.)

This was a case of simplicity of heart and mind, perhaps not often found. Since the work on the cross, anyone can appropriate just as simply the whole benefit of Christ's work.

CHAPTER EIGHT

The Holy Spirit's Work in the Believer: as Against the Flesh, verses 1-13; as Witnessing our Sonship and Heirship—even though Suffering, verses 14-25; As Helping our Infirmity by Intercession, verses 26, 27.

God's Great Purpose in His Elect: Conformity to Christ's Image, and Association with Him: Their Heavenly Destiny. All Earthly Providences for their Good. Verses 28-30.

Triumphant Response of Faith to These Things! Verses 31-34.

No Separation from God's Love, since it is IN Christ Jesus our Lord! Verses 35-39.

1 There is therefore now no condemnation to
2 them that are in Christ Jesus. For the law of the Spirit of life in Christ Jesus freed me from the law of sin and of death.

3 For, (the thing the Law could not do, because it was powerless on account of the flesh) God, having sent His own Son in the likeness of sinful flesh, and
4 for sin, condemned sin in the flesh: that the righteous result of the Law might be fulfilled in us, who walk not according to flesh, but according to Spirit.

5 For those who are according to flesh, the things of the flesh do mind; but those according to Spirit,
6 the things of the Spirit. For the mind of the flesh is death: but the mind of the Spirit is life and
7 peace. Because the mind of the flesh is enmity against God: for it is not subject to the Law of
8 God, neither indeed can it be: and those being in the flesh cannot please God.

9 But ye are not in flesh but in Spirit, if so be that the Spirit of God dwelleth in you. But if any man hath not the Spirit of Christ, he is none of His.

10 And if Christ is in you, the body, indeed, is dead on
account 'of sin; but the Spirit is life on account of
11 righteousness. But if the Spirit of Him that raised
up Jesus from the dead dwelleth in you, He that
raised up Christ Jesus from the dead shall give life
also to your mortal bodies through His Spirit that
dwelleth in you.

WE HAVE NOW COME to that great chapter which sets
forth that part in our salvation which is exercised by the third
Person of the Godhead, the blessed Holy Spirit. Without
Christ's work on the cross there would be no salvation, and
without the presence and constant operation of the Holy Spirit,
there would be no application of that salvation to us,—indeed,
no revelation of it to us!

Let us therefore with the profoundest reverence, and greatest
gladness, take up the study here in Romans Eight of that work
of the Holy Spirit which is directly concerned with our salvation: for Romans is a book of salvation. Jesus Christ and Him
crucified is the message that concerns salvation. Christ Jesus
and Him glorified is that which concerns our perfecting as
believers. The latter, other epistles will unfold more fully.
But the teaching of the work of the Holy Ghost in Romans
regards His fundamental operations,—just as it is fundamental
phases of Christ's work that are presented here.

The Eighth Chapter of Romans is the instinctive goal of the
Christian. Whether or not he can tell why—whether or not he
can give the great doctrinal facts that give him comfort here, he
is, nevertheless, like a storm-tossed mariner who has arrived at
his home port, and has cast anchor, when he comes into Romans
Eight!

The reasons are:

1. He finds himself in the hands of the blessed Comforter,
the indwelling Spirit, in whose almighty and loving ministry he
finds "life and peace."

2. He finds himself, without cause in himself, called "God's
elect,"—involved in a great Divine purpose, that will end in his

being conformed to Christ's image, Christ being "the First-born among many brethren."

3. He finds himself beloved *in Christ;* and therefore never to be "separated" from that love.

And these are both the "upper and nether springs" of eternal comfort.

This Eighth of Romans, then, comes after the work of Christ —after His atoning blood has put the believer's sins away; after he has seen, also, that he died with Christ,—to sin, and also to that legal responsibility he had in Adam; after the words, "Sin shall not have dominion over you, for ye are not under Law, but under *Grace";* and, finally, after the hopeless struggle of the apostle has shown "the flesh" to be incurably bad; and that there is a blessed deliverance, which, though not changing "the body of this death," nevertheless gives freedom therefrom "through our Lord Jesus Christ."

Verses 1,2: There is therefore now no condemnation to them that are in Christ Jesus. For the law of the Spirit of life in Christ Jesus freed me from the law of sin and of death.

Therefore looks back to the struggle of Chapter Seven, and the thankful shout of verse 25; and not to the expiatory work of Christ for us in Chapters 3.21 to 5.11. **Those that are in Christ Jesus,** and none others, can be before us in all this section.

It is on account of the Spirit's acting as a *law* of life, delivering the believer from the contrary law of sin and death in his yet unredeemed members, that **there is no condemnation.** It is of the utmost importance to see this. The subject here is no longer Christ's work for us, but the Spirit's work within us. Without the Spirit within as a law of life, there would be nothing but condemnation: for the new creature has no power within himself apart from the blessed Spirit,—as against a life of perpetual bondage to the flesh,—"the end of which things is death" (6.21).

Now the work of the Holy Spirit in the believer as set forth in Chapter Eight is fundamental, essential to the believer's salvation, and must be understood by all of us, for Romans is the book of foundation truth.

In Christ Jesus—Here the verse should end, as see note below.* The words **in Christ Jesus** express that glorious place God has given the believer. The question is not at all now one of justification, but one of position, in Christ Risen, "where condemnation is not, and cannot be." There cannot be degrees here: men either are in Christ, or not in Him.

There is no condemnation—Those in Christ Jesus have more than justification from all things by His blood. They have "justification *of life*," which means that they share His risen life. **No condemnation**—means, no condemnatory judgment. The question of rewards for work for our Lord will indeed come up at His judgment seat—*bēma* (II Cor. 5.10); but it is after the Church is caught up that this judgment occurs, when Christ comes, "apart from sin, to them that wait for Him." Blessed hope! (See Heb. 9.28.)

---

*The Revised Version correctly omits "who walk not after the flesh but after the Spirit." Since the King James translation, over 300 years ago, many, and the best, most accurate, ancient Greek manuscripts which we have, have been recovered; and earnest, godly men have gone steadily ahead with the tedious but fruitful work of correcting errors that had crept in in copying. For, as we all know, we have not the original manuscripts of Scripture: God has been pleased to withhold these from creatures so prone to idolatry as the sons of men.

We must close verse 1 with the words "in Christ Jesus," for four reasons: (1) The evidence of the Greek manuscripts is overwhelmingly in favor of the omission of the clause "who walk not after the flesh but after the Spirit" from verse 1,—as the evidence is universally for including these words in Verse 4. (2) Spiritual discernment also agrees, for the introduction of these words in verse 1 makes our safety depend upon our walk, and not upon the Spirit of God. But all in Christ Jesus are safe from condemnation, as is plainly taught throughout the epistles. Otherwise, our security depends on our walk, and not on our position in Christ. (3) The clause is plainly in proper place at the end of verse 4,—where the manner of the believer's walk, not his safety from condemnation, is described. (4) That the clause at the end of verse 1 in the King James is a *gloss* (marginal note by some copyist) appears not only from its omission by the great uncial manuscripts, Aleph, A, B, C, D, F, G; A, D (corr.); with some good cursives and ancient versions (see Olshausen, Meyer, Alford, J. F. and B., and Darby's excellent discussion in his *Synopsis, in loc);* but it also appears from the similarity of this gloss to like additions made through legal fear, found in other passages.

That God chose to have His Word translated and still authoritative is seen from the use in the New Testament of the Greek translation of the Hebrew Old Testament, the Septuagint.

We should thank God for those devoted men who have spent their lifetimes in profound study of the manuscripts God has left us, and who have given us so marvelously perfect a translation as we have. We should distinguish such scholars absolutely and forever from the arrogant "Modernists" (or, in former days, the "Higher Critics"), who undertake to tell us what God *ought* to say in the Bible, rather than with deep humility seeking to find out what God *has* said.

For* the law of the Spirit of life in Christ Jesus, freed me from the law of sin and of death. "The law" in both occurrences here indicates "a given principle acting uniformly." Now, as to "the law of sin and of death," the latter part of Chapter Seven made abundantly clear what that was—the power of sin working in our unredeemed bodies against which even man's renewed will was powerless.

But now, another "law" has come in: not only has the believer life in the Risen Christ, but to him has been given the Holy Spirit as the power of that life: so that the Spirit becomes the Almighty Agent within the believer, securing him wholly, making effectual in experience that "deliverance which Paul saw when he cried in Chapter 7.24,25: "Who shall deliver me out of the body of this death? I thank God [for deliverance] through Jesus Christ our Lord." Of course, the deliverance† is through Christ, for it is Christ's own risen life the believer now shares. But it is the blessed Holy Spirit as "the Spirit of life in Christ Jesus," who makes the deliverance an experience. That is, the constant operation of the Spirit makes effectual in those who have life in Christ Jesus, that deliverance which belongs to those in Christ.

How wonderful, how limitless, the patience of the blessed Spirit of God! Moment by moment, day by day, month by month, year by year, through all the conscious and unconscious processes of tens of thousands of believers, the Spirit acts with

---

*Here we have at the very beginning of the chapter, one of the most common words of argument in Paul's epistles—for (Gr. *gar*). It occurs some 17 times in this Eighth Chapter, and about one half as many in Chapter Seven, etc. In general, it *assigns the reason*. Let us not be among those who avoid Paul's epistles because of the mental attention they demand. Most people would rather read a novel or go to the picture shows than study. A chapter with 17 "fors" in it, is closely knit, and must be patiently followed. Unmeasured blessing will result.

†John Wesley's testimony is well known, concerning the beginning of his life of real faith (in his 35th year, after 13 years in a relatively common-place ministry): "In the evening I went very unwillingly to a society in Aldersgate Street where one was reading Luther's preface to the Epistle to the Romans. About a quarter before nine, while he was describing the change which God works in the heart through faith in Christ, I felt my heart strangely warmed. I felt I did trust in Christ, Christ alone, for salvation; and an assurance was given me, that He had taken away *my* sins, even *mine*, and saved *me* from the law of sin and death." For the next 53 years Wesley was "the outstanding figure and the greatest force in the English speaking world." But notice that he realized at Aldersgate Street, the two great elements of our salvation: (1) forgiveness of sin's guilt; and (2) deliverance from sin's power—from the law of sin and death!

a uniformity that is called "the *law* of the Spirit of life in Christ Jesus." In the newest convert, in the oldest saint, He gives freedom from the law of sin and of death! "Sin in the flesh, which was my torment, is already judged, but in Another; so that there is for me no condemnation on account of the flesh. . . . We lose communion with God, and dishonor the Lord by our behavior, in not walking, according to the Spirit of life, worthy of the Lord. But we are no longer *under the law of sin,* but, having died with Christ, and become partakers of a new life in Him and of the Holy Spirit, we are delivered from this law."

Verses 3, 4: **For, (the thing the Law could not do, because it was powerless on account of the flesh), God, having sent His own Son in the likeness of flesh of sin, and for sin, condemned sin in the flesh: that the righteous result of the Law might be fulfilled in us, who walk not according to flesh, but according to Spirit.**

Several things appear at once from this passage:

1. God did a thing that the Law could not do.

2. The thing that God did was to make possible a holy life for those walking by His indwelling Spirit.

3. The reason that the Law was unable to bring about this holy life, lay in the flesh (Greek, *sarks*), the "mind" of which (verse 7) is enmity against God, and not subject to His Law or Will. Thus, though the Law was holy, just, and good, in itself, it only irritated by its commands a sinful flesh that was not subject to it.

4. God's plan (which, we must remember, is "apart from law," without law's help or "rule," but the very opposite—3.21; 6.14; 7.4,6) was to send His own Son, who had a body "prepared for Him" (Heb. 10.5), and was born according to the angel's words to Mary in Luke 1.35:

"The Holy Spirit shall come upon thee, and the power of the Most High shall overshadow thee: wherefore also that which is to be born shall be called holy, the Son of God." So, although sinless, our Lord Jesus Christ was born in the likeness of "flesh of sin,"—in the likeness of the bodies of the children of Adam, bodies under bondage to sin.

5. God's purpose, as revealed in this passage, was to *get at sin as connected with human flesh,* and deal with it at the cross in the way of righteous condemnation, so that sin would no longer have rights in human bodies. The preposition "for" (Gr. *peri*) in the words **and for sin** is the common word in the Septuagint for sacrifices *for sin.* But it refers here in Romans 8.3 not so much to atonement for sin's guilt before God,—that has already been fully set forth in Chapters Three to Five. The question here(and in Chapters Six to Eight entire) regards the thing Sin itself rather than its guilt.*

It is of the very first importance for the believer to recognize the two great facts which Paul develops concerning Christ's work on the cross:

First, His blood shed *for* us in expiation of our guilt. Considering this, one always thinks of the righteous claims of God's throne against us, and of their being satisfied, fully met, by Christ's shed blood; and of our being thus brought nigh to God.

Second, Our death with Christ, as "made sin for us." Because of our condition of sinfulness, as connected with Adam, and thus "in the flesh," we died *with* Christ. When we believed upon Him, Christ became our Adam, and God dated our history back to Calvary, and commanded us to reckon ourselves dead to sin because we died with Him federally,—thus our history in Adam was ended before God: so that He plainly says to us, "Ye are not in flesh"—where once we were: Chapters 8.9 and 7.5. Compare Ephesians 2.1-3.

Now, in Chapter 8.3, God goes more explicitly into having Christ identified with us, made to become sin on our behalf, our old man crucified with Him. It was that God might thus **condemn sin in the flesh,** dealing with it judicially: as connected potentially with the whole human race, and actually with believers.

When Adam sinned, his federal relationship involved all his posterity in condemnation (5.18,19), but he also "begat a son

---

*"The expression is purposely a general one, because the design was not to speak of Christ's mission to atone for sin, but, in virtue of that atonement, to destroy its dominion and extirpate it altogether from believers. We think it wrong, therefore, to render the words (as in margin) "by a sacrifice for sin" *(peri hamartias)* for this sense is too definite, and makes the idea of expiation more prominent than it is"—Jamieson-Fausset-Brown.

in His own likeness." ALL since Adam have participated in the fallen nature of Adam. "Who can bring a clean thing out of an unclean? Not one." "Behold, I was shapen in iniquity, and in sin did my mother conceive me." "We [now believers] *were* by nature children of wrath."

Now, human thoughts and philosophies, being under, and recognizing, this proneness to evil, and referring it to the body as the conscious abode of sin and source of sin's lusts and temptations, have praised a disembodied state as the only desirable one. Not only the Manicheans and the Buddhists, but real Christians who ought to know better, have regarded a disembodied spiritual state as their hope: "This robe of flesh I'll drop, and rise," etc. "Modernists" today, generally,—as unbelievers in all periods, deny the resurrection of the material body.

But in Romans 8.3 God tells us that sin as connected with flesh has been *condemned, dealt with;* although it has not yet been removed. Some pious and very earnest people have spoken of and sought after "eradication of the sin-principle from the body." But the redemption of the body lies in the future, at Christ's coming. Meanwhile, "We that are in this tabernacle do groan, being burdened; not for that we would be unclothed, [disembodied spirits] but that we would be clothed upon . . . with our habitation which is from Heaven" (our glorified bodies at Christ's coming): "that what is mortal may be swallowed up of life" (II Cor. 5.4).

But the foundation both for the resurrection of the sleeping saints when Christ comes, and for the changing of living believers, lies here in Romans 8.3: *sin has been condemned as connected with human flesh.* This gives God, speaking reverently, the righteous right to transform and catch up into glory the bodies of His saints.

It also gives the Risen Christ the glorious right to live in these bodies of ours while they are on earth; and to walk in us, therefore, daily, in resurrection victory! The only condition of such victorious life, is that we ourselves walk by that indwelling Spirit which has been given to us.

Again, speaking reverently, the Spirit has no commission in this dispensation to go beyond the work done by our Lord on the cross. But that work on the cross was perfect, and far-reaching indeed. Not only did Christ there put away our guilt before God by His blood, but there our old man was crucified with Him: sin was condemned as having any connection with human flesh!

And for sin—The evident reference to the second phase of the sin-offering is apparent in these words. The question in this verse is not one of atonement for guilt, but of the dealing in judgment with that which was not to be atoned for! The evil of our natures is not atoned for, but *judged,* at the cross. The first phase of the sin-offering of Leviticus Four is the sprinkling of the blood before Jehovah, outside the veil of the most holy place, and the putting of the blood upon the horns of the altar of sweet incense before Jehovah, which golden altar, according to Hebrews 9.3,4 pertained to the holy of holies, the Shechinah presence of God; and the pouring out at the base of the brazen altar at the door of the tabernacle, the rest of the blood; together with the burning of the fat—symbol of the inner affections—upon that brazen altar.

This first phase is seen to represent the power of the shed blood of Christ to bring us nigh to God—always the first thing.

Then the second phase is seen in verses 11 and 12 (Lev. 4), where

—"the whole bullock shall he carry forth without the camp unto a clean place, where the ashes are poured out, and burn it on wood with fire: where the ashes are poured out shall it be burnt."

Here, surely, is something further than the putting away of guilt by the shed blood. The fire, burning to ashes that sin-offering, seems to indicate God's holy dealing with sin itself, after the shed blood has made the offerer nigh. It surely has a most solemn significance, for there is no atonement to be made for our evil nature.

At the cross, God having sent His own Son in the likeness of sinful flesh, and having laid on Him as our Substitute our sins, now secures that opportunity which He sought—to deal with sin itself as connected with flesh. And He did deal in judgment. Sin, as connected with flesh, is a condemned, though not yet removed, thing.*

The thing the Law could not do—was accomplished by God! The law was **powerless on account of the flesh.** The Law, holy, just and good, could command; but the flesh was not subject to it, and could not be. Therefore the Law could forbid, rebuke, reprimand, and curse, sin; but could not effectually condemn it, as connected with the flesh. When Christ comes, thank God, we shall be freed from the very presence of sin. But it has already been **condemned in the flesh,** and should be reckoned so by us all. Just as really as our sins were put away by the blood of Christ, so was sin in the flesh condemned, judgment executed on it.

In Romans 8.3, God so "condemned" sin,—so dealt with it, that it was thereafter a *convict*—as regards the flesh.

This had no more been done before, than our *sins* had been borne before! Not until the Cross were *sins* borne, and not until the cross was Sin *judicially dealt with* in the flesh. Sin has thus no more *rights* in us now, than it will have in our glorified bodies!

As we shall see in verse 9, believers are *not in the flesh before God,* at all. This is the second glorious truth; the first being that because sin as connected with human flesh has been dealt with by God, all danger from it, *all possible condemnation for those in Christ Jesus, is over.*

Verse 4: **That the righteous result of the Law** [which the Law sought in vain] **might be fulfilled in us**—Now let us say at once that a righteous state of living, while it is to be brought about in the Christian, is not what God primarily seeks; but rather "that we should be holy and without blame before Him IN LOVE." This will begin to be developed in Romans,

---

*"God condemned, or, as you might say, executed sin in the flesh for us by the death of Christ. He did not die only for my sins (though that's true), but for my sin. The root of sin that is in my nature, and that which worries and distresses the heart of the sincere believer daily, is put away for faith by death, and we are dead to it . . . God has settled the question, condemned the sin in you, which you condemn. But where has He done it? Outside of yourself altogether. . . He takes away the condemnation of sin in the nature, by God's judgment being executed on the sinless flesh of His own Son. Thus sin in my flesh is judged, as well as my committed sins"—Darby, *Notes on Romans, in loc.*

but more thoroughly in other epistles. Nevertheless, our first occupation must be with the truth as set forth in God's order. The Law commanded a wholly righteous walk toward God and toward our neighbor. But David said:

> "I have seen an end of all perfection;
> Thy commandment is exceedingly broad."

Throughout the Psalms, and all the Old Testament Saints' experiences, we find that there is under the Law, an almost constant striving and groaning after a righteous state,— seen, but not experienced, because the Law consisted of outer enactments, to be fulfilled by man. The Law furnished no power. Now in Romans 8.4 we have three things: first, this **righteous state** or result; second, the fact that it was not fulfilled *by* us—we have no more power in ourselves than had the Old Testament saints: but it is **fulfilled *in*** us—it is the passive voice: **be fulfilled.** Third, it is **fulfilled in us** as we consent to reject the flesh and **choose to walk according to** the Spirit. In the Spirit lies all the power. With us, the responsibility of *choice*—a blessed, solemn one!

Verse 5: **For those who are according to flesh,* the things of the flesh do mind; but those according to Spirit, the things of the Spirit.**

The word *phronousin,* "mind," does not here have reference to intellect or understanding, but to the attention or occupation of the being, caused by its natural disposition. And we find thus two classes; first, **those according to flesh.** This we believe includes here all those not born of God, that is, still in a state of nature, in which class Ephesians 2.3 shows believers once to have been: "We also once

---

*We find the definite article "the" in the Greek before the word *Spirit,* where the Holy Spirit's person or personal action is emphasized. But where His power, or nature as a sphere of being, and not His person, is before us, the article generally disappears. To translate literally several instances in this chapter: The Holy Spirit is introduced in verse 2 as "the Spirit of life in Christ Jesus"; but in verse 4, it is "who walk not according to flesh but according to Spirit." In verse 5, "they that are according to Spirit, the things of *the* Spirit." Here "according to Spirit" is a matter of characterizing; whereas in "the things of the Spirit," the Holy Spirit's person is brought to the fore. He has certain *things*—"the things of God none knoweth save the Spirit of God" (II Cor. 2.11). Again, in Romans 8.9, "Ye are not in flesh but *in Spirit*."

lived in the lusts of our flesh, doing the desires of the flesh and of the thoughts." Second, **those according to Spirit.** These are God's true children, the Holy Spirit, of whom they were born, indwelling all of them.

The distinction between these two classes is as real as that between the sheep and goat nations at Christ's coming, or between those written in the book of life and those not written, at the last judgment. An unconquerable sadness rises in our hearts at the fact that after these centuries upon centuries of Divine dealing with man, and especially since the gospel has been preached, as Paul declares, "in all creation under heaven" (Col. 1.23), there are yet those like Cain, Esau, Balaam, Saul, Judas, that are **according to flesh.** Alas, this description includes the mass of our race, for it is only "a little flock" that can be described as being **according to Spirit.**

Now all those **according to flesh** cherish, desire, are occupied with, and absorbed in, talk of, think of, follow after, **the things of flesh; those according to Spirit,** likewise discern, value, love, are absorbed in, **the things of Spirit.**[*]

Those **according to flesh** "mind" the flesh's things: its physical lusts,—gluttony, uncleanness, slothfulness; its soulical lusts,—mental delights, pleasures of the imagination, esthetic indulgences, or "tastes"—whether art, music, sculpture, or what not; its spiritual lusts,—of pride, envy, malice, avarice: in a word, every unclean thing, and every good thing used by unclean persons,—that is, persons not cleansed by the blood of Christ, not new creatures in Him. Then, too, there is the "religion" of the flesh, which includes all not of and in the Holy Ghost.

And there are those who are **according to Spirit,**—who "mind" the Spirit's things: salvation, the person of Christ, the

---

[*]Man earthy, of the earth, an hundred feeds
  On earth's dark poison tree—
Wild gourds, and deadly roots, and bitter weeds;
  And as his food is he.
And hungry souls there are, that find and eat
  God's manna day by day;
And glad they are, their life is fresh and sweet,
  For as their food are they!

—Ter Steegen.

fellowship of the saints, the Word of God, prayer, praise, prophecy, the blessed hope of Christ's coming, walking as He walked before men. True, many, many of these fall woefully short (as they well know); yet they **mind the things of Spirit,** the things of God, to some degree, while others will have nothing of them.

The reason immediately appears:

Verse 6: **For the mind** *(phronēma*—noun form of the verb of verse 5) **of the flesh is death; but the mind of the Spirit, life and peace.** It is terrible to contemplate a mind, disposition, purpose, so set on death (which is its end) that it can be said to be death. It is a most solemn contemplation that we who are in Christ were once in the flesh, the mind and disposition of which we could not and would not change, and which was death itself!

The King James rendering in this verse is hopelessly obscure. God does not say that "to be carnally minded" is death, but that **the mind of the flesh,** in which they are, **is death.** Further, He does not say, "to be spiritually minded is life and peace," as if it were a state into which the believer came; but He does say, **the mind of the Spirit is life and peace.** In neither case does God speak of people, but of the flesh and of the Spirit. If you are **according to Spirit,** having been born of God, there is indwelling you a mighty One, the Comforter, whose whole mind, disposition, and manner of being and ruling within you, is life and peace. This "life" is the life of the Risen Christ, which the Spirit, as "the Spirit of grace," supplies (Heb. 10.29, Gal. 3.5); and this "peace" is that of Christ as spoken of in Isaiah: "Of the increase of His government and peace there shall be no end."

Verse 7: **Because the mind of the flesh is enmity against God: for it is not subject to the law of God, neither indeed can it be.** Here the disposition (mind) of the flesh is shown to be the reason why that disposition is death. Perhaps no one text of Scripture more completely sets forth the hideously lost state of man after the flesh. For the disposition (mind) of the flesh is *enmity itself* toward God! There was indeed, as we saw in Chapter 5.10, reconcilement to God while we were enemies,.

but it did not in any wise consist in changing the nature of the flesh. On the contrary, we were transferred by death with Christ, into the Risen Christ, the flesh remaining unchanged. Your estate while in the flesh was as lost by nature as that of the demons. For nothing worse could be said of them than that they are enmity toward God and are not able to be subject to His law. God certainly has given the flesh up, and nothing but sovereign mercy ever redeemed a human being.*

Verse 8: **And those who are in flesh cannot please God—** This is God's sweeping announcement concerning all mankind that are out of Christ. In this sense, all in the flesh are out of Christ. Those in the flesh, even if, like Cain, they would worship God, would come in their own way,—the flesh's way, which God cannot accept. Terrible prospect! in a state forever displeasing to Him in whom is all blessing. Such are all not born of God.

Verse 9: **But ye are not in flesh but in Spirit, if so be that the Spirit of God dwelleth in you.** Here the great mark of a true Christian is, that the Spirit of God dwells in him. If he is indwelt by the Spirit of God, he is not "in flesh," but instead an entirely different kind of being,—"in Spirit." The Spirit becomes now the element in which the believer lives, like water to the fish, or air to the bird, vital, supplying, protecting.

Practically, there are those, like the men of Ephesus—"about twelve (Acts 19.1), who were disciples," but did not have the Holy Spirit,—a fact Paul instantly discerned. Their answer to his question in verse 2, is wrongly translated in the King James. They really said, "We did not so much as hear whether the Holy Spirit *was*" (or, "was given": it is exactly the same form as John 7.39, "The Spirit *was* not yet; because Jesus was not yet glorified"). John the Baptist had constantly taught about the Holy Spirit, that He that should come after him

---

*Very many years ago a deep revival was in progress in New Haven, Conn., and in Yale College there. Many, especially of the society class, were falling under profound conviction. Several young ladies who had found peace in the blood of Christ, went to a very prominent friend,—a young woman whose generosity, grace and kindness had endeared her especially to her circle of friends. They besought her to come to the revival meetings. When she objected, they protested, "But God has a claim on you. He loves you. He gave His Son to die for you." Fiercely she burst forth, stamping her foot: "I *hate* God!"

would give them the Holy Spirit. It was concerning the coming of the Holy Spirit at Pentecost that these at Ephesus were ignorant. They were honest: they were converted men; they had been baptized with John's baptism of repentance. John had said that they should, however, believe on Him that should come after him—on Jesus. Now Paul takes them and instructs them that Christ's redeeming work having been fully finished on the cross, the Holy Spirit was come, and was given to all believers.

"And when Paul had laid his hands upon them, the Holy Spirit came on them; and they spake with tongues, and prophesied" (vs. 6).

Now they were in the full Christian position. Thousands upon thousands of earnest, professing Christians have, we believe, like these, not yet heard "that the Holy Spirit *was*," that is, had definitely come on the scene at Pentecost, to be given to every believer. He is *here!* The gift of Him and His indwelling constitutes the distinctive mark of Christians.

Many sincere people are yet spiritually under John the Baptist's ministry of repentance. Their state is practically that of the struggle of Romans Seven, where neither Christ nor the Holy Spirit is mentioned, but only a quickened but undelivered soul in struggle under a sense of "duty," not a sense of full acceptance in Christ and sealing by the Holy Spirit.*

---

*Of earnest "church members" today have all the Holy Spirit? Here and there is one who has the witness, "Abba, Father"; who testifies boldly that Jesus Christ is his Lord; who has a burden of prayer for the lost; who has a yearning for the fellowship of the saints, and a hunger for God's Word. What about the rest? They are occupied with various "Christian" activities. Or, having in most cases, (I speak of earnest souls) a Seventh of Romans experience, not knowing themselves fully accepted of God on the ground of Christ's work, and not knowing the deliverance that is through Christ Jesus by the indwelling Holy Spirit from the power of sin and selfishness and worldliness, and sometimes—awful to say! not willing to come out and be separate from that world which crucified their Lord (and is not sorry!), they become part of the present ecclesiastical system,—as Jews were of that system.

You ask, are such people Christians? If they have finally broken with sin, and are "praying to God alway," they belong, indeed, in the company of Cornelius (Acts 10), who was a devout man, but was not yet in the Christian position. Two steps led him to the Christian position: first, faith in Christ that his sins were remitted, (Acts 10.43); second, the gift of the Holy Ghost, which followed (Acts 11.15-18.)

Of course, we cannot agree with the Pentecostal people that only those that speak with tongues have the Holy Ghost. We believe that gift was given at Cornelius' house to convince Peter, as we read in the following chapter (Acts 11.17) that

But if any man hath not the Spirit of Christ, he is none of His.

Now this sentence would seem at first to rule out what we have been saying in the foot-note on the Holy Spirit. But, that the apostle is not speaking of those who will shortly have the Spirit of Christ, they being sincere, godly souls, is at once evident when we remember that Cornelius, and those twelve men at Ephesus, were sincere disciples as far as their light went: and in them God is simply showing us the processes of the work of salvation in real saints. Whereas, when Paul says **none of His,** he is speaking in an absolute way of those who are Christ's and those who are not. Those who are Christ's either have or will have the Spirit. Sad to say, it may not be until on a death-bed, when at last the soul renounces all hope but the shed blood of Christ, and is then sealed by the Spirit. Notice also here that the Spirit is called **the Spirit of Christ.** This is, of course, the Holy Spirit, (not the mind or disposition of Christ).* He is called the Spirit of *Christ,* because Christ promised and sent Him: "The Comforter, whom I will send unto you from the Father,—the Spirit of truth, which proceedeth from the Father," (John 15.26); "Having received of the Father the promise of the Holy Spirit, He [Christ] hath poured forth this which ye see and hear" (Acts 2.33). And

---

*It is astonishing to find many commentators insisting on "Spirit" with a small "s" here, stating that it is "the human spirit, . . . essentially that part of man that holds communion with God" (Sanday). But such a notion defeats the whole meaning of the passage, which is, that that possession by the believer of the Holy Spirit in person is the seal and mark of a true believer over against those that are merely "soulical" (literally, "psychical"); as in Jude 19: "These are they who make separations, sensual, [Greek: *psychikoi*], *having not the Spirit."* Paul says to the Ephesians concerning Christ: "In whom, *upon believing,* [aorist] ye were sealed with the Holy Spirit of promise, which is an earnest of our inheritance" (Eph. 1.13,14). Having the Holy Spirit is the unvarying apostolic sign of the true Christian. "Hereby we know that He abideth in us *by the Spirit* which He gave us" (I John 3.24). Compare Gal. 3.2,3; I Cor. 12.3,13.

---

they had "the like gift," that had been conferred on the hundred and twenty on the Day of Pentecost. That gift was the Holy Spirit; and not a gift—*charisma*—which the Spirit Himself afterwards conferred. The same thing applies to Acts 19.6: "The Holy Spirit came on them; and they spake with tongues, and prophesied." The essential thing was the conferring of the Holy Spirit, and not the Spirit's operations thereafter.

(What we say does not mean that we "forbid to speak with tongues"—which God forbids us to forbid:—I Corinthians 14.39;—and concerning "prophesying" we comment in Chapter Twelve.)

also because He manifests Christ: "He shall glorify Me; for
He shall take of Mine, and shall declare it unto you" (John
16.14). Those therefore who belong to Christ have thus His
Spirit given to them, always, as we said above, (if they are
not still in the preparatory states of repentance, or legal struggle against sin, as in Romans Seven) when they rest believingly
in Christ and His work!

Dwelleth in you—This word **dwelleth** is a touching word,
used five times of the Spirit's making His home within us, in
every redeemed one!

Verse 10: **And if Christ is in you, the body indeed is
dead, on account of sin; but the Spirit is life, on account of
righteousness.**

Here in this tenth verse we have the answer to our Lord's
prayer in John 17.21, 22: "I pray . . . that they may all be
one; even as Thou, Father, art in Me, and I in Thee, that they
also may be in us: . . . that they may be one, even as we
are one."

We have seen in an earlier chapter how we came to be in
Christ: that God, having ended our history before Himself as
connected with the first Adam, at the cross, created us in
Christ, the Last Adam, the Second Man. Thus was the one
part of our Lord's intercession answered. *We are in Christ.*
But the other part of the great mystery is here before us in
Romans 8.10: *Christ is in us.* Although, as we know, He
is within us by His Spirit, yet it is Christ Himself who is in us.
That the Spirit can make Christ present in us, we see in the
beautiful words of II Corinthians 3.17, 18: "Now the Lord
is the Spirit: . . . We . . . are transformed into the same
image from glory to glory, even as from the Lord the Spirit."
Or, as Paul says in the solemn words of II Corinthians 13.5:
"Know ye not as to your own selves, that Jesus Christ is in
you?"*

---

*"Christ in you, the hope of glory" (Col. 1.27), is called by the apostle there
"the riches of the glory of this mystery"—the great revelation which Paul's gospel
contains.

But it is a terrible error to confine the revelation of that mystery to what are
called "the prison epistles," beginning with Ephesians. The two sides of the gospel, We in Christ, and, Christ in us, are constantly set forth from Romans on.
The very words of our verse in Romans (8.10): If Christ is in you, are as won-

Our Lord said in John 14.10, 11: "Believe Me that I am in the Father, and the Father in Me." Christ and His Father were distinct persons, yet one, in being, life, love, and purpose. "I and the Father are one." "The living Father sent Me, and I live because of the Father." "The Father loveth the Son . . . I love the Father." "I glorified Thee . . . glorify Thou Me with Thine own self." A similar marvelous union our blessed Lord asked and obtained for us with Himself: "That they may be one, even as We are one!" "That they may be in Us" (John 17.21-23).

Returning to Romans 8.10: There is a double fact stated concerning those in whom Christ by His Spirit is. First, **the body is dead.** Second, **the Spirit is life.** It is evident that our bodies here are contrasted with our spirits, and these as *in* the Holy Spirit. It is well that we thoroughly understand and believe that our bodies are in no sense redeemed as yet. They are "dead" as regards any emotion Godward; and this "because of sin." Those who teach and seek "eradication of the sinful principle," as they call it, would do well to ponder this tenth verse.

The other blessed fact, that **the Spirit is life because of righteousness,** is enough for our present walk. "Him who knew no sin God made to become sin on our behalf, that we might become the righteousness of God in Him." Not only are our sins put away and we ourselves "justified from all things"; but we have been created in Christ Jesus. The new creature, Paul tells us, "hath been created after God in righteousness and holiness of truth" (Eph. 4.24). It is striking in Romans 8.10 that the noun **life** is opposed to the adjective **dead.** Our spirits before they were new-cre-

---

derful as we find! In Galatians also (2.20): "It is no longer I that live, but Christ liveth in me." And in II Corinthians 13.3: "Christ that speaketh in me"; and in Galatians 1.16: "To reveal His Son in me." (These last two refer especially to testimony.) In Ephesians 3.14 to 21 we have the great prayer, "that Christ may make His home down in your hearts through faith." He lives in all saints (II Cor. 13.5), just as all saints are in Him. But the Ephesians passage is like Revelation 3.20: "Behold, I stand at the door and knock: if any man hear My voice and open the door, I will come in to him, and will sup with him, and he with Me." Let us beware of the false teaching, that only the so-called "prison epistles" are "church truth." For in all Paul's epistles we find this great double truth, we in Christ, and Christ in us. Each epistle has its particular object and phase of truth, certainly, but they are *one;* and are *all* for the Church, the **one** Body!

ated in Christ, were alive so far as existence is concerned, but had no life as God counts life—for that is only in Christ, and by the Spirit.

We read "Spirit" in this verse, meaning the Holy Spirit. The sense being, that the Spirit, by whose power we were made partakers of the risen life of Christ, acts constantly as "the Lord the Spirit," (as quoted above from II Cor. 3.17) as the maintainer and supplier of that life of Christ in us. The Holy Spirit alone could be called *life!* We recognize that the human body and the human spirit seem to be contrasted in the verse before us.* Yet we remember Galatians 5.25: "We live by the Spirit"; and Romans 8.2: "The law of the Spirit *of life* in Christ Jesus"; and "The mind of the Spirit is life" (verse 6). Our spirits are now alive—and that to God! But "Christ is our *life";* and the Administrator of that life in us is the Spirit of God.

Verse 11: **But if the Spirit of Him that raised up Jesus from the dead dwelleth in you, He that raised up Christ Jesus from the dead shall give life also to your mortal bodies, through His Spirit that dwelleth in you.**

The body—the mortal body—is the subject of this verse. Our spirits have been shown to have *life,—now*: while the body is still *dead*—as to God: But now God announces that to *these bodies,* so dead to God, holiness and heaven, is by and by to be *given life!*

First, we are reminded that the Spirit of that God who raised up *Jesus* is dwelling in us. Now, *Jesus* is our Lord's personal name: "Thou shalt call His name Jesus." It was *Jesus* whom they crucified, and buried in Joseph's tomb. With Jesus, before His death and resurrection, we were not joined; but with *Christ Jesus,* the Risen One! This is His resurrection Name: indeed, He is never named thus until the Epistles.

Now we are asked to reflect on that place of weakness and deadness in which Jesus once was. But God raised *Him* up from the dead. And the Spirit of the God who thus raised Jesus is dwelling in *us!*

---

*It is "body" *(soma),* not flesh *(sarx).* If it were *sarx,* we would at once know the Holy Spirit is meant,—from Galatians 5.17.

So that, although our bodies are yet dead on account of sin,—dead to God,—the Spirit of Him who raised up *Christ Jesus* from the dead,—Christ Jesus, in whom we now are,— this God will give life also to these poor mortal bodies of ours! And it will be by His Spirit who now indwells us! (This word *"mortal"* means, *subject to physical death;* and is used in Scripture only of *the body.*)

What an unutterable comfort! "Whether we wake or sleep," this blessed indwelling Spirit of God will give life to these mortal dead-to-God bodies of ours, so that they shall be as *alive Godward* as our redeemed spirits now are!

It is present comfort beyond measure to know that when the day comes, God will do this blessed giving of life to our bodies through His Spirit that is now dwelling in us!

Mortal bodies—"Mortal" and "immortal," always, as we note above, in Scripture refer to the body. It is "this mortal" which will "put on immortality" when Christ comes. "What is mortal shall be swallowed up of life" (I Cor. 15.35,54; II Cor. 5.4).

What blessed phases of our salvation lie in the hands of the indwelling Spirit!

"Who shall deliver me?" That question of Chapter Seven is abundantly answered here in Chapter Eight! Not only from guilt, by the shed blood of Christ (in Chapter Five); but from the "law of sin" in the members, over which even man's quickened will was so impotent; and from a "mind" that is death, into the mind and walk of the blessed indwelling Spirit Himself: into a mind that is "life and peace." But further, now, we find that God, by that same indwelling Spirit, will bring our very mortal bodies,—now dead to God, and subject to death, to share that life in Christ which our spirits now have!

12   So then, brethren, we are debtors, not to the
13   flesh,—according to flesh to be living! For if ye
      live according to flesh, ye are about to die: but if,
      by the Spirit, ye put to death the doings of the
14   body, ye shall live. For as many as are led by

15 [the] Spirit of God, these are sons of God. For
ye received not a spirit of bondage again unto
fear; but ye received a Spirit of adoption, whereby
16 we cry, Abba, Father. The Spirit Himself beareth
witness with our spirit, that we are children of
17 God: and if children, then heirs: heirs of God,
and joint heirs with Christ; if so be that we suffer
with Him, that we may be also glorified with Him.

Verse 12: So then, brethren, we are debtors, not to the
flesh—according to flesh to be living. "So then" has all
the great truths in mind from Chapter 6.1 to this verse!
Identified with Christ, our old man was crucified with Him,
our connection with Adam the first being thus broken by
death. Next we share His newness of life as being in Christ
Risen. Next the Spirit of life is caused to indwell us, by
His almighty power setting us free from the law of sin and
of death—because all rights of sin as connected with flesh
were cancelled at the cross. Finally, although our body is
still dead to God, yet the Spirit of Him who raised Jesus
personally dwells within us, guaranteeing that He who
raised Christ federally and caused us to share His risen
life will make our bodies also alive toward Him when
Christ returns. And meanwhile the indwelling Spirit becomes an "earnest" of the coming redemption of our
bodies. "So then"—let the power of all these mighty truths
govern our thoughts here.

Now note the form of statement in verse 12: **We are
debtors**—(indeed we are) to God, to Christ and to the
indwelling Spirit! But this debtorship to God is not here
pressed at all. But rather the negation of any debtorship
whatever to the flesh! in view of our wonderful deliverance
just recited. We are indeed debtors, but **not to the flesh—
according to flesh to be living.** God formed man's body,
first, calling him *man* (Gen. 2.7). Then he breathed into his
nostrils the breath (literally, *spirit*) of life; and man became
a living *soul*. His bodily functions we all know. His soul-life
put him in touch with the world into which by Divine creation
he had now been introduced, but man was essentially a *spirit,*

living in a *body,* possessing a *soul.* It was with his *spirit* that God communed and in which alone man was God-conscious.

Now when man sinned, all was overthrown! The body, that was to be the tabernacle of this Divinely inbreathed or created spirit, took immediate lordship. The life of God was withdrawn from man's spirit. He had *died to God!* The spirit became the slave of the body; and the propensities of the latter, normal and controlled before, became the whole urge or driving force of man's existence! His *soul,* also, which included his five "senses,"—which perceived and enjoyed the external universe; with his reason and imagination, became controlled by what God called "the flesh." "The thoughts of man's heart," became "only evil and that continually."

Now in the new birth the dead spirit (dead to God) is by Divine creation made alive, or enlifed with Christ; and the Holy Spirit becomes the sphere of man's newly created spirit; for whatever the believer's progress may be, he is no longer in flesh but in Spirit!

The body's demands are the same as ever, because the body is not yet redeemed; and to live after the desires of the body— "according to flesh" Paul warns:

Verse 13: **For if ye live according to flesh, ye are about to die**—Here is a terrible warning: (1) It is one of the great red lights by which God keeps His elect out of fatal paths. (Compare I Cor. 15.2, Col. 1.23.)   (2) It shows how those who have received a knowledge of the truth and are addressed by the apostle as among God's people, may yet be choosing a flesh-walk—which involves the refusal of the Spirit—refusal to be led by Him, as are all God's real sons (verse 14). (3) Death, here, is of course eternal death, as in Chapter Six: "The end of these things is death"; and here in Chapter Eight: "The mind of the flesh is death." (4) Note that expression "about to die" *(mellete).* Those following a flesh-walk are not yet viewed as dead, so let them hear and repent quickly, lest they become as those professing Christians became in Jude 12: "Autumn trees without fruit, twice dead, plucked up by the roots,"—summer ended, a fruitless autumn, and Divine cursing. For "twice dead" means that there was an awakening, a quickening, and a tasting, as in Hebrews Six; tasting of the heavenly gift—eternal life; then, final apostasy, and withdrawal of all gracious influences; the very roots, as in the barren fig tree, plucked up and withered. Born again? No. Yet "escaping the defilements of the world," only to choose to go back to a "twice-dead" condition. Surely the mind of the flesh is death!

But if, by the Spirit, ye put to death the doings of the body, ye shall live—Here is a most definite word that the body is under the control of sin; and a most definite statement as to the manner of a holy life.

1. The deeds, or doings of the body are naturally selfish, and so, evil, for the body is not redeemed. (See same word "deed" in Luke 23.51.) The body would have its every desire gratified—because it so desires. It has no governor in itself but the sin by which it is still dead—to God and all holiness. Even the lawful needs and desires of the body become sinful and deathful if the body is allowed to rule. In Chapter 6.12 we hear: "Let not sin reign in your mortal body that ye should obey the desires of it" (the body). The beasts and birds follow the instincts and desires of their bodies, being without spirit, conscience or sin. But man cannot do so. For he has,—yea, he is, essentially a spirit,—though he dwells in a bodily tabernacle, and has a conscience, under the eye of which all his consents or refusals pass, and that constantly. And to let his unredeemed body govern him, is to fall far below the very beasts: for he lets sin reign in his mortal body, when he lets the lusts of the body control his decisions.

2. Now God says the "doings" of the body are to be put to death. Not that our bodies are not dear to God. They are,—and if we are Christ's our bodies are members of Christ (I Cor. 6.15). But they are not redeemed as yet. And God has left us in these unredeemed bodies, that we may learn—(1) the badness of our old self-life, as we see that in our flesh there dwelleth no good thing; (2) the exceeding sinfulness of sin,—and learn to hate and abhor it; (3) the sweet and blessed path of relying on the indwelling Holy Spirit,—nay, even of using His Almighty and willing power by acts of simple faith;

for it reads, "If WE, by the Spirit, put to death the doings of the body."

For we must note most carefully that a holy life is to be lived *by us*. It is not that we have any power,—we have none. But God's Spirit dwells in us for the express object of being called "upon by us to put to death the doings of the body." Self-control is one of that sweet cluster called "the fruit of the Spirit," in Galatians 5.22.

How confidently Paul walked in this power of the Spirit! "In the Holy Spirit," he says, in II Corinthians 6.6,—"in pureness," etc. And again, "I will not be brought under the power of any" bodily desire,—however lawful. And again, "I buffet my body, and bring it into subjection; lest, having preached to others, I myself should be rejected" (I Cor. 6.13; 9.27).

A holy life without a controlled body is an absolute contradiction; not to be dreamed of for a moment. Indeed, God goes further here, and says, "Ye shall live,—if ye by the Spirit put to death the doings of the body": the opposite path being, "If ye live according to flesh, ye are about to die!"

When we announce that the Scripture teaching is that walking by the Holy Spirit has taken the place of walking under the rule of the Mosaic law, there remains to be examined, and that most carefully, just what walking by the Spirit means.

1. It does not mean to desert the use of our faculties of moral perception or of moral judgment.

Although there doubtless are occasions in which the believer, being filled with the Spirit, acts in a wholly unanticipated way; and although there may be times when he will be carried quite out of himself in ecstasies of joy or love; and although the believer walking by the Spirit will normally be conscious of the almighty power within, of triumph over the world and the flesh: nevertheless the feet of the believer will never be swept from the path of conscious moral determination. He will always know that so far as decisions of moral matters are concerned, he has still the sense of moral accountability, or, perhaps better, responsibility. The believer's own conscience will protest against any such letting go of himself as has been unfortunately found throughout Church history when people have submitted themselves to such ecstatic states that moral judgment and self-control were cast to the winds.

We do indeed read of most remarkable experiences, and that in deeply approved saints, in which their spirits were overwhelmed by the vision of Divine things, and we must adduce that in such experiences they were rapt and ecstatic; but never to the losing of that self-control which, we read in Galatians 5.22, is a fruit of the Spirit. Even in the exercise of the gifts spoken of by the apostle in I Corinthians 12 to 14, it is definitely declared, "The spirits of the prophets are subject to the prophets."

It is in the abandonment of the sense of moral responsibility into unscriptural surrender of the mental and spiritual faculties, —into other control than self-control directed by the Holy Spirit, that such awful extravagances have occurred in Church history.

2. To be led by the Spirit does indeed involve the surrender of our wills to God. But God, on His side, does not crush into fatalistic abandon those very faculties with which He has endowed men. On the contrary, the surrendered saint immediately finds His faculties marvelously quickened,—his faculties both of mind and of sensibility. All the powers of his soul-life (which include his intellect, tastes, feelings, emotions, and recollective memory) are renewed. His will being yielded to God, God now "works in Him to will" as well as "to do of His good pleasure,"—in which the surrendered saint rejoices.

But while it is indeed God who works in us even to will, yet it is true that walking in the Spirit is still our own choice: "If ye by the Spirit put to death the doings of the body"— we read. The Holy Spirit is infinitely ready, but God leads rather than compels.

There is deep mystery, no doubt, in the great double fact of God is working in us to will, and on the other hand, of our choosing His will, moment by moment. We can only affirm that both are taught in Scripture, and we ourselves know both to be blessedly true.

Verses 14, 15: **For as many as are led by [the] Spirit of God, these are sons of God. For ye received not a spirit of bondage again unto fear;**—Let us look first at the words "sons of God"; and second at what is meant by being "led by the Spirit"; third, let us see that our being thus in the Spirit's sphere and control is the proof of the reality of our sonship.

1. "Sons" means "adult-sons," sons come of age (see footnote, verse 15). The term, when referring to saints, is applied in Paul's epistles both to Christ (Rom. 1.3, 4, 9); and to those associated with Him since His resurrection (Gal. 4.4-7); therefore to His own saints, sealed by the Spirit—those sons whom God is "bringing unto glory."

2. Being "led by the Spirit" does not refer here to service, nor to "guidance" in particular paths. It refers to that general control by the blessed Spirit of those born of the Spirit, living by the Spirit, in the Spirit. He is the sphere and mode of their being, and is their seal unto the day of redemption.

3. That our being thus in the Spirit's sphere and control is the proof of the reality of our sonship, is evident from what has been said; but let us avoid the thought that assurance of our sonship is based on our perfect obedience to the Spirit. Nothing is based upon *us*. If one of God's true saints disobeys, it is the office of that same Spirit to convict him of his sin, interceding in Him "according to God" (Rom. 8.27), while Christ intercedes for him above (I John 2.1).

Israel received a **spirit of bondage** when they were placed under the Law. And how sad that perhaps the most of Christians regard themselves as under the Law and so under bondage. In this they are like the world, which fears Christ as (they think) a hard taskmaster. Now the result of a spirit of bondage was **fear.** When Israel walked in the wilderness with Jehovah dwelling in darkness in the holy of holies in the tabernacle, they were taught to fear. For Jehovah was teaching a sinful people His holiness and separateness from them, and how to draw near Him only by sacrifices.

But when Christ came, all was different. He came not noticing or marking sin. Quickly the common people became glad. Proud religion called Him "a friend of publicans and sinners"—and He was. We have no words to express the limitless graciousness of God manifested in the flesh—in Christ.

But how much beyond even those favored to see "the days of the Son of Man" on earth is the position of those in Christ Risen: sin put away forever, released from the old Adam life and responsibilities, and now the Spirit sent witnessing in our hearts—the very Spirit of God's Son. A spirit of fear and bondage is as out of place now as if one caught up with Christ in the Rapture were afraid to face God, in whose Son he is!

Ye received a spirit of adult-sonship,* whereby we cry Abba, Father!

Verse 16: **The Spirit Himself beareth witness with our spirit that we are born-ones of God.**

The manner of communication between the Holy Spirit and our spirit is a profound mystery. Indeed all man's vaunted knowledge is challenged by Jehovah's word to Job: "Who hath given understanding to the mind?" We do not speak now

---

*We have sought in vain for some simple English expression to set forth the Greek word so poorly rendered "adoption." This word is *huio-thesia*: from, *huios,* "son come of age"; and *thesia,* a placing, or setting a person or thing in its place. In earthly affairs, "adoption" is the term applied to the selection as child and heir of one not born of us; and the execution of legal papers making such child our own, inheriting legal rights, etc.

But God's children are begotten and born of God, and are called *tekna,* "born-ones," of God. Thus are they directly related to God, "partakers of the Divine nature" (II Pet. 1.4). All God's children, whether in Old Testament days or to-day, are thus born. But the word *huios* means, a child come of age: no longer "as a servant" (Gal. 4.7). And *huiothesia* means God's recognizing them in that position! This will be consummated fully at the coming of Christ, when our *bodies,* redeemed, and fashioned anew, shall be conformed to Christ's glorious body.

Meanwhile, because we are already adult sons *(huioi),* God has given us a spirit of adult-sonship! No Jew called God "Father," or "Abba"; but "Jehovah." (Indeed, fearfulness, even prevented, generally, the use by the Jews of God's memorial-name—Jehovah—for that nation: they called Him *Adonai*—"Lord." And the English translations of the Old Testament, except the A.R.V., do the same thing,—only printing Jehovah as "LORD"—in capitals! But this is no translation; and is legal fearfulness.)

"Because ye are adult-sons *(huioi)* God sent forth *the Spirit of His Son* into our hearts, crying, Abba, Father" (Gal. 4.6, 7).

Even as to the strong Roman law concerning "adoption" of those *not* born in the family, (and Paul is writing to Romans) the following is instructive:

"The process of legal adoption by which the chosen heir became entitled not only to the reversion of the property but to the civil status, to the burdens as well as the rights of the adopter—made him become, as it were, his other self, one with him ... We have but a faint conception of the force with which such an illustration would speak to one familiar with the Roman practice; how it would serve to impress upon him the assurance that the adopted son of God becomes, in a peculiar and intimate sense, one with the heavenly Father." (Merivale, quoted by Vincent.)

with the mere purpose of ridiculing man's vaunted knowledge, but simply to state facts. Human philosophy and science know absolutely nothing about the quality or nature of spirit.

God, in this passage in Romans, does not address Himself at all to human intellect, but to the consciousness of His saints.* **The Spirit Himself beareth witness with our spirit.** There is no certainty comparable with this!

"With our spirit"—We are not told that the Spirit bears witness *to* our spirit, as if the knowledge that we are God's children were some unheard of, undreamed matter to our own spirits. But He **beareth witness *with* our spirit,** showing that the child of God, having had communicated to him God's own nature (II Pet. 1.4), Christ's own life (I Cor. 6.17), is fundamentally, necessarily conscious of the glorious fact of filial relationship to God. Along with this consciousness, the Spirit indwelling witnesses, enabling us, moving us, to cry, "Abba, Father." There is life before this, just as the new-born babe has life and breath before it forms a syllable. It is significant that the Spirit indwelling is the power whereby we cry, Abba, Father,—by His enlightenment, His encouragement, His energy.

*Much unnecessary and unfruitful questioning as to what is the **witness of the Spirit** has arisen.

It is plain both in this passage (verses 15, 16) and from the great verse in Galatians 4.6: "Because ye are sons, God sent forth the Spirit of His Son into our hearts, crying, Abba, Father," that the "witness of the Spirit" is the producing of the consciousness of being born of God, of belonging to His family, in Christ. And for us today who are in Christ, there should be the consciousness, not merely of babes, but of adult-sons. "God sent forth *the Spirit of His Son* into our hearts, crying, Abba, Father." It is a sense of the very relation to the Father which Christ Himself has as Son! Mark, in this we do not "know" the Son, for He is the second person of the Deity; but we do know the Father, and the Son "willeth to reveal Him" by sending the blessed Spirit for that purpose. (See Matt. 11.27.)

How beautifully sweet is the recognition of its parents by a babe, a child! unconscious, instinctive, yet how real!

Now the witness of the Spirit is to the fact of our relationship. How foolish it would be, and how sad, if a child should fall into the delusion that it must have certain "feelings" if it is to believe itself a child of its parents. The unconscious certainty of the relationship is the beauty of it. There are, indeed, certain tests Divinely given us, by which to assure ourselves. Most of these, perhaps, are in the great Epistle of Fellowship, First John;—"fellowship with the Father and with His Son Jesus Christ": "I have written unto you, little children, because ye know the Father (2-13). Beloved, now are we children of God, and it is not yet made manifest what we shall be. We know that, if He shall be manifested, we shall be like Him; for we shall see Him even as He is (3.2). Hereby we know that He abideth in us, by the Spirit which He gave us" (3.24).

The operations of a man's mind either in philosophy or in science constitute an eternal quest for certainty. The conclusions of philosophy are based upon theories and hypotheses, and are always being challenged and perpetually overthrown by succeeding new schemes of philosophy. And even the dearest discoveries of science await new explanations—of the very constitution of the universe they are invented in.

But with the child of God—the born-again family, there is no such uncertainty! A child of God *knows*. And the blessed Holy Spirit, by whose inscrutable power he was born again, keeps forever witnessing with his consciousness,—and that through no processes of his mind, but directly, that he is a born-one of God.

This is most natural and could not be otherwise. Children in an earthly family grow up together as a family, their parents addressing them as children, their brothers and sisters knowing them to be such. It is the most beautiful thing in the natural world!

How much more certain, yea, how much more wonderful and beautiful, is the constantly witnessed relationship of His children to God: **the Spirit Himself beareth witness with our spirit, that we are born-ones* of God.** Believers will find themselves calling God *Father,* in their prayers and communion. This witness will spring up of itself in the heart that has truly rested in Christ and His shed blood.

Conversely, if we find ourselves always in our prayers saying Lord, Lord, and never Father, we should be concerned, and should go back to the beginnings of things,—that is, to the record concerning our guilt, in Romans Three, and our helplessness, and to the fact that God has set forth Christ as

---

*This word *tekna* means "born-ones," offspring. The several other Greek words for child are used accurately in Scripture: *brephos,*—an unborn child or a new-born child (Luke 1.44 and 2.12 and 16); *nepios,* babes or small children,—children not come of age (Matt. 21.16; I Cor. 3.1; 13.11; Gal. 4.1, 3; Eph. 4.14), as over against adults or those come of age; *pais, paidion* and *paidarion,* children, generally; and with regard to their need of training and teaching. (The verbal form *paideo* means to train children, or to cause any one to learn; thus arises its use in Hebrews 12.6.) Finally, *huios,* which is the word of sonship, of adult understanding: Paul contrasts this word, with *nepios* in both Galatians 4.6, and I Corinthians 13.11, as adulthood over against childhood, or infancy.

These distinctions are not absolute, but practically so.

a propitiation; and resting there, in His shed blood, we should boldly call God Father, and cultivate that habit.

Nor, in our judgment, should Christians permit themselves habits of address in prayer not authorized and exemplified in Scripture. Our Lord Jesus prayed saying, "Father," "My Father," "O righteous Father." He did not say, "Almighty God," nor did He use the name "Jehovah," as Israel did in the Psalms and elsewhere. He said, "Father." And He said to us, "When ye pray, say, Father." (Note Luke 11.2 in the Revised Version.) "We have our access," says Paul, "in one Spirit unto the Father." "To us there is one God, the Father" (I Cor. 8.6). Today, also, some devoted Christians address God as "Father-God." But why not say, "Father," as our Lord directed and the Spirit witnesses? To say "Father-God," makes the first word an adjective!

Some may say, "It is foolish and unnecessary to make such discriminations." But if God "sent forth the Spirit of His Son into our hearts, crying, Abba, Father," we speak to the Father as did our beloved Savior Himself. This is infinite grace, and should be appreciated and cultivated by us. Moreover, if you were going into the presence of the King of England, you would take thought for a proper form of address. How infinitely rather when you address God!

Verse 17: **If born-ones, then heirs**—We have noted that the word for children here, *tekna,* is different from the word for adult-sons *(huioi)* of verse 14. The word indicates the fact that we are really begotten of God through His Word by His Spirit, and are partakers of His nature. Heirship is from relationship. The young ruler who came running to the Lord saying, "What good thing shall I *do* that I may inherit eternal life?" was a perfect example of a legalist. Indeed, Nicodemus, beloved man, "understood not these things"—of being born again. Now, if a man is really a child of God by begetting and birth, he becomes indissolubly God's heir! This is a fact of such overwhelming magnitude that our poor hearts hardly grasp it. It is said of no angel, cherub, or seraph, that he is an heir of God. Believer, if you will reflect, meditate deeply, on this, *I am born of God; I am one of His heirs!* earthly things will shrink to nothing. Now, J. D. Rockefeller, Jr., has inherited his father's wealth: why? Because he was his father's *born son*. The young ruler said, "What must I *do* to inherit?" a contradiction in itself!

Heirs of God, and joint-heirs with Christ—I could not have the presumption to write these words if they were not in God's holy Book. That a guilty, lost, wretched child of Adam the First should have written of him, **a joint-heir with Christ,** the Eternal Maker of all things, the Well-beloved of the Father, the Righteous One, the Prince of life—only God, the God of all *grace* could prepare such a destiny for such a creature!

And, we may humbly say, perhaps, that God could only do this by joining us in eternal union with His beloved Son, as the Last Adam, the Second Man; having released us from Adam the First and all his connections, at the cross, and having placed us in Christ Risen, in all the boundless and everlasting rights of His dear Son, whom He has "appointed heir of all things!" Ages after ages of ever-increasing blessing forever and forever and forever, lie in prospect for believers—for the joint-heirs!

If so be that we suffer with Him, that we may be also glorified with Him—Here two schools of interpretation part company, one saying boldly that all the saints are designated, and that all shall reign with Christ; the other, that reigning with Christ depends upon voluntary choosing of a path of suffering with Him. Well, the Greek word *eiper* translated "if so be," will support either of these interpretations.*

"That we may also be *glorified together*." This is the key to our question: WHO are to be glorified with Christ when He comes? In Chapter Five Paul says (and that of, and to, all the saints), *"We* rejoice in hope of the *glory* of God." And in

---

Eiper—"if so be that," is used six times in the New Testament: Rom. 8.9 and 17; I Cor. 8.5; 15.15; II Thess. 1.6; I Pet. 2.3. An examination of these references shows that this word *eiper* can only be interpreted in one passage, I Cor. 15.15, as introducing a non-existent state of things; and here it is only most evidently for the sake of argument only: "if so be that the dead rise not." This use in Rom. 8.9, the text proves to be in connection with a positive asserted fact: "if so be the Spirit of God dwelleth in you." This word *eiper* can be rendered in all six passages by "if, as is supposed." I would suggest the rendering, "inasmuch as," for Rom. 8.17.

II Thessalonians 1.10 we read, "When He shall come to be glorified *in His saints,* and to be marveled at *in all them that believed."* And in I Corinthians 15.23 : "Christ the firstfruits ; then *they that are Christ's,* at His coming." And again (Col. 3.4) : "When Christ our life shall be manifested, then shall *ye* also [evidently all the saints!] with Him be manifested in glory." Again (I John 3.2) : "Now are *we* [all the saints] children of God . . . We know that, if He shall be manifested, *we* [all the saints] shall be like Him ; for we shall see Him even as He is !"

Such passages leave *no room at all* for a "partial rapture !" *All* the saints will share Christ's glory.

Now, as to *places* in the Kingdom, what *reward* we shall have, what responsibilities of kingdom government (in the 1000 years), we shall each be able to bear, or be entitled to, our "suffering with" Christ Jesus, seems to determine. "If we died with Him [as did all believers] we shall [all] also *live* with Him [in glory] ; if we endure, we shall also reign with Him" (II Tim. 2.12, R. V.).

Now the Greek word used in Romans 8.17 for "suffer with" *(sumpascho)* is used just once more in the New Testament : in I Corinthians 12.26 : "If one member suffer, all the members *suffer with* it." Here Paul is speaking of the Body of Christ into which all believers have been baptized by the Spirit (I Cor. 12.12,13) : "As the [human] body is one, and hath many members, and all the members of the body, being many, are one body ; so also is Christ ; For in one Spirit were we all baptized into one Body." Here note all believers are in this Body. And then, verse 26 : "Whether one member suffereth, all the members suffer with it." Here (and mark again this is the only occurrence of the word besides Rom. 8.17) "suffering with" is not a voluntary matter, but one necessitated by the relationship. If someone should tread upon your foot, your whole body would be exercised. So it is with Christ and His members.

Now as to the other word, of II Timothy 2.12 : "If we endure, we shall also reign with Him" ; this word is entirely different : but (and note this), the subject of which it treats is different. Being a joint-heir with Christ, and being a member of His Body, and therefore, sharing necessarily those sufferings that every member of a living Christ will suffer in a world where Satan is prince, is one thing; gaining the ability to have victory over Satan and the world, entering gladly into the conflict those sufferings involve, and *enduring,* is perhaps an additional thing, fitting one for reigning with Christ, though all His members are joint-heirs with Him.

(Notice "endure"—(Gr. *hupomeno)*—of II Timothy 2.12 in several instances: Heb. 12.2,3,7; Jas. 1.12; 5.11; I Cor. 13.7.)

18   For I reckon that the sufferings of this present time are not worthy to be compared with the glory
19   which shall be revealed to us-ward. For the earnest expectation of the creation is waiting for the revealing of the sons of God.
20   For the creation was subjected to vanity, not of its own will, but by reason of Him who subjected
21   it in hope: because the creation itself also shall be delivered from the bondage of corruption into the
22   liberty of the glory of the children of God. For we know that the whole creation groaneth and travaileth in pain together until now.
23   And not only so, but ourselves also, who have the first-fruits of the Spirit, even we ourselves groan within ourselves, waiting for our adoption, to-wit,
24   the redemption of our body. For unto [a state of] hope were we saved: but hope that is seen is not hope: for who hopeth for that which he seeth?
25   But if we hope for that which we see not, then do we with patience wait for it.

Verse 18: The word **I reckon** *(logidzomai),* is a favorite with Paul. It expresses faith in action. Paul had known abundant sufferings: read II Corinthians Eleven, and all his epistles. But like our Lord, "the File-Leader" *(archegos*—Heb. 12.2) of the column of believers, who endured the cross in view of the joy set before Him, despising the shame, Paul "reckoned" in view of the coming glory: which should be the constant attitude of all of us.

The sufferings of this present time—"This present time"; it is necessary to have God's estimate of these days in which we live or we will be deluded into man's false thoughts. Note: "this present *evil* age" (Gal. 1.4); "the days are evil"; "this darkness" (Eph. 5.16; 6.12); "the distress that is upon us"; "the fashion of this world is passing away" (I Cor. 7.26,31).

Are not to be compared with the glory—These words need to be pondered in view of passages like Hebrews 11.35-38; "tortured . . . mockings and scourgings . . . bonds and imprisonment, stoned . . . sawn asunder . . . tempted . . . slain with the sword . . . went about in sheepskins, in goatskins . . . destitute, afflicted, evil-treated . . . wandering [through] the earth." In spite of the horrors of the days of Nero, Diocletian and the rest; and the nameless terrors of the Spanish Inquisition: the "glory which shall be revealed" so swallows up these brief earthly troubles, that they shall not be named nor remembered in that day when Christ shall come.

It is difficult, impossible, to depict in language all of, or any real measure of, what is meant by the glory which shall be revealed toward us. In fact, as we know, we are to be glorified with Christ, to share His glory, and appear with Him in glory.* In Colossians 3.4 we read, "When Christ, who is our life, shall be manifested, then shall ye also with Him be manifested in glory"; and in II Thessalonians 1.10: "When He shall come to be glorified in His saints, and to be marveled at in all them that believed." Such passages show that not only will the saints behold Christ's glory, but, beholding, they will share that glory, and be glorified with Him. This is the great object before God's mind now, to "bring many sons unto glory" (Heb. 2.10), that they may be conformed to Christ's image (Rom. 8.29).

In constant view of that glory to be revealed in and through the Church, the sufferings which God called the saints to go through, no matter what they were, seemed as nothing.

---

*The expression "the glory which shall be revealed toward us," is translated "in us" in the King James. This preposition *(eis)* is used twice, for example, in II Thess. 2.14: *"Unto* which also He called you through our gospel *unto* the obtaining of the glory of the Lord Jesus Christ." This "glory" is to be revealed "to usward": not only to us, but in us, and therefore through us, to an astonished universe; and that forever!

Verse 19: **For the earnest expectation of the creation is waiting for the revealing of the sons of God.**

The world knows nothing of this astonishing verse. All the saints should always have it in remembrance! Man's philosophy and science, taught in their schools, continually prate of "evolution" and "progress" in the present creation. And they go back in pure imagination millions of years and forward millions of years, telling you confidently how things came to be, and when, and what they will come to be; but they know nothing. Here God tells us unto what creation is coming—for what it is waiting: "earnestly." Whether inanimate things on earth (for even the rocks and hills shall sing for joy shortly!) or whether the moving creatures on earth or sea; or whether, may we say, the hosts on high—all are waiting in expectation for that "unveiling of the sons of God." For the word here translated "revealing" is *apokalupsis,* a removal of a covering,—as when some wonderful statue has been completed and a veil thrown over it, people assemble for the "unveiling" of this work of art. It will be as when sky rockets are sent up on a festival night: rockets which, covered with brown paper, seem quite common and unattractive, but up they are sent into the air and then they are revealed in all colors of beauty, and the multitude waiting below shout in admiration. Now the saints are wrapped up in the common brown paper of flesh, looking outwardly like other folks. But the whole creation is waiting for their unveiling at Christ's coming, for they are connected with Christ, one with Him, and are to be glorified *with Him* at His coming.

Verse 20: **For the creation was subjected to vanity, not of its own will, but by reason of Him who subjected it in hope:**

Now God, in His infinite wisdom, thus subjected the creation,*—that is, the earth. "The whole creation" must refer to

---

*The expression creation seems to refer to this earth, even although the words in verse 22 are the whole creation. In Colossians 1.23, Paul speaks of the gospel having been preached "in all creation under heaven." God announced as a result of man's sin, "Cursed is the ground for thy sake; thorns and thistles shall it bring forth unto thee." The creation—the old version here reads "creature," which is not accurate or clear. The reference is especially to the present world and the order of life upon it.

the earth, for the Cherubim, the Seraphim, and the holy angels were not "subjected to vanity"!

Vanity—Here look back to the garden of Eden, and to Adam's first sin, the judgment of which fell not upon the man, but we read: "Cursed is *the ground* for thy sake; in toil shalt thou eat of it all the days of thy life; thorns also and thistles shall it bring forth to thee." Here we find God subjecting the whole creation to "vanity,"—that is, to unattainment. The book of Ecclesiastes dwells long, with a mournful tone upon this vanity, this unattainment; things "putting forth the tender leaves of hope" only to have the "sudden frost" of disease and death end earthly hopes. "Our days on the earth are as a shadow, and there is no abiding," as David said in his great prayer (I Chron. 29.15).

Not of its own will, but by reason of Him who subjected it in hope—God had a vast plan, reaching on into eternity, and "hope" lies ahead for creation: for the Millennium is coming, and after that, a new heaven and earth.

Verse 21: **Because the creation itself also shall be delivered from the bondage of corruption**—Now although we who are in Christ are new creatures, yet God has left our bodies as the link with the present "groaning" creation. Meanwhile, how "the bondage of corruption" appears on every side! Death —are not all creatures in terror of it, seeking to escape it? Every decaying carcass of poor earth-creatures speaks of the "bondage of corruption." What ruin man's sin has effected throughout the creation, as well as upon himself! It was God's good pleasure, that when man sinned and became estranged from his God, all creation, which was under him, should be subjected to the "bondage of corruption" along with him, in decay and disease and suffering, death, and destruction, everywhere,—of bondage, with no deliverer.

Into the liberty of the glory of the children of God—As Paul shows, we already have liberty in Christ,—the liberty of *grace*. The "liberty of the *glory* of the children of God" awaits Christ's second coming. How blessed it is to know that into that glorious liberty, creation, which has shared "the bondage of corruption," will be brought along with us!

Contrast the state of creation now with the Millennial order described in Isaiah 11.6-9: The wolf dwelling with the lamb, the leopard with the kid; the calf, the young lion, and the fatling together, and the little child leading them. The cow and the bear feeding, their young ones lying down together; the lion eating straw like the ox; children playing over the serpent's hole: "They shall not hurt nor destroy in all My holy mountain; for the earth shall be full of the knowledge of Jehovah, as the waters cover the sea."

Verse 22: **For we know that the whole creation groaneth and travaileth in pain together until now.**

We know—Always this is the expression of *Christian* knowledge. This earth's poets, philosophers, scientists, face to face with *death* with a capital D,—in every crushed ocean shell, in every rotten log, in the very minor keys in which the voices of beasts and birds are pitched, seem never even to get a glimpse of the *bondage of corruption* in which all creation is groaning; but talk in sprightly ways of "progress," of "evolution"! How far from understanding the creation around them are human beings all,—except Spirit-taught Christians! "Their own poets" write thus,—of a "groaning creation":

> "The year's at the spring,
> And day's at the morn;
> Morning's at seven;
> The hill-side's dew-pearled;
> The lark's on the wing;
> The snail's on the thorn;
> God's in His heaven—
> All's well with the world!"

To think of writing "All's well," in a world where all are dying! Christians, and only Christians see the present creation with new vision, as the work of their dear Father. As Wade Robinson's hymn says,

> "Heaven above is softer blue,
> Earth around is sweeter green!
> Something lives in every hue
> Christless eyes have never seen:

> Birds with gladder songs o'erflow,
> Flowers with deeper beauties shine,
> Since I know, as now I know,
> I am His, and He is mine."

Groaneth and travaileth in pain together until now—Ever since Adam's sin, the curse lies on all the earth. The earth and the creatures are away from God. All is estranged, consequently "groaning" and "travailing" are everywhere. (But travailing, though painful, looks toward a birth!)

Until now—No "evolution," "progress,"—but the opposite,—until Christ shall come with the "liberty of the glory."

Verse 23: **And not only so, but ourselves also, who have the firstfruits of the Spirit, even we ourselves groan within ourselves, waiting for our adoption, to-wit, the redemption of our body.**

Let us note that the Spirit does not take us out of sympathy with groaning creation, but rather supports us in such sympathy! Being ourselves, as to the body, in a groaning condition,— "longing to be clothed upon with our house which is from heaven" (II Cor. 5.2) we are able to sympathize with the creatures about us, which is a precious thing! No one should feel as tender as should the child of God toward suffering creation. No one should be as gentle. Not only should this be true about us as concerns unsaved people: as Paul says, "Be gentle, showing all meekness toward all *men*," but, I say, we should be tender and patient toward animals, for they are in a dying state—until our bodies are redeemed.

What a marvelous position, then, is the Christian's! On the heavenly side, the side of grace, *in Christ,* sharing in His risen life, delivered from sin and law and all worldly things. On the other hand, not yet partaker of glory (though expecting and awaiting it), but kept in an unredeemed body,—not fitted yet for heaven: and in which the longing spirit, knowing itself "meet to be partaker of the inheritance of the saints in light," can only "groan"!

This groaning is not at all that of the "wretched man" of Romans Seven. For not only is spiritual victory known; but the "redemption body" is longed for and awaited as that which the Lord's coming will surely bring!

Thus, then, does the Christian become the true connection of groaning creation with God! He is redeemed, heavenly; but his body is unredeemed, earthly. Yet the blessed Holy Spirit, as the "firstfruits" of coming bodily redemption, dwells in him. Thus the believer and the whole creation look toward one goal— the liberty of the coming glory of the sons of God!*

Ourselves also, who have the firstfruits of the Spirit, even we ourselves groan—Here then is a wonderful scene: (1) new creatures in Christ, whose citizenship is in heaven; (2) the presence of the Spirit within them as "firstfruits" of their coming inheritance—witnessing of it, giving them to taste of its glory; (3) a state of groaning despite all this; (4) a waiting for bodily redemption.

Waiting for our adoption, to-wit, the redemption of our body—The instructed Christian, knowing that his body belongs to the Lord, and is not yet redeemed, longs for, yearns for, groans for that day when his body will be placed in a position of openly acknowledged sonship and glory, even as his spirit now, is. Till that day he cannot be satisfied.

This scene is deeply touching. One who, redeemed, belongs in heaven, yet kept in a body in which he groans with groaning creation. Then—amazing goodness! the blessed Spirit, we may say, represents God's tender feeling toward His creation, abiding, as He does, in us the while our bodies are not redeemed. We repeat and repeat that the Christian's hope is not disembodiment, or mere "going to heaven." For, knowing that "our citizenship is in heaven; we patiently wait for a Savior, the Lord Jesus Christ: who shall fashion anew the body of our humiliation, that it may be conformed to the body of his glory." There is an element, we fear, of cowardice, as well as of unbelief in

---

*Major D. W. Whittle—of blessed memory! used to say, "The trouble with most Christians is that they are not willing to groan! Unwilling to face constantly the fact of being 'in a tabernacle,' our earthly body, in which we groan, being burdened; and thus to long for the coming of Christ in the redemption of their bodies, most Christians get weary and long for death—disembodiment, which is not the Christian's hope. Or else they turn back for some kind of satisfaction ,to the things of this poor wretched dying world. Or they seek to have sin 'eradicated' from their bodies."

setting our hope on "getting to heaven," and leaving, so to speak, our body behind. God began with man's body in Eden (Gen. 2); and He will end with redeeming our bodies. The heart of God and of Christ,—yea of the indwelling Spirit (Rom. 8.11) is set upon that. Let our hearts, also, be set upon it.

Verse 24: **For unto [a state of] hope were we saved: but hope that is seen is not hope: for who hopeth for that which he seeth?**

This places us, along with all creation, **in hope.** For, as verse 24 announces, **unto** [a state of] **hope were we saved.** There is a longing for and expectation of something better, no matter what spiritual blessing comes to the believer. This that is longed for, is, of course, "the liberty of the glory," that belongs, by God's grace, to the children of God (verse 21). Creation will share this "liberty." Therefore we have a double feeling toward creation: sympathy with its suffering, and joy in its prospect of sharing the "liberty of the glory" into which we shall shortly come.

Verse 25: **But if we hope for that which we see not, then do we with patience wait for it.**

Now **hope** is expecting *something better!* The very fact that we have not seen it realized as yet, begets within us that grace which is so precious to God—**patience.** But note, it is not patience in the abstract that is set forth here: but patient *waiting for* the coming liberty of the glory of the children of God.

26   And in like manner the Spirit also helpeth our
        infirmity: for we know not how to pray as we
        ought; but the Spirit Himself maketh intercession
27   for us with groanings which cannot be uttered! and
        He that searcheth the hearts knoweth what is the
        mind of the Spirit, because He maketh intercession
        for the saints according to God.
28   And we know that to them that love God all
        things work together for good, to them that ac-
29   cording to His purpose are called ones. For whom
        He foreknew He also foreordained conformed to
        the image of His Son, that He might be the First-

30 born among many brethren! and whom He fore-
    ordained, them He also called: and whom He
    called, them He also justified: and whom He justi-
    fied, them He also glorified.

Verse 26: **And in like manner also**—We have just read
that "we that have the firstfruits of the Spirit groan within
ourselves," waiting for that blessed day of "the liberty of the
glory of the sons of God." These words "in like manner," refer
to that operation within us of the Spirit, which makes us, in
real sympathy, one with the groaning creation about us. "In like
manner," then, with this truly wonderful help, the Spirit "helps
our infirmity,"—in its ignorant and infirm dealing with God.
Note, the word "infirmity" is singular number: for we have
nothing but infirmity! **We know not how to pray as we
ought.** Oh, beware of the glib and intimate chatter of the
"Modernist" preacher in his *prayers!* He would flatter both the
Almighty and his hearers, and most of all, himself, in his "beautiful" and "eloquent" addresses to God! Not so with Paul, and
the real saints of God, who have the Holy Ghost. There is with
them the sense of utter and boundless *need,* and along with this
the sense of *ignorance* and *inability.* Yet, still, bless God! there
is, with all this, the sense of the limitless help of the Holy
Spirit!

**The Spirit Himself maketh intercession for us with
groanings which cannot be uttered**—We know that Christ
maketh intercession for us at the right hand of God, but
here the Spirit is making intercession within us: The
Spirit, who knows the vast abysmal need of every one of
us, knows that need to the least possible particular.

Groanings which cannot be uttered—expresses at once
the vastness of our need, our utter ignorance and inability,
and the infinite concern of the blessed indwelling Spirit
for us. "Groanings"—what a word! and to be used of the
Spirit of the Almighty Himself! How shallow is our ap-
preciation of what is done, both by Christ for us, and by
the Spirit within us!

Which cannot be uttered—Here then, are needs of ours,
of which our minds know nothing, and which our speech

could not utter if we could perceive those needs. But it is part of God's great plan in our salvation that this effectual praying should have its place—praying, the very meaning of which we cannot grasp. Men of God have testified to the spirit of prayer prostrating them into deep and often long-continued "groanings." We believe that such consciousness of the Spirit's praying within us is included in this verse, but the chief or principal part of the Spirit's groaning within us, perhaps never reaches our spirit's consciousness.

Verse 27: **And He that searcheth the hearts knoweth what is in the mind of the Spirit, because He maketh intercession for the saints according to God.**

It is God the Father here that is "searching the hearts." How we used to shrink from the thought of such Divine searching! But here God is "searching hearts" to know what is the mind of the indwelling, holy Spirit concerning a saint, to know what the Spirit groans for, for that saint; in order that He may supply it.

For in the plan of salvation, God the Father is the Source, Christ the Channel, and the Spirit the Agent.

Because He maketh intercession for the saints according to God—We feel that the introduction of the words "the will of" before the word God, merely obscures the meaning. "According to God"—what an all-inclusive, blessed expression, enwrapping us as to our salvation and blessing, wholly in Divine love and power. We know not how to pray as we ought; but the Spirit makes intercession in us, "according to God," according to His nature (of which we are partakers); according to our needs, which He discerns; according to our dangers, which He foresees—according to all the desires He has toward us.

Verse 28: **And we know that to them that love God all things work together for good**—The words **we know** are used about thirty times as the expression of the common knowledge of *the saints of God as such,* in the Epistles: (in Romans, five times)—indicating always *Christian* knowledge; also I Corinthians 8.4, I John 5.19,—and John 21.24, are perfect examples. Lodge members, having been "initiated," go about as those that "know." The Christian is traveling to glory along with a blessed company that can say "We know," in an infinitely higher and surer sense.* And here, what a knowledge! **that to them that love God all things work together for good!**

Now as to **them that love God** John tells us in his first Epistle, "We love, because He first loved us"; and, "Herein is love, not that we loved God, but that He loved us"; and, *"We know* and have believed the love which God hath in our case." Real faith in the God who gave His Son, will, Paul tells the Galatians (5.6), be "working through love." Only those can and do really love God whose hearts have been "sprinkled from an evil conscience"—delivered from fear of God's just judgment. The question therefore, comes right back to this: Have we believed, as guilty lost sinners, on this propitiation by the blood of God's Son on the cross? Is that our only hope? If so, I John 4.16 becomes true: "We know and have believed the love which God hath in our case," and verse 19 follows: "We love, because he first loved us." We cannot work up love for God, but His redeeming love for us, believed in, becomes the eternal cause and spring of our love to God.

Now we find in Romans 8.28 a great marvel: **all things work together for good** to these believing lovers of God. This involves that billion billion control of God's providence,— of the most infinitesimal things—to bring them about for "good" to God's saints. When we reflect on the innumerable "things" about us,—forces seen and unseen of the mineral, vegetable, and animal worlds; of man at enmity with God; of Satan, and his principalities and powers, in deadly array; in the uncertainty and even treachery of those near and dear to us, and even of professed Christians, and of our own selves, —which we cannot trust for a moment; upon our unredeemed

*As for the "Modernist," his shallow, ignorant, blatant boast is, "We do *not* know; we are *not* sure," thus giving continual open evidence that he does not be- long to that company of whom John writes: *"We know* that the Son of God is come, and hath given us an understanding, that *we know* Him that is true, and we are in Him that is true, even in His Son Jesus Christ. This is the true God, and eternal life."

bodies; upon our general complete helplessness:—then, to have God say, "All things are working together for your good,"— reveals to us a Divine providence that is absolutely limitless! The book of Proverbs sets forth just such a God: for it describes the certain end, good or bad, of the various paths of men on earth—every *minute detail* ordered of God. So also Ephesians (1.11): "The purpose of Him who worketh all things after the counsel of His will"; and David: "All things are Thy servants" (Ps. 119.91); as also the whole prophetic Word,—yea, the whole Word of God; for the God of Providence is in all of it!

For good—Dark things, bright things; happy things, sad things; sweet things, bitter things; times of prosperity, times of adversity. The "great woman," the Shunammite, with her one child lying at home dead, answers Elisha's question, "Is it well with the child?": "It is well." "A soft pillow for a tired heart," Romans 8.28 was called by our beloved Brother R. A. Torrey.

To them that are called according to His purpose—We come now up on the high, celestial mountains of Divine Sovereign election, and find those who love God are further defined as those that are "called" (not "invited,"* but given a

---

*"Called" here does not mean *invited*,—as in Proverbs, for instance. "Unto you, O men, I call"; for this would be an appeal to man's will instead of a description of those who are the objects of God's will, His *purpose*. "Called," in the sense of Romans 8.28, is illustrated in I Corinthians 1.24: where "Christ crucified" is declared to be a "stumbling-block" to Jews (to people whose thought was religion) and "foolishness" to Greeks (to those whose life lay in philosophy): but to "the called themselves" (Gr. margin) "Christ the power of God and the wisdom of God." Here "the called" are seen to be a company whose mark is neither religious response nor intellectual apprehending; but the electing grace of God which has so marked out the sphere of their being, that they are named "the called." They are called according to His (God's) purpose!

Now, that purpose is not merely an expressed Divine desire, but a fixed and vast will, that itself subordinates, necessarily, all things; submerges all opposition; effects its object. God's purpose, in regard to "the called," His "elect," does, indeed, arise out of His desire, as well as being according to His infinite wisdom. This is shown in:

"Jehovah hath chosen Zion;
He hath desired it for His habitation.
Here will I dwell; for I have desired it" (Ps. 132.13, 14).

Also, "Because He [Jehovah] loved thy [Israel's] fathers, therefore He chose their seed after them" (Deut. 4.37). Even those "chosen in Christ before the foundation of the world," are said to be "loved in Christ Jesus our Lord." "God is love," and acts according to that nature. Out of His infinite, holy desire arose His purpose. Reverse this order, and you have the god of the fatalist, not of the Bible.

Divine elective calling) according to His Purpose. Meditation upon the purpose of the eternal God greatens every soul thus occupied. God is infinite; man, a bit of dust. If God had a purpose, a fixed intention, it will come to pass, for He has limitless resources,—as David says, "All things are Thy servants."

We have been dealing in the first part of the chapter with the human will and its consent to walk by the Spirit. Not so from the 28th verse to the chapter's end. It will be *all God* from now on! **Purpose** means an intelligent decision which the will is bent to accomplish. The Greek word, *prothesis,* is used twelve times in the New Testament. As to man, the word is seen to indicate what he is entirely unable to carry through, as in Acts 27.13: They supposed "that they had obtained their purpose," but the ship was wrecked. In the saints, their purpose is carried on by Divine grace, often with many failures: Acts 11.23, "He exhorted them all that with purpose of heart they would cleave unto the Lord." And in II Timothy 3.10, Paul refers Timothy to that "manner of life, purpose, faith," which the apostle had shown at Ephesus, a purpose carried out to final victory in finishing his course. But, as he says, "By the grace of God I am what I am."

In God, however, purpose is absolute,—wholly apart from contingencies. In the very next occurrence after Romans 8.28 we read, "that the purpose of God according to election might stand"—everything subordinated, and the end predicted. We read also in Ephesians 3.11 of a "purpose of the ages" which God has ordained and will carry through, just as our salvation is referred to as "not according to our works, but according to His own purpose and grace, which was given us in Christ Jesus before the times of the ages" (II Tim. 1.9).

Therefore we beg the reader in examining the great verses 29 and 30, to distinguish the things that differ, utterly refusing to confuse or mix them: (1) First, we shall find many Scriptures in which the consent of man's will is asked, and blessing is contingent upon his consent; and some ("rocky ground" people) will receive the Word "immediately with joy, and for awhile endure," but in time of tribulation or persecution "fall away." (2) Second, we shall find plainly written in Scripture the purpose of God according to which He works effectually; and all His elect are brought safely in, and there is no separating them from His love which was given them in Christ Jesus, in whom they were "chosen before the foundation of the world."

Now do not seek to mix these two things; and still more emphatically we say, do not try to "reconcile" them! Profitless controversy and partisan feeling will be the only result. Who told us to "reconcile" in our little minds, these seemingly contradictory things? Have we ceased to believe where we do not understand?

Every system of theology undertakes to subject the words of God to categories and catalogs of the human intellect. Now, if you undertake to "reconcile" God's sovereign election with His free offer of salvation to all, you must sacrifice one truth or the other. Our poor *minds* may not "reconcile" them both, but our *faith* knows them both, and holds both, to be true! And Scripture is addressed to faith, not to reason.

Verse 29: **For whom He foreknew He also foreordained conformed to the image of His Son, that He might be the First-born among many brethren.**

For whom He foreknew—This *for* looks back at the word *purpose,* and opens out that great word before us.

And first we have, **foreknew.** This foreknowledge of God —what is it? In seeking its meaning we dare not turn to men's ideas, but to Scripture only.* In Amos 1.2 to 2.8, Jehovah gives in detail His exact knowledge of the sins and of the coming judgments of Syria, the Philistines, Tyre, Edom, Ammon, Moab; and then also of Israel. But to Israel He says, "You only have I *known,* of all the families of the earth." What did such language mean? That He had *acquaintanceship* with "the whole family which He brought up out of the land of Egypt." Of Israel again—especially the godly Remnant, He speaks: "God did not cast off His people which He fore-

---

*"It is important to observe that the apostle does not speak of a passive or naked foreknowledge, as if God only saw beforehand what some would be, and do, or believe. His foreknowledge is of persons, not of their state or conduct; it is not *what,* but 'whom' He foreknew" (Kelly).

knew." Now, even of Christ it is written in I Peter 1.20,
"He was *foreknown* indeed before the foundations of the
world." This is the same Greek word as in Romans 8.29.
Now Christ was the Eternal Son of God, the Eternal Word.
But, "The Word become flesh": that occurred when He came
into the world. And as thus manifested, "He was *foreknown.*"
It was not a mere Divine pre-knowledge that He would be
manifested; but a pre-acquaintanceship before His manifestation,—*with Him as such!* From which "foreknowledge," or
pre-acquaintance, flowed the most intimate prophecies of
Him, His lowly coming, His rejection, and the manner of His
death. All this is wrapped up in this word *foreknowledge!*

He also foreordained—Foreknowledge is first—by the
God that "calleth the things not being, being" (4.17, Gr.).
Then, the marking out a destiny befitting such foreknown
ones. The words "to be" need not be here: but we may
read, **foreordained conformed to the image of His Son.**
Here we come to words of plain meaning, but limitless reach!
Christ the Son, for whom and by whom all things were made;
Christ the Son, the appointed Heir of all things; Christ the
Son—center of all the Divine counsels! Christ the Son, God's
Son, the Son of *His love!* Conformed to *His* image,—nothing
lacking, nothing short: like Christ—conformed to His image:
in glory, in love, in holiness, in beauty, in grace, in humility,
in tenderness, in patience! Our very bodies at last *alive unto
God!* For we know that this also shall be: "When Christ, our
life shall be manifested, then shall ye also with Him be manifested in glory!" And thus to be with Christ, like Him forever and ever! Only God can show, and only simple faith
respond to, grace such as this!

That He might be the First-born among many brethren
—In Christ, like Christ, brethren there with the First-born! This
is the highest place, shall we not say, that God *could* give creatures! God puts us there: and of Christ it is written, "He is not
ashamed to call them brethren"; because we are "all of one"
with Christ! (Heb. 2.11). "This, in fact, is the thought of
grace, not to bless us only *by* Jesus, but to bless us *with* Him."

Verse 30: And whom He foreordained, them He also called—Since we are here considering God's unfolding of His *purpose* (of verse 28), we must regard **called** from God's side,—who counts things not being, being. Further, calling is here that determination by God of the sphere and mode of life those should have whom He foreknew and foreordained. This "calling" belongs to Eternity past; as "calling," for example in II Thessalonians 2.14, and Galatians 1.6, belongs to experience in present time.

And whom He called, them He also justified—God does not here speak of that entering upon justification *by faith*—of which this Epistle is full. For only believing souls are accounted righteous, justified, as we well know. Yet in God's counsels are all His elect already before Him, accounted righteous—*justified*. This is wonderful truth: and its power to stay the soul will be seen in the last part of this great Chapter!

And whom He justified, them He also glorified—This is the necessary end of this amazing series—*glorified!* Thus must these foreknown ones be ever, before God, since God foreknew them in Christ. None has yet been glorified in manifestation. Indeed, Christ Himself has not yet been "manifested"; although He has entered into His glory. And it is in this glorified Christ that God chose us long ago,—before the foundation of the world! God, who could thus connect us with Christ, can also say of us, I have glorified them! And so the saints go on to a glory already true of them by the word of their God!

31   What then shall we say to these things? If God
32   is for us, who is against us? He that even spared
       not His own Son, but delivered Him up for us all,
       how shall He not also with Him freely give us all
33   things? Who shall lay anything to the charge of
34   God's elect? [It is] God that justifieth: who is he
       that condemneth? Christ Jesus [God's own Son]
       is the one that died,—yea rather, that was raised
       from the dead, who is at the right hand of God,
35   who is also making intercession for us! Who shall

separate us from the love of Christ? shall tribulation, or anguish, or persecution, or famine, or
36 nakedness, or peril, or sword? Even as it is
written,

On account of thee we are killed all day long:
We were reckoned as sheep for the slaughter.

37 Nay, in all these things we are more than conquerors through Him that loved us!

38 For I am persuaded, that neither death, nor life,
nor angels, nor principalities, nor things present,

39 nor things to come, nor powers, nor height, nor
depth, nor any other created thing, shall be able
to separate us from the love of God, which is in
Christ Jesus our Lord.

Concerning this great passage, Bengel says, "We can no
farther go, think, wish." Olshausen emphasizes "the profound and colossal character of the thought"; and Brown
says: "This whole passage, to verse 34 and even to the end of
the chapter, strikes all thoughtful interpreters and readers as
transcending almost everything in language."

Paul here arrives at the mountain-height of Christian position! And that, so to speak, by way of experience. He does,
indeed, in the word "us" bring all the saints with him. There
was first our state of awful guilt—and Christ's work for us,
and justification thereby. Then came the knowledge of indwelling sin, and the Spirit's work within us, and deliverance
from sin's power thereby. Now he has arrived upon the im-
movable mountain-top of Divine sovereign election, and he
sees God Himself for us! Not at all meaning, here, God
merely on our side in our struggles, but God's uncaused
unalterable attitude with respect to those in Christ. God is *for*
them: nothing in time or in eternity to come has anything
whatever to do with matters here. Our weak hearts, prone to
legality and unbelief, with great difficulty receive these mighty
words: *God is for us*. Place the emphasis here where God
places it—on this great word "for." God is *for* His elect.
They have failed, but He is *for* them. They are ignorant, but
He is *for* them. They have not yet brought forth much fruit,

but He is *for* them. If our hearts once surrender to the stupendous fact that there are those whom God will eternally be *for,* that there is an electing act and attitude of God, in which He eternally commits Himself to His elect,—without conditions, without requirements; whose lives do not at all affect the fact that *God is for them*—then we shall be ready to magnify the God of *all grace!*

Verse 31: **What then shall we say to these things?** By "these things" Paul evidently indicates not only the whole process of our salvation by Christ, from Chapter Three onward, with that great deliverance by the help of the Holy Spirit set forth in this Eighth Chapter; but he also points most directly to what He has been telling us of the *purpose* of God: "Whom He foreknew, foreordained, called, justified, glorified!" Now it is a sad fact that many dear saints have said many poor, even lamentable things, to **these things** of Divine sovereign foreknowledge and election. Some, indeed, will not hear "these things," as Paul sets them forth. Let us not be of this company! **What shall we say to these things?** To doubt them is to deny them: for God asserts them—from foreknowledge to glorification. To question whether they apply to us is to question—not election, but the words "whosoever will," of the gospel invitation. You can let God be absolutely sovereign in election, and yet, if you find the door opened by this sovereign God, and "whosoever will" written over it by that same sovereign God, by all means *enter!* Set your seal to this, that God is true, by receiving His witness (John 3.33). Do not allow any "system of theology" to disturb you for one moment! *What will you say to these things?* Say, with Paul: God is for me: He spared not His own Son—for me! This question, **What shall we say to these things?** is a testing word, as well, as a triumphant word.

Concerning "these things," if we simply rejoice, with Paul, saying, "God is for me, who is against me?" it is well! But if we cannot rejoice in Divine, sovereign foreknowledge, foreordination, and calling, this also is the fruit of subtle unbelief and self-righteousness. "I know," said Spurgeon, "that God chose me before I was born; for He never would have chosen me afterwards!" Let us not be of the Little-faiths, or of the Faint-hearts; but let Mr. Greatheart himself, even Paul, set forth the case: **If God be for us, who is against us?** This "if" does not imply doubt, but amounts to *since*. We are expected to have heard, understood, and believed all the previous marvels of our salvation written in this epistle. The conclusion is: GOD IS FOR US. The Creator of the universe, the Upholder of all things, the Redeemer God Himself, *for* us!

Therefore the challenge: **who is against us?** Paul knew, as none have ever known, the power and malignity of Satan and his hosts, the persecuting energy of the haters of the gospel, the relentless watchfulness of the Roman Empire—that had flung justice to the winds, and crucified Paul's Lord, and ever stood ready, upon occasion, to seize him. Yet he challenges all! It is not a question of logic, as the King James puts it: "Who *can be* against us?" But it is a direct challenge in the lists: to all and any in the whole possible universe: literally, **If God for us—*who* against us?**

Verse 32: **He that even* spared not His own Son, but delivered Him up for us all**—This is the God who is for us; and this is the proof! *Spared* not—what that word shows! Of the infinite price of redemption! of the measureless unconquerable love of God that would not be stopped at such frightful cost! "His own Son"; His only Son; His well-beloved Son,—from all eternity! And for *us!* Ah, how wretched we are, even in our own sight! guilty, undone, defiled, powerless, worthless,—*for us all!* Verily, "the most miserable of sheep!" (Zech. 11.7).

Then, **delivered Him up**—We remember immediately the same word in Chapter 4.25: "delivered up for our trespasses." Yea, we know for why: but *unto* what? gainsaying, mocking, spitting, scourging, crucifying—by *men;* and to the awful cup of wrath for our sin at *God's* hand—infinitely more appalling

---

*Both the R.V. and the King James neglect to translate the little particle (Gr. *ge*) which gives this passage its peculiar emphasis: Literally: "God for us . . . . who even spared not His own Son!" went even that length.

that any creature stroke! Yet God *spared not*—His own Son, but *delivered Him up!*

For us all—Here the saints are spoken of. (Paul never uses *"us"* of any others!) And who are the saints? *Sinners* who have heard God's good news concerning His Son, and have simply *believed!* Only faith can walk here! Unbelief, coming to the fearful gulf between the infinitely holy God and the awful guilt of the sinner, shrinks back; while faith, seeing Christ crucified, cries, God is for me! and passes gladly over the bridge God made—who spared not His own Son!

How shall He not also with Him freely give us all things?—The great gift, the unspeakable gift, being made, all must follow! "How shall He *not,* with *Him?*" If you buy a costly watch at the jeweller's, he sends it to you in a lovely case which he gives you freely—with your purchase. It is as in Chapter Five, with the "much mores." God has not spared His Son: what are all else to *Him?* God has opened to us His *heart,* He has spared not,—giving us His best, His all— even Christ. Now, with Him, all things come! God cannot but do this. Shall He give us His dear Son, and then hold back at trifles? For "all things" of this created universe,—yea, even all gifts or blessings God may give us, here or hereafter, are but nothing, compared with *Christ!*

"All things": It will greatly please God for us boldly to beg Him for this or that, saying: Thou didst not spare Thy Son, but gavest Him for me. Now I need a thing from Thee; and I ask it as *one to whom Thou gavest Christ!* "How shall He not?" not, "How shall He?"—as doubt would put it! Let "all things" be *all things indeed* to thee,—only seeking wisdom in asking. This verse is a great feeder of faith!

Verse 33: Who shall lay anything to the charge of God's elect? Note (1) It is *God's elect* whom this passage concerns. (2) God's elect not only believe, but are *confident!* For there can be no charge laid against them. (3) They boldly *challenge* any and every foe, concerning any possible charge against them before God! It is not that those triumphing are without fault in themselves—they know that! But *God* is *for* them!

They are His "elect," and we know from the next chapter that the purpose of God according to election is *not of works":* but on the contrary, "of Him *that calleth"* (Romans 9.11). As absolutely as righteousness is "not of works," so neither is election! Both have God Himself as the only Source! So, "the purpose of God according to election stands!"

It is God that justifieth:* **who is he that condemneth?—** Here the emphasis is upon *God.* He is the Judge; and He has declared His elect,—those "of faith in Jesus," *righteous.* Now will any condemn? Shall any stand before God's High Court and condemn *whom He has justified?* Never! Satan may accuse us in our consciences; but the day of our condemnation was past forever—when Christ our Substitute "bore our sins in His own body on the tree!" When it is announced as toward all possible foes: "It is God that justifies," we feel in our hearts *God taking our part!*

Verse 34: **Christ Jesus [God's own Son] is the one that died,—yea, rather, that was raised from the dead, who is at the right hand of God, who is also making intercession for us!**

Some would render the answer to the question of verse 33, "Who shall lay anything to the charge," etc., entirely in the question form: "Shall God that justifieth? Shall Christ that died?" We have not yielded to rendering it thus; for this question-form does not fit the bold challenge here: for this whole passage is governed by the great word: **Who shall lay anything to the charge of God's elect?** And further, verse 35, **Who shall separate us from the love of Christ?** God then, is seen "for us," as *justifying;* His own Son Christ Jesus as dying and as interceding for us. All of which commits God to us irreversibly! The **Yea, rather, that was raised from the dead,** follows the exact order of the development of the truth of Christ's work in this epistle: set forth as a mercy-seat through faith in His blood in Chapter Three; God seen raising

---

*Note that the last statement of verse 33—"It is God that justifieth," is connected with the opening question of verse 34. The verse division is unforunate, and beclouds the meaning. The second sentence of verse 34, **Christ Jesus is the one that died,** etc., is entirely separate from and an advance upon, the preceding verses.

Him who was delivered on account of our trespasses in Chapter Four. There is no crucifix, no Romanism, here; no dead Christ, but One raised.

Nay, more, **Christ Jesus is at the right hand of God,**—We have here the first of seven historical statements in the Epistles that He is there,* and not merely there in the place of honor and power, but occupied (as ever) for our benefit: **who also is making intercession for us.** In verse 22, the indwelling Spirit is making intercession *for* the saints; in verse 31, God is *for* us; in verse 34, Christ Jesus is making intercession *for* us. What a wonderful salvation this is, in which all three persons of the Trinity are constantly occupied in our behalf!†

Verse 35: When Paul says, **Who shall separate us from Christ's love?** and then begins to enumerate *things,* it is plain that in the word "Who" he has in mind the great enemy who opposes "things" to God's saints! Satan is "prince of this world," and "god of this age": this the apostle always has before him: "that no advantage may be gained over us by Satan; for we are not ignorant of *his* devices." So he says: **Who shall separate us? shall tribulation?** Thirty-seven times this word rendered "tribulation" *(thlipsis)* and its verb are used to denote those direct troubles that afflict the saints,— *because of the gospel!* Satan has sought,—and, oh, how desperately,—but has never succeeded in separating *one saint* from Christ's love by tribulations! (See this word in Matt. 13.21; I Thess. 1.6; 3.3; John 16.33.) And God sees to it that the

---

*The other instances: Ephesians 1.20; Hebrews 1.3; 8.1; 10.12; 12.2; Col. 3.1.

†Christ Jesus making intercession for us at the right hand of God in Heaven, is not properly Romans truth, but is brought in here simply to show His eternal commitment to our cause. We say this because the remnants of Romish unbelief lie in most or all of us. For instance, take the lines,

> "O blessed feet of Jesus, weary with seeking me,
> Kneel at God's bar of judgment, and intercede for me!"

What a mixture and hodge-podge such words are! Christ is not "appeasing God" in Heaven. That was all done forever on the cross where our sins were put away. Our Lord as our High Priest in Heaven now leads our worship and praise, and looks after us in our infirmity. The book of Hebrews opens out this. But it is that same book which says, "He, when He had offered one sacrifice for sins forever, sat down on the right hand of God" (10.12). The work on which faith rests has been done, and those who rely on Christ's work on the cross will find their needs taken care of by Christ in Heaven.

path of the Christian is a narrow, "straitened one! (Matthew 7.14 has the same word—"narrow." See also II Cor. 4.8; 7.5.)

And now the next word—**distress.** This word *(stenochoria)* is rightly translated "anguish" in Chapter 2.9; for there it evidently means a fixed place in which "every soul of man that doeth evil" is held while Divine judgment is visited. The word means a narrow, cramped place, where one is "in straits." For the lost this is unendurable; for the saved, it only affords room for God's help, when naught else can avail. So, *distresses*— how terrible soever—cannot separate from Christ's love. (See the note on the Russian women in Chapter Five.) Remember, Christ, the Lord of glory, had not a place to lay His head: He knows what *distresses* are!

Or persecution—*(diōgmos).* This is a word used ten times in the New Testament, and always in reference to the gospel. Its verb means, "to make to run," or "to run swiftly to catch" those pursued; so, to *persecute.* No saint thus persecuted has yet been forsaken by Christ,—nor ever will be! "If they persecuted Me, they will also persecute you." Christ never forsakes, but has the sweetest fellowship with those persecuted by the world,—directed (under God's permissive decree only!) by Satan. Christ is always saying, "Be of good cheer!" (Acts 23.11.)

Famine—comes next. And you would think that the Lord of all would ever provide liberally for His saints. Not always! The "present distress" is on. Christ the Heir was cast out of Israel's vineyard and slain! The Head of the new Body has indeed been glorified. But why should not the members of His Body know by experience what the Head passed through and thus find fellowship with the Head? Thus they come to have one heart with Him! "Famine?" Yes. But not to separate us from Christ's love! "I know how to be in want," says Paul. Twelve times is "famine" *(limos)* mentioned in the New Testament: though only twice (here in Rom. 8.35, and in II Cor. 11.27— this last concerning an apostle!) does it directly touch the saints. In Acts 11.28, indeed they get *relief* (though by other saints, not by government agency!). Yea; you may be hungry in this Christ-rejecting world, and yet be beloved of your Lord!

"The meek shall inherit the earth"—but not yet! Not till *He* comes back!

> "All here is stained with blood!—
> Thy blood, O glorious Christ!
> And man and Satan do today
> Whate'er they list!"

(Yet do not forget that, amidst it all, God lives! The God of Elijah still looks after His own!)

Or nakedness—In I Corinthians 4.11, Paul says, "Even unto this present hour we both hunger, and thirst, and are naked, and are buffeted, and have no certain dwelling-place." (Read the whole passage.) How ashamed we feel, who are not as devoted to our Lord as was Paul, to hear him speak thus! This whole part of Romans Eight shows us as partakers with a Christ the world cast out.

Or peril—Eight times in one verse, II Corinthians 11.26, does Paul use this word. Read that verse, remembering the same word in I Corinthians 15.30: "We stand *in jeopardy* [peril] *every hour.*" In Paul's bringing you this gospel, Jewish hatred, Roman jealousy, pagan blindness (Acts 14.8-20) and false brethren (Acts 15) beset him round,—striving that "the truth of the gospel" might come unto *us!* God grant we cherish it! Many have suffered, that we might have these wondrous truths!

Or sword—The first use of this word *(machaira)* is connected with our Lord Himself: Matthew 26.47: "A great multitude with *swords* and staves" to take Him; while Acts 12.2 ("Herod . . . killed James the brother of John with the sword"), and Hebrews 11.37 ("They were slain with the sword"), give only examples of the attitude of this world toward Christ and His saints. The world hates the saints; though sometimes those making most hideous use of the sword have worn "the sign of the cross." That was the world's religion; and, like Cain, it killed God's people. But, even in the hour of death most terrible, Christ was there: they were not separated from His love!

Verse 36:

Even as it is written,

On account of Thee we are killed all the day long:

We were reckoned as sheep for the slaughter.

Here, then, is the description of God's saints: "killed perpetually," and "sheep for slaughter." We know that this quotation is taken from a Psalm (44.22) which describes that terrible hunting down by the Antichrist of the godly remnant of Israel in the days of the Great Tribulation. But today—all the day [of grace] long, this is the real state of real saints: killed, and slaughter-sheep! To the student of God's Word, the many years of outward peace—from persecution, horrors, and death,—that have come to *us* is the unusual, the astonishing thing. Look at the "deaths oft" of the early Church, the martyrs; and again when truth burst out afresh at the Reformation! (See footnote p. 475.)

But now again! look at Russia, look at Germany, look all around! Ruthless hatred of God's saints is breaking out everywhere, as of old!

Now, we ought not to view such things with alarm, but, on the contrary, to remember that Christ has not yet set up His kingdom,* nor will till His second coming! Satan is the prince

---

*As we say elsewhere, the mouthings of the "Modernist" who knows not the prophetic Word (and would not bow to it if it were shown to him) must not be listened to for a moment. The "Stone" of the Second of Daniel strikes that great prophetic Image of Gold, Silver, Brass, Iron, and Iron-Clay feet, with a sudden unexpected *impact*, destroying the whole Gentile order of things,—away down in the feet and toes period. The Kingdom of the Most High is then, and not till then, set up. We all know that those born again shall "see the Kingdom of God" —indeed, are in that Kingdom, as spiritually existing. But no others, no "social order," no man-made conditions, are in the Kingdom! Further, to those born again, God says, "The Kingdom of God is righteousness and joy and peace, *in the Holy Ghost.*" Outside the Spirit, the Kingdom of God does not exist. Indeed, the Kingdom has not yet been given to Christ in heaven by the Father. When it is given to Him (Rev. 5; Psalm 2.7-9), He will Himself come and *set up* His Kingdom in power according to Matthew 13.36-43; 25.31-46. Read these words of Christ, and believe them,—hearkening to no "peace, peace" words of the "Modern" dreamers.

of this world, and shall yet be exhibited as the "god of this age"—see Revelation Thirteen. For,

> "The whole earth wondered after the Wild Beast [Satan's man, the Antichrist] ; and they worshipped the dragon [Satan] . . . and there was given to him authority over every tribe and people and tongue and nation. And all that dwell on the earth shall worship him, every one whose name hath not been written from the foundation of the world in the book of life of the Lamb that hath been slain."

Let the saints rouse quickly from these false dreams of "peace." The saints are **sheep for slaughter!** Name yourself among them, and cease contending for your "rights" in a world that has cast out Christ! Persecution is shaping itself up again throughout Christendom—yea, even in the United States. Intolerance unto death for any who will not bow to a totalitarian state is ready, as in the days of the Roman emperors (who demanded worship) to assert itself,—is asserting itself, throughout the world. This "totalitarian" movement is setting the stage for Antichrist more rapidly than you dream! Therefore get ready. Put up over your mirror the motto: "I am Christ's: a sheep for slaughter."

Verse 37: **Nay, in all these things we are more than conquerors through Him that loved us!**

What a wonderful book this Word of God is! "Sheep for slaughter" naming themselves **more than conquerors!**[*]

Now note three things in this verse: (1) We are conquerors in all this terrible situation, **in all these things.** (2) We are **more than conquerors.** (3) It is altogether **through Him that loved us,** and not through human energy of any kind, that we are **more than conquerors.**

Now, what is it to be "more than conquerors?" (a) It is to come off conqueror in every difficulty. (b) It is to know that

---

[*] It is evident that those whose description is "killed all the day long," "sheep for slaughter," will never become **more than conquerors,** or conquerors at all, through "moral influence," human "merits," "the ballot box," "the betterment of humanity," "inter racial understanding"! No, not with Satan prince and god, here! And he will be such until cast into the abyss (Rev. 20) at Christ's coming.

Divine, and therefore infinite, power has been engaged for us
in the conflict. (c) It is the absolute confidence that this infinite
and therefore limitless Divine help is granted to us against any
possible future emergency. (d) It is to "divide the spoil" over
any foe, after victory! (Isa. 53.12.)

Him that loved us—Note first the past tense. That preaching which always emphasizes the present love of God or Christ
for the soul, as the great persuading power over the human
heart, falls sadly short. When our Lord described God's love
for the world, it was, "God so *loved* that He *gave* His Son."
Again, "Herein is love, that God *loved* us, and sent His Son."
Again, when Paul describes Christ's love for His own it is by
pointing to His sacrifice. Here (in Rom. 8.37) the cross is
indicated, as in verse 32 of our chapter: "He that *spared* not
His own Son."

Further, when Christ's love for the Church is described,
it is again the past tense—"Christ *loved* the Church and gave
Himself up for it" (Eph. 5.25). And, "The Son of God *loved*
me and *gave* Himself for me" (Gal. 2.20). It is this past tense
gospel the devil hates,—for "the Word of the Cross is the power
of God." Let a preacher be continually saying, "God loves you,
Christ loves you," and he and his congregation will by and by
be losing sight both of their sinnerhood and of the substitutionary atonement of the cross, where the love of God and of
Christ was *once for all* and *supremely* set forth,—and in
righteous display!

Now whether God or Christ is indicated in **Him that
loved us** in this verse, what we have said holds true.

Frankly we personally feel that the rendering "the love of
God" in verse 35, is correct. And this because it is the love *of
God* that is emphasized throughout this passage, from verse 31
to the end. For note, it is God that is for us, God spared not
His Son; God justifieth. And it is Christ Jesus whom He had
"not spared," that died, that was raised, who is at the right
hand of God, and who intercedes. From such love *of God* (as
good authorities read in verse 35), no difficulties can separate us.

We know, however, that verse 39 definitely declares that it is "the love of God which is *in Christ Jesus*" from which nothing can separate us.

Therefore, we are also quite strongly drawn to read "the love *of Christ*" in verse 35, because (1) Christ's work for us has just been described in the immediately preceding verse; and also (2) because of the glorious historical fact that the martyrs were directly conscious, in the midst of the flames and when they were thrown to the beasts, of the presence and love of Christ, their Redeemer, Lord and Head.

But, however we read, both are correct!

Verse 38: **For I am persuaded**—Before we quote the last two verses of this triumphant paean, let us lay to heart this word **persuaded**, for it is the key to Paul's triumph as he goes shouting up these mountain heights of Christian faith. "Persuaded" is a heart word. The difference between knowing a truth and being heart-persuaded of it, Paul brings out in Chapter 14.14: "I know, and am persuaded in the Lord Jesus, that nothing is unclean of itself." (See that passage.) Many people know, for example, that in this dispensation all distinctions of meats have been removed; yet their consciences are not relieved. Weakness and fear still trouble them—about meats and days and many things. To know a Bible truth, you have only to read it: to be "persuaded of it in the Lord Jesus" involves the fact, first, that the truth in question touches your own personal safety before God; and, second, that your heart has so been enlightened by the Holy Spirit, and your will so won over—"persuaded"—that *confidence,* heart-satisfied *persuasion,* results.

Now Paul says in Romans 8.38: **I am persuaded**—Dear saints, had not Paul passed through all these terrible things of verse 35, tribulation, anguish, persecution,—all? Look at the scars on his body! Assurance? He had it: "In the sight of God speak we in Christ" (II Cor. 12.19) ; "Seeing that ye seek a proof of Christ that speaketh in me" (II Cor. 13.3). Confidence? Hearken to his last epistle: "The Lord will deliver me from every evil work, and will save me unto His heavenly kingdom: to whom be the glory unto the ages of the ages" (II Tim. 4.18). "Persuaded?" His mind, his conscience, his heart, his whole being, were sublimely committed to what he is about to say. The days of doubt and uncertainty were forever passed for him!

Verses 38,39: **For I am persuaded, that neither death, nor life, nor angels, nor principalities, nor things present, nor things to come, nor powers, nor height, nor depth, nor any other created thing, shall be able to separate us from the love of God, which is in Christ Jesus our Lord.**

How we do misquote this verse, putting it according to natural thought, "neither life nor death." But God says, **neither death nor life.** To the instructed believer, the fear of death is gone (see Hebrews 2.14,15). Christ partook of it: "That through death He might bring to nought him that had the power of death, that is, the devil; and might deliver all them who through fear of death were all their lifetime subject to bondage."

But **life!** Ah, life is so much more difficult than death!— life with its burdens, its bitternesses, its disappointments, its uncertainties; often with its physical miseries,—as Job said, "My soul chooseth strangling and death rather than these my bones." But just as death cannot separate us from this unchangeable love of God in Christ, neither can any circumstances of life do it!

Nor angels—Whether we speak of the elect angels—the angels of God's power, in the presence of whom the saints have felt overwhelmed by their utter unworthiness (as Daniel, Dan. 10.8-17); or whether it be the malignant angels, who chose Satan's captaincy, and are a unity with him in evil;—*no* angels can separate us from that love of God which is fixed forever in Christ.

Nor principalities—Here we touch a mysterious word. We know from Ephesians 1.21 that there is an ordered realm of unseen authorities whether of good or of evil (Eph. 2.2; 6.12). But with none of them have we anything to do, for whatever they are, they cannot separate us from God's love in Christ.

Nor things present nor things to come—In Job's case, Satan dealt in "things present"—and they were as bad as hellish enmity could make them. But they did not separate from God's love, for look at "the end of the Lord," with Job. In the cases of David and Elijah, Satan dealt in "futures": David said, "I shall now one day perish by the hand of Saul." Yet shortly he sat on the throne! And Jezebel threatened, "I will make thy life as the life of one of them [the slain prophets] by *tomorrow* about this time." When Elijah saw *that,* (alas, these "thats" of the devil!) "he arose, and went for his life." Yet God took him up by a chariot of fire into heaven!

Nor powers—The word translated "powers"* here is *dunamis,* energy: and has reference evidently to those uncanny and horrible *workings* of Satan and his host seen in spiritism, theosophy, and all kinds of magic. Indeed, this very word is used in Acts 8.10 concerning Simon the Magician: "They said, This man is that power *(dunamis)* of God which is called Great." All kinds of bewitchment, sorcery, necromancy, "evil eye," and "mystic spells" cast upon people are included. Now I know that sorcery, the "evil eye," "spells," are potent over the unsaved. But, it is a sad fact that many dear saints are troubled by these things. They are *afraid*—of Friday the thirteenth, of passing under a ladder, of seeing a black cat, of breaking a mirror! Now this simply leaves *God* out! Who rules in earth's affairs, Satan or God?

People say to me, "Do you believe there is anything in spiritism?" I say, "I certainly do,—the devil's in it!" But none of these "powers" can separate us from the love of God, which is in Christ Jesus, our Lord. There is no such thing as "luck." Let us cease to dishonor God by mentioning it! "God worketh all things after the counsel of *His will.*" I have seen professing Christians "knock on wood" if making some confident statement! (I am ashamed as I write this.) Let us be "persuaded" of the love which God, without cause in us, has unchangeable toward us in Christ Jesus our Lord. No matter how real, insidious, terrifying these demon powers may be, we are safe in Christ! If you want to be free from superstition and fears,

---

*In Ephesians 6.12, in the expression "principalities and powers," the first word, *(archai)* is the word translated "principalities" in Romans 8.38, meaning one in high position in the unseen world. The second word, "powers," in Ephesians 6.12, is the Greek *exousia,* and is directly connected with "principalities," being a word indicative of authority, rather than energy. See Matthew 10.1; Acts 26.10, 12.

do as James directs: "Ye ought to say, If the Lord will, we shall both live and do this or that." That brings God in!

Verse 39: **Nor height, nor depth**—The astronomers would frighten us with their figures of the vastness of the universe. But Christ has passed through *all* the heavens, and is at the right hand of God! And God has loved us *in Christ*—there is no separation from that love. But "depth"—Ah, poor mortals, we are afraid, even of earthly cliffs and chasms. Yea, but Christ *descended* into "the lower parts of the earth," into "the abyss" at "the heart of the earth" (Eph. 4.9; Rom. 10.7; Matt. 12.40). Moreover, He has said that His Church would not enter the gates of Hades (Matt. 16.18). And they shall not! But even if God had arranged that they should, Christ says to John, "Fear not; I am the First and the Last, and the Living One; and I was dead, and behold, I am alive forevermore, and *I have the keys* of death and of Hades!" This is indeed a glorious salvation! No "depth" can separate us from God's love in Christ.

Nor any other created thing—There! That should banish all our fears, no matter what they be. The ability of the human heart to conjure up possible trouble and disaster is without limit, it seems: but this word gives us peace. **No created thing shall be able to separate us from the love of God, which is in Christ Jesus, our Lord.**

Notice that this love of God is *in* Christ Jesus our Lord. Why God set His love upon us, we cannot tell. Why He chose us *in Christ* before the foundation of the world, connecting our destiny eternally with Christ His beloved Son, we cannot tell. But, "Whatsoever Jehovah doeth, it shall be forever." We must therefore hold in mind this fact, that God has loved us even as He loved Christ (John 17.26): for He loved us *in Him*.

Some dear saints seem to think that it is a mark of humility to doubt the security of God's elect. But *Romans* has surely shown us the way to be *certain!* Do not try to assure your heart that you are one of God's elect. If you are troubled with doubts, go and sit down on the sinner's seat, and say, "God declares righteous *the ungodly* who trust Him. I renounce all thoughts of my own righteousness, and *as a sinner* I trust the

God who raised Christ from the dead,—who was delivered up for *my trespasses.*" This is the path our God in Romans shows us. Uncertainty about election arises from some kind of *self-righteousness!*

As we have elsewhere noted, the saints are those who have received Him whom God in His great love gave to the world, and they by Divine grace welcomed this only-begotten Son whom God has given. Therefore the love of God in Christ Jesus is forever theirs. However the world of men may treat this astonishing unspeakable *gift* which God has proffered, and may go on rejecting Christ till a day when it must be eternally withdrawn; yet God's elect, the saints, "those who have *believed,*" find themselves borne upon the irresistible tide of this Divine affection which "is in Christ Jesus," out into an eternity of bliss! "God is love," and "the Father loveth the Son." And now these *connected with Christ* find themselves wrapped in this same *eternal affection* shown by God to His dear Son.

When we fail utterly, and are overwhelmed, then is the time to say: We have been accepted in Christ—only in Christ, wholly in Christ. Our place is unchanged by our failure. We are ashamed before God, but not confounded. Just now His eyes are on us in Christ, as they ever have been. His love is as deep and wonderful as ever, being "the love wherewith He loved Christ"! We do not resolve to "do better," for we are weak. We trust the grace of God in Christ and cast ourselves anew, and all the more wholly, upon His grace alone. We trust Him never to forsake or fail us: for He hath loved us in His beloved Son; and God will never forsake Christ! For His sake will He deal with us now and ever.

How hard it is to turn away from its object the love even of a *man,* a creature, a bit of dust! How eternally impossible, then, that the infinite God should be turned away from His love to those that are in Christ Jesus!

The wonderful text of this passage, GOD IS FOR US, fills our amazed and grateful hearts more and more.

MY HIGH TOWER

By PAUL GERHARDT: A. D. 1676

IS GOD FOR ME? I fear not, though all against me rise;
I call on Christ my Savior, the host of evil flies.
My friend the Lord Almighty, and He who loves me, God!
What enemy shall harm me, though coming as a flood?
I know it, I believe it, I say it fearlessly,
That God, the Highest, Mightiest, forever loveth me;
At all times, in all places, He standeth at my side,
He rules the battle fury, the tempest and the tide.

A Rock that Stands forever is Christ my righteousness,
And there I stand unfearing in everlasting bliss;
No earthly thing is needful to this my life from Heaven,
And nought of love is worthy, save that which Christ hath given.
Christ, all my praise and glory, my Light most sweet and fair,
The ship wherein He saileth is scathless everywhere!
In Him I dare be joyful, a hero in the war
The judgment of the sinner affrighteth me no more!

There is no condemnation, there is no hell for me,
The torment and the fire mine eyes shall never see;
For me there is no sentence, for me death has no stings,
Because the Lord Who saved me shall shield me with His wings.
Above my soul's dark waters His Spirit hovers still,
He guards me from all sorrow, from terror and from ill;
In me He works and blesses the life-seed He hath sown,
From Him I learn the Abba, that prayer of faith alone.

And if in lonely places, a fearful child, I shrink,
He prays the prayers within me I cannot ask or think;
In deep unspoken language, known only to that Love
Who fathoms the heart's mystery from the Throne of Light
      above.
His Spirit to my spirit sweet words of comfort saith,
How God the weak one strengthens who leans on Him in faith;
How He hath built a City, of love, and light, and song,
Where the eye at last beholdeth what the heart had loved so long.

And there is mine inheritance, my kingly palace-home;
The leaf may fall and perish, not less the spring will come;
As wind and rain of winter, our earthly sighs and tears,
Till the golden summer dawneth of the endless Year of years.
The world may pass and perish, Thou, God, wilt not remove—
No hatred of all devils can part me from Thy love;
No hungering nor thirsting, no poverty nor care,
No wrath of mighty princes can reach my shelter there.

No Angel, and no Heaven, no throne, nor power, nor might,
No love, no tribulation, no danger, fear, nor fight,
No height, no depth, no creature that has been or can be,
Can drive me from Thy bosom, can sever me from Thee.
My heart in joy upleapeth, grief cannot linger there—
While singing high in glory amidst the sunshine fair!
The source of all my singing is high in Heaven above;
The Sun that shines upon me is Jesus and His Love!

CHAPTER NINE

Paul's Great Sorrow for Unbelieving Israel—Unbelieving Despite an Eight-Fold Preëminence. Verses 1 to 5.

The Real Israel, however, were an Elect, not a Natural Seed: God's Sovereignty in Election Defended. Verses 6 to 29.

The Astonishing Conclusion! The Gentiles, not Following after Righteousness, Attain to it by Simple Faith; Israel, Following after a Law-Method, Stumble at the By-Faith Way,—at Christ! Verses 30 to 33.

IN ROMANS NINE, Ten, and Eleven, Paul turns aside from that glorious exposition of Grace, in the first eight chapters, to the explanation of God's present dealing with Israel. God had committed Himself to bless this nation; and lo, now it is nationally set aside, while Paul's message goes out to all nations without distinction between Jew and Greek! Where, then, is the Divine faithfulness? How reconcile God's former condition of blessing,—through circumcision, the Law with its observances, the temple with its presence of Jehovah in the Holy of Holies, and the *separateness* of the elect nation, Israel, *from* all others:—how reconcile all this with such a by faith "no difference" message as Paul has been preaching to us— in the first eight chapters? A message, indeed, which he resumes from Chapter Twelve to the close, magnifying God's present mercy to the Gentiles; and ending up the Epistle as he began it, with the words: "My gospel, (revealing a heretofore hidden secret), is sent forth unto *all the nations* unto the simple obedience of *faith*"!

The question, therefore, is, how to reconcile the "no distinction between Jew and Greek" message that Paul is here preaching, with God's former manner of speech to Israel, concerning which the Psalmist sings:

> "He showeth His word unto Jacob,
> His statutes and His ordinances unto Israel.
> He hath not dealt so with any nation;
> And as for His ordinances, they have not known
>   them" (Ps. 147.19,20).

And not only so, but the whole book of Psalms, for that matter; yes, and the prophets, also!

Now it will not do merely to go back to Israel's idolatrous history, and denounce the nation; or even to our Lord's awful utterance, as He finally left their temple:

> "O Jerusalem, Jerusalem, that killeth the prophets, and stoneth them that are sent unto her! how often would I have gathered thy children together, even as a hen gathereth her own brood under her wings, and ye *would not!* Behold, your house is left unto you desolate" (Luke 13.34, 35).

It will not do to say they were a disobedient people, and God has rejected them entirely, and has brought blessing out to the Gentiles instead. Nor will it do, in these three chapters, merely to go forward to Ephesians (2.14-16) and say, "Christ is our peace, who hath made both [Jew and Gentile] one, and has *broken down* the middle wall of partition, having abolished in his flesh the enmity [between them], even the Law of commandments in ordinances; that He might create in Himself of the two *One New Man,* so making peace; and might reconcile them both in *One Body* unto God through the cross." Furthermore, it will not do to go on into Colossians and say concerning this new man, the Body of Christ, that "there *cannot be Greek and Jew,* circumcision and uncircumcision, barbarian, Scythian, bondman, freeman; but *Christ is all, and in all"* (Col. 3.11). All these things are true for us who are in Christ. But it is the facts as they are set forth *in Romans,* that we must examine, if we are to study *Romans.* And God, here in Romans, sets forth His ways in the past, and His ways in the future, *with this chosen earthly nation, Israel.*

That God should so signally honor this nation Israel as to reveal His awful presence on Sinai, and speak in an audible voice to them, giving to them and them alone His holy "fiery Law,"—this fact must have its true place with us.

> "For ask now of the days that are past, which were before thee, since the day that God created man upon the earth, and from the one end of heaven unto the other, whether there hath been any such thing as this great thing is, or hath been heard like it? Did ever a people hear the voice of God speaking out of the midst of the fire, as thou has heard, and live? Or hath God assayed to go and take Him a nation from the midst of another nation, by trials, by signs, and by wonders, and by war, and by a mighty hand, and by an outstretched arm, and by great terrors, according to all that Jehovah your God did for you in Egypt before your eyes?" (Deut. 4.32-34.)

I say, for God to do all this, and then publicly set this nation aside, and send a Paul to all nations without distinction of Jew or Gentile, preaching salvation apart from the Law, and by simple faith, instead of by "the Jews' religion"; promising blessings, and that even heavenly blessings, inconceivably beyond those promised to Israel,—this was an astounding thing! The trouble with us Gentiles is, that we have become accustomed to it, we take it for granted. God's plans and ways with Israel do not concern most Christians.

There is no more striking example of the deadly and deadening self-confidence into which human beings so quickly drift when they find themselves objects of Divine goodness: "Man that is in honor, and understandeth not, is like the beasts that perish" (Ps. 49.20).

One has only to look about Christendom to see at once the evidence of this fateful delusion. Behold the "state" churches, the great cathedrals, the vested choirs and magnificent music; and the "church calendars" with their man-invented feast days, "holy" days, "Christmas-tides," "Lenten" periods, "Easter" services,—all that goes to make up the so-called "Christian religion"! And the high talk of the Gentiles about Israel as God's *"ancient* people": whereas God has never had and never will have any *people,* any elect *nation,* but earthly Israel!

When we reflect that, after He has "caught up in the clouds" His Church saints, our Lord is coming back to this earthly people Israel, and will establish them in their land, with a glorious millennial temple and order of worship, to which the Gentile nations must and will submit: then we see that the present time is altogether anomalous! It is a *parenthesis,* in which God is making a "visit" to the Gentiles, to "take out of them a people for His name";—*after* which, James tells us, our Lord "will Himself return," and "build again the tabernacle of David, which is fallen" (Acts 15.16), on Mount Zion, in Jerusalem, where David lived.

Romans Nine, Ten, and Eleven become an essential part of Christian doctrine in this respect: that while they do not set forth our salvation or our place in Christ, as do the first eight chapters, yet they unfold to us our relative place in God's plans, along with national Israel's place. They also reveal to us several matters absolutely essential to our proper estimate of God and His ways; and, properly believed, they "hide pride" from us: bringing in as they do the great fact that both ourselves and (in the future), the saved Remnant of Israel, are the objects of sovereign Divine *mercy.* We discover ourselves in Chapter 9.23 to be "vessels of *mercy,*" as will future Israel discover themselves to be, by the example of the mercy shown to us. The *grace* of God has been spoken of in this Epistle often before; but not until these chapters is *mercy* named; and until mercy is understood, grace cannot be fully appreciated.

In Luke 1.78 (margin) we read of the "heart of mercy" of our God; and in Ephesians 2.4, that God is "rich in mercy." God proclaimed His name to Moses: "Jehovah, Jehovah, a God merciful and gracious, slow to anger, and abundant in loving-kindness and truth" (Ex. 34.6). God's *mercy* is the sovereign going forth of His heart to us sinful wretched creatures; His *grace* follows, in His pardoning our guilt; and His *loving-kindness* is His proceeding with us in abundant goodness thereafter.

1   I speak the truth in Christ, I lie not, my con-
     science bearing witness with me in the Holy Spirit,
2   that I have great sorrow and unceasing pain in my

3 heart. For I could pray that I myself were [cast
   out] accursed from Christ for my brethren's sake,
4 my kinsmen according to the flesh: who are Israelites; whose is the [Divine national] adoption and
   the [earth-manifested] glory, and the covenants,
   and the custodianship of the law, and the sanc-
5 tuary service, and the promises; whose are the
   fathers, and of whom is Christ as concerning the
   flesh, who is over all, God blessed unto the ages.
   Amen.

This most remarkable paragraph naturally divides itself into
two parts:

1. Verses 1 to 3: Paul's constant yearning pain for the unbelieving Israelites, his brethren and kinsmen,—a yearning to
which he declares the Spirit bears witness, which could, were
it right, go the length of his being lost if they could be saved!
Thus Moses prayed: "If thou wilt not forgive them, blot me,
I pray thee, out of Thy book, which Thou hast written!" (Ex.
32.32,33.)* Dear old Bengel searchingly says, "It is not easy
to estimate the measure of love in a Moses and a Paul. For
our limited reason does not grasp it, as the child cannot com-
prehend the courage of warriors!"

2. Verses 4 and 5: The rehearsing of eight matters which
belonged to Israel,—yea, and yet belong to Israel, in spite of
all their unfaithfulness. As Jehovah says to Jeremiah:

> "If these ordinances [of the sun, of the moon, of the
> stars and of the sea] depart from before Me, saith Jehovah,
> then the seed of Israel also shall cease from being a nation
> before Me forever. Thus saith Jehovah: If heaven above
> can be measured, and the foundations of the earth searched
> out beneath, then will I also cast off all the seed of Israel
> for all that they have done, saith Jehovah" (Jer. 31.35-37).

---

*Bishop Moule remarks upon the impossibility of Paul's really *making* such a
prayer: "To desire the curse of God would be to desire not only suffering, but
moral alienation from Him, the withdrawal of the soul's capacity to love Him. Thus
the wish would be in effect an act of 'greater love for our neighbor than for God.'
Again, the redeemed soul is 'not its own': to wish the self to be accursed from
Christ would thus be to wish the loss of that which He has 'bought and made His
own.' But, the logical reason of the matter apart, we have only to read the close
of Chapter 8, to see how entirely a moral impossibility it was for Paul to complete
such a wish."

Therefore, first, let us deeply reflect on this thing of Paul's unceasing pain over Israel, lest in our Gentile shallowness we miss the correct judgment of the importance of this event before God, that Israel, among whom He had dwelt, became disobedient, and were broken off from blessing; and lest in our own affections we become so narrowed as to have no yearning over Israel. Shall we let Paul, our great apostle, have this "unceasing pain," this "great sorrow," in his heart, all alone? Nay, for Paul would not have shared the fact with us except he expected our sympathy in the Spirit. Let us not be like those thousands of grace-hating Jews in Paul's day who kept following him in his blessed ministry, declaring that he was an apostate Jew, one really denying the faith of his fathers, bitter against his own race in order to curry favor among the despised Gentiles. They spread the report that Paul "taught all men everywhere against Israel and the Law and the temple" (Acts 21.28). How Christ-like was the love in Paul's heart, that persisted even to be willing to be *lost,* for the unbelieving Israelites who were reviling him!

Second, let us enumerate and examine the eight respects in which the apostle here declares the nation of Israel differed before God from all other nations:

1. **The** Divine national **adoption**—"Thus saith Jehovah, Israel is my son, my first-born" (Ex. 4.22). "Thou art a holy people unto Jehovah thy God: Jehovah thy God hath chosen thee to be a people for His own possession, above all peoples that are upon the face of the earth" (Deut. 7.6). "You only have I known of all the families of the earth" (Amos 3.2). Let the nations, British, Americans, French, Germans, or whatever they be, lay this to heart before it is too late! For as to God's election of Israel as His chosen nation, it is absolute and eternal,* as He says in Isaiah 66.22: "As the

---

*The envy of other races and nations towards God's elect nation Israel has always existed. But there is a mild phase and a virulent phase of this Gentile sin-disease that should be noted:

First, the mild phase: this is Anglo-Israelism, the teaching that the Anglo-Saxons, especially Britain and America (Britain as Ephraim and America as Manasseh!) are the "lost ten tribes" who, carried away East across the Euphrates in God's judgment,—turned East into West and landed at the British Isles! No; British and Americans are *lost,* but they are *not* The Ten Tribes!

new heavens and new earth [of Rev. 21 and 22] shall remain before Me, so shall your seed and your name [Israel] remain."

2. **The glory**—We all know how God's presence accompanied Israel as a pillar of cloud by day and of fire by night through the sea and through the wilderness, and then filled the tabernacle! No other nation has had or will have God's presence thus. God said:

> "And let them make Me a sanctuary, that I may dwell among them . . . And thou shalt put the mercy-seat above upon the ark; and in the ark thou shalt put the testimony that I shall give thee . . . And there I will meet with thee" (Ex. 25.8,21,22).

And concerning the dedication of Solomon's temple we read,

> "It came to pass, when the trumpeters and singers were as one, to make one sound to be heard in praising and thanking Jehovah, and when they lifted up their voice with the trumpets and cymbals and instruments of music, and praised Jehovah, saying, For He is good; for His lovingkindness endureth forever; that then the house was filled with a cloud, even the house of Jehovah, so that the priests could not stand to minister by reason of the cloud: for the glory of Jehovah filled the house of God" (II Chron. 5.13,14).

3. **The covenants**—With "covenants" Gentiles have absolutely nothing actively to do.* In Genesis Fifteen God made

---

*It is indeed an infinitely blessed fact that all who believe share in the benefits of that "everlasting covenant" of Hebrews 13.20, made between the Father and the Son, on these conditions: that if the Son would come to earth and die for our sins, the Father would bring Him again from the dead as the great Shepherd of the sheep. Paul says in I Corinthians 11.25, "In like manner also the cup, after supper, saying, This cup is the new covenant in My blood." (The "New Covenant with the house of Israel and with the house of Judah" has not yet been made; for we read that it will be made after these [Gentile] days. See Acts 15.13-16.) When our Lord said therefore, "This cup is the new covenant in My blood," He must, we believe, refer to that covenant of Hebrews 13.20; to which covenant, as we have said, the Father and the Son were parties. Even concerning the New Covenant to be made in the future with Israel, God says in Romans 11.27: "And this is the covenant *from Me* unto them, when I shall take away their sins." It is no longer blessing conditioned on their obedience, but it is the day of Jehovah's "power" to Israel (Ps. 110.3), not merely a "visitation" (Luke 19.41-44).

Second, the virulent phase of this jealousy and envy towards elect nationⁱ Israel appears in "anti-Semitism," or anti-Jewism; and has lately been carried to new depths of pagan infamy by Hitler in Germany. For this phase of Gentilₑ

a covenant with Abraham, and gave to his earthly seed the token of circumcision. In Genesis Twenty-two, God "confirmed" the promise to Abraham's *Seed,* which is *Christ* (Gal. 3.16). With David God made an earthly kingdom-covenant,—that one of David's descendants should sit upon his throne forever (II Sam. 7.13); as we find Gabriel announcing to Mary in Luke 1.32,33. God says He will make a New Covenant in the future with the house of Israel and with the house of Judah (Heb. 8.8-12 , quoted from Jer. 31.31,ff), in connection with which He promises to "bring Israel back into their land," to "take away the stony heart out of their flesh, and give them a heart of flesh, to put His Spirit within them, to *cause* them to walk in His statutes, and keep His ordinances, and do them" (Ezek. 36.24-27).

4. **And the custodianship of the Law**—It was a great thing to be entrusted with God's holy Law, as we have seen in Chapter 3.2. Let me here repeat that every writer of Scripture is an Israelite. No other nation has ever been even directly spoken to, as a nation, by God: except to be *warned,* as were Egypt by Moses, and Nineveh by Jonah. There were written messages,—as Isaiah 13-23; but these were given to Israel, *concerning* other nations.

5. **And the sanctuary-service**—The Greek word here *(latreia),* refers to those religious ordinances prescribed to Israel by God in connection with the tabernacle-worship, and afterwards the temple-worship, which will be resumed in the Millennium, as we read in the last nine chapters of Ezekiel. (The ordinances and offerings then will be *memorial,* rather than prophetic, as in the days before Christ died.)

Note carefully that such outward form-worship belongs to the nation of Israel, and not to Christianity. To introduce it

---

envy rejects Scripture. Mr. Hitler hates the Jews and declares for "pure Aryan blood"—(pray where would you find it?). Carrying his boasting hatred to its logical conclusion, he rejects the Word of God as authority, and turns back to the old pagan gods of Northern Europe.

Now all hatred of national Israel arises from rebellion against Divine sovereign election. We know that Israel has failed God: but God declares He will not fail them finally, whereas the hate of modern Gentiles (wiser than God—for are they not the "moderns"?) would seek to crush Israel and exalt Gentiledom. Of course, it will end in the Antichrist, but the Lord Jesus will end him, and all Gentile boasting, at "the forthshining of His arrival" (II Thess. 2.8, Rotherham).

into Christianity is to return to paganism. For Paul plainly classifies the forms and ceremonies of Judaism as now belonging with "the weak and beggarly religious principles" which heathen Gentiles engage in! (Gal. 4.9,10.)

Until the "Aryans" (whoever they are) have been led out from all other races by God Himself in manifest presence, and have had a "fiery law" given them from heaven as had Israel, let them stop their mouths, and also stop their ears from any vain pagan prophet! And let the Gentiles all humble their miserable pride. What have they to do with the Law that God committed to Israel? or with the Jewish Sabbath, which God said was a token of His covenant with that chosen people? (Ex. 31.12-17.)

6. **And the promises**—God's salvation-promises were lodged in Abraham; His kingdom-promises, in David. No promises were made to Gentile nations as such. For the gospel now proclaimed is not a promise, but the announcement of a fact to be believed; and it is not preached to nations as such, but to individuals—good news to sinners everywhere. But to Israel, promises, thousands of them, were committed,—as *a nation*.

Now we do not have to become "Israelites" in any sense whatever to enjoy God's salvation in Christ.* The nation of Israel has been set aside for the present as the vessel of Divine blessing to the world, while the Gentiles, as set forth in Chapter Eleven, have now the privileged place, and Jews and Gentiles come individually, upon believing, into a *heavenly* inheritance. Nevertheless, "the promises" pertain nationally to Israel, and to no other nation as such.

7. **Whose are the fathers**—Abraham, Isaac, and Jacob, are directly referred to; and Jacob's sons also, especially Joseph, and Judah the vessel of *royal* promise and blessing to Israel (Ps. 77.15; 80.1; 81.5; Gen. 49.8,10; Heb. 7.14). Our hearts include Moses, Samuel, David, and the prophets when we think of Israel and remember "the fathers." But it is

---

*Some accurate book setting forth the absolute difference between the Church and Israel should be read, such as *Israel and the Church*, by James H. Brookes; or Mr. Blackstone's (W. E. B.) always excellent *Jesus Is Coming*.

especially to Abraham, "the father of all them that believe," that our grateful memory turns; for, although we have no connection with Israel, we do have indeed a vital connection with Abraham, as his "children."

8. **And of whom is Christ as to the flesh—who is over all, God blessed unto the ages! Amen.*** In Chapter 1.3 God's Son is said to be "born of the seed of David according to the flesh"; in John 1.14, we read: "The Word became flesh"; in Hebrews 2.16: "He taketh hold of the seed of Abraham"; and in Matthew 1.1, it is: "The book of the generation of Jesus Christ, the Son of David, the Son of Abraham."

Now this is an astonishing honor to Israel,—infinitely outranking all others: our Lord, "the Mighty God" (Isa. 9.6), is, "according to the flesh," an *Israelite!* For two other things are immediately affirmed of Him: He is **over all,** and He is **God blessed unto the ages.** The words "over all" are partly explained in I Corinthians 15.27: "He [God the Father] put all things in subjection under His [Christ's] feet." But in John 1.1,3: "The Word was God. All things were made through Him." As in Colossians 1.16,17: "All things were created through Him and unto Him; and by Him all things consist" (hold together); so that Christ is indeed "over all, God blessed forever"! (As to this ascription of deity to Christ, see Kelly's Notes on Romans, pp. 165-171.)

And now Paul falls back upon the sovereignty of God, accomplishing thereby three things:

First he defends himself (and all of us) against the charge of teaching that God had been unfaithful in His promises toward Israel; (2) he shows that Israel's own Scriptures had foretold their temporary rejection, and the salvation of the

---

*The questions concerning both Romans 9.5 and I Timothy 3.16 have arisen from the mists of doubt rather than from the heights of childlike faith in God's revelation of the deity of Christ. See Alford's excellent and exhaustive note on 9.5, from the end of which we quote:

"No conjecture arising from doctrinal difficulty is ever to be admitted in the face of the consensus of mss. and versions. The rendering given above is, then, not only that most agreeable to the usage of the Apostle, but the only one admissible by the rules of grammar and arrangement. It also admirably suits the context: for having enumerated the historic advantages of the Jewish people, he concludes by stating one which ranks far higher than all,—that from them sprung, according to the flesh, He who is God over all, blessed forever."

Gentiles; and (3) he shows the great future blessing which
will come to Israel, in God's sovereign MERCY. Let us read
the text:

6   But it is not as though the word of God hath
     come to nought. For they are not all Israel, that
7   are of Israel; neither, because they are Abraham's
     seed, are they all children: but, In Isaac shall thy
8   seed be called. That is, It is not the children of
     the flesh that are children of God; but the children
9   of the promise are reckoned for a seed. For this
     is a word of promise, According to this season will
10   I come, and Sarah shall have a son. And not only
     so; but Rebecca also having conceived by one,—by
11   our father Isaac: for [the children] being not yet
     born, neither having done anything good or bad,
     that the purpose of God, according to election
     might stand, not of works, but of Him that calleth,
12   —it was said unto her, The elder shall serve the
13   younger. Even as it is written, Jacob I loved, but
     Esau I hated.

The great revealed truth of the sovereignty of God perplexes
many, disturbs others, and some take occasion to stumble at it.

Verse 6: But it is not as though the word of God hath
come to nought—Paul here refers to those great promises
God had made to Abraham, then to Isaac, then to Jacob; conferring blessing upon their seed, announcing Himself as God of
Israel, giving them by oath the land of Palestine, placing in
David's line the promise of perpetual royalty on earth; prophesying a great and glorious future for Israel, not only in the
coming Millennium, or 1000 years kingdom here, but in the new
earth which follows that (Isa. 66.22). Paul's immediate explanation (for it looked as if these Divine promises had lapsed)
was that not all that are of Israel are really Israel before
God.

Verse 7: Neither, because they are Abraham's seed, are
they all children: but, In Isaac shall thy seed be called. I
know, said our Lord, that ye are Abraham's descendants; but

if you were Abraham's children you would do the works of Abraham. "If God were your Father, ye would love Me. Ye are of your father the devil" (John 8.37 to 44). To regard religious privilege as spiritual reality is the very deadliest delusion. The real sons of Abraham are defined in Galatians 3.7: "Know therefore, that they that are *of faith,* the same are sons of Abraham." However, in the present passage, the point is not that Abraham's real children are those that believe, but that Divine sovereign *calling* lies behind all. As God said to Abraham concerning Ishmael, "Nay, but Sarah thy wife shall bear thee a son; and thou shalt call his name Isaac: and I will establish my covenant with him for an everlasting covenant for his seed after him. And as for Ishmael, I have heard thee: behold, I have blessed him and will make him fruitful, and will multiply him exceedingly. But *My covenant* will I establish with *Isaac,* whom *Sarah* shall bear unto thee at this set time in the next year" (Gen. 17.19-21). The direct quotation is from Genesis 21.12, when Ishmael was cast out. "In Isaac shall thy seed be *called.*" This is Divine sovereign action. Now Paul explains it:

Verse 8: **That is, it is not the children of the flesh that are children of God; but the children of the promise are reckoned for a seed.** What does the apostle mean by "The children of the promise are reckoned for a seed"? It is most necessary that we perceive that Paul is speaking here, not of man's believing a promise and therefore being written down as one of God's children; but on the contrary, of the promise (of God to Christ) that characterizes the existence and calling of all the real children of God. He expounds this in the next verse.

Verse 9: **For this is a word of promise, According to this season will I come, and Sarah shall have a son**—The quotation is from Genesis 18.10. Read the connection there carefully. Isaac, the coming child, did not believe the promise in order to be born! But, God promised Isaac to Abraham, and kept His promise by a miracle. When Isaac was born, therefore, he was a child *of promise,—a promised* child, in God's sovereign will.

Verses 10,11: **And not only so, but Rebecca also having conceived by one, even by our father Isaac—for the children being not yet born, neither having done anything good or bad, that the purpose of God according to election might stand, not of works, but of him that calleth,—**

In the former passage it is brought out that Isaac was a child of promise, not merely of natural generation. In the present passage the Divine sovereignty—"the purpose of God according to election"—is seen extending still further than birth, to the disposition of the condition and affairs of the children thus promised. **The elder shall serve the younger,** is not only a prophecy that Jacob would inherit and obtain the Divine blessing, and that his seed (as in the days of David and Solomon) would be temporarily triumphant over the Edomites, Esau's descendants; but also looks far into the future beyond the brief triumph of the Herodians, the Edomites, in the days of Christ and the apostles, to the day when, as Balaam was forced against his will to prophesy:

"There shall come forth a Star out of Jacob,
And a Sceptre shall rise out of Israel,
And shall smite through the corners of Moab,
And break down all the sons of tumult.
And Edom shall be a possession;
Seir also shall be a possession, who were his enemies;
While Israel doeth valiantly" (Num. 24.17,18).

"And they [Israel and Judah when the Lord returns, agrees Isaiah], shall put forth their hand upon Edom and Moab, and the children of Ammon shall obey them" (Isa. 11.14).

Verses 12,13: **The elder shall serve the younger,** and, **Jacob I loved, but Esau I hated**—These words are chosen from the first and from the last books of the Old Testament. As to "Jacob I loved, but Esau I hated," a woman once said to Mr. Spurgeon, "I cannot understand why God should say that He hated Esau." "That," Spurgeon replied, "is not my difficulty, madam. My trouble is to understand how God could love Jacob!" All men being sinners, we must allow God to "retreat into His own sovereignty," to act as He will. You and I may say, Esau proved himself entirely unworthy of the covenant blessings, for he despised them. This, however, will be seen to be a shallow view of the statement of the eleventh verse, that the prophecy of their future was told to their mother while the children were yet in her womb, **not having done anything good or bad.** For the Divine statement concerning His own election, and His providence that carries out that election, is very plain, that it is **not of works** but of Himself, who gives the creature his calling. We have already in Romans seen and believed that righteousness is not of works but of Divine grace—uncaused by us. Now let us just as frankly bow to God's plain statement that His purpose according to election is likewise not of human works. That is to say, the favor of God to the children of promise (to those whom He has given to Christ) is not procured by their response to God's grace, but contrariwise, their response to God's grace is because they have been given to Christ.

14   **What shall we say then? Is there unrighteous-**
15   **ness with God? Far be the thought! For He saith**
       to Moses, I will have mercy on whom I have
       mercy, and I will have compassion on whom I have
16   **compassion. So then it is not of him that willeth,**
       nor of him that runneth, but of God that hath
17   **mercy. For the Scripture saith unto Pharaoh, For**
       this very purpose did I raise thee up, that I might
       show in thee My power, and that My name might
18   **be published abroad in all the earth. So then He**
       hath mercy on whom He will, and whom He will
       He hardeneth.

We have now come upon that passage of Scripture against which the human mind—or rather heart, rebels most of all. For it sets the creature as he really is before God; not, indeed, as an automaton, nor in fatalistic compulsion,—otherwise there were no morals, and no appeal in the gospel.

Nevertheless, it will be our only safe path to receive *just as God writes it down,* the truth we find here.

Verses 14,15: **What shall we say then? Is there unrighteousness with God? Far be the thought! For He saith to**

Moses, I will have mercy on whom I have mercy, and I will have compassion on whom I have compassion. We have only to remember the circumstances under which God thus spoke to Moses, to see the righteousness of God's sovereignty in mercy. There had been the awful breach at Sinai: Israel had "changed their glory for the likeness of an ox that eateth grass." The eternal ineffably glorious Jehovah in His indignation had said to Moses: "Let Me alone, that My wrath may wax hot against them, and that I may consume them: and I will make of thee a great nation" (Ex. 32.10). Moses pleads for the people, and the next day offers, if God will forgive them, to be himself blotted out of God's book! He said to the people: "I will go up unto Jehovah; peradventure I shall make atonement for your sin" (Ex. 32.30). Forty days and forty nights this devoted man lay on his face interceding for Israel, and God brought about, as we know, Moses' mediatorship for Israel. (Study carefully Ex. 33 and 34: especially 33.12-17; 34.1,27,28,32.) God shows Moses himself favor; and finally extends it to all the people. And note, it is in this connection, and under these circumstances, and in answer to the personal request of His beloved servant: "Show me, I pray thee, thy glory," that Jehovah says, "I will make all My goodness pass before thee, and will proclaim the name of Jehovah before thee; and I will be gracious to whom I will be gracious, and will show mercy on whom I will show mercy" (Ex. 33.18,19).

Now who can find fault with that? Unless Jehovah shows mercy, Israel must all righteously perish. There was no resource left in *man!* God, whose name is Love, must come out to man and come in mercy, or all is over! And here we earnestly ask you to read the remarkable words of Darby, in the foot-note below.* It will accomplish in the heart which weighs it

---

*"Here the apostle shows Israel from their own history that *they must leave God to His sovereignty or else they must lose their promises;* and then that in the exercise of this sovereignty He will let in the Gentiles, as well as the Jews. If, says Paul, you Israelites will take your promises by descent, we will just see what comes of it. You say, we be Abraham's seed, and have a right to the promises by descent; for these Gentiles are but dogs, and have no right to share with us in God's promises. Well, if God has His sovereignty, He will in grace let in these Gentile dogs! But now I will prove to you that you cannot take the promises by descent. In the first place, 'They are not all Israel which are of Israel'; yet if it is by descent you must take in all Abraham's seed. And if you take in Abraham's

carefully that reconciliation of the sovereignty of God with God's love and grace which is possible alone to faith; and it will also enlighten the mind concerning God's dealings with Israel as recorded in these three great chapters of Romans.

Verse 16: **So then it is not of him that willeth, nor of him that runneth, but of God that hath mercy**—Oh, that this great verse might sink into our ears, into our very hearts! Perhaps no statement of all Scripture so completely brings man to an utter end. Man thinks he can "will" and "decide," Godward, and that after he has so "decided" and "willed," he has the ability to "run," or, as he says, to "hold out." But these two things, deciding and holding out, are in this verse utterly rejected as the source of salvation,—which is declared to be *God that hath MERCY*. Human responsibility is not at all

---

children, then you must take in Ishmael—those Arabians! Oh no, say they, we cannot allow that; what! Ishmaelites in the congregation of Israel, and heirs of promise? Yes, if by descent! You *must* take it by *grace;* and if it is by grace, God will not confine this grace to you, but will *exercise it toward the Gentiles.*

"But now, to go further down in your history, you have Jacob and Esau; and if you go by descent, you must let in the Edomites by the same title as yourselves. But in verses 5 and 9, it says, 'The children of the promise are counted for the seed': so that it must rest on Isaac and Jacob, and Ishmael and Esau remain outside: therefore your mouth must now be closed as to descent, for your mouth is bound up by God's saying, 'Jacob have I loved, but Esau have I hated.' He has chosen, according to His sovereign title, to bless you, and on that alone your blessing depends; as your own history shows, and your own prophetic testimony proves. You cannot rest it on a mere title by descent. But further, see how their (the Jews') mouth is stopped: for *when* did God say, 'I will have mercy on whom I will have mercy'? *When every Israelite had lost all title to everything God had to give, then God retreated, if I may use the expression, into His own sovereignty, that He might not cut them off.*"

[See Exodus 33.19, after the great breach made by Israel's worshipping the golden calf, while Moses was standing in the mount with Jehovah!]

"By this act, Israel had forfeited everything; they had cast off the promises, which they had accepted on the condition of their own obedience (Ex. 19.8), and the God who made the promises, and who alone could fulfil them. *Could God overlook this sin?* Israel had undertaken to have the promises by their obedience; if God had dealt with Israel in righteousness, every one must have been cut off. What could *God do, but retreat, as I said, into His own sovereignty? There He had a resource; for if any of them are to be spared, it must be in this way of mercy.* 'I will have mercy on whom I will have mercy.' Man is entirely lost, so now God says, I will act for Myself. Taking a truth in connection with all other truth gives it its right and proper place, and its own Divine force.

"*Say now, you Jews, (and you, my reader, ask yourself the question), will you be willing to be dealt with in righteousness? No, you would not! Then do not talk about it, until you can go to God on that footing. But if you have such a conviction of sin as stops your mouth about righteousness, and so excludes all boasting, you will rejoice in the 'mercy' and 'compassion' of God, who retreats into His own sovereignty, that He may know how to spare; because in this sovereignty He can show mercy.*"

denied here: man ought to will, and ought to run. But we are all nothing but sinners, and can do,—will do, neither: unless God come forth to us in sovereign mercy.*

Verses 17 and 18: **For the Scripture saith unto Pharaoh, For this very purpose did I raise thee up, that I might show in thee My power, and that My name might be published abroad in all the earth. So then He hath mercy on whom He will, and whom He will He hardeneth.**

Now in Pharaoh's case, it is customary to emphasize the fact that he said: "Who is Jehovah, that I should hearken unto His voice to let Israel go? I know not Jehovah, and moreover I will not let Israel go" (Ex. 5.2).

But we must go back of that to Exodus 4.21: "And Jehovah said unto Moses, When thou goest back into Egypt, see that thou do before Pharaoh all the wonders which I have put in thy hand: but I will harden [lit., make strong] his heart, and he will not let the people go."

"And I will harden Pharoah's heart and multiply My signs and My wonders in the land of Egypt. But Pharaoh will not hearken unto you, and I will lay My hand upon Egypt, and bring forth My hosts, My people the children of Israel, out of the land of Egypt by great judgments" (Ex 7.3,4).

Now it is not necessary nor right to make God the author of Pharaoh's stubbornness. No more is it right to insist that if God be a God of love He must save everybody, as all sorts of Universalists claim. Exodus 7.13,14 records Pharaoh's attitude after the first "wonder"; and then God's report of Pharaoh's heart-condition,—for God sees the heart: "And Pharaoh's heart was hardened [lit., was strong], and he hearkened not unto them; as Jehovah had spoken."

---

*God has come forth at Calvary! He has set forth Christ as a propitiation through faith in His blood. Here is infinite love, displayed when human sin was at its topmost height of frightful guilt and malignity. "Father, forgive them; for they know not what they do" (Luke 23.34) were the words spoken in tenderness to God the Father by God the Son at the moment wicked hands were nailing Him to a cross of agony—spoken by One whose face was "marred more than any man."

Therefore in the gospel is power to turn men's hearts, for it is the *goodness* of God that leadeth us to repentance. "That repentance and remission of sins should be preached *in my Name*," said our risen Lord, He of the pierced hands and feet and side!

"And Jehovah said unto Moses, 'Pharaoh's heart is heavy.' " Now the Hebrew word translated "heavy" or "hard" here, is frequently used of that which *weighs down,* as in Exodus 17.12: "Moses' hands were heavy"; and in I Kings 12.10: "Thy father made our yoke heavy." See especially Isaiah 1.4: "A people laden [lit., *heavy*] with iniquity." On the whole, therefore, we are compelled to see that Pharaoh's heart was left by God simply in its natural state,—heavy with iniquity. Unlike Jehoshaphat (II Chron. 17.6), his heart had never been "lifted up in the ways of Jehovah." Unlike David, he had not even felt the weight of his sins, for David complains, in Psalm 38.4:

> "Mine iniquities are gone over my head;
> As a heavy burden they are too heavy for me."

The word *heavy* here is the same Hebrew word which God uses to describe Pharaoh's heart, in Exodus 7.14.

God had a perfect right to allow Pharaoh to remain (where we all would have remained, apart from Divine sovereign mercy!), in a disobedient, God-defying attitude: "Who is Jehovah that I should obey Him?" Pharaoh fulfilled the Divine counsels. The plagues his rebellion brought on, and his overthrow at the Red Sea, are celebrated in Exodus 15.14: "The peoples have heard, they tremble." The pagan Philistines, even in Samuel's day said: "These are the gods that smote the Egyptians with all manner of plagues in the wilderness" (I Sam. 4.7,8). Jehovah's name was indeed through this unregenerate rebel, Pharaoh, "published abroad in all the earth," just as He said!

What God's Word tells us as to His dealing with Pharaoh, explains "He hardeneth." But nothing else than a subject heart of faith will enter, with reverent footstep, into the twice repeated words, "whom He will," here. And we say boldly, that a believer's heart is not fully yielded to God until it accepts without question, and without demanding softening, this eighteenth verse.

Paul in the Spirit forestalls the natural operations of man's proud heart:

19   Thou wilt say then unto me, Why doth He still
20   find fault? For who withstandeth His will? Nay,
      but, O man, who art thou that repliest against
      God? Shall the thing formed say to Him that
21   formed it, Why didst Thou make me thus? Or
      hath not the potter a right over the clay, from the
      same lump to make one part a vessel unto honor,
      and another unto dishonor?

In His infinite wisdom and knowledge God reads with un-
erring accuracy the operations of the human heart: "Man
looketh on the outward appearance, but Jehovah looketh on
the heart." Man says, If I am not one of God's elect, an
object of His mercy, then I cannot do right, and God should
not blame me. I asked an intelligent man in western Michigan
if he had believed on the Lord Jesus Christ. He burst out
into loud laughing, saying, "If I am elect, I will go to heaven;
and if I am not elect, there is no use in my worrying about
the question!" I rebuked him sternly, with these words: " 'God
commandeth men that they should *all everywhere repent*: inasmuch as He hath appointed a day in which He will judge
the world in righteousness by the Man whom He hath ordained.' 'God's commands are God's enablings,' and if you
will hearken to Him, you will be saved. But you will not dare
to say to God in that day, I could not come because I was not
of the elect; for that will not be true! The reason you refused to come, will be found to be your *love of sin,* not your
non-election!" God says, "Whosoever will," and the door is
open to *all,* absolutely *all. God means "Whosoever":* and that
is the word for *you,* sinner; and not *election,* which is God's
business, not yours!

Verse 20: **Nay, but, O man, who art thou that repliest
against God? Shall the thing formed say to Him that
formed it, Why didst thou make me thus?** Literally, this
reads: "O man, yes! but rather,—you! who are you, replying
against God?"

Alford well says: "The words 'yea, rather,' take the ground
from under the previous assertion and supersede it by another:
implying that it has a certain show of truth, but that the proper

view of the matter is yet to be stated. They thus convey, as in Luke 11.28, a rebuke,—here, with severity: 'That which thou hast said may be correct human reasoning,—but as against God's sovereignty, thy reasoning is out of place and irrelevant; the verse implying, Thou hast neither right nor power to call God to account in this matter.' These verses are a rebuke administered to the spirit of the objection, which forgets the immeasurable distance between us and God, and the relation of Creator and Disposer in which He stands to us."

And Stifler warns: "He who replies against God must mean that it is God's hardening that deprives a soul of salvation; that if God did not interpose with an election and take some and leave others to be hardened, all men would have at least an equal opportunity of salvation. This is false. If God did not elect, none would be saved, for there is 'none that seeketh after God' (Rom. 3.11). And, men are not lost because they are hardened; they are hardened because they are lost; they are lost because they are sinners.

"God is not responsible for sin. He is under no obligation to save any one. Obligation and sovereignty cannot both be predicated of God. If He saves any one it is a sovereign act of mercy."

Shall the thing formed say to Him that formed it, Why didst thou make me thus?

Thus speaks also Jehovah by Isaiah:

"Woe unto him that striveth with His Maker! a potsherd among the potsherds of the earth! . . . Ye turn things upside down! Shall the potter be esteemed as clay; that the thing made should say of him that made it, He made me not; or the thing formed say of him that formed it, He hath no understanding?" (Isa. 45.9; 29.16.)

In the Scriptures, those who meet God, fall into the dust. "I am but dust and ashes," said Abraham. and Job: "Mine eye seeth Thee, and I abhor myself, and repent in dust and ashes."

A "thing," yea, and a *formed* thing, owing its very being to a Creator! Have we thus considered ourselves? Our only proper creature-attitude is one of faith, not questioning. As

> "Frail creatures of dust,
> And feeble as frail,
> In Thee do we trust,
> Nor find Thee to fail."

These are days of man-vaunting, and God-despising. But they shall soon end, and the very earth on which man's legions marched in such pride, shall flee away "before the face of Him who sits upon the Throne"! (Rev. 20.11.)

Verse 21: **Or hath not the potter a right over the clay, from the same lump to make one part a vessel unto honor, and another unto dishonor?** As concerns the right of the Divine Potter over the human clay, we need to go with Jeremiah to "the potter's house": "I went down to the potter's house, and, behold, he was making a work on the wheels. And the word of Jehovah came to me, saying, O house of Israel, cannot I do with you as this potter? Such as is the clay in the potter's hands, so are ye in my hand, O house of Israel" (Jer. 18.3-6). God called man "dust" in Eden (Gen. 2.7; 3.19). And, "The nations are as a drop of a bucket and are accounted as the small dust of the balance" (Isa. 40.15). When the apothecary would weigh an article accurately, he whisks out with a breath from the balances any former dust remaining therein: and there go the nations, all,—as regards greatness before God! Yet here is one atom of this "small dust" replying against God, saying, "What right has He to do thus with me?"

Now it will not do to answer, "God is love"; "God so loved the world." True, indeed. But God is God, and the nations are "less than nothing, and vanity," as you read in Isaiah 40.17, and in many other Scriptures. God has rights high above all our poor comprehension. We know that God will always act righteously. We are not God's judges! God has a right "from the same lump of human clay to make one part a vessel unto honor, another unto dishonor." No godly person challenges that right. Nay, godly people most reverently bow to it! "What would the ability to fashion be worth, if it were under the dictation of that which is to be fashioned?"

22   What if GOD, willing to show His wrath, and
     to make His power known, endureth with much
     longsuffering vessels of wrath fitted unto destruc-
23   tion: and that He might make known the riches of
     His glory upon vessels of mercy, which he afore
24   prepared unto glory, even us, whom He also called,
     not from the Jews only, but also from the Gentiles?

Verse 22: **What if GOD**—the greatness of the Creator
and the nothingness of the creature! God's will is supreme
and right, even to His being **willing to show publicly His
wrath**—both at the day of judgment, and on through eternity. His holiness and righteousness will be exhibited to
all creatures in His visitation of wrath upon the wicked:

And to make His power known—Job in astonishing
words describes God's power as seen in creation and providence, but adds:

"Lo, these are but the outskirts of His ways:
   And how small a whisper do we hear of Him!
   But the thunder of His power who can understand?"
   (Job 26.14.)

But the day is coming when His power will be publicly exhibited in overwhelming and eternal visitation upon the vessels
of wrath. Let us ponder this great passage:

**What if GOD, willing to show His wrath, and to make
His power known, endured with much longsuffering vessels of wrath fitted unto destruction?**

Here we find:

1. That certain were fitted unto destruction. It is not
said that God so fitted them.* But in Chapter Two we find

---

*Nevertheless, we must let certain Scriptures lie just as they are, whether or
not they consort with our conceptions, or whether we find ourselves able to "reconcile" them with our "theological system" or not. We quote a few of these
Scriptures:

"The wicked are estranged from the womb;
They go astray as soon as they are born, speaking lies" (Ps. 58.3).
"Jehovah hath made everything for its own end;
Yea, even the wicked for the day of evil" (Prov. 16.4).
"They stumble at the word, being disobedient: whereunto also they were ap-
pointed" (I Pet. 2.8).
"Again, when a righteous man doth turn from his righteousness, and commit

those who "despise the goodness and forbearance and long-suffering of God, not knowing that the goodness of God was meant to lead them to repentance." Of such it is said that they "treasure up for themselves wrath in the day of wrath."

2. God had, we next read here, in their earth-life dealt with these with much longsuffering. They never learned, however, as Peter urged, to "account that the longsuffering of our Lord is salvation" (II Pet. 3.15). This longsuffering is the enduring on earth of ungrateful rebels by a God surrounded in Heaven by the glad, obedient hosts of light!

3. They thus became vessels of wrath: those in and through whom God could publicly and justly display His holy indignation against sin and godlessness,—for a warning to all ages and creatures to come.

4. Thus these came to that destruction unto which their sin had duly fitted them. Now this "destruction" is not at all that *cessation of being,* of which we hear so much from Satan's false prophets in these days. But it is, according to II Thessalonians 1.7,9, an eternal visitation of Divine anger "in flaming fire" from the very presence of the Lord Himself! It not only involves the final withdrawal of all mercy and long-suffering, but the eternal infliction of Divine punishment upon the bodies of the damned.

5. The terribleness of this is seen in the fact that this "destruction," this visitation of punishment upon the persons of the lost, will be made the occasion of God's exhibiting publicly both His holy wrath against sin, and also His power in the punishment of it. His hatred of sin is absolute,—and these will be made to experience it; His power is infinite, and these will be compelled to be an example of it.

iniquity, and I lay a stumblingblock before him, he shall . . . die in his sin, and his righteous deeds which he hath done shall not be remembered (Ezek. 3.20).

"Because they had not executed Mine ordinances, but had rejected My statutes, . . . I gave them statutes that were not good, and ordinances wherein they should not live" (Ezek. 20.24,25).

However, even in these passages, solemnly terrible as they are, we must separate God's actions from man's responsibility. God is not the author of evil; He tempteth no man; "He would have all men to be saved and come to the knowledge of the truth."

6. In the words **What if GOD**—should proceed thus? all creature-questionings are stilled into awful silence, *if not today, some day!*

Verse 23: Then at the next words: And that **He might make known the riches of His glory upon** vessels **of mercy,** we are just as silent as before, though in boundless, endless gratitude: for apart from mercy, we too had become "vessels of wrath." As Paul says in verse 29: Except the Lord had dealt in mercy with us, we also "had become as Sodom!"

Note carefully that while it is God's wrath and power that are to be made known in the "vessels of wrath"; and though the glory of God would be thus in His justice exhibited, He yet does not use the word *glory* in connection with the damnation of the wicked. In Exodus 15.11 Moses and the children of Israel do indeed celebrate the overthrow of Pharaoh, as setting forth God's praise, saying,

"Who is like unto thee, O Jehovah, among the gods?
Who is like thee, glorious in holiness,
Fearful in praises, doing wonders?"

Yet we must ever remember that God is love, from past eternity, and now, and forever. So that it is written: "He delighteth in mercy"—lovingkindness: (Micah 7.18); and, "As I live, saith Jehovah, I have no pleasure in the death of the wicked; but that the wicked turn from his way and live" (Ezek. 33.11). God will not exult over the lost! witness Christ weeping over Jerusalem, and sorrowing over Judas (John 13.21); and the "lamentation" even over the fall of Lucifer (figured in the King of Tyre, in the remarkable passage of Ezekiel 28.11ff.).

But when God speaks in verse 23 of the **vessels of mercy,** it is at once said that He **afore prepared them unto glory,** that is, for entering into His own glory (Romans 5.2), and that they will be the means of making known through eternity to come **the riches of His glory.** So He speaks in Ephesians 2.4 to 7 of His being "rich in mercy." If it is true of us that where our treasure is our hearts will be; it is infinitely more true of God! God's treasured riches are mercy and grace. Judgment, the execution of wrath, He calls His "strange work," His "strange act" (Isa. 28.21). Mercy is the work dear to His heart!

Mark well here this word "afore." For the whole process of our salvation is viewed from that blessed future day when we shall enter, through Divine mercy, into that glory unto which God "afore" appointed us, and for which He "afore" prepared us, in the work of Christ for us, and the application to us of that work, by the blessed Holy Spirit. All was "afore" arranged by God!

Verse 24: **Even us, whom He also called, not from the Jews only, but also from the Gentiles.** How constant, in Paul's consciousness, the owing all to God's sovereign grace. "Prepared unto glory"*—in past eternity, in sovereign election, and having a calling befitting that "preparing." Surely no one can miss, in this apostle, the supreme consciousness that he is God's,—not by his choice, but God's own choice,—an eternally settled thing, uncaused by Paul! All believers will have the same consciousness, when they find, (as Paul found), along with their Divine election, that there is in them, in their flesh, "no good thing"!

Now the apostle, having declared that these "vessels of mercy" were "called," both from Jews and Gentiles, adduces several plain Scriptures (which the gainsaying Jews should have laid to heart).

25 As He saith also in Hosea,
> I will call that my people which was not my
> people;
> And her beloved, that was not beloved.
26 > And it shall be, that in the place where it was
> said unto them, Ye are not My people,
> There shall they be called sons of the Living God.

---

*Hodge's remarks here are excellent: "The passive participle may be taken as a verbal adjective, *fit* for destruction. Of the vessels of wrath, it is simply said that they are fit for destruction; but of the vessels of mercy, that God prepares them for glory. Why this change if the apostle did not intend to intimate that the agency of God is very different in the one case from what it is in the other? God does not create men in order to destroy them. God did not make Pharaoh wicked and obdurate; but as a punishment for his sin, he so dealt with him that the evil of his nature revealed itself in a form, and under circumstances, which made him a fit object of the punitive justice of God."

27 And Isaiah crieth concerning Israel,
   If the number of the children of Israel be as the
      sand of the sea,
   The Remnant shall be saved:
28 For He is bringing the matter to an end, and cut-
      ting it short in righteousness;
   Because a matter cut short will the Lord make in
      the earth.
29   And, as Isaiah hath said before,
   Except the Lord of Sabaoth had left us a seed,
   We had become as Sodom, and had been made like
      unto Gomorrah.

Verse 25: I will call that my people which was not my
people; and her beloved that was not beloved. Paul here,
in a most remarkable way, takes from the prophet Hosea (2.23)
a passage that distinctly refers to Israel: as Peter, quoting the
same place says: "Ye are an elect race, a royal priesthood, a
holy nation, who in time past were no people, but now are the
people of God." For here we see the "Remnant according to
the election of Grace," addressed by Peter, their Apostle. The
nation after the flesh was apostate; but God views believing
Israelites as perpetuating—not the national place, which has
been forfeited for the present—but His lovingkindness to those
which He had called His "people"; His "elect nation." "To
you first," Peter said to Israel after Pentecost, "God, having
raised up His Son, sent Him to bless you." So that Paul and
Peter are in perfect agreement that Hosea 2:23 fits believing
Israelites.

And then we have Hosea quoted again! But now it is
Chapter 1:10, last part.

Verse 26: And it shall be, that in the place where it was
said unto them, Ye are not my people, there shall they be
called sons of the living God. Here now come the Gentiles,
—according to verse 24. No Gentile nation was ever called a
people of God! Nor are the Gentiles today called such. Although
in the Millennium all the Gentiles "upon whom the Lord's
Name is called," will seek Him (Acts 15:17); yet Israel are
his elect people, always.

But now "some better thing" has been provided for us (Heb. 11:40) both Jewish and Gentile believers of this "day of salvation": *Sons of the Living God!* See Galatians 4:1-7. The Spirit of God's Son cries Abba, Father, in our hearts, who "partake of the heavenly calling."

God's infinite grace takes up those who were once (and that by our Lord Himself) called "dogs"—as compared with the "children"—nation of Israel, and gives them a *heavenly* calling: far above that of earthly Israel,—even when restored! "Sons of the Living God"—oh, let us give praise unto Him!

Verse 27: **And Isaiah crieth concerning Israel, If the number of the children of Israel be as the sand of the sea, the Remnant shall be saved.** Here the apostle takes another prophet, Isaiah, and quotes again from two passages; and again from the later one first. The 27th verse is from Isaiah 10:22. Some estimate the Jewish population as 20,000,000 (though that probably is too high). If we read Ezekiel 20:33-38, we see the Lord Jehovah, "with wrath poured out" bringing Israel out from the nations (He is beginning this now!); and *cutting off* "the rebels" amongst them,—the rebels against the national Divine calling as a separate nation to Jehovah. Only the *Remnant* will be left; for, as Isaiah says, "a destruction is determined!" How solemn these words! And let them sink into our foolish Gentile hearts; for only a "few men left" of all the nations, will enter the Millennium.

Verse 28: **For He is bringing the matter to an end, and cutting it short in righteousness: Because a matter cut short will the Lord make in the earth.** The ways of God should be the study of the saints. He waits long,—He forbears—He is silent: then He suddenly puts into execution an eternally-formed purpose! Thus it was at the Flood, and in the destruction of Sodom, and afterwards of the Canaanites. Also now, for a long season, God has been letting the nations go on in comparative quiet, filling up the earth with much the largest population ever known; and despite their various persecutions the Jews have also been relatively secure from that Divine "indignation" which all students of Scripture know is yet to be brought to a terrible "end" upon them. The awful words of Ezekiel 20:35,36 are to be fulfilled—"cut short in righteousness." The expression there "the wilderness of the people,"—where the Jews will have no national friend or refuge whatever, except Palestine; and Jehovah "entering into judgment" with them, "like as He entered into judgment with their fathers in the wilderness of the land of Egypt" (when he turned them back from Kadesh-barnea to die in the wilderness) —all this remains to be done,—and in "a short work."

The Remnant shall be saved [the majority having been slain in the Great Tribulation] **for He is ending up the matter** [of His dealing with Israel] **and cutting it short** [in the time of "Jacob's trouble"—the "forty-two months"; the "time, times, and a half";—three and a half years, of Daniel's Seventieth Week] **in righteousness, because a matter cut short will the Lord make on the earth.**

Every student of Scripture should be familiar by this time with the general "mould of prophecy." Therefore we have boldly inserted in brackets the evident meaning here. It is the great crisis of prophecy here in view, the closing up not only of the times of the Gentiles, but of God's dispensational dealings with national Israel, the Remnant of whom—a "very small Remnant"—will be saved; preserved through the Great Tribulation to bless the earth after the Lord returns. Any reader of Scripture will be astonished, and deeply edified if he will take a concordance and study God's Word about the Remnant.*

God is now letting matters run on in general, both among the Gentiles and Israel. This will shortly be utterly changed, even to what scientists call the "laws" of the powers of the heavens—and **a short work will the Lord make upon the earth.** (See Author's book on *The Revelation,* p. 140,ff).

This involves, of course, that the most of the natural children of Israel will be cut off; that it will be only the elect Remnant who will be saved and share in the Millennial Kingdom; which, as the prophecies concerning the "Remnant" abundantly testify, that Remnant will enjoy. (See last nine

*See Genesis 45.7; Isaiah 1.9; 10.21,22; 11.11,16; 46.3; Jer. 23.3; Ezek. 6.8; Amos 5.15; Mic. 2.12; 5.7,8; Zeph. 2.7,9; 3.13; Zech. 8.6,11,12.

chapters of Ezekiel; Isa. 10.21,22; and Chapter 35; Jer. 31.1-14.)

Verse 29: Israel might object to the doctrine of "the Remnant," the "election of grace" by God; but the quotation in verse 29, from Isaiah 1.9 shows that if God had not intervened in sovereign grace, they would have all become as Sodom [in iniquity], and been made like unto Gomorrah [in their damnation]. It was sovereign goodness that saved* any Israelites,—just as it is sovereign goodness that saves any Gentiles.

Thus it becomes plain (for Israel is but a sample of the human race) that opposition to the truth of Divine elective mercy arises from ignorance of or blindness to the utter sinfulness and wholly lost state, of mankind. All would go to perdition unless God in mercy intervened!

30   What shall we say then? That Gentiles, those not at all pursuing after righteousness, attained to righteousness, even the righteousness which is of
31   faith: but Israel, pursuing after a law [which should give] righteousness, did not arrive at [such
32   a] law. Wherefore? Because they sought it not by faith, but as it were by works. They stumbled at
33   the Stone of stumbling; even as it is written,

Behold, I lay in Zion a Stone of stumbling, and a Rock of offence:

And he that believeth on Him shall not be put to shame.

---

*In these passages brought by the Spirit from the Old Testament and fitting present times precisely, we are again face to face with the marvels of God's inspiration. William Kelly well says:

"What a witness of Divine truth, of indiscriminate grace, that the gospel, in itself unprecedented and wholly distinct both from what was seen under the Law and what will be when the Kingdom appears in power and glory, does nevertheless find its justification from words both of mercy and of judgment uttered hundreds of years before by the various servants God sent to declare His message to His people! But, as they blindly despised them and rejected His word then for idols, so now they fulfilled them yet more in the rejection of Christ and hatred of the grace which, refused by them, was sought and received by Gentiles, and thus yet more proved the word Divine, to the confusion of the unbelief which is as blind as it is proud and selfish" (Kelly, *Notes on Romans, in oc*).

We here have a most remarkable passage, full of the deepest consolation on the one hand, and warning on the other.

Here were the Gentiles, deep in the sin described in Chapters One and Two, occupied with superstition and idolatry. Paul said in Athens, a city full of idols, "I perceive that in all things ye are very religious" (lit., "demon-fearing"). There was no seeking after righteousness before a holy God! Paul quotes in Chapter Three those Psalms which declare there is "none that seeketh after God." **For the Gentiles,** of Antioch in Pisidia, for example, **were not pursuing after righteousness;** but here come Paul and Barnabas, preaching; and "the whole city is gathered together to hear the Word of God." And when the Jews reviled the blessed gospel of grace,

> "Paul and Barnabas spoke out boldly, and said, it was necessary that the word of God should first be spoken to you. Seeing ye thrust it from you, and judge yourselves unworthy of eternal life [How terrible!—dying men refusing life!] lo, we turn to the Gentiles. For so hath the Lord commanded us, saying,
>
> I have set thee for a light of the Gentiles,
> That thou shouldest be for salvation unto the uttermost part of the earth.
>
> And as the Gentiles heard this, they were glad, and glorified the word of God: and as many as were ordained to eternal life believed. And the word of the Lord was spread about throughout all the region" (Acts 13.44,46-49).

Here is good news for bad men!—men who had never read the Old Testament Scriptures, nor "pursued after righteousness"; yet, though Gentiles, hearing the gospel and believing, they walk right into righteousness by faith, past **the Jews,** who had been **pursuing after**—what! **a law** that should give them **righteousness.** Note, we are not told that even the Jews were pursuing after *righteousness,* but after **a law** by which, through their self-efforts, they hoped to attain righteousness! They did not, like the Gentiles, as sinners, simply believe the good news of a God of grace. But although their own Law would have convicted

them of sin if they had really *heard** it, yet they kept pursuing after a Law whose requirements they could not meet,
but in possessing and pursuing after which, they gloried!
It was all as-it-were-works,—a dream!

They did not arrive at that law,—it was always just
ahead, out of reach! Why? Because they never directly
trusted God! Having the conceit of the self-righteous,—that
some day they would attain God's final acceptance of their
works, they never thought of needing God's *mercy,* or of "simply trusting" Him as they were,—as David does in Psalm
Fifty-one!

So when Christ came, saying, "Transfer your trust from
yourselves to *Me!* Moses gave you the Law, but none of you
keepeth the Law":—they turned in fury and slew the Righteous
One!

So the Jews stumbled. Now, it takes a spiritual mind
and a subject heart to read with profit what is here. Were
there Divine commands in the Law? Certainly. Were there
hopes connected with fully keeping them? Certainly. "The
man that doeth the righteousness which is of the Law shall
live thereby" (Lev. 18.5; Rom. 10.5). Were there those that
professed righteousness by the Law? Yes, on every side:
Pharisees, priests, scribes,—who also became the crucifiers of
Christ! But what else do we read in the Old Testament?
We read from Genesis 3.15 throughout Scripture that there
was a *Seed,* the *Seed of the woman,* the Seed of Abraham, the
Seed of David, through whom alone salvation and blessing
would come. "This is the name by which He shall be called,
Jehovah our righteousness." As David cried, "I will make
mention of Thy righteousness, even of Thine only" (Ps. 71.16).
But also it was also plainly written of Him, "They shall smite
the Judge of Israel with a rod upon the cheek"; and that He
would "hide not His face from shame and spitting"; that He
would be "despised and rejected"; that His hands and feet

---

*So Paul to the Galatians: "Tell me, ye that desire to be under the law, do ye
not HEAR the law?" (Gal. 4.21.) Paul himself, he tells us, was "alive apart
from the Law once,"—although he knew the Law and gloried in it and observed its
outward ordinances. But the day came, as he showed in Chapter 7, when he
"heard" it: it became a distinct spiritual command to his soul to do the righteousness commanded.

would be "pierced," but that *"through the knowledge of Himself,* God's Righteous Servant, [Messiah] should *constitute many righteous"* (Isa. 53.11). So He, Christ, the meek and lowly One, who went about doing them good, who healed them, loved them, and finally died for them,—became to them the **Stone of Stumbling!** And it was **in Zion,** where they had the Law, that this **Stone of stumbling** was to be laid. Now the only way to have Him is to believe on Him: otherwise, He was a **Rock of offence.** He offended all the claims of the Jews as "children of Abraham"; He offended all their false claims of righteousness, by the light which He was,—the H,oly One. He offended the leaders of Israel, by exposing their sin. He offended the hopes of an immediate, carnal, earthly kingdom, by showing that only those poor in spirit and pure of heart would be in that kingdom. In short, He offended the nation by overthrowing its whole superstructure of works built on sand,—as-it-were-works!

However, there were those that **believed on Him**—the "poor of the flock," and they were not then, and **shall not be put to shame.** (See comment on Chap. 10.11.)

Even so, today, the true gospel of Christ crucified, bringing out our guilt and the danger of Divine wrath, offends men who would like to come and "join the church" in their *respectability!* Respectability of what? Of filthy rags!*

It is a humanly incurable delusion of the human heart that salvation is within the natural reach; and that at any time if a man will "make up his mind like a man," and "hold out to the end," God will certainly accept him. But this conception

---

*Sir Robert Anderson relates: "A lady of my acquaintance, well known in the higher ranks of London society, called upon me one day to ask for police help, to relieve her from certain annoyances. Her evident distress at my inability to give her the protection she sought, led me to remark that the peace of God in the heart was a great antidote to trouble. "Ah," said she, "if I were only like you!" "If it depended on my merit," I replied with real sincerity, "it is you who would have the peace, not I." Presently her manner changed, and with tears in her eyes she told me something of her spiritual struggles. If she could be more earnest, more devout, more prayerful, she was sure that God would accept her.

"I was greatly interested," I remarked, "by what I heard about the supper you gave the tramps last week. Did they offer you anything for it? Of course, they had no money, but they might have brought you some of their coats and shirts!"

"If you had only seen their coats and shirts!" she exclaimed with a smile.

"Filthy rags they were, I'm sure," said I, "and what you don't believe is that in God's sight *'all our righteousnesses are as filthy rags.'* "

leaves out entirely the word "mercy." The very name of this plan is Vain Confidence. It has doomed and damned its millions. For, salvation being altogether of God, the soul who is hugging the delusion that it is "of him that willeth," "of him that runneth," is making God a liar and walking in blind pride.

You ask, Is there not a place for human responsibility? Does not God command all men to repent? Does He not say: "Whosoever will, let him take the water of life freely?" He does. But the Ninth of Romans is no place to discuss that subject, and that because God does not here discuss it. You say, If Christ "gave Himself a ransom for all"; and God "would have all men to be saved"; if Christ "tasted death for every man," if "God was in Christ reconciling the world unto Himself, not imputing unto them their trespasses," and is now sending out His ambassadors to beseech men to be reconciled to God—how can these statements be reconciled with God's words in verse 18: "So then He hath mercy on whom He will, and whom He will He hardeneth"?

Friend, who set you or me to "reconcile" (which means to reduce to the compass or our mental grasp) the sayings of the infinite God of truth? If I wait to believe the statements of God the Creator until I can "reconcile" them with my creature conceptions, that is not faith, but presumption.

Moreover, unless you receive both doctrines: on the one hand, that of the death of Christ for all, and the actual, *bona fide* offer of salvation through His cross, to all who will believe; and, on the other hand, that of the absolute sovereignty of the God who "hath mercy on whom He will, and whom He will, hardeneth," you will neither believe Scripturally either doctrine, nor clearly preach either. You will be either preaching a "limited atonement"—that Christ died only for the elect; or, on the other hand, refusing to surrender to God's plain statement of His sovereign election, you will preach that Christ having died for all, God's election depends on man's will. A shallow preacher in California cried, "It is election day: God is voting for you and the devil is voting against you, and you cast the deciding vote!" Of such antiscriptural statements the folly is evident. God distinctly says in Chapter 9.16: "It is not of him that willeth"; and in verse 11: "That the purpose of God according to election might stand, not of works, but of Him that calleth."

You say, "What then shall we teach?" We answer: *Teach the words of Scripture and let it go at that.* God can "reconcile" His own Word!

Many years ago a widely-known and beloved teacher of God's Word said to me, "I do not like to assert a truth too positively; I like always to teach a truth modified by any seemingly contradictory truth." I had myself observed in his discussion of a Scripture doctrine his citation of "authorities": "So-and-so says this; on the other hand, So-and-so says that: now take your choice." But in his later years, because he was a constant and devoted reader of God's Word, his manner of teaching quite changed: he was willing to take such a passage as the Ninth of Romans and teach it *as it is,* and say, "Thus saith the Lord"; *and leave it there.* And when there came up another line of truth that could not be "reconciled" with the first, in the mind of men, he taught this second truth also just as God stated it, *and left it there.*

Now if there is any passage of God's Word in which He seems to say: *I am Myself assuming all responsibility for what I here announce,* it is this same Ninth of Romans.

But remember its closing words: "He that believeth on Him [Christ] shall not be put to shame!" God's simple-hearted, trusting saints are quite ready, having received God's great gift of Eternal Life in Christ, to await the day when they shall "know fully"—as they have been known. Meanwhile, they walk *by faith,* with humble hearts, *subject to what God says.*

GOD NECESSARILY SOVEREIGN IN SALVATION

1. Man was lost—he could not save himself.
2. He was guilty—none could pardon him but the God he had sinned against.
3. He was by nature "a child of *wrath*" not deserving good; nor being able to change his nature.
4. He was allied with God's Enemy; and had a mind at

enmity against God: a mind not subject, nor able to be subject to God's law or will.

5. He knew he was doing things "worthy of death"; but not only persisted in them, but was in league-approval with those of like practice; he was "of the world," not of God.

6. Therefore, if any move be made toward man's salvation, it must come from God, not man.

7. God, being God, knew beforehand that the attitude of every man by nature toward his overtures would be to oppose them.

8. Since any real response to those overtures, therefore, must come from God's grace, He must elect to overcome effectually man's resistance, either

    (a) In no case,

    (b) Or, in every case,

    (c) Or, in certain cases.

9. To hold God unable to overcome man's resistance in any case is to limit His power.

10. But to hold that God is unwilling to have certain saved is to deny His repeated word—"Who would have all men to be saved and to come to the knowledge of the truth"; "As I live, saith the Lord Jehovah, I have no pleasure in the death of the wicked; but that the wicked turn from his way and live."

11. Therefore, it would seem that only in those cases in which it would no longer be consistent with God's glory—that is, consistent with His holiness and righteousness, and His just government of His creatures, would God withhold, or refuse longer to employ, His gracious operations in behalf of any creature.

12. But, when we consider Election, we must remove our thoughts wholly from this world, the first Adam, the sin of man, and his "attitude" toward God. The purpose of God according to Election is "not of works, but of Him that calleth." It is outside human history altogether. It is *of God*.

CHAPTER TEN

Paul's Prayer for Israel, who had Zeal, without Knowledge of, or Subjection to, God's Righteousness: Fundamental Contrast between the Righteousness of Doing and That of Believing. Verses 1-10.

The Believing Method was According to Israel's Own Scriptures,—unto which They did not Hearken: as God had Foretold. Verses 11-21.

1 Brethren, the dear wish of this heart of mine, and my prayer to God for them, [Israel] is for
2 [their] salvation. For I bear witness to them that they have a zeal for God, but not at all according
3 to knowledge. For being ignorant of God's righteousness, and seeking to establish their own, they did not subject themselves to God's righteousness.
4 For Christ is the end of the Law unto righteousness, to every one that believeth.

BRETHREN,—HERE PAUL addresses all saints concerning his yearning for national Israel's salvation. The words **my heart's desire** are literally, "the dear pleasure of my heart." Israel's salvation was to Paul a thing of delight to contemplate and hope for. Moreover, as always, Paul puts his wish for them into **prayer to God:** in which all spiritual longings should end!

Verse 2: He bears them this witness, and gladly, that they had a **zeal for God,** but he most strongly denies that there was any real knowledge of God and His ways in that zeal. Mohammedans have zeal. When I passed through the Azhar Mosque, in Cairo, a Moslem merchant was kneeling, forehead on the carpet, in prayer. Four hours later I saw him still kneeling! And outside were over 10,000 students, diligently learning the Koran! Zeal must not be mistaken for knowledge in Divine things. See Josephus, quoted below.* It is perhaps unkind in this place, (so tender with Paul), to cite the religious zeal of pagan or Mohammedan. But Paul himself classes the "beggarly elements" of Jew and pagan together! (Gal. 4.8-10), since the cross.

Verse 3: But it is certainly a terrible thing we see. Here is the Jew with God's own Book, the Old Testament Scriptures, in his hand, and blind to that Scripture's revelation of his guilty, lost state before God. The Jews were in a fearful condition in two ways:

First, they were **wholly ignorant** of the one great, vital fact sinners must know: that righteousness, life, and all things are a free gift of the grace of God; and that the Law was meant only to make them discover their sin and their own helpless need of the outright *gift* of righteousness from God. The expression **ignorant of God's righteousness,** does not mean that the Jewish people were ignorant of holiness and righteousness as attributes of God,—in fact, they prided themselves on the knowledge of such a God as over against the hideous pagan gods. But the righteousness of which they were wholly ignorant was that while "God Himself was just," He was also *"the Justifier of the ungodly"* of all *who "believed on Jesus."* As we said in Chapter Nine, the Jews had seized upon their possession of the Law as in itself giving them a standing with God. Our Lord could have spoken to almost any Jew as He did to the woman at Sychar's well: *"If thou knewest the gift of God, and Who it is that saith to thee!"* For of a *gift* of righteousness they had *no conception.*

The Law dispensation was necessarily unfruitful, "making nothing perfect," because it neither imparted life, nor gave

---

*"The Jew knows the Law better than his own name . . . The great feasts were frequented by countless thousands. . . . Over and above the requirements of the Law, ascetic religious exercises advocated by the teachers of the Law came into vogue . . . Even the Hellenised and Alexandrian Jews under Caligula died on the cross and by fire, and the Palestinian prisoners in the last war died by the claws of African lions in the amphitheatre, rather than sin against the Law. What Greek wuold do the like? . . . The Jews also exhibited an ardent zeal for the conversion of the Gentiles to the Law of Moses. The proselytes filled Asia Minor and Syria, and—to the indignation of Tacitus—Italy and Rome."
Surely the Jews of Josephus' day had a "zeal for God."

strength to fulfil its demands. As Paul writes to the Hebrews, there was a "disannulling" of it, and a "vanishing away" of the legal covenant (Heb. 7.18; 8.13).

When Christ came, although born under the Law in order to redeem Israel (Gal. 4.4,5), yet He Himself, from the very beginning, took the place of the Law! In the Sermon on the Mount (Matt. 5, 6, and 7) He declared: "It was said . . . but *I say*." He came, indeed, not to destroy but to fulfil, and inasmuch as Israel was under the curse of the Law, He redeemed them that were under the Law by becoming Himself a curse for them (Gal. 3.13).

Although Christ in His ministry, ("lest we cause to stumble," —Matt. 17.27) paid due heed to Moses' directions (as in the case of the leper—"Go show thyself to the priest"), yet He never, for example, enforced the *Sabbath*: indeed He freely wrought healings on that day, in the face of the murderous hatred of the legalists.

The Law was designed not to bring about self-righteousness or self-hope, but contrariwise, self-despair. The law witnessed to a man his need of a mediator—as at Sinai (Deut. 5.23-27). Christ Himself is the righteousness of God. When He died, bearing the sin of the world, the Law's demand for human righteousness was over, ended, closed up, set aside. *Christ* has now been "made of God unto us righteousness": we want no other. But it is not easy to subject ourselves unto God's righteousness: for God justifies the *un*godly. Justification is a gift for very beggars, the only hope for the guilty, lost and undone.* The Jews, ignorant of God's gift of righteous-

---

*"This is what God calls 'subjecting ourselves to God's righteousness': finding a righteousness which is neither of nor in ourselves, but finding Christ before God, and the proud will, through grace, submitting to be saved by that which is not of or in ourselves. It is Christ instead of self,—instead of our place in the flesh."

Rowland Hill, at the close of a great meeting, saw a lady riding in an elegant carriage, who commanded her coachman to halt, and beckoned Mr. Hill to approach her.

"Sir," she said, "my coachman came to your meetings and says you told him how to be saved; so that he is now very happy. Please tell me how a lady of the nobility is to be saved, for I also desire to be happy."

"Madam," said the preacher, "Christ died for the whole world. God says there is no difference. All are to be saved through simple faith in Him."

ness utterly refused thus to subject themselves. They said, "We know that God has spoken to Moses, but as for this man [Jesus], we know not whence He is!"

John the Baptist's ministry is full of meaning here. It is both a precious and an awful thing—the results of John's testimony. Luke tells us: "All the people, when they heard [John], and the publicans, justified God [when John preached repentance and confession of their sins], being baptized with the baptism of John. But the Pharisees and the lawyers rejected for themselves the counsel of God, being not baptized of him" (Luke 7.29,30). It is touching to the spiritual heart to find, for instance, that all five of those converted in the first chapter of John were John's disciples.

Second, to this day they seek to "establish their own righteousness." But in this path that "seemeth right unto a man" is the way of death, yea, of direct rebellion against God.*

They (the Jews) were desperately set on establishing, building up that which God had cast down, that is, human righteousness. They heard with deaf ears their own prophets' voices: "There is none righteous, no not one." "All our righteousnesses are as filthy rags." Therefore, the Jews were, and are today, worse off than the heathen. Their Law—"whensoever Moses is read, a veil lieth upon their heart" (II Cor. 3.15). According to Isaiah 25.7, there is "a covering that covereth *all* peoples, a veil that is spread over *all* nations" (to be removed in Millennial days, thank God!). But over the face of the Israelite there is now not only the common blindness of man to his own condition as a sinner, but, added to that,

---

*As Stifler so well says: "The Jews claimed that in following the Law they were submitting to God, for He gave the Law. No, says Paul; in so doing you are not submitting to the righteousness of God. 'For Christ [whom God gave and you reject] is the end of the Law for [with a view of] righteousness to every one that believeth.' The Jew's system was one of doing; but God's was one of believing, one of grace. Law and grace are mutually exclusive and antagonistic systems. Because the Jew held to Law he was not in subjection to God. The proof that he was not is the great principle of grace here recorded."

"Do you mean," she said haughtily, "that I must be saved in the same way as my coachman?"

"Precisely. There is no other way."

"Then," she said, "I will have none of it!" and she made her coachman drive away.

the false confidence the Jew has in his own righteousness because the Law was given by Jehovah to his nation.*

Verse 4: **Christ is the end of the Law unto righteousness to every one that believeth.** There has been much discussion of the meaning of the word "end" here. Let us see if Scripture does not clear up this matter for us. When Christ died, He bore for Israel the curse of the Law, for they, and they alone, were under the Law. Divine Law, being broken, does not ask for future good conduct on the part of the infractor; but for his *death*,—and that only. Now Christ having died, all the claims of the Law against that nation which had been placed under law were completely met and ended. So that even Jews could now *believe,* and say, "I am *dead* to the Law!"

To him that believeth, therefore, Jew or Gentile, *Christ,* dead, buried, and risen, is the end of law for righteousness,— in the sense of *law's disappearance from the scene!* Law does not know, or take cognizance of believers! We read in Chapter Seven (verse 6) that those who had been under the Law were discharged from the Law, brought to nought, put out of business *(katargeo),* with respect to the Law! The Law has nothing to do with them, as regards righteousness.

The Scripture must be obeyed with the obedience of 'belief: "Ye are not under law [not under that principle] but under grace" (the contrary principle). "Ye are brought to nothing from Christ [literally, "put out of business from Christ"], ye who would be justified by the Law; ye are fallen away from grace" (Gal. 5.4). Paul writes in Hebrews 7.18,19: "There is a *disannulling* of a foregoing commandment, because of its weakness and unprofitableness (for the Law made nothing perfect), and a bringing in thereupon of a 'better hope, through which we draw nigh unto God." Again, "Christ abolished in His flesh the enmity [between Jew and Gentile], even the Law of commandments contained in ordinances" (Eph. 2.15); again, speaking as a Hebrew 'believer, Paul says, "Christ

---

*It is with unutterable sadness that we contemplate the even worse condition of the Laodicean *Church* of today! "Wretched, poor, miserable, blind, naked"—and knowing it not! Christ on the *outside* of the door! Yet *outwardly* rich, and increased with goods!

blotted out the bond written in ordinances that was against us, which was contrary to us: and He hath taken it out of the way, nailing it to the cross" (Col. 2.14).

If these Scriptures do not set forth a complete closing up of any believer's account toward the Law, or to the whole legal principle, I know nothing of the meaning of words.

The words **Christ is the end of the Law,** cannot mean Christ is the "fulfilment of what the law *required*." The Law required obedience to precepts—or death for disobedience. Now Christ *died!* If it be answered, that before He died He fulfilled the claims of the Law, kept it perfectly, and that this law-keeping of Christ was reckoned as over against the Israelite's breaking of the Law, then I ask, Why should Christ *die?* If the claims of the Law were met in Christ's earthly obedience, and if that earthly life of obedience is "reckoned to those who believe" the curse of the Law has been removed by "vicarious law-keeping." *Why should Christ die?*

Now this idea of Christ's keeping the Law for "us" (for they will include us among the Israelites! although the Law was not given us Gentiles), *is a deadly heresy, no matter who teaches it.* Paul tells us plainly how the curse of the Law was removed: "Christ redeemed us," (meaning Jewish believers), "from the curse of the Law, having become a curse for us" (Gal. 3.13). And how He became a curse, is seen in Deuteronomy 21.23: "He that is hanged is accursed of God." It was on *the cross,* not by an "earthly life of obedience," that Christ bore the Law's curse!

There was no law given "which could make alive," Paul says; "otherwise righteousness would have been by it." Therefore those who speak of Christ as taking the place of fulfilling the Law for us,—as "the object at which the Law aimed" (Alford); or, "the fulfilment or accomplishment of the Law" (Calvin); give the Law *an office that God did not give it.* There is not in all Scripture a hint of the doctrine that Christ's earthly life—His obedience as a man under the Law, is "put to the account" of any sinner whatsoever! That obedience, which was perfect, was in order that He might "present Himself through the eternal Spirit without spot unto God," as a sin-offering. It also was in order to His sacrificial death, as "a curse," for Israel.

The gospel does not begin for any sinner, Jew or Gentile, until the cross: "I delivered unto you *first of all,* that Christ *died* for our sins" (I Cor. 15.3).

And for those under the Law, that was the end *(telos)* of the law. The Law had not been given to Israel at the beginning as a nation. They came out of Egypt, delivered from Divine wrath by the shed blood of the passover; and from Egypt itself by the passage of the Red Sea; Jehovah being with them. Go now to Elim with its "twelve wells of water and three score and ten palm trees": there the nation is encamped with their God. They have yet not been put under law at all. The Rock is smitten, giving them drink, and Manna, the bread of heaven, is given, all before Sinai!

Therefore we must believe God when He says in Romans 5.20: "The Law came in [not as an essential, but] as a circumstantial thing." (The Greek word, *pareisēlthe,* "came in alongside," can mean nothing else.)

In Paul's explanation of God's dealing with Israel in 9.31-33; 10.5-10, and 11.5,6, the meaning of this word *telos* "end," appears: that, when an Israelite believed on Christ he was as completely through with the Law for righteousness as if it had never been given. He had righteousness by another way!

The vast discussion among commentators concerning the expression "the end of the Law," would never have been, had it been recognized: (1) that God gave the Law only to Israel— as He said; (2) that it was a temporary thing, a "ministration of death," to reveal sin, and therefore the necessity of Christ's death; (3) that Christ having come, the day of the Law was over—it was "annulled" see Heb. 7.18.

It is because Reformed theology has kept us Gentiles under the Law,—if not as a means of righteousness, then as "a rule of life," that all the trouble has arisen. *The Law is no more a rule of life than it is a means of righteousness.* Walking in the Spirit has now taken the place of walking by ordinances. God has another principle under which He has put his saints: "Ye are *not under law,* but, *under grace!"*

5   For Moses writeth that the man that doeth the righteousness which is of the Law shall live there-
6   by. But the righteousness which of faith saith thus, Say not in thy heart, Who shall ascend into
7   heaven? (that is, to bring Christ down:) or, Who shall descend into the abyss? (that is, to bring
8   Christ up from the dead.) But what saith it? The word is nigh thee, in thy mouth, and in thy heart:
9   that is, the word of faith, which we preach: because if thou shalt confess with thy mouth Jesus to be [thy] Lord, and shalt believe in thy heart that God raised Him from the dead, thou shalt be saved:
10 for with the heart man believeth unto righteous-ness; and with the mouth confession is made unto salvation.

The apostle now takes us into a great contrast between the way of the Law and the way of faith. He first quotes Leviticus 18.5, where God said to Israel: "Ye shall therefore keep My statutes, and Mine ordinances; which if a man do, he shall live in [or by] them: I am Jehovah." You ask, Why did God make such a statement if no one was to obtain life by the Law? The answer is two-fold. First, in the plain utterance of Galatians 3.21: "If there had been a law given which could *make alive,* verily righteousness would have been of the Law": God never placed in the Law the *power to give life!* Second, the Law is called a ministration of death and condemnation: "But if the ministration of death, written, and engraven on stones, came with glory . . . if the ministration of condemnation hath glory¨ (II Cor. 3.7-9). It was never intended that people should gain hope by it, but rather that they should despair and be driven to cast themselves upon God's mercy, as did David (Psalm 51). Thus the Law becomes a "youth-leader" leading unto Christ (Gal. 3.24). Now, we humbly beg you, permit these Scriptures to "shut *you* up,"—according to Gal. 3.22! God had a right to put Israel under the Law for 1500 years from Moses to Christ; and He did so, knowing they could obtain neither righteousness nor life by that Law, since both were through faith in Christ only: and, "the Law is *not of* faith" (Gal. 3.12).

Now follows a most remarkable use by Paul of a Scripture out of Moses' own mouth which he spake to Israel concerning the Law, and which Paul here applies to Christ. It will be best to quote the passage from Deuteronomy 30.11-14 in full:

> "For this commandment which I command thee this day, it is not too hard for thee, neither is it far off. It is not in heaven, that thou shouldest say, Who shall go up for us to heaven, and bring it unto us, and make us to hear it, that we may do it? Neither is it beyond the sea, that thou shouldest say, Who shall go over the sea for us, and bring it unto us, and make us to hear it, that we may do it? But the word is very nigh unto thee, in thy mouth, and in thy heart, that thou mayest do it."

Moses, who had been with Israel forty years, and had been their mediator in bringing the Law down from Mount Sinai unto them, is about to die. He is leaving with them not only the ten commandments, but also all the statutes, ordinances, precepts and judgments connected with them. Now what will be the natural reaction in the hearts of Israel, when Moses goes up to the top of Pisgah and dies, and Jehovah buries him? It will be this: "Moses, who brought us this Law, is gone! Moses received this Law from Jehovah, who *came down from heaven* to the top of Sinai in great majesty and display of glory. Now Moses is dead; and all we have left is, these written words! Our circumstances are altogether different from those of our fathers, who *saw* the awful presence of Jehovah on Sinai and heard His voice. Who will go up to heaven for *us* now, and come down, and make *us* hear this Law, in the same way our fathers heard, that we may do it? Or, if there be someone away beyond the sea, some wonderful teacher (like Moses) whom we can send for, to come across the sea and bring it to us, and make us hear it, that we may do it—."

Now Moses' answer to all this is, "*The word* is nigh unto thee,—in thy mouth, and in thy heart, that thou mayest do it." That is, the written words of the Law the people knew: they could repeat them; they were told to teach them diligently unto their children, and, as David did, "hide them in their hearts," that they might not sin. It was all simple, indeed. And, of course, there were those, like Joshua, who said, "As for me and my house, we will serve Jehovah"; or who, like Zecharias and Elisabeth in Luke 1.6, were "righteous before God, walking in all the commandments and ordinances of the Lord blameless."

But the great point Moses makes with Israel is that there was the Law, in simple, plain *words*. They needed no sign, no manifestation; that had all been done at Sinai. But the great difficulty in the human heart (with Israel just as with us), is simple *subjection* to God's words. See how the Jews in our Lord's day kept asking of Him, "Show us a sign from heaven."*

Verse 6: Now Paul knows the human heart to be the same today as in the days of Moses, so he lifts out of Deuteronomy Moses' words about the Law and applies them to faith in Christ: **The righteousness which is of faith** [instead of asking a sign] **saith thus, Say not in thy heart, Who shall ascend into heaven? (that is, to bring Christ down:).** This would be the natural working of the heart of a Jew. The Messiah, Christ, was to be sent to him from God; in fact, the nation had kept looking for Him. But the perpetual rising of unbelief, apart from "a sign from heaven," was there.

It is very striking, as has been observed by others, that the Spirit of God should select the verses quoted above from Deuteronomy. For this chapter plainly prophesies that the Jews will be scattered among the nations because of their despising of God's Law. So that all hope from the Law will have perished, and they will be cast wholly upon the mercy of God:

> "among all the nations, whither Jehovah thy God hath driven thee, and shalt return unto Jehovah thy God, and shalt obey his voice . . . with all thy heart, and with all thy soul; that then Jehovah thy God will turn thy captivity, . . . and will bring thee into the land which thy fathers possessed, . . . and He will do thee good."

---

*It is so to this day, and sad to say, the tendency to demand "signs" is increasing rather than lessening. If a man come announcing "healing meetings" (although no such "meetings for healing" are known in Scripture), the place will be crowded. History is full of spiritual wreckage caused by "Lo, here," and "Lo, there!"

Into this dead, hollow shell, then, of legal hope, Paul here in Romans Ten, takes verses 11 to 14 of Deuteronomy Thirty, and puts *faith in Christ* in place of the Law! Israel will at last, at the end of the age, be cast upon the *mercy* of God! And then they will understand these great chapters, Romans Nine, Ten and Eleven, were written concerning *them!*

Verse 7: So that the Jew said in his heart, **Who can ascend to heaven to bring Him down unto me?** Then further, Christ being proclaimed that He had been sent already, and had borne their iniquities according to prophecy,—that He had died,—there would come the question in the Jewish heart: **Who shall go down into the abyss and bring Him up from the regions of the dead*** that I may see Him and thus believe on Him?

Verse 8: Now, answering all these inquiries, these sign-askings, came the simple **word of faith preached** by Paul. This expression, "the word of faith," involves the whole story of the gospel: that Jesus was the Christ, that He had come, died for sin, been buried, been raised, and been seen by many witnesses after His resurrection (I Cor. 15.3-8).

Verses 9 and 10: Paul speaks, then, in these verses—as if addressing a Jewish hearer: **If thou shalt confess with thy mouth Jesus as Lord** [literally, Jesus, Lord; or, Jesus to be (thy) Lord], **and shalt believe in thy heart that God raised Him from the dead, thou shalt be saved.** It is assumed the whole gospel has been preached to this hearer. And now is he persuaded that this Risen Jesus, was really the Messiah? And, though rejected by Israel, that He is Lord over all,—the Deity? And is *his* Lord? And is he willing so to confess Him as his own Lord before men?

---

*Our Lord plainly said he would be three days and three nights in the heart of the earth (Matt. 12.40). This was not Joseph's tomb (which was on the surface of the earth), but the Hebrew *Sheol* (Greek, *Hades*), which is always in Scripture located below the earth's surface—even "the lower parts of the earth" (Eph. 4.9). To another compartment of these "lower parts" the wicked also went; as see Ps. 63.9. That this was in the general region called Hades, the rich man of Luke 16.22,23 proves. (Always read the Revised Version about the words *Sheol—Hades:* for it transliterates them. The King James simply obscures them by various renderings.) While Christ's body lay in Joseph's tomb "not seeing corruption," His soul (or quickened spirit, I Peter 3.18)—as Peter and Paul, quoting Ps. 16.10, plainly show (Acts 2.31; 13.34,37) was duly brought up again "from the depths of the earth" (Ps. 71.20).

With thy mouth—We remember that in our Lord's
ministry among the Jews, "Even of the rulers many believed on
Him; but because of the Pharisees they did not confess Him,
lest they should be put out of the synagogue: for they loved
the glory of men more than the glory of God" (John 12.42,43).

Then does this Jewish hearer, in short, being persuaded of
Jesus' Lordship and confessing it, believe in his very heart that
God raised Him from the dead? For Christianity, as we have
said, "begins with the resurrrection." No matter how thoroughly
persuaded a Jew might be that Jesus fulfilled the prophecies in
His birth, life, ministry, and death; there remained this stupendous task of faith, to **believe in the heart that God had
raised** Him from the power and domain of death, of that
which was the wages of sin,—the "King of Terrors" (Job
18.14) of the whole world!

Those thus confessing Christ's Lordship, and believing in
the heart that God had raised Him, would be saved! The
explanation of the apostle of what has happened in such a
case is, that **with the heart the man believed unto righteousness; while with the mouth** the faith of the heart is boldly
followed in confession, resulting in salvation.

You may ask, would not a Jew (for these chapters particularly concern Jews) who had "believed unto righteousness"
have, thus, salvation?* It is better to let the Scripture language

---

*Faith is directly connected with the word "righteousness" or "justification,"
about twenty times in the New Testament, but faith is directly connected with the
word "salvation" only four times; and these four instances (Rom. 1.16, I Pet.
1.5,9,10) themselves show that whereas righteousness expresses the present
standing of a believing one; salvation is a larger and more inclusive word—in the
sense of Romans 13.11: "Awake out of sleep, for now is our salvation nearer to
us than when we believed." (In this verse our bodily redemption at Christ's
coming, is included). And, I Peter 1.5: "Guarded through faith unto a salvation
ready to be revealed in the last time." This shows that although we do "receive
the end of our faith, the salvation of our souls" (I Pet. 1.9), the word salvation
in general includes not only the salvation of our souls, but also the consummation
of our final deliverance at Christ's coming.

I do not find "salvation," then, connected in Scripture with any but those who
shall thus be found in Christ at His coming. The words of Paul in Corinthians
(I Cor. 15.1-4) outlining His gospel, are, "Ye are saved, if ye hold fast the word
which I preached unto you." In the preceding verse, he declares that they had
"received" the gospel which he had preached unto them. But this gospel was
not to be let go. As our Lord says concerning the good ground hearers in Luke
8.15: "These are such as in an honest and good heart, having heard the word, hold
it fast, and bring forth fruit with patience." In I Thess. 5.21 the same word is
translated "hold fast that which is good." It is solemnly used also in Heb.

stand. God here connects the word salvation with the word confession, not with the word faith. Peter, in his second epistle,
speaks of those who "had known the way of righteousness,"
which is always faith,—and then afterward "turned back from
the holy commandment delivered unto them" (II Peter 2.20,
21); while our Lord in Luke Eight says of the rocky-ground
hearer that he "believed for a while, and in time of temptation
fell away." Therefore, while in both parts of Romans 10.10,
Paul refers to the man of verse 9 as one who is to be "saved,"
it is well to let the verse remain as it is. The Lord when on
earth among the Jews asked that they *confess Him publicly;*
the Spirit still asks this. Not only Jews but Gentiles must confess Him; although the form of presentation of the truth in
Chapter Ten is as it would apply to a Jew, to whom had been
offered a Messiah, concerning whose claims he had to decide,
according to several Old Testament Scriptures. The Gentiles
did not have the Scriptures, and the matter of the presentation
of the gospel to them was much more simple. But "confession
with the mouth" will follow "the faith of God's elect," Jew or
Gentile.

Now, as ever when dealing with the Jews, Paul turns to their
Scriptures, and quotes eight times from the Old Testament,

3.6,14 and 10.23. This is no argument against Divine election, or the eternal
security of the saints. But it is a truth that must be, and really is, faced by
every godly soul.
   Over and over, of course, in the Gospels, the word for saved (*sodzo*) is used.
The word of our Lord is, "Thy faith hath saved thee," (or, A.V. "made thee
whole"—same Greek word). It is also used concerning salvation: Matt. 19.25,
Acts 2.21, 16.30,31. Paul also uses this word in Rom. 5.9,10; 10.13, etc.
   What we are urging is that we connect in our own thinking, and confession of
our Lord,—the word "faith" with *righteousness,* as Scripture in the Epistles so
constantly does. In times of darkness and weak faith such as this, the rescue
from doom is uppermost in the believer's mind; whereas God would have *his
standing in Christ uppermost!* How constantly we hear in a testimony meeting,
"I have been, or I was, *saved* ten years," etc.; and how very seldom, if ever,
the testimony is: I have been *declared righteous* by faith, and have peace with
God. I am *righteous before God,* through my Savior's death. I thank God I
have been made *the righteousness of God in Christ.* The old Methodists used to
testify to their justification,—"justified state," they called it. But then old-
fashioned Methodist preachers, preached of coming judgment, of eternal punishment,
of the sinner's terrible danger; and they boldly spoke of *pardon* as what the
sinner needed. We believe God has given still more light upon Scripture since
those days, but would God we had the moral earnestness and the wonderfully bright
experiences of the old-fashioned Methodists!
   Again we say, God generally connects faith with righteousness. Let us do
likewise.

before this Tenth Chapter is out—thirty times altogether in these three chapters (9, 10, and 11)!

11 For the Scripture saith, Whosoever believeth on
12 Him shall not be put to shame. For there is no distinction between Jew and Greek: for the same Lord
is Lord of all, and is rich unto all that call upon
13 Him: for, Whosoever shall call upon the name of
14 the Lord shall be saved. How then shall they call
on Him in whom they have not believed? and how
shall they believe in Him whom they have not
heard? and how shall they hear without a preacher?
15 and how shall they preach, except they be sent?
even as it is written, How beautiful are the feet of
them that bring glad tidings of good things!

Verses 11 and 12: **The Scripture saith**: the believer learns to love this word, "the Scripture" (our old word *graphē!*). The manner in which its Author, the Holy Spirit, makes the Scriptures of the Old Testament speak, in the New, is comfort without limit! And here is Isaiah 28.16 again, which was quoted (from the Septuagint) in the last verse of Chapter Nine. The Jews should have seen from that word **whosoever believeth** that simple faith in their Messiah was God's way, and that the message meant "whosoever."

They should have been warned also that inasmuch as *believing* was God's way—the path in which those who walked would not be put to shame; those who chose the way of works, of self-righteousness, would surely be put to shame. This word "ashamed" or "put to shame" is in the Hebrew, to flee—from *fear*. Those who have exercised simple faith in Christ, and abide thus in Him, shall "have boldness: and not be ashamed before Him [Christ] at His coming"—"boldness in the day of judgment; because as He is, even so are we in this world" (I John 2.28; 4.17).

This "whosoever" message is further developed in verse 12, where we see the familiar words **no distinction between Jew and Greek.** We remember this as the exact expression used as to universal sinnerhood in Chapter 3.22; which is now used as to salvation. For, first, He is **Lord of *all*,** and second, He is **rich unto *all*** that call upon Him.

These great words must be laid to heart. They bring great comfort, directly to any Jews who desire the Savior, and also to the hearts of all of us, Jew and Gentile, because the universal availability of salvation is so gloriously opened out here, based as it is upon the universal lordship of Christ. As Peter said at Cornelius' house to Gentiles, "The word which He sent unto the children of Israel, preaching good tidings of peace by Jesus Christ (He is Lord of all)." It is a great day when a human heart turns to this Savior who is Lord of all, for he immediately finds Him "rich unto all."

Verse 13: And then the great word by the prophet Joel is brought forward: **Whosoever shall call upon the name of the Lord shall be saved** (Joel 2.32). Now who could miss the meaning of this simplest of all messages? Now, (if we should preach on this verse!) First, salvation is promised. Second, it is a *be*-saved, not save-yourself, salvation. Third, it is *the Lord* who is to do it. Fourth, He does it for those who **call upon His Name.** Fifth, He does it for the **whosoevers,** for *anybody.* What a preacher, Joel! But note that Paul is writing to Jews, and is giving Old Testament texts. For Paul's great gospel message is to *hear and believe* "the word of the cross, which is the power of God." This message goes away beyond that of the Old Testament. Paul preached the good news of a work *finished.* It was *for* the "whosoevers": and Joel's use of that word should have convinced any Jew of God's purpose of salvation to any one, to all. But Paul does not mean that his gospel was "Call on the Lord." His gospel was, Christ died for our sins: He was buried, and was raised, for *you: hear* and *believe.*

These "whosoevers" should have taught the Jews that the way of salvation was not by their Law or any special way for them, but for any and all. Alas, the word "whosoever" was too wide for the narrow Jewish mind in Joel's day and Paul's day, and is so today.*

Verses 14 and 15: But now Paul takes these two "whosoever" verses, and from them answers the Jew, who not only relied on his law-keeping instead of on simple faith to save him, but also denied that either Paul or any of the apostles had any right to proclaim salvation by a simple message,—a message that left out the Law and Judaism. If salvation were to come unto them that "call on the name of the Lord" argues Paul, calling is impossible to one who has not believed on the Lord; and believing is impossible to one who has not heard the message about the Lord; and hearing is impossible unless some one comes preaching the message; and preaching is impossible except the messenger be Divinely sent! And again Paul clinches it with the Scripture (Isa. 52.7): **How beautiful are the feet of them that bring glad tidings of good things!** Moses' Law was not glad tidings, but a ministration of death and condemnation. "The Law worketh wrath." But the gospel— "Glad tidings! Good things!" And God who knows, calls

---

*And alas, also, there are those who insist that the Jew has a special place right through this dispensation; that he must always be "first," that there *is* a difference, although God says plainly in Chapter Three that there is *no difference* between Jew and Greek as to sinnership, guilt; and *no difference* as to the lordship of Christ and the availability of salvation to the "whosoevers," Jew or Gentile. If Paul were among us today, he would abhor and decry the special, esoteric methods of approach to the Jew in vogue in some pretentious quarters today. Become all things to the Jew, to win him, certainly. Paul did. But tell him the truth, that he is just a whosoever, and nobody else!

The terrible prophecy of Ezekiel 20.33-38 (read R. V. only, here) is about to be fulfilled concerning the scattered millions of Israel:

"As I live, saith the Lord Jehovah, surely with a mighty hand, and with an outstretched arm, and with wrath poured out, will I be king over you. And I will bring you out from the peoples, and will gather you out of the countries wherein ye are scattered, with a mighty hand, and with an outstretched arm, and with wrath poured out; and I will bring you into the wilderness of the peoples, and there will I enter into judgment with you face to face."

What the poor, wretched Jewish exiles need this hour is a Paul to go right in amongst them with a "whosoever" message for sinners, not a "literary-approach" Paul, but the exact opposite, with perhaps "bodily presence weak and speech of no account," but "provoking them to jealousy" by boasting in a Messiah whom their nation has lost,—a nation to whom God is *not now offering a Messiah,* but instead salvation, as common whosoevers, no-distinction people, ordinary guilty sinners. I protest that in Acts 28 God through Paul officially closed the door to the national offer of the gospel to the Jews, and that thereafter to treat the Jew as having a special place with God, is to deny Scripture.

"beautiful" the feet that carry such news. Are our feet "beautiful"—in God's eyes?

Paul now, with a saddened heart, goes back to the record of Israel's refusing the glad tidings:

16   But they did not all hearken to the glad tidings.
      For Isaiah saith, Lord, who hath believed our re-
17   port? So faith is from a report, but the report
18   through the word of Christ. But I say, Did they
      not hear? Yea, verily,
           Their sound went out into all the earth,
           And their words unto the ends of the world.
19   But I say, Did Israel not know? First Moses saith,
           I will provoke you to jealousy with that which
           is no nation,
           With a nation void of understanding will I anger
           you.
20   And Isaiah is very bold, and saith,
           I was found of them that sought Me not;
           I became manifest unto them that asked not
           of Me.
21   But as to Israel he saith, All the day long did I
           spread out My hands unto a disobedient and
           gainsaying people.

Verses 16, 17: Astonishing thing,—refusing good news! Men will hearken to good news along all other lines,— business, pleasure, social preferment, ambition, physical health. Go to any stock exchange and see them watch the ticker tape; or behold the political candidates sitting up all night for election news favorable to them. But the apostle mourns along with Isaiah (53.1): **Lord, who hath believed our report?** Probably men's unbelief is the greatest final burden before God of every man who speaks for God, "Lord, they do not believe." They said to Moses, "You take too much upon yourself!" (Num. 16.3); to Ezekiel, "Is he not a speaker of parables?" (Ezek. 20.49); to Amos, "The land is not able to bear all your words: Flee away to Judah and eat bread"—you are just looking for money! (Amos 7.10-13); to Jeremiah, "As for the word that thou hast spoken unto us in the name of Jehovah, we will not hearken unto thee" (Jer. 44.16-19). And hear that weeping prophet tell of his trouble:

"Hear ye, and give ear; be not proud; for Jehovah hath spoken. Give glory to Jehovah your God before He cause darkness, and before your feet stumble upon the dark mountains, and while ye look for light, He turn it into the shadow of death, and make it gross darkness. But if ye will not hear it, my soul shall weep in secret for your pride; and mine eyes shall weep sore, and run down with tears, because Jehovah's flock is taken captive" (Jer. 13.15-17).

Our Lord said to those of the multitudes that gathered to hear Him,

"This people's heart is waxed gross,
And their ears are dull of hearing,
And their eyes they have closed;
Lest haply they should perceive with their eyes,
And hear with their ears,
And understand with their heart,
And should turn again,
And I should heal them" (Matt. 13.15).

And He prophesied that His preachers would find "wayside hearers," "rocky ground hearers," "thorny ground hearers"; and then, in one out of four cases, a "good ground hearer."

Verse 17: **So faith is from a report; but the report through the word of Christ**—The Greek term here for "word" is *hrēma*, not *logos*. It literally is, "saying," "speech," as in John 3.34; 14.10; Acts 11.14. Faith, indeed, however, does come from a report; and there must be a *message* and a *messenger*, sent of God; as we have seen. But Christ accompanies this preachèd word by His Almighty "voice," as we know from John 5.25: "The hour cometh, that the dead shall hear the voice of the Son of God, and they that hear shall live." It is a "quickened" word, that creates living *faith*.

It is here that the missionary urge comes! Christ must, indeed, utter His creating word from Heaven to the dead soul, saying, Live! But in II Corinthians 5.18,19,20, we see that while "God was, indeed, in Christ reconciling the world unto Himself," He has "committed to us [Greek, "placed *in* us"] the word of reconciliation." So that God is entreating *by* us: we beseech (people) on behalf of Christ, "Be ye reconciled to God!"

Faith, indeed, comes of *hearing*. Do not imagine men will be saved in any other way. Earnest, prayerful Cornelius is commanded (and that by an angel) to send for "Simon whose surname is Peter, who shall *speak to thee words* by which thou shalt be saved" (Acts 11.14). "It pleased God by the foolishness of preaching [lit., the *preached thing*—Christ crucified] to save them that believe" (I Cor. 1.21 marg.). Note also that "faith *cometh*." If you hear, with a willing heart, the good news, that Christ died for you; that He was buried; that He was raised from the dead:—by truly "hearing," faith will "come" to you. You do not have to do a thing but hear! So there is God's part—He gave, by the Spirit, the written Word. And Christ's part,—He speaks, quickening the Word. And your part: "He that hath ears, hear."

Verse 18: But Paul goes on to mourn: **But I say, Did they** [Israel] **not hear? Yea, verily.** And then he makes a quotation from a wholly unexpected Scripture, even Psalm 19.4:

> **Their sound went out into all the earth,**
> **And their words unto the ends of the world.***

---

*The use of the plural "their"—"their sound," "their words," here, is immediately evident in the familiar Psalm itself:

> "The heavens declare the glory of God;
> And the firmament showeth his handiwork.
> Day unto day uttereth speech,
> And night unto night showeth knowledge.
> There is no speech nor language;
> Their voice is not heard.
> Their line is gone out through all the earth,
> And their words to the end of the world."

"Their" voice is the vast chorus of the created universe, and of course plural. But Paul has just been speaking here of *hearing* coming by *Christ's* word. But, Christ is Himself the Creator of all this universe! For "all things were created by Him and for Him." We must keep this fact in mind and allow the words of the Psalm to witness to the universality of the testimony concerning Christ. The emphasis on into all the earth; unto the ends of the earth must have included Israel. The "invisible things of God were clearly perceived from the creation of the world, even His everlasting power and divinity,"—as we saw concerning all men in Chapter One,—but the Jews had immeasurably more! God had come down and spoken to them on Mount Sinai; then their prophets, and then the Son, the Heir, had come; yea, and through the apostles and Stephen they had had the testimony of the Holy Spirit directly from Christ on high! So Israel had indeed "heard"! Therefore, in quoting Psalm Nineteen, Paul holds Israel to the "voice" of creation as if no other people existed. It was their Psalm!

Verse 19: Paul proceeds: **Did Israel not know?**—concerning this *whosoever*-plan, this *believing*-plan, this *calling* upon the Lord's name and being saved? Yea, even about this constant warning by their own Scriptures that if they were unfaithful God would extend His mercy to the Gentiles? First, he calls Moses to witness (Deut. 32.21):

I will provoke you to jealousy with that which is no nation,

With a nation void of understanding will I anger you.

That which is no nation—compared with the marvelous place and privileges of the race of Israel, it could be said of every other people, "It is no nation, a nation **void of understanding**" (of the things of God). **I will anger them** —for Israel can be reached in no other way—either then or now! God seeks to provoke them to jealousy: beware how you palaver over them.

Verse 20: Now finally Paul calls Isaiah again to the witness stand; and Isaiah gives a double testimony: he is indeed **very bold** in his prophecy of Gentile salvation:

I was found of them that sought me not;

I became manifest unto them that asked not of me.

Then Isaiah becomes exceedingly mournful as to wretched Israel's **disobedient and gainsaying** attitude (see verse 21).

How Jews could read this passage and remain unmoved, in their traditions, formalities, and unbelief, only faithful preachers can imagine,—who have had to deal with the titanic possibilities of evil and unbelief in the human heart.

As showing how far Christendom has lost the whole spirit of the gospel, we remind you that everywhere people have the idea they *ought* to "seek" salvation; they are everywhere told they *ought* to "go to church."*

How many now reading these words believe that Romans 10.20 is God's program for this Gentile day? You say, Should we not seek God? No! You should sit down and hear what

---

*It is an excellent thing to go where God's saints gather; and to "meetings" for unsaved people. But attending meetings saves no one. There is a Savior! And *good news* about Him to be *believed* for *yourself!*

is written in Romans: first, about your guilt, then about your helplessness, and then about the inability of the Law to do anything but condemn you; and then believe on Christ whom God hath sent; and then praise God for righteousness *apart* from works, *apart* from ordinances! hear how God laid sin, your sin, on a Substitute, His own Son, Jesus Christ our Lord, and that now, sin being put away, God has raised Him from the dead. Seek God? No! God is the Seeker, and He has sought and is now seeking *those that asked not of Him,* and has been found of those who *sought Him not!*—but simply *heard* the good news and *believed!* Praise His Holy Name!

Verse 21: But, alas, poor Israel! Jehovah, through Isaiah, speaks thus of them: **All the day long did I spread out my hands unto a disobedient and gainsaying people** (Isa. 65.2). What yearning, what love, what pleading, what patience! And it is *The Creator, God Himself,* here, spreading out His hands! Towards whom? Towards a disobedient people; a people that, being rebuked, did deny and gainsay their prophets, and even their own Messiah,—as they do unto this day!*

It should astonish and warn us—every unbelieving Jew we see! Astonish us, that the human heart should treat God so! And warn us: for, as we shall see in the next chapter, we Gentiles are now being "visited" by God,—this same God of Love: and He is stretching out His hands to usward! May we early yield to Him!

And here, lest we miss the lesson for *us,* in considering wretched Israel's rejection of their Messiah, let us read a message to our own hearts:

---

*"And he (Manasseh) set the graven image of the idol, which he had made, in the house of God, of which God said to David and to Solomon his son, 'In this house, and in Jerusalem, which I have chosen out of all the tribes of Israel, will I put My name forever': . . . And Manasseh seduced Judah and the inhabitants of Jerusalem, so that they did evil more than did the nations whom Jehovah destroyed before the children of Israel."

"All the chiefs of the priests, and the people, trespassed very greatly after all the abominations of the nations; and they polluted the house of Jehovah which He had hallowed in Jerusalem. And Jehovah, the God of their fathers, sent to them by his messengers, rising up early and sending, because He had compassion on His people, and on His dwelling-place." But alas, we read: "They mocked the messengers of God, and despised His words, and scoffed at His prophets, until the wrath of Jehovah arose against His people, till there was no remedy" (II Chron. 33.7,9; 36.14-16).

THE GREAT UNKNOWN

WHY dost Thou pass unheeded,
  Treading with piercèd feet
The halls of the kingly palace,
  The busy street?
Oh marvellous in Thy beauty,
  Crowned with the light of God,
Why fall they not down to worship
  Where Thou hast trod?
Why are Thy hands extended
  Beseeching whilst men pass by
With their empty words and their laughter,
  Yet passing on to die?

Unseen, unknown, unregarded,
  Calling and waiting yet—
They hear Thy knock and they tremble—
  They hear, and they forget.
And Thou in the midst art standing
  Of old and forever the same—
Thou hearest their songs and their jesting,
  But not Thy name.
The thirty-three years forgotten
  Of the weary way Thou hast trod—
Thou art but a name unwelcome,
  O Savior God!

Yet amongst the highways and hedges,
  Amongst the lame and the blind,
The poor and the maimed and the outcast,
  Still dost Thou seek and find—
There by the wayside lying
  The eyes of Thy love can see
The wounded, the naked, the dying,
  Too helpless to come to Thee.
So Thou art watching and waiting
  Till the wedding is furnished with guests—
And the last of the sorrowful singeth,
  And the last of the weary rests.

                    —C. P. C. (in *Hymns of Ter Steegen*).

CHAPTER ELEVEN

Israel not Finally Cast Off: an Election Saved—Paul Being Proof. Verses 1-6.

Others Hardened,—as Scripture Foretold. Verses 7-10.

"Fulness of Gentiles" Comes in Meanwhile. Verses 11,25,28.

Gentile Salvation to Provoke Israel to "Jealousy"— Since They are the "Natural Branches" of the Tree of Promise. Verses 11-18.

Gentiles Must Continue in Divine "Goodness"; Otherwise Gentiles to be "Cut Off" from Place of Present Blessing. Verses 19-25.

All Real Israel to be Saved at the Return to Them of Christ Their "Deliverer." Verses 26-32.

Rapturous Praise of the Ways of God's Wisdom and Knowledge; God the One Source, Channel and End of All Things! Verses 33-36.

ALL THE SAD RECORD of Chapters Nine and Ten concerning Israel having been shown, the apostle now turns to that question which naturally arises in our Gentile hearts (for in 11.13 he says, "I am speaking to you that are Gentiles").

1 I say then, Did God cast off His people? Far be the thought! For I also am an Israelite, of the seed
2 of Abraham, of the tribe of Benjamin. God did not cast off His people which he foreknew. Or understand ye not what the Scripture saith in [the portion concerning] Elijah? How he pleadeth with
3 God against Israel: Lord, they have killed thy prophets, they have digged down thine altars; and
4 I am left alone and they seek my life. But what saith the answer of God unto him? I have left for Myself seven thousand men, who have not bowed

5   the knee to Baal. Even so then at this present time
    there is a Remnant according to the election of
6   grace. But if it is by grace, it is no more of works:
    otherwise grace is no more grace.

Verse 1: Here Paul rejects with horror—**Far be the
thought!** that God had finally abandoned, "cast off" His
people Israel.* Let every Christian reject the suggestion
with equal horror.

First, Paul says, **I myself** am proof: **an Israelite;** not a
proselyte either, but **of the seed of Abraham,** and a **Ben-
jamite,**—not one of the ten tribes which separated from
Judah!

Verse 2: Then Paul defines the Israel that is not rejected: **God's people whom He foreknew.** In "You only
have I known," He is not speaking of knowing about them or
their affairs, but of the fact that to them only had He made
Himself known; because they were foreknown of Him; that is,
acquainted with beforehand,—before their earthly history began!

(See note on Romans 8.29.) In Amos 3.1,2 we read:

"Hear this word that Jehovah hath spoken against you,
O children of Israel, against the whole family which I
brought up out of the land of Egypt, saying, You only
have I known of all the families of the earth: . . . "

---

*The Eleventh of Romans should at once and forever turn us away from the
presumptuous assertions of those who teach that God is "through with national
Israel,"—that it has "no future as an elect nation" in Palestine.

Mr. Philip Mauro makes the astounding statements: "The last word of prophecy
concerning this people Israel as a nation was fulfilled at the destruction of
Jerusalem by the Roman armies," and "the 'all Israel' of Rom. 11.26 is the
whole body of God's redeemed people." . . . "Zion is where the Lord Jesus is."
While in utter blindness to the prophetic message he claims, "Paul quotes the
words, 'Behold, I lay in Zion' as being fulfilled in this present era (Rom. 9.33)"!
"Those who insist upon what they call 'literal fulfilment' of the promised blessings that were to come to Israel through Christ, have completely missed the
mark!"

Yet even Augustine, back in the fourth century, said, "Distinguish the dispensations, and all is easy."

That there is a future for the nation of Israel in their land upon this earth,
all faithful believers know very well. Let the saints steadily go forward into the
increasing light, of these last days, no matter who turns about and takes the back
track into the darkness of ignorance of medievalism or even the relatively faint
dispensational light of the Reformation.

I would earnestly commend those who desire a full discussion of Mauro's
attack on "Dispensationalism" (for it is a typical one!) to read Dr. I. M. Halde-
man's review of Mauro's book, *"The Kingdom of God."* It is able and unanswerable.

Now in the preceding chapter of Amos, there is a remarkable series of messages of judgment concerning the various nations surrounding Israel. In each case the exact reasons for the judgment are detailed by God, beginning with Damascus (1.3), then Gaza (1.6), Tyre (1.9), Edom (1.11), Ammon (1.13), Moab (2.1), then Judah (2.4); and finally, the northern kingdom, (to which Amos spoke), Israel (2.6): showing that God knew the exact conduct of each nation. Therefore, when God says concerning Israel, "You only have I known," He is not speaking of knowing about them or their affairs, but of the fact that to them only had He made Himself known;* (as Paul says to the Galatians: "Now ye have come to know God,—or rather, to be known by God"). But here we have a fore-acquaintance-ship with Israel. This foreknowledge is described in Romans 8.29 (which see), where the term is used in a wider sense, and therefore must include the foreknowledge of the Remnant "according to the election of grace"—of the nation of Israel, spoken of here.

Verses 3,4: Again Paul lets the Scripture "speak," and here we find Israel's greatest prophet pleading against Israel! Because they had **killed Jehovah's prophets** and **destroyed Jehovah's altars,** Elijah believed himself **left alone,** and believed they were **seeking his life.**† But how utterly outside and beyond Elijah's conception of things was God's reply that He had left for Himself a "Remnant" (even 7000!) who had utterly refused Baal-worship. Here is Divine sovereignty mar-

---

*God calls the Church His "saints," not a "people"; see Rom. 1.6,7; I Cor. 1.2; Eph. 1.1. He never refers to the Church as a "people," or nation. I Peter 2.9 is not an exception, but rather a proof of this fact, for Peter is writing to the elect of the Diaspora, (the individual Jewish believers of the Jewish Dispersion), in Asia Minor, just as James also wrote, "To the twelve tribes which are of the Diaspora." In both James and Peter, there is still the suffer-ance by God of Jewish things; as in Acts they are allowed to keep the feasts, and are in the temple: although these were all past, in God's sight, and the temple left "desolate." God was acting in great patience with Jewish believers. But Paul brought a new message, that the Church was not earthly, nor national, nor Jewish, in any sense; but a "new body," and altogether heavenly. So the Jewish saints now are called "partakers of a *heavenly* calling" (Heb. 3.1).

†There is always the tendency, in a faithful man of God in dark days, (a tendency diligently cultivated by the devil!) to imagine himself *alone.* So he hunts the solitude befitting his imagined solitariness. But the voice of God came to Elijah, "What doest thou here?" Embarrassing question, that! It should bring out every Christian monk from his monastery!

velously illustrated! The nation is apostate, under Ahab and Jezebel; Baal's prophets number hundreds; and Elijah had fled the land,—back to Horeb, where the Law was given! Now comes the revelation that Divine sovereign intervention has been timely, ample, definite and perfect. God has preserved seven thousand. This reminds us immediately of the sealing of 144,000 of Israel in Revelation Seven. Unbelief or shallow interpretation would say this merely indicates some indefinite number. Well, then, go on to say, the 7000 of Elijah's day were an "indefinite number,"—and see where your false wisdom (which is really *unbelief*) will bring you!

Verse 5: Even so, says Paul, **at this present time also there is a Remnant** (of Israelites) being preserved by God, although the nation has crucified their Messiah, and rejected the testimony concerning Him by the Spirit through the apostles—an infinitely worse condition of things than Ahab's Baal worship! Only sovereign grace will do here; so it is a **Remnant according to the election of *grace*.** This "Remnant" are put now into the Body of Christ: they become "partakers of a heavenly calling" (Heb. 3.1). Every saved Israelite has abandoned his Israelitish hopes, and believed on Christ as a *common sinner!* Of course only a few Israelites—a "remnant," do this.

Verse 6: Paul insists, (as he does continuously throughout his Epistles): **If it is by grace, it is no more of works: otherwise grace is no more grace**—Here is perhaps the most direct and absolute contrast in Scripture of two principles: for *grace* is God acting sovereignly according to Himself; *works* is man seeking to present to God a human ground for blessing. The two principles are utterly opposed. As Paul, in his conflict with Peter in Galatians 2.15,16 and 21, says: "Even we, Jews by nature, and not 'sinners of the Gentiles' believed on Christ Jesus. I do not make void the grace of God, for if righteousness is through law, Christ died for nothing!" And as Peter said at the first Church council, "We [Jews] believe that we shall be saved through the grace of the Lord Jesus, in like manner as they" (Gentiles) (Acts 15.11).

7   What then? That which Israel is in search of
     [righteousness], that he [the nation] obtained
     not; but the election obtained it, and the rest were
8   hardened: according as it is written, God gave
     them a spirit of drowsiness, eyes that they should
     not see, and ears that they should not hear, unto
9   this very day. And David saith,
          Let their table be made a snare, and a trap,
          And a stumblingblock, and a recompense unto
            them,
          Let their eyes be darkened, that they may not
            see,
          And bow Thou down their back always.

Verse 7: Here, then, in this chapter, is the very height
of Divine sovereignty: not only electing people, but even
deciding the very time when they should come on the
scene of this world's history. "Israel after the flesh" nationally was in search of righteousness,—that was their
very business, in the preservation and application of the
Law. But that was not the way of righteousness. We
have seen that their own Scriptures set forth that "calling
on the name of the Lord," and believing on the "Stone"
(Christ) at whom others in legality "stumbled," was the
true way. So the nation obtained not righteousness. But
the election obtained it. And, as to the rest? God's answer
is, they were hardened.

But remember Chapter Nine and do not "reply against" God,
—and hear a "Thou—who art thou?" from Him; but note carefully, how and why they were thus "hardened."

Verse 8: Paul now says (quoting Isa. 29.10): **According as it is written, God gave them a spirit of stupor, eyes
that they should not see, and ears that they should not
hear, unto this very day.**

The process of that awful thing, spiritual hardening, is thus
depicted in Israel as nowhere else, for hearts harden most
quickly when men are trusting in their place of special privilege, without fellowship with the God who gives it. (Thus, we
fear, it is with thousands in Christendom, and even among those

who have the Lord's table most frequently before them. What but a deadly snare to the soul is the table of the Lord, without real communion with the Lord of the table!)

Verse 9: So it is written of Israel's "table": **Let their table be made a snare.** This is quoted from David, in Ps. 69.22, and evidently refers to the "table" at which the Israelites were privileged to eat with Jehovah. This was indeed a high and special privilege which Israel had: they ate with God. In Exodus 24.11, we read: "They saw God and did eat and drink"; and from the Passover of Exodus 12 onward, they ate in their sacred feasts. We know the priests "ate before God": Leviticus 6.16; 7.18,20. But not only was this true of the priests, but of the people in their peace offerings (Lev. 7.18,19; 23.6); and in their feasts, as in Leviticus 23.6 and Numbers 15. 17-21; 18.26,30,31; Deuteronomy 12.7,18; 14.23; 27.7.

For the "table" of the Israelite was connected by Jehovah with Himself. Certain things the Israelite might eat, others not; because he was one of a holy nation unto Jehovah. But the Israelite quickly began to trust not in Jehovah, but in his manner of eating, as did Peter: "Not so, Lord; for I have never eaten anything that is common and unclean." Without true faith, therefore, their very table of privilege became a snare.*

It is to be noted carefully that each time the solemn Sixth of Isaiah is quoted, the sovereignty of God in hardening whom He will is increasingly emphasized. We see in Matthew 13.15, that it is the people's heart that had "waxed gross": their ears were

---

*An ominous comment on this—this "table made a snare,"—is the story of the Last Supper: Judas was, it appears, sitting so near to Jesus, that "the sop," which should mark the betrayer, was handed to him without attracting the attention of the rest. (It has been my own belief that, while John was sitting on one side of our Lord, Judas was on the other side! It was the hideous presumption of callous sin.) "And after the sop, then entered Satan into him." And, "having received the sop, he went out . . . and it was night" (John 13.21-30). Judas typifies Israel. Indeed, he so became the spiritual representative of apostate Israel that rejected Christ, that we need only turn to that 69th Psalm, (Christ's great "reproach" Psalm) from which Paul is quoting here in Romans 11.9,10, to see this. The 21st verse of this Psalm says, "In My thirst they gave Me vinegar to drink." Evidently it is Christ speaking. Then verse 22, and following: "Let their table become a snare,"—and through verse 28, that wicked generation, symbolized in Judas, is shown. And just as Satan entered into Judas at the table,— when he presumed most on his place as a chosen apostle, so it was Israel's very relationship to, knowledge of, and communion with, Jehovah, at their feasts and temples, *that they presumed upon!* Read Jeremiah 7.1-11.

"dull of hearing" because of lack of interest; their eyes *they* had closed,—not *desiring* to turn and understand, lest they should perceive, and hear, understand, turn, and be healed of God! Then, in the fourth Gospel, at the end of our Lord's public testimony, (John 12.39): "They could not believe, for that Isaiah said,

"*He* hath blinded their eyes, and *He* hardened their heart;
Lest they should see with their eyes, and perceive with their heart;
And should turn,
And I should heal them."

This is judicial action, following the people's attitude.

In the third occurrence of the words of Isaiah Six (in Acts 28), Paul *officially shuts the door* to national Israel: "Well spake the Holy Spirit through Isaiah the prophet unto your fathers,"—quoting this Isaiah Six, and declaring: "Be it known therefore unto you, that this salvation of God is sent unto the Gentiles: they also will hear."*

Verse 10: As to Israel, nationally, it is written, **Let their eyes be darkened, that they may not see, And bow Thou down their back always.** It will be so until that future day, described in Zechariah 12.10, when God "pours upon them the Spirit of grace and of supplication, and they look unto Him whom they have pierced."

We dare not believe in any of the modern reports of national Jewish "turning to the Lord." They will go into yet greater darkness (after the Rapture of the Church). There will be the former evil spirit of idolatry "taking with itself seven other spirits more wicked than itself," entering in and dwelling in this present evil generation of Israel! (Matt. 12.45). Do not be deceived. At our Lord's coming, and not until that be-

---

*Since this awful use of Isaiah 6, the gospel has no Jewish bounds or bonds whatever! And it is presumption and danger, now, to give the Jews any other place than that of common sinners! "No distinction between Jew and Greek," says God. Those that preach thus, have God's blessing. Those that would give any special place whatever to Jews, since that day, do so contrary to the gospel; and, we fear, for private advantage. Tell Jews *the truth!* Their Messiah *was* offered to their nation, and *rejected.* And *God is not offering a Messiah to Israel now,* but has Himself rejected them: all except a "remnant," who leave Jewish earthly hopes, break down into *sinners only,* and receive a sinner's Savior,—not a "Jewish" one! Then they become "partakers of a heavenly calling."

leagured nation *sees* "the sign of the Son of Man in Heaven"
(Matt. 24.30),—which will be that "looking upon Him whom
they pierced" of Zechariah 12, will they have faith. Thomas, in
John 20, who "would not believe except he see in Christ's hands
the print of the nails," is an exact type of the coming conversion
of Israel. Until then, let us "provoke to jealousy" all of them
we can, by boasting in Christ and His Salvation; and so we
may save a few of them,—*as sinners,* the "Remnant according
to the election of Grace."

11   I say then, Did they stumble that they might
      fall? God forbid: but by their fall salvation is
      come unto the Gentiles, to provoke them to jeal-
12   ousy. Now if their fall is the riches of the world,
      and their loss the riches of the Gentiles; how much
13   more their fulness? But I speak to you that are
      Gentiles. Inasmuch then as I am an apostle of
14   Gentiles, I glorify my ministry: if by any means
      I may provoke to jealousy them that are my flesh,
      and may save some of them.

15   For if the casting away of them is the recon-
      ciling of the world, what shall the receiving of them
16   be, but life from the dead? And if the firstfruit
      is holy, so is the lump: and if the root is holy, so
      are the branches.

17   But if some of the branches were broken off,
      and thou, being a wild olive, wast grafted in among
      them, and didst become partaker with them of
18   the root of the fatness of the olive tree: glory not
      over the branches: but if thou gloriest, it is not
      thou that bearest the root, but the root thee.

19   Thou wilt say then, Branches were broken off,
20   that I might be grafted in. Well: by their unbelief
      they were broken off, and thou standest by thy
21   faith. Be not high-minded, but fear: for if God
      spared not the natural branches, neither will He
22   spare thee. Behold then the goodness and severity
      of God: toward them that fell, severity; but toward
      thee, God's goodness, if thou continue in His good-

23 ness: otherwise thou also shalt be cut off. And they also, if they continue not in their unbelief, shall be grafted in: for God is able to graft them
24 in again. For if thou wast cut out of that which is by nature a wild olive tree, and wast grafted contrary to nature into a good olive tree; how much more shall these, which are the natural branches, be grafted into their own olive tree?

Verse 11: Did they stumble that they might fall? Some individuals, alas, do,—both of Jews and Gentiles. Some are offended and turn away forever. But not finally the Israelitish nation! Banish the thought! We shall soon in this chapter see God's future salvation for that nation. But here the apostle notes that **their fall was made the occasion of salvation to the Gentiles**; and this again is **to provoke them to jealousy**—that they may be saved. God's manifest blessing to Gentiles causes the careless, self-satisfied Jew to *awake*,—first to ridicule Gentile testimony; then,—seeing the reality of Divine visitation to the despised Gentile, to arouse to a deep *jealousy*:* "They have what we ought to have; but we have lost God's favor!"

Verse 12: **Their fall is the riches of the world; their loss the riches of the Gentiles.** Before they fell, if a Gentile wanted to know the true God, he must become a "proselyte." He must journey up to Jerusalem three times a year; and even then he could not worship directly. He must have Levitical priests and forms. Contrast with this the day of Pentecost. Every man heard *in his own tongue in which he was born*, the wonderful works of God! And by and by Paul goes freely

---

*How amazingly different Paul's method of "provoking the Jews to jealousy," from that pursued by many Jewish mission workers today! The Jew must have a "special" place as a Jew! In some quarters they are even organizing "Jewish assemblies," and in other quarters advocating "the literary method of approaching Israel"! All this, we cannot but feel, is abominable kow-towing to Jewish *flesh,* and hinders their salvation. Jews now are common sinners, who have for the present been set aside nationally, and must come to rely, as *individual sinners,* hopelessly guilty and helpless, upon the shed blood of Christ, and upon Him risen from the dead.

It is an awful thing to make present day "Jewish" claims, when God says Jews are, for the present, *no different from Gentiles,* before God: but are just— *sinners!*

forth, apart from the Law, and "religion," to all the Gentiles:

"Christ the Son of God hath sent me
Through the midnight lands:
Mine the mighty ordination
Of the piercèd hands!"

See Ephesus, and Corinth, and then Rome, and the whole world, "rich," by Israel's fall! Wherever you are, you can call on the Lord, and walk by the blessed Holy Spirit, and witness of a free salvation to all and any who will listen! No "going up to Jerusalem" to keep feasts, and worship Jehovah afar off, but drawing nigh to God in Heaven through the blood of Christ, at any time, any place, under all circumstances! In everything, invited to "let your requests be made known unto God!" That is riches, indeed! If you do not now hold it so, you shortly will: for you will need the Lord, ere long! And He is so nigh!

Alas, how much Israel lost in refusing Christ's "day of visitation" to them. How He wept over that! (Luke 19.41-44). We cannot blame God for Israel's rejection of their Messiah, and their "fall." He foretold it, indeed: but Christ said, "Ye *will* not come to Me, that ye may have life!"

But rather, let us see in the blessing that has resulted to us, "the heart of mercy" of God! (Luke 1.78, margin.) He will show "kindness" *somewhere*. And, if the invited guests have had themselves "excused," let us who belong in "the highways and hedges" run quickly to the feast when we are bidden!

If their fall is the riches of the world, and their loss *has* been "riches to the world" and to the Gentiles, how much more their fulness?

In the days of David and Solomon, there were prodigal riches,—both of God's glorious presence (II Chron. 5.11-14) and of worldly wealth and honor (I Kings 10, entire). But this presence, and this blessing, was for Israel. Now, as our Lord told the Samaritan woman, the hour has come, when "neither in this mountain nor at Jerusalem" do men go to worship the Father: but salvation has come out as "riches" to the whole world and to Gentiles, who had the place of "dogs" before (as compared with Israel).

Now if this blessing be so great for the world, with Israel "fallen," how much more, when the time of restoration, and of fulness for Israel, be come!

Verses 13,14: **I speak to you that are Gentiles***—There were many Jewish saints at Rome. But these three chapters of Romans (9, 10 and 11), are peculiarly fitted to our Gentile instruction. And particularly so is this word: **Inasmuch as I am an apostle of Gentiles, I glorify my ministry: if by any means I may provoke to jealousy them that are my flesh, and may save some of them.** I boast, before the Jews, of how God works among the Gentiles, of His saving them, filling them with His Spirit, and with peace; using them in saving others, establishing them in heavenly joy. And why do I thus magnify my Gentile ministry? **To provoke my fellow-Jews to jealousy**—of an inward peace they have not, that they may desire it: and, perhaps, choose it!

Verse 15: **The casting away of them ... the reconciling of the world**—As long as God held fellowship with Israel on the ground of the old legal covenant, Gentiles were out of His direct favor, unless they became Jewish proselytes. Upon

*The moment Paul says this, we know he is not addressing either Jewish believers or Gentile Christians *as such*—those "in Christ," for in Christ is neither Jew nor Greek. So he must be speaking to us Gentiles as having at present (not as the Church, but the Gentiles as over against the Jews) come into God's general favor—which the Jews had, but of which they are at present deprived. Gentiles, not Jews, at present are the field of God's operations on earth. They are favored, as Israel once was. And they have, therefore, like responsibilities. If Israel was "cut off" through unbelief, Gentiledom must beware lest not abiding in that "goodness" in which God has set the Gentiles (that is, in that direct Divine favor,—without law, or religion, in which God has put Gentiledom), it also shall be cut off! For God did not give Gentiledom a Law, with its "10,000 things," as He gave Israel. He gave Gentiledom the gospel only. He gave them Paul; and the message of GRACE.

Now, if they go back to "religion," or if they forget or neglect God's great salvation, it is to desert God's "goodness"; and thus to be shortly "cut off."

And they have done just that,—as we know too well! If Gentiledom has "continued" in God's uncaused grace and goodness, what meaneth then this bleating in our ears—of liturgies, masses, holy days, even prayers for the dead? What meaneth all this buzz of "administering sacraments," of "vestments," of "holy orders," of priestcraft? Why these vast cathedrals? This lavish outpouring for great "religious" establishments? The apostles had none of this! God commanded none of it. Nay, He forbade it! "The Most High dwelleth not in temples made with hands"! The Jews stoned Stephen, who dared to say so! And see the Popes burning like witnesses! And "Modern" Denominations turning faithful preachers out of churches!

No; Gentiledom has deserted the "goodness" of God, for a Judao-pagan system with "Christian" names. *And Gentiledom will be cut off.*

Israel's rejection of their Messiah and not until then (for
Christ came first to Israel,—as see Matt. 10.5) could God
"reconcile" the world to Himself. See II Corinthians 5.19:
"God was in Christ reconciling the world unto Himself."

**The casting away of them—reconciling the world; re-
ceiving of them—life from the dead!**—Paul speaks God's
words; and God never exaggerates! Therefore, in understanding (so far as we may) these great words, we have only to
compare our wretched Gentile state before the blessed reconciliation news, with our present Gentile blessing under the
gospel,—as the fruit of the "casting away" of the Israelites;
and then judge what blessing will come when God "receives"
them! It will indeed be "life from the dead"! For this world
has never seen what shall then be seen: "The earth shall be
full of the knowledge of Jehovah, as the waters cover the sea"
(Isa. 11.9). Not even in Eden, before man's sin, was that seen!
And all this waits the "receiving" of God's earthly people, elect
Israel! God must have them back in their land, to become "a
joy to the whole earth." When Jehovah finally speaks everlasting comfort to His people Israel and to Jerusalem, it is
written, "And the glory of Jehovah shall be revealed, and all
flesh shall see it together"* (Isa. 40.1-5).

Verse 16: **And if the firstfruit is holy, so is the lump:
and if the root is holy, so are the branches**—The firstfruit
here seems to me to be the believing Israel of the old days,
as in Jeremiah 2.2,3: "Thou wentest after Me in the wilderness, . . . Israel was holiness unto Jehovah, the firstfruits
of his increase"; and **the lump** to be the whole "Israel of
God," of Galatians Six; that is, Israel, in God's sight as an
always beloved nation; though now the saved "Remnant according to the election of grace" comes out of that nation into a
risen, heavenly Christ, into a higher calling, where there is
neither Jew nor Gentile. And, as has been said, the Gentile "is
placed upon the *root,*" not upon the trunk nor upon the branches.

---

*It must ever be remembered that the calling of the Church, the Body of
Christ, is a heavenly one; as Israel's is not. Though by God's grace partakers
of an ineffably higher place—members of Christ Himself, yet we, more than
any, should regard Israel's coming blessing: for we have, as they will have,
mercy: the sweetest conferment of God on sinners!

He became *neither a Jew,* nor *of Israel.* Blessing, however, had been promised *through Abraham* to *"all* the families of the earth."

Now it is important to see that **the root** is Abraham, the depositary of the promises. The tree of Divine blessing grows up by these promises to Abraham, and His Seed, which is Christ. The natural branches, that is, those who first partook of the tree's root and fatness, were Jews. You cannot say that the tree is the Jewish nation, but rather that it is those partaking of the Divine blessing from Abraham through Christ. The most of the Jews were thus, because of unbelief, broken off. Those Jews who believed, as we know (the election of grace), came to partake of the heavenly calling in the Church "the assembly of God." Again, when that assembly is taken away to heaven, and God grafts back the·remnant of the Jewish people, into their former ("their own") olive tree, Divine blessing on earth will have the earthly character it had before Church days: Israel will be the land, Jerusalem the city, and the temple-worship the form (see Ezek. 40-48).

Verse 17: **Some of the branches were broken off, and thou, being a wild olive, wast grafted in.** This simply means that we, as Gentiles, have been set in the place of blessing from Abraham. It does not mean that all Gentiles are in the Body of Christ,—for it is not of that Body as such that Paul is here speaking: but of Gentiles as having been put into that place of Divine blessing where Israel once stood. Nor do the words **some of the branches** mean that any whole tribe of Israel will be wholly lost; for all twelve tribes appear in Ezekiel, in the millennial kingdom. The word **thou** is generic, of Gentiles: but of course is addressed to individuals—those of the Gentiles who would hear. "The warnings here are addressed not to brethren in Christ, but as being *of the Gentiles.*"

Verse 18: **It is not thou that bearest the root, but the root thee**—How few of us Gentile believers understand and bear in mind that we are beneficiaries of those promises which God lodged in Abraham as a *root* of promise,—all the promises we inherit in Christ! This is illustrated by Galatians 3.7: "They

that are of faith, the same are sons of Abraham"; and even the
gift of the Holy Spirit is "the blessing *of Abraham* in Christ
Jesus" coming upon the Gentiles (Gal. 3.14).

There is a very great danger, as Paul shows in Romans
11.18, that we Gentiles **glory over** the Jewish branches, and
forget it is not thou that bearest the root, but the root thee.
Abraham was the root, the vessel of promise, and we (if we
are in Christ) are his children.

Verse 19, alas to say, voices the general consciousness
and the consequent conduct of Christendom through the
so-called "Christian centuries": **Branches were broken off,
that I might be grafted in!** The despising of the Jews, and
the horrid persecuting of them by Christendom, is one of
the three great scandals of history.*

Verses 20,21: The only wise attitude for Gentiles is
now prescribed by our apostle—**Well, by their unbelief they
were broken off, and thou standest by thy faith. Be not
high-minded, but fear;†**—In other words, it was not the

---

*The *first* scandal was the persecution of their own prophets by the Jews,
God's own nation; the *second* was the hatred unto death against the witnesses
and truth of the gospel by papal Rome (the professed church of God!) with its
Inquisition tortures and stake; the *third* I have named above, the hatred of the
Jews by professing Christians,—by those who professed faith in a Savior who
is Himself "an Israelite after the flesh."

I do not here mention pagan persecutions, either of Jews or of Christians,
for such were to be expected. Dean Milman, in his History of the Jews, (and
such a book could be read with great profit in these days of rising anti-Semitism),
calls the persecution of the Jews during the middle ages "A most hideous chronicle
of human cruelty (as far as my researches have gone,—fearfully true). Perhaps
it is the most hideous," he goes on, "because the most continuous to be found
among nations above the state of savages. Alas! that it should be among nations
called Christian, though occasionally the Mohammedan persecutor vied with the
Christian in barbarity . . . Kingdom after kingdom, and people after people,
followed the dreadful example, [of hatred and persecution of the Israelites], and
strove to peal the knell of the descendants of Israel; till at length, what we blush
to call Christianity, with the Inquisition in its train, cleared the fair and smiling
provinces of Spain of this industrious part of its population, and self-inflicted
a curse of barrenness upon the benighted land."

We may remark that the present fratricidal slaughter in Spain is simply a
fulfillment of God's words to Abraham and his seed: "Him that curseth thee will
I curse." In its persecutions both of Jews and of Christians, Spain sowed the
wind: it is now reaping the whirlwind!

†Some, who deny the eternal safety of the saints, apply the warning of
verses 20,21, as if it were a personal, instead of a generic one,—a warning
to individual believers, instead of to Gentiledom as such. But this is not only
bad theology, but a missing of Paul's whole point here. It is bad theology, for
our Lord says of His sheep, that they "shall never perish" and when Paul warns
believers of being "high-minded" (compare I Tim. 6.17 with Rom. 11.20) it is

Gentiles' importance over that of the Jews, but the Jews' unbelief, that caused some—for the present all but a "remnant"—to be broken off: and the Gentile "stands" by his faith,—not by his superiority to the Jews! "High-mindedness" is the contrary of the "fear" here enjoined (the root of which is humility,—consciousness of unworthiness). And why fear? Verse 21 tells plainly: **God spared not the natural branches** [the Jews], **neither will He spare thee** [Gentiledom]; if Gentiledom walks in forgetfulness of its sinnerhood, and of God's "goodness,"—in self-importance, pride, and high-mindedness.

Verse 22: **Behold then the goodness and severity of God: toward them that fell, severity; but toward thee, God's goodness, if thou continue in His goodness: otherwise thou also shalt be cut off**—This is a most solemn word, indeed! It calls the Gentile world to behold **the goodness and** [its opposite] **severity of God! Toward them that fell, severity:** in spite of what had been the privileges of having Jehovah's temple among them; and the former faithfulness of the nation, and afterwards of individuals, Israel fell into self-righteousness, pride, and rejection of their Messiah. Toward such, "severity." Christ beheld Jerusalem and wept

not to threaten doom to them, but to counsel them how to walk. Then, it is bad interpretation: for the whole passage in Rom. 11.19-24, deals not with the Church, (where there is no distinction between Jew and Greek!) but with Jew-position and Gentile-position in God's affairs on earth. Israel, unbelieving, was cut off for awhile from his place of Divine favor and blessing. Gentiledom comes into favor instead of Israel, for a while; and "the Church came into the administration of the promises in the character of Gentiles, in contrast with Jews." It is to a characteristic Gentile, that Paul speaks in Rom. 11.19: "Thou wilt say, Branches were broken off, that I might be grafted in." He speaks generically, to this characteristic Gentile, when he warns, in verse 22: "Toward thee, God's goodness, if thou continue in His goodness; otherwise thou also shalt be [as was Israel before Gentiledom] cut off." Now we know, from God's prophetic Word, that Gentiledom will, indeed, be cut off, as was Israel, and Israel be restored to his former place, as the sphere and channel of God's blessing to earth.

So that, when Paul says, "I speak to you that are Gentiles," he is talking, not to God's saints as such, much less to the Church which is the Body of Christ; but to Gentiledom, which has been given to be, in God's "goodness," the place of His blessing, while Israel is for the time set aside.

Another proof of this is in the very admonition itself: "Be not highminded, but fear." If this (as some claim) is merely a warning to individual saints to avoid pride, why should it be addressed to Gentile saints only? Had Jewish believers no danger of pride?

No; it is not of the Church at all, nor of His real saints, that God speaks here: but of Gentiledom.

over it, for judgment is God's "strange work." But, we beg you, get Josephus, or any history, and read what befell the Jews when Titus took Jerusalem; and see Matthew Twenty-three, and our Lord's anguished words: "O Jerusalem, Jerusalem, that killeth the prophets, and stoneth them that are sent unto her! Behold, your house is left unto you desolate!"

Now it is the common talk through Christendom that the Jews were God's "ancient" people; and that now the Gentiles are God's favored ones. People love to hear sermons on the "goodness" of God, but resent talk of Divine severity toward the Gentiles! But have the Gentiles proven themselves different from the Jews in their conduct toward God? Christendom is today sinning against greater light than ever Israel had!

God says to the Gentile: **Toward thee, God's goodness, if thou continue in His goodness**—Now what is "the goodness" referred to here?

We remember our Lord's saying to the twelve apostles, when He first sent them out to the "lost sheep of the house of Israel," "Go not into any way of the Gentiles, and enter not into any city of the Samaritans" (Matt. 10.5). He had come as "a minister of the circumcision" to His own. But when they had rejected and crucified Him, the Risen Lord said: "Go ye into *all the world,* and preach the gospel to *the whole creation*" (Mark 16.15); "Ye shall be My witnesses, both in Jerusalem, and in all Judea and Samaria, and unto *the uttermost part of the earth*" (Acts 1.8).

So, the Holy Spirit having been given at Pentecost, Peter is shortly sent to the house of the Gentile, Cornelius: who believes the simple gospel of Christ, and, on "all them that heard the Word the Holy Spirit fell." Then Barnabas and Saul, Silas and Timothy, and the rest, go on to the Gentiles, turning the world "upside down" with the gospel of *grace.* No need for a "religion" now; they had *Christ.* No need for a temple,—they, the assembly, were "the temple of God"; for, as Stephen witnessed—and was stoned for it—"The Most High is not [now] dwelling in temples made by hands." No need for a ritual: they had the Holy Spirit, and worshipped by Him instead of forms! No need of a special priesthood,—all believers were alike priests, and drew near unto God by the shed blood, Christ Himself, over the house of God, leading their worship, as the Great High Priest in heaven. No need of seeking "merit,"—they were *in Christ,* already accepted in Him,—yea, made the very *righteousness of God in Him!*

Now this was God's **goodness** toward Gentile *believers.*

And, as for the Gentiles *all:* they were no longer called "dogs," as contrasted with the favored race of Israel (Matt. 15.26). There was a complete change in the relationship of Gentiles as such toward God. They were put into the place of privilege and opportunity of Divine blessing: an "acceptable time," a "day of salvation," in God's "goodness" was extended to them. If one had sought to instruct a Gentile in the Old Testament days, he must have said, "God is the God of Israel: become a proselyte; go up to Jerusalem; keep the feasts according to the Law." If one should go to a Gentile in the coming Millennium, the like instruction would be necessary, for all the nations must then go up to Jerusalem by their representatives "to worship the King, Jehovah of Hosts" (Zech. 14.16-18).

But *now?* No! An ambassador for God says anywhere, to the worst heathen, "Believe on the Lord Jesus Christ, and thou shalt be saved."

This is *the Divine goodness.*

Now, have the Gentiles continued in that goodness?

For if the Gentiles have not so continued, God's severity must be shown to them, as before to Israel: **thou SHALT BE CUT OFF.**

What then is the record? It is ghastly!

First, as to sending out the gospel: After nearly 2000 years, much of the human race knows nothing of Christ.

Then, as to salvation by grace preached to lost men, apart from law and from ordinances, we see, instead, "good character" preached up as the way of acceptance; the simple supper of the Lord called "these holy mysteries," and baptism, instead of a glad confession of a known Savior, relied on as a "means of regeneration."

Instead of simple gatherings (as at the first), of believers
unto the Name of Christ their Lord, relying on the presence
of the Holy Spirit solely, (as at the first), we see great Judao-
pagan temples, and an elaborate "service." And would this were
in Rome only!

Instead of the free, general common priesthood of believers,
in the fellowship of prayer and faith (as in apostolic days) we
see thousands upon thousands of professing Christians that
have never prayed nor praised openly in the assembly of His
saints; myriads who do not have even the assurance of salvation
(though Christ, who bore sin for them, has been received up
on high). Contrast with this Acts 2.42: "They continued steadfastly in the apostles' teaching and fellowship, in the breaking
of bread and the prayers."

We see open, general, horrible *idolatry,* in both the Greek
and Roman cathedrals; and a growing tendency to put up
"crosses" instead of preaching *"the word* of the cross," in so-
called "Protestant" places!

We see great State Churches, a thing unknown and impossible in Scripture; and we see professing Christians divided
into "denominations," each with its own "program,"—ignoring
wholly Paul's words in I Corinthians 1.12,13 and 3.2-4; and
not at all walking in the consciousness of *the One Body.* Indeed,
instead of the *unity of the Spirit,* they are ready to establish
horrible outward earthly *union,* of all "professing Christians,"
"modernists," and *Jews*—in short, all "religionists."*

So that the Gentiles will be "cut off" from that place of
Divine privilege which they now have (and which Israel
nationally has lost), and Israel will be restored to the privileged
place, as before. Of course this "cutting off" does not mean
that individual Gentiles cannot be saved! But, as in the Old

---

*That God is withdrawing from "denominational" Christianity is very evident.
"Modernists" control some denominations completely and the hideous unbelief of
"modernism" is infiltrating slowly every denomination. Honest souls familiar with
the facts all know this and are perplexed what to do. But God will take care
of His testimony,—indeed is doing so, by means of Bible conferences, Bible classes,
and gatherings for prayer in private homes—more and more after the early
Church pattern. As for Laodicean "property," the great churches, schools,
libraries, and what not, the devil is falling heir to them fast,—which need not
alarm the saints, for the early Church had none of these things, but Christ and
the Holy Ghost and God's Word only!

Testament, and in Matthew, Mark, and Luke, Israel will be honored as the center and spring of Divine blessing on earth; the Gentiles becoming again subordinate to Israel,—as to spiritual things; and having again to "go up to Jerusalem" to worship Jehovah. The Church, the Body of Christ, will of course have been translated to heaven before this order of things comes in. The Church is "the fulness of the Gentiles," of Romans 11.25.

Thus, instead of continuing in God's goodness, Gentile "Christendom" has set up the "Christian religion"; and has settled down upon earth as if the Church belonged here; and as if Christ might not come at any moment! If you dream Christendom has continued in the humble gospel of *grace,* and the *goodness* of God in giving His Son to shed His blood for lost sinners, just examine the "religious" pronouncements in the press!

Verse 23: **They also, if they continue not in their unbelief, shall be grafted in again**—We know from a multitude of prophecies that Israel will not continue in unbelief! Thank God for this! They must, of course, *see* to believe. But Zechariah 12.10 declares that in a future day they shall "look on Him whom they pierced"; while the eighth and ninth verses of Zechariah's very next chapter say, that, while "two parts of the nation shall be cut off and die," the third part shall be left,— "refined as silver" and "tried as gold is tried. They shall call on My name, and I will hear them: I will say, It is My people; and they shall say, Jehovah is my God."

"O earth, earth, earth, hear the word of the Lord!"—and not the false dreams of men that tell you "God is through with Israel forever." They make God a liar when they say that! For read Jeremiah 31.23-40: What does God mean otherwise than *what He plainly says in that passage?** Thank God, that while the Gentiles are going into darker unbelief every day, there will be a spared Remnant of Israel!

*It is a blessed fact that God's real saints, the true Church, are coming more and more, daily, into the light, and back into the simple faith of the beginning. This is most especially evident in the attitude of true believers in their expectancy of the coming of the Lord—a spirit that characterized the early Church for 300 years! Nevertheless, what we say is true, as reads Isaiah: "Darkness shall cover the earth, and gross darkness the peoples."

Verse 24: **Thou, a wild olive, grafted contrary to nature into a good olive tree**—In the process of grafting we select a shoot of a fruit-bearing limb of a desirable tree, and opening the bark of an inferior tree of the same species, we insert the shoot, tying it in well. Then, behold, this inferior tree supplies sap to this good shoot, but the engrafted shoot goes on to bear its own good variety and class of fruit, and not that of the inferior tree. This is *nature*.

Now, the exact contrary has been wrought by God in taking us Gentiles (who, God says, are "by nature a wild olive tree"), and grafting us into the good olive tree to "partake of the root and of the fatness" of the tree of Divine blessing,—of the promises given to Abraham and to his Seed. Thus, behold instead of the natural process of the shoot's producing its own quality of fruit, we produce that "fruit unto God," which belongs to the good olive tree, and not to the wild olive Gentile tree!

Now if this **contrary to nature** process has been wrought by God, how much rather, **how much more, shall the natural branches be grafted** back into their own olive tree? Of course, as Paul emphasizes in verse 13: "I am speaking to you that are Gentiles,"—that is, to you *as* Gentiles. Now in Christ, as Paul has plainly taught us elsewhere (Col. 3.11), "there cannot be Greek and Jew, circumcision and uncircumcision, barbarian, Scythian, bondman, freeman; but Christ is all and in all." Unless we clearly see that Paul in this chapter is not discussing Church truth, we shall become hopelessly mired. The apostle is not declaring here either the character, calling, destiny, or present privileges and walk of the Church, the assembly of God, the Body of Christ, the present house of God, the Bride for which the heavenly Bridegroom is coming,—none of these things.

The whole question in Romans Nine, Ten and Eleven is one of reconciling God's special calling and promises of Israel, the earthly people, with a gospel which sets aside that distinction, sets aside Israel's distinctive place for the present dispensation; and places the Gentiles in the place of direct Divine blessing, once enjoyed by Israel.

It is for this reason that Paul addresses us here as "Gentiles."* Paul is claiming nothing for the Jewish believer as over against the Gentile believer,—in Romans Eleven. He even says to the Galatians: "I beseech you, brethren, become as I am, for I also am as ye are." But inasmuch as God had lodged His promises in Abraham and in his Seed ("which is Christ"), Paul in all faithfulness must not only tear up by the roots the Jewish hopes based on natural descent, and refer all to God's sovereign grace; but he must also tell us Gentiles the *facts*. Those eight wonderful points of advantage spoken of by Paul at the beginning of Chapter Nine as pertaining to Israel (and which still do pertain to them), he cannot allow us Gentiles to ignore, lest we come into a sense of personal importance (such as puffed up Israel), and say, **Branches were broken off that we might be grafted in.**

Now God did not, does not, make Israelites out of us Gentiles! He had a secret purpose kept from all the ages—of giving to His Son a Bride composed of Jewish and Gentile believers who should be received as mere guilty sinners, on purely *grace* grounds; and should have the highest calling of any creatures— to be *members of Christ Himself*,—a thing never promised to Israel.

While not speaking here of our heavenly calling in Christ, Paul yet must tell us plainly that Israel were the natural, earthly

---

*In discussing the heavenly calling of the church in Ephesians 2.11-15 Paul refers to us thus: "Remember that once ye, the Gentiles in the flesh, who are called 'Uncircumcision' by that which is called 'Circumcision,' in the flesh, made by hands; that ye were at that time separate from Christ, alienated from the commonwealth of Israel, and strangers from the covenants of the promise, having no hope and without God in the world. But now in Christ Jesus ye that once were far off are made nigh in the blood of Christ. For He is our peace, who made both one, and brake down the middle wall . . . having abolished in His flesh the enmity, the Law of commandments . . . that He might create in Himself of the two ONE NEW MAN, so making peace."

In the first part of Ephesians 2, we are seen "dead through our trespasses and sins," and are "made alive together with Christ, and raised up with Him and made to sit with Him in the heavenlies, in Christ Jesus"; but in the second part of the same chapter, our Gentile place as "far off," "aliens," is contrasted with the place of Israel, who were "nigh." But mark: God does not *Himself* recognize in Ephesians the distinction between circumcision and uncircumcision: He merely says that the Gentiles are *called* "Uncircumcision" by that which is *called* "Circumcision." For the circumcision had become in God's sight uncircumcision. "For he is not a Jew who is one outwardly"; so that it is merely a distinction circumcised sinners made with regard to uncircumcised sinners. In the real fact, "There is no distinction (between Jew and Gentile), for all have sinned and come short of the glory of God."

branches of the tree of promise, some of which, through their unbelief, were broken off. It is the matter of sharing Divine mercy, and not of the Christian calling, which is being discussed.

Let us ask ourselves, and frankly answer, these questions:

Did God once have a house on earth?

The answer must be, Yes.

Where? At Jerusalem, certainly. Our Lord at the beginning of His ministry called that temple "My Father's house"; and at the end of His ministry "My house"; and finally said to the blind leaders of Israel: *"Your* house is left unto you desolate."

Will God restore to Israel His earthly House?

He will, as we know, at Christ's coming back to earth. And we are told it will be upon Mount Zion in Jerusalem. See James' prophecy in Acts 15, quoted from Amos 9.11,12.

But meanwhile, between our Lord's absence in Heaven and His second coming, does God have a house?

We know that He does.

What is that house? Paul says that the Church *(ekklesia)* is now God's House. "But if I tarry long, that thou mayest know how men ought to behave themselves in the house of God, which is the Church of the living God, the pillar and ground of the truth" (I Tim. 3.15). The house of God is the Church of the Living God. Here God the Holy Spirit dwells both in individual believers, Jew and Gentile; and also, in a corporate way, in the Assembly of God's saints.

This House was formed first on the day of Pentecost, when the Holy Spirit came down to dwell in those believers. And from thence: "From Jerusalem and in all Judea and Samaria, and unto the uttermost part of the earth"—"where two or three are gathered" in the name of Christ.

Will this Church or Assembly ever be connected with Israel?

In no wise! Christ has built His Assembly, the Church, and is building it. But He first *broke down* the middle wall of partition, "the Law of commandments, in ordinances"—the thing which differentiated Israel from Gentiles: and in which Israel gloried. From both Jewish and Gentile believers Christ is now creating ONE NEW MAN!

But whence do these blessings come?

From the promises made to Abraham! Abraham was the root, and from the promises to him comes the fatness.

But after the Church has been taken to Heaven, God will again bless Israel.

25   For I would not, brethren, have you ignorant of
      this mystery, lest ye be wise in your own conceits,
      that a hardening in part hath befallen Israel, until
26   the fulness of the Gentiles be come in; and so all
      Israel shall be saved: even as it is written,
          There shall come out of Zion the Deliverer;
          He shall turn away ungodlinesses from Jacob:
27   And this is the covenant from Me unto them,
      When I shall take away their sins.
28   As touching the gospel, they are enemies for your
      sake: but as touching the election, they are be-
29   loved for the fathers' sake. For the gifts and the
30   calling of God are not repented of. For as ye in
      time past were disobedient to God, but now have
31   obtained mercy by their disobedience, even so have
      these also now been disobedient, that by the mercy
      shown to you they also may now obtain mercy.
32   For God hath shut up all unto disobedience, that
      He might have mercy upon all.

Verse 25: For I would not have you ignorant, brethren, of this mystery—Note that in saying "brethren," Paul is speaking now to the saints as such: for even real saints, while not to be "cut off," may become "puffed up." Now we have elsewhere remarked that God had certain *secrets,* which He tells His saints,—and of which they do not well to be ignorant,—as, alas, so many of them are! Here then, is stated to us one of these Divine mysteries, or secrets: and it will protect us from Gentile pride, in these days of the dazzling greatness of the Gentile times depicted in Daniel (e.g., Dan. 2 and 3)—lest ye be wise in your own conceits (as behold the vauntings of a blind Hitler* and his Gentile "Aryans," and the boastings of a Mussolini of Roman-Gentile-greatness!) **that a hardening in part hath befallen Israel, until the fulness of the Gentiles be come in.**

Note here:

1. There is a definite **fulness** of Gentiles—the very number of which God knoweth—to "come in," that is, to be saved: for this word "fulness" is not spoken as to privilege, but as to election.

2. In order for these Gentiles to come in, a "hardening," judicial and sovereign, hath befallen national Israel.

3. All talk, therefore, of Israel's national turning to the Lord, until this Gentile **fulness** be come in, is vain. The fearful days of Armageddon will have to come, ere Israel, nationally turns to God. Read Zechariah 12-14.

4. Israel's **hardening** is *in part,*—for some, "the Remnant according to the *election of grace,*" are now being saved. National hardening is in view here.

And so—after this Divinely revealed order, we read,

Verse 26: **And so all Israel shall be saved**—This is the real, elect, spared nation of the future,—"those written unto life" (Dan. 12.1; Isa. 4.3, margin). The *mystery* comprehends this fact (as we have said above, and as the apostle amplifies in verse 31) for the salvation of national Israel was *impossible,* except on purely *grace* lines. God had given them the Law: that was necessary to reveal sin. But they utterly failed. Now comes in the fulness of the Gentiles—by

---

*We find in Scripture (Ezekiel 38 and 39) a horrid confederation of evil headed by the "prince of Rosh, Meshech and Tubal," which Bible students commonly accept as Russia, Moscow and Tobolsk; with which is allied Persia, Cush, Put, Gomer, and the house of Togarmah—"even many peoples with thee." They go to cut off re-established Israel, just before the Millennial days described in Ezekiel 40 to 48. Now we know from the Second Psalm and many other Scriptures, that the nations of earth will all finally rebel, and that intelligently, against Jehovah, and against His Anointed, saying, "Let us break Their bonds asunder, and cast away Their cords from us."

We do not wonder, then, that these North-European nations are first to come out into open God-defying: Russia with its atheism, and then Hitler, with his arrogant anti-Scripture conceit concerning Aryans, willing to go back to the pagan deities of Northern Europe. The word of prophecy connects these northern nations —including Germany—in a great confederacy: however far apart they may seem to be at present.

grace: and so, after that, and on the same grace line as were the Gentiles, **all Israel shall be saved!** Most of that earthly nation will perish under Divine judgments, and the Antichrist: but *the Remnant* will be "accounted as a generation." Our Lord told His disciples that this present unbelieving generation of Israel would not pass away till all the terrible judgments He foretold would be fulfilled. But that that generation—"Israel *after the flesh*" will pass away we know; and a believing generation take their place. See Psalm 22.30; 102.18. Jehovah at last "arises, and has pity on her,—for the set time has come!" So we read the Psalmist's words:

"This shall be written for *the generation to come;*
And a people which *shall be created* shall praise Jehovah."

This is the real *Israel of God,* of whom it is written, "All Israel shall be saved."

Verses 26,27: And now, as is usual with Paul, the Old Testament prophecies of Isaiah throng into his mind, by the Spirit:

There shall come out of Zion the Deliverer;
He shall turn away ungodliness from Jacob:
And this is the covenant from Me,
When I shall take away their sins.

There are three aspects of Christ's second coming: (1) For the Rapture of the Church; (2) For the Judgment of the Nations; (3) For the Deliverance of Israel.

The second of these aspects, Christ's coming to judge the nations, has been recognized through the centuries, almost to the exclusion of the first and third aspects of our Lord's coming. Christ has been regarded as the Judge; and this of course He will be, as Revelation Nineteen shows Him,—"King of kings, and Lord of lords—in righteousness judging and making war," "treading the winepress of the fierceness of the wrath of God, the Almighty." But the creeds of Christendom have taught one "general judgment," and thus they have overlooked two most essential things: first, The special relationship of Christ's coming to His real Church; and second, The relationship of His coming to the nation of Israel, and to the elect spared Remnant of that nation—to the real *Israel.*

Concerning the first, the Rapture of the Church, we have only to read I Thessalonians 4.13 to 17:

"— The Lord Himself shall descend from heaven, with a shout, with the voice of the archangel, and with the trump of God: and the dead in Christ shall rise first; then we that are alive, that are left, shall together with them be caught up in the clouds, to meet the Lord in the air: and so shall we ever be with the Lord." And also: "— We all shall not sleep, but we shall all be changed, in a moment, in the twinking of an eye, at the last trump: for the trumpet shall sound, and the dead shall be raised incorruptible, and we shall be changed" (I Cor. 15.50 ff).

To whom does this phase of His coming refer? We read in Ephesians Five that Christ will "present the Church unto Himself, a glorious Church, not having spot or wrinkle, or any such thing"; and that "we wait for a Savior from heaven, the Lord Jesus Christ, who shall fashion anew the body of our humiliation, that it may be conformed to the body of His glory" (Phil. 3.20,21); and that Paul called those whom he had won to Christ as his "hope and crown of glorying before our Lord Jesus, at His coming" (I Thess. 2.19). Now the calling of the Church and that of Israel are *never confused in Scripture.* Israel as a nation does not belong to heaven, but to the land which God has given them forever, by a solemn covenant with Abraham, Isaac, and Jacob. And this "Rapture," or catching of the Church up to Christ, is a hope belonging to the Church: not to Israel.

The third stage of our Lord's return is for the restoration of Israel to that Divine favor connected with the "New Covenant" and the national "taking away their sins." This presupposes the absence from earth of the Church: for God cannot have the two testimonies on earth at the same time! In the Church there is no distinction of Jew or Greek, neither has the Church outward religious ceremonial service (*latreia*), which belongs to Israel (Rom. 9.4). Furthermore, the Church has a commission to all nations, including Israel, to evangelize them. None of these things can belong to the Church when Israel shall have been restored. The Church will have been caught up to meet the Lord in the air (I Thess. 4.17), and will have glorified bodies like Christ's; while Israel will be His nation upon the earth, in Palestine.

Then what about Israel's *hope*? All through the prophets, we find their hope is to be *gathered back to their own land,* and established there with their Messiah in their midst—Jehovah "dwelling with them in majesty"; their eyes "seeing the King in His beauty"; and complete and eternal deliverance there from all their enemies and from all their own iniquities. So verse 26 reads: **There shall come out of Zion the Deliverer.** Hear what James tells us in Acts 15 in giving the dispensational program of God (which no denominational "standards" nor "a millennial" sophistry can change!) : "Brethren, hearken unto me: Simeon hath rehearsed how first God visited the Gentiles, to take out of them a people for His name." (The present dispensation). "And to this agree the words of the prophets; as it is written:

"After these things I will return,
And I will build again the tabernacle of David, which
  is fallen;
And I will build again the ruins thereof,
And I will set it up:
That the residue of men may seek after the Lord,
And all the Gentiles upon whom My name is called,
Saith the Lord, Who maketh these things known from of
  old." (From the First Church Council Records: Acts
  15.13-18.)

Now even instructed Christians, who know about the Rapture of the Church, and the Judgment of the Lord upon the nations shortly after that Rapture, when He comes on down to earth, are apt to neglect or under-emphasize the fact that He comes to earth for *the Deliverance of His people Israel*. But the prophets are full of this subject. Perhaps no passage is more overwhelming than the last chapter of Habakkuk—the prophet's marvelous vision of our Lord's glorious return!*

---

*God came from Teman,
And the Holy One from Mount Paran.

It is a picture of the Remnant of Israel, who put their trust in Jehovah amid the overwhelming awfulness of the "Great Tribulation"; the stupendous signs in sun, moon, and stars at the end of that Great Tribulation; and the unutterable glory and majesty of the Day of Wrath. Read the 46th Psalm (R. V. is better). It is again the godly Remnant of Israel, in those days.

We have just listened to the coronation ceremonies of the King of England (1937), and have been deeply moved, and filled with thanksgiving that God has preserved to this day an Empire that publicly acknowledges the Name of the Father, Son, and Holy Ghost. We pray for the continuance of that Empire as long as it be God's will, for the British flag wherever flown has protected the gospel of Christ.

Nevertheless, dark days are coming, when all nations, under the direct influence of demonic powers, will be "gathered together unto the war of the great day of God the Almighty," "into the place which is called in Hebrew Har-Magedon"—gathered "to cut off Israel from being a nation" (Rev. 16.12-16; Ps. 83.4; Zech. 14; Joel 3.9-15). But while we read:

His glory covered the heavens,
And the earth was full of His praise.

. . .

He stood, and measured the earth;
He beheld, and drove asunder the nations;

. . .

Was Jehovah displeased with the rivers?
Was Thine anger against the rivers,
Or Thy wrath against the sea,
That Thou didst ride upon Thy horses,
Upon Thy chariots of salvation?
Thy bow was made quite bare;
The *oaths to the tribes* were a sure word.
Thou didst march through the land of Israel in indignation;
Thou didst thresh the nations in anger.
Thou wentest forth for the *salvation of thy people* [Israel],
For victory with Thine Anointed [Christ].

And then (Verse 13) there is the smiting of "the wicked man" (Antichrist), and the piercing of "the head of his warriors." This is exactly what we find, of course, in Revelation 19.19 to 21! And see the faith even in those terrible days preceding Christ's return.
"I heard, and my body trembled, . . .
Because I must wait quietly for the day of trouble [the Great Tribulation].
For the coming up of the people that invadeth us [all nations: see Zechariah
    14.1,2; Joel 3.9-17].
For though the fig-tree shall not flourish,
The vines . . . the olive, . . . the fields . . . the flock [be] cut off,
Yet I *will rejoice in Jehovah*,
ᵀ ᵚill joy in the God of my salvation!"*

"Multitudes, multitudes in the valley of decision! for the day of Jehovah is near in the valley of decision! The sun and the moon are darkened, and the stars withdraw their shining. And Jehovah will roar from Zion, and utter His voice from Jerusalem; and the heavens and the earth shall shake" (Joel 3.14-16),—

We also read these words of comfort from God to Israel:

"But Jehovah will be a refuge *unto His people,* and a stronghold to the children of Israel. So shall ye know that I am Jehovah your God, dwelling in Zion my holy mountain."*

We make no excuse for spending time here, for the Holy Spirit devotes very many pages to this exact subject of Jehovah's Deliverance of His people Israel by the coming back to earth to them of their Messiah in great power and glory.

Let us then study these three phases or aspects of our Lord's return with balanced time and care: the Rapture of the Church; the Judgment of the Nations; and the Deliverance of Israel.

Verse 27: **This is the covenant from Me when I shall take away their sins**—we give the literal rendering. It will be no longer a conditional covenant, as at Sinai; but one of *grace*— "from ME!" See Jeremiah 31;† Ezekiel 36 and 37; and Daniel

---

*The words "out of Zion shall come forth a Deliverer" have puzzled many, and indeed there are real difficulties here. The quotation is from Isaiah 59.20, "a Redeemer will come to Zion." But let us look at certain facts: There are two mountains in Jerusalem, one Mount Moriah, where the former temple was built; and the other, the higher, Mount Zion. Here, when David became king, the Jebusites had a stronghold. David's first desire when made king over all the people was to take this stronghold of the enemy (II Sam. 5.7; I Chron. 11.5). It was thereafter called "the city of David, which is Zion" (I Kings 8.1). Now in the quotation from James in Acts 15, we find that the Lord upon His return "will build again the tabernacle of David," meaning on Mount Zion, not Moriah (for typical things shall have passed away). And concerning Zion we read in Isaiah 4.3,4: "And it shall come to pass, that he that is left in Zion, and he that remaineth in Jerusalem, shall be called holy, even every one that is written among the living in Jerusalem; when the Lord shall have washed away the filth of the daughters of Zion, and shall have purged the blood of Jerusalem from the midst thereof, by the Spirit of justice, and by the Spirit of burning." The expression of Rom. 11.26,27: "There shall come out of Zion the Deliverer; He shall turn away ungodlinesses from Jacob" becomes clearer, verse 26 showing Christ delivering Israel from their ungodlinesses, and verse 27 showing Christ establishing His earthly Temple and Throne on Mount Zion, and "uttering His Voice" from thence. See Amos 1.2.

†There is a beautiful view of God's mercy to His people in the time of the Tribulation, in Jeremiah 31.2: "Thus saith Jehovah, The people that were left of the sword found favor in the wilderness; even Israel, when he went to find him rest" (margin). In Revelation 12.14 we see the woman, Israel, fleeing into the wilderness and nourished for three years and a half in a marvelous way, as

9.24,—in which we see six distinct blessings come to Israel at the end of the Divine "indignation" against His nation; Isaiah 32.1,8,16,20; all of Isaiah 35. This is the "New Covenant" of Jeremiah 31, quoted in Hebrews 8.8 to 12. It will not be "according to the covenant that God made with their fathers." Blessing will not depend then on man's obedience; but it will be *sovereign mercy,* at last extended to a whole spared nation (Jer. 31.33,34; Rom. 11.28,29).

Verse 28: We should remember two things, always, when we see an Israelite: first, **As touching the gospel, they are enemies for your sake**; and second: **As touching the election, they are beloved for the fathers' sake** (Abraham, Isaac, and Jacob). Gentile believers are so prone to forget both these things, especially if they behold a poor wretched son of Israel, or a proud and self-vaunting one, or even a wealthy one! Anti-Semitism, or Jew-hatred, arises, first, from Gentile rebellion against the Divine national election of Israel; and second, from envy toward them because of their wealth and power. Let no Christian give way to anti-Semitism. Of course, we must "judge righteous judgment," form unbiased opinions, of their beliefs; for many of them, like Spinoza in rationalism, and Marx and Engels in Communism, have been peculiarly used of the devil. Nevertheless, we dare not yield to Gentile hatred of Israelites. For our Lord is, after the flesh, of Israel; and God has vast gracious blessing for them shortly!

Verse 29: **For the gifts and the calling of God are not repented of** (by Him). These words are a source of endless joy. We may trust a God who refuses to allow the utter failure

during the 40 years in the wilderness in Sinai after Egypt. Note that Jeremiah says, "The people that were *left of the sword.*" This cannot refer to Israel as coming up from Egypt, but must look toward that "Remnant" left after the terrible cutting off of the most of fleshly Israel, as seen in Ezek. 20.32-38, R. V.; Isa. 10.22,23. This Remnant flees when Antichrist is revealed, and escapes death at his hands. Isaiah 16.3 and 4, the Moabites are commanded by God to protect these fleeing ones of Israel: "Make thy shade as the night in the midst of the noonday; hide the outcasts; betray not the fugitive. Let Mine outcasts dwell with thee; as for Moab, be thou a convert to him from the face of the destroyer." The words immediately following, "For the extortioner is brought to nought, destruction ceaseth, the oppressors are consumed out of the land. And a throne shall be established in lovingkindness; and One shall sit thereon in truth, in the tent of David, judging, and seeking justice, and swift to do righteousness"— these words (Isa. 16.4,5) reveal the Deliverance that is about to come at that time.

of Israel—nay, the idolatrous wickedness and apostasy of Israel —to alter His determination of blessing. The "gifts" are such as were recited in Chapter 9.4,5; and the "calling" is, that Israel is a holy nation unto God Himself. And He will see that it is so, not only in the coming kingdom, the Millennium; but in the new creation: "For as the new heavens and the new earth, which I will make, shall remain before Me, saith Jehovah, so shall your seed and your name Israel remain" (Isa. 66.22).

Verses 30-32: **For as ye in time past were disobedient to God, but now have obtained mercy by their [Israel's] disobedience, even so have these also now been disobedient, that by the mercy shown to you [Gentiles] they also may now obtain mercy. For God hath shut up all unto disobedience that He might have mercy upon all**—God brings in the principle upon which He will bless Israel when He makes His New Covenant with them at Christ's second coming. It seems that we Gentiles are to be to Israel an example of Divine *mercy*, by which at last they will understandingly see the "heart of mercy" of their God! (Luke 1.78, margin).

Our Gentile history is summed up in the words "disobedient to God"; our present position in the words: "have obtained mercy by their [Israel's] disobedience"; and now Israel nationally have been more disobedient even than the Gentiles: disobedient to God's Law, to His warning prophets, to His own dear Son, their Messiah, whom they crucified; to the witness of the Spirit through Stephen and the apostles of the resurrection of the Messiah. But at last they will "obtain mercy,"* a new principle for them!

---

*To render verse 31 (as the Latin Vulgate, Luther, Darby, and others, insist on doing), "been disobedient to our [Gentile] mercy," not only is a straining of the text, but also wholly defeats understanding of the passage. The Gentile world in verse 30 is seen as disobedient to God, that is, living in sin and idolatry. But the disobedience of the Jews, (verse 31), was the rejection of their Messiah and particularly of the apostolic testimony of His resurrection. When the Jews believed, it was called "being obedient to the faith" (Acts 6.7); and, "God hath given the Holy Spirit to them that obey Him" in believing (Acts 5.32).

Notice that the question of Gentile salvation had not at that time come up at all! In the synagogue at Ephesus some of the Jews were "hardened and disobedient, speaking evil of *the Way*" (Acts 19.9). It was rejecting the way of salvation by faith apart from works, and faith in God's message concerning the Christ whom their nation had rejected and crucified—this constituted Jewish disobedience.

Having proved utterly disobedient, having lost all claim on God, they will at last be met by God on the same great principle of *mercy,* and *mercy alone.* So that in the future age, the Millennium, and on forever,* this nation will carry in its heart the two great principles that give God all the glory: first, that they were beloved of Jehovah, who had set His love upon them, the only reason being in Himself. "Because Jehovah loveth you, and because He would keep the oath which He sware unto your fathers" (Deut. 7.7,8). Second, the consciousness of their own complete failure: of a history of ingratitude, rebellion,

---

*But there is another deep truth also: Christ was made to become sin, and died unto sin, and unto all connection with man in sin. When our Lord was raised as the First-born from among the dead, it was in the "power of an endless life." He showed Himself alive, indeed, to His disciples, saying, "Handle me and see; for a spirit hath not flesh and bones, as ye behold me having" (Luke 24.39), and He even ate with them. Nevertheless, His body was on resurrection ground, as heavenly as His spirit. And we shall have bodies like unto His glorious body, but it will be only when we shall be "changed," at our Lord's coming; when "this corruptible puts on incorruption, and this mortal puts on immortality."

Even as regards God's counsels toward the spared Remnant of Israel during the Millennium, as well as toward all the earth,—while the eyes of the Remnant shall "see the King in His beauty," and His glory shall be seen over the millennial temple by all nations; yet, as it seems to me, not until after the Millennium, will even Israel share that new creation place that the Church now, and the saints of Revelation 20.4, enter on before and during the Millennium. See Isaiah 65.17,18; 66.22.

Of course, both the Remnant and those of the nations who bow in real worship during the Millennium, will share spiritual life in Christ, for then will be completely fulfilled Pentecost, which Isaiah describes as the time when "the Spirit is poured out on us from on high" (Isa. 32.15); but it is not until "the new heaven and the new earth" wherein the seed and name of Israel shall remain (Isa. 66.22), that even that nation will be fully on new creation ground, such as the Church, members of Christ, are now as to their spirits, and will be shortly, as to their bodies, at the Rapture.

When today poor blinded Jewish rabbis and elders claim "Jesus of Nazareth" as belonging to them, as "one of their prophets," "perhaps the greatest one," it causes in the heart of the instructed Christian, only a lament. Christ was indeed, as to His flesh, born of them; but they rejected and crucified Him; and He is passed into a new creation, and is the last Adam, a Second Man, *with whom the Jewish nation as such has as yet no connection,* any more than have unbelieving Gentiles. "Except a man be born from above he CANNOT SEE the kingdom of God!"

Romans 11.32 must be connected with Galatians 3.22: "The Scripture shut up all things under sin, that the promise of faith in Christ Jesus might be given to them that believe," with "God hath shut up all unto disobedience, that He might have mercy upon all." This does not make God the author of disobedience: —man, whether Gentile or Jew, is responsible for that. As for the Gentiles, God, since Babel, "suffered all the nations to walk in their own ways" (Acts 14.16). Then He met them in the way of sovereign mercy, which they were *not seeking.* As for the Jews, God brought them unto Himself, gave them His Law, sent His prophets and His Son, and they despised all, even the offer of national pardon. Thus, the Jews were "disobedient" to God's way with *them.* But, by the example of Gentile mercy, they also will obtain mercy.

wickedness, idolatry, refusal of instruction and correction, and finally, of despising and rejecting their own Messiah (II Chron. 36.14-16; Ps. 106). They will be brokenly conscious forever of being the objects of the absolute *uncaused mercy* of Jehovah their God! Thus they will be able to trust and rejoice in Jehovah, as the true Church-saint now trusts and rejoices and glories in God as the Father of our Lord Jesus Christ who associated us with His own Son in the same sovereign mercy!

It must be carefully marked and deeply pondered, this great account of sovereign mercy,—mercy first to us, and by and by to Israel,—"the MERCIES of God," by means of which God will win our hearts, "beseeching us" by His apostle, to present our bodies a living sacrifice to Him (12.1). It is not only that God has dealt with us in *grace*,—unearned favor; but that He has shown *mercy* when all was hopeless! We may venture to say that it is only in those who learn to regard themselves as the objects of the Divine mercy, of uncaused Divine compassion, that the deepest foundations for godliness of life will be, or can be, laid.

Now the apostle bursts forth into most rapturous utterance concerning the ways of God—in view of His mercies;—as shown to us as traced in Chapters One to Eight; and yet to be shown to Israel, as told in Chapters Nine to Eleven:

33   **O the depth of the riches both of the wisdom and the knowledge of God! How unsearchable are His**
34   **judgments, and His ways past tracing out! For who hath known the mind of the Lord? or who**
35   **hath been His counsellor? or who hath first given to Him, and it shall be recompensed unto Him**
36   **again? For of Him, and through Him, and unto Him, are all things! To Him be the glory unto the ages! Amen.**

When one turns from the contemplation of what we have been reading in Romans to man's poor books,—there is immediate revulsion and constant weariness! The poverty! the shallowness! of this world!—whether its philosophy, its science, its poetry, yea, or its religion, all is vanity! As Paul says, "The wisdom of this world is foolishness with God"; "The Lord

knoweth the reasonings of the wise that they are vain" (I
Cor. 3.19,20).

Verse 33: Paul is overwhelmed at **the depth of the riches
both of the wisdom and the knowledge of God;**—and here
is where we all join Paul: in adoring contemplation of God's
counsels,—the wisdom with which He brings them forth, and the
knowledge of man and of his heart and his history, past,
present, and future, that He displays in it all.

Verse 34: **For who hath known the mind of the Lord?**
None, till He choose to unfold it! We are, as we see in verse
25, ignorant of God's secrets; and we have no means, except
He please to tell us, of discovering His mind. Bless God that
He has "made known unto us the secret ["the mystery"] of
His will, according to His good pleasure which He purposed in
Christ" (Eph. 1.9). Men today come from Italy and boast
loudly if they have had a talk with the "dictator" there; or from
Germany, and say, The great "leader" of Germany let me in
to his plans; or from Washington, and boast that they have had
"inside information" concerning those that are prominent there.
But what are these rulers all? Bits of dust! God declares that
in His sight the nations are "accounted as the small dust of the
balance," and that "the rulers of this age are coming to nothing"
(Isa. 40.15; I Cor. 2.6).

Now may God give us grace to realize at least a little of our
mighty privilege in having revealed to us the mind of the Lord,
the God of hosts.

> "Thus saith Jehovah,
> Let not the wise man glory in his wisdom,
> Neither let the mighty man glory in his might,
> Let not the rich man glory in his riches;
> But let him that glorieth glory in this,
> That he hath understanding, and knoweth Me,
> That I am Jehovah who exerciseth loving kindness,
> Justice, and righteousness, in the earth:
> For in these things I delight,
> Saith Jehovah" (Jer. 9.23,24).

Or who hath been His counsellor? As God said to Job: "Where wast thou when I laid the foundations of the earth?" We know, if we are Christ's, that we are in Him, of whom Isaiah wrote, "His name shall be called Wonderful, Counsellor, Mighty God, Father of Eternity, Prince of Peace" (Isa. 9.6). Of Christ God speaks: He is "The Man that is my Fellow, saith Jehovah of hosts" (Zech. 13.7). Christ has been made the Wisdom of God unto us: there is no other real wisdom! When the present creation has passed away,—with the very "laws" that are said to "govern" it; and God creates a new heaven and a new earth, all but God's saints will be *eternally ignorant!* For all the natural man knows is the present creation: whereas of the new creation God says, "Behold, I make *all things new!*" This will include the very mode and manner of existence: and what does "science" know about *that?* Of our Lord's resurrection *body,* for example! And with none of God's saints, or of His angels, or of the seraphim or the cherubim, took He counsel, when He created all things! Nor does He take counsel of any, in the New Creation!

Verse 35: **Or who hath first given to Him and it shall be recompensed unto Him again?** How beautifully this puts us in our place! "What hast thou that thou didst not receive? And if thou hast received it, why dost thou glory as if thou hadst not received it?" (I Cor. 4.7). Men love to think of themselves as "creators" of this and of that. But man has created nothing. He is the user, for a few days, of this present creation of God. He may even "discover" some substance or force that God long since created. Man must needs boast of his "inventions," his "creations," his greatness, and especially his "progress." But alack, the undertaker comes along and hauls him away!

Yes, says Paul, if somebody has actually supplied something to God, God will quickly recompense him! He will be in no creature's debt!

Verse 36: **For of Him** (God)—as the one great Cause and Source; **and through Him** as the mighty Worker who without creature-assistance brings into effect, into realization, one by one, His counsels; **and unto Him** as the right and proper, and necessary object and end—(for how could a *crea ture* be a *final object?*—it would ruin the creature—make a Satan of him; and it would be unrighteous for the creature to be made the end or object of the glory of the Creator!)—**are all things**—note, **all things!** In this the saints exult! Against this, the serpent and his seed constantly fight and war. If Satan cannot get himself worshipped, he will beget in man's wicked mind a philosophy of "evolution"—a theory that all things came about by blind uncaused "development." But men, professing themselves to be wise, always become "fools."*

All things—The sun, the moon, the stars of light, the earth, the atmosphere, the trees, the animals, our bodies,—for those who study the human frame agree with David, "I am fearfully and wonderfully made!" Our minds,—with powers, as Locke says "capable of almost anything."

> "Who hath put wisdom in the inward parts?
> Or who hath given understanding to the mind?"
>
> (Job 38.36).

Our spirits also,—which can be spoken to directly by the Spirit of God Himself, putting us thus into intelligent conversation with the infinite Creator of all things: Yea, "of Him, through Him, unto Him are *all things!*"

And now the ascription of His proper honor forevermore: **To Him be the glory unto the ages!** What a prospect for a redeemed sinner! In the ages to come—ages of worship without end, in which glory will be ascribed to God,—and that with ever-increasing delight! And the word of eager, glad heart-consent ends it all: **Amen.**

---

*Hear Voltaire, the brilliant French infidel in the eighteenth century, speak of Sir Isaac Newton (one of the greatest minds and godliest men of history): "Look at the migthy mind of Newton. When he got into his dotage he began to study the book called the Bible; and it seems, in order to credit its fabulous nonsense, we must believe (says Newton) that the knowledge of mankind will be so increased that we shall be able to travel at fifty miles per hour. The poor dotard!" (Newton had been studying and writing upon Daniel 12.4: "Many shall run to and fro, and knowledge shall be increased," when he made this prediction.)

At Daytona Beach, in Florida, a few miles from my home, a man recently traveled nearly six times fifty miles per hour! So it seems Voltaire was the fool, the "dotard," and not Newton! And the very room in which Voltaire asserted, "A hundred years after I am dead the Bible will be an unknown book"—is now a wareroom of the British and Foreign Bible Society!

We find, then, in Romans Eleven:

1. That God has not cast off Israel, a Remnant being always preserved—this Remnant now, "the election of grace."

2. That all but the election were hardened,—to let the fulness of the Gentiles come in: for the purpose of provoking Israel to "jealousy,"—that they might discover Jehovah's mercy.

3. That although broken off from the stalk of blessing, they will be grafted back into "their own olive tree."

4. That this will be at the coming to Zion in Jerusalem of the Lord Jesus Christ; and that then a New Covenant will be made with Israel.

5. That the Gentile will be cut off from the present privilege-place, for not continuing in God's "goodness" (His grace to sinners); and the place of direct Divine blessing again be taken by Israel, who will return from their unbelief.

6. That this most solemn fact should warn Gentiles against individual self-confidence, and especially against the fearful delusion that Israel has been "cast away" forever, and that the Gentiles have taken their place! God has made no covenants with any nation but Israel; and that nation He will restore, the Gentiles becoming then dependent on blessing, through Israel, throughout the future.

7. That instead of being unfaithful to His promises to Israel, God has simply exercised His sovereignty (1) in cutting off Israel for the present; (2) in calling in the fulness of the Gentiles on the principle of mercy only; (3) in taking away from Israel, whom He exalted and to whom He gave His law, all claims upon Him either by national descent, personal righteousness, or any covenant commitments (for they rejected their promises and crucified their Messiah): thus shutting them up to the one great principle of *mercy*.

It cannot be too much emphasized that Chapters Nine, Ten, and Eleven do not teach that the *Church as such* has succeeded the Jews in the place of blessing; but do show that Gentiledom has received the place of privilege and opportunity, and consequently of responsibility, that Israel once had. Through not continuing in the Divine "goodness," Gentiledom will be cut off as directly blessed of God, and will be blessed through restored Israel only, in the future, after Christ's return, the Rapture of the Church, and the setting up of the Millennial Kingdom.

This blessing of Gentiles will be much wider and greater when Israel is restored. But the blessing will be of *another order,*—and *not so high an order* as that enjoyed by believers today, who are members of Christ's Body! Now, "there is no difference between Jew and Greek." But, when the Lord returns to Zion: "In those days ten men shall take hold, out of all the languages of the nations, they shall take hold of the skirt of him that is a Jew, saying, We will go with you, for we have heard that *God is with you!*" (Zech. 8.23).

To gather, as we now may do, in the name of the Lord Jesus and with the conscious presence of the Holy Spirit, and with direct communion with God through our Lord Jesus Christ, as the Assembly of God, the Church, is indescribably a greater privilege than going as part of a national delegation up to Jerusalem to "worship the King, Jehovah of Hosts"; although at that time the glory will be openly manifest at Jerusalem. Then it will be walking by sight, which is ever a lower path than walking by faith. No Gentile—nor Israelite either, for that matter,—will say in the Millennium, "For me to live is Christ!" God has today "made us alive together with Christ, and raised us up with Him, and made us sit in the heavenlies in Christ Jesus." We are in Christ, and Christ is in us, "the hope of glory!"

Alas, alas, how little do we appreciate our place as Church saints!

CHAPTER TWELVE

Paul's Great Plea for Personal Consecration to God, in View of His Mercies; God's Perfect Will for Each Believer thus Discovered. Verses 1 and 2.

For We are One Body in Christ, with Varying Gifts. Verses 3-8.

Our Walk toward Others, whether Believers, or Enemies. Verses 9 to 21.

1   I beseech you, therefore, brethren, by the mercies of God, to present your bodies a living sacrifice, holy, acceptable to God, which is your spirit-
2   ual service.   And be not fashioned according to this age: but be ye transformed by the renewing of your mind, that ye may prove [in experience] what is the good and acceptable and perfect will of God.

Verse 1: **I BESEECH YOU** — What an astonishing word to come from God! From a God against whom we had sinned, and under whose judgment we were! What a word to us, believers,—a race of sinners so lately at enmity with God,— "I beseech you!" Paul had authority from Christ to command us,—as he said to Philemon: "Though I have all boldness in Christ to enjoin thee that which is befitting, yet for love's sake I rather beseech." Let us give heart-heed to this our apostle, who often covered with his tears the pages whereon he wrote. As he said of his ministry, "We are ambassadors therefore on behalf of Christ, as though God were entreating by us: we beseech—!"

And what does he cite to move us to hearken to the great appeal for our devotion to God which opens this section of Romans—this part that calls for our response to the great unfoldings of God's salvation in the previous chapters? **I BESEECH YOU BY THE MERCIES OF GOD!**

447

Let us call to mind these MERCIES of which Paul speaks:

1. JUSTIFICATION,—including pardon, removal of sins from us, trespasses never to be reckoned, a standing in Christ,—being made the righteousness of God in Him!

2. IDENTIFICATION—taken out of Adam by death with Christ,—dead to sin and to law, and now IN CHRIST!

3. UNDER GRACE, NOT LAW—Fruit unto God,—unto sanctification, made possible.

4. THE SPIRIT INDWELLING—"No condemnation," freedom from law of sin; witness of Sonship and Heirship.

5. HELP IN INFIRMITY, and in any present sufferings, on our way to share Christ's glory.

6. DIVINE ELECTION: Our final Conformity to Christ's Image as His brethren; God's settled Purpose,—in which, believers already glorified in God's sight!

7. COMING GLORY—beyond any comparison with present sufferings!

8. NO SEPARATION POSSIBLE—God loved us *in Christ*.

9. CONFIDENCE IN GOD'S FAITHFULNESS confirmed by His revealed plans for national Israel.

Present your bodies—This has been used to divide believers harshly into two classes,—those who have "presented their bodies" to God, and those who have not. But this is not the spirit of the passage. For God "beseeches" us to be *persuaded by His mercies*. He does not condemn us for past neglect, nor drive us in the matter of yielding to Him. We must believe that these Divine mercies *have persuasive powers* over our wills. It is not that we can move our own wills; but that faith in God's mercies, personally shown us, has power. It is "the goodness of God" that moves us,—when we really believe ourselves the free recipients of it!

So Paul beseeches us to **present our bodies** to God. We might have expected, Yield your spirits, to be controlled by the Holy Spirit. But Paul says, *bodies*. Now if a man should present his body for the service of another, willingly, it would carry all the man with it.* In the case of a slave, his master owns his body; so he does what his master says: often with inner reluctance. We are besought to present our bodies,— that is, willingly to do so. God, who made and owns us, and Christ, whose we are (see chapter 1.6, — "called as Jesus Christ's")—God, I say, might have said, Come, serve Me: it is your duty. That would have been law. But instead, *grace* is reigning, over us, and in us; and Paul says to us, I beseech you, present your bodies. And there and then, in a believing view of God's mercies, we find our hearts going forth. For there is great drawing power in the knowledge that someone has loved us, and given us such Divine bounties as these mercies!

A living sacrifice—This is in contrast with those slain offerings Israel brought to God. God's service is freedom, not slavery; life, not death. **Holy, acceptable unto God**—We remember that God said of Israel's offerings: "Whatsoever toucheth the altar shall be holy" (Ex. 29.37). It is very blessed to know that any believer's yielding his body to God is called a "holy, acceptable sacrifice,"—well-pleasing unto God Himself! That any creature should be able to offer what could "please" the infinite Creator, is wonderful; but that such wretched, fallen ones as the sons of men should do so, is a marvel of which only the gracious God Himself knows the depth!

Which is your spiritual service—Here "spiritual" or "intelligent" religious service *(logikē latreia)* is contrasted with that outward religious service Israel had in former days. They had the temple, with its prescribed rites, its "days, and months, and seasons and years," its ordinances and ceremonial observances. Indeed, it was right that they should carry out these ordinances as God directed. But, while it was "religious serv-

---

*A man desiring to enlist in the British army comes, after the physical examination, to present himself to the enlisting officer. He is still his own man. Then the enlisting officer gives him "the king's shilling"—as enlistment money. He signs an attestation as to his age, place of birth, trade, etc., and takes the oath of allegiance: "To be true and faithful to the king and his heirs, and truth and faith to bear of life and limb and terrene honour, and not to know or hear of any ill or damage intended him without defending him therefrom." Having accepted the king's money, and taken this oath, he is now legally the king's ~wn soldier.

ice" (which is what *latreia* means), it was not intelligent service. It was not *logikē latreia*; but consisted of "shadows of
the good things to come" (Heb. 10.1-14). There was a cease-
less round of "services"; but God dwelt in the *darkness* of the
Holy of Holies; and sin was not yet put away. But now
Christ has come, propitiation has been made; Christ has been
raised; the Holy Spirit has come; and "intelligent service" is
now possible. And giving over our bodies to God is the path
into it.*

Verse 2: **And be not fashioned according to this world**
(literally, age, *aiōn*). This present age, Paul calls "evil," declaring in Galatians 1.4 that our Lord Jesus Christ "gave Himself for our sins, that He might deliver us out of this present
evil age *(aiōn)* according to the will of our God and Father."
Believers, before they were saved, "walked according to the
course of this world [literally, "according to the age *(aiōn)*
of this world-order"—*cosmos*] according to the prince of the
power of the air" (Eph. 2.2). Here you have the *cosmos,*
or world-order, since Adam sinned; and since then each particular phase of the Satanically arranged and controlled world-
order now on, called the *aiōn.* In I Corinthians 7.31, this is
called the "fashion,"—literally, *scheme,* of this world-order.
"We know," writes John, "that we are of God, and the whole
world [lit., *world-order*], lieth in the evil one." It is necessary
to grasp intelligently this fearful state of things, in order to
obey the apostle's exhortation not to be conformed to it: a
world-order without God!

We read that Cain "went out from the presence of Jehovah
and builded a city" (Gen. 4), which became filled with inven-

---

*It is sad and terrible to see how professing Christianity has departed from all
this blessed "intelligent service" in the Holy Spirit, back into the darkness of
man-prescribed religion! Imagine Peter setting up holy days, in the Book of
Acts: as, "Ash Wednesday"; "Good Friday"; "Lent"; "Easter"! It would all
have been denial of their new connection with a Risen Christ, and of the
Presence of the Comforter! It would have been turning back to Judaism, yea, to
Paganism, for the name "Easter" is simply "Ishtar," the great goddess of Babylon!
(See on all these things, Hislop's *Two Babylons.*)

We will either yield ourselves to God, and be led by the Holy Spirit into the
"intelligent service" that belongs to this dispensation and to the true Christian;
or we will be hiding away from God in the false "Christian" forms and ceremonies "Christendom," with its religion, has taken on.

God abhors "ceremonies,"—since the blessed Holy Ghost has come, and has
brought liberty!

tions—"progress": music, arts; its whole end being to forget God,—to get along without Him. And ever since, Satan has developed this fatal world-order, with its philosophy, (man's account of all things,—but changing from time to time); its science (ever seeking to eliminate the supernatural); its government (with man exalting himself); its amusements (adapted to blot out realities from the mind); and its religion (to soothe man's conscience and allay fears of judgment).

The Spirit by Paul asks the saints **not to be fashioned* after this** [Satanic] **order of things, but on the contrary to be transformed by the renewing of their mind.** The word for "transformed" is remarkable: our word "metamorphosis" is the same word, letter for letter! In Matthew 17.2 it is used of Christ: "He was *transfigured*," which Luke 9.29 explains: "The fashion of His countenance was altered." That is, from the lowly, despised One in whom was "no beauty" to attract the eye of man, He was transformed to appear as He will appear at His return to this earth (for of His coming and kingdom the transfiguration was a figure, II Pet. 1.16-18). Thus Psalm 45 depicts Him at His second advent:

"Thou art fairer than the children of men:
      Grace is poured into Thy lips!"

Infinite, endless grace, beauty, and glory, will then be publicly displayed in Christ.

Now, to be "transformed" or "transfigured" into the image of Christ is the blessed path and portion of the surrendered believer in the midst of this present evil world. "But we all, with unveiled face beholding as in a mirror the glory of the Lord, are transformed into the same image, from glory to glory, even as from the Lord the Spirit" (II Cor. 3.18). Note that neither in world-conformity, nor in Christian transformation, are we the actors: the verbs are passive, in both cases. It is, "*Be* not fashioned," and "*Be* transformed." In the first case, Satan and the world have abundant power, they know to fashion anyone found willing; But how are we to be transformed? The

---

*"Fashioned" is literally, schemed-together-with. It is the very word of I Corinthians 7.31: *scheme* (Greek, *schema*), made into a verb, with the conjunction along-with (*sun*), for prefix. The devil will rope you into his "scheme," **unless** you surrender your body to God to be by Him delivered.

answer is, **By the renewing of your mind**; and here we
come again upon that wonderful part of our salvation which is
carried on by the Holy Spirit; and we must look at it atten-
tively.

Paul sweepingly describes this salvation as follows (Titus
3.5): "God according to His mercy saved us, through the
washing of regeneration (1) and (2) renewing of the Holy
Spirit." Here the first action signifies the whole application to
us of the redemptive work of Christ,—the "loosing from our
sins in His blood" (Rev. 1.5), and the imparting to us of
Christ's risen life so that we were made partakers of what is
called here "regeneration."* Then the second action is called
a "renewing," and is carried on by the Holy Spirit. Now what
does this signify? It cannot refer to our spirits, for our
spirits were born, created anew, under the first action here described; so that we were put into Christ, as says II Corinthians
5.17: "If any man be in Christ, he is a new creature: the old
things are passed away; behold, they are become new." And,
"That which is born of the Spirit, is spirit" (John 3.6). Nor
can this "renewing" refer to our bodies; for, although they are
indeed quickened and sustained by the indwelling Spirit, according to Romans 8.11; yet there is never a hint (but quite
the contrary), that the believer's body will be "renewed" during this present life.

There remains then to be the object of this "renewing," *the
soul,* which includes the mind, with its thoughts; the imagina-

---

*The Greek word for "regeneration" (*palingenesia*), occurs only twice in the
New Testament, here in Titus 3.5, and in Matthew 19.28. Mr. Darby's contention that this word is "not used in Scripture for a communication of life, but for
a change of state or condition," seems refuted by the fact that the Greek word
for renewing (*anakainōsis*) in this same verse, is also used but twice—Titus 3.5
and Romans 12.2. Its cognate verb is also used twice: II Cor. 4.16, and Col.
3.10. In all four instances, it has to do with the operation of the Holy Spirit upon
one already born again. So that, if the word translated *regeneration* in Titus 3.5
does not have in it any reference to the "communication of life," there is no real
definition of salvation at all in this verse: but the verse claims to be such a
definition!

As to the use of "regeneration" in Matt. 19.28, and the assertion that the
word here is "evidently a change of state and condition, and not communication of
life," the very opposite is what Scripture asserts concerning Israel at that time,
for this passage concerns the saved Remnant at the opening of the Kingdom.
Of this Remnant, God says, "They shall be *all righteous,*" "they shall be those
written unto life" in Jerusalem. It will certainly be the communication of life,
yea, the receiving of them will be "life from the dead," when they shall have
"looked on Him whom they have pierced."

tion,—so untamed naturally, the sensibilities or "feelings"; the "tastes," or natural preferences,—all which, since the fall of Adam, are naturally under the influence and power of the sinful flesh, and must be operated upon by the Holy Spirit, after one's regeneration. The memory, also, must be cleansed of all unclean, sinful recollections. And that it is the soul that is renewed,* is abundantly confirmed both from Scripture and from human experience.

Man, we remember, "became a living soul," after his body had been formed, and there had been communicated to him a spirit, by God's direct in-breathing (Gen. 2.7). Man's spirit dwelt in his body; but the body itself could not contact understandingly the world into which Adam had been introduced. Nor could his spirit do so directly. The *soul*-life, however, put him in touch with creation. It had five "senses": sight, hearing, feeling, smell, and taste. Man's spirit was thus put into intelligent relationship with the creation about him. He had also another faculty,—reason. The spirit of man perceives things directly,—apart from a "process of thought." But God placed man in circumstances in which he could use this faculty of observation and discrimination,—of *reasoning*,—which faculty he was to employ as to the creation about him. There were also the "sensibilities," and the esthetic faculty,—to see the beautiful and enjoy it. Imagination, too,—what a fertile field for unspiritual, earthly life! Memory, also, we must not overlook, for although memory belongs to the spirit (even to lost spirits,—Luke 16.25), yet since man sinned, the memory of saved people must be "renewed," so that freedom from horrid recollections shall be given, and the blessed inclination to retain that which is good, remain.

The whole "mind," therefore must become the object of the Spirit's renewing power. The entire soul-life, in human existence, must come under the Spirit's control.

---

*The word for "renew" (*anakainŏŏ*) is used only by Paul. It mans to "grow up new, afresh" (Thayer),—like foliage in the spring. Man's spirit having already been *created* anew, and being joined to the Lord; and witnessed to and eared for by the Holy Spirit; man's soul-faculties are now to be taken over by that same blessed Spirit; so that the whole mind and disposition and tastes of the man will become conformed to the fact that he is a new creature.

Paul's word, "the renewing of the mind," takes in the whole sphere of conscious life for the child of God. This also appears from the use of the word "renew" by Paul in other places. The "new man" being a new creation in Christ, all the graces and beauties of Christ belong to him; just as, before, the evil he inherited from the first Adam was his, because he was federally connected with him. Now, however, he is to "put on" the new man by simple appropriating faith. But, in order that he may do this, his soul-life must be laid hold of, "renewed," by the Holy Spirit: "That ye put away, as concerning your former manner of life, the old man, that waxeth corrupt after the lusts of deceit: and that ye be renewed in the spirit of your mind, and put on the new man,* that after God hath been created in righteousness and holiness of truth" (Eph. 4.22-24).

Paul further develops this in Colossians 3.9 and 10:

> "Ye have put off the old man with his doings, and have put on the new man, that is being renewed unto knowledge, after the image of Him that created him."

The Colossians are viewed as having put off the old man (when they were created in Christ), and put on the new man (which hath been created in righteousness and holiness of truth), and is now ever being renewed unto perfect knowledge *(epignōsis),* that experimental, spiritual revelation of the Risen Christ which Paul so coveted for the Ephesians, as we see in his great prayer ending thus:

> "That ye may know the love of Christ which passeth knowledge; that ye may be filled unto all the fulness of God" (Eph. 3.19).

These three distinct aspects of sanctification therefore appear:

1. That effected and perfected once for all by our Lord in His death: "We have been sanctified through the offering of the body of Jesus Christ once for all . . . For by one

---

*This new man is not Christ personally, any more than our old man was Adam personally. However, we sustained such a relation to Adam that the "old man" was ours, as much as "by nature" we were Adam's children. So since we are in Christ, the "new man" belongs to us,—being that sum total of the marvelous Divine graces and dispositions "created" for, and to be realized in, the believer in union with Christ. Note that believers *have* "put off" the old man; but are here told to "put him *away*,"—be not influenced by him.

offering He hath perfected forever them that are sanctified" (Heb. 10.10, 14). This is the effect of the shed blood of Christ: it has satisfied all Divine claims against us, and has redeemed us from sin unto God, separating us unto God forever with an absolute, infinite tie.

2. That which results necessarily from our being *in Christ Risen,*—"new creatures" in Him. Thus the Corinthians, though in their spiritual condition and experience yet "babes in Christ," are addressed by the apostle as those "sanctified in Christ Jesus" (I Cor. 1.2).

3. That wrought in the mind, the soul-life, and its faculties, by the Holy Spirit, who seeks to bring "every thought into captivity to the obedience of Christ" (II Cor. 10.5).

The first two aspects are fundamental, and equally true of all believers. The third, Paul longed to have brought about fully in all believers: "Admonishing every man and teaching every man in all wisdom, that we may present every man perfect in Christ" (Col. 1.28).

"Come ye out from among them [unbelievers] and be ye separate, saith the Lord,

And touch no unclean thing,

And I will receive you [in the way of fellowship]

And will be to you a Father [in fellowship, as I am in relationship],

And ye shall be to Me sons and daughters, saith the Lord Almighty."

"Having therefore these promises, beloved, let us cleanse ourselves from all defilement of flesh and spirit, perfecting holiness in the fear of God" (II Cor. 6.17, 18; 7.1).

"And may the God of peace Himself sanctify you wholly; and may your spirit and soul and body be preserved entire, without blame at the coming of our Lord Jesus Christ" (I Thess. 5.23).*

---

*A "clean heart" is taught in the Scripture most plainly. Even in the Old Testament David prays, "Create in me a clean heart." In Acts 15.9, Peter speaks of the occasion of the Holy Spirit's falling upon those of Cornelius' household, as, "cleansing their hearts by faith." And Paul says in his charge to Timothy, "The end of the charge is love *out of a pure heart* and a good conscience and faith unfeigned" (I Tim. 1.5). And further, to Timothy, "Flee youthful

That ye may prove what is the good and acceptable and perfect will of God—This word "prove" means to put to the proof, as in Ephesians 5.8 to 10: "Walk as children of light, proving [or finding out by experience] what is well-pleasing unto the Lord." The man in Luke 14.19 used the same word: "I have bought five yoke of oxen, and I go *to prove* them." The "will of God" here may be rendered "what is willed by God" (Meyer); or, as Sanday says, "The will of God is here not the Divine attribute of will, but the thing willed by God, the right course of action." This passage involves two facts: first, that God had a plan for our lives, which He is very willing and desirous we should discover; and, second, that only those who surrender themselves to Him, rejecting conformity to this age, can discover that will. All of us in times of desperate need, or crisis, are anxious to find God's path for us. And, in answer to the cry of even His unsurrendered saints, He may and often does graciously reveal the path of safety and even of temporary blessing to them. But only those who have surrendered their bodies as a living sacri-

---

lusts and follow after righteousness, faith, love, peace with them that call on the Lord *out of a pure heart*" (II Tim. 2.22).

Now it will not do, in interpreting the Bible, an infinitely accurate Book, to deal loosely or confuse terms. When David said, in Psalm 108.1, "O God, my heart is fixed," repeating it in Psalm 57.7, "My heart is fixed, O God, my heart is fixed: I will sing, yea, I will sing, yea, I will sing praises"—I say in such an utterance the Psalmist is not claiming that there was not iniquity present with him, but that his *heart* was by Divine grace *fixedly choosing* God and His will; as he says in Psalm 18.23, "I was also perfect with Him, and I kept myself from mine iniquity." Here he recognizes evil present with him, but his heart is fixed for God.

To confuse the flesh with the heart is a vital mistake. Paul says we have no confidence in the flesh. But on the other hand we may have complete confidence toward God, at least when our faith has been "perfected" (I Thess. 3.10). The heart is the throne-room of the being. When it is really handed over to God, "the peace of Christ rules" therein. If no provision is made for the flesh, but instead the Lord Jesus Christ is put on (Rom. 13.14); if we obey II Cor. 6.14 to 7.1, refusing "unequal yokes" with unbelievers, refusing to have "portions" with unbelievers, "keeping ourselves from idols," "cleansing ourselves from all defilement of flesh and spirit," "perfecting holiness in the fear of God," and consenting to be "separated" to God and "touch no unclean thing,"—then God "walks in us." Our hearts are wholly given to Him and "do not condemn us."

Such a surrendered believing heart is called in Scripture, a "pure heart." To be among those thus "cleansed" by simple faith, and to have such a pure heart, should be the longing desire and purpose of every believer.

Do not confuse, therefore, a clean, perfect heart toward God as taught in Scripture with the supposed "eradication of the sin-principle" from the flesh. The flesh is unchanged until Christ comes. But God will cleanse our *hearts*, by faith, and the Holy Spirit will form Christ fully within us.

fice to Him, enter upon the discovery of His blessed will as their very *sphere and mode of life.*

That ye may prove—Note that it is not that you are seeking after "victory," or "blessing," or even instruction in truth; but you are to enter into *the will* of Another,—even *God.*

Note, further, that in order to "prove," or experimentally enter into, God's will, there must be "the renewing of the mind" by the indwelling Holy Spirit. It is all-important to understand that *only a yielded will can desire, discover, or choose God's will.*

Further, we should, along with this, be impressed continually with the blessed fact that God's will for us is infinitely loving, infinitely wise, and gloriously *possible of fulfilment;* while our own wills are selfish and foolish and weak: for often we are impotent of accomplishing even our own poor objects!

Good, acceptable, perfect—Good for us, acceptable to God; and that which, being itself perfect, leads to our perfecting, as Epaphras prayed for the Colossians: "That ye may stand perfect and fully assured in all the will of God" (4.12).

Some would render it, "The will of God, even the thing that is good, acceptable and perfect": as if we entered upon it all, once we yielded our bodies to God. Also, it has been suggested that we enter first into God's *"good"* will: for, although we are ignorant and clumsy at first, God in His goodness gladly calls our work "good." Then, when we learn further, our work becomes in a higher sense *"acceptable."* Finally, we stand "perfect and fully assured in all the will of God."

Both these views are true. God's will is always good, acceptable and perfect; and, when we begin to surrender to it, it is all that, at once, for us. On the other hand, we do progress in it! It takes faith to surrender our wills. We must be brought to believe in our very heart that God's will is better for us than our own will. And, as we once heard a man earnestly testify, "If you can't trust One who died for you, whom can you trust?"

We beg you to seek out some saints (for there are some!) who have yielded themselves to God, and study their faces:

you'll discover a light of joy found on no other countenances.
Cling to such. Converse with them. Learn their secret. Be
much with them. And follow such as follow Christ. Blessing
lies that way!

> 3   For, I say, through the [apostolic] grace that
>   was given to me, to every one that is among you,
>   not to be estimating himself beyond what he ought
>   to estimate; but to be so estimating himself as to
>   have a sober estimate, according as God to each
>   one of us divided a measure of faith.

We have used here Rotherham's rendering, "estimate," instead of the common rendering, "think." It is remarkable that
God crowds (in the original) this one word, "have an opinion,"
or "estimate," four times into this one sentence! It is also
striking that this command, not to have a higher opinion of
ourselves than we ought to have, is the first, the opening one
of all the exhortations which follow. Let us lay this to heart!

Note what this proves: (1) That over-estimation of one's
importance among the saints is a fundamental temptation. (2)
That God has granted to each one of His saints a certain allot-
ment, or "measure," of faith,—that is, of the ability to lay hold
on the mighty operations of the Spirit of grace. And note carefully that God does not say, according to the measure of
knowledge, but "of faith." (3) That only the one who comes
into a personal discernment of God's special will through surrender to Him, will come to have a "sober estimate" of his own
place. (4) That it is a distinct command of the apostle (emphasized by allusion to the mighty apostolic charge and grace
given by God to him direct to us), that being surrendered to
God, we come into a sober estimate of our place,—of our
"measure of faith." This great verse is now to be followed by
its explanation:

> 4   For even as we have many members in one body,
> 5   and all the members have not the same office: so
>   we, who are many, are one Body in Christ; and as
> 6   to each one, members of all the rest! And having
>   gifts differing according to the grace that was
>   given to us, whether prophecy, let us prophesy ac-

7   cording to the proportion of our faith; or ministry,
     let us give ourselves to our ministry: or he that
8   teacheth, to his teaching; or he that exhorteth, to
     his exhorting: he that giveth, let him do it with
     liberality; he that ruleth, with diligence; he that
     showeth mercy, with cheerfulness.

Verses 4 and 5: **For even as we have many members in
one body, and all the members have not the same office: so
we, who are many, are one Body in Christ; and as to each
one, members of all the rest!**

Here is Paul's first mention of this great doctrine of the
Body of Christ, a doctrine which he alone, among the apostles,
sets forth, he being the one chosen "minister of the Church"
(Col. 1.24,25),—as to its real, heavenly, corporate *character*.
Note now the comparison: (1) Our human bodies have many
members. (2) These members, however, constitute a unity:
they are one *body*. (3) Each member is a member of all the
others. (4) All our members have not the same work to do.

Even so with us in Christ: (1) We are many, but (2) we
are one Body in Christ. "Body" is not here an illustration, but
an actuality. "He that loveth his own wife, loveth himself,
. . . even as Christ also the Church; because we are members of His Body. For this cause shall a man leave his father
and mother, and shall cleave to his wife; and the two shall become one flesh. This mystery is great: but I speak in regard
of Christ and of the Church" (Eph. 5.28-32): "The Church
which is His Body, the fulness of Him that filleth all in all"
(Eph. 1.22,23). This union is so absolute that Paul writes:
"As the body* is one, and hath many members, and all the mem-

---

*Of course there is all manner of looseness of talk by those who do not
discern, hold, and continually speak in terms of, the one Body of which Christ
Risen is the Head. We do not have any right to use the word "body" of any
but the true, mystical Body of Christ: those who have been "by the one Spirit
baptized into One Body." The confusion of the Scripture doctrine of the true
Church, *the Body* of Christ, with the Church's outward relationships, responsibilities,
and testing, as *the House of God on earth,* has given rise to innumerable evils.
The *Church* which is Christ's Body is the blessed company of all true believers
from Pentecost to its Rapture at Christ's coming. The House of God is "the
pillar and stay of the truth" upon earth, just as Israel was before the cross. But
just as there was an elect Remnant, Simeons and Annas, Zachariahs and Eliza-
beths,—the true Israel—in our Lord's day; while the temple, the House of
God, had been invaded by all manner of corruption and merchandising, having

bers of the body, being many, are one body; SO ALSO IS CHRIST" (I Cor. 12.12). We deceive ourselves and delude others when we use the word "body" as connected with the Church of God, of any but the true, elect members of Christ, indwelt by the Spirit. And that consciousness (that is, the consciousness of the One Body of Christ of which Christ Risen in glory is the Head and they, the living, Spirit-indwelt members, are the fulness), should be held by us continually to the exclusion of anything earthly or merely local or sectarian. Thus we should find ourselves at once in fellowship with true believers everywhere, for they with us are *members of Christ,* and they and we are *members one of another.*

(3) We are individually "members one of another." Compare I Corinthians 12.27: "Now ye are the Body of Christ, and individually members thereof." Being members of the Body of Christ, we necessarily are members of one another; as my right hand, being a member of my body, is a member of my left hand. Mark that Paul makes this "membership one of another," an additional (though necessary) truth to the fact of the one Body in Christ. Note carefully that Scripture never speaks of "church members," as men today do; nor of "membership" in or of a local assembly; but only of membership *in the Body of Christ,* and of membership *one of another.* We are members of the heavenly Head, Christ, and therefore members one of another by an operation of the Spirit of God, not by action of man. In local assemblies, according to Scripture, we have *fellowship,* as *already* members of Christ and of one another. The importance of seeing this is immeasurable. For the great fact that we are *one,* actually *members* of other believers, is made by the Spirit of God the basis of our love toward one another! As Paul says in Ephesians 4.25: "Putting away falsehood, *talk truth* each one with his neighbor; for we are *members* one of another." Your right hand has never yet

been built up by Herod the Great, a son of Esau;—so, today, the true Church is not what you see gathering into meetings all about you, but that company of true believers known to God, all of whom have been baptized by the Spirit into One Body, and who also are indwelt by the Spirit. All others, however prominent "church members" they may be, are simply part of the "great house" of II Timothy 2.20, where vessels "unto dishonor" as well as those "unto honor" exist; which the "house of God" set forth in I Timothy 3.15 has, through man's failure, become,

had a fight with the left: on the contrary, each constantly helps the other! And, as to suffering, "Whether one member suffer, all the members suffer with it."

Verse 6: **And having gifts, different according to the grace that was given unto us**—For each believer there is some particular "gift," to be bestowed by the already indwelling Spirit, (as those yielding themselves to God find) to make each believer a direct benefit to the Body of Christ: "To each one is given the manifestation of the Spirit to profit (the whole Body) withal, . . . the Spirit dividing to each one severally even as He will." The various gifts are bestowed by the Spirit for "ministration" to the Lord Jesus, and the "working" in each case is by God Himself. Read I Corinthians 12.4 to 11.

Now, these differing gifts are "according to the grace that was given unto us." In Romans 12.3 Paul speaks by the apostolic grace given unto him, and to each believer there is also an individual differing "grace," given to each for the particular service to which God calls him. In accordance with this "grace," there is, therefore, a "gift," by the indwelling Spirit. (This is not the gift of the person of the Spirit, but is a gift communicated by the already given Spirit.)* For the receiving and using of these gifts, there is necessary the element of *faith,* which is bestowed by God in exact accordance with the gift given each one. The bestowal is called, "the *grace* that was given to us."† It will not do to say, if we find ourselves not in possession of certain gifts, "They are not for us: they belonged only to the 'Early Church.'" This is a three-fold presumption! (1) It is excusing our own low state; and worse: (2) It is blaming the result of the failure of the Church upon God,—an awful thing! (3) It is setting up the present *man*-dependent, *man*-sufficient state of things as superior to the days when the Holy Spirit of God was known in power.

---

*Of course, it will be to many, as it was to the author, a startling revelation, that the Spirit is ready to engift each believer for Divinely appointed service! Those mentioned as "unlearned" in I Corinthians 14.23 were evidently believers, but ungifted; or, as Alford says, "plain believers," persons unacquainted with the gifts of I Corinthians 12.

†Alford well says, "The measure of faith, the gift of God, is the receptive faculty for all spiritual gifts; which are, therefore, not to be boasted of, nor pushed beyond their province, but humbly exercised within their own limits."

It is true that God, in His infinite grace, accepted, at the hands of the Jews, at the end of the 70 years' captivity, the temple of Zerubbabel, saying: "Build the house, and I will take pleasure in it, and I will be glorified." It is true that our Lord called that temple (though built in its grandeur by Herod, the Edomite—descendant of Esau, not Jacob!) "My Father's house," and "My house," for He had not yet finally deserted it, (as He did at last in Matthew 23.38). But the Jews of our Lord's day gloried in that temple: though there was in it neither the Ark of the Covenant nor the Shechinah Presence of Jehovah. The glory had departed; but the Jews forgot all this, just as many Christians today, though often quite "Bible students,"—practically forget or ignore *the immediate Presence of the Holy Ghost, with His all-necessary gifts:* saying, "These belonged to the 'early days'; but we have the written Word now, and do not need the gifts, as did the Early Church."

And this self-sufficiency is leading, has led, to the same form of truth-without-power, that the Jews had in Christ's day.

We are not hereby saying, Let us bring back these gifts. But we are pleading for the self-judgment and abasement before God that recognizes our real state. The outward church today is Laodicean, "wretched, poor, miserable, blind, naked"—and knows it not! And the Philadelphian remnant have only "a *little* strength." Let us be honest! We have substituted for the mighty operations amongst us of the Holy Ghost, the pitiful "soulical" training of men. We look to men to train, to "prepare" preachers, and teachers, and "leaders," for a heavenly company, the Church, among whom the Holy Ghost Himself dwells as Administrator. Let us not dare to claim that the Holy Ghost is no longer willing to work in power amongst us. Because, for Him to do so is *God's plan!* Indeed, He is so working where not hindered. Let us confess the truth. Our powerlessness is because of unbelief,—the inheritance of the sins of our fathers, the inheritance of a grieved Spirit. It may be true that He does not work as He once did; but let us admit two things: we dare not say, He is not willing so to work; and, we dare not say, It is God's plan that He does not! We can only say, *We have sinned!* So did Daniel (Dan. 9). So did

Ezra (Ezra 9). So did they of Nehemiah's day (Neh. 9). Our days are days of failure, just like those. Nor will it do, (as with so many enlightened saints), merely to "see and judge the failure of the professed Church" and gather in the name of the Lord, and remember His death in the breaking of bread every Lord's day. All this is good. But we must judge ourselves if we do not have real power amongst us. And the power of the Spirit, in a day of apostasy like this, will bring us into *a deep burden over the state of things, and into prayer,* such as the great men of God made in the three great chapters to which we have just referred!

—Whether prophecy [let us prophesy] according to the proportion of our faith—Paul's exhortation, as we shall see, is here devoted to the believer's exercising any gifts "according to the proportion" of his God-given confidence, or "faith," in the exercise of it: not over-estimating himself, but soberly estimating, and thus proceeding. (It is taken for granted, of course, that all are fully willing to exercise any gift; and will not, through unbelief or false humility, hold back therefrom.)*

---

*"An apostle was sent direct, as an architect, authorized by Christ to build His Church. Apostles were authorized, on the part of Christ, to found and to build, and to establish rules in His Church. In this sense there are no longer apostles.

"But it appears to me, that in a lower sense, there may be apostles and prophets in all ages. Barnabas is termed an apostle. Junius and Andronicus are called apostles, and it is said of them that they were 'of note amongst the apostles' (Rom. 16.7); so that there are others who were not named.

"As regards the revelation of God, it is complete; as regards any authority to found the Church it no longer exists: neither the twelve nor Paul have had any successors. The foundation cannot be twice laid. But one may act under an extraordinary responsibility as sent by God. We may cite as examples, without pretending to justify all that they did, a Luther, a Calvin, a Zwingli, and perhaps others. So for prophets; although there be no new revelations of truth, there may be, as proceeding from God Himself, a power of applying to the circumstances of the church, or of the world, truths hidden in the Word; such as, in practice, might render the ministry prophetic. Moreover all those who expressed the mind of God 'to edification' were called prophets, or at least, 'prophesied.'

"Prophets, who were associated with apostles as the foundation, because they revealed the mind of God, may, it appears to me, in a subordinate sense, be believed to exist,—those who not merely teach and explain ordinary and profitable doctrine,—but who by a special energy of the Spirit can unfold and communicate the mind of Christ to the Church where it is ignorant of it (though that mind be treasured up in the Scripture)—can bring truths, hidden previously from the knowledge of the Church, in the power of the testimony of the Spirit of God, to bear on the present circumstances of the Church and future prospects of the world, and thus be practically prophets (though there be no new facts revealed, but all are really in the Word already), and thus be a direct blessing and gift of Christ to the Church for its emergency and need, though the Word be strictly adhered to, but without which the Church would not have had the power or that Word" (Darby).

We can easily see in a Luther or a Calvin, in the sixteenth century, in a Bunyan in the seventeenth century; in a Wesley in the eighteenth, in a Moody in the nineteenth, such apostolic operation. Wesley spoke from God to all England, as did Luther to Germany. Moody, we know, was first an evangelist, loving and reaching the lost. But God, who is sovereign, gave him spiritual authority in the consciences of Christians throughout the whole world. We know what debt under God all those who have the truth today owe to Darby, through whom God recovered more truth belonging to the Church of God, than through any other man since Paul, and whose writings are today the greatest treasure of truth and safeguard against error known to instructed believers. Such men had more than an evangelist's or teacher's gift. There was spiritual authority they themselves did not seek, attending their ministry. This fact discerning believers,—those free from tradition's bias, readily see and gladly admit. Paul defines the prophetic gift in I Corinthians 14.3: "He that prophesieth speaketh unto men edification, and comfort, and consolation." New Testament prophets and apostles laid the foundation of the Church,—the prophets speaking directly by inspiration from God. But while the early apostles and prophets had their peculiar ministry in a foundational way, yet both gifts remain in the Church (see Eph. 4.11-13) along with evangelists, pastors and teachers. Now since the prophet speaks under the moving of the Spirit, he is to do so "according to His faith." Dean Alford makes the evident distinction, "The prophet spoke under immediate inspiration; the teacher *(didaskalos)*, under inspiration working by the secondary instruments of his will and reason and rhetorical power." We have ourselves sometimes heard those speaking in "testimony" or "praise-meetings" whose words were not, properly speaking, teaching; but yet entered in the power of the Spirit directly into the heart of the hearers, edifying, exhorting, and consoling, — a high ministry indeed, though in the "secondary character" of it, as compared to the words of the early apostles and prophets. Such an one could, of course, speak profitably only when speaking in the Spirit, and thus, "in proportion to his faith."

The remarkable foot-note above, from J. N. Darby, is a frank and explicitly plain statement of truth. Mr. D. repeats over and over (seven times, at least, in the pages from which our excerpts are taken—Coll. Writ. I, 350; III. 217-9) that the written Word is complete. No honest heart, however, knowing history, can fail to admit that God has, in mercy, raised up, from time to time, men who have administered His Word in such apostolical and prophetic power. That He will again do so, we do not doubt. For there is an ever-recurring need of these gifts. Probably, a *constant* need!

Verse 7: **Or [personal] ministry, let us occupy ourselves in our ministering** [to the needs of the saints]—God graciously places this word "ministering" [*diakonia*] between prophesying and teaching. In Acts Six we have the word twice, applied first to physical things: "the daily ministration" (of food to the widows); and second to spiritual things: "We will continue . . . in the ministry of the Word." But here in Romans Twelve, its being placed as it is, indicates that those who, like the house of Stephanas, in I Corinthians 16.15, minister to the saints' *material* needs, should set themselves to such ministering. It is the whole-hearted exercise of this gift, when it is given, that is urged by the apostle. Perhaps there is no gift so liable to lapse into haphazard exercise, as this Christ-like gift!

Or he that teacheth, to his teaching—Proper Christian *teaching* is not mere "Bible study"; but, first of all, clear explanation direct to believers' hearts, of Christ's work for us, and of the Pauline Epistles that directly concern the Church of God as the Body of Christ, indwelt by the Spirit, one with Him. Proper teaching would see that the saints become familiar with the wonders of the Old Testament, and love it. The prophecies, both of the Old Testament and of the book of The Revelation should also be taught, remembering that "the testimony of Jesus is the spirit of prophecy"; and that every true Christian teacher should be able to say: "It was the good pleasure of God to reveal His Son in me, that I might preach *Him*" (Gal. 1.16); "that in all things Christ might have the preëminence"; "that we may present every man perfect in Christ

Jesus." This is the kind of work that was done by Priscilla and Aquila, when they had heard Apollos in the Ephesian synagogue: "They took him unto them, and expounded unto him the Way of God more accurately." It is being done whenever one who knows the truth really brings another into it. Oh, for more such teaching! We leave so much unapplied,—so much that the dear saints never really enter into!*

Verse 8: Or he that exhorteth, to his exhortation—The gift of exhortation is distinct from that of teaching (though both may be found in the same person). Exhortation is an appeal to the will; teaching, to the mind. Exhortation is a precious gift—invaluable! whereby the Holy Spirit directly persuades the hearing heart into obedience to the truth which it has heard. A true exhorter, also, must be walking the path he calls others to follow!

He that giveth, with singleness [of heart toward God]— The literal meaning of giving here is that of imparting, of sharing our substance with others; and the manner of such giving is to be without secret reluctance, for "God loveth a cheerful giver" (II Cor. 9.7); also without false pretense, such as Ananias and Sapphira had; finally, with an eye single to God. In fact, in Ephesians 6.5 this same word "singleness" is used in the phrase "in singleness of your heart, as unto Christ."

He that ruleth, with diligence—Ruling is first a gift, then an office, like those of elders and deacons (I Tim. 3.4, 12),

---

*Many years ago, at the Keswick Convention, in England, I was returning, about seven o'clock, from an early morning walk. I passed the "Drill Hall," and down came MacGregor (G.H.C.) and greeted me. I said, "Your face looks pale; are you not well?" "Oh yes,—only a bit weary," said he. Then, by questioning further, I found he had just then finished with the last case left from the previous night's meeting! *That was teaching indeed.* He had patiently labored all night long to expound to one after another "the Way of God more perfectly!"

It is our privilege just now to have beneath our roof a beloved sister in her eighty-fourth year whose energies for over forty years have been constantly used in teaching others. Although having to support herself by public school teaching, yet with a steadfastness that is deeply touching, *one thing she does* with every one with whom she comes in contact: she teaches each the gospel. Many people, and even preachers, have come to her for instruction, even when she was confined to her bed in sickness or infirmity. There they sat patiently listening to her words concerning Christ. Her great passion is to "make all men see" Paul's wonderful explanation of our identification with Christ in His death, burial, and resurrection.

[Later: Alas for us,—not for her! our beloved Mrs. S—— has gone triumphantly Home!]

who must, of course, first "rule well their own house." Just as prophesying, teaching, and exhorting were gifts by the Spirit; and as giving is a grace given of God (II Cor. 8.1, 4, 7) ; so the work of elders and deacons were offices: "If a man seek the office of a bishop"—or overseer: called also "elder," as see Acts 20.17, 28;—as being more matured in Christian faith and experience; while the term "bishop" or "overseer" designates the duties of the office—to oversee). Dean Alford objects to interpreting "ruleth" here (Rom. 12.8) of rulership in the Church, saying, (as a true churchman would), "It is hardly likely that the rulers of the Church, as such, would be introduced so low down in the list, or by so general a term, as this!" But in the enumeration of the gifts in I Corinthians 12.28, we have this order: "Apostles, prophets, teachers, miracles, healings, helps"; and then, "governments," next to the last term in the list! Of course man, who glories in office, would want this order changed.

Gifts were a direct bestowment *(charisma)* of the Spirit; moreover, they were general, while the "rulers" were confined to their own assemblies. Prophets, evangelists, pastors and teachers (Eph. 4.11) were that wherever they were; but an elder or deacon held his own office in his own assembly only.

The ruler was to attend, with constant diligence, to his work; not, indeed, "lording it over" the Lord's heritage, but according to Peter's direction: "The elders among you I exhort . . . tend the flock of God which is among you" (that was their *business*—to take care of the Lord's sheep in the assembly where they were), "exercising the oversight, not of constraint, but willingly." They were to watch; to be ready at any sacrifice of personal comfort to look after needy sheep: "nor yet for filthy lucre." (They were not to have money in mind, although elders that "ruled well" were to be "counted worthy of double honor," especially if they were able to instruct in the Word; God would look after their financial needs): "neither as lording it over the charge allotted to you, but making yourselves ensamples to the flock."

Truth to tell, Christ's sheep are ill-tended these days! they are "scattered upon the mountains." Elders that "rule well," with humble diligence, day and night, are desperately needed. Every believer has a right to the consciousness of being personally shepherded by Divinely raised-up elders; and cared for even in material things by faithful deacons. "And when the Chief Shepherd shall be manifested," the rulers who have ruled with godly diligence shall receive a crown of glory! (I Peter 5.1-4.) Concerning false shepherds, see the awful words of Jeremiah 23.1-4, Ezekiel 34—the whole chapter! and Isaiah 56.10 to 12. (These chapters make us tremble!)

He that showeth mercy, with cheerfulness—Showing mercy is of course the bounden duty of those to whom God has shown mercy. But mercy toward others may be shown with the long, sombre face of one driven by a duty in which he is not happy. Yet the joyfulness of spirit in which one helps another is often of more real blessing than the help itself. Godet well remarks, with many others, that the words "he that showeth mercy" denote the believer who feels called to devote himself to the visiting of the sick and afflicted. There is a gift of sympathy which particularly fits for this sort of work, and which is, as it were, the key to open the heart of the sufferer. The phrase "with cheerfulness" literally reads *in hilarity!*

9   Let love be without hypocrisy. Abhor that
10 which is evil; cleave to that which is good. In love of the brethren be tenderly affectioned one to
11 another; in honor preferring one another; in diligence not slothful; fervent in spirit; serving the
12 Lord; rejoicing in hope; patient in tribulation;
13 continuing steadfastly in prayer; communicating to the necessities of the saints; pursuing hospital-
14 ity. Bless them that persecute you; bless, and
15 curse not. Rejoice with them that rejoice; weep
16 with them that weep. Be of the same mind one toward another. Set not your mind on high things, but be carried away with things that are lowly. Be not wise in your own conceits.

17   Render to no man evil for evil. Take thought
18 for things honorable in the sight of all men. If it be possible,—as much as in you lieth, be at peace

19 with all men. Avenge not yourselves, beloved, but give place unto the wrath [of God] : for it is written, Vengeance belongeth unto Me; I will recompense, saith the Lord. But if thine enemy hunger,

20 feed him; if he thirst, give him to drink: for in so doing thou shalt heap coals of fire upon his head.

21 Be not overcome of evil, but overcome evil with good.

Verse 9: **Let love be without hypocrisy**—The world is full of effusive expressions of affection,—and so, we fear, are many professing Christians—without real love in the heart: "Talking cream and living skim milk," as Mr. Moody phrased it. "Let us not love in word, neither with the tongue; but in deed and truth" (I John 3.18). **Abhor that which is evil**— This is impossible to the unregenerate, and only intermittently possible for the carnal Christian; but to one who has obeyed the first two verses of this chapter and surrendered to God, it is a holy instinct! "Ye that love Jehovah, hate evil" (Ps. 97.10). To be a good Christian, a man must be a good hater! **Cleave to that which is good**—Here is not only the negative, the abhorrence of evil; but the positive, the discerning and holding fast that which is good. As Paul says in Philippians 4.8: "Brethren, whatsoever things are true, whatsoever things are honorable, whatsoever things are just, whatsoever things are pure, whatsoever things are lovely, whatsoever things are of good report: if there be *any* virtue, and if there be *any* praise, [in a person] take account of *these* things." Trust the anointing which you have received (I John 2.20, 27) for discernment; and trust the study of the Word of God, to teach you what is really *good*.

Verse 10: **In love of the brethren be tenderly affectioned one to another**—Of course all Christians "love the brethren"—that is a sign of spiritual life (I John 3.14). But to be *tenderly* affectioned—how few are! "Be ye kind one to another, tenderhearted, forgiving each other, even as God also in Christ forgave you." Beloved, are we willing to be made tender? It is God's will for all believers. **In honor preferring one another**—How beautiful a grace! Really to *prefer* from your heart other believers before yourself, to be glad when others are honored above you.* Farrar well renders, "Love the brethren in the faith, as though they were brothers in blood." Vincent prefers the A.V. rendering, "kindly affectioned," perhaps properly, since our word *kind* was originally *kinned,* and "kindly affectioned" is, having the affection of kindred!

Verse 11: **In zeal not sluggish**—The words have no reference whatever to worldly "business" or affairs, but wholly to spiritual matters. Luther renders, "In regard to zeal, be not lazy," which is the meaning. Alford renders, "In zeal not remiss,"—saying, "Not 'business,' as in the Old Version, which seems to refer it to the affairs of this life; whereas, it relates as in all these verses (11 to 13), to Christian duties *as such.*" Satan would use the doctrine of grace, or the assurance of faith, to settle down believers into spiritual slothfulness. Watch against that. **Fervent in spirit, serving the Lord**—The word translated "fervent" (used of Apollos in Acts 18.25), means ardent, or burning. Be ardent in spirit in our Lord's service. It is the opposite of dignified, cold, unemotional. Christ has loved us with infinite fervency. Let us serve Him in the same spirit.

Verse 12: **In hope rejoicing**—Our hopes are bound up with our Lord's coming, in prospect of which we should constantly be filled with exultation. **In tribulation remaining patient**—Patience in trial is the only path to our perfecting; wherefore James says we should count "manifold trials to be *all joy";* and, "let patience have its perfect work, that we may be perfect and entire, lacking in nothing." **In prayer steadfastly continuing**—So did the early Christians (Acts 2.42, 46, 47; 6.4; 12.5, 12). But do not forget to *watch* expectantly, and to give *thanks* in your prayers. (Col. 4.2.) Ten will attend Bible teaching, and one hundred Sunday preaching, to two or three who "in prayer steadfastly continue": but be thou of that two or three; for they prevail, and to them Christ reveals

---

*For "love of the brethren," and "tenderly affectioned" there are two beautiful words in the Greek: *philadelphia,* and *philostorgos,* the latter used of the closest family ties.

Himself; and they become channels of blessing to countless others.

Verse 13: **To the needs of the saints contributing**—"So to make another's necessities one's own as to relieve them."

When you obey this injunction and begin wisely to inquire about the saints' *needs,* you will be astonished at two things: first, at the actual pressing necessities of many saints all about you; and second, at the way God will supply your own necessities as you minister to them. When the Holy Spirit took complete possession of the early Church, "Not one of them said that aught of the things which he possessed was his own; but they had all things common"; with the result that "neither was there among them any that lacked." Now this shows the basal spirit of Christian giving. It is not "saying in our hearts" that what we have is "our own," but holding all in stewardship to the Lord, ready to be ministered, as He shall direct. It is true that Paul, in his epistles, which give the constitution of the Church of God, does not direct those that are rich in this world's goods to "sell all that they have"; but to "do good, to be rich in good works, *ready* to distribute, *willing* to communicate." This passage (I Tim. 6.17-19) should be most carefully regarded as at once the Divine protection against the awful "community of goods" of socialism and communism, because the Bible teaches constantly *the rights of personal, private property;* and also as the foundation principle of our giving.

Pursuing hospitality—Here the word for hospitality is literally love to strangers, "stranger-loving," and the translation "given to" is not strong enough. In its forty or fifty occurrences in the New Testament, this word is very frequently translated "pursuing," which is the literal meaning. You have it three times in Philippians 3: in verse 6, *"persecuting* the church"; in verse 12, "I *follow* after"; and in verse 14, "I *press on."* The meaning here, then, is, *pursuing* hospitality,—*persecuting* folks, even strangers, with kindness! What a wonderful testimony of love, hearty obedience to this simple exhortation to pursue hospitality would be! We have in Hebrews Thirteen three uses of this Greek root *phil* (meaning *love*): (1) "Let love of the brethren *(philadelphia)* continue";

(2) "Forget not to show love unto strangers" *(philoxenia)*; and, (3) in verse 5, "Be free from silver-loving" *(philarguros)*. If you are tempted to *philarguros, philadelphia* and *philoxenia* will cure you! "Given to hospitality," then, means far more than being "willing to entertain" those who may call on you. It indicates *going after* this business, pursuing it, following it up! The Lord will reward some day even a cup of cold water given in His Name. Let us make "Strangers' Inns" of our homes. We are not staying here long. And the Lord may send "angels" around when we least expect! "Forget not to show love unto strangers, for thereby some have entertained angels unawares."*

Of course it is taken for granted in all these exhortations that we have presented our bodies to God according to the opening verses of the Chapter; and thus by the indwelling Holy Ghost are *enabled* to walk in His revealed will, as those could not who were under law.

Verse 14: **Bless them that persecute you: bless, and curse not**—Here is a verse that needs no comment, in view of our Lord's words of Luke 6.27,28: "Love your enemies, do good to them that hate you, bless them that curse you, pray for them that despitefully use you"; and of His blessed example. But note, in our present verse it is not mere outward blessing that is commanded, but refraining from inward reservations, or private expressions, for sometimes we speak sweetly to opposers, but our after words prove that we did not allow our hearts to go out in love to those enemies. And by the way, do not stumble if you find other Christians speaking ill of you, even persecuting you. Bless *them,* too!

Verse 15: **Rejoice with them that rejoice; weep with them that weep**—Now here is a verse that takes us out of ourselves. The literal rendering is, Rejoice with rejoicing ones, and weep with weeping ones. Believers, of course, are especially meant in both cases. There will always be some that are weeping. Blessed is he who, like the Lord at Lazarus' grave, can enter into others' sorrow even unto tears!

---

*I doubt if the reference in "unawares" is to Abraham in Genesis 18. For he at once recognized the Lord, and knew His attendants. The statement seems rather an absolute one of inspiration, involving such a possibility for any of us!

"Alas, there is such a phenomenon, not altogether rare, as a life whose self-surrender, in some main aspects, cannot be doubted, but which utterly fails in *sympathy*. A certain spiritual exaltation is allowed actually to harden, or at least to seem to harden, the consecrated heart; and the man who perhaps witnesses for God with a prophet's ardor is yet not one to whom the mourner would go for tears and prayers in his bereavement, or the child for a perfectly human smile in his play. As to the Lord Himself, the little child, the wistful parent, the widow with her mite, the poor fallen woman of the street, could 'lead away' his blessed sympathies with a touch"—Moule.

Verse 16: **Minding the same thing one toward another**— Let us quote several comments by beloved writers: "Be of one mind amongst yourselves"—Conybeare. "The harmony which proceeds from a common object, common hopes and common desires"—Sanday. "The loving harmony when each in respect to his neighbor has one thought and endeavor"—Meyer. "Aspiring after the same aims, aiming at the same object for one another as for ourselves. Having the same solicitude for the temporal and spiritual welfare of the brother as for one's own"—Godet. "Actuated by a common and well-understood feeling of mutual allowance and kindness"—Alford. Evidently the reference is not to uniformity of thought, but to charity of attitude.

Not minding high things, but being carried away along with the lowly—This sixteenth verse is in close connection with the spirit of verse 15. It is the spirit of Philippians 2.2 to 5: "Be of the same mind, having the same love, being of one accord, of one mind [not of one opinion, but one heart-intent]; doing nothing through faction or through vainglory, but in lowliness of mind each counting other better than himself; not looking each of you to his own things, but each of you also to the things of others. Have this mind in you which was also in Christ Jesus." "High things" are a continual temptation. Carefully read here the excellent remarks of Godet: "There frequently forms in the congregations of believers an aristocratic tendency, every one striving by means of the

Christian brotherhood to associate with those who, by their gifts or fortune, occupy a higher position. Hence small coteries, animated by a proud spirit, and having for their result chilling exclusiveness. The apostle knows these littlenesses and wishes to prevent them; he recommends the members of the church to attach themselves to all alike, and if they will yield to a preference, to show it rather for the humble." Lay these words well to heart. They are *continually needed*.

The word rendered "carried away with" really means the opposite of its King James rendering "condescend to." The idea of one pardoned sinner's thinking of "condescending" to another! The word really means "to be carried away along with," as has been every Bernard, Assisi, Luther, Zinzendorf, Bunyan, Wesley, Whitefield, Spurgeon, Moody. All the saints filled with the Spirit have found themselves among the lowly of this earth. For that matter, there is not, and never has been, a real assembly of God of wealthy upper class people only! "Not many mighty, not many noble are called." The rich have to come *where the poor are* to hear the gospel. Once received, the gospel of Christ is the blessed and only real leveler of us all. Beware always of any "religious" movement cultivating the rich!

Be not wise in your own conceits—Paul in Chapter 11.25 used exactly the same expression, warning us as Gentile believers of the danger of being "wise in our own conceits." This searching expression, "wise in one's own eyes," or "conceit," occurs five times in the Old Testament, and two here in Romans,—seven in all. Of such a one, Solomon says, "There is more hope of a fool than of him." He is first cousin to the sluggard, and to a blind rich man; and all of these are related to "them that know not God." See Proverbs 26.5,12, 16; 28.11; 3.7. The self-conceited are not among those who are "weeping with them that weep."

Verse 17: Render to no man evil for evil—This takes for granted that some will do you evil. Satan and the world hate God's saints who walk with Him; and will do them all permitted evil. Now do not lay it up against the doer, if evil has been done you. Alas, some real believers are thoughtless; some jealous, some envious, some possibly even spiteful. Put far away the expectation of "getting even" with anybody. "If any man have"—really *have*—"a complaint against any, even as the Lord forgave you, so also do ye" (Col. 3.13). The Lord forgets, as well as forgives! (Heb. 8.12).

Taking care by forethought for comely [or seemly] **things before every one** (literally, *all men*,—whether Christians or not)—"Before the eyes of all men taking care for what is good" (Meyer). This exhortation has no special reference to "making provision for ourselves or our families in an honest manner," as some have thought (from the Old Version). It means to take careful forethought for such a course of Christian behavior ("honorable things") as will commend itself to all—whether Christians or not. We forget, most of us, thus to view our lives as a whole, day by day, detecting and rejecting whatever in ourselves others might criticize as not honorable.

Verse 18: **If it be possible—as much as in you lieth—be at peace with all men**—Paul himself did cause trouble everywhere, as did our Lord, who said, "Think not that I came to send peace on the earth: I came not to send peace, but a sword." But neither Paul nor his Lord was ever the selfish cause of trouble. It is not always possible for a Christian to be at peace with all men, but he can be a peace-lover; a peace-liver; and often a peace-maker, among men. As James says, "The fruit of righteousness is sown in peace by them that make peace." Perhaps the most fruitful cause of trouble for a Christian is his claiming "his rights," forgetting Paul's description of us Christians throughout this dispensation:

"For Thy sake we are killed all the day long;
We were accounted as sheep for the slaughter."*

Verse 19: **Avenge not yourselves, beloved; but give place unto the** [coming] **wrath** [of God]—Believers are

---

*One who had visited the Chicago stock yards on a slaughter-day said to me, "Our guide took us to where the swine were being slaughtered. Here there was squealing and grunting everywhere, and the moment the men laid hold of one for slaughter, it gave a wild shriek, and the uproar was terrible. By and by we approached another building and heard no sounds; and we found that here the sheep were being slaughtered, without complaining—in silence!"

here seen sorely tempted to seek to bring about by their own hand that righting of matters which belongs to God only. The motto of Scotland, *"Nemo me impune lacessit"*—"No one treads on *me* unpunished!"—applies to man in the flesh throughout the world. Note Paul's word, "Give place unto the wrath,"—to the coming wrath of God in the day of wrath, of Chapter 2.5. As for "the wrath of man," we know it "worketh not the righteousness of God" (James 1.20). Oh, how hard, yea, how impossible, for those who have not yielded their bodies a living sacrifice to God, to leave the visitation of wrath wholly in God's hand!

For it is written, Vengeance belongeth unto Me; I will recompense, saith the Lord—Let us not dare seek to steal from God what He so distinctly asserts to be His province alone,—vengeance,*—the dealing out just desert to evil action.

God's "vengeance" must require that infinite knowledge of conditions, of motives, of results upon others, which God, the just Judge, alone possesses. And He has faithfully promised to "recompense." The Greek of this word is startling: it means to *pay back,* personally and accurately. Both Romans 12.19 and Hebrews 10.30 quote the passage in Deuteronomy 32.35 which prophesies the coming *vengeance* of God. The word is also used in II Thessalonians 1.6. In these shallow, sinful days, men have forgotten that there is a day of reckoning; but the saints must not forget. "Forestall not God's wrath," says Meyer, "by personal revenge, but let it have its course and its sway. The morality of this precept is based on the *holiness* of God. Hence, so far as wrath and love are the two poles of holiness, it does not exclude the blessing of our adversaries and intercession for them."

Verse 20: **But if thine enemy hunger, feed him; if he thirst, give him to drink: for in so doing thou shalt heap coals of fire upon his head**—Here are specific directions for active love toward an enemy,—praying for him meanwhile, as Christ commanded: "Bless them that persecute you, pray for them that despitefully use you." There is no more terrible

---

*Quaint old John Trapp says: "In reason, revenge is but justice; Aristotle commends it. The world calls it manhood; it is doghood, rather!"

danger than that of cherished revenge; and nothing marks out so blazingly a Christian path as love toward a foe. The Indians who inhabited America when the white man came, hated one another, tribe against tribe. The war paint, the warpath, the tomahawk, the scalp lock,—and pride in it all! was the hell-mark wherewith Satan branded these poor heathen, —and where are they today? No less devilish are the ghastly family "feuds" in certain parts of America. No less significant is the kind of man admired in some regions: "He won't take a word from anybody"; "He'll fight at the drop of the hat," and the like.

Now the promise is most striking indeed, that in a deed of kindness to an enemy we shall "heap coals of fire upon his head." Of course, as always, when the literal statements of God's judgment are made, we are apt to shrink in timidity and unbelief, and seek to evade the actualities. But remember exactly what we are dealing with: we are asked to step aside from self-avenging, and "give place" to God's coming vengeance and recompense. Of course, we continue loving our enemies and praying for them, hoping they may repent. Thus we are sharing the feeling of God Himself, who "takes no pleasure in the death of the wicked, and would have all men to be saved." Nevertheless, we know in our hearts that many will refuse Divine mercy, and go on to that day of vengeance. And what do we read in the Scriptures about "coals of fire" at that time?

Let burning coals fall upon them:
Let them be cast into the fire,
Into deep pits, whence they shall not rise (Ps. 140.10).
Upon the wicked He will rain snares;
Fire and brimstone and burning wind shall be the portion of their cup (Ps. 11.6).

It is a trifling exposition that would make the "coals of fire" of Romans 12.20, quoted from Proverbs 25.21,22, a mere *figure* —and meaning, really, *nothing!*

The knowledge and constant remembrance by the saints of the coming literal doom of the wicked, is both a deep incentive to a holy walk, and a strong motive for loving and praying for them. But let us not forget that the more we are "a sweet savor of Christ unto God" as we preach the gospel, the more we become "a savor from death unto death in them that are perishing" (II Cor. 2.14-16). Paul significantly, just here, adds the words: "And who is sufficient for these things? For we are not as the many, corrupting the Word of God" (II Cor. 2.17). Our Lord Himself said, "If I had not come and spoken unto them, they had not had sin: but now they have no excuse for their sin." It is a fearful thought that in our kindness to enemies—enemies of our Lord and of ourselves for the gospel's sake, we may be increasing their doom: but the responsibility is theirs; the obedient kindness, ours!

Verse 21: **Be not overcome of evil, but overcome evil with good**—"Evil" here directly connects itself with that hatefulness in others of verse 20; but it also includes all the evil in the world, through which the Christian walks as a stranger and a pilgrim. This plan of setting forth a positive path of "good" before His saints, instead of a mere negative "Thou shalt not," is the constant way of God in grace. Compare, "Let him that stole steal no more; but rather let him labor, working with his hands the thing that is good, *that he may have whereof to give* to him that hath need" (Eph. 4.28). It is not merely, Stop stealing; but, Begin giving! Just as in the following verse of Ephesians we read: "Let no corrupt speech proceed out of your mouth, but such as is good for edifying as the need may be, *that it may give grace* to them that hear." Merely to stop doing wrong things will finally make a monk out of you; doing good, will put you in Paul's company. No one is "overcoming" in the sense of Romans 12.12, save those whose time is *filled with good*: praise, prayer, and thanksgiving towards God; and loving ministry towards men!

> "There is a faith unmixed with doubt,
>   A love all free from fear;
> A walk with Jesus, where is felt
>   His presence always near.
> There is a rest that God bestows,
>   Transcending pardon's peace,
> A lowly, sweet simplicity,
>   Where inward conflicts cease.

"There is a service God-inspired,
   A zeal that tireless grows,
Where self is crucified with Christ,
   And joy unceasing flows.
There is a being 'right with God,'
   That yields to His commands
Unswerving, true fidelity,
   A loyalty that stands."

CHAPTER THIRTEEN

Subjection to Rulers, as Ordained of God. Verses 1 to 7.

No Debt but Love: What that Achieves! Verses 8 to 10.

Awake! Christ's Coming Nears! Put on Christ Now! Verses 11 to 14.

1   Let every soul be in subjection to the authorities in power. For there is no authority save from God; and those that exist are put in place by God.

2   Therefore he that sets himself against the authority, withstandeth the ordinance of God: and those [thus] withstanding shall receive for themselves judgment.

3   For rulers are not a terror to the good work, but to the evil. And wouldest thou have no fear of the authority? Practice that which is good and thou

4   shalt have praise from the same. For it is God's servant to thee for good. But if thou dost practice that which is evil, be afraid! For not in vain doth it bear the sword! For God's minister it is, an avenger for wrath to him that doeth evil.

5   Wherefore ye must needs be in subjection, not only because of the wrath, but also for conscience'

6   sake. For this cause ye pay tribute also; for they are God's ministers, attending continually upon

7   this very matter. Render to all their dues: tribute to whom tribute [is due]; custom to whom custom; fear to whom fear; honor to whom honor.

WE HAVE HERE a passage of great importance in these lawless days!

Verse 1: Let every soul be in subjection to the authorities in power [or, the constituted authorities]. For there is no

480

authority but from God; and those that exist are put in place by God.

Every soul here, of course, means every believer: this Epistle is addressed only to believers (see 1.1-8). The **authorities in power** are the civil **authorities ordained of God** into whose hands God has committed external human government. (We say external, as opposed to inward, spiritual, which lies outside Caesar's province.)

To be **in subjection** to the higher powers, means to render them their due respect and obedience according to verse 7: **tribute to whom tribute,** etc.

There is great necessity at this hour to emphasize to all Christians this solemn exhortation of the apostle. Lawlessness,—contempt for authority—is upon us like a flood. This lawlessness *(anomia)* is the *essence* of sin. We have already called attention to the fact that the Old Version translation of I John 3.4: "Sin is the transgression of the Law," is wholly astray. Not *parabasis,* transgression; nor *paraptoma,* offense; but a much deeper word, *anomia,*—literally, *lawlessness:* the spirit of refusing control,—this does God define as sin! Sin was in the world 2500 years before the Law. Already existing sin caused the Law's "Thou shalt not." *Lawlessness* is behind and below all law-breaking!

That the lawlessness of the last days is coming upon us, we see everywhere! In the contempt of treaty obligations on the part of nations; in the disregard for old-time honesty in private contracts; in the "breaking loose" of "flaming youth" from parental restraint, and the rush to "expressionism," whether in school "dramatics" or in disdain of "old fogy" morals; in the calling the sin of lasciviousness and adultery by "modern" names,—such as "petting," "sex-experience"; in the flood of murder magazines and "mystery" novels; in the unwillingness of the public to have crime really *punished,*—showing public sympathy with sin!

It is because of this latter that law-enforcement breaks down. For, on the whole, judges, prosecuting attorneys, sheriffs, and police, would have criminals dealt with firmly: but the "technicalities" of legal procedure are seized upon by evil, unscrupulous men to defeat law. And who would be so foolish as to claim that things could be so if the entire community were, in their hearts, righteously abhorrent toward all law-breaking?

Perhaps the most glaring of all instances of last-days lawlessness, is the tolerance of Red Communism. We do not now speak of Russia; but of the fact that Communistic doctrines (which openly declare war upon all Divinely appointed order) are held,—even by professing Christians! in England, the United States, Canada, and all over the world. You have no more right to "sit down" upon another's property, against his will, than any common thief has to enter your home to plunder! God's Word defends the rights of property, just as the right to life. "Thou shalt not steal" and "Thou shalt not kill," are in the same code of law. Christians need to read and heed Matthew 20.1 to 15. The "householder" there "agrees" with the "laborers": these had the right to sell their labor at an "agreed" price; while he had the right to decide what he could profitably pay them, and "agree" to pay it. And he recognizes what they had earned as theirs: "Take up that which is *thine,* and go thy way" (verse 14). But as concerning that which was his, and which they had not earned, he says, "Is it not lawful for me to do what I will *with mine own?*" He paid them what they had earned, and sent them off his property! Now Christ gave this lesson! And He calls the eye "evil" (verse 15) that would covet what it had not earned!

No wonder Marx and Lenin and the Communists hate the Bible! It convicts them of covetousness and thievery! Read Matthew 20.1 to 15 again; and see what you think our Lord would have said of those laborers, if they had "sat down" in that vineyard, claiming, "It really belongs to *us,* 'the workers'; and we will not move until this householder raises our wages to *what we ask!*" You see, the only way for Communism to exist, is to destroy all hold of the Bible on men! Communism is *the devil's opium* for a people willing to let go the Word of God!

Let Christians beware of the specious lies of all movements of force ("direct action," the Reds call it!) to right the wrongs of this present world. There are wrongs, as James tells us

(Jas. 5.1-6), but the Christian is told to be "patient until the coming of the Lord" (Jas. 5.7,8). *Pray* and *wait*. Things will get worse and worse, until "violence fills the earth," as in "the days of Noah." But God will deliver you—if you trust Him, and do not put forth your hand with "violent men." I pray you, read Proverbs 1.10-15, where you have a vivid picture of all the "share the wealth" movements! Let the Lord's people avoid them as the very plague! If, instead of "godliness with contentment," earthliness and covetousness seize your heart, you are really setting in on Lenin's and Stalin's path—which ends in hell! and makes a land a bloody horror meanwhile.

The "restlessness" of today is really that deep "lawlessness" which God calls *sin:* "SIN IS LAWLESSNESS!" The Man of Sin is called "the lawless one" in II Thessalonians 2.7 and 8, where we are told that "the mystery of lawlessness" is already working, but that there is One (the Holy Spirit, we believe), that "restraineth now" until He be "taken out of the way." "And then shall be revealed the lawless one." This is the coming Antichrist.

Now since God's saints know that lawlessness and violence, lust and covetousness, are characteristic of the last days, and know from Daniel's prophetic interpretation of the Great Image Nebuchadnezzar saw, that we must be nearing the time of the end of the age, how peculiarly needful that we all lay to heart these instructions concerning magistrates!

Magistrates are **put in place, set up, or ordained, of God.** Never mind if they are bad ones, the word still stands, "There is no power but of God." Remember your Savior suffered under Pontius Pilate, one of the worst Roman governors Judea ever had; and Paul under Nero, the worst Roman Emperor. And neither our Lord nor His Apostle denied or reviled the "authority!"

The authority is called a **servant** [*diakonos*] **of God to us for good** (verse 4): and those exercising this authority, are called **ministers** [*leitourgoi*] **of God** for good: He [the power or authority set up by God] **is a minister of God, an avenger for wrath to him that doeth evil** (verse 4 and again in verse 6). Against the evil-worker, the ruler is an avenger for wrath, not bearing a vain sword like some lodge officer on parade, but bearing a sword given to him by the covenant of Genesis Nine, —a sword with, necessarily, the death penalty wrapped up in it, to be exercised when necessary: "Whoso sheddeth man's blood, by man shall his blood be shed," God said to Noah, when He lodged governmental authority in human hands. For the support of this governmental work, we pay "tribute"; for **They are God's ministering officers, attending continually upon this very thing** (verse 6).

Thus there is in this passage to be considered, the governmental authority as an abstract thing established by God; and then the personal ruler's exercising his rights and duties under the authority. God established human government, and then appointed certain men to administer it.

Verse 2: **Therefore he that sets himself against the authority, withstandeth the ordinance of God: and those [thus] withstanding, shall receive to themselves judgment.**

It is only in spiritual matters—"things that are God's"— that "to obey God rather than men" is our path. The things pertaining to God are those that concern our obedience to our confession of the faith of our Lord Jesus Christ,—that is, all matters of our Christian conscience. Caesar has no right to touch my conscience. If I yield to him there, I am a traitor to the truth. We should emulate the old martyrs here, and even those who are suffering for the truth under Caesar's wickedness in our own day: for instance, under pagan Hitlerism in Germany, or atheist communism in Russia, where, often, the most noble witnesses of Christ are found. But, as to our persons and our property and our lives, that is, as regards earthly things, we are subject to the powers that God has put in place or ordained; and should not "withstand" them. Those who do so withstand, will bring on themselves guilt and Divine chastening. The Christian, above all men, should be in quiet subjection to constituted authority.

Verse 3: **For rulers are not a terror to the good work, but to the evil. And wouldest thou have no fear of the authority? Keep practicing that which is good, and thou shalt have praise from the same.**

This is the rule in general. Of course, Satan will stir up special trouble against those who are proclaiming the gospel, which he desperately hates; as he stirred up unjust accusation and persecution against the apostles and the Lord Himself. Also, "the will of God may so will," that some may suffer for well-doing (I Pet. 3.17). This whole passage, however, regards the general path of the believer with reference to Divinely constituted authorities; rather than the peculiar enmity of Satan and the world toward the message of the gospel. Every Christian, in his life, should be praiseworthy in the eyes of rulers, and, if consistent, he generally is so.

William Kelly well says: "'Authorities in power' is an expression that embraces every form of governing power, monarchical, aristocratic, or republican. All cavil on this score is therefore foreclosed. The Spirit insists not merely on the Divine right of kings, but that 'there is no authority except from God.' Nor is there an excuse on this plea for change; yet if a revolution should overthrow one form and set up another, the Christian's duty is plain: 'those that exist are ordained by God.' His interests are elsewhere, are heavenly, are in Christ; his responsibility is to acknowledge what is in power as a fact, trusting God as to the consequences, and in no case behaving as a partisan. Never is he warranted in setting himself up against the authority as such."*

Verse 4: For it [the authority] **is a servant of God to thee for good. But if thou do that which is evil, be afraid; for not in vain does it bear the sword.**

To "bear" is, literally, to bear constantly, illustrated in the provincial Roman magistrates' habitual wearing of the sword. It was also borne before them, in public processions, as a symbol of their right to punish by death. This is in accordance with God's covenant with Noah, after the Flood, which covenant remains in force: "Whoso sheddeth man's blood, by man shall his blood be shed." Those who decry "capital punishment," are

*In those cases where Christians have been able to withdraw from intolerable situations, this rule is in no wise broken. The Huguenots fled from France to England, and the Puritans from England to America, for freedom of conscience, —much as the Lord said, "If they persecute you in one city, flee to another." Escape is sometimes possible, and is not rebellion.

themselves withstanding the Word of God as to the very foundation of human government.

For a minister of God it is! an avenger for wrath to him that doeth evil.

There are people in every community who live in constant terror of government, because of their evil-doing. Let no Christian be in such a position! You say, Would the magistrate have a right to deal with a real Christian, if he became an evil-doer? Most certainly; and would be bound to do so. Peter says: "Let none of you suffer as a murderer, or an evid-doer, or as a meddler in other man's matters," showing that Christians as such, have no protection from human law. But Peter's exhortation has not kept some true Christians out of these things; insomuch, indeed, that God's established government on earth would not or should not permit them to go unpunished here, (if murder or crime had been done) ; although the blood of Christ was their entrance into Heaven!

Verse 5: **Wherefore ye must needs be in subjection,— not only because of the wrath, but also for conscience' sake.**

Believers are to be in subjection, not only to avoid earthly governmental dealing, but because of a loving conscience toward God,—knowing that in being subject, they are doing right, as well as avoiding trouble.

The constituted authorities include all the civil officers, state, county, and municipal; together with the police, militia, and military forces. There are many indeed in these foolish days who call themselves "pacifists," and decry the work and office of the soldier. Yet we believe they would with alacrity telephone for the police if they found marauders breaking into their houses! Police protect towns and cities. State constabulary and militia, under the hand of the governor, protect life, liberty, and order in the state; and a national army does likewise for the nation.

It is God who has allowed the formation and growth of nations, and given them "the bounds of their habitations"; and the "authorities" who govern them do so by Divine command. They "bear the sword,"—whether for order within the nation,

or for defense toward an outward enemy. Therefore it is folly
to call the work of a soldier evil, and to confuse personal murder with the public execution of justice. When "soldiers on
service" (Luke 3.14, margin), asked John the Baptist: "And
we, what must we do"? his answer was not, Resign your com-
missions, or, Leave the army. On the contrary he recognized
their work as honorable, saying to them only: "Extort from
no man by violence, neither accuse anyone wrongfully; and be
content with your wages" (generally, with soldiers, small
enough!)

Cornelius, the centurion of Acts 10, "a devout man, one that
feared God with all his house, who gave much alms to the
people, and prayed to God always," heard the gospel at Peter's
mouth and believed it, and was filled with the Holy Spirit; and
he kept right on being a soldier, a minister of God's service
along the line of government. Such men as General Havelock,
General "Chinese" Gordon of the British Army; General O. O.
Howard and General "Stonewall" Jackson, of American Civil
War fame; and General Allenby, in the World War, have performed nobly and ably their soldier's duty,—the while maintaining a Christian's walk with God.*

---

*Pacifists and "Internationalists" are (sometimes doubtless ignorantly) deadly
enemies of God's order. It is a cowardly and a decadent generation that is willing to enjoy a heritage purchased at the cost of blood and tears, and then with
an ignorant or basely perverted conscience say, "I do not believe in war or in
fighting,"—a generation ignorant, first, of the very Scripture we are now studying, which tells us that magistrates, bearing no vain swords, are ministers of God;
ignorant, second, of the lessons of history.

> "Ill fares the land, to hastening ills a prey,
> Where wealth accumulates, and men decay."

Effeminacy, dilettantism, and loss of patriotism, have always gone together. The
hordes of barbarians from the North came down on a Rome enfeebled by luxury
and hideous sin, and we know the result! Today America is filling up with the
same sort of moral weaklings! We abhor war; but war there will be. We say to
"pacifists": Study the Scriptures and history, and be awakened from a fool's dream
of unrealities.

To those "conscientiously objecting" to bearing arms, we say: Study God's
Word here in Romans 13. The magistrates, the rulers, are ministers of God,
"bearing not the sword in vain." Pacifist principles are doomed to defeat, for
they are anti-Scriptural. You ask me, Would you fight? If called to military
service by my government, I should answer that my ministry is preaching God's
gospel of grace; but that I should gladly go to the battle front, and be placed
in any position of danger, and should minister the gospel even to an active
enemy, or to a prisoner from the enemy's ranks, with the same earnestness which
I should hope to show toward men of my own country. On the other hand, I
should abhor even the thought of divulging my country's secrets to my country's

Verse 6: For this cause ye pay tribute also; for they are ministers of God, attending continually upon this very matter.

Here the apostle uses the word from which we get "liturgy" *(leitourgoi)* in describing these "authorities." God uses the same word in Hebrews 1.14 regarding the angels, calling them "ministering spirits"; and also concerning the "ministering" of the Old Testament priests (Heb. 10.11). In these days of restlessness toward restraint, and flouting of authority, we need to meditate much on the fact that the constituted authorities are *liturgists of God*: not indeed at all in spiritual things, but none the less God's own ministers in governmental things. It is on this account that those governed pay tribute; for these ministers of government must be supported.

Verse 7: Render to all their dues: tribute to whom tribute [is due]; custom to whom custom; fear to whom fear; honor to whom honor.

Here "tribute" (taxes) comes first. How great the temptation to avoid rendering this that is due! Next, "custom"; "tribute" *(phoros)* is generally a tax paid by subjects to a ruling nation (Luke 20.22); while custom *(telos)* is a tax on us, or duty on our goods, by our own nation. Alas, how we loathe having the customs officers "go through" our effects!

---

enemy. This would be rebuked by God Himself, who established nations, and gave them the duty of protecting their citizens and their borders.

Strange dupes are American "pacifists" and "internationalists!"

Christians who desire to know the conditions of the age, and how rapidly "The iniquity of the end" is rushing toward us should read pages 68 to 140 of A. C. Gaebelein's *Conflict of the Ages*. While we are not to be perplexed by the terrible things happening in the world: for the Lord said, "When ye hear of wars and rumors of wars see that ye be not troubled; for all these things must needs come to pass." Nevertheless, we should not be as the leaders of Israel—blind to the days in which they lived. All these new forms of power—Communism, Facism, Naziism; and also the subtle powers of evil working in America are preparing the way for the Antichrist.

Several easily procurable books, such as *Tainted Contacts* by Col. E. N. Sanctuary; *The Red Network*, by Elizabeth Dilling; and *Pastors, Politicians, and Pacifists*, by L. F. Smith and E. B. Johns, expose the poison of this "deadly white snake," pacifism; and should be in the possession of every believer.

In parallel columns on pages 100 to 107, in *Tainted Contacts*, Communists, Socialists, Internationalists, and Pacifists, are shown to be bed-fellows of common aims. The "Federal Council of Churches," (perhaps the most insidiously serpentine in its operations of any organization in America) is seen to be hand-in-glove with all these evil influences.

Again we say, *Read the Scriptures, and re-read them! They alone enlighten, reprove, correct, instruct.*

But let us remember that even customs are "dues," by God's appointment. **Fear to whom fear**—"Fear" does not here designate terror, but (which removes terror) a conscientious regard for and awe of men in whose hands God has placed governmental authority,—whether police, magistrates, judges, governors, presidents, or kings.*

Honor to whom honor—Honor is our attitude of reverence for the persons of those who have authority over us; as also toward those who stand in any place of earthly dignity. As Peter says so beautifully, "Honor all men [for they are made in the image of God]. Love the brotherhood [of saints]. Fear God [with whom you have constantly to do]. Honor the king" [whom you may never see, but whom you hold in due regard in your heart] (I Pet. 2.17). Not only law-officers, but those men to whom God has committed wealth, or outstanding ability; or who have risen honorably among their fellows, should receive the honor due them. Let Christians be first to give "honor to whom honor is due." Leave to the base the despising of others!

8   To none owe anything, except to love one another: for he that loveth the other hath fulfilled
9   law. For this, Thou shalt not commit adultery, Thou shalt not kill, Thou shalt not steal, Thou shalt not covet, and if there be any other commandment, it is summed up in this word, namely,
10 Thou shalt love thy neighbor as thyself. Love

---

*"This ideal of the apostle neither confounds church and state, nor places them in antagonism, but properly co-ordinates them in Christian ethics. Romanism subordinates state to church; Erastianism [as today Fascism and Communism—W. R. N.], subordinates the church to the state, usually confounding them; Puritanism also confounded them, but with more of an acknowledged theocratic principle"—Schaff and Riddle.

We may add that the Reformation did not fully escape, in this respect, from Romanism and Judaism. Calvin established a theocratic state at Geneva, holding fast to civil powers in religious things, which led to the burning of Servetus! While Zwingli, in Switzerland, took the sword, and perished by it. We may further add that in our own day the perpetual meddling with governmental affairs carried on at various government centres by the church lobbies (I write in America) reveals that ignorance of the Church's heavenly calling, and that vain hope to "mend" this present world, which so darkens the counsels of government itself, and increases daily that deep-seated resentment by the powers that be against those who claim *spiritual directive* authority over government. The upshot has always been and will always be disastrous; for the State finally rises up and wades to independence of "religious" interference through rivers of blood!

worketh no ill to one's neighbor: love therefore is
law's fulness.

Verses 8 to 10: **To none owe anything, except to love
one** another—The word "owe" here is the verb of the noun
"dues" in verse seven. The connection is direct: when you
pay up all your dues, whether private debts or public, and have
only this constant obligation before you,—to love one another,
"Love must still remain the root and spring of all your actions; no other law is needed besides. Pay all other debts; be in-
debted in the matter of love alone." So Paul continues: **For
he that loveth the other hath fulfilled law.** Notice carefully that it is love, and not law-doing which is the fulness
(Greek, *plerōma*) of law! The one who loves *has* (without
being under it) exhibited what the Law sought! For the law
said: **Thou shalt love thy neighbor as thyself**; and lo, love
has, *from another principle,* even *love and grace,* zealously
wrought no ill to others. Love, therefore, is shown to be the
fulness (not, "the *fulfilling*") **of the law.** It is only those not
under law that are free to love others. Love, and not righteousness, is the active principle of Christianity. And lo, one
loving, has wrought righteousness! Thus, only those not under law show its fulness. Of course, the believer is in a "new
creation," and is to walk by that infinitely higher "rule of life"
(Gal. 6.15, 16), and not by the Law. Nevertheless, in *loving*
he *has* fulfilled the lower law!

11 And this, knowing the season, that already it is
    time for you to awake out of sleep: for now is our
    salvation nearer to us than when we [first] believed.
12 The night is far spent, and the day is at hand! Let
    us therefore cast off the works of darkness, and let
13 us put on the armor of light. Let us walk becom-
    ingly, as in the day; not in revelling and drunken-
    ness, not in chamberings and wantonness, not in
14 strife and jealousy. But put ye on the Lord Jesus
    Christ, and as for the flesh,—do not make provi-
    sion to fulfil its lusts!

Verse 11: **And this, knowing the season, that already it is time for you to awake out of sleep: for now is our salvation nearer to us than when we [first] believed.**

The hope of the imminency of our Lord's coming, with the consummation of salvation in bodily redemption and glorification, is constantly used by the apostles in exhorting believers to a holy walk in love. This present verse sets before us the awful tendency to sink down (as did the ten virgins!) into slumber and sleep,—into a state of spiritual torpor in which no Christian duties are effectively done. Believers are to "know the season." Our Lord sternly arraigned the Jews of His day for their ignorance concerning "the time"; "When ye see a cloud rising in the West, straightway ye say, There cometh a shower; and so it cometh to pass. And when ye see a south wind blowing, ye say, There will be a scorching heat; and it cometh to pass. Ye hypocrites, ye know how to interpret the face of the earth and the heaven; but how is it that ye know not *how to interpret this time?* And why *even of yourselves* judge ye not what is right?"

There their Messiah was, in their midst, and they knew Him not! Why? Because they did not *apply themselves to know* the time they were in, although they could have known it, both from the prophetic Word which was being fulfilled before their eyes in Christ; and also "of their own selves," if they had set themselves to judge truly of the moral conditions about them and the necessities of action involved therein. If the Jews even then were called by our Lord "hypocrites," for applying their God-given discernment to the signs of the weather, and neglecting to apply it to spiritual things, and so going on blindly to judgment; how much more this should arouse us who have so much greater light and knowledge, in view of Christ's death and resurrection, and the presence of the Holy Spirit; and the certainty of our Lord's coming, and our uncertainty as to the day and hour!

Verse 12: **The night is far spent, and the day is at hand! Let us, therefore, cast off the works of darkness, and let us put on the armor of light**

As long as our Lord was on earth, He was the light of the world (John 9.5). Since He is gone, it is spiritual night. But He now says, "*Ye* [believers] are seen as lights in the world, holding forth the word of life" (Phil. 2.15,16). Of course, it was night for the human race from the moment Adam sinned; and deeper night, as sin increased.

Our Lord's coming brought a brief day—a "day of visitation," and of actual blessing, if they received Him. His return to earth is spoken of as "the Sun of Righteousness arising with healing in His wings," when it will again be *day!* It is good to know, in our wrestling with "the principalities and powers, the world-rulers of this darkness," that **the night is far spent, the day is at hand.** The word translated **at hand** is from the verb to "draw nigh," as in Matthew 21.1. Paul uses it in Hebrews 10.25: "So much the more as ye see the day *approaching*": and it is the same word in I Peter 4.7: "The end of all things is *at hand*" (drawing nigh). No matter what others say about the second coming of Christ, the apostles and the early Church lived in the expectation of it! Read Dean Alford's excellent comment below: remembering that as an expositor of Scripture he is rightly held in the very highest regard with respect to scholarship, sanity, and honesty, as well as devotedness to God.*

Let us therefore cast off the works of darkness—In Ephesians Five, after speaking of the "sons of disobedience,"

---

*"A fair exegesis of this passage can hardly fail to recognize the fact that the Apostle here as well as elsewhere (I Thess. 4:17; I Cor. 15:51), speaks of the coming of the Lord as *rapidly approaching*. Prof. Stuart, (Comm. p. 521), is shocked at the idea, as being inconsistent with the inspiration of his writings. How this can be, I am at a loss to imagine. 'OF THAT DAY AND HOUR KNOW-. ETH NO MAN, NO NOT THE ANGELS IN HEAVEN, NOR THE SON: BUT THE FATHER ONLY' (Mark 13:32). And to reason, as Stuart does, that because Paul corrects in II Thess. 2:1-3, the mistake of imagining it to be *actually come*, he did not himself expect it soon, is surely quite beside the purpose. The fact that the nearness or distance of that day was *unknown to the Apostles,* in no way affects the prophetic announcements of God's Spirit by them, concerning its preceding and accompanying circumstances. The '*day and hour*' formed no part of their inspiration:—the *details of the event, did*. And this distinction has singularly and providentially turned out to the edification of all subsequent ages. While the prophetic declarations of the events of that time remain to instruct us, the *eager expectation* of the time, which *they expressed in their day,* has also remained, a token of the true frame of mind in which each succeeding age *(a fortiori)* should contemplate the ever-approaching coming of the Lord. On the *certainty of the event,* our faith is grounded: by the *uncertainty of the time* our hope is stimulated, and our watchfulness aroused."

Paul says: Be not ye therefore partakers with them; for ye once were darkness, but are now *light in the Lord*: walk as *children of light*. Now Paul had said the saints *had* put off the old man (when they were put into Christ). Now they are to put away, or cast off as not of their new life, all evil things. See Colossians 3.8,9,; and Hebrews 12.1,—for it is the same Greek word as the one there rendered "lay aside." The "works of darkness" are to be "put away," "cast off." And since "our old man was crucified with Christ," we see we *can* put them away! **Let us put on the armor of light.** This is a marvelous exhortation! Modern warfare has contemplated throwing upon the enemy mighty electric lights of such overwhelming brilliancy as to completely dazzle them. We all know how approaching automobile lights often blind us. In the remarkable passage of Luke 11.33-36, our Lord says: "If therefore thy *whole body* be full of light, having no part dark, it shall be *wholly* full of light, as when the lamp with its bright shining shall give thee light." This is the redeemed one whom Satan hates and fears, —one *filled* with light, *armored* with light. A blaze of light is harder to approach than swords or bullets. Our Christian armor, piece by piece, is described in Ephesians 6.11-18. But here it is more our *"walking* in the light, as God is in the light," that is in view. Since we are "light in the Lord," let us so walk and war!

Verse 13: **As those in the day, let us be walking becomingly**—Men choose the night for their revels; but our night is past, for we are all "children of the light and of the day" (I Thess. 5.5). Let us therefore do only what is fit for the light and for the day. We belong to that "day" which our Lord's coming will usher in,—and that *shortly!* Therefore, let us walk as those already in the daylight of that day! **Not in riotings and drunkennesses**—Nocturnal revels such as characterized the Roman Empire of Paul's day, and the myriad drunkennesses of modern "night parties," are in view here. How needful the warning to keep clear of these things in this hour when the time of "the iniquity of the end" (Ezek. 21.25,29) is drawing nigh! Young people, rushing on to damnation, with "dates" beginning at 10 or 11 or even midnight, and ending perhaps at dawn, know well what "revellings and drunkennesses" are. Let the saints in horror shun them!

And the next things of the text follow these, as they have always followed them: **Not in chamberings and wantonness**—The word translated "chamberings" occurs three other times: Luke 11.7, Romans 9.10, Hebrews 13.4. Its being in the plural number here, and associated with the word generally rendered "lasciviousness," suggests its horrid meaning. Schaff and Riddle well say: "Various forms of secret vice are here indicated by the plural. These sins are closely connected with the preceding (revellings and drunkennesses), often caused by them. The word translated 'wantonness' points to an abandoned sensuality." David said: "The floods of ungodliness (Heb.: *Belial*) made me afraid" (Ps. 18.4). So earth's steadily increasing tide of Noah's-day wickedness would terrify us, did we not know that *the Lord is coming,* to deliver His saints and to judge this very wickedness!

Not in strife and jealousy—Brawls, troubles, "wounds without cause"; hatreds and jealousies, follow this train of self-indulgent sins. "Strife and jealousy," here, may also particularly indicate those strifes, envyings, and jealousies which so frequently remain not put away among believers: "Wherefore let us keep the feast, not with old leaven [that is, revellings and vices of the world of the wicked], neither with the leaven of malice and wickedness," (I Cor. 5.8)—which, alas, Paul has to warn against over and over among Christians: "Whereas there is among you jealousy and strife, are ye not carnal, and do ye not walk after the manner of men?" (I Cor. 3.3). "Put away anger, wrath, malice, railing" (Col. 3.8).

Verse 14: **But on the contrary, put ye on the Lord Jesus Christ, and for the flesh,—do not make provisions, to fulfil its lusts.**

The full title of our Lord Jesus Christ awakes, almost startles us, here: *Jesus* is His *personal* name (Matt. 1.21); as *Christ,* the anointed One, He does His *saving work;* as *Lord,* He is *over all things.* The full title was announced by Peter at Pentecost: "God hath made Him *both Lord and Christ,* this *Jesus* whom ye crucified." All true believers have put on

Christ (Gal. 3.27) for He is their life; and the Corinthians were told that Jesus Christ was in them (II Cor. 13.5). It is striking that the first use of our Lord's full title is by Peter in Acts 11.17, in connection with the gift of the Holy Spirit in the upper room: "The gift God gave unto us, when we believed on the *Lord Jesus Christ.*" They had before believed on *Jesus,* as the Jewish Messiah, the Christ, the Son of God: but evidently when He had ascended into glory, God led them to a surrendering of earthly hopes, and an appropriating of *their Lord,* in His now exalted and glorified character, as *the Lord Jesus Christ,* in a phase of faith never know before. It is this Christ Paul commands us to put on—the Lord Jesus Christ! Not as our righteousness are we to "put Him on": for He is Himself the righteousness of all believers. But it is as to our walk and warfare that we put Him on. We are to be panoplied with Christ!

There is an instructive passage in Colossians Three, giving light on this command to "put on." In verse 3 there, the Holy Spirit says through Paul, "Ye died." (It is an aorist tense, asserting a fact.) The believer now shares Christ's risen life, and is told (as we have repeatedly seen) that he is "alive from the dead," a *new creation.* In the ninth verse of the same chapter, we have the words, "Ye *have* put off the old man"; and in verse 10, "Ye *have* put on the new man"! Then, in verses 5 and 8, "put to death," "put away," your "members which are in the earth: fornication, uncleanness, passion; anger, wrath, malice," and all such things. It is in and by the fact that we died with Christ that we have "put off the old man": as is said in Colossians 2.11, also, concerning our participation in "the circumcision of Christ"* (His cutting off in death), we put off "the body of the flesh."

Then, (and not until our realization by faith of this federal death with Christ), are we ready in confidence to "put away" all those things that belong to our former manner of life, the

---

*The circumcision with hands, of our Lord, when He was a babe eight days old (Luke 2.21), is here distinguished from His death, as cut off from natural life,—a "circumcision made without hands," and in which we have such part that we are now called "the circumcision" (Phil. 3.3). Jewish circumcision was a striking token of that death to the flesh which was executed at the cross.

old things, and to "put on, as God's elect, holy and beloved (of Him), a heart of compassion, kindness, humility, meekness" (Col. 3.12, ff).

"Putting on the Lord Jesus Christ" is, therefore, our path, not only prescribed, but gloriously attainable. For we are *in* Him! and that federal "new man which hath been created in righteousness and holiness of truth" (Eph. 4.24) belongs now to us. Even as "the old man" belonged by natural birth to us in the First Adam, so does the "new man" belong to us who are in Christ, the Last Adam!

Make not provision for the flesh—The word "provision" here is literally "forethought." It denotes the attitude of mind we used to have toward the flesh, as secretly expecting to gratify it, if not immediately, yet at some time. It is the opposite of the spirit of Galatians 5.24; it is Saul sparing Agag.

To fulfil its desires — The flesh has endless lusts and desires,—all clamoring for indulgence. Besides the lower lusts, and our natural self-sparing slothfulness, there are all the forms of self-pleasing: self-esteem, "sensitiveness," love of praise, man-fearing, fleshly amiability, flattery of others for selfish ends, pride, "dignity," impatience of non-recognition by others, sheer empty conceit, and a thousand other "desires of the flesh," for which **no provision** is to be made. Often we can, if we will, see beforehand and shun circumstances that would give the flesh an advantage to indulge itself. But it is only by **putting on the Lord Jesus Christ** as the positive attitude of the soul, that we shall find ourselves able and willing to refuse any provision for the flesh.*

---

*Bishop Moule beautifully says: "Put on, clothe, and arm yourselves with the Lord Jesus Christ, Himself, the living Sum and true Meaning of all that can arm the soul. It is by living our life in the flesh by faith in the Son of God (Gal. 2:20), that is, to say, in effect, by personally making use of the crucified and living Savior, Lord, Deliverer, our Peace and Power, amidst all the dark hosts of evil can do against us. Full in the face of the realities of sin—of Roman sin, in Nero's day—St. Paul has written down across them all, this spell, this Name: 'Put ye on the Lord Jesus Christ.' Take first a steady look, he seems to say, at your sore need, in the light of God; but then at once look off, look here. Take your iniquities at the worst; this can subdue them. Take your surroundings at the worst,—this can emancipate you from their power. It is the 'Lord Jesus Christ' and the 'putting on' of Him. We can 'put Him on' as Lord, surrendering ourselves to His absolute, while most benignant, sovereignty and will,—deep secret

CONCERNING CAPITAL PUNISHMENT

1. God for His own reasons forbade any human hand to execute Cain, the first murderer. Iniquity increased, and God brought the Deluge.

2. After the Deluge, God announced a complete change of earth's governmental affairs. In the words of Genesis 9.5 and 6, "Surely your blood, the blood of your lives, will I require; at the hand of every beast will I require it; and at the hand of man, even at the hand of every man's brother, will I require the life of man. Whoso sheddeth man's blood, by man shall his blood be shed; for in the image of God made He man." God here puts the sword of the magistrate into man's hand as not before. Furthermore, the "everlasting covenant" with Noah, of which the above quoted words were a part, God said would last "while the earth remaineth" (Gen. 8.20-9.7).

3. Under the Law of Moses, 1000 years later, God reaffirmed the governmental duty of punishing murderers with death: "Ye shall take no ransom for the life of a murderer that is guilty of death. For blood, it polluteth the land, and no expiation can be made for the land for the blood that is shed therein, but by the blood of him that shed it" (Num. 35.31,33).

4. Note that in the above quotation, the crime of murder is said by God so to pollute the land, that there can be "no expiation made for a land" for this crime, save by the execution of the murderer.

5. It is said that upwards of 200,000 known man-killers are alive in America. "To realize," said Judge Kavanagh of Chicago, "the prevalency of this invisible class (murderers at large in the United States), it is only necessary to consider that they are more than we have of clergymen of all denominations, or male teachers in our schools; or all lawyers, judges, and magistrates, put together; and three times the number of our editors, reporters, and writers; and 52,000 more unconfined killers than we have policemen." Only by the stern carry-

---

of repose. We can put Him on as 'Jesus,' clasping the truth that He, our human Brother, yet Divine, saves His people from their sins. We can put Him on as 'Christ,' our Head, anointed without measure by the eternal Spirit, and still sending of that same Spirit into His happy members,—so that we are indeed one with Him, and receive into our whole being the resources of His life."

ing out of the command of God regarding the murderer, can this crime be checked.

(In England, where more than 90% of murderers are executed after a fair but speedy trial, even the police do not carry revolvers except by special license!)

6. To claim that it is "not Christian" to execute murderers, is to deny directly Paul's plain word here in Romans Thirteen, that the magistrate "beareth not the sword in vain," being "a minister of wrath to him that doeth evil," and one of whom evil-doers are commanded to be afraid.

7. It is therefore an appalling disservice to home, state, and nation, to call that *murder* which God has *commanded to be done*—the execution of shedders of human blood. It is a libel on Christianity to claim that the current anti-capital-punishment cry is Christian. It is not Christian, but rebellion against God. "We suffer," said the penitent thief to his impenitent companion on the cross, "the due reward of our deeds!" That penitent thief said to Jesus, "Lord, remember me"; and our Lord's answer, "Today thou shalt be with me in Paradise," shows anew the great truth that government in this world, and salvation in the next, are two absolutely distinct things. Only the ignorant confound them.

CHAPTER FOURTEEN

Strong and Weak Believers Neither to Despise nor to Judge Each Other. Verses 1 to 12.

Perfect Liberty in this Dispensation; but Each Must Walk According to Conscience. Verses 13 to 23.

1   But him that is weak in faith, receive ye, yet not
2 for decision of [his] scruples [for him]. One man hath faith to eat all things: but he that is weak
3 eateth herbs. Let not him that eateth set at nought him that eateth not; and let not him that eateth not judge him that eateth: for God hath received him.
4 Who art thou that judgest the house-servant of another? to his own Master he standeth or falleth. Yea, he shall be made to stand; for the Lord hath power to make him stand.
5   One man esteemeth one day above another: another esteemeth every day [alike]. Let each man
6 be fully assured in his own mind. He that regardeth the day, regardeth it unto the Lord: and he that eateth, eateth unto the Lord, for he giveth God thanks; and he that eateth not, unto the Lord he eateth not, and giveth God thanks.
7   For none of us liveth to himself, and none dieth
8 to himself. For whether we live, we live unto the Lord: or whether we die, we die unto the Lord: whether we live therefore, or die, we are the Lord's.
9 For to this end Christ died and lived again, that He [and none else] might rule over both the dead and the living.
10   But thou, why dost thou judge thy brother? or thou again, why dost thou set at nought thy brother? for we shall all stand before the judgment-seat of God.

11   For it is written,
            As I live, saith the Lord, to Me every knee
                shall bow.
            And every tongue shall confess to God.
12   So then each one of us shall give account of him-
            self to God.

PAUL, IN THIS Fourteenth Chapter, and the following
one, directs his instruction chiefly "to the 'strong,' who can
bear it, while indirectly showing the state of the 'weak'"! Those
weak in faith, like babes, are not able to take much nourish-
ment at once; while those who are strong are often not willing
to receive what seems to reflect upon their vigor. To have faith
before God, secretly, hiding it from the weaker brother, *for his
sake,* until he becomes stronger, is not easy: it requires walking
in love, which is always costly to the one loving!

Verse 1: **But him that is weak in faith receive ye, yet
not for decison 'of [his] scruples [for him]**—As to receiving
and welcoming into our fellowship believers less instructed or
with weaker faith than ourselves, let us note what our attitude
should be, (1) toward those less instructed or of weaker faith
than ourselves; and (2) toward those with greater knowledge,
and liberty of conscience, than ourselves.

There are those who are "weak" in faith. They have true
faith, they have Christ; but, because of traditional or legal
teaching; or perhaps through Satan's accusations on account of
former sins; or through not grasping the fact of their death
with Christ and their present and eternal union with Him; or
possibly because of habits of introspection and self-accusation,
or even through unsubdued sin,—for some or all of these reasons, they are "weak."

Such weak ones are to be *received.* Of course, in these days,
when that sweet powerful fellowship of the early Christian
assemblies, that consciousness of the presence in the assembly
of the Holy Spirit, and so of the Risen Christ, is rare, there is
difficulty in making clear the meaning of the word "receive."
Ecclesiastical procedure has so usurped the place and preroga-
tives of the saints' acting by the conscious will of the Holy

Spirit, as largely to obliterate the meaning of these words, "receive ye." People say, Was not so and so received into the church by the pastor and officers? "Official action" has supplanted the saints' blessed ministry of receiving, as described here.

Nevertheless, we must go directly to Scripture in this serious, practical matter. By "receiving" the weak brother, is not meant allowing him to "join the church"; but acknowledging him, by the discernment of the Spirit, to be a man of faith (even though his name be Mr. Ready-to-halt). Thus he and we are members one of another, being in Christ. And there is the same welcome in the assembly to this feebler member as to the most gifted teacher of the Word among us. It is not that he has been "officially recognized," but that he has been discerned generally and welcomed, in the Spirit.

He is to be *received,*—but not to decide for him his conscientious scruples. No one's conscience but his own can direct him. He may be taught the Word, however, and God will bring him along. He must not be forced. If he have faith, though it be but weak faith, he is among us not by our action, but by Christ's.

What a terrible contrast to the teaching of this Scripture is presented by the "close communion" people, and the "exclusivists," of all sorts. Unless a man pronounces "shibboleth" their way, there is not the thought of receiving him. This is the Pharisaism of the last days. And sad to say it is most found among those most enlightened in the truth, for "knowledge puffeth up, but love buildeth up." We are profoundly convinced that if those who now "exclude" so readily those differing from them were filled with love, filled with the Holy Ghost, not only would there be deliverance from the awful wickedness of "exclusiveness," but there would be hundreds, even thousands, of hungry believers flocking into fellowship, where they would be lovingly greeted *just as they are!* Further teaching for them can wait: but receive them!

Where faith in Christ in the least degree is found, we should be thankfully delighted, and should welcome such believers.

All believers have not the same knowledge, nor the same freedom from tradition, nor the same strength of appropriating
faith. We have no right to say to believers, "Sit back, until we
are satisfied about you." This puts your will between believers
and fellowship with God's saints.

Verse 2: **One man hath faith to eat all things: but he
that is weak eateth herbs.**

In this verse Paul illustrates the strength and weakness of
faith in a way that not only the Jewish believers of his day,
but also people in our day, instantly understand. **Faith to
eat all things:** "Faith" here means knowledge and heart-
persuasion that Jewish distinctions of meats do not exist in this
dispensation, which knowledge, one having, could eat any food
with thankfulness, and with no scruples. Though certain flesh
had been forbidden to an Israelite, and may be still regarded
as an improper food by many, yet the strong believer remembers
how our Lord Himself "made all meats clean" (Mark 7:19);
and how Peter, insisting on regarding "all manner of four-
footed beasts and creeping things and birds" as "common and
unclean," heard God say thrice over, "What God hath cleansed,
make not thou common."*

To eat all things—At man's creation, God gave him the
"green herb" and the fruits of "trees yielding seed." After the
Flood, God gave man "every moving thing that liveth," to be
food for him (Gen. 9.3). Today, all these foods are for us:
herbs, fruits, flesh (and that of "all manner of four-footed
beasts and creeping things of the earth and birds of the heaven"
—Acts 10.12); and Paul also commands Timothy to "use a
little wine for his stomach's sake, and his often infirmities."

Christian freedom, then, takes no account of former restrictions of either food or drink, *except for the weak brother's sake.*

---

*Our Lord taught with sunlight clearness, "There is nothing from without a man,
that entering into him can defile him" (Mark 7.15). The word "nothing" is de-
cidedly emphatic and embraces what we drink as well as what we eat. And the
weak in faith must remember this before they condemn the saints who use the
liberty here given to them.

On the other hand, Paul teaches that this liberty of the stronger believer will
limit itself by love. There has not been a time since he wrote when it was more
necessary to heed this than today. For now there is abundant teaching, in zeal
without knowledge, that contradicts and nullifies the principle laid down by Christ.
This false teaching binds, without enlightening, the conscience.

"All things are clean" must be allowed to cover *all* things, whether of food or drink. The only restricting thought is of the "weak" brother who does not see this.*

But he that is weak eateth herbs—Mark this! The "vegetarian," if so by conscience, is a "weak" brother. There even are those today who esteem themselves particularly "strong," in abstaining from eating flesh, although God says, meats were "created to be received with thanksgiving, by them that believe and [also] *know the truth*. For *every* creature of God is good, and *nothing* is to be rejected, if it be *received with thanksgiving*: for it is sanctified through the Word of God and prayer" (I Tim. 4.3-5). To make distinctions of meats where God has set aside such distinctions, is sad weakness indeed,—and sometimes presumption. However, presumptuous people are not in view in Romans 14.2, but simply those whose faith is not strong enough to enable them to eat the food they have been accustomed to regard as "forbidden."

Verse 3: **Let not him that eateth set at nought him that eateth not**—Here is a solemn charge to the stronger brother. He that is strong in the liberty of faith is directed not to "set at nought" the weaker one. This applies not to eating only, but to the matter of regarding days, and to any other things people have "scruples" about. How a strong man loves to walk with a little child, holding his hand gently, and not ridiculing or scorning his weakness! Let us walk thus with weaker brethren!

And let not him that eateth not judge him that eateth—The weaker brother is not to "judge" the stronger. And note, in the case of the stronger, are used the words, **For God hath received him.** Doubtless God has received the weaker brother also. But do you know it is much more difficult for us really to believe in our hearts that God approves a man of wide Christian liberty, than to believe that God approves a man of

---

*There is, of course, to be temperance in the use of all things. "The bishop must be temperate," even as the deacon must not be "given to much wine" (I Tim. 3.2,8).

Nor is the man who has intelligent faith deceived by the wily pretenses of these last days, whether of the "vegetarians," or of the don't-eat-starch-and-protein-together people. He remembers that God sent the ravens with *bread* and *flesh* twice a day to Elijah!

many conscientious scruples? Yet the man of wide, strong faith, is honoring the work of Christ, as the man of trembling conscience has not yet come to do!

Verse 4: Paul writes this verse directly regarding this judging, whether secret or open, of Christ's stronger servants by weaker ones; and thus he encourages Christian freedom: **Who art thou that judgest another's house-servant? to his own master he standeth or falleth. Yea, he shall be made to stand; for the Lord hath power to make him stand**—despite the criticisms and judgings of those who have not his faith.

It is striking, and tenderly suggestive, that the word "servant" in this verse is "household servant," or, as we have shortened, "house-servant." How would we, as masters of houses, feel, if, having invited a number of guests to dinner, we should overhear one of these guests criticizing the servant who waited upon him! Now Christ is Head over God's house, and all believers are servants of *Christ*. Let no one undertake to judge, therefore, a servant of Another—before whom we shall all shortly stand!

And meanwhile, no matter what are our failures, or the attitude of others toward us, the fact remains that our Lord "hath power to make us *stand*," before Him,—our only Judge. What a deep comfort these words are!

Verse 5: **One man regardeth one day to be above another: another regardeth every day [alike]. Let each man be fully assured in his own mind.** Here Paul takes up the "day question,"—a live one to this hour! You instantly say, Is not the Lord's Day above others? No, not in itself, as a "holy" day, in the sense that the Sabbath was and will be to Israel. Paul shows this plainly in his exhortation of Colossians 2.16: "Let no man judge you . . . in respect of . . . a sabbath day." For, says he, you died with Christ unto earthly religious things; and must not now "observe" them. This passage shows that the first day of the week is not the "sabbath" at all. All those days of Judaism were "shadows." "But the body is Christ's." But you say, I am not a Jew; the day has been *changed*. To which I answer, you speak as might a

Jew; for the day has *not* been "changed." There is but one weekly Sabbath known in Scripture and that is *the seventh day*. It will even be observed again weekly, in the land of Israel, after "the six working days," of every week in the coming age, the Millennium (Ezek. 46.1,3,4). Because men have been wrongly taught or influenced, whether by Judaizing believers in the early Christian centuries, or alas, by Reformers and Puritans since the Reformation, most Christians regard the first day of the week as "the weekly Sabbath," a "holy day,"—which entirely defeats its proper Scripture use. It substitutes a stern legal *must* for grace's sweet word, *privilege*. "The so-called Puritan teaching here has been rightly called 'an adulterous theology'; because it sought to marry believers to both husbands, to the Law and to Christ" (Scofield).

Howbeit, let us remain in the spirit of this fifth verse, which is one of love: **Another regardeth every day** (alike). The weak brother, still influenced in his conscience by legal considerations, held the first day of the week* as peculiar and sacred *in itself*. He invested it with the restrictions of a Jewish *sabbath*, insead of hailing it with fresh joy each week as an opportunity for remembering, with other Christians, his Lord; and our place in the new creation with Him.

Now, the strong believer regarded every day alike. Each day alike was an opportunity for him to be filled with the Spirit, and in everything by word or deed giving thanks unto God the Father through Him. No day, thus, was holy *in itself*, above another! Privilege there was on the Lord's Day, but no

---

*Paul is evidently *not* speaking here of "various Jewish feasts and festivals," as some claim. Paul has nothing but the severest reprimands for those who turn to "observing days, and months, and seasons and years" (Gal. 4.10), and calls Judaism "weak and beggarly rudiments," now,—like the old idolatry (vv. 8.9); and in Colossians 2.14: "The bond which was contrary to us" having been nailed to the cross, he classes feast days and new moons along with "a sabbath day"; and asks believers not to let themselves be "judged" about them.

With such observances, the Christian had nothing to do. But as to the first day of the week, marked out by the resurrection of our Lord, and His appearings to the disciples, as also by the breaking of bread (Acts 20.7,8), and the Christian's systematic giving (I Cor. 16.2), the matter was different. The Christians gathered on the first day, they remembered the Lord at His table on that evening, weekly. (I say, "evening," for it was so at the beginning—John 20.19, Acts 20.7). God has indeed graciously so ordered things now, that we have the whole day. Yet look at Russia! And the same godlessness is spreading over the whole earth. Living faith in Christ,—not any kind of bondage, can sustain us.

bondage. Paul's instruction is, **Let each man be fully assured in his own mind.** Moses never could have said a thing like that! There is a sense in which these words reveal our liberty in Christ as does no other single passage. The Law allowed no liberty of action in such things: its very spirit and essence was bondage to a letter. Conscience was judged beforehand by the letter of the Law; conduct was prescribed. When a man gathered sticks on the Sabbath, he was stoned! Not so, now! Not being under the Law, or the legal principle, but in the Risen Christ, under God's eternal favor, we have entered upon what the Spirit, in Chapter Twelve, calls our "intelligent service." Here is an amazing sphere of holy freedom in which each of us, learning the truth, is treated as a king in the realm of his own mind. Instead of being told what he must or must not do, he is freely exhorted to assure his own mind and heart fully, and walk as Christ's free man. Read Alford's trenchant note below.*

6   He that regardeth the day, regardeth it unto the
     Lord: and he that eateth, eateth unto the Lord, for
     he giveth God thanks; and he that doth not eat,
     unto the Lord he doth not eat, and giveth thanks
     to God.

---

*"The Apostle *decides nothing;* leaving *every man's own mind* to guide him in the point. He classes the observance or non-observance of particular days, with the eating or abstaining from particular meats. In both cases, he is concerned with things which he evidently treats as of *absolute indifference in themselves.* Now the question is, supposing the Divine obligation of one day in seven to have been recognized by him *in any form,* could he have thus spoken? The obvious inference from his strain or arguing is, that *he knew of no such obligation,* but believed *all times and days to be,* to the Christian strong in faith, ALIKE. I do not see how the passage can be otherwise understood. If any one day in the week were invested with the sacred character of the Sabbath, it would have been *wholly impossible* for the Apostle to commend or uphold the man who judged all days worthy of equal honour,—who, as in verse 6, paid *no regard* to the (any) day. He must have visited him with his strongest disapprobation, as violating a command of God. *I therefore infer, that sabbatical obligation to keep any day, whether seventh or first, was not recognized in apostolic times.* It must be carefully remembered, that this inference does not concern the question of the observance of *the Lord's Day as an institution of the Christian Church, analogous to* the ancient Sabbath, but not in any way inheriting the Divinely-appointed obligation of the other, or the strict prohibitions by which its sanctity was defended. The reply commonly furnished to these considerations, viz., that the Apostle was speaking here only of JEWISH festivals, and therefore cannot refer to Christian ones, is a quibble of the poorest kind: its assertors themselves distinctly maintaining the obligation of one such Jewish festival on Christians. What I maintain is, that had the Apostle believed as they do, he could not by any possibility have written thus. Besides, in the face of 'every day' the assertion is altogether unfounded." (Alford: New Test., *in loc.*)

7   For none of us liveth to himself, and none dieth
8   to himself. For whether we live, we live unto the
     Lord; or whether we die, we die unto the Lord;
     whether therefore we live or die, we are the Lord's.
9   For to this end Christ died and lived again, that
     He might rule over both the dead and the living.

Verse 6: These verses, of course, contemplate true believers
only, those who "give God thanks."

Here we have some **regarding the day** as holy in itself.
Jewish believers especially, not fully delivered from the Law,
would have tender consciences about days. But if they knew
the Lord, it would be **toward the Lord** their consciences could
be exercised, and they must be considered in love on that account; love would see through their eyes!

Again, there were those with greater knowledge and liberty
who "regarded not the day," knowing that every day, for those
risen in Christ, is alike: the first day of the week being not a
sabbath, but rather the celebration of our Lord's resurrection
which delivered us from legal things. Ignatius (martyred
about 115 A.D.) said, "Those who were concerned with old
things have come to newness of confidence, no longer keeping
Sabbaths, but living according to the Lord's Day, on whom our
life, as risen again, through Him, depends." And Justin Martyr, (martyred about 168 A.D.) when reproached by Trypho
with "giving up the Sabbath," said, "How can we keep the
Sabbath, who rest from sin all the days of the week?"

Let those of legal tendencies mark this: that a man may
regard not what we *regard,* and do so "unto the Lord." Then
the man who has liberty to eat all things, eats "unto the Lord,"
and gives God thanks. And again, (let the stronger brother
consider) there are those that *eat not* as "unto the Lord," giving
God thanks.

Verses 7, 8, 9: The argument of verses 7, 8 and 9 is that
each one of us is living or dying absolutely *unto the Lord,*—
whose we are. We are not in any sense one another's lords!
but belong to Christ alone, who died and lived that He might
rule over us all,—and not we be lords of each other! or of the
faith of others! Therefore comes the searching question:

Verses 10-12: But thou, why dost thou judge thy
brother? or thou, again, why dost thou set at nought thy
brother? for we shall all stand before the judgment-seat of
God.

For it is written:

As I live, saith the Lord, to Me every knee shall bow,
—[not to men].

And every tongue shall confess to God.

So then each one of us shall give account concerning himself to God—[not to men].

The best manuscripts read "the judgment-seat of God" in
verse 10: thus accommodating the words to the quotation from
the Old Testament (Isa. 14.23). This word "God" is also used
in Romans 14.12, as we see; although we know from II Corinthians 5.10, it will actually be before the judgment-seat of
Christ that believers will be called. (Always remembering that
Christ is God the Son.) Also, that "the Father has given *all*
judgment to the Son" (John 5.22).

Of course we know from our Lord's words in John 3.18 and
5.24, that condemnatory judgment cannot be applied to believers
here, for, "He that believeth on Him is not judged"; "Verily,
verily, I say unto you, He that heareth my word, and believeth
on Him that sent Me, hath eternal life, and cometh not into
judgment, but hath passed out of death into life." In Revelation 20, also, the saved, the "blessed and holy," partake of the
first resurrection; and over them the second death, the penalty
of the lost, 1000 years later, has "no authority." Nevertheless,
we must not allow this blessed fact to dull the force of the
solemn question propounded to us by our beloved apostle Paul,
as to *how we dare* either judge or despise our brother? seeing
that such action involves presumptuous forgetfulness both of
the fact that *we are not judges;* and of the other fact that we
shall all, though saved, stand before the judgment-seat of God
and each "give an account of *himself*" to *Him.* In II Corinthians 5:10, of this judgment-seat (*bema*) for believers this
is said: "We must all be made manifest before the judgment-
seat of Christ; that each one may receive the things done in
the body, according to what he hath done, whether it be good

or bad." In I Corinthians 3.13-15, we see that "if any man's work shall abide . . . he shall receive a reward." It is a matter of reward for our service, and not salvation, that is here in question. "If any man's work shall be burned, he shall suffer loss; but he himself shall be saved; yet so as through fire"— that is, losing, as one whose house is burned, all his goods, though himself delivered. The whole emphasis here in Romans 14.12, is that each gives an account concerning *himself*—not of others; and to *God* instead of to man!

The reading "judgment-seat of Christ," Romans 14.10, would seem to agree both with II Corinthians 5.10, and the whole spirit of the preceding verses here, especially verse 9. We know also that the Father has committed to the Son all judgment, both of believers and unbelievers (John 5.22,27; Acts 17.31). But that it is before *God* (instead of a fellow-man) that all will bow, is being emphasized; and Christ is God, and will, we believe, as Man be the Judge, even at the Great White Throne of Revelation 20.11-15.

13   No longer, therefore, let us [Christians] be judging one another. But do judge ye this, rather, that no man put an obstacle in his brother's way,

14   or a snare. I [personally] know and am persuaded in the Lord Jesus, that nothing is unclean of itself: save that to him who reckoneth anything to be

15   unclean, to that one it is unclean. For if because of thy food thy brother is grieved, thou walkest no longer in love. Destroy not with thy food that one for whom Christ died!

16,17   Let not then your good be evil spoken of. For the kingdom of God is not eating and drinking, but righteousness and peace and joy in the Holy Spirit.

18   For the one herein serving Christ is well-pleasing to God, and approved of men.

19   So then let us pursue things which make for peace, and things whereby we may edify one

20   another. Overthrow not for food's sake the work of God! All things indeed are clean; howbeit it is

21 evil for that man who eateth with stumbling. It
is noble not to eat flesh, nor to drink wine, nor
[to do] anything whereby thy brother stumbleth,
22 or is offended or is made weak. The faith which
thou hast, have thou to thyself before God. Blessed
is he that doth not judge himself in that which he
23 alloweth! But he that doubteth is condemned if
he eat, because he eateth not of faith; and whatsoever is not of faith is sin.

Verse 13: No longer, therefore, let us [Christians] be
judging one another. But do judge ye this, rather, that no
man put a stumbling-block in his brother's way, or an occasion of falling.

Here now is indeed a field for *judging!* and it is ourselves,
not our brother, which we are to judge! And it is ours to see
to it that no one of us is, or is doing, aught that hinders or
stumbles any brother. If these comments persuade any Christian to stop judging others and begin to judge himself, it
will indeed be a fruit unto God! A stumbling-block is
something in us that grieves a weaker brother; an occasion of falling, signifies that which we may freely do, but
which another, undertaking, may in doing act against his
own conscience, and therefore sin. Literally, the word means
"snare," or "trap."

Verse 14: I know [personally], and am persuaded in the
Lord Jesus, that nothing is unclean in itself: save that to
him that reckoneth anything to be unclean, to that one it
is unclean.

Paul states in verse 14 his own knowledge and liberty,—
which is our pattern. Note carefully that knowledge comes
first: "I know." "Persuasion in the Lord Jesus," that is, full
heart liberty, or freedom of conscience, is *second*. There must
be *both*,—not only knowledge of the Christian's freedom, but
heart and conscience *persuasion,* if we would *walk* in the liberty that belongs to the Christian. To such a one, nothing is
unclean "of itself." Distinction of meats (as under Judaism)
is entirely gone; distinction of days (as under Judaism) is
entirely gone. It is only to those whose lack of knowledge or

weakness of conscience "accounts" or holds a thing to be *un-clean,*—or, as we say, "wrong," that it is so. What a glorious deliverance! No place is left for "religious fussing." Christ, and the freedom that is in Him, fills all heaven, our whole horizon, at every moment: "To me, to live is *Christ.*"

But to the conscience not yet delivered (and real freedom of conscience is more rare than we think!) many things seem to be "unclean" *in themselves*: that is, Christians feel it is "wrong" to do them. You and I may have full light to the contrary: yea, these also may see the written Word that "nothing is unclean in itself" in this dispensation. But the conscience cannot be commanded. It must be *persuaded,* by the blessed Spirit—*in the Lord Jesus.* When one is thus set free, his walk is not forced, but happy and natural.

Verse 15: **For if because of meat thy brother is grieved,* thou art no longer walking according to love. Do not with thy meat destroy that one for whom Christ died.** "If Christ so loved as to die for him, how base in you or me not to submit to the smallest self-denial for his welfare!" This verse often occasions the question, How could a "brother" be in danger of destruction? Let me quote on this passage from Charles Hodge, one of the greatest Calvinistic writers: "Believers (the elect) are constantly spoken of (in Scripture) as in danger of perdition. They are saved only if they continue stedfast (in faith). If they apostatize, they perish. If the Scriptures tell the people of God what is the tendency of their sins as to themselves, they may tell them what is the tendency of such sins as to others. Saints are preserved not in spite of apostasy, but from apostasy." To this agree Paul's words: "Ye are saved *if* ye hold fast the word which I preached unto you" (I Cor. 15.2). "If so be that ye continue in the faith, grounded and stedfast, and not moved away from the hope of the gospel" (Col. 1.23). Before us, in verse 15, lies the awful fact that the destruction

---

*"Two stages are noted in the words 'grieved' and 'destroy.' When one man sees another do that which his own conscience condemns, it causes him pain (he is grieved); but when he is further led on from this to do *himself* what his conscience condemns, he is in danger of a worse fate; he is morally ruined and undone (destroyed). The work of redemption that Christ has wrought for him is cancelled, and all that great and beneficent scheme is hindered of its operation by an act of thoughtlessness or want of consideration on the part of a fellow-Christian"—Sanday.

of one who is called a brother lies within the power of our use of our liberty—if it causes him to "stumble."

This does not touch the security of those born of God and "sealed to the day of redemption." God says even of the carnal Corinthians, that "God was faithful, through whom they were called," "who would confirm them unto the end" (I Cor. 1.8,9). But we are not saved as *automatons!* God gives us a gospel to be believed, and a walk to be walked, corresponding to that gospel. That God can (and often does) rescue those whose walk is a failure is seen in the stern, but saving dealing with the brother of I Corinthians 5.1-5. But this same epistle records the solemn warning quoted above: "Ye are saved *if ye hold fast the words.*" Modernists, like all infidels, make light of "holding fast the pattern of sound words" (II Tim. 1.13). But God told earnest, praying Cornelius to send for Peter, who should "speak unto him *words,* by which he should be *saved*" (Acts 11.13,14). Faith begins and lives by God's words only!

Verse 16: **Let not then your good be evil spoken of**— (literally, *blasphemed*): "Good" here refers to the use of Christian liberty by those who are strong of faith, which is indeed good and delightful to God in itself; but in the use of which one must take heed that it be not judged and spoken evil of by the weaker brethren. We must always have the weaker in mind. You may have very blessed liberty in Christ; and that is *good!* But watch, in using your freedom, lest some one not having your freedom calls your path wickedness! Don't *lose* your liberty, but *use* it carefully. (See verse 22.)

Verse 17: Now Paul writes a great verse, giving such a reason for this careful walk as ought to win all of us:

For the kingdom of God is not eating and drinking, but righteousness and peace and joy in the Holy Spirit. For the one thus serving Christ, is well pleasing to God, and approved of men.

In saying **the kingdom of God is not eating and drinking,** Paul at one word sweeps the whole Christian platform clear of the rubbish of all the traditions of men. Men bow, for example, to the Pope's "no-meat-on-Fridays." But let these mark well that all such things have nothing whatever to do with the *king-*

dom of God! The kingdom of God **is righteousness, peace and joy in the Holy Spirit.** Man cannot even *see* the kingdom of God except by a new, "down from above" *(anothen)* BIRTH (John 3.3)! And, since the Holy Spirit came at Pentecost, believers are said to be *in the Spirit*—no longer in *the flesh*—to which the earthly distinctions of meats and days pertained.

And note, that the words here are not, righteousness *in Christ*—referring to our standing; but **righteousness in the Holy Spirit**—referring to our *walk!* Also, **joy in the Holy Spirit.** We cannot too strongly emphasize this fact—that "the kingdom of God," now, is altogether in the Spirit! This leaves forms and ceremonies, days and seasons, unclean meats and clean meats, absolutely *out!* Such things are *not Christian.* They are Jewish or pagan, now! Such "religious" distinctions as these concerning eating and drinking are certainly not at all in *the Holy Ghost*—where all the saints now are (Rom. 8.9), and in whose energy *all* the real operations of "the kingdom of God" now are!

Verse 18: **The one herein serving Christ**—This word **herein** refers to the state of righteousness of life, peace of heart, and joy in God which those walking in the Spirit display. And the words **serving Christ** further prove that verse 17 has reference to practical walk, not to our standing in Christ. One thus walking, we see, **is well-pleasing to God, and approved of men.** Our Lord said, "If any man serve Me, him will the Father honor" (John 12.26). Nothing really pleases God, (since Christ the Son has been manifested, and become obedient to the Father even unto death), but to have men know and serve Christ—whose yoke is easy! But such service is made possible only since the coming of the Holy Spirit: therefore, "righteousness, peace, joy, in the Holy Spirit" is that service of Christ which delights God. **And approved of men**—Men will not always admit it, but they approve a believer who walks righteously, in Divine peace, and joy. Mere religious professors, men despise: but, while they may and often do persecute the one who walks in the Spirit, they at heart approve such,—yes, and only such! Let us ask ourselves, Does *my* walk please God? Is it approved in the hearts of men?

Verse 19: **So then let us pursue the things that belong to peace, and things whereby we shall build up one another.**

The word "pursue" is a strong word, generally used for *persecute,* follow hard after, as in hunting. Compare Chapter 12.13b, "given to (literally, *pursuing*) hospitality": Philippians 3.14: "I press toward the mark." Peter says, "Let him seek peace and *pursue* it"—same word. See also I Timothy 6.10, and II Timothy 2.22. So let us *pursue* the things of peace and of helping others. There is no more direct and effectual path away from yourself!

"Pursuing peace" is the negative side—refusing to engage in selfish conflict. Pursuing "edifying things" is the positive side. You must study the state and need of others, and "build up their need." See Ephesians 4.29, margin.

Verse 20: **Overthrow not for food's sake the work of God!** Let us not be as unregardful of our brother as was Esau of God Himself! The "work of God" here refers to the opera-tions of the Spirit of God within the soul—"the fabric which the grace of God has begun, and which the edification of Chris-tians by each other may help to raise." Or, which the selfish refusal to walk in love may pull down! For we find more people stumbling at the inconsistencies, and lack of love, in pro-fessing Christians, than at all things else. Let us follow Paul: "Though I was free from all men, I brought myself under bondage to all, that I might gain the more . . . Let no man seek his own, but each his neighbor's good . . . even as I also please all men in all things, not seeking mine own profit, but the profit of the many that they may be saved" (I Cor. 9.19; 10.24,33).

All things indeed are clean; howbeit it is evil for the man who eateth with stumbling—All meats, all food, is indeed (in itself) clean, but to him that eats with a bad conscience, everything is evil. God indeed plainly says, concerning those who "command to abstain from meats," that such are "giving heed to seducing spirits, and doctrines of demons, because He Himself created meats to be "received with thanksgiving by them that believe and know the truth" (I Tim. 4.1-5). But if one have not the assurance in his own conscience freely to obey this "command" of God, let him not violate his conscience; but wait humbly upon God, by His Word to strengthen him, and bring him into true Christian liberty. Otherwise his eating or drinking is not "with thanksgiving," but in mere self-indulgence.

Verse 21: **It is noble not to eat flesh, nor to drink wine, nor [to do] anything whereby thy brother is made to stumble, or is ensnared, or is [made] weak**—It has been remarked that in each of these three things, the effect is less than in the preceding one,—thus greatly strengthening and enlarging the exhortation. First, do not cause thy brother, by thy use of thy liberty, or in any conduct of thine, to have his fatal fall; second, do not even obstruct his Christian course by doing what might act as a snare to your brother, inducing him to act beyond his conscience; third, do not use your liberty, if your weaker brother, although he sees you are right, is not yet strong enough to follow you: and would therefore become disappointed and discouraged if he see you do so. "Wait for me!" did not your childhood's brother often call out to you? So let us *"wait* for one another" in the spiritual life! Be conformed to his weakness for the present, and accommodate your walk to his, lest he remain weak.*

Verse 22: **Hast thou faith? Have [it] to thyself before God. Blessed is he that doth not judge himself in the acts which he alloweth** [in his own life].

"It is much more blessed to have a liberty before God which we do not use on account of our brother's weakness, than to insist on our liberty, though it be distinctly given. The man whom Paul declares 'happy' is he who can eat what he pleases and drink what he pleases, without any qualms of conscience to condemn him while he does so." These words (from Sanday)

---

*Brown (in Jamieson, Fausset & Brown) well says, "This injunction to abstain from flesh and wine and whatsoever may hurt the conscience of a brother, must be properly understood. Manifestly the apostle is treating of the regulation of the Christian's conduct with reference simply to the prejudices of the *weak in faith;* and his directions are not to be considered as principles for one's entire lifetime, but simply as caution against too free use of Christian liberty in matters where other Christians, through weakness, are not persuaded that such liberty is Divinely allowed."

are true. The word translated "allows," or "permits," or "approves," is literally, "puts to the test." The picture is of a man having before him a question of conscience (of days, meats, or whatever), whose decisions in the use of his liberty are such that he *does not go beyond his knowledge, and persuasion in the Lord Jesus* (verse 14). For, though he have in his mind that he is free in such or such a matter, if his conscience check him, he "judges" himself if he rushes ahead in an action. To the strong believer the apostle speaks this word: "Hast thou faith? Have it to thyself before God." You have probably known people whom in this sense you did *not* know! They had learned, yet were content *not publicly to use,* that great liberty of faith into which God had led them. It is blessed to have faith. It is yet more blessed to have that faith "before God"—when using the freedom it gives might perplex another!

Verse 23: **But he that doubteth is condemned if he eat, because he eateth not of faith; and whatsoever is not of faith is sin.**

Of course the word "damned" (for "condemned") of the King James Version, is not the meaning here. But what is meant is the state of conscious condemnation into which one falls who goes beyond his faith in the exercise of his liberty. For he who acts thus enters the realm of self-will, the lawlessness *(anomia)* which God declares is *sin* (I John 3.4).

The apostle's definition of sin here as "what is not of faith" is most searching. It will drive us to our knees. It reaches everything in our lives concerning which our conscience is not at rest, in which we do not have faith to proceed, in which we cannot walk with God.

CHAPTER FIFTEEN

Believers to Receive One Another, as Christ (after His Jewish ministry), Received the Gentiles,—TO GOD'S GLORY. Verses 1 to 13.

Paul's Great "Priestly-Ministry" of the Gospel to the Gentiles. Verses 14 to 21.

His Purpose (long-hindered) to Come to the Roman Christians,—after the Great Jerusalem Contribution. Verses 22 to 33.

1   Now we that are strong ought to bear the infirmities of the weak, and not to please ourselves.
2   Let each one of us please his neighbor for that
3   which is good, unto edifying. For Christ also pleased not Himself; but, as it is written, The reproaches of them that reproacheth Thee fell upon
4   Me. For whatsover things were written aforetime were written for our learning, that through patience and through comfort of the Scriptures we
5   might have hope. Now the God of patience and of comfort grant you to be of the same mind one with
6   another according to Christ Jesus: that with one accord ye may with one mouth glorify the God and
7   Father of our Lord Jesus Christ. Wherefore receive ye one another, even as Christ also received you, to the glory of God.

THESE SEVEN VERSES should have closed the preceding chapter, as they continue and close up the subject there considered.

Verse 1: **Now we that are strong ought to bear** [literally, *are in debt to bear*] **the infirmities of the weak, and not to please ourselves.**

In Chapter 13.8 the word here translated "ought" (Greek, to owe), is used in forbidding a Christian to be in debt to others except in the way of love. Paul here addresses the "strong," being himself of that number; in which company may we also be found! It is those who are "spiritual" who can show love to others (Gal. 6.1). Note most carefully that it is not bearing *with* the infirmities of others that Paul is speaking of. The old lady said in the testimony meeting, "I have always got a lot of help out of that Bible verse that says, 'Grin and bear it!'" And the little California girl was heard singing, "When all my *neighbors* and trials are o'er!" We are apt to think of others' weaknesses and infirmities as a burden we must put up with, for the Lord's sake,—as "our particular cross," for the present! Instead, God's Word here teaches us gladly to bear, to take over as our own, these infirmities! *"Bear ye one another's burdens,"* is the "law of *Christ"!* (Gal. 6.2). How our blessed Lord bore the infirmities of His disciples!—infirmities of ignorance, of unbelief, of self-confidence, of jealousy among themselves,—until the disciples came into a state of loving trust in their Lord which made even Thomas say, "Let us also go, that we may die with Him"; and Peter: "Lord, I will lay down my life for Thee." Our Risen Lord again set the example of such "bearing." For even after they had forsaken Him in Gethsemane, in the upper room the Risen Lord appeared to them with, "Peace be unto you,"—and never a mention of their utter failure! It is this ability, manifested by Divine grace in us, constantly and without end to bear the infirmities of others, to take thought for, and excuse their weaknesses; and to endure for them anything and everything, that manifests *Christ;* and wins the trustful devotion of our fellow-saints.*

---

*It is this heart-hunger for sympathy,—for some one to take over our burdens, that has always made Romanism such a refuge (albeit a false one!); and is now making Buchmanism, commonly known as the "Oxford Movement," such a deadly danger. The Romanist unloads the story of his sins and failures in the ready ear of his "father confessor": while the Buchmanites gather in so-called "house parties," and "share" their inner secrets with their deluded comrades. Both the Romanist and the Buchmanite feel a great sense of "relief," after the confessions. Indeed, the Buchmanites make a great parade of testimonies of those whose lives have been "changed" through this process of "sharing." Certainly! But John Bunyan, in the seventeenth century gave the right name to Buchmanism: "Changing Sins";—that is, exchanging one sin for another. It is not by unburdening my conscience to my fellow man, whether "priest" or friend, that peace with God, and eternal safety come; but by deep conviction of both my guilt and my helplessness—of my lost state; and revelation to me, by the Spirit, of the shed blood of Christ as my only refuge and hope,—a Christ who bore *God's wrath against sin,* and provided the only ground on which a holy God can deal

Meyer well says, "In themselves strong and free, the strong become the servants of the weak, as Paul, the servant of *all.*" "Pleasing *ourselves*" is the exact thing each of us will do unless we set ourselves to pursue, to follow after, *love,* until our Lord comes back!

Verse 2: **Let each one of us please his neighbor, in what is good, for [his] edification.** Of course Paul does not mean here to exhort us to man-pleasing in the way of selfishly seeking man's favor. He himself says, "Am I now seeking the favor of men, or of God? or am I striving to please men? if I were still pleasing men, I should not be a servant of Christ" (Gal. 1.10). There is a man-pleasing spirit that is very obnoxious to God. We may be "nice" to people for our own selfish benefit. But remember that this exhortation to please our neighbor "for *his* benefit unto edifying," indicates a studied care for others; laying aside our own preferences, and pleasing them in every way that will in the end benefit them spiritually. This, of course, does not mean that we are to compromise with any evil our neighbor may be doing, by having fellowship with him in a worldly path in order to "win" him. The expression "unto that which is good," shuts out that. Paul puts it beautifully in I Corinthians 10.32 to 11.1: "Give no occasion of stumbling, either to Jews, or to Greeks, or to the Church of God: even as I also please all men in all things, not seeking mine own profit, but the profit of the many, *that they may be saved.* Be ye imitators of me, even as I also am of Christ."

Verse 3: **For Christ also pleased not Himself: but, as it is written, The reproaches of them that reproached Thee**

---

with guilty man. Resting in God's Word about His Son whom He raised from the dead, I have *salvation.* Salvation is not at all by "confession,"—either to God or man; but by faith in the vicarious sacrifice of Christ. Even the thief on the cross made no "confession" of his sins, either to God or to Christ:—for lo, Christ was just then *bearing* his guilt! and it was not by means of his confessing it that sin was put away, but by God's *placing it on Christ.* Although this thief, in speaking to the impenitent one, recognizes his crimes in the words, "We suffer the due reward of our deeds"; yet he simply hands himself over to Christ as he is,—"Lord, remember *me*": and our Lord's words are, "Today thou shalt be with Me in Paradise." (By the way, friend, that thief not only did not "confess" his sins; but he never was baptized; he never "joined the church"; he never went to "mass"; and he did not go to any "purgatory"; but he *went straight to Paradise,*— that day! And, further, Mary the mother of Jesus was standing right there: but our Lord never mentions her to this thief! But says, "Today thou shalt be with *Me.*" What do you say to that! That thief is a perfect picture of you and me, as regards salvation!)

fell upon Me—Christ never "looked after" Himself: the whole world knows this! "The foxes have holes, and the birds of the heaven have nests; but the Son of man hath not where to lay His head." Yet His whole life, from early morning till late at night, and often into the night, was occupied in ministry to others! The multitudes found out with joy that here was One whose whole business was "going about doing good." The constant drawing upon Him by the multitudes,—upon His time, His love, His teaching, His healing, was a marvelous proof that they could count on the *absolute absence of self-pleasing, in Him!*

The Psalms, which give the inner heart-history of our Lord, reveal, (as, for instance, does the Sixty-ninth Psalm, from which Paul here quotes,—the great "Reproach"* Psalm), how difficult was our Lord's path in a sinful, selfish, God-hating world. Yet it is written of Him: "He pleased not Himself."

Verse 4: **For whatsoever things were written aforetime were written for our learning, that through patience and through comfort of the Scriptures† we might have hope.**

Note these four words that God has joined together: *"learning . . . patience . . . comfort* of the Scriptures . . . *hope"*: "learning" is heart knowledge, as our Lord said: "Every one

---

*Let us follow this word, "reproach," in this 69th Psalm and others:

Verse 7: "For Thy sake I have borne *reproach."*

Verse 9: "The *reproaches* of them that *reproach* Thee are fallen upon Me."

Verse 10: "When I wept, and chastened My soul with fasting, that was to My *reproach."*

Verse 19: "Thou knowest My *reproach,* and My shame, and My dishonor."

Verse 20: *"Reproach* hath broken My heart."

Our Lord upon the cross cries that He is a *"reproach* of men" (Ps. 22.6). In Ps. 31.11, as we find so carried out in the gospels:—

"I am become a *reproach,*
Yea, unto My neighbors exceedingly,
And a fear to Mine acquaintance";

while in Ps. 109.22-25, He says He is "poor and needy," heart-wounded, gone like a shadow, tossed up and down, weak through fasting, His flesh failing, "a *reproach* unto them."

But it was always, "For *Thy* sake I have borne *reproach,"*—the reproaches that fell *upon God*—upon the Father, whose will and works Christ was doing, and whom man was learning the more to hate as "the beauty of Jehovah" was manifest more and more in Him. Now, if it were so with Christ, whose goodness was constantly reproached, shall we complain or stumble if even our good be evil spoken of? Let Christ dwell within us, as the Father dwelt in Christ, and let us cease from self-pleasing!

†"Those who neglect the Old Testament Scriptures may well remember that this expresses the Christian experience of an inspired apostle!"—(Schaff and Riddle). For it was the Old Testament Scriptures of which Paul spoke here.

that hath heard from the Father, and hath *learned,* cometh unto Me" (John 6.45). "Patience" follows, for, knowing God, we can wait for Him to work. Next is "comfort of the Scriptures." It is astonishing—something beyond human conception, this "comfort of the Scriptures"! We have all seen saints poor in purse, accounted nothing at all by men, and perhaps suffering constant physical pain, sad bereavement of loved ones, and complete lack of understanding by other professing Christians: yet *comforted* by poring over the Scriptures! Hearts happy and hopeful, despite it all! You can step from any state of earthly misery into the glorious halls of heavenly peace and comfort! Praise God for this! "Be ye *comforted,*" writes Paul in II Corinthians 13.11.

It is ever good to be going over God's dealings, not only with Christ, but with His Old Testament saints; marking how He is continually bringing them into hard places, where they learn to trust Him more! Joseph, in prison for righteousness; David, anointed of God, but hunted for years "like a partridge in the mountains"; Jeremiah in the miry dungeon; the three in Nebuchadnezzar's furnace, and Daniel in the den of lions: not to speak of the New Testament story—James and Stephen killed, the apostles in prison. You may ask, How does "hope" spring out of such trials? We do not ask such a question if we have learned the lesson of Romans Five: "Knowing that tribulation worketh steadfastness; and steadfastness, approvedness; and approvedness, *hope,*"—witnessed to by the shedding abroad of God's love for us in our hearts! Therefore let us seek that comfort and hope which this verse tells us the Scriptures work in us if we patiently *learn* them. When we get thus *learningly* to verse 13 in this chapter, we shall find ourselves *abounding* in hope!

Verses 5 and 6: **Now the God of patience and of comfort grant you to be of one mind together according to Christ Jesus; that ye may with one accord, with one mouth, glorify the God and Father of our Lord Jesus Christ.**

Paul asks here that the same God who gave to the Old Testament saints and to the apostles "endurance" and "comfort of the Scriptures," may grant that we may be "like-minded, loving as brethren" (I Pet. 3.8). "Behold, how these Christians love one another!" was the amazed but constant testimony of paganism, yea, of Judaism, also, regarding believers in the early days of the Church. *And this Spirit-wrought unity and tender affection is by far the greatest need amongst believers today.* New "movements," new "educational programs," great contributions of funds—what are these worth while Christians are divided in mind, more in discord than accord? Such a state cannot "glorify the God and Father of our Lord Jesus Christ." "By this," our Lord said, "shall all men know that ye are my disciples, if ye *have love* one to another" (John 13.35).

And this accord, this unity, is not brought about by outward organization. There is, incited by the devil, a great cry that all professing Christians today "get together," form themselves into a great "charitable" unity, inclusive of Romanists, Protestants, and well-intended Jews. Meanwhile, in answer to the earnest, persistent cry of God's people that He would revive His Church, the real saints are being drawn more and more by His Word into the true fellowship of the Holy Spirit. Bible conferences, unsectarian Bible schools, gatherings and even leagues for prayer, and increasing intelligent fellowship with truly godly missionary effort, are the real sign that God is granting Paul's desire that believers may **with one mouth glorify the God and Father of our Lord Jesus Christ.**

People generally make one of two mistakes concerning Christian unity. First, that there must be absolute unanimity of opinion on all points of doctrine; and second, that there must be external unity of all so-called "Christian bodies."

We have alluded to the second of these ideas as of Satanic *origin,* and deluded human *consent.* But now, as to the first, the desire of the apostle in verse 5, that **the God of patience and of comfort grant you to be of the same mind one with another according to Christ Jesus,** does not have reference to opinions or views of doctrines, but does have reference to gracious dispositions of spirit; for God is not spoken of here as the God of wisdom and knowledge, but as **the God of patience and of comfort.** It is God's acting in these blessed graces toward the saints that will enable them to be "of one mind together according to Christ Jesus."

When the Spirit of God is freely operating among a company of believers, the eyes of all of them, first, are toward Christ Jesus. They are thinking of Him, of His love, of His service, and of what will please Him. They are conscious of their blessed place in Him. Then follow, naturally, patient dealing with one another, comforting one another. Some of the company may know much more truth than others; many may hold varying judgments or opinions concerning particular matters. But this does not at all touch their unity—their conscious unity, in Christ; and it does not in the slightest degree hinder their being of one mind, and working together with one accord, and, in the vivid words of Scripture, be **with one mind together according to Christ Jesus.**

Rome has undertaken to compel unity in both these evil senses (for she knows not the blessed unity of the Spirit): and rivers of martyrs' blood have flowed because they dared to express an opinion contrary to the edicts of "the Church." The doctrine, too, is constantly promulgated, that to be outside "Mother Church," outside the fold of Rome, is to be without the pale of salvation!

Both these things are fearful perversions of the truth.

Verse 7: **Wherefore receive ye one another, even as Christ received you, to the glory of God.**

Strong and weak believers alike are here exhorted to **receive one another,—for God's glory.** This not only includes formal welcoming of other believers into the fellowship of the church, the Assembly of the Saints; but, what is far more and deeper, exercising constant careful love to one another; —and all this done with a view to *the glory of God!* For **Christ received us to that end!** As He says, "All that which the Father giveth Me shall come unto Me; and him that cometh unto Me I will in no wise cast out. For I am come down from Heaven, *not to do Mine own will, but the will of Him that sent Me*" (John 6.37,38). It is Christ's delight to welcome sinners, for that *glorifies God;* and there is joy in Heaven over it! Let there be like joy over our Christian love,—our "receiving" one another; for it glorifies God!

Verses 8 and 9: **For I say that Christ hath been made a minister of the circumcision for the truth of God, that He might confirm the promises unto the fathers, and that the Gentiles might glorify God for His mercy—**

Here Paul defines in a single phrase our Lord's character as a "minister," in His earthly life: He was a "minister of *the circumcision.*" That is, He came "unto *His own.*" He said, "I was not sent but unto the lost sheep of the house of Israel," (Matt. 15.24). Tell this to the ordinary professing Christian, and he regards you with amazement, if not with anger. When our Lord sent out the Twelve, in Matthew Ten, He said, "Go not into any way of the Gentiles, and enter not into any city of the Samaritans: but go rather to the lost sheep of the house of Israel." Now people resent that, because of their sad *ignorance* —both of the Divine sovereignty, and revealed plan. So, the first thing to clear away in our minds is the uncertain or false teaching, about the mission of Christ on earth. He was **made a minister of the circumcision for the truth of God; that He might confirm the promises unto the fathers.**

Now we know that Christ came to declare the Father—to reveal God as He is. Also He came to give His life a ransom for many, to become "the propitiation for the whole world." Thus He "came not to be ministered unto, but to minister."

But, if we are to understand the story of His ministry, in the Gospels, we must remember that He was first a "minister of the *circumcision,*" as the Jewish Messiah, fulfilling, "confirming" the Divine promises of the Old Testament to that nation.* And what was this "ministry of the circumcision?

---

*It is essential to understand and submit fully to this remarkable expression concerning our Lord's ministry to Israel, taking great care, however, that we do not allow ourselves to be drawn into the high folly of the Bullingerites, and others, who, because Christ was made a "minister of the circumcision," therefore regard as "transitional," and as not concerning the Church, the Body of Christ, the Gospels, the Acts, the present Epistle (to the Romans), the Corinthian Epistles,—in fact, all but the "prison epistles"! Some of these mistaken teachers, indeed, do not go to this length, but many are even more extravagant than this, claiming that Christ did not begin to build His Body on the day of Pentecost, but that there was a "transitional" time and state, after Pentecost, with a "Jewish Body"; and that the Body revealed by Paul in Ephesians and Colossians begins with Paul's revelation of it in "the prison epistles"! Now everyone knows

What was it meant to accomplish? Paul here says, It was for the sake of God's truth, God's faithfulness, His veracity, "to confirm the promises that had been given to the fathers"— Abraham, Isaac, and Jacob. It was on God's behalf, to show that when God makes commitments and promises, He forgets them not, but fulfils them. He had promised a Messiah to Israel, and He sent the Messiah.

But God had made no promises, no commitments, **to the Gentiles.** Consequently, upon Israel's rejection of their Messiah, **mercy,** sovereign **mercy,** flows out to us **Gentiles:** and for this we **glorify God,** for that is the purpose of this mercy—*that God may be glorified.*

The prophet Micah, in the last verse of his prophecy (7.19, 20), illustrates exactly this distinction between "the truth" of God toward Israel, and "the mercy" of God toward the Gentiles: "Thou wilt perform the truth to Jacob and the loving

---

that there was a gradual entering upon the *full truth* of what *Gentile grace* was, upon the part of the twelve apostles,—as witness Peter in Acts 10; and the Council of Acts 15. But to say that because they did not know fully the calling and hopes of the Church until Paul had revealed them (as indeed was true, by Christ's appointment) therefore the Body of Christ did not *exist* from Pentecost on, is idle, shallow folly!

The object of the devil in causing these delusions, is practically the same as in his inspiring "higher criticism" and "modernism." It is to break the moral effect upon the conscience of certain books and certain passages of the Bible, by teaching believers to say, "That Scripture is not for us—it is not for the Church." Now the account of the creation is not "Church Truth," yet Paul takes great comfort from it, saying, "It is God that said, Light shall shine out of darkness, who shined in our hearts to give the light of the knowledge of God, in the face of Jesus Christ" (II Cor. 4.6). Paul also takes great delight in pointing out, in quoting Genesis 2.24, that a man's leaving father and mother to cleave to his wife, was a type and picture of, and really concerned the union of, Christ and the Church! (Eph. 5.29-32.) The book of Job was not written "for the Church," yet we learn in that great book things of our God and of His ways not fully revealed elsewhere.

I deem it not only folly, but presumptuous wickedness to speak as do these self-appointed wise men of our Lord's earthly ministry as "not concerning the Church," saying we must therefore leave the gospels and go to the epistles alone for instruction. Paul, on the contrary, continually quoted even the Old Testament Scriptures; even adducing *the Law* for our "instruction" (although telling us we are not under it: I Cor. 9.9; 14.34; Eph. 6.1,2).

Likewise the Psalms: Of course they were written with Israel's Messiah in direct view,—His sufferings, (and the Remnant's) with His ultimate earthly Kingdom-triumph in the 1000 years.

Yet, recalling always the facts of our heavenly calling and place, the Psalms become full of blessing to the spiritual mind! The Holy Spirit makes them the quickened vehicle of guiding us into unexpected truth. And the four Gospels:— "the words of our Lord Jesus Christ" have a use and beauty of blessing for us, all the greater because we know we are enlifed in, and risen with, Christ, new creatures in Him, and seated with Him in the heavenlies, in Christ Jesus! Indeed, we find our Lord, in John 17, *praying for that marvelous oneness* which

kindness [or, mercy] to Abraham, which Thou hast sworn
unto our fathers from the days of old." To Jacob the blessings were announced by God (above that ladder of Genesis 28)
with the words: "I am Jehovah, the God of Abraham thy
father, and the God of Isaac" (Gen. 28.13). The birthright
which Esau despised and forfeited, Jacob had; and the promises were to be fulfilled in faithfulness. But to Abraham it was
sheer *mercy*. His father was a Chaldean idolater, and probably he had been so (Josh. 24.2,3,14,15). But "the God of
glory" appeared to him out of hand, without cause, right in
the midst of Chaldean iniquity there at Ur. This was *mercy*
(Acts 7.1). Jehovah "redeemed" Abraham (Isa. 29.22).

Now for the present a "hardening in part" has befallen
Israel, "until the fulness of the Gentiles be come in," as we
saw in Chapter Eleven.

---

was realized in the Church as revealed in all Paul's Epistles: "that they may
be one—even as thou, Father, art in Me, and I in Thee." *There is no higher
truth about the Church than this!* "The Mystery," the Church as such, was not
yet revealed,—as it begins to be in Romans and onward: but we have the great
petitions *that made the Church possible, here in John.*

When we step into The Acts, only those who *leave the simplicity of Christian
consciousness* (as does Bullinger) dare affirm that in those earliest Christians
there was not the very life and unity belonging to the one and only Body of
Christ which it was later given Paul to "minister," as to its character, calling,
destiny, and walk.

Of course Romans is as much "church truth" as Ephesians! Avoid Bullingerism
as you would the plague! The Church *did* begin at Pentecost; there is but *one*
Body of Christ known in Scripture,—and no special "Jewish" Body; the Lord's
words to the Seven Churches of Rev. 1-3 are solemn warnings to *present*
assemblies, and not imaginary "Jewish" assemblies, after the Body of Christ is
raptured to heaven, as Bullinger teaches! How anyone can be captured by
such fantastic nonsense, is only explainable by the appalling ignorance of Pauline
truth, and the hunger for it, (an ignorance and hunger of which Bullinger takes
advantage!) Bullinger called the great Welsh Revival of 1904-5 "Spiritism,"—
attributing to the devil what the whole Church of God knows was God's work.
(See Bullinger's *Foundations of Dispensational Truth*, p. 259.) And he taught
"Soul-sleeping," calling Sheol and Hades "only *gravedom.*" (See on Revelation,
Chap. 1.) To follow such a presumptuous and blind leader, is to fall into the
ditch. Only, Bullingerites *think* everyone but themselves in the ditch: and that
they are mountain-top dwellers! Have you heard of a Bullingerite Bible conference
for the deepening of the spiritual life? No; and you will not: for they are
"*sick* about questionings, and disputes of words" (I Tim. 6.4). The reason we
warn of Bullingerism so repeatedly is, that it endangers the earnest souls who,
desiring to escape the intolerable bondage of Protestant denominational ecclesi-
asticism (now daily becoming more Romish in fact and papal in process), hail
Bullinger's system as freedom. But it is a much worse danger than what they
have escaped! You may call it dispensational modernism, or modernistic dispensationalism: for it is both.

It is difficult to deal in patience with presumption that takes an attitude
much like that of Theosophy, of a "higher wisdom." It is a striking thing,
(though from history it might be expected) that these errorists like others, are
consumed by their error! They must harp on it at all times!

It is striking that in the present passage, Chapter 15.9-29, Gentiles are named *ten* times, the Gentile number! Five of these instances are from the Old Testament prophecies themselves. Let us study these quotations with especial attention:

9   Therefore will I give praise unto Thee among the Gentiles,
     And sing unto Thy Name (Ps. 18.49).

10 And again He saith,
     Rejoice, ye Gentiles, with His people (Deut. 32. 43).

11 And again,
     Praise the Lord, all ye Gentiles;
     And let all the peoples praise Him (Ps. 117.1).

12 And again, Isaiah saith,
     There shall be the root of Jesse,
     And He that ariseth to rule over the Gentiles;
     On Him shall the Gentiles hope (Isa. 11.10).

There are three remarkable points about these passages:

I

They are selected from the three great divisions of the Scripture: the Law, the Prophets, and the Psalms (Luke 24.44).

II

There is a progress in the selections.

1. Christ Himself gives **praise unto God** from among the Gentiles. The quotation is from Psalm 18.49, where David becomes a distinct type of Christ, David's coming Seed, as see next verse. See also Psalm 22.22, where, after the awful description of the cross in the first part of that Psalm (verses 1-21) —the Divine forsaking, pierced hands and feet, parted garments—the Lord begins thus the resurrection praise:

"I will declare Thy name unto My brethren:
   In the midst of the assembly will I praise Thee."

This "assembly" began, of course, with those Jewish believers in that upper room, to whom He first appeared; but that "assembly" shortly included *Gentiles* (Acts 10 and on). But we note here in Romans 15.9 that Christ Himself is celebrating Jehovah's work,—giving praise "among the Gentiles."

2. Verse 10: The next step is, **Rejoice, ye Gentiles, with His people.** Now, in Scripture, "His *people*" are always Israel; and, for awhile, as we find in the Acts, the Gentiles were "rejoicing *with* His people": it was with Jerusalem as the center, and the apostles and elders there recognized even by Paul, even after preaching to the Gentiles had begun (Acts 15).*

3. Verse 11: The next passage calls for direct praise from the Gentiles, with no distinct notice taken of Israel as a people; for the Greek reads: **Praise the Lord, all ye Gentiles; and let all the peoples** [plural] **praise Him** (as the R.V. correctly translates).

III

Verse 12: There is a looking forward to the Millennial reign in the quotation from Isaiah 11.10: **the Root of Jesse, He that ariseth to rule over the Gentiles. On Him** [who shall thus reign] **shall the Gentiles hope.** Gentiles, thank God, may *now* freely "hope," and look to Him who *will rule* all the earth, during the Millennium. All nations then will be directly dependent upon the Lord, enthroned in the Millennial temple at Jerusalem. How blessed is the Gentile who now learns to "hope in Christ" (Eph. 1.12) *before* He "arises to reign"! Verily there will be a reward!

As Paul says in II Timothy 2.8: "Remember Jesus Christ, risen from the dead, *of the Seed of David,* according to my gospel." How few Christians connect their Savior with *David!* They remember Romans 1.4, but not 1.3. So they forget His royal earthly claims!

In this passage we saw (in verse 8) a setting forth of Christ as a "minister of the circumcision"; but this ministry was duly

---

*Of course, the Church, the Body of Christ, was begun at Pentecost. But, though God would by and by send Paul to show the *heavenly* calling and character of the Church, yet God, in great patience and grace, called upon Israel first to repent and believe (Acts 3.26). So that, for a while,—even to Paul's officially closing Israel's *national* door, in Acts 28.25-28,—the Gentiles rejoiced "with" God's people Israel: it was "to the Jew first." But it is not so now! "There is no difference between Jew and Greek" *must be preached,* if God's Word is to be followed. Movements that put the Jew, now, in a place of preference, as "first," do the poor Jew,—a common sinner, undistinguished from the Gentile,— the greatest disservice possible! They protect him from judgment as guilty before God (Rom. 3.19). Instead, Paul went about to "provoke to jealousy" the Jews, by boasting in Christ, as himself the very "chief of sinners," saved by grace, not by the Law!

accomplished. It did not extend to the Gentiles, for no promises had been made to the Gentiles. Consequently, Gentiles are brought under Divine "mercy," and "hope" in Christ, wholly apart from Jewish connections; though recognizing our Lord's past and future ministry to the circumcision.*

Verse 13: **Now the God of hope fill you with all joy and peace in believing, that ye may abound in hope, in the power of the Holy Spirit.**

Look at this great thirteenth verse: how it blossoms out before us! Here is a verse packed full!

1. The name here given to God thrills our hearts: **The God of Hope.** Hope looks forward with exultation for ever and ever! We remember Chapter 5.2: "We rejoice in hope of the glory of God"; and Chapter 12.12: "rejoicing in hope"; and also that hope, along with faith and love, abides forever, for God will be opening up new treasures of grace to us through all the ages to come! See Ephesians 2.7.

God is called the "God of peace" in Romans 15.33 and 16.20; and in Philippians 4.9, I Thessalonians 5.23, II Thessalonians 3.16, and Hebrews 13.20; and, of course, peace is fundamental: Christ made peace by the blood of His cross. But we are not to be content with peace alone. Many would stop at Romans 5.1, "Being justified by faith, we have peace with God." But in this present verse God speaks as the God of *hope;* and He wants us **filled with all joy** as well as **peace,** so as to be **abounding in hope, in the power of the Holy Spirit.**

Now, if God is the God of hope, looking forward with expectancy and delight to the certain, glorious things of

---

*God had made arrangements with Israel at Sinai, had given them promises conditioned on their obedience. This limited God's action to the fulfilment of these commitments to Israel. "Christ hath been made a minister of the circumcision for the truth of God, to confirm the promises made unto the fathers."

But, at the cross, all was ended. Sin rose to its height, and transgression of the Law to its climax. When the Jews "killed the Lord Jesus" (I Thess. 2.15,16), that Law which distinguished the "circumcision in the flesh" was "abolished" (Eph. 2.14,15; Col. 2.14).

God having thus wound up matters with Israel, and being, of course, entirely free from any covenant with or commitment unto the Gentiles, could act according to the movements of absolute Love, which He is.

The highest action of Love, consequently, succeeded the highest action of human sin: man crucified God's Son; God sends the Holy Ghost, baptizing believers into vital union with that Son raised from the dead and glorified. The Church, the Body of Christ, stands in the nearest possible relation to God of any creature!

the future, then a dejected, depressed, discouraged saint of His is yielding to a spirit directly contrary to His will, which is, for each of us, that we **abound in hope.**

2. It is God Himself alone who can **fill us with all joy and peace,** making us to abound in hope. We cannot transform ourselves!

3. It is by **the power of the indwelling Spirit** that we are to "abound in hope." Some human beings are naturally introspective and gloomy. Others are naturally jovial and buoyant: but the joy in which we as believers are to abound does not in any wise flow from nature, but from the direct, inworking energy of the Holy Ghost. Some of the most naturally "happy" people of the world, have been thrown into desperate trouble of soul either by the Spirit's convicting them of their sin, or, perhaps, by the withdrawal of natural supports on a death-bed without hope; while some of those whose tendency was discouragement and despondency almost to hopelessness have, "by the power of the Holy Ghost," been filled with all joy and peace, and have abounded in hope day by day and hour by hour!

4. It is in a **believing heart** that these blessed results are brought about. When asked by the Jews in the Sixth of John, "What must we do that we may work the works of God?" our Lord replied, "This is the WORK of God [the one thing He asks of you], that ye BELIEVE on Him whom He hath sent." The "believing" of Romans 15.13 is, of course, that "living by faith in the Son of God" of which Paul speaks in Galatians 2.20. It is stepping out on the facts God reveals about us; and learning to live the life of *trust.*

The verse we are considering is the highest development of Christian experience revealed in this great, fundamental Epistle of Romans. Deeper things will be elsewhere unfolded,—as, for instance, the Indwelling *Christ* of Ephesians 3.14 to 21. But, as Jude 20 tells us, we must "build up ourselves on our most holy *faith.*" Paul declares that the "law" that prevails in this dispensation is a "law of *faith*" (Rom. 3.27) ; and that the obedience into which we are called is the obedience of *faith* (Rom. 1.5; 16.26).

5. It is the *will of God* that you and I—all believers—be "filled with all joy and peace in believing,"—blessed spiritual state! that *we* may "abound in hope in the power of the Holy Ghost." Some are content if they merely find the way of salvation through faith in the blood of Christ. They are much given to talk about being "saved by grace," but they are not much exercised about holy living. A second class of believers become deeply exercised as to a life of "victory over sin." These, of course, if instructed aright, accept the wondrous fact that they died with Christ, and are now on resurrection ground, freed from sin, and from that which gave sin its power,—the Law. A third class go further, to the Twelfth of Romans, and enter on true Christian *service,* by presenting their bodies a living sacrifice to God; and discovering thereby His good, acceptable, and perfect will for them—whatever measure of faith He may give them, and to whatever gift or peculiar service He may call them. But here, in this great fountain of water in Chapter 15.13, we find that a daily, hourly life "filled with all joy and peace in believing, abounding in hope," is the normal state for every one who is in Christ!

It will not do for us to make excuses for ourselves: God is the God of hope! His yearning is to fill you and me with all joy and peace, if we will just launch out and believe. Others just as unworthy as we have believed; we will never become "more worthy" of believing. "This poor earth is a wrecked vessel," as Moody used to say. Man is drifting on into the night, and judgment is coming. All the more, then, may the God of hope fill YOU with all joy and peace in believing, that YOU may abound in hope!

Many cherish their doubts, even adducing them as a proof of their humility, which is sad indeed. As Charles F. Deems used to say, "Believe your beliefs, and doubt your doubts; most people believe their doubts, and doubt their beliefs." *You* can believe. What a wonderful thing to be among those (sadly few!) believers who are *filled* with all joy and peace, and *abound* in hope!

We can enter into the benefit of our great apostle Paul's benedictory prayer in this matter: "Now the God of hope fill you"

—for Paul yearned over, prayed over, and had effectual prayer, even, for "those that had not seen his face in the flesh" (Col. 2.1); and we may assume that God will answer this mighty believing prayer of his on our behalf. And our Great High Priest, who moved Paul to pray, is at God's right hand, making constant intercession for us!

14   And I myself also am persuaded of you, my brethren, that ye, yourselves, are full of goodness, filled with all knowledge, able to admonish one
15   another. But I wrote the more boldly unto you in a measure, as putting you again in remembrance on account of the [especial] grace that was given me
16   of God, that I should be a minister of Christ Jesus unto the Gentiles, administering as priest the gospel of God; that the offering up of the Gentiles might be made acceptable, being sanctified by the Holy Spirit.

Verse 14: Although Paul had never been in Rome, he kept track of believers throughout the whole Roman world! Now he had said in our first Chapter (1.8) that he "thanked God through Jesus Christ for them all, that their faith was proclaimed throughout the whole world." This was a remarkable condition,—it was early freshness and vigor of faith! Our present verse has especially to do with those inner engiftments of the Spirit which enabled them with loving hearts and discerning knowledge to look after one another's spiritual needs without any apostle's help. For neither Paul, nor Peter, nor any apostle, had as yet preached the gospel at Rome! Of the Corinthian church also, Paul testifies: "In everything ye were enriched in Christ, in all utterance and all knowledge; even as the testimony of Christ was confirmed in you: so that ye come behind in *no gift.*" Now he says of these believers at Rome that he is **persuaded that they are full of goodness, filled with all knowledge,** and therefore really **able to admonish one another!** But Paul takes the very occasion of their remarkable pristine vigor in the Spirit, to bring before them that special and wonderful commission given him of God to the nations.

The ministry of the chosen apostle to the Gentiles was just as needful to establish the Romans (1.11,12; 16.25) as it was for the Corinthian church, of which Paul himself was directly the "father." So Paul says to the believers at Rome, as he retraces in his mind the contents and manner of the great Epistle God has enabled him to send to them,—and which he is preparing to close:

Verses 15,16: **All the more boldly, therefore, in a measure, I wrote unto you** [in this epistle] **on account of the** [peculiar] **grace that was given me of God, that I should be a minister of Christ Jesus unto the Gentiles, officially administering the gospel of God; that the offering up of the Gentiles might be made acceptable, being sanctified by the Holy Spirit.**

And now Paul is reminding these Roman Christians—"putting them again in remembrance," of this great special *grace* that had been given him of God, that he should act toward the Gentiles as God's official administrator, ministering as such the gospel of God. This "grace" was God's mighty outfitting of His servant Paul for this ministry among the Gentiles, or nations, to whom he was sent.

Paul always carried about the consciousness that he was Christ's chosen vessel to the Gentiles. Most people are ignorant that he was so, and regard Paul simply as *"an* apostle," "one of the twelve," and so forth. But observe that the words of verses 15 and 16 go far beyond mere apostleship.

The word which characterizes Paul's ministry here is, in Greek, *leitourgos.* It is difficult to convey the meaning of it by any one English word. Alford renders it "ministering priest" (of Christ Jesus for the Gentiles); Darby, "an administrator officially employed"; Thayer, in his Lexicon, shows its original meaning to be, "a public minister, a servant of the state." The simple translation "minister of Christ Jesus" will scarcely do, because every preacher (and in a sense rightly) would deem himself to be thus described.*

---

*We cannot press the *liturgical* meaning in the sense of a literal *priestly* function here; for the same Greek word is used in Chapter 13.6 concerning public officials; they are said to be God's ministers (*leitourgoi*). Again, in verse 27 of

1. It is evident from Peter's preaching, in Acts 10.35 and 11.18, that Gentile salvation had begun,—apart from Jewish things altogether. "In every nation he that feareth God and worketh righteousness is *acceptable* unto Him": though not, of course, accepted, *saved,* except through the preachèd name and work of Christ (Acts 11.14). "To the Gentiles also God hath granted repentance unto life."

2. It is also evident from Paul's words in Romans 15.16, that he had a special ministry toward the Gentiles: **that I should be a minister** *(leitourgos)* **of Christ Jesus unto the Gentiles.** Just as when Israel, already God's people while in Egypt, had sent to them Moses, who brought them out, and with whose ministry they were Divinely connected by God; so Paul was sent to the Gentiles, to whom the door of salvation had already been opened. And as God laid Israel on Moses, so laid He the Gentiles on Paul. Paul it is whose gospel, without mixture of even those Jewish things permitted in measure back at Jerusalem (Acts 21.20), was **administered in priestly fashion** among the nations, telling of the One Great Offering for sin for *the whole world* (and not for Jews only); that **the offering up** *(prosphora)* **of the Gentiles might** [thus] **be made acceptable** *(euprosdektos).* This last is the same word as in II Corinthians 6.2: "Now is the *acceptable time*": the time when God freely accepts, without Law, convenant-conditions, or religious forms, any and all!

3. It is also evident from Romans 15.16 that apart from this full-grace gospel of Paul, the **offering up of the Gentiles** could not be "gladly acceptable" by God. For Israel had had a Law, with forms and ordinances. The Gentiles had had *nothing*: and to them as having nothing, Paul's grace-gospel came,—asking nothing, but bestowing everything!

4. Finally, it is evident that this acceptance of the Gentiles involved the presence and sanctifying power of the Holy Spirit. This began at Cornelius' house in Acts Ten:

---

our present chapter (15), we find that the Gentiles owed it to the Jerusalem saints "to *minister* unto them in carnal things." Here the verb form of the same word is used. See its use further in II Corinthians 9.12, and Philippians 2.17,25, 30. But that its use here makes Paul a special *official of God* no one should doubt.

"The Holy Spirit fell on all them that heard the Word." It was continued in Samaria, in Acts Eight. Paul's question to those at Ephesus in Acts Nineteen was: "Did ye receive the Holy Spirit when ye believed?" Even of the Galatians, mixed up in mind as they were, it was said: "He that supplieth to you the Spirit"!

Ah, we do not realize our privileges! Such an apostle as *Paul*— is not only ours, but *God laid us Gentiles upon this man* as He laid Israel upon Moses. Alas, Moses complained of the burden (Num. 11.11-15). But Paul complained not, even of "that which presseth upon me daily, anxiety for all the churches" (II Cor. 11.28,29). Paul it was who "most gladly would spend and be spent out for our souls" (II Cor. 12.15). Paul it was who longed "for fruit in us also, as in the rest of the Gentiles"; who also "prayed with *agonizing* for as many as had not seen his face in the flesh" (Col. 1.2, Gr.).

So, as God hearkened to Moses regarding wretched Israel at Sinai (Ex. 32.7-14),—for he had made Moses responsible for them, may we not believe that God yet remembers the prayers for the Gentiles of this devoted servant Paul?

We know, from Romans Eleven, that the day will come when Gentiledom will be "cut off" as the sphere of God's direct blessing (through their unbelief and refusal of Divine "goodness"), and Israel, the natural branches, will be grafted in again. But we cannot but feel that some (and that in prominent places) are forgetting Paul with his "offering up of the Gentiles," and turning slavishly back, with flattering words, to Jews,—if not to Judaism! The glorious grace of the Pauline gospel to the Gentiles may be corrupted, despised, rejected, by fawning upon the Jew as being a *special* being,—different from common sinners. When God said, "There is *no distinction*" between Jew and Greek, that matter was *settled!* The wall of partition is *down,—broken down by God!* Woe to those who, under any claim, build it up! When God's time comes, *after "His whole work"*—of indignation toward Israel, He will Himself build up Zion. Meanwhile hearken to *Paul!**

---

*A certain Jewish mission worker declared that when God caused the birth of Isaac from barren Sarah, He "infused into the blood-stream of his descendants *new life*," which differentiated them from the rest of the human race!

Now this is not merely twaddle, but an accursed *lie*, which denies the whole

Romans 15.16 has been passed lightly over at this Gentile end of the dispensation. Gentiles have taken over "religious" things, such as the Jews and heathen had, and have not regarded that peculiar "offering up" of them, through Paul's priestly ministering of the Gospel of God to them. But this is a great verse. It must not be "spiritualized" away into mere figurative speech.

The necessity of bowing to this Scripture's teaching that the unclean Gentiles are "sanctified by the Holy Spirit" through their being offered up by Paul, by means of the Gospel, is brought out in Chapter 11.17. Today, the Gentiles feel as proud and self-sufficient before God as the Jews of old came to be. And just as the Israelitish branches were "broken off," so will the Gentiles be, by and by, according to the passage just referred to. When the Gentiles are broken off, and the natural branches (Israelites), grafted in again to the root of promise and blessing in Abraham, then, as formerly, the Gentiles, not being "sanctified by the Holy Spirit," can no more worship God as they do now, freely; but they will have to go up from all over the earth, to keep the Feast of Tabernacles, and be subordinated to the priestly nation of Israel. This is brought out in Zecha-riah 14.16-19.

Ministering the good news of God, and thus making **the offering up of the Gentiles acceptable, sanctified by the Holy Spirit,**—must cease when the Church is raptured and the gospel which Paul preached has ended its ministry. The Gentiles then are immediately, as before, far away, unclean; Israel, forgiven, cleansed, restored, becomes the priestly nation, unto which the nations must resort as of old for the knowledge of the true God. Not today do the nations have to come "as crawling things licking the dust before Jehovah's glory," as they will do in the Millennium. Words fail us to express the glory of the privilege that today prevails in the humblest gospel meeting as a means of access to God, with an amazing free gospel-welcome to God *direct,* through the shed blood of Christ, that will cease in-

---

gospel of God in this book of Romans! For if God iterates and re-iterates one thing, it is *universal equal human sinnerhood!* Nay, if there are *special* sinners in Romans they are Jews: "For the name of God is blasphemed among the Gentiles because of you" (Jews).

stantly upon the rapture of the Church, when the Gentiles will no longer be under the astonishing blessing which has been theirs during the present gospel dispensation through the apostle Paul. In priestly ministration of the gospel he offered up* the Gentiles, by which God made them "acceptable"; and upon believing, "sanctified by the Holy Spirit" (not as Israel had been, by circumcision and outward religious ordinances).

In view of this astonishing ministry of Paul, it is no wonder that he writes "boldly,"—*very* boldly, to the Christians in Rome, although he had not been there. Being "full of goodness and knowledge," they would be ready to be "put in remembrance" that there was one, although absent, who had, as their apostle, acted on their behalf in a general offering of them to God, as Gentiles; and now was lovingly and particularly concerned about their condition as saints,—such an one as made continual prayer concerning them and longed after them (1.9-11).

17 I have therefore my glorying in Christ Jesus in things pertaining to God.

18 For I will not dare to speak of any of those things which Christ did not work through me, in order to the [believing] obedience of the Gentiles,

19 by word and deed, in the power of signs and wonders, in the power of the Holy Spirit; so that from Jerusalem, and round about even unto Illyricum, I have fully preached [lit. fulfilled] the gospel of

20 Christ; yea, making it my ambition so to preach the gospel, not where Christ was already named, that I might not build upon another man's founda-

21 tion; but, as it is written,

They shall see, to whom no tidings of Him came, And they who have not heard shall understand.

Verse 17: The word **therefore** refers us to that peculiar ministry of verse 16 just described: **I have therefore my glorying in Christ Jesus in things pertaining to God.** How

*Meyer thus comments here: "In priestly fashion administering the gospel of God. The gospel is not indeed the *offering*, but the Divine *institute*, which is administered (is in priestly fashion served) by the presenting of the offering. The Gentiles, converted, and through the Spirit consecrated as God's property, are the offering which Paul, as the priest of Jesus Christ, has brought to God."

different from that of Moses was Paul's ministry! Moses operated under God, beneath the eye of all the nations, humbling the proudest of them, and leading Israel in the wilderness, by a marvelous, continuous, physical miracle, for forty years; with God defending him publicly even to opening the earth to swallow his opposers! There is something overwhelmingly magnificent, outwardly, about Moses' whole life and ministry. Not so with Paul! He shared (and gloried in it) the place of earthly rejection and despising His Lord had; his great desire being to be "conformed unto His death" (Phil. 3.10). Therefore it requires spiritual discernment to see Paul's place and ministry. Over and over Paul makes statements like that of the present verse, insisting that he and his glorying were before (the unseen) God, and not before men. "God is my witness, whom I serve in my spirit in the gospel of His Son"; "We persuade men, but we are made manifest unto God; and I hope that we are made manifest also in your consciences" (II Cor. 5.11).

Here then, is this "least of all the apostles,"—nay, "less than at least of all saints," to whom God has given this greatest place of all (as Christ promised to the "least"); not only a ministry of being "an apostle of the Gentiles" (11.13), "a teacher of the Gentiles in faith and truth" (I Tim. 2.7); but also the official presentation of the Gentiles to God, "offering them up." No wonder that Paul has a "glorying in Christ Jesus" in these things,—things "pertaining to God" indeed! There was no outward pillar of cloud and fire, no visible temple or formal worship; but just as really as God committed Israel to Moses' hands, so did God give this liturgical ministry toward the Gentiles to Paul, a priest-like office exercised by this "unknown" though "well-known" apostle. This explains the verses which follow:

Verse 18: **For I will not dare to speak of any of those things which Christ did not work through me, in order to the** [believing] **obedience of the Gentiles, by word and deed**—Paul means to indicate here the absolute distinctiveness of his calling and work. He does not confuse it with, or take glory for, the wonderful work of God at Jerusalem

on the day of Pentecost and thereafter (Acts 2 to 12) by
the twelve apostles, whose ministry was to the circumcision:
of which twelve Paul was not! (I Cor. 15.5). He will speak
only of what Christ has done through *him,* through preaching,
and attesting miracle, and the attending presence and power
of the Holy Spirit. An example of the "signs" of verse 19,
was the "special miracles" at Ephesus: Acts 19.11,12; and an
instance of a "wonder" was Paul's shaking off the viper which
had bitten him: Acts 28.3-6. All these things set seal to the
gospel which Paul preached, as *of God.* The whole passage
needs to be compared with its parallel in II Corinthians
10.13-17.

Verse 19: **In the power of signs and wonders, in the
power of the Holy Spirit; so that from Jerusalem, and round
about even unto Illyricum, I have fully preached [lit., ful-
filled] the gospel of Christ.**

What a marvelous, absolutely tireless love-laborer was this
man Paul. Illyricum was the next province to Italy. Between
Jerusalem and Illyricum lay the province of Syria, with its
capital at Damascus, but its spiritual capital Antioch; and next
to it Cilicia, with its great center Tarsus, Paul's own home,
whither he had been sent by the brethren away from Jerusalem
persecution (Acts 9:30); and whence Barnabas brought him to
the work at Antioch (Acts 11.25,26); next province Pamphylia
with Perga and Attalia; and above that Pisidia, centered at another Antioch; then Lycaonia, and above that the great and difficult Galatia with the churches Paul founded there; next proconsular Asia, centered at Ephesus, of course, and the mighty work
there and the "fighting with beasts"; then at Troas across the
Agean came the call from Macedonia, and its cities Philippi,
Berea and Thessalonica, the saints of which lay so close to the
apostle's heart; then Achaia, centered at Corinth, whence he
wrote this present letter to the Romans—vast city, vast wickedness, but much people for the Lord. And so we arrive at Illyricum. And through all these regions just traced, Paul has
fulfilled the gospel of Christ: insomuch that verse 23 in-
forms us that he **had no more any place in these regions.**

Verses 20-23: **Yea, making it my ambition so to preach
the gospel, not where Christ was already named, that I
might not build upon another man's foundation; but, as it
is written,**

> **They shall see, to whom no tidings of Him came,
> And they who have not heard shall understand.**

**Wherefore also I was hindered these many times from
coming to you: but now, having no more any place in these
regions, and having these many years a longing to come
unto you—**

Hindered—These many labors from Jerusalem to Illyricum
had "hindered" Paul from seeing Christians at Rome as he
longed to do. In I Thessalonians 2.18 he said, "We would fain
have come unto you, I Paul once and again; and Satan hindered us,"—by some direct, desperate stand. But here, mul-
titudinous labors have hindered. Compare Romans 1.13.

These many times shows how continually Roman Christians were on his mind and in his desire.

And now let us enter into the astonishing statement of verse
23, **having no more any place in these regions.** Everybody
converted? No. All the saints established and perfected? No.
Yet there was the urge to go on where no tidings of Him had
come. This is the highest, deepest, widest, most Christ-like
emotion that ever filled a human breast. How we should weep
over our far departure from the whole spirit of Christ and His
great apostle in this matter of preaching on and on and on!
Instead of the passion to pay our debt to every creature by
carrying the good tidings to them, we are rather churlish if
they do not come to the buildings we have set up. We say,
Why do they not come to church? and we talk of the "un-
churched masses."

But God did not tell them to "come to church." He told us
to *carry* the glad tidings to *them!* Let us cease chiding men
for failing to come to hear the gospel, instead of our obeying
the Lord and going with it to them where they are! The church
at Jerusalem "settled down," until God drove the saints out after
Stephen's martyrdom, so that they "went about preaching the
Word." It is, indeed, the unusual Christian who has written in

his soul, as had Paul, **the ambition to carry the gospel where the name of Christ had never been on the tongue,** and thus, **not merely to build on an already laid foundation!** To such missionaries verse 23 is fulfilled! When they return to England, or America, or Sweden, it is ever in their hearts, "I have no more any place in these regions."*

And, by the way, **a longing to come** unto any field (prayed over persistently), will probably land one in that field! So it was with Paul.

Verse 24: **Whensoever I proceed** [on my course] **unto Spain for I hope** [proceeding thus] **to see you, and by you be brought on my way thither, after I have in some measure satisfied my long-cherished desire for your company.**

Proceed unto—The same Greek word is used of Christ's pursuing His path: "He set His face to proceed [on His course] to Jerusalem" (Luke 9.51); "I must proceed [on my course] today and tomorrow" (Luke 13.33); "The Son of Man proceedeth [on His course] as it is written of Him" (Luke 22.22).

We see here Paul's consciousness of his "course," appointed by the Lord, which he had not finished even at his first imprisonment (Phil. 3.12-14); but which he had finished at his second imprisonment (II Tim. 4.7,8).

Unto Spain—Paul's purpose to go to Spain, where Christ had not been named, is re-affirmed as a fact in his Divinely-purposed course, in verse 28: "I will go on by you unto Spain." Meanwhile his longing to have fellowship with, and be a blessing to, those who were already believers at Rome, is very strong. He cannot bear to go on to Spain without being, for a while,

---

*A letter from a missionary just returned "on furlough" from China, reads: "I asked the Board as a special favor to allow me to take a *short* furlough, and I am hoping to return to China in September. My heart is longing more every day to get back to China. The things I miss here in others, the ways in which I see time, energy, and money wasted for the things that do not satisfy,—all these things and others make me realize more than ever how subtly Satan works to steal away our hearts and keep us from God's *best,* and makes me desire more than I ever did in my life that I shall not fail of His grace, and that as He works in me and deals with me, these days I may respond fully, so that as I go back to China, if He wills it so,—I may go in the fulness of the grace of Christ, to fulfil all His will in and through me. How the world needs Christ!"—L. S.

at least, comforted with their fellowship. **In some measure***
—Paul's meaning is evidently not brought out in either the
A.V. or R.V.   Conybeare's rendering is, "After I have in some
measure satisfied my desire for your company," or, "I must to
some extent at least have my fill of your company." It is a
wholly loving expectancy!

Paul also hopes, not only to see these Christians at Rome,
but, **to be brought on my way** [to Spain] **by you.** Thus was
the Gospel "furthered" in those days,—yea, and even yet! For
we find today companies of saints who by prayer and gifts, send
the preacher on to other fields!†

25   But now, (I say), I am proceeding unto Jeru-
26   salem, to minister unto the saints. For [the saints
      in] Macedonia and Greece have gladly undertaken
      to make a certain contribution for the poor among
27   the saints that are in Jerusalem. Yea, they have
      gladly done it; and they are indeed their debtors.
      For if the Gentiles have been made partakers of
      their [Jewish] spiritual things, they owe it also to
28   minister unto them in earthly matters. When
      therefore I have accomplished this, and have sealed
      to them this fruit, I will go on by you unto Spain.
29   And I know that, when I come unto you, I shall
      come in the fulness of the blessing of Christ.

Verses 25,26: Paul now announces the purpose of his visit
to Jerusalem (to carry a love-gift to the saints there), which was
brought out only in a general way in Acts 24.17. This was no

---

*" 'In some measure' (*apo merous*) is an affectionate limitation of *emplestho*,
implying that he would wish to remain much longer than he anticipated being
able to do," says Dean Alford.

†"This phase, 'brought on the way,' or 'sent forward,' refers to a semi-official
custom of the apostolic churches in furnishing an escort to go some or all the way
with a departing minister or missionary. Paul is here most likely asking that one
or more of the Roman brethren be sent with him to Spain. See Acts 15.3; 20.38;
21.5; I Cor. 16.6-11; II Cor. 1.16; Tit. 3.13; III John 6"—Stifler.

Paul is not asking for a "collection" from the Roman believers, but asking that
blessed *fellowship in all things* of the Spirit which pertained then and now pertains
to every servant of Christ and to all believers; to set forward in every way
those who are going forth with the blessed gospel.

hasty journey. In II Corinthians 9.1,2 he had written to the Corinthians in Greece:

> "As touching the ministering to the saints, I know your readiness, . . . that Greece hath been prepared for a year past; and your zeal hath stirred up very many of them" (Christians north of them, in Macedonia,—Philippi, Thessalonica, Berea).

It was a deliberate act of love on the part of the Gentile saints. It is called a special "grace" from God at least six times by Paul in II Corinthians Eight and Nine. It led the Gentile Christians into special consecration. Paul himself, together with other brethren, took this great offering back to Jerusalem, to seal in person unto them this fruit of the blessed gospel! This was probably in God's sight the highest act of Paul's whole ministry, fulfilling our Lord's words: "If ye know these things, blessed are ye if ye *do* them"; "By this shall all men know that ye are my disciples, if ye have *love* one to another."

Not only was this offering for the poor in Jerusalem the "good pleasure" of the Gentile Christians, and gladly given, but Paul recounts that in Macedonia this grace of grateful giving to the poor among the saints in Jerusalem, whence the gospel first came, led to their "beseeching Paul with much entreaty" to take what they gave—"of their own accord and even beyond their power"; "in much proof of affliction the abundance of their joy and their deep poverty abounded unto the riches of their liberality!"—they first, "having given their own selves to the Lord"—evidently in special meetings for prayer and consecration to this ministry of giving!

Here, then, we have the *original* order of "foreign" missions: The grace of God so abounds in the hearts of those in the unreached lands when they hear the gospel, that they joyfully insist, amidst persecution and poverty, on *sending back*, to those whence the gospel first went forth, a ministry of money, in grateful love! Instead of asking to be "supported" from the "home field," they entreat to be permitted to send back a love gift for any poor saints there!*

Verse 27: **Yea, they have gladly done it; and they are indeed their debtors. For if the Gentiles have been made partakers of their [Jewish] spiritual things, they owe it also to minister unto them in earthly matters.**

Here then is the reason for our special ministry toward Jewish Christians, and, as Gentiles, to help the Jews in any way possible: we have been made partakers of their "spiritual things." It is not that they are at present recognized, nationally, by God: they are not. But we are "their debtors." So we should be ready to "minister" to them, as we are able.

"Their Spiritual things" does not mean that our *calling* is Jewish or earthly, in any sense. See Chapter Eleven.

Here is announced also the principle which Paul states concerning himself to the Corinthians: "If we sowed unto you spiritual things, is it a great matter if we shall reap your carnal things?" . . . And although he "did not use this right," he declares that "the Lord ordained, that they that proclaim the gospel should live of the gospel" (I Cor. 9.11,12). To the Levites only, among the tribes, was given no inheritance, Jehovah saying, "I am their inheritance." But others were to minister unto them of their substance, so that, when the Israel-

---

*One wonders what the re-action would be in some comfortable church in America or England, Holland or Scandinavia, if some morning it were publicly announced, "Gifts for the poor among us have just arrived from the persecuted, poor, but happy saints in China, and India, to whom we have sent out the gospel!" Would we really have humility enough to receive such gifts? On the other hand, as regards the poor among the saints at Jerusalem, Olshausen trenchantly remarks that the community of goods of Pentecostal days "evidently had not lasted long!" However, in answer to this, let us remember that even in those days *absolute right of possessing private property was recognized*: "While it remained, did it not remain thine own? and after it was sold, was it not in thy power?" (Acts 5.4); and that the community of goods was evidently Divinely set forth at the time as a sign to the Jews of the power of the love of Christ which completely set aside private claims; and, finally, that the epistles of Paul, which are the charter of the Church of God, indicate the path for "them that are rich in this present age, that they do good, that they be rich in good works, that they be ready to distribute, willing to communicate" (I Tim. 6.17-19). They may continue, in comparison to others, rich, having thus the responsibility of *stewards*, as some must have. Finally, we must remember our Lord's words: "The poor ye have always with you."

But would even poor saints here be willing to be known as having *received* a contribution from "the foreign mission field"?

ites were faithful, the Levites had plenty; and when Israel forgot Jehovah, they forgot the Levites.

Verse 28: **When therefore I have accomplished this, and have sealed to them this fruit, I will go on by you unto Spain.**

Note Paul's confidence of the success of his ministry; also that giving is regarded as the proper "fruit" which "seals" to other believers the reality of our confession. See II Corinthians 9.13 about this same matter: "Seeing that through the proving of you [Grecian Christians] by this ministration they [the Jerusalem poor] glorify God for the obedience of your confession unto the gospel of Christ." Confession of Christ that does not result in ministering to others, is not an obedient confession.

Verse 29: **And I know that, when I come unto you, I shall come in the fulness of the blessing of Christ.**

This verse should put to silence those who claim that Paul was "below" his apostolic calling in this journey to Jerusalem. First, Paul had a holy, inspired knowledge that he would get to Rome; second, he had the same knowledge that when he should come, it would be not on a lower plane than his full apostolic message, but "in the fulness of the blessing of Christ."

30   **Now I beseech you, brethren, by our Lord Jesus Christ, and by the love of the Spirit, that ye strive [lit., _agonize_] together with me in your prayers to**
31   **God for me; that I may be delivered from them that are disobedient in Judea, and that my ministration which I have for Jerusalem may be acceptable to**
32   **the saints; that I may come unto you in joy through the will of God, and may refresh myself**
33   **in your fellowship. Now the God of peace be with you all. Amen.**

Here Paul makes the most solemn appeal for the supplications of the saints to be found in all his epistles. "Prayer changes things!" And many things needed to be wrought by God, if Paul's Divinely-guided journey to Jerusalem was to be successful.

First, there was the inveterate hatred of the Jews toward
Paul as the minister of grace to the Gentiles; the Jews were
indeed "disobedient." Paul describes them in I Thessalonians
2.15,16.*

Second, there was the natural disinclination even on the part
of Jewish Christians, through prejudice and pride, to accept for
their poor an offering at the hands of Gentiles.

Third, there was the constant willingness on the part of the
Roman governors of Judea to "gain favor" with the Jews by
yielding as far as possible to their demands in matters of their
religion. All these difficulties had to be overcome,—and by what
means? By God's appointed way—through *prayer*.

Paul therefore in verses 30-33, **beseeches** and that **by
our Lord Jesus Christ** Himself, and **by the love** wrought in
believers by the **Holy Spirit,** that they agonize (Greek,
agonidzo, the word used of contestants wrestling in Greek
games), together with Paul in their prayers to God for these
things: for, the Jews being entrenched in Satanic opposition
to Christ and His gospel, Paul asks the Christians at Rome to
pray **that he may be delivered from them that are disobedient in Judea;** again, he asks them to pray that his
ministration for Jerusalem may be acceptable to the saints;
and that, that he **may come** to the Roman Christians **in joy
through the will of God, and together with them be
refreshed.**

Now God answered these prayers, though bearing long; for
Paul was imprisoned at Caesarea two years; and came a prisoner
to Rome, suffering shipwreck by the way! Yet in due time *all
three things were brought about by prayer!*†

---

*"The Jews, who both killed the Lord Jesus and the prophets, and drove out
us, and please not God, and are contrary to all men; forbidding us to speak
to the Gentiles that they may be saved; to fill up their sins always; but the
wrath is come upon them to the uttermost."

†It is astonishing (and the more so the more we study it) how God makes His
work in this world *depend on the prayers of His saints!* Even His processes of
judgment wait for "the prayers of the saints" (see author's Revelation, p. 121).
And we know, from I Tim. 2:1,2, that the saints' living "a tranquil and quiet
life, in all godliness and gravity" is brought about through their faithful prayers
"for all men, for kings, and all that are in high place." Alas, how sadly this
duty has been neglected,—and with consequences of what dire national unrest
and trouble and disturbance of that outward tranquility and quietness wherein the
gospel best is proclaimed, and the church built up! (Acts 9:31.) Paul begs the

The beautiful benediction of verse 33, **The God of peace
be with you all,** shows how fully at peace was the apostle's
heart, and how fully in God's will! Also, His overflowing
love for the saints. For the "God of peace" to be *with* us,
is more than salvation: it is to be *conscious* of him—in peace!
Amen!

prayers of all the churches to whom he writes (except the Galatians!) "Doors for
the word" were to be opened through their prayers; "boldness," "utterance," that
the gospel might be "made manifest,"—all waited on their *prayers!*
   Epaphras, the Colossian, was a good example of what kind of praying we
should do! See Col. 4.12,13: "A bondservant of Christ Jesus, *always* agonizing for
you in his prayers, that ye may stand perfect and fully assured in all the
will of God."

CHAPTER SIXTEEN

Phoebe the Deaconess, Carrying the Epistle, Earnestly Commended to Roman Christians. Verses 1, 2.

Loving Salutations to Particular Saints and Assemblies in Rome. Verses 3 to 16.

Warnings against Those Causing Divisions and Stumbling. Verses 17 to 20.

Salutations from Paul's Fellow-workers. Verses 21 to 23.

Ascription of Praise through Jesus Christ to God only Wise: Who is Revealing through Paul's Establishing Gospel the Mystery Heretofore Concealed. Verses 25 to 27.

1 I commend unto you Phoebe our sister, who is a
2 deaconess of the church that is at Cenchreae: that ye receive her in the Lord, worthily of the saints, and that ye assist her in whatsoever matter she may have need of you: for she herself also hath been a helper of many, and of mine own self.

THIS SIXTEENTH CHAPTER is neglected by many to their own loss. It is by far the most extensive, intimate and particular of all the words of loving greeting in Paul's marvelous letters. No one can afford to miss this wonderful outpouring of the heart of our apostle toward the saints whom he so loved—which means all the real Church of God!

Verses 1, 2: **Phoebe, a deaconess of the assembly,** in the town **of Cenchreae,** the eastern seaport of Corinth, (about nine miles distant from that important city) is to carry to Rome this great Epistle! She had business in Rome,—probably legal or official business. (See Conybeare's note here.) She was evidently a devoted and prominent Christian,—a deaconess of the Cenchrean assembly. This, together with her evident business ability (for she is traveling to the world metropolis in connection with her affairs), made this entrustment to her of this great Epistle to the Romans humanly safe;—and through the Apostle's prayers and those of the saints at Corinth (where Paul is writing the Roman Epistle) absolutely safe. She is **commended** to the saints at Rome,—with all which that beautiful word "commended" contains (cf. Rom. 5.8 and II Cor. 10.18); and the saints are not only to **receive her in the Lord, worthily of saints** (for the saints should be devoted to receiving one another!) but they are asked to **assist her in her affairs in any way that they may find her needing help**; for, says Paul, **she herself hath been a helper of many and of mine own self.** Let us also mark those who, like Phoebe, are "helpers," and give ourselves to assisting them, both by prayer and by personal service; for the Lord will approve this, in His Day!

As to Phoebe's being called a **deaconess** *(diakonon)* of the Cenchrean assembly,* note that she was recognized by that church as designated of the Lord to her ministry, and was called by the name "deaconess." Let us not shun Scripture terms. Dorcas, in Acts 9.36, was "full of good works which she did," yet she is not called a deaconess. It is plain that

---

*Why both the King James and the Revised Versions should translate the same word *deacon* when it applies it to men (I Tim. 3.8, 10), and *servant* or *minister* when applied to women, let others explain. I Tim. 3.11 describes women-deacons evidently. As William Kelly (Romans: p. 274) says, "We know from elsewhere that elderly females held a position in which they rendered official or quasi-official service in the assembly where they lived. Phoebe was one of these of the port of Corinth, Cenchreae."

In our indignant rejection of papal pretenses and ecclesiastical man-made officialdom, we are apt to swing the pendulum too far, and refuse to recognize those whom God raises up as elders, deacons, and deaconesses. To claim that Timothy and Titus "have no successors" as direct apostolic delegates with authority "to appoint elders in every city," and that therefore eldership is no longer possible, is to ignore two great facts: first, that it is *the Holy Spirit Himself* Who makes men elders (Acts 20.17, 28), and second, that the Lord gave to Paul to write public letters describing the qualifications of both bishops (that is, elders), and also deacons (I Tim. 3; Titus 1). If the ministry of Timothy and Titus as "apostolic delegates" was purely personal and ended with them, then the instructions would have been in private, and not have been left to the Church at large! For what profit would instructions about the selection of elders, deacons, and deaconesses be, if there were to be none such, after Timothy and Titus?

We accept fully all those directions concerning women given by Paul. Women are not to be arbiters of doctrine, nor to usurp authority over men. This, however, does not hinder their praying publicly, and testifying (prophesying), if they have their heads obediently covered; nor does it hinder their being recognized,— as was Phoebe, as deaconesses. And it should humble the pride of some of us to find Phoebe, *a woman*, carrying this mighty fundamental Epistle of the gospel of God—more important than the Law of Moses!—to the center of the Gentile world!

both deacons and deaconesses were known in the early Church. (Elders, who would "rule,"—I Timothy 5.17—were, always, of course, men.)

3   Salute Prisca and Aquila, my fellow-workers
4 in Christ Jesus, who for my life laid down their own necks; unto whom not only I give thanks, but
5 also all the churches of the Gentiles; and [salute] the church that is in their house. Salute Epaenetus my beloved, who is the first fruits of Asia unto Christ.
6 Salute Mary, who bestowed much labor on you.
7 Salute Andronicus and Junias, my kinsmen and my fellow-prisoners, who are of note among the apostles, who also have been in Christ before me.
8 Salute Ampliatus my beloved in the Lord.
9 Salute Urbanus our fellow-worker in Christ, and
10 Stachys my beloved. Salute Apelles, the approved in Christ. Salute them that are of the [household]
11 of Aristobulus. Salute Herodion my kinsman. Salute them of the [household] of Narcissus, that
12 are in the Lord. Salute Tryphæna and Tryphosa, who labor in the Lord. Salute Persis the beloved,
13 who labored much in the Lord. Salute Rufus the chosen in the Lord, and his mother and mine.
14 Salute Asyncritus, Phlegon, Hermes, Patrobas, Hermas, and the brethren that are with them.
15 Salute Philologus and Julia, Nereus and his sister, and Olympas, and all the saints that are with
16 them. Salute one another with a holy kiss. All the churches of Christ salute you!

Verses 3,4: **Prisca** (Latin name of which Priscilla is the diminutive), who, with her husband Aquila (Acts 18.1-3) had toiled with Paul, had, at some time untold, **laid down their own necks**, risking their lives in such fashion as to call forth the thanks, not only of Paul, but of all the assemblies of the Gentiles.

Verse 5: There was also **an assembly of saints** [which gathered] **in their house.** We see here, in God's naming Priscilla first, that she was probably superior in spiritual intelligence and activity to her husband. Of course Aquila is recognized as the head of his house, as we see from Acts 18.2: "A certain Jew, named Aquila, with his wife Priscilla." But in Acts 18.26, when they are inviting eloquent, poorly-instructed Apollos to their home, it is Priscilla whose humble discernment and gospel earnestness seem to be foremost: "When Priscilla* and Aquila heard him, they took him unto them, and expounded unto him the Way of God more accurately." Compare II Timothy 4.19: "Salute Prisca and Aquila,"—personal salutations. But where the assembly is concerned, as in I Corinthians 16.19 (for this devoted pair had their house open in Ephesus, also, for an assembly of the saints), Aquila, as head of the house, is named first. The position and ministry of sisters in Christ is not at all unrecognized or suppressed in Paul's Epistles!†

---

*For this order, see Lachmann, Tischendorf, Tregelles, Alford, and R. V.

†The ministry of women in the early Church is strikingly brought out in this 16th Chapter. The list includes Phoebe, Prisca, Mary, Tryphæna, Tryphosa, Persis, Rufus' mother, and Julia. We read that they labored "in the Lord"—"labored *much* in the Lord," facing dangers generously, and were intrusted (as Phoebe) with the deaconess' office.

Now in what did their "labor" consist? Certainly not merely in getting chicken dinners for preachers! It is a *spiritual* activity here spoken of! As Paul says of Euodia and Syntyche, in Philippians 4.2,3, "Help these women, for they *labored with me in the gospel*, with Clement also, and the rest of my fellow-workers, whose names are in the book of life."

Just so Philip the evangelist had four virgin daughters who prophesied (Acts 21.8,9). They did so, of course, with covered heads, according to I Corinthians 11.4,5, where the distinct direction to women is, not to refrain from the exercise of the gift of prophesying, or praying, but to prophesy *with covered head*. To claim that these women took public part only in meetings of *women*, is a pitiful recourse to which many have resorted. "Your sons *and your daughters* shall prophesy," Peter quoted on the day of Pentecost.

In these matters three evils have sprung up, (1) The suppression of woman's voice entirely in the assembly of the saints. (2) The expression of women's earnest desire to serve the Lord, in the forming of independent women's organizations not controlled by the assembly. (3) Where men were fearful in faith, or ungifted, the bold pushing of individual women out to the front into leadership and government, even as "pastors" of assemblies,—leaders of "movements" which have swept into their ranks many untaught souls, to their great harm.

Now concerning the first, let any unbiased man study I Corinthians 11.4 and 5, and he must see that the gift of "prophecy,"—speaking unto others unto "edification, and comfort, and consolation," was shared alike by men and women. And to claim that it was exercised by women *only before other women*, is a twisting of Scripture worthy of a modernist! For when Paul in I Corinthians 14.34 says, "Let the women keep silence in the assemblies: for it is not permitted unto them to speak," the word for "speak" is not *didasko*, which means to teach authoritatively, involving dominion over men (I Tim. 2.11, 12); but the word is to "talk," to "talk out,"—Greek, *laleo*, which would indicate a woman's requesting *publicly* an answer to some *personal* inquiry: "If she would learn anything," etc. It does *not* have to do with that participation in the operation of the Spirit which

Salute Epaenetus my beloved . . . the first-fruits of Asia unto Christ—probably converted in Paul's great three years' mission in Ephesus, the capital of proconsular Asia, which is here referred to. We always specially treasure first converts!

Verse 6: **Salute Mary,—for she bestowed much labor on you.** Mary is a Jewish name, from Miriam. "Much labor" means great spiritual toil on behalf of all the saints and assemblies.

Verse 7: **Salute Andronicus and Junias, my kinsmen, and my fellow-prisoners, . . . such ones as** *(hoitines)* **are of note among the apostles, who also were in Christ before me.** From verse 21, we learn that three others of Paul's kinsmen were with him at Corinth when he wrote Romans. It is precious to note how, like our Lord Himself, he won his relatives! (See Acts 23.16-22.) But here we have two kinsmen converted *before Paul!* but who had, however, shared his hardships. Having the apostolic gift (though not among the twelve,) they were "of note" in it. Bishop Moule remarks, "Not improbably these two early converts helped to 'goad' (Acts 26:14) the conscience of their still persecuting kinsman, and to prepare the way of Christ in his heart."

---

prophesying and *praying* do. In I Timothy 2.8-10, also, it is evident, as in I Corinthians 11.4, 5, that women engaged in prayer in the assemblies. The words "in like manner," of I Timothy 2.9, are connected with the words, "that the men pray"; while the women, as instructed in I Corinthians, are to adorn themselves modestly *in their praying*.

I have often wondered how an "exclusive brother" would have felt when the woman of Luke 8.43 to 48, after touching the Lord and being healed, and shrinking back, was *called out by the Lord Himself* to "declare *in the presence of all the people* for what cause she touched Him, and how she was healed immediately." I once asked certain of them about this. The reply was,—"The Church had not yet begun!" Aye, but these very "exclusives" are very ready to bring in the Law ("as also saith the Law") when they are seeking to suppress woman's laboring in the gospel, by a passage which refers to keeping order in the assemblies. And what temerity to say that our Lord would have called out that woman of Luke 8 to testify in public—if her testifying had been contrary to that order in creation which the Church was to set forth!

No one has, I think, greater horror than we, of woman's breaking loose from the place of quietness to the place of publicity and even, alas, to the rulership of men. Isaiah cried concerning the apostate state of Israel, "As for my people, children are their oppressors, and women rule over them!" That is the state in the world today, and the devil ever seeks to bring it about in the assembly of God. But because some, even many, cast to the winds Paul's distinct direction that a woman take *not* the place of authoritative teaching or dominion over a man, but remain in quietness,—far be it from us because of these excesses, to shut our eyes to the operation of the Holy Spirit in women, whether it be in

Verse 8: **Salute Ampliatus, my beloved in the Lord:** Probably a convert of Paul's own, dear to him.

Verse 9: **Salute Urbanus our fellow-worker in Christ, and Stachys my beloved.** How wonderfully does the heart of this apostle retain personal names and maintain special love!

Verse 10: **Salute Apelles the approved in Christ.** Here is a tried and true saint—well known of all men: "the Lord knows, not we, the tests he stood." **Salute them that are of the household of Aristobulus.** Bishop Lightfoot holds that this Aristobulus was the grandson of Herod the Great, brother of Herod Agrippa of Judea; "his household," therefore, would be his retainers and servants, who would still, after his death, hold their master's name. This may be true also of the **household of Narcissus,** in verse 11. The word "household" does not appear in the Greek, but only "those from" or "of" Aristobulus and Narcissus. It should be noted, also, that in Philippians 4.22, where "the household of Caesar" is mentioned, the word for household *(oikia)* is expressed in the Greek. So that Aristobulus and Narcissus may have been prominent Christians, with numerous families connected with them,—children, relatives, retainers, servants. God loves to save whole households!

---

testimony or in prayer, and that in the assembly of the saints.

There was a wonderful old saint in St. Louis, Mother Gray, humble, teachable, earnest, and mightily filled with the Holy Spirit. When she rose, with her back bowed with many, many years of physical and spiritual labor, and her reverent head covered with her little black bonnet, and began to testify, to exhort, or to pray, every one was moved, and even the Plymouth Brethren (my best helpers not only in St. Louis, but generally, wherever it has been my privilege to preach), said to me, "Mother Gray seems an exception!"

No, she was not an exception, any more than was dear old "Auntie" Cook, in Chicago, who with another sister prayed unceasingly for D. L. Moody till he was mightily anointed with the Spirit of God.

And there was "Holy Ann," in Toronto, her little, feeble frame bent with years, but filled with the Spirit of God. Standing up to testify in the great Cooke's Church one afternoon, being very short, she gave her hand to be lifted, and stood on the pew! And we shall never forget her exhortation, *for God was in it!*

"The letter killeth, the Spirit giveth life." Ministry in the Spirit by a woman is different altogether from her taking over authority, or infringing upon the order of the assembly of God:

"The Lord giveth the Word: The women that publish the tidings are a great host" (Ps. 68.11 R. V.).

The general secretary of a well-known faithful missionary society told us recently that they had 20 women volunteers for missionary work, to one man! These are indeed days of terrible declension, or the proportion would not be such!

Verse 11: From his name some think **Herodion, Paul's kinsman,** would be connected with the Herodian retainers (see above).

Verse 12: **Salute Tryphæna and Tryphosa, who labor in the Lord. Salute Persis the beloved, who labored much in the Lord.** Not all of God's saints are real laborers in His vineyard. Persis was one whom the saints especially loved, and who gave them *much* service in her Lord. Note that Paul speaks of the men to whom he is especially attached, (like Stachys in verse 9), as "my beloved," and of a woman as *"the* beloved." He is careful in these matters.

Tryphæna and Tryphosa were, perhaps, sisters; and "almost certainly, by the type of their names, female slaves"; but Paul would send them a special greeting. For in the Church of God, as James says, "the brother of low degree glories in his high estate; and the rich that he is made low": both which things are impossible for the world!

Verse 13: **Salute Rufus the chosen in the Lord, and his mother and mine**—Perhaps the Rufus of Mark 15.21, the son of Simon of Cyrene, who bore our Lord's cross! "And his mother—*and mine."* How great the privilege this unnamed woman had that she should be regarded by this great apostle as a mother to him! And Paul, having left all for Christ, has a "mother" in this saint! See Mark 10.30. Let Christian mothers find here a great field for that wonderful heart of instinctive loving care given by God to mothers,—that they extend their maternal care beyond their own family circle, to all Christians, and especially to all laborers for Christ. The Lord will remember it at His coming!

Verse 14: Here we have five brethren greeted by name, and also the **brethren who are with them: Asyncritus, Phlegon, Hermes, Patrobas, Hermas.** This is the second of the three gatherings of saints in Rome here mentioned. For we must remember that in the early days of the Church believers gathered in great simplicity, according to our Lord's word: "Where two or three are gathered together in My Name, there am I in the midst of them" (Matt. 18.20). It is fast coming to this, in these last days, also, where the Laodicean spirit claims the property and ecclesiastical importance in this world, of that which is known as "the Christian religion"; while humble saints, finding themselves unfed and very often unwanted in the great "establishments," are gathering more and more as the early Christians did,—in homes, in Bible Conferences—wherever Christ and His Word and real fellowship in the Spirit are the only drawing powers (and how sufficient!).

Verse 15: Next comes another such assembly: **all the saints that are** *with* **Philologus and Julia**—a precious couple!—**and Nereus and his sister.** It is a growing wonder that Paul in his multitude of burdens, his "care for all the churches," remembers, each and all, these beloved individuals!

Verse 16: **Salute one another with a holy kiss.** It is remarkable that this direction should be repeated five times: here; in I Thessalonians 5.26; in I Corinthians 16.20; in II Corinthians 13.12; and in I Peter 5.14. In the first four, the word "holy" is used, and in the passage in I Peter, "a kiss of love." Sanday declares, "The earliest references to the kiss of peace as a regular part of the Liturgy is in Justin Martyr; then mentioned by Tertullian and others."

The simplicity and warmth of early Christian devotion cannot be brushed aside as an "Orientalism" by the colder hearts and more formal and "reserved" manners of our day. "Behold, how these Christians love one another!" was the constant remark in the early days. The word **beloved** is used four times by Paul in these few verses.

All the churches in Christ salute you. Paul knew these assemblies; the burden of all of them he says pressed upon him daily (II Cor. 11.28). He was familiar with their feelings toward the saints in the great world center, and in their name he sends the Christians in Rome their greetings of love. How beautiful, how good and pleasant, were those early days of first love! The mustard seed was yet little—"least of all seeds"; later it was to grow in outward form into the "great tree," where "the fowls of the air" (Satan's very own) were to find lodging (Matt. 13.31,32,4,19). Would it not be wonderful in our eyes to come upon some community today where the saints were *all one!* loving one another and thus fulfilling our Lord's great prayer in John 17? Surely the world has much to stumble at in our divisions and lack of tenderness one toward another.

And now, as Bishop Moule beautifully writes in his tender remarks on this Chapter: "The roll of names is over, with its music, that subtle characteristic of such recitations of human personalities, and with its moving charm for the heart due almost equally to our glimpses of information about one here and one there, and to our total ignorance about others; an ignorance of everything about them, but that they were at Rome, and that they were in Christ. We seem, by an effort of imagination, to see as through a bright cloud, the faces of the company, and to catch the far-off voices; but the dream 'dis-solves in wrecks'; we do not know them, we do not know their distant world. But we do know Him in whom they were, and are; and that they have been 'with Him, which is far better,' for now so long a time of rest and glory. So we watch this unknown but well-beloved company with a sense of fellowship and expectation impossible out of Christ. This page is no mere relic of the past; it is a list of friendships to be made hereafter, and to be possessed forever in the endless life where personality indeed shall be eternal, but where also the union of personalities in Christ shall be beyond our utmost present thought."

17   Now I beseech you, brethren, mark them that are causing the divisions and occasions of stumbling, contrary to the doctrine which ye learned:
18   and turn away from them. For they that are such serve not our Lord Christ, but their own belly; and by their smooth and fair speech they beguile the
19   hearts of the innocent. For your obedience is come abroad unto all men. I rejoice therefore over you: but I would have you wise unto that which is good,
20   and simple unto that which is evil. And the God of peace shall bruise Satan under your feet shortly. The grace of our Lord Jesus Christ be with you

Verses 17,18: Already, at Rome, we find men willing to bring about **divisions** among the saints and to become **occasions of stumbling.** Alas that such an unearthly wonder of beauty as the love and unity of the saints in Christ should be hated and attacked by deadly foes! But so it is, and Paul must write, **I beseech you, brethren, mark such ones!** And there is the ever present danger of our very Christian charity making us unwilling to deal with righteous sternness toward others who are doing deadly work. If any one was known to be causing selfish divisions, or had become an occasion for others' falling, **contrary to the doctrine which they had learned of Paul,** their only path was to **turn away from them.** Compare II Thessalonians 3.6, Titus 3.10, II John 10. Such evil workers were not **serving our Lord Christ, but their own belly.** What an unutterably fearful spiritual state!—to be amongst those filled with holy love toward the Lord Jesus Christ, and toward one another as fellow members of His Body, and yet be bent on altogether selfish business! Concerning many professors of Christianity John Bunyan said, "A man will go far for his own belly's sake." Compare Philippians 3.18,19,20:

"Many walk, of whom I told you often, and now tell you even weeping, that they are the enemies of the cross of Christ: whose end is perdition, whose god is the belly, and whose glory is in their shame, who mind earthly things: for our citizenship is in Heaven."

Just as in Eden God did not prevent the serpent from tempting Eve,—"beguiling her in **his craftiness"**; so God does not forcibly prevent false teachers, division-makers, evil workers, stumbling producers, from coming among His saints. But He warns His saints, and expects them to exercise both their discernment and their holy hatred of evil in turning away from such. Also, they "have an Anointing from the Holy One,"—these saints of God; and this Anointing "teacheth them concerning all things." The saints do not have to depend on their own understanding, but to consult constantly God's Word, and *trust* the indwelling Spirit. God warns concerning these evil workers that **by their smooth and fair speech they beguile the hearts of the innocent.** Beautiful testimony of an all-seeing God to the blessed "innocence" of His own children toward the subtle wickedness of evil doers!

Verse 19: Indeed, Paul declares of these Roman Christians, whose obedience was come abroad unto all men: I rejoice, therefore, over you! Everywhere throughout the Roman world, the simple wholehearted faith and love of the Christians at Rome was talked of (See Chapter 1.8). But Paul expresses his concern in the remarkable words, I would have you wise unto that which is good, and simple unto that which is evil. Here is a Divinely safe path for the believer! "Wise unto that which is good," will include: the constant study of God's Word of truth, and careful observation and valuing what is good in the lives about us, and of those whose lives and works we read. Paul sums it up to the Philippians (4.8):

"Whatsoever things are true, whatsoever things are reverend whatsoever things are just, whatsoever things are pure, whatsoever things are lovely, whatsoever things are of good report (concerning anything or any person); if there be any virtue, and if there be any praise, take account of these things."

Oh, for such a habit of mind—to be constantly "wise unto that which is good!"

But the other side, "simple unto that which is evil," must accompany wisdom toward the good. "Simple" here literally means *unmixed,*—used of wine or metals: *pure;* and so, "free from guile," "like a little child." We are in the midst of a world of evil, but the Spirit of God will bring us into an attitude of a babe's simplicity toward it all,—as Paul says in I Corinthians 14.20: "in malice, be ye babes." That whole verse reads, "Brethren, be not children in mind: yet in malice, be ye babes; but in mind be *of full age.*" You see it is wholly possible to grow up from spiritual infancy (in which were the Corinthians, for instance: I Cor. 3.1), into spiritual adulthood, without becoming mixed up at all with the "deep things of Satan, as they say" (Rev. 2.24). Indeed, Paul distinctly warns us against a "knowing" spirit as to worldly things: "If any man thinketh that he is wise among you in this age, let him become a fool that he may become wise, for the wisdom of this age is foolishness with God." "Sophisticated" is what many young people today so desire to be considered:

but it is a horrible term, implying experimental knowledge of the unclean things of this world, with all its evil ways. Malice, along with pride, are valued by the world, as exhibiting what they call "spirit"! Let us remember, therefore, that Paul would have us "simple" unto that which is evil. He says in I Corinthians Thirteen, "Love thinketh no evil,"—literally, "taketh not account of evil." Evil is all about one, but the believer, abiding in Christ, is kept in sweet simplicity toward it.*

There has been much conjecture as to the character of these early evil workers (of verses 17,18) at Rome: some regarding them as evil teachers, probably of a Jewish character (Sanday); others as early Gnostics, which insidious Satanic philosophy developed itself fully later (Moule). It is not, however, as necessary to know their historic setting, as to take the moral lesson here, and to discern such characters, whatever they be, in our own day among the saints; and turn away from them. The inability to turn resolutely and holily away from false teachers and evil workers, is a mark of spiritual ill-health, decadence, and possibly of the state of spiritual death itself!

Mad dogs are shot; infectious diseases are quarantined; but evil teachers who would divide to their destruction and draw away the saints with teaching **contrary to the doctrine** of Christ and His Apostles are everywhere tolerated! How ghastly and ruinous is this false toleration! Let us take heed lest we "partake in the evil deeds" of such evil workers! Remember II John 9,10,11.

"Whosoever goeth onward [lit., 'taketh the lead'—into such 'progressiveness' as Modernism, Theosophy, New Thought], and abideth not in the teaching of Christ, hath not God: he that abideth in the teaching, the same hath both the Father and the Son. If any one cometh unto you, and bringeth not this teaching, receive him not into your house, and give him no

---

*Satan has deceived some good preachers into "personally investigating evil people and conditions," in order to "preach against them"; but God says "The things that are done of them in secret, it is a shame even to speak of." Preach the *Word;* therein will be found abundant discoveries of evil and denunciations thereof; but, being the Word of God, it is holy, and may safely be used in exposing evil. It is like the sunshine that lights up the foulest alley without being itself defiled! Don't go down the alley "personally," lifting the lids of their garbage-cans; or you will *smell* of it!

greeting: *for he that giveth him greeting partaketh in his evil works."*

Verse 20: **The God of peace shall bruise Satan under your feet shortly.** The same word here translated "bruise" is used of Christ's breaking the nations at His second coming (Rev. 2.27). Note that it is **the God of peace** who will do this blessed delivering! And it is **Satan,** the great dragon of Revelation Twelve, against whom Michael and his angels go forth to war, that shall be bruised. Note further that it will be **under the feet of His saints** that God will do this bruising; and note finally that it is to be done **shortly.** This corresponds to the "quickly" of "Behold, I come,"— in Revelation 22.7,12,20; and is the very phrase used in Revelation 1.1! This is to be held fast by our faith, despite all seeming delays and apparent Satanic victories. Meanwhile, let it astonish us and fill us with exultant joy that the great foe of God, who will have the hardihood to war against Michael and his angels, flees before the saints on earth today who, in heart-subjection to God, "resist" him "steadfast in their faith"! (James 4.7; I Pet. 5.9.)

How glorious the prospect of the complete overthrow of Satan, whose unlimited pride will be abased, and that under the very feet of those he now despises, hates, and seeks to overthrow!

Satan's ruin began (as traced in Ezekiel 28) in heaven, where he was the "anointed cherub," walking up and down in the midst of "the stones of fire,"—perhaps leading all others in worship. But his heart became lifted up by very reason of his beauty; he corrupted his wisdom by the very reason of his brightness, and he was "cast as profane out of the Mountain of God"—that is from the heavenly council-place of Divine Majesty. Now, though he still has ability to accuse the saints before God (Rev. 12.10), and with his host is in "the heavenlies" (Eph. 6.12)—that is, not confined to earth, but still permitted the freedom of certain heavenly regions as a heavenly being—yet he will be cast down (after the Church's Rapture, or taking up,) to this earth. And in his rage, therefore, he will inaugurate the Great Tribulation to obliterate God's nation Israel from the earth.

Upon Christ's coming down to earth with His saints and angels, Satan will be cast into the abyss at the center of the earth for a thousand years—The Millennium, (Rev. 20). At the end of that he will be released for a little season and lead the last great warfare against God and His people. Thence he is cast into the lake of fire and brimstone to be tormented forever (Rev. 20,10). Every believer should be familiar with these facts concerning his great enemy. Shortly, he will be "bruised" by Christ; according to the first prophecy and promise in the Bible: Genesis 3.15: "He" [the seed of the Woman] "shall bruise thy head" (the Serpent's, Satan's). This is a heartening promise, indeed! Further, there will be no peace, no truce, until it is done. The word "shortly" should fall on our hearts with constant hope, as it did on Paul's.

Then comes the "benediction," as we call it, pronouncing, promising, to the Saints: **the grace of our Lord Jesus Christ be with you.** In the last verse of II Corinthians (13.14) Paul says, "The grace of the Lord Jesus Christ, and the love of God, and the communion of the Holy Spirit, be with you all"; but seven times "the grace of our Lord Jesus Christ" is pronounced on the saints in the Epistles! Even in the verse from Corinthians quoted above, when the three persons of the Godhead are mentioned, it is still "the grace of the Lord Jesus Christ"! Now the "grace of the Lord Jesus Christ" is defined in II Corinthians 8.9:

"Ye know the grace of our Lord Jesus Christ, that, though He was rich, yet for your sakes He became poor, that ye through His poverty might become rich."

It is as the Head, from whom all the Body is supported and nourished, that Christ thus constantly supplies grace to all believers: For "God gave Him to be Head over all things to the Church"—the Assembly of God. It may be said that grace has God the Father as its Source; with Christ as its Bestower; and the Holy Spirit as its Communicator.

21   Timothy my fellow-worker saluteth you; and
22   Lucius and Jason and Sosipater, my kinsmen. I
       Tertius, who write the epistle, salute you in the

23 Lord. Gaius my host, and of the whole church, saluteth you. Erastus the treasurer of the city saluteth you, and Quartus the brother.

Verse 21: Now come the salutations to the Christians at Rome from Paul's fellow-workers, from his gracious host, and others. Bishop Moule with his fervid imagination pictures the Epistle to the Romans as written in Gaius' house in one day! "They began at morning on the themes of sin, righteousness, and glory of the present and the future of Israel, of the duties of the Christian life, of the special problems of the Roman Mission; carried their hours along to noon, to afternoon . . . But before he bids his willing and wonderful secretary, Tertius, rest from his labor, he has to discharge his own heart and affections which have already lain in it all the while! And now Paul and Tertius are no longer alone—other brethren have found their way to the chamber—Timothy, Lucius, Jason, Sosipater, Gaius himself, Quartus, and no less a magistrate than Erastus, Treasurer of Corinth. A page of personal messages yet to be dictated from St. Paul and his friends."

Now while we cannot agree that the Epistle was written in one day, the words above bring vividly to our mind the closing scene.

Timothy, my fellow-worker, saluteth you. "I have no man likeminded," wrote Paul to the Philippians (2.19-22), "who will truly care for your state. Ye know that as a child serveth a father, so he served with me in the furtherance of the Gospel." I can think of no higher honor than to be counted by Paul a "fellow-worker." Although Paul's name alone must stand at the beginning of this Epistle to the Romans, as it sets forth the foundation of Christian doctrines as the Lord committed them to him, yet here at the end is Timothy, his "true yokefellow," faithful from the beginning on. Then we have **Lucius, Jason and Sosipater, kinsmen of Paul's.** Lucius was perhaps, even probably, the "Lucius of Cyrene" of Acts 13.1; and Jason that Jason who had received Paul in Acts 17.5-9; while Sosipater is in all likelihood Sosipater, the son of Pyrrhus, of Berea. These last three, being relatives of Paul's, were, doubtless, Jewish Christians.

Verse 22: Then we have a direct word from Tertius, who transcribed the Epistle for Paul: **I, Tertius, who am writing the Epistle, salute you in the Lord!**

Next that gracious and generous hearted believer, who kept open house for the whole Church of God, and was at present entertaining Paul, gives his greeting: **Gaius, my host, and of the whole church, saluteth you.** This doubtless is the Gaius of the very next chapter of the New Testament I Corinthians 1 (verse 14), whom Paul himself had baptized,—as a man prominent and well known. God gave Solomon "largeness of heart as the sand upon the sea shore," and here is a brother whose hospitality welcomes all the saints. Brother, if you have a longing to be helpful to God's saints, be a Gaius! Count not the things you have as your own, but as belonging to Christ; and, therefore, to be used freely by Christ's own. Our Lord, while on earth, found *one* home,—that at Bethany, thus open fully to Him, and He said to His disciples, "He that receiveth you, receiveth Me, and he that receiveth Me, receiveth Him that sent Me."

Verse 23: **Erastus, the City Treasurer, saluteth you.** Sanday thinks that Paul mentions Erastus because of his being "the most influential member of the community." But that would not be like Paul! And the salutation of Erastus is just as genuine as that of Gaius, or of the saint next mentioned here as simply **Quartus the brother.** Quartus was not a city official, nor prominent, but along go his warm greetings to the Christians at Rome, with Paul's and all the rest!

These tender salutations, both to the Christians at Rome, and from the Christians gathered about Paul in Corinth where he writes, arouse both joy and grief in our hearts today,—joy that in that early day there existed such unity of consciousness in Christ, such brotherly solicitude, such friendly, loving greetings, between those who knew themselves one company, one Body, one band of pilgrims through the dark and dreary desert of this world! and grief that our own day sees such sad divisions, jealousies, contentions, such earthly-mindedness; such loss of the *mighty truths* of this great Epistle to the Romans,—that our sin has been put away forever by the one sacrifice of

Christ, that we died with Him and have been raised into newness of life with Him, and are no longer of this world! Not
only grief at the awful Babylonish ecclesiastical structure, worse
than paganism, which Satan has built, beginning at this very
city of Rome; but deeper grief at the indifference and uncon-
cern at increasing Romish abominations of those calling themselves "Protestants"; at their willingness to be divided—their
even glorying in it; at the lack of that burning love so evident
in Paul and those with him, and at the loss of separation from
this world that crucified our Lord!

25   **Now to him that is able to establish you accord-
        ing to my gospel and the heralding of Jesus Christ,
        according to the revelation of the mystery which**
26   **hath been kept in silence through times eternal, but
        now is manifested, and [now] by prophetic Scrip-
        tures, according to the commandment of the
        eternal God, is made known unto all the nations**
27   **unto obedience of faith: to God alone wise,
        through Jesus Christ, to whom be the glory unto
        the ages. Amen!**

Verses 25 to 27: All agree that the Epistle to the Romans
is the foundational Epistle. Consequently the great doctrines
of Christianity appear there. But it is not generally recognized
that in verses 25 to 27 preparation is made by the Apostle Paul
for the unfolding in his further epistles of that great secret of
God called "The Mystery,—kept in silence through the times
of ages"; the Special revelator of which Paul is. It is necessary to see clearly that in the words **to establish you** of
verse 25, Paul refers to truth beyond that which the Romans
already knew. He says in Chapter One he "longs to see them
. . . that they might through his teaching, ministry, and fellowship, be *established*." Those to whom Paul writes in this
Epistle had believed; they had become "obedient from the
heart to that pattern of doctrine whereunto they were delivered"
(6.17). Therefore when Paul speaks to them of **my gospel**
and of **the heralding of Jesus Christ according to the revelation of the mystery,** he cannot be referring to that revelation of God's righteousness which had been "witnessed by

the Law and the prophets" (3.21). Furthermore, these two expressions, **my gospel** and **the preaching of Jesus Christ according to the revelation of the mystery,** seem to be two coördinate terms, or possibly we should say, the second characterized the first: for we know that to some (like the Corinthians), who were babes, not full grown, Paul preached only "Jesus Christ and Him *crucified.*" Whereas he himself tells us, as we have before observed, of higher, heavenly truth, connected with Christ Jesus and Him *glorified,* which he preached to "fullgrown" believers.

The Greek word translated **establish** is used about ten times in the New Testament concerning a settled, stable spiritual condition. We find this first in our Lord's words to Peter: "When once thou hast turned again, *establish* thy brethren" (Luke 22.32). It includes not only a knowledge of the truth, and a settled persuasion in Christ of that truth; but also obedience in the power of the Spirit, to the truth: "to the end He may establish your hearts unblamable in holiness before our God and Father, at the coming of our Lord Jesus with all His saints" (I Thess. 3.13) ; and it also involves our testimony: "establish your hearts in every good word and work" (II Thess. 2.17).

We shall find the Greek construction of the great doxology of verses 25 to 27, involved and difficult, unless we place ourselves in the position of Paul himself. He has been writing with the hand of the Spirit upon him, those stupendous truths which we find in this great, fundamental Epistle: the glory, holiness, and righteousness, of the infinite, eternal God; the awful guilt and helplessness of man; the story of the astonishing intervention of a Grace that not only pardoned and justified, but made believing sinners partakers in Christ of the very glory of God Himself; the absolute consistency of all this with God's promises to His earthly nation, Israel; the openness of all Heaven now to all nations, and that on the simplest possible condition—*Faith alone!* And the Apostle has God in view as the Giver, Christ in view as the means, and the saints in view as the receivers of this mighty bounty!

Therefore this great passage becomes both a doxology, and a commendation with a doxology, of praise to this great God, and a commendation of the saints unto Him. Paul thus commended the saints in Ephesus (Acts 20.32) : "And now, brethren, I commend you to God, and to the Word of His grace." Therefore, if we must seek for grammatical regularity (which we do not need to do in such an overwhelming passage as this!) we may read: Now I commend you to Him that is able to establish you . . . To the only wise God, through Jesus Christ: to whom be the glory unto the ages!

The last words, to whom be the glory unto the ages must, it seems, be taken, in view of all other Scriptures, to refer to God. It is to Him the glory comes, through Jesus Christ. This is the constant voice of Scripture. Furthermore, Paul at the beginning declares this gospel to be the Gospel of God concerning His Son, and as we have noted throughout the Epistle, God is the Actor—setting forth Christ as a propitiation. He is the God, "not of Jews only, but of Gentiles also,—seeing that God is One." "We have peace with *God* through our Lord Jesus Christ." "It is *God* that justifieth," and "O the depth of the riches both of the wisdom and knowledge of *God!*" and "We present our bodies living sacrifices to *God.*" Right through the Epistle goes the message of the gospel of God concerning His Son.

Also the double mention of God, first (verse 25), to Him that is able to establish you; and second (verse 27) : to the only wise God, draws our minds irresistibly to God the Father as the Source of all this grace and blessing—to whom the ascription of praise goes up.

We notice also that it is *God* who establishes us according to the preaching of Jesus Christ (verse 25) ; that the message concerning the mystery is brought forth according to the commandment of the eternal God (verse 26) ; and that the glory goes up to God through Jesus Christ (verse 27), much as the King James Versions reads: to God only wise, be glory through Jesus Christ forever.

Our blessed Lord Himself insisted beyond all others that the Father be glorified in and through the Son! and thus we find it in Romans.*

"THE MYSTERY WHICH HAD BEEN KEPT IN SILENCE"

God had a sovereign purpose to take certain creatures *into His own glory,* to share in that Glory. And He desired also that these should know Him in His nature as Love, and be with Him, before Him, in that blissful atmosphere of pure love, forever.

These happy creatures were not to be taken from among the "elect angels,"—holy, blessed beings that these are.

It was God's purpose to manifest *Himself,* all that He is,—not in holiness and righteousness and truth only; but in His infinite Love, Grace, Mercy, Tenderness, Gentleness, and Patience.

God therefore sent His Son, and lo! *God* was manifest in the flesh! Christ declared God—all God was: which had not ever been done before, to any of His creatures!

But, after revealing God's love, mercy, and gracious tenderness toward sinners, the Son of God goes to the cross. And there is revealed the eternal unchangeable holiness of God in hatred of sin, together with that love capable of giving the Son of His delight to bear sin for a world that rejected, despised His Son!

But *the mystery* of which Paul speaks was not yet revealed. Was it not prophesied in the Psalms and prophets, and witnessed in the types of all the offerings, that the Son of God, the Messiah, would suffer, and that for human sin? "Thus it is written in the law, the prophets and the psalms, that Christ should suffer, and rise again from the dead the third day," our Risen Lord said to His disciples in Luke 24.44-46. And "the

---

*Yet while we feel sure that we should read in verse 27: "Glory to God, through Jesus Christ"; let us never forget that Christ is *God the Son*: as we read in Chapter 9.5: "Christ—who is over all, God blessed forever!" The question in the last verse of Romans is not at all concerning the deity of Christ, but of the Divine order—both of blessing to us, and of thanksgiving by us.

mystery" had been "hid in God who created all things,"—hid "from the ages and from the generations."

What then, is the *mystery?*

It is wrapped up, (though not revealed) in our Lord's words in His great heavenly prayer of John 17: For here we find Him praying for a company given Him by the Father out of the world.*

Now in verse 22, our Lord Jesus says plainly: "The glory which Thou hast given Me I have given unto them." So that this glory into which Christ was to enter was to be shared with these whom the Father had given Him.

This, then, is the foundation for the revelation of "the Mystery." Certain were to be brought, in Christ, *into the Divine glory!* They were to be "manifested with Him *in glory,"* at His appearing. But that would be because they had *entered into* a glory never before given creatures! It was not given to angels, seraphim, or cherubim, but to blood-bought sinners as *members of Christ!* Nor was such a union proposed to earthly Israel. Saved Israel will, indeed "see the glory of God": "Thine eyes shall see the King in His beauty," is promised to that beloved, restored nation (Isa. 33.17): and also that over restored Jerusalem "the glory shall be spread a covering" (Isa. 4.2-6). But there was never a hint in the Old Testament that there would be a *heavenly* calling,—a company who would enter into that glory—be glorified with this glorious One!

This is the secret, the mystery, "kept in silence through times of ages," the unfolding of which Paul declares will *establish* the saints!

For it must involve the revelation to us that we were *"chosen in Christ* before the foundation of the world"! That we were foreknown, and foreordained to be "conformed to the image of

---

*Our Lord asks five things for them in John 17: (1) That they may be kept—in the Father's name, and from the evil one (Verses 11-15); (2) That they might be sanctified—as not of the world, first in the truth, and second by our Lord's identification with them—"For their sake I sanctify Myself" (set Myself apart to the cross) (Verses 16-19); (3) That they may be "one," "perfected into one," and that in a wondrous union only to be defined "as Thou, Father, art in Me and I in Thee, that they may be in Us" (Verses 21-23); (5) That these may be *with Him*—and that forever, where He is, to behold His glory into which He would enter upon His ascension (Verses 5, 24).

God's Son, that He might be "The First-born among many brethren"!

That we, having a sinful history in Adam the first, would not only have our sins put away, in God's grace, by the blood of Christ; but would be so identified with Him, by God's astonishing act, as to be cut off from all connection with the first Adam and be created in His Son, now risen from the dead!

That we would not only be enlifed with Him, but be raised up with Him, and made to sit with Him in the heavenlies in Christ Jesus! Thus passing out of earthly connections, and becoming citizens of heaven!

That, in "the riches of the glory of this mystery, Christ would be in us, dwelling in our hearts by faith, in the energy of the Holy Spirit!" (Col. 1.27; Eph. 3.14-21).

That thus, our hearts being as a "mirror," we would behold the glory of the Lord, and be transformed into His image, "from glory to glory," here below (II Cor. 3.18).

That, at our Lord's second coming, our bodies would be in an instant redeemed, (I Cor. 15.51-53); so that "these bodies of our humiliation," would be, by Christ's "fashioning them anew," be at once "conformed to the body of His glory"; so that "we should be like Him, for we shall see Him even as He is"!—which not even Paul has yet done! (Phil 3.20,21; I John 3.3).

That, in "the ages to come," God will "show the exceeding riches of His grace, in kindness to us, in Christ Jesus" (Eph. 2.7).

And that, as Eve shared with the first Adam the dominion given him, being one with him (she having been taken out of his side and "builded into" a woman) and even sharing with him his name Adam (Gen. 1.28; 2.21-23, and 5.1,2): just so the Church, the wife of the Lamb, as one with Christ, having been created in Him and sharing with Him His name! (I Cor. 12.12) will share His dominion! See, reverently, Ephesians 1.23; 2.10 and I Cor. 12.12,13. That thus Christ and His Bride, the Church, shall be forever: "That they may be with

Me where I am; that they may behold My glory which Thou hast given Me; and the glory which Thou Hast given Me I have given unto them."

Creatures—only creatures we, and forever will be, but given the highest place which the Word of God gives to creatures: "For we are *members of Christ's Body"!* and, "We rejoice in the hope of *the Glory of God.*"

Now although on the Day of Pentecost, God baptized into Christ in glory those in the upper room and all true believers thereafter; and although it is true that God thus in their *experience* made known to "His holy apostles and prophets in the Spirit," "this mystery of Christ which in other generations was not made known unto the sons of men"; yet He chose Paul to open out before God's saints the doctrine of this heavenly mystery or secret; and to write in "all his Epistles" these things for us. All the apostles knew, for example, on that Day of Pentecost that Christ had been glorified in heaven and that they were in the boundless joy of the revelation of this glorious Christ to their souls. They had all entered into the enjoyment of the blessedness belonging to this great thing concealed by God from all creatures before that moment. But it was Paul to whom the Lord revealed *the whole doctrine* of the mystery; and we firmly believe he thus became the revelator to all men of these glorious things connected with this mystery.

Not that God subjected James, Cephas and John, the apostles of the circumcision, to Paul in their ministry. In their spheres of ministry, Paul went to the Gentiles and they to the circumcision. But as to the unfolding of the great facts of the mystery, the Lord chose Paul,—who writes himself down (and that by an inspired pen), as "less than the least of all saints"; so that "by the grace of God" Paul himself said, "I am what I am." And we give all glory, therefore, to God.

Now no one is able to read, understand, believe and meditate, upon this, God's great secret, of our heavenly calling, our connection with Christ Himself and with the glory that shall be revealed, without becoming himself heavenly minded!

So that the heralding of Jesus Christ according to the unfolding of the mystery is the preaching by which God establishec

His heavenly saints. For if indeed we are heavenly; if our "citizenship" is in heaven; if our worship is by the Spirit; if through Christ by that Spirit we have "our access to the Father"—unto God in heaven; how utterly unable is any "religious" earthly system to establish us! Nay, says Paul; "We are the circumcision who worship by the Spirit of God and glory in Christ Jesus and have no confidence in the flesh!" (Phil. 3.3).

We recognize fully that the "mystery" is not developed in Romans, though set forth and implied in Chapter 12.5: "We who are many are one Body in Christ." Paul is here speaking as if the Roman Christians were expected to understand the expression, or were at least to expect Paul to reveal and fully explain it to them when he should get to Rome. Inasmuch, therefore, as some of our readers may not have access to those writings Scripturally setting forth what the mystery is and our participation in it, or may even neglect to read the other remarkable Scriptures which open it out, we have thought it best to speak briefly upon the mystery, even in a work on Romans.

And we would remind the reader that unless this "revelation of the mystery" becomes indeed *revelation* to his own soul, he must fall short entirely of understanding what the present dispensation is; and what is the Church's (or Assembly's) real character, calling, destiny, and present walk. As the prayer of Paul for us is realized in us: "That you may know what is the hope of His calling" (Eph. 1.18,19,ff), these things will be brought to pass in you and me:

1. We shall see and realize that our history in the first Adam was ended at the cross.

2. We shall see that the Christ with Whom God has now connected us is wholly a heavenly Christ, and that neither Christ nor those in Him have anything to do with Israel after the flesh, to whom the Law was given, and to whom the Messiah came.

3. We shall see ourselves vitally connected with, joined to, this heavenly Christ, so that we have been received in Christ as belonging to heaven, "even as He"; that we are "the righteousness of God in Him"; that we are loved even as He; and that

our citizenship is in heaven. Our hearts must be convinced that these things are *facts,* not figures of speech, or things to be realized in some far future. We wait, indeed, for the redemption of our bodies, but we ourselves are already in the new creation, and for us old things (all earthly things, "religious" or worldly), have passed away.

4. We shall see that blindness has befallen Israel; that the mystery of lawlessness is working; that the earthly testimony of the Church has failed; that iniquity will abound and "evil men and seducers wax worse and worse" in professing Christendom—of all these things we shall be certain: but knowing them beforehand, and understanding that the course of things on earth has nothing to do with our heavenly calling, we shall continue steadfast in faith.

5. An ever-deepening humility will be wrought in us by the knowledge that we have been called into this Divine union, so that there is fulfilled in us what our Lord prayed for: "That they may all be one; even as Thou, Father, art in Me, and I in Thee, that they also may be in us": as Paul writes to the Thessalonians: "The assembly of the Thessalonians *in God our Father and the Lord Jesus Christ.*"

6. Not only humility, but hope—the true hope of the instructed Christian, will rise and well up in our hearts: "Looking for the blessed hope and appearing of the glory of our great God and Savior Jesus Christ" (Titus 2.13).

7. Thus the believer walks consciously justified from all things, and in newness of life (Romans); as a new creature in Christ (II Corinthians); as made alive together with Christ, raised up in Him, and made to sit with Him in the heavenlies (Ephesians); thus with Paul as the example, he runs His course toward Christ Himself (Philippians); as walking through many dangers on this earth, yet "holding fast the Head," in Whom is all fulness, and in Whom, in constant appropriation of His fulness, the believer is being made full (Colossians); and thus with ever-absorbing hope he expects the day when Christ shall appear, and he become "in a moment" "like Him,"—seeing Him as He is (Thessalonians).

SPIRITUAL ORDER OF PAUL'S EPISTLES

We believe that the order of arrangement of Paul's Epistles to the Churches was Divinely established; and that there is a *progress of spiritual experience* from Romans to II Thessalonians.

(1) In *Romans* man is shown without righteousness: "There is none righteous, no, not one." This involves man's fundamental relation to God. Christ is set forth a propitiation, meeting all Divine claims, and by His death releasing man from the necessity of a righteousness and holiness of his own: *Christ becomes his righteousness,* and a believer has the witness of the Spirit that he is God's child.

(2) *I Corinthians.* Here the subject is not righteousness but *wisdom.* The words "wisdom" and "wise" occur in the first four chapters twenty-five times, and the words "foolish" and "foolishness" some eight times! In 1.30 we are seen as of God —we that are in Christ Jesus who was "made unto us wisdom from God": which indeed includes "Righteousness, Sanctification and Redemption" but *Christ is looked at as our Wisdom.* Indeed, in 2.16, "We have *the mind* of Christ." Those declared righteous in Romans, and become children of God, are now brought to school,—as children should be. But lo! the wisdom of the world is "foolishness,"—therefore *God's* "wisdom" is revealed to these children of God by the Spirit, the Holy Spirit indwelling them (2.6-16).

(3) *II Corinthians.* Here we find Christ our *sufficiency.* Declared righteous in Romans, instructed by the Spirit in I Corinthians, the believer has yet to learn his utter weakness. The key-verses here are 12.9-10: "When I am weak then am I strong," and, "My grace is sufficient for thee." Many believers never find that God alone is their strength along every line. Paul found it! Read 1.8-10. Again: "We have this treasure in earthen vessels, that the exceeding greatness of the power may be of God, and not from ourselves" (4.7-11). Again:

"Our outward man is decaying, yet our inward man is renewed day by day" (4.16). Again: "Our flesh had no relief, but we were afflicted on every side; without were fightings, within were fears. Nevertheless he that comforteth the lowly, even God, comforted us by the coming of Titus" (7.5,6). Again: "Most gladly therefore will I rather glory in my weaknesses that the power of Christ may rest upon me" (12.9).

(4) *Galatians.* The Epistles are linked together, each leading on to the following. So, in II Corinthians 13.11, Paul exhorts, "Be *perfected*" (Compare 6.14 to 7.1). Now the Galatians are seeking to be perfected, but it is by turning back to "religion," by observing "days, seasons, months, years" (4.10,11). "Are ye so foolish, having begun in the Spirit, are ye now perfected in the flesh?" But Paul goes clear back to Romans Six, and testifies to these Galatians, "I have been crucified with Christ; and it is no longer I that live, but Christ liveth in me: and that life which I now live in the flesh I live in faith, the faith which is in the Son of God, who loved me and gave himself up for me" (2.20). He goes back to II Corinthians 5.17: "If any man be in Christ he is a new creation; the old things are passed away; behold, they are become new"; and he sets before us the proper "rule of life" of the believer in words which completely set aside "religious" life, whether Jewish, Romish, or Protestant. "Neither is circumcision anything, nor uncircumcision, but *a new creation.* And as many as shall *walk by this rule,* peace be upon them, and mercy and [when the future time comes for blessing the real Israel] upon the Israel of God" (6.5,16). Thus far we have seen *righteousness without works, in Romans; wisdom without education, in I Corinthians; power without strength, in II Corinthians; perfecting without "religion," in Galatians.*

(5) *Ephesians. Men on earth seated in the heavenlies.* For although named as "the saints that are at Ephesus," and "all true ['faithful'] believers in Christ Jesus" yet that marvelous secret is opened out by which we are made alive with the raised and glorified Christ—raised up with Him and made to sit in the heavenlies [no longer in the *earthlies* as were Israel]

and made indeed to become the fulness of Christ our Head, who filleth all in all. We are not yet in Heaven but are "sealed with the Holy Spirit of promise, which is an earnest of our inheritance, unto the redemption of God's own possession unto the praise of His glory." [An "earnest" is a foretoken of our inheritance.]

(6) *Philippians.* Here we see *Paul as a sample believer* of all these glorious truths, *running the wonderful "course"* toward that coming "day of Christ"! (1.6,10). Saying, as he runs, "To me to live is Christ, and to die is gain" (1.21); exhorting, "Have this mind in you, which was also in Christ Jesus" (2.5-8); crying, as he runs, "I count all things to be loss for the excellency of the knowledge of Christ Jesus my Lord: for whom I suffered the loss of all things, and do count them but refuse, that I may gain Christ, and be found in Him not having a righteousness of mine own, even that which is of the Law, but that which is through faith in Christ, the righteousness which is from God by faith: that I may know Him, the power of His resurrection, the fellowship of His sufferings, becoming conformed unto His death. *I press on,* if so be that I may lay hold on that for which also I was laid hold on by Christ Jesus. *I press* on toward the goal unto the prize of the high calling of God in Christ Jesus. Let us therefore, as many as are perfect, be thus minded. For our citizenship is in heaven. I can do all things through Him that strengtheneth me: And my God shall supply every need of yours, according to His riches in glory in Christ Jesus." (Chapter 3, entire; 4.13,19). Paul's word in 3.17: "Brethren, *be ye imitators together of me,* and mark them that so walk as *ye have us for an ensample,*" is the key of Philippians. By the grace of God certainly, but none the less truly, Paul was enabled to run the Christian race *in all its fulness!*

(7) *Colossians. Heavenly men on earth*—yet *holding fast the Head* in heaven, and *becoming filled with His fulness,* is what we see here. All the fulness of the Godhead dwelling bodily in Christ, with whom believers' lives are hid in God, Christ becomes the object of all the believer's thoughts and

affections. Since you are raised together with Christ, "Set your mind on the things that are above, not on the things that are upon the earth. For ye died, and your life is hid with Christ in God." The believer awaits Christ's coming—content not to be known or manifested till the glory comes. Four desperate foes oppose this mystery of faith of holding fast the Head in Heaven while walking on earth. See them in 2.4,8,16,18.

(8) *I Thessalonians.* The Thessalonian Epistles set forth *the Personal Return of our Lord Jesus Christ*—the end of the earthly path of God's dear saints!

I Thessalonias gives *The Church's hope, the Rapture:* "The Lord Himself shall descend from Heaven with a shout, with the voice of the archangel, and with the trump of God: and the dead in Christ shall rise first; then we that are alive, that are left, shall together with them be *caught up in the clouds, to meet the Lord in the air:* and so shall we ever be with the Lord! Wherefore comfort one another with these words" (4.16-18).

The believer who knows himself righteous (Romans), having the mind of Christ (I Corinthians), who has learned to glory in his weakness (II Corinthians), and to walk by the "rule of the new creation" knowing that he was crucified with Christ, who is now living in Him (Galatians), and who sees with Spirit-enlightened eyes the heavenly character and calling of the Church (Ephesians), and is really becoming an imitator of Paul in the race—running the course unto Christ—"the day of Christ" (Philippians), who is really holding fast the Head, paying no attention to those who would delude him with persuasiveness of speech and make a spoil of him through "philosophy" and would judge us in "religious" things or rob us of our prize by turning us to a self-humility that fails to hold fast the Head (Colossians): such a believer is ready indeed for I Thessalonians! And he is sincerely eager in *daily, hourly watching for His coming*—for the Rapture of the Church!

(9) *II Thessalonians* gives the second phase of our Lord's Return, the "revelation of the Lord Jesus from Heaven in

flaming fire rendering vengeance to them that know not God and to them that obey not the gospel of our Lord Jesus Christ." It is the great Day of Wrath of Revelation 19.11-21. In II Thessalonians Paul guards the saints from confusing the Rapture with that Day of Wrath,—called "the Day of the Lord" (R.V. 2.1-3). The church at Thessalonica was being tempted by its troubles to confuse the coming of the Lord Jesus Christ and our gathering together unto Him [the Rapture] with the Day of the Lord—which sees the manifestation of the Antichrist. Which terrible days, thank God, the Church is not appointed to see! I Thessalonians 5.9, Revelation 3.10.

"For God appointed us not unto wrath, but unto the obtaining of salvation through our Lord Jesus Christ" (I Thess. 5.9).

"Because thou didst keep the word of my patience, I also will keep thee from the hour of trial, that hour which is to come upon the whole world, to try them that dwell upon the earth" (Rev. 3.10).

INDEX TO
ROMANS VERSE BY VERSE

Exhortation, gift of, 466.

'Exclusivists', 501.

Experience, Christian, 334, 530.

Faith, not in intellect, 18, note; condition of our being accounted righteous, 23, note; 63; not meritorious, 105, 131, note; not trust, 108-9; 'most holy', 126; contrasted with unbelief, 149, note; how understood, 150, note; why God prescribes f, 152, note; f only takes hold of God, 153, note; is Satan's target, 155, note; appropriating f, 209; always against appearances, 225; is living, acting, 141, note; f connected with certain words, 398, note; is by God's words, 512; is the condition of Heaven, 565.

Fascism, 488-9, notes.

Fatherhood, three-fold, of believers, 145.

'Federal Council of Churches', 488, note.

Field, Marshall, 107.

Flesh, the, four points about, 211-12; the unsaved are in f, 257, 259; impulses of f, 266; hopes in f, 269; evil of f, 276; what f wants, 282; f unchanged, 284; f versus holiness, 291; sin connected with f, 294-5 and note; religion of f, 297; the f is not the heart, 456, note; lusts of f, 296-7, 496.

Freedom, heavenly, in Christ, 103, 234.

Freud, 30 and note.

'Friends of God', 103.

Ghandi, Mahatma, 31, note.

Gatherings, of early believers, 554-5.

Gentiledom, 419, note; warned, 422-3, note.

Gentiles, objects of mercy, 525-6; never under Law, 25, note; 64, note; 258; God's program for, 406; summary of Gentile history, 438-9; ghastly record of, 425-7; now the 'good olive tree', 428; Paul, Gentiles' official administrator, 533-8.

Gerhardt, Paul, 103.

Gifts, 301, 461-4, notes.

Giving, 466, 545.

GOD, a person, 52; too good to punish sinners? 62, note; God's holiness, 122, 172; His love, 169-70; three degrees of His kindness, 56; Sovereignty of God, 364-7; 371, 412-4; 385-6; mercy of, 355, 367, 380, 441; purpose of, 330, 333; God the Seeker, 81, 407; His plan for us, 456; His judgment, wrath—see words. God's righteousness, 98-9; apart from Law-keeping, 105.

'Golden age' of Grecian and Roman letters, 32.

Gospel, glory of and power of, 4, 18-21; Paul's Gospel, 2; heart of g, 92; first point of, 157; Rom. 7.4 and 6, 253; second truth of, 280; reveals (four points), 282; begins at the Cross, 393-7; only real leveler, 474.

Government, Divine, 125.

Grace of God, 9, 81, 115, 162; grace versus works, 136, 412; **reign of grace**, 176; abundance of, 185; for Israel, 193; examples of, 194-6; **g** rejected, abused, 201; four points about, 245-7; three, 561; **g** and eternal life, 244; enemies of, 264; when appreciated, 355; **g** of our Lord Jesus Christ, 561; what **g** did, 565.

Greek words, several important: **aionios, anomos,** 62, note; **charis,** 116; **dikaioma,** etc., 185 and note; **eiper,** 316, note; **dorean,** 114-5; **graphe,** 5, note; **gignosko,** 210, note; **hilasterion,** 117, note; **huiothesia,** 312, note; **katargeo,** 143, note; **logia,** 75, note; **logidzomai,** 223, note; **nekros** and **thnesko,** 223; **palingenesia,** 452, note; **pistia,** 75, note; **prasso,** etc., 272, note; **syneudokouso,** 39; **tekna,** etc., 314, note; **zoe,** 146, note. See also 35 note, 36 (#6), 37 (#10), and note; 339-341.

Guilt, and 'church members', 78; sentence of, 87; **g** and law-keeping, 89; universal, 178. Grissom, Capt., story of, 134-5, note.

Hades, 44, 60-1, 181, note; **Hades** and **Sheol** explained, 348, 397, note.

Heart, natural, 81; 396; defined, 456, note.

Heirs of God, 315-6.

Heresy, judged from Paul's writings, 2.

Hebrew and Greek languages, use by God, 196-7, note.

Hitler, 432, note.

'Holy days', 88, 450, note.

Holy Scriptures, two words for, 5, note.

Holy Spirit, His work and power, 200, note; 214, 274, 282, 287, 290, 298-9; who gave Him, 300-1, note; 'dwelleth' in believers, 302, 305; Administrator, 304; renews, 452-3; controls believers, 311; walking by the Holy Spirit, 239, 254-5, 284 and note, 296 and note;

Holy walk, 200, 226, 283.
303, 309-12, 393; witness of the Spirit, 313 and note; first-fruits of, 324.

Human Government, 484-5.

Human race, facts about, 80-6.

'I' in Ch. 7, 251, note.

Identification with Christ, 161, 200, 202-3, 213, 216, 235, 255 and note; 292, 569; idenification and death, 220; identification taught before 'surrender', 275; new revelation, 279.

Idolatry, origin and result, 29; since the Flood, 33, note.

Intellect, 18, note.

'Internationalists', 487, note.

Israel, God's elect earthly nation; 357, note; God's 'olive tree', 421-2; of whom according to the flesh, is our Lord, 361; how differing from other nations, 357-362; not finally abandoned, 359, 410, 445-6; Remnant of, 342, 355, 377, 411-2, 416; deliverance of Remnant, 379, 437, 440, 525-6.

Israelite, described by Ch. 7.5, 257; believing Israelites (in Hos. 2.23), 377.

Jehovah, God's name as toward Israel, 312.

Jesus Christ, see CHRIST.

Jews, their natural 'advantages', 74-5; have lost special place, 22, 402, note, 415 and note, 417 and note, 528 note; their 'faithlessness', 75; sinners and transgressors, 86; trusted in circumcision, 139; 'killed the Lord Jesus', 529 note, 546 note; fearful condition, 388-90; must confess Christ, 397-9; way to reach J, 406, 416-7, 419; had most testimony concerning Christ, 405; persecutions by and of Jews, 422, note; why Gentile believers should minister to, 544; Hebrew believers 'partakers of heavenly calling', 411, note; 415, note.

John's baptism, 300, 390.

Jones, E. Stanley, 47.

Judaizers, 8, note.

Judas, typifies apostate Israel, 414, note.

Judgment of God, principles of, 54-71; a consequence of death, 181, note; wrath at the last judgment, 173; j's in O.T. days, 182. Divine judgment fell on Christ at Cross, 173 note, 244; wicked souls held under Divine j, 340.

Judgment Day at the Cross, 125, 295; j d in Eden, 188, 190; three j d's, 116, note.

Judgment seat of Christ, 508-9.

Justification through faith in Christ, 91-129; greatest verse on, 114; cause of is in God, 115; j of life, in Christ, 105 note, 156; 188 and note, 289; j is by the Last Adam, 183, 198, 267; an act of God, 147; most direct statement on, 178; summary of, 159-61.

Justified from sin, 215 note, 216-7; God's elect already j, 333.

Katargeo, 143-4, note; meaning of, 214; in Ch. 7.6, 258.

Kingdom of God, 342 note, 512-3.

Kings, the two, 176.

Know, Gr. words for, 210.

Lamb of God, the, 116, 158; why sent, 120, 192; Substitute, 123; ground of Abraham's justification, 154; overcoming by the blood of, 227, note.

Law and 'The Law', 86, note; 'established', 127-8; 'incidental', 178, 193, 393; 'vicarious law keeping', 191-2; believers not under Law, 231-4; 259 and note; contrasted with Grace, 247 (IV.7); 390, note; terrible and 'fiery', 268; Paul and Law, 265-270; Law is spiritual, 271-2. THE LAW, to whom given, 64, 192-3; does not make righteous, 93; our death to, 251-9; the two "laws", 290-1; the Jew and the Law, 388, note; Christ, the Cross and the Law, 389, 391; three points about, 291, 393; two points, 394; Moses' Law not "glad tidings," 402.

Lawlessness, 237, 481-3.

Legal dispensation, 240; legal principle, **231 and note:** 252, 278, 282; 1 restraint, **257**, responsibility, 288

Legalists, 143, note; 213, 315.

Leper, cleansing of, 278.

Liberty, how to use, 200; Law allowed none, 506; of grace, of glory, 321; 1 in Christ, 512, 515.

Life, newness of, 207-9, 219, 222, 237. Christ laid His life down, 173; note; 208. Christ's risen life, 174.

Living, compared with believing, 153 and note.

Lord's day, see Sabbath.

Love of God, 118, note; three-fold view of, 169-71; 328. Love as motive, 243; principle of Christianity, 490; walking in 1, 500.

Man: Spirit, soul, body, 11, 211, 306-8; man's soul-life, 310, 453; man's condition, 114; no hope in, 27; knew God's power, 29; worships demons, 81; history of fallen **m**, 84-6; **m** brought to end, 367-8.

McCheyne, Robert Murray, 195.

Martyrs, the, 167, 187, 345.

'Membership', in Scripture, 70, note.

Men, The Two, 176.

Mercy of God, 355, 367, 380.

MESSIAH, 402, note; 415, note.

Millennium, coming, 321-2; order of, 322, 377, 446, 536; Remnant of Israel in, 379, 440; nations in the **M**, 425, 440, 528.

Methodists, early, 103.

Minister (diakonos), 3, note; gift of, 465.

Modernists are Sadducees, 60; 128 note, 293; arrogant, 289 note; beware of, 326, 342, note.

MOSES, mediator for Israel, 193, 356, 535; 'baptized unto **M**', 205; life and ministry, 538.

Mystery, The, 13, 526 note, 564; summary of, 567-72.

Mystics, 103.

New Man, does not sin, 202 and note; to be put on, 454.

Observances, Jewish, 505, note.

'Old Man', our, crucified with Christ, 207, 211-3, 222, 226-7 and note, 259; still exists, 226, 274, note; Christians were in, 248; was crucified with Christ at Cross, 211, 255, note; to be put away, 211, 274, note.

O. T. believers, how God passed over sins of, 116, 126; God's dealings with, 521; offerings of, 120.

Ordinances, set aside, 139, 141, 449.

Pacifists, 486-8, note.

'Partial Rapture', 317.

Paul, stands alone, 2; authority of, 3, note; greatest of men, 2-4; apostleship, 8; prayers and power, steward's consciousness, unconquerable heart, preaching, 2-22; tasks in ROMANS, 92; struggle (Ch. 7), 261-3, 267, 273, 280; 'Paul's struggle not Christian doctrine', 281-5; conversion, 266-7; 277; love for Israel, 357; Paul, minister of the Church, 459; vessel to the Gentiles, 533-7 and notes, 538; his epistles, 572 (#7); "Spiritual order of Paul's epistles', 573-7; Paul's place and ministry, 538; missionary passion, 540; journey to Jerusalem, 542-6; Paul a sample believer, 575.

Peace, 9-10, 529; everlasting peace, 61; false peace, 342, note.

Pentecost, things done there, 233 note (#4-7), 430; Church began there, 459 note, 526 note.

Persecution, in N.T., 340; shaping up again, 342-3. Pharaoh, 60; God's dealing with, 368-9, 375, 376, note.

Philosophy, a delusion, 18, note; uncertainty of, 314.

Plymouth Brethren, 103.

Prayer, Scriptural address in, 315; saints' sense of need in, 326; spirit of, 327; God's work depends on, 546-7, note.

Prophets; prophecy, gift of, 463-4.

Propitiation, meaning of, 116-7, note; 173, note; includes, 118-9, 255; defined, 124; is through faith, 225; result of, 450.

Puritans, 187.

Rapture, Jews after r, 415; at Christ's coming, 459, note; not the Day of wrath, 577.

'Reckon' (logidzomai), 131, note; 223, note; a word for faith, 225, 318.

Reconciliation, illustrated, 171, note; result of, 171-5 and note.

Redemption of the body, 241, note; 293, 308, 325.

Reformers, theology of, 106, 173 note, 191, 255, 313, 393; not an authority, 112 note; 'reigned in life', 187; faint light of, 410 note; R's and the state, 489 note.

Regeneration, is not justification, 159; what it is, 452 and note; re-generate and unregenerate man, 273, 276-7.

Relationship, new, the, 202 note; our r Christ's, 214, 222; our r to God 249; our r to Adam, 259, note.

Religion, meaning of, 8, note; 'religious' privilege, 363; 'religious' distinctions, 513; Christendom's 'religion', 450, note.

Representative, Adam was our, 179; how a r acts, 180, 181; Christ is our Representative, 223.

Responsibility, according to privilege, 62; in Adam, 96, 101, 221, 259, note.

Resurrection, purpose of, 156-7; of Christ, 96, note; Christ's risen life, 207-8, 220-2. Deniers of, 293.

Reward, in the Kingdom, 317; for service, 508-9.

Right, of property, 471, 482, 544, note.

Righteous, declared r, 105; meaning, 114, 133-5, 141, note; basis of, 147, 154.

Righteousness, God's, what it is, 23 and note; Law has no place in, 93; three views of, 98-9; defined, 99, 100, 104 and note, 105; Ref-ormation statements of, 101; on the faith principle, 108; Mr. Darby on, 111, note; a relative term, 121; believers are the r of

586

God in Christ, 189; see God's Righteousness.

Righteousness 'without works', 129; what it is, 131, note; words connected with r, 185, note; faith connected with r, 398, note.

Risen ones, 230.

Roman Empire, 241-2, 336, 493; R world, 252.

Romanism, Romanists, 3, 19 note, 110, 143, 165 note, 173 note, 208-9 note, 214, 426, 518 note, 523.

Romans, Epistle to, 249, 289; addressed to believers only, 481; more important than Law of Moses, 549 note; has message of gospel, 566; believers' walk in R, 572 (#7); place in Paul's epistles, 573 (#1).

Russia, testimony from, 167-8; future of, 432 note.

Sabbath, when revealed to man, 67 note; never enforced by Christ, 389; is the seventh day, 504-7.

'Sacraments', 139 note.

Sacrifice, Christ's, 173 note, 192, 234.

SAINTS, meaning, 3; connected with Christ, 9, 349; attacked, 556-7; what establishes s, 568.

Salvation, is wholly of God, 144, 384, 386 (#5); five parts to, 200 note; distinguished from surrender, 243; Christ's Name in, 245; facts of, 273; Christ's and Holy Spirit's work in, 287; source of, 367; plan of, 327; is by faith, 225, 519, note.

Sanctification, fruit unto, 224, 243, 256; three aspects of, 454-5.

Satan, his program, 155, note; history, 560-1.

Scandal of universe, 116; of history, 422.

Scripture, compared with 'sacred writings', 5; our use of, 116; set forth Christ's death, 117; written by Israelites, 359; to be taught, 385; O.T. S speaks in N.T., 400, 520, note.

Second Coming of Christ, 321, 433, 492, 572 (#6, 7).

Second chance, 62, note.

Sectarianism, 70, notes; 107, note.

Self-Righteousness, 171; merciless, 268; causes uncertainty, 348-9.

Sheol, see Hades.

Sinai, 183, 393.

Sin, God's arraignment of, 25; has ben soft-pedalled, 31; woman had lead in, 33; 'life choice of sin', 61 note; judgment days of, 116 note, 125; s between Adam and Moses, 182; God's definition of, 182, 516; Israel's s at Sinai, 183; effect of Adam's s, 183; Christ's death to s, 200-1; 'justified from s', 215; its lordship, 231; strength of s, 238; its birth, end, wages, 243; indwelling s, 261, 265, 267, 270-1-3-4, 277-9; evil desire is s, 265; no human power against s, 266; Paul died to s and Law, 279; sin's guilt compared with s itself, 292; s as connected with flesh, 294-5.

Sins, what they are, 46-7.

Sinner-consciousness and revival, 125.

Sinnerhood, three stages of, 169-70; by Adam's guilt, 181-90.

Women as deaconesses, 549 and note; ministry of in early Church, 551-3, note.

Work of Christ, finished, 126, 143, note (#4).

Works, 88, note; 141.

World, God's wrath in, 26; world and believer, 256.

Wrath, of God, reason for, 29; in ROMANS, 40-46; Day of Wrath, 56-7; God's mind toward wicked, 60; is righteous, 76; Christ bore w on the Cross, 173; men are children of w, 277; vessels of w, 373-7.

Zeal, in Divine things, 387-8.

Index of Authors Referred to

589